The
Neoconservative
M I N D

W9-BHG-667

The
Neoconservative
MIND

*Politics, Culture, and the
War of Ideology*

GARY DORRIEN

Temple University Press

PHILADELPHIA

Temple University Press, Philadelphia 19122
Copyright © 1993 by Temple University. All rights reserved
Published 1993
Printed in the United States of America

The paper used in this publication meets the minimum requirements of American National
Standard for Information Sciences—Permanence of Paper for Printed Library Materials,
ANSI Z39.48-1984 ∞

Library of Congress Cataloging-in-Publication Data
Dorrien, Gary J.
    The neoconservative mind : politics, culture, and the war of
ideology / Gary Dorrien.
        p.   cm.
    Includes bibliographical references and index.
    ISBN 1-56639-019-2 (cl : alk. paper)
    1. Conservatism—United States. I. Title.
JA84.U5D67   1993
320.5'2'0973—dc20   92-11187

For my parents,
Jack and Virginia Dorrien,
with ineffable love

Contents

Preface

Prefaces are written last, usually to introduce the subject or make personal remarks, or both. This will be mostly personal. I began to track the progress and varieties of neoconservatism as an undergraduate in the early 1970s, not long after the movement acquired its name. Among the handful of journals that introduced me to subjects not covered in my undergraduate curriculum, *Commentary* was perhaps the most instructive and certainly the most provocative. The magazine's extensive letters section introduced me to the politics of intellectual combat. The magazine's often ferocious attacks on modern liberalism caused me to open each new issue with roughly equal foreboding and fascination. Neoconservatives criticized, with particular vehemence, the modern liberal Christianity with which I identified.

My interest in neoconservatism intensified during my seminary and graduate career, partly because neoconservative writings frequently seemed more interesting to me than conventional academic fare, but especially because neoconservatives criticized feminism, the antiwar movement, political liberalism, and the mainline churches with a perceptiveness apparently gained from close acquaintance. The in-your-face polemical style that neoconservatives perfected made a striking contrast to modern theological scholarship, which typically exalted ecumenical dialogue and called for the relinquishment of exclusivistic claims. The neoconservatives seemed less interested in promoting dialogue with opponents than with demolishing them. Their journals, to be sure, also offered scores of lower-voiced, number-crunching studies in social science and politics. In both cases, however, neoconservatives refused to compromise or apologize for their beliefs, but rather proclaimed the superiority of their convictions over available alternatives. Their arguments were advanced with distinctive energy and power. The same qualities later made neoconservatism a powerful intellectual movement.

Neoconservatives have often claimed that nearly everything written about them has been wrong or unfair. The complaint was voiced in every interview that I conducted with them. Norman Podhoretz told me that 95 percent of the literature about neoconservatism was "worthless." "I never recognize myself in the things they write about me," he reported. I have taken this complaint to heart. Like most of those who have written about neoconservatism, I am not a follower. However, I have taken particular care to explicate the movement's arguments accurately. My respect for the neoconservatives, which was high at the outset, has only grown through the course of writing this book. Michael Walzer has rightly observed that neoconservatism is the only intellectual movement in recent American politics to successfully unite theory and practice. No other contemporary intellectual movement comes close to this achievement.

My own political perspective blends liberal, social democratic, feminist, and communitarian elements and is chastened by conservative criticism. No single tradition of moral or political theory is, to me, sufficient as a guide to conceiving the common good or making concrete gains toward it. The morally imperative effort to strive for freedom, equality, and ecologically sustainable development is, by necessity, guided by provisional theories. From this perspective, the essential theoretical task is to refashion parts of a complex social inheritance into a politics that serves the common good. Neoconservative arguments—especially those concerning the moral ravages of modern nihilism—contribute to this reconstructive project. My version of this project is closer to the pluralist/social democratic politics of Walzer, Amy Gutmann, and Robert Bellah than to neoconservatism. My deepest disagreements with neoconservatives center on their opposition to feminism. My aim in the present work, however, is not to refute neoconservatism or to belabor the points on which I especially disagree with neoconservatives, but to offer a critical examination of neoconservatism's history, its arguments, and its future prospects. I shall argue that there is such a thing as neoconservatism, that it grew out of the Old Left, and that it retains the marks of its origins in the factional New York Intellectual debates of the 1930s. More importantly, I shall describe the different ideological currents within neoconservatism, track the movement's attainment of political power in the 1980s, explain how the collapse of communism has fractured neoconservatism's foreign policy consensus, and analyze the movement's subsequently heightened concern with cultural politics. I shall finally argue that neoconservatism is not yet, but has the potential to become, America's first genuine conservative intellectual tradition.

Neoconservatism is distinctive among American conservatisms partly

because it seeks to conserve the social order that actually exists. Neoconservatism does not (for the most part) attempt to restore a real or imagined
conservatism of the past, but defends the existing modern commercial
order from its various critics. In Berger's phrase, neoconservatism faces up
to modernity. The importance of the term *modernity* in neoconservative
thought compels a definition of this term at the outset of the book. In
accordance with neoconservative usage, I shall define modernity as the
social order and ethos created by Enlightenment criticism, modern science
and technology, and especially capitalist economics.

In the course of this project I have accumulated considerable personal
debts. I am deeply grateful to numerous colleagues whose comments on
early drafts helped me improve the manuscript. They include Michael
Ames, Bogdan Denitch, Lisa Freeman, Amy Gutmann, Harvey Kaye,
Russell Kirk, Alane Salierno Mason, Joseph Schwartz, Peter Steinfels,
Clare and Lester Start, David Updike, and several anonymous reviewers.
I am equally grateful to several co-workers for their invaluable assistance
in tracking down hard-to-find articles and references. They include Jen-
nifer Adams, Laura Packard-Latiolais, Steve Purvis-Smith, Carol Smith,
and especially Pam Sotherland. My Religion Department colleagues at
Kalamazoo College— J. Mark Thompson, Waldemar Schmeichel, and
Paul McGlasson—generously supported my work through their friendship
and encouragement. I am grateful, above all, to the principal subjects of
this book, all of whom unfailingly responded to my queries and provided
me with background information about their careers and work. For their
gracious cooperation with this endeavor, many thanks to Peter Berger,
Irving Kristol, Michael Novak, and Norman Podhoretz.

1

What Is Neoconservatism?

In the early 1970s, Michael Harrington and the editors of *Dissent* magazine began to look for a term to describe an assortment of former liberals and leftists who had recently moved to the Right. Most of these new conservatives were former radicals; all of them had supported the early civil rights movement. Some were opposed to America's war in Vietnam; all were repulsed by America's antiwar movement. Most were Democrats who supported a limited welfare state; all had turned against the politics and culture of American liberalism. Most of them claimed to be true liberals in the Democratic party's forsaken Cold War tradition. What was now called liberalism, they insisted, was a countercultural perversion of traditional Democratic politics. They had not changed, they claimed, but were reminders of what American liberalism stood for before it was radicalized by the Movement.

The claim was at least partially justified for those who had opposed the sixties movements from the outset. Most of the new conservatives, however, had changed more than they acknowledged. Many of them were bitterly attacking long-time friends who remained in the Left. Former freedom-riders were repudiating the black nationalist "degeneration" of the civil rights movement. Recent proponents of Lyndon Johnson's War on Poverty were denouncing the Great Society for creating a "New Class" of parasitic bureaucrats and social workers. Former contributors to *Dissent* were making socialist arguments for Richard Nixon's re-election. *Commentary* was running furious assaults on anti-interventionist, feminist, and environmentalist beliefs it once promoted. The phenomenon was worth naming.

Harrington, Irving Howe, and Lewis Coser recognized that the kind of conservatism showing up in *Commentary*, *The Public Interest*, and *The New*

1

Leader was significantly different from previous American conservatisms. The new conservatives were modernists. Most of them were trained in the social sciences. Some of them still considered themselves socialists or social democrats. Most of them were Jews. They expressed little nostalgia for the lost glories of medieval Catholicism, seventeenth-century orthodoxy, nineteenth-century capitalism, or the Old South. The Fall had occurred, not with the Reformation, the French Revolution, the Enlightenment, or the rise of the welfare state, but only yesterday, with the triumph of something they called the New Class. Some of the new conservatives would later attempt to deepen the philosophical basis of their politics by claiming linkages with older political and cultural traditions. But in the beginning, they seemed to be nearly as different from established conservatisms as they were from the liberalism they attacked. "We finally started calling them 'neoconservatives' because we recognized that they represented something new in American politics," Harrington later explained. [1]

THE FRACTURED LEFT

There was a further reason. Many of the neoconservatives were Harrington's former comrades. In 1972, the Socialist party—the party of Eugene Debs and Norman Thomas—was ripped apart by a long-simmering dispute over the antiwar movement and the politics of "New Class liberalism." It would be the last schism of the Old Left. More than half of the party's leaders were right-wing social democrats and trade unionists who despised the antiwar movement and the dovish "New Politics" represented by George McGovern's presidential campaign. They included such long-time anti-Stalinists as Sidney Hook, Max Shachtman, Emanuel Muravchik, Arnold Beichman, Arch Puddington, John Roche, Bayard Rustin, Harry Overstreet, and Frank Trager. Some were veterans of the struggle in the 1930s to drive Communists out of the unions, when the struggle was fought with guns and clubs. Their anti-Stalinism had hardened over the decades into a fierce anticommunism; their socialism was reduced to the AFL-CIO's immediate demands. The emergence of the New Left in the 1960s repulsed these Old Leftists from the outset—and eventually drove them further to the Right. They were deeply alienated from what they called the "liberal intelligentsia" or the "fashionable liberal elite." This alienation would later fuel their war against the New Class. The 1972 presidential election was a watershed for the Old Leftists. Though they still regarded themselves as socialists, their revulsion for McGovern's antiwar liberalism drove them into unfamiliar territory. Many of them found themselves supporting Nixon; others joined George Meany on the sidelines, holding their noses at both sides. To all of them, the McGovern candidacy represented the triumph of appeasement and New Class isolationism. For most of them, even Nixon was preferable to this betrayal of the Democratic party's Cold War tradition.

Harrington pressed for a different kind of social democracy. He feared that the party of Debs and Thomas was reducing socialism to "laborism"— that is, to the politics of the existing labor movement—and consequently squandering an opportunity to broaden its constituency. Though he assured the Old Left that he would support "the merest laborism against middle-class liberalism," Harrington insisted that any viable progressive movement in America needed to embrace the "New Class" intellectuals and activists whom the Old Left spurned. Though his own relationship to the sixties generation was strained by his vehement rejection of the New Left's anti-anticommunism, Harrington worked throughout the decade to bridge the chasm between the Old Left and the student radicals. He believed that a redefined social democratic politics could blend the best of both sides. He tried to explain the Old Left's visceral anticommunism to the founders of Students for a Democratic Society (SDS), though, as he later recalled, "my notion of a progressive, Leftist anti-Communist made as much existential sense to them as a purple cow."[2] America's military escalation in Vietnam and the growth of a student-based antiwar movement in the mid-sixties made this project imperative to Harrington. He recruited several hundred activists and intellectuals to democratic socialism through this effort. His faction of the Socialist party opposed the war in Vietnam and worked with sympathetic segments of the Democratic party to attain what Harrington called "the Left-wing of possibility." They supported the progressive New Politics movement in the early 1970s and endorsed McGovern's presidential candidacy. Their support for the Democratic party's liberal wing drove them, in turn, into a bitter factional fight for control of their own party.

This conflict had a complicated background, not least because both of the Socialist party's major factions were led by Shachtmanites. Max Shachtman had been a Communist in the 1920s, a co-founder of American Trotskyism in 1929, a close associate of Leon Trotsky throughout the 1930s, the founder of "Third Camp" revolutionary socialism in 1940, and the chief theorist of American "democratic Marxism" in the later 1940s and 1950s. A brilliant, charismatic autodidact and spellbinding orator, Shachtman trained several generations of American radicals in the literature and lore of Marxism while moving from Soviet-style communism to

Trotskyism to quasi-Trotskyism to right-wing social democracy. In 1958, in a move that required all of his immense sectarian skills, he folded his Independent Socialist League into Norman Thomas's Socialist party. Most of Shachtman's followers thought that he (and therefore, they) were scheming to attract disaffected Communists to their movement. They supported the merger with Thomas's Socialists on that basis. Their ranks included Harrington and Bogdan Denitch. Shachtman, however, was secretly, perhaps even unconsciously, moving to the Right.

The Shachtmanites were tactical Bolsheviks. Most of them disdained the Socialist party's indiscriminate anticommunism. Their ferocious anti-Stalinism bore a closer kinship to their organization's Trotskyist past than to social democracy. Many of them were not finished with revolutionary Marxism. Thomas's social democrats were no match for them. Trotsky once called Thomas's group a party of dentists. Faced with the prospect of merging with the Shachtmanites, Thomas feared that Shachtman's highly disciplined followers would devour his party. The Shachtmanites therefore pledged not to run a full slate of candidates for party offices, and further agreed to exile their most threatening operator—Denitch—to Berkeley, where he promptly took over the local chapter.

The Socialist party's attempts to control the Shachtmanites proved to be futile. Shachtman's followers soon dominated the party. Their conquest did not confirm Thomas's fears about them, however, because Shachtman was finished with ultraleftism. Upon entering the Socialist party, he quickly made alliances with the party's most conservative elements. He adopted the party's hardline anticommunism and its unfailing support for the AFL-CIO. His turn to the Right eventually drove several of his key followers, including Denitch and Deborah Meier, to leave the party in the early 1960s. Shachtman continued to attract impressive young disciples, however—some of whom found jobs working for Al Shanker's United Federation of Teachers. And he retained Harrington's loyalty until the mid-sixties. "Mike stuck with Max longer than some of us, partly because he was closer to Max's politics, and partly because he refused to acknowledge how much Max was changing," Denitch later recalled. [3] The differences between Shachtman and Harrington finally broke open after Lyndon Johnson massively escalated America's intervention in Vietnam. While Harrington opposed the war and tried to recruit the New Left to democratic socialism, Shachtman supported the war and despised the anti-intellectualism and utopianism of the New Left. His last generation of followers embraced these views. Shachtman brought Carl Gershman, Rachelle Horowitz, Tom Kahn, Penn Kemble, and Joshua Muravchik into the Old Left just before it collapsed. These young recruits would lead the

Old Left's final schism. Though they considered themselves Marxists, they would soon hear themselves being called neoconservatives.[4]

The schism began in October 1972, when Harrington resigned as the Socialist party's national co-chair at the party's pre-election National Committee meeting. "I listened in stunned amazement as an old friend and comrade announced that she hoped Nixon would smash McGovern," he later recalled.[5] It was a defining moment. The friend was a longtime Socialist and veteran of the civil rights movement. Though the committee declined to endorse her position, Harrington was shaken by the support it received from key party leaders. The general tone of their discussion convinced him that the party of Debs and Thomas was turning into a reactionary force. This conclusion was reinforced by the prospect of the party's imminent reunification with the Democratic Socialist Federation (DSF), the descendant of the "Old Guard" faction that broke from the Socialist party in 1936. Harrington feared that a merger with the DSF would greatly strengthen the party's right wing. He therefore resigned his chairmanship and prepared for a factional showdown at the party's national convention, which took place in December 1972. His group demanded a vote on the party's future. "Mike enticed several of us back to the party for that convention," Denitch recalled. "He convinced Meier, Irving Howe, and several others to come back for a final stand against the reactionaries."[6] For the first time, the Shachtmanites were allowed to operate without restrictions. The youngest Shachtmanites led the fight against Harrington's challenge. The crucial vote took place over the right wing's proposal to change the name of the party to Social Democrats, U.S.A. Harrington's opponents won the vote and took control of the party. The party of Eugene Debs renounced the Left. Harrington's group walked out of the party and, the following year, formed the Democratic Socialist Organizing Committee. This group would soon dwarf the Social Democrats in numbers—but not in influence.

"My friends had turned themselves into a fanatically anti-Communist clique of people with staff jobs in unions and related institutions," Harrington explained. "But the real corruption was not careerist or opportunist, it was political and ideological. Socialism was programmatically reduced to the immediate demands of the American labor movement; morality became a sophisticated adaptation to tactical necessity; the socialist function of practical prophecy was dismissed as dilettantish. All this was done by people with the best socialist will in the world. They were not scoundrels who were bought and paid for. That is why they are tragic."[7] His personal trauma was that he was forced to break from many of his closest friends and teachers, including his chief mentor, Shachtman. Sixteen years later,

very symbol - like Life of Brian

he remarked that the notion he found most difficult to explain to his students was the concept of socialists for Nixon.[8]

DEFINING THE MOVEMENT

The neoconservative phenomenon was already more complicated than the politics of the Shachtmanites when the editors of *Dissent* began to muse about neoconservatism. Not all of the neoconservatives came from the Old Left, and Harrington never restricted the label to his former comrades. *Commentary* and *The Public Interest* were already publishing neoconservative critiques of the Great Society by figures with little background in radical politics. Harrington acknowledged that some of the new conservatives were disaffected liberals. The influence of this group within neoconservatism would increase throughout the 1970s. Most of the movement's original partisans, however, came from the Old Left. They were labeled "neoconservatives" partly for factional reasons. Harrington and his followers needed to distinguish their form of social democracy from the hawkish, increasingly antiliberal politics of their former comrades. It was an exercise in dissociation. Their message was: These people are no longer with us. They are not the right wing of the Left, but the left wing of the Right.

The difference was crucial. The neoconservatives were well acquainted with the sociological phenomenon of labeling. For that reason they initially rejected their label and its insinuations. They would not be tagged by the likes of Harrington and thus allow themselves to be excommunicated from the Left. Their antipathy for America's liberal intelligentsia soon brought them unexpected company, however. The label stuck, mainly because most of the so-called neoconservatives did go on to align themselves objectively with the politics and institutions of the American Right. Their emergence signaled that a realignment in American politics was taking place.[9]

Harrington later defined the neoconservatives as "those who came to their position from a liberal or socialist background, after being disillusioned of their Great Society dreams."[10] This did not describe Irving Kristol, who opposed most of the Great Society from the beginning. Yet it was Kristol who first accepted the designation "neoconservative" and who ensured that neoconservatism would become a more complex phenomenon than Harrington had envisioned. Throughout the 1970s, most of the neoconservatives bristled at their consignment to the Right. Having long since renounced his own radicalism, however, it was easier for Kristol to acknowledge that he had, indeed, become some kind of conservative.

He later explained that the parallel with neo-orthodox theology helped him to accept the term. "Neoconservatism is a current of thought emerging out of the academic-intellectual world and provoked by disillusionment with contemporary liberalism," he observed in 1979. "Its approach to the world is more 'rabbinic' than 'prophetic.'" [11] Kristol's eight-point definition oddly failed to mention communism, but his declaration opened the door for others to explain why they were neoconservatives.

"A neoconservative is a person brought up as a person of the left, who grew dissatisfied with the ideas and the spirit of the left," Michael Novak offered. "Typically, this dissatisfaction arose because the way of life of the left seemed to demand so many forms of false consciousness and, above all, a loathing for the American system." [12] Norman Podhoretz similarly defined neoconservatism as a repudiation of "the anti-Americanism that by the late '60s had virtually become the religion of the radical movement in which we ourselves had actively participated in the earlier years of the decade." [13] The theme of disillusionment was common to the neoconservatives' self-definitions. The first generation of neoconservatives became conservatives not by inheritance, but by conversion. Their turn to the Right was a surprise to themselves. The social movements of the sixties and seventies drove them into positions they hadn't expected to defend. Nathan Glazer thus defined a neoconservative as "someone who wasn't a conservative."

The movement's critics frequently seized upon the same theme. Peter Glotz defined neoconservatism as "the net into which the liberal can fall when he begins to fear his own liberalism." [14] Peter Steinfels similarly reported that he had difficulty taking Novak's capitalist enthusiasms seriously because he was haunted by the memory of Novak "posed in white turtleneck and lovebeads, advocating a 'revolution of consciousness' which would reintroduce freedom into an industrial, technological state.'" [15] The conversion theme, with all of its religious connotations, dominates the literature on both sides. Whether neoconservatives have seen the light or merely lost their compassion is a debate repeatedly taken up in the literature by and about them.

If conversion is a central theme in the writings of the movement's major figures, however, it is not an absolute prerequisite of neoconservatism itself. Neoconservatism is now long enough established to have gained numerous followers by inheritance. Many of the movement's younger intellectuals have never been anything but neoconservatives. Until the collapse of Soviet communism, the politics they inherited was centrally preoccupied with fighting communism and with resisting the political and cultural influence of the New Class. It is rare that an intellectual movement significantly affects American politics. Neoconservatism has been such an exception. With the disintegration of the Soviet Union and the election of a Democratic president, it is unlikely that neoconservatism can regain in the 1990s the political influence it achieved in the 1980s. Neoconservatism remains, however, a potent intellectual movement in American politics.

The neoconservative mission to thwart the New Class encompasses a host of political, economic, and cultural concerns. The movement's twofold agenda has been aptly captured by Jürgen Habermas, who defines neoconservatism as a movement dedicated to opposing communism and to supporting the theory of democratic rule by elites.[16] Whether this definition adequately describes what most neoconservatives call "democratic capitalism" is an arguable point. Other neoconservatives reject the concept of "democratic capitalism," arguing that capitalism is inherently undemocratic and that so-called "democratic capitalism" rationalizes presumptuous foreign policy goals.

It is possible, however, to identify several elements common to all neoconservatives. Expanding Habermas's definition, I shall define neoconservatism as an intellectual movement originated by former leftists that promotes militant anticommunism, capitalist economics, a minimal welfare state, the rule of traditional elites, and a return to traditional cultural values.

Intellectual Roots and Branches

This is not another book on the New York Intellectuals. Neoconservatism is more heterogeneous than the storied New York Intellectual tradition in which it is rooted.[17] A number of the movement's theorists are not from New York; some are not Jewish; some have little background in leftist politics. Novak, Peter Berger, and Richard John Neuhaus, for example, came to neoconservatism from backgrounds considerably removed from the Marxist/Freudian/literary culture of the New York Intellectuals. A substantial portion of this book will be devoted to their work.

Neoconservatism is unarguably rooted, however, in the factional politics of Harold Rosenberg's fabled "herd of independent minds." In 1937, William Phillips and Philip Rahv refashioned the formerly Communist *Partisan Review* as an independent Marxist journal. Though the magazine's political militancy steadily diminished over the next two decades, its attempt to blend an anti-Stalinist politics with a modernist aesthetic marked nearly all of the New York Intellectuals long after they gave up on Marxism. The founding generation of New York Intellectuals included Sidney Hook, James Burnham, Lionel Trilling, Diana Trilling, and Lionel Abel. A group of writers younger by ten to fifteen years later joined them, which included Saul Bellow, William Barrett, Irving Howe, Irving Kristol, Alfred Kazin, and Delmore Schwartz. A third generation would subsequently include Hilton Kramer, Steven Marcus, and Norman Podhoretz. The forerunners and founders of neoconservatism came from this tradition. An intellectual history of neoconservatism must therefore begin with the New York Intellectual saga.

Howe once observed that the New York Intellectuals were radicals or former radicals with a fondness for polemic and a highly developed sense of politics as tournament. The marks of neoconservatism's roots in this tradition—and particularly, its roots in the Trotskyist debates of the 1930s—would become evident in the movement's rhetorical style, its chief concepts, and its character. Neoconservatism marks the last stage of the Old Left, being the last surviving faction in American politics to define itself principally by its opposition to communism. It may also represent the first stage of a genuine intellectual tradition of American conservatism.

The neoconservatives are generalists in an age of specialization. Though they often exalt the knowledge of experts over the opinions of mere intellectuals, most of them are intellectuals. Many of them came early to the New Class world of foundations, think tanks, journals, and consulting. Their journals typically range on a nonspecialist's level over politics, literature, art, economics, history, theology, philosophy, and social theory. No other intellectual movement in America has established as many high-quality journals as the neoconservatives. *Commentary* and *The Public Interest* head the list, but the list also includes Hilton Kramer's *The New Criterion*, Neuhaus's *First Things*, Myron Kolatch's *The New Leader*, Owen Harries's *The National Interest* (published by Kristol), Dinesh D'Souza's *Crisis* (co-published by Novak), Melvin Lasky's *Encounter* (in England), Jerome Hanus's *Current*, Karlyn Keene's *The American Enterprise*, Patrick Clawson's *Orbis*, R. Emmet Tyrell's *The American Spectator*, Joseph Epstein's *The American Scholar*, Marc F. Plattner and Larry Diamond's *Journal of Democracy*, Seymour Martin Lipset and Ben Wattenberg's *Public Opinion*, and (with contributing dissenters) Martin Peretz's *The New Republic* and Irving Louis Horowitz's *Society*. Neoconservatives frequently appear in *Partisan Review*, *Foreign Policy*, *Foreign Affairs*, *The Washington Quarterly*, *Policy Review*, *National Review*, *Problems of Communism*, *Ethics and International Affairs*, and *Forbes*. They control or substantially influence numerous corporate-funded policy centers, including the Institute for the Study of Economic Culture, the Institute for Contemporary Studies, the Institute on Religion and Public Life, the Manhattan Institute, the American Enterprise Institute, the Ethics and Public Policy Center, the Center for Strategic and International Studies, the National Forum Foundation, and the Center for Security Policy. Among these institutions, the most important is the American Enterprise Institute (AEI), which was established in 1943 to promote free-enterprise economics in opposition to the New Deal. AEI took a neoconservative turn in the early 1970s, and has since grown into one of the largest and most influential think tanks in America.

During the 1970s and 1980s, neoconservatives fought against what they called "the culture of appeasement" through such organizations as the Committee on the Present Danger and the Committee for the Free World. These organizations repeatedly condemned the "pacifism" and "human rights moralism" of the Carter administration and claimed that America was losing the Cold War to a militarily superior enemy. It was nearly too late to prevent the Soviet Union from dominating the world, they claimed. The present danger was that America lacked not only the means, but the will to impede Soviet expansionism. Neoconservatives rang this alarm with fervent certainty throughout the 1970s—and found themselves making surprising alliances along the way. For most of the 1970s, the neoconservatives had tried to change the Democratic party. They organized the Coalition for a Democratic Majority to purge the party of McGovernism. With the election of Ronald Reagan, however, they were presented with more gainful opportunities. As Podhoretz put it, many neoconservatives found themselves joining forces "with those in the *other* party who wanted to be our friends."[18]

Their ideological stridency perfectly suited the new president during the early years of his presidency. Neoconservatism hit its political high-water mark in the mid-1980s. Reagan appointed Jeane Kirkpatrick as ambassador to the United Nations after reading her article in *Commentary* on the differences between dictatorial and totalitarian regimes.[19] Podhoretz's son-in-law, Elliott Abrams, was named assistant secretary of state for international organizations, then moved to the Human Rights division, and later directed Reagan's Central America policy as assistant secretary of state for inter-American affairs. Richard Perle became assistant secretary of defense; Eugene Rostow and Kenneth Adelman successively served as directors of the Arms Control and Disarmament Agency; Max Kampelman headed the administration's arms control negotiations; William Bennett chaired the National Endowment for the Humanities and later directed the Department of Education; Richard Pipes directed the East European and Soviet Affairs division of the National Security Council; Chester Finn and William Kristol worked for the Department of Education; Linda Chavez served as staff director for the U.S. Civil Rights Commission; Ben Wattenberg received advisory posts in the international communications apparatus; Gertrude Himmelfarb obtained an appointment on the Council of the National Endowment for the Humanities; and Novak led the American delegation at the Bern Conference on Security and Cooperation in Europe. Though Podhoretz failed to get the post he wanted at the U.S. Information Agency (USIA), his book *The Present Danger* was rewarded with a glowing endorsement from the new president, and he was subsequently appointed chairman of the USIA's New Directions Advisory Committee. Neoconservatives filled numerous lesser positions as well. *The New Republic* half-seriously warned that "Trotsky's orphans" were taking over the government.[20] Gershman was hired by Kirkpatrick as a staff aide, served as an adviser to the Kissinger Commission on Central America, and was later named president of the National Endowment for Democracy. Puddington worked for Radio Free Europe/Radio Liberty. Kemble became director of Prodemca, an organization that mobilized support for Reagan's Central America policy.

Many of the neoconservatives became Republicans and flourished. Though their tainted backgrounds and their heresies on the welfare state prevented them from obtaining posts affecting economic or welfare policy, they dominated the foreign, defense, and educational policy areas of the Reagan administration.[21] They established new journals and policy institutes and expanded their corporate contacts throughout the eighties. Kristol explained the neoconservatives' success. "We had to tell businessmen that they needed us," he recalled. Though neoconservatives were forced to overcome considerable cultural differences between themselves and business leaders, he noted, they became increasingly effective throughout the 1970s and 1980s at making alliances with the corporate class and the political Right. "Business understands the need for intellectuals much more than trade unionists understand it, but not enough," said Kristol. "Basically, it wants intellectuals to go out and justify profits and explain to people why corporations make a lot of money. That's their main interest. It is very hard for business to understand how to think politically."[22] The neoconservatives would teach the business class how to think politically, just as they would tell a conservative president how to run the country's domestic and, especially, foreign policy.

Neoconservatives and Paleoconservatives

The neoconservatives rarely inspired affection. Their ascension in the early 1980s was viewed with mounting resentment by the old-style conservatives they outmaneuvered. This resentment flared into an outright backlash during Reagan's second term. The so-called "paleoconservatives" harbored their own factional differences, principally between the Old Right elitists clustered around William F. Buckley, Jr.'s *National Review* and George Panichas's *Modern Age* and the more populist, hard-edged conservatism represented by Thomas Fleming's journal, *Chronicles*. Neither of the paleoconservative Right's main factions warmed to its neoconservative allies, however. In the mid-eighties, though Buckley and a few others tried to mediate the dispute, paleoconservatives from both sides attacked the neoconservatives for a mounting litany of offenses. The dean of American intellectual conservatism, Russell Kirk, rebuked the neoconservatives for their "ideological infatuations" ("the neoconservatives are often clever, but seldom wise") and wryly commented on their industry. "How earnestly they founded magazine upon magazine!" he noted. "How skillfully they insinuated themselves into the councils of the Nixon and Reagan Administrations!" The real conservatives were not fooled. The neoconservatives behaved like the cadre of a political machine, "eager for place and preferment and power, skillful at intrigue, ready to exclude from office any persons who might not be counted upon as faithful to the Neoconservative ideology," Kirk argued. They were "clever creatures, glib, committed to an ideology, and devious at attaining their objects." Many of them were also, in his view, cultural and economic imperialists. [23] They had begun as Marxists and were now reverse-Marxists. They were ideologues who thought they had invented conservatism. Their style was hard to take. "It is splendid when the town whore gets religion and joins the church," Stephen J. Tonsor told the Philadelphia Society. "Now and then she makes a good choir director, but when she begins to tell the minister what he ought to say in his Sunday sermons, matters have been carried too far." [24]

The neoconservatives had gone way too far for the traditional Right. The conservatives charged that the neoconservatives were ideological, obnoxious, imperialistic, boring, and opportunistic. The last trait gave particular offense. Fleming and Paul Gottfried bitterly observed that the neoconservatives not only had developed close ties with the Scaife, Smith Richardson, and John M. Olin Foundations, but were also taking over such previously Old Right institutions as the American Enterprise Institute, the Heritage Foundation, and the Hoover Institution. [25] They were also preventing conservatives from obtaining positions they deserved. Clyde Wilson expressed the conservatives' resentment at this injustice. "We have simply been crowded out by overwhelming numbers," he cried. "The offensives of radicalism have driven vast herds of liberals across the border into our territories. These refugees now speak in our name, but the language they speak is the same one they always spoke. . . . Our estate has been taken over by an imposter, just as we were about to inherit."[26]

At first, neoconservatives uncharacteristically resisted the temptation to respond in kind. Though they often muttered off the record about the costs of working with reactionaries, they bit their tongues in public and waited for the furor to pass. This was an argument they couldn't win. The resentment they inspired during the Reagan presidency did not pass, however—even after a new president wiped the appointment slate clean. With few exceptions, George Bush studiously avoided the neoconservatives, the Old Right paleoconservatives, the populist paleoconservatives, the Straussians, and the various factions of New Right and libertarian intellectuals when he made his administrative appointments. The new president had little use for quarrelsome intellectuals of any kind. The prescriptions of the party's assorted ideological factions were useless to a president with no agenda. Several neoconservatives became key advisers to Vice President Dan Quayle, who needed their intellectual ballast. A few others, notably Bernard Aronson, Constance Horner, and Paul Wolfowitz, landed positions in the Bush administration. Most of the neoconservatives, however, returned to their journals, think tanks, universities, and syndicated columns to resume their political battles. Their ongoing feud with "paleoconservatives" would constitute one front. (This conflict will be discussed in Chapter 7.) The neoconservatives viewed their feud with the traditional Right, however, as an unfortunate diversion from their chief mission. This was their fight against New Class liberalism.

The Concept of the New Class

As Chapter 2 will explain, the concept of the New Class is a product of anarchist and Trotskyist history, which was later popularized by James Burnham and Milovan Djilas.[27] As a critique of the role of intellectuals in modern society, the neoconservative conception of the New Class extends arguments developed by Joseph Schumpeter and F. A. Hayek in the 1940s.[28] However, the notion was first recycled in its contemporary form by long-time New York Intellectual critic David Bazelon in 1966. A former writer for Dwight Macdonald's iconoclastic *Politics*, Bazelon updated the theory of bureaucratic collectivism to explain modern American politics. "The chief effect of the creation of the corporate order, apart from the fact that it has worked so devastatingly well, is that it has also fairly fully undermined the previously existing system of private property," he observed.

Bazelon argued that corporate capitalism had created a New Class of non-property-owning managers, bureaucrats, and intellectuals "whose life conditions are determined by their position within or in relation to the corporate order."[29] Owning property was no longer the key to attaining status or power. The New Class was not out to accumulate capital. It gained status and power not through economic productivity, but through organizational position. To understand what was happening in America, Bazelon argued, one needed to grasp the peculiar interests of this recently burgeoning class. What was called "liberalism" in America was largely a rationalization of the interests of New Class managers, lawyers, bureau-crats, social workers, consultants, and academics. Liberalism rationalized the creation of an ever-expanding welfare state, providing meaningful employment and ego gratification for the hordes of newly educated consumers. It also rationalized massive investments in higher education, and thus provided prestigious employment for the scribbling set. Conser-vatives fought the welfare state in the name of commerce and traditional values—while playing the same game in their own ways. From his perch at the radical Institute for Policy Studies, Bazelon put a Macdonald-like spin on his argument, claiming that liberals and conservatives alike were creating a vast bureaucratic state designed "to administer everybody and everything."[30]

The neoconservatives, however, found more partisan uses for the idea of the New Class. They took their cue from Harrington. In his 1968 book, *Toward a Democratic Left*, Harrington argued that the idealism of Bazelon's newly educated New Class could lay the foundation for a new American liberalism. Having come to political consciousness during the 1960s, America's postwar baby-boom generation was nearing the point at which it could change traditional power relations. The ranks of the New Class were massively expanding as the sixties generation came of age. Huge numbers of newly educated baby-boomers were entering the professional middle class. Harrington wanted to recruit them to progressive politics. Though he conceded that Bazelon's fears about the New Class were amply founded, he argued that the new generation's experiences of the civil rights and antiwar movements predisposed them to an egalitarian, anti-imperialist politics. The children of the sixties were receiving a distinctive education. They were now presented with the opportunity to use their education to build a good society—or to protect their own new privileges. Rather than become the sophisticated enemy of the poor and working classes, Harrington argued, the New Class's next generation could be-come the "conscience constituency" for a new American progressivism.[31]

This was red meat for the neoconservatives. Novak launched the first attack on Harrington's overture to the New Class. Harrington's alternatives were bogus, he claimed, since "progressive politics" itself was fast becoming a vehicle for New Class interests. The New Class masked its own drive for power and prestige under the banner of compassion.[32] Kristol and Podhoretz quickly picked up the theme, arguing that the triumph of McGovernism in the Democratic party was attributable to the conceits and ambitions of the New Class. The battle cry of the Shachtmanites entered America's political mainstream as Novak, Kristol, and Podhoretz recycled the argument behind the Old Left's final schism. Virtually all of the neoconservatives soon invested great significance in the notion of the New Class. The amorphous nature of the concept gave them little pause. They repeatedly cited the same quotations from Bazelon and Harrington over the next twenty years. After the Soviet bloc imploded, many of them argued that the war against New Class culture comprised the essence of neoconservatism.

Neoconservatism germinated in the New York Intellectual tradition and soon developed into a variegated ideological movement. The structure and style of this book are designed to emphasize the movement's origins and its subsequent diversity. The book features a sustained tension between these themes. I shall equally emphasize that neoconservatism grew out of the Old Left and that much of the movement subsequently retained only an indirect relationship to its Old Left origins. Chapter 2 recounts the careers of neoconservatism's two most important New York Intellectual precursors, James Burnham and Sidney Hook, whose polemics against American moralism, appeasement, and New Class liberals laid the ideological groundwork for what was later called neoconservatism. Their work not only directly influenced many of the movement's original partisans—including Kristol, Shachtman, and the Shachtmanites—but also prefigured the politics of neoconservatism's dominant tradition in the 1980s, represented in this book by Podhoretz. The influence of neoconservatism's New York Intellectual background is therefore emphasized in the book's early and later chapters.

Neoconservatism would become a rich tapestry of many colors, however. Apart from their common revulsion for the sixties' antiwar protesters, the movement's chief figures came to neoconservatism by markedly different paths. Kristol broke from liberalism in the 1950s; Podhoretz turned Right at the end of the 1960s; the right-wing social democrats became neoconservatives in the early 1970s. Many neoconservatives were never part of, or significantly influenced by, the New York Intellectual tournaments of the 1930s and afterwards. Their role within neoconservatism is represented in this book principally by Novak and Berger.

I have taken a narrativist approach to neoconservatism on account of its diversity. This account focuses on Kristol, Podhoretz, Novak, and Berger, both because they are the movement's most influential theorists, with large bodies of published work to their credit, and because they represent different currents within neoconservatism. In his otherwise excellent book, *The Neoconservatives*, Peter Steinfels focused on Kristol, Daniel Bell, and Daniel Patrick Moynihan.[33] Moynihan has since reverted to his earlier liberalism, however, and Bell has convincingly maintained that he is not a neoconservative at all, but a liberal-socialist-conservative.[34]

If neoconservatism first became a force in American politics as an antidote to the antiwar New Politics of the late 1960s and early 1970s, the movement's earliest literature was, nonetheless, at least equally concerned with the direction of the welfare state. Neoconservative misgivings about American domestic policy predated the movement's name and the development of its infrastructure. Moynihan's warnings about the "law of unintended consequences" defined the movement's chief domestic concerns from the late sixties to the mid-seventies. These concerns were epitomized by *The Public Interest*, which doggedly catalogued the unintended consequences of the Great Society's antipoverty and welfare policies. Moynihan, Bell, Kristol, and Glazer repeatedly claimed that liberalism was transgressing the limits of social policy. Samuel P. Huntington warned that an "excess of democracy" was overloading the public sector with demands it could not fulfill.[35]

Steinfels's account of neoconservatism emphasized this side of the movement's agenda, which was amplified during the 1970s by such figures as Aaron Wildavsky, Roger Starr, Edward C. Banfield, Lewis Feuer, Edward Shils, James Q. Wilson, Seymour Martin Lipset, Paul Seabury, and Midge Decter. The neoconservatives never renounced unemployment insurance or Social Security. Most of them continued to support legislation for health and safety regulation. In the 1980s, their continued support for a minimal welfare state distinguished them from such conservatives as Charles Murray and George Gilder, who called for the dismantling of the welfare state. The neoconservatives were trying to repeal the 1960s, not the New Deal.

Throughout the 1980s, however, both Murray and Gilder published their attacks on the welfare state in neoconservative journals.[36] This development represented more than a venture in ecumenism. Neoconservatives opened their publications to social policy conservatives because, though they continued to distinguish themselves from America's antigovernment Right, their own grievances against the New Class were consuming their identification with Keynesian economics. Neoconservative disquisitions on the evils of welfare dependency, busing, affirmative action, progressive taxes, and (sometimes) even the minimum wage became increasingly difficult to distinguish from traditional conservative rhetoric against social engineering. Though they repeatedly reaffirmed their support for the welfare state, neoconservatives during the 1980s increasingly claimed that the *chief* consequences of government action were the unintended ones. The New Class not only was obstructing America's effort to fight communism, it was sapping America's vital entrepreneurial energies. The New Class wanted government to be strong and America to be weak. Neoconservatives fought the New Class on both fronts. Their skepticism about government efforts to promote greater equality hardened into principled opposition. The social democratic wing of the movement that Bell once represented was thus eclipsed. Bell and Moynihan distanced themselves from a movement that, to them, exaggerated the failures of the Great Society and the need for greater military spending and foreign military intervention. [37]

Neoconservatism was reshaped by the political debates of the 1980s and early 1990s. The figures examined in this book have been the movement's most influential theorists during this period, if not always its most widely recognized proponents. Due to their high-profile service in the Reagan administration, Kirkpatrick and Bennett became more widely known than any of their neoconservative colleagues. However, neither of them published major works that compared in scope or influence to the writings of Kristol, Podhoretz, Novak, or Berger. The substance and varieties of neoconservative thought are best represented by these four figures. Their writings have defined the movement's politics and vision. Their elaboration of a modernized conservatism has made conservatism intellectually respectable to many intellectuals.

The leftist background of neoconservatism aided this achievement. If the Old Left origins of neoconservatism faded during the 1980s, they never disappeared. Sidney Hook, Arnold Beichman, Arch Puddington, Bayard Rustin, Carl Gershman, Penn Kemble, Joshua Muravchik, and other refugees from American Marxism filled the pages of neoconservative organs throughout the 1980s, usually to claim that America was losing its war against communism. [38] The hatred for liberalism that neoconservatives expressed was only explicable against neoconservatism's Old Left background. The style and character of neoconservatism were also incomprehensible apart from the history of New York Intellectualism. "The neocons are the real heirs of the New York Intellectuals," Paul Berman observed. "They're the ones who still believe in the power of ideas—the conviction that if you can get the analysis of society straight, you'll accomplish great things."[39] Whether they can fashion an intellectual tradition lasting more than one generation is an open question.

2

The Struggle for the World:
The Forerunners

The forerunners of neoconservatism began their careers as communists. In the early 1930s, Sidney Hook and James Burnham were close friends and colleagues in the philosophy department at New York University. They were also propagandists for a de-Stalinized, American-style communism. Hook had studied at the Marx-Engels Institute in Moscow, was personally acquainted with numerous Communist party officials, and moved easily among the Stalinist, Trotskyist, and Bukharinist factions of the international communist movement. In 1932, he signed the declaration by radical American intellectuals, "Culture and Crisis," which endorsed the Communist party's presidential ticket. Like Sherwood Anderson, who supported the Communists "because they mean it," Hook was contemptuous of what was then called Norman Thomas socialism. The Communists alone stood for revolution.

Hook and Burnham were put off, however, by the Communist party's intellectual sterility. While they accepted the party's chief political and economic principles—including the dictatorship of the proletariat and the need to abolish political dissent—they were offended by the party's unscientific spirit and the crudeness of its dialectical materialism. The following year, when A. J. Muste founded the American Workers party as an independent communist alternative to the Communist party, Hook and Burnham became the new party's chief ideologists. "Despite its best revolutionary intentions," they declared, "the Communist Party has neither advanced the cause of revolutionizing the situation of the masses, nor has it done anything to advance the immediate interests of the producing classes." The party had, rather, "brought disgrace to the term Communism."[1]

Their project was to complete the task at which William English

19

Walling, Eugene Debs, and Max Eastman before them had fallen short: to translate revolutionary Marxism into an American idiom. They believed that Marxism had few followers in America mainly because it lacked an American vocabulary and style. Hook addressed the problem by recasting Marxist categories into the language of American philosophical pragmatism. In his brilliantly didactic, logic-chopping reformulation of Marx's dialectic, *Towards the Understanding of Karl Marx*, he contended that Marxism and American pragmatism shared the same essential methodological empiricism. Like American pragmatism, Marxism was realistic and materialistic, basing itself on the stream of human experience rather than on metaphysical or other abstract constructions of reason. Marxism was a theory of social revolution "based on the observable tendencies of social development."[2] It was not impartial, but was nonetheless objective by virtue of its empirical orientation. "The objective truth of Marxism realizes itself in the informed revolutionary act," Hook explained. "Marxism is neither a science nor a myth, but a realistic method of social action."[3]

Hook was straightforward about the kind of social action that Marx had in mind. For Marx, he observed, the state was "an expression of the irreconcilable class antagonisms generated by the social relations of economic production."[4] As Marx himself put it in *The Communist Manifesto*, "The modern state power is merely a committee which manages the common business of the bourgeoisie." The aim of Marxism was to smash the state and establish the dictatorship of the proletariat. This aim could only be achieved, Hook instructed, by a revolutionary party "free from the twin faults of sectarianism and opportunism, and therefore capable of properly exploiting every lead towards the seizure of power." This was revolutionary realism. The Marxist attitude toward violence was similarly objective. "For Marx, the use of force in a revolutionary situation was no more a moral problem than the use of fire in ordinary life," Hook explained. "It was only the *intelligent* use of force which constituted a problem." To use force in a revolutionary struggle to overthrow the state was only morally degrading if it was done badly.

It was axiomatic for Hook that all existing forms of government must be abolished ("Wherever we find a state, there we find a dictatorship") and that the ultimate end of the revolution must be to establish a classless society. For those who suffered the "dictates of revolutionary necessity," he granted, the violence and terror of the revolution would undoubtedly seem to be "spawned of hell," but these dictates were nonetheless uncompromising. "The first task the proletarian dictatorship must accomplish is to crush all actual or incipient counter-revolutionary movements," he declared. "Revolutionary terrorism is the answer of the proletariat to the political terrorism of counter-revolution." Before any proletarian dictator-ship could pave the way to communism, it first needed to crush the advocates of other ways. Hook ascribed a scientific status even to Marx's vision of a stateless revolutionary society. Under communism, the state would be unnecessary, because the state functioned only to rationalize and defend class privilege.[5]

Towards the Understanding of Karl Marx carefully avoided current factional debates. In the early months of 1933, Hook was still hoping to influence the direction of the American Communist party. He thus refrained from criticizing recent developments in the Soviet Union, and was rewarded with an invitation to meet Earl Browder, the national party chief, at the party's national headquarters. Browder went straight to the point. Hook was an intellectual and therefore had romantic misconceptions about the revolution. This explained his occasional criticisms of Engels and Lenin. The intellectuals always thought they could teach the party how to run the revolution. Browder nonetheless took him seriously. Even an unaffiliated intellectual like Hook could perform real services for the party, he observed. Browder proposed that Hook set up a national network of fellow-travelers to assist the party's propaganda effort (Hook pleaded lack of time) and organize government workers into "independent associations" (Hook was slow to realize that this meant dual unionism). Browder saved his chief proposal for last: He asked Hook to set up a national spy apparatus at American universities that would report to the party on new military and industrial experiments.

Hook was both honored and repelled by the requests. He protested that he wasn't a party member, but Browder assured him that these were tasks best performed by a fellow-traveler. The meeting shook him. If he believed his own writings, did he have good reasons for turning Browder down? His bizarre encounter with the party chief forced Hook to rethink his relationship to the communist movement. He had assumed, while writing his book on Marxism, that a new movement was needed to save communism from the Communist party. His book had been written to give voice to the realistic and emancipatory social vision that was needed. The pragmatic core of Marxism had been buried, he believed, under the dogmatism of the Stalinist regime and its affiliated national parties. But his writings backed away from making this argument.

In the fall of 1933, Hook resolved to clarify his position. He began to argue for an alternative communist movement and to devote himself to building one. With Muste, he founded a new communist party, the American Workers party (AWP). His widely reprinted article, "Why I Am a Communist," presented the rationale for the new party. "It seems to me that only communism can save the world from its social evils; it seems to me to be just as evident that the official Communist Party or any of its subsidiary organizations cannot be regarded as a Marxist, critical, or revolutionary party today," he declared. "The conclusion is, therefore, clear: the time has come to build a new communist party and a new communist international."[6] The literature of the AWP would present Marxism as a revolutionary form of American pragmatism, mixing Marx and Lenin with the formulations of Hook's mentor, John Dewey.

Though he had only recently converted to the revolutionary movement, Burnham immediately became a party theorist and official, writing for the AWP paper, *Labor Action*, and serving briefly as party secretary. He was quick to absorb the world view of his new associates, writing in 1934 that Hitler was "no Teutonic accident," but was, rather, "the cultural price we pay for the preservation of private property." The same year, however, Burnham showed a stronger sense of reality while contemplating the fortunes of his new party. Faced with the party's failure to build a serious national organization, he began, on Hook's urging, to campaign for a merger with the Communist League of America (the American Trotskyist party). The new party would be called the Workers party.

Hook encouraged Burnham's overtures to the Trotskyists and agreed to lead the AWP's negotiations with them. When the merger was completed, however, Hook chose not to join the new organization that he instigated. During the previous year, he had convinced AWP leaders that Marx's references to the dictatorship of the proletariat were primarily economic and could be replaced by the phrase "workers' democracy."[7] Marx had envisioned a society run by the workers themselves, who constituted an overwhelming majority. But the Trotskyists were unreconstructed Leninists. For them, the dictatorship of the proletariat meant the dictatorship of a revolutionary vanguardist party *over* the proletariat and all other groups. They had no concept of democracy for anyone, except themselves. They assumed that socialism required a one-party dictatorship (Hook favored a pluralism of revolutionary workers' parties) and that the workers' councils would hold no authority over the party. When the Trotskyists belatedly embraced the principles of workers' democracy in the later stages of their negotiations with the AWP, Hook was not fooled. He had worked to build a de-Stalinized communist party in the United States, but he eschewed the company and the practical tasks it would bring. Having backed away from the embrace of the Communist party, he was now backing away from his alternative to it. Though he would claim an affinity with Marxism for the rest of his life, his decision not to join the Workers party marked the beginning of his journey toward the far side of the anticommunist divide.

Hook's decision also left the intellectual guardianship of the Workers party to Burnham, who joined Max Shachtman as co-editor of the party's theoretical organ, *The New International*. The Workers party quickly turned into a vehicle for Trotsky's crusade for a Fourth International, and Burnham became the oddest figure in American Trotskyism's colorful history.

Burnham was the son of a wealthy, British-born Chicago railroad industrialist. He had delivered a Latin valedictory address at Princeton—where he studied under T. S. Eliot—and he later studied neo-Thomism under Martin D'Arcy at Oxford. His intently upper-class lifestyle and his well-bred manners went unaffected by his conversion to communism. His melodramatic broadsides against Stalinism and the New Deal were ferried to party offices by functionaries not otherwise acquainted with high society. Hook later recalled the embarrassment that Burnham's wife regularly experienced upon finding a seedy-looking Trotskyist at her Sutton Place door, waving an urgent telegram from Trotsky or the proofs of an article for *The Militant* or *The New International*. The embarrassment was apparently mutual, since these messengers often found Burnham in formal dinner dress, partying with his hard-drinking upper-class guests. "Burnham would excuse himself, have a hurried whispered consultation with his comrades, and then return to his dinner party," Hook recounted. It was not unusual for Burnham to arrive at cell meetings dressed in a tuxedo, en route to cocktails with the Rockefellers or other friends. Like Hook, William Barrett would later recall that Burnham's personal manners were unfailingly gentlemanlike. If Burnham's fellow revolutionaries could never reconcile his lifestyle with his flaming communist polemics, Hook recounted, his family and friends could only have been relieved when, "in the course of his evolution toward anticommunism, then anti-Marxism, and finally antisocialism, his social life suffered from no embarrassing lapses."[8]

Burnham's communist phase was a serious affair, however. He was a philosopher of literature and Eliot enthusiast when he arrived at New York University in 1930, having served as editor of the *Nassau Literary Review* at Princeton. During his early career he avoided politics, devoting himself to literary criticism. With his senior colleague, Philip Wheelwright, he wrote a widely admired philosophical textbook that used passages from literature to explain epistemological problems.[9] He and Wheelwright also edited *The Symposium*, a literary journal that prefigured *Partisan Review* in certain respects. Burnham's early writings focused on Eliot's poetry, the epistemological status of poetry and literature, the literary metaphysics of William Faulkner, the literary criticism of I. A. Richards and the "New Critics"—and Trotsky's *History of the Russian Revolution*. His review of Trotsky offered the first hint of his inner struggle over politics. Burnham found the book intoxicating. He raved about Trotsky's dazzling literary style and method, confessing that reading his remarkable account of the Bolshevik revolution had been an exciting experience. [10]

He was determined not to become a Marxist, however. Though he never shared the New Critics' claims for the autonomy of art, Burnham's early writings were often criticized by Marxists for avoiding politics. He ventured a first response in January 1933. "Marxism and Esthetics" staked out a middle ground between the New Criticism's "art for art's sake" fetishism and the crude reductionism of the Marxist demand for social relevance. With his customary precision and emotional detachment, Burnham argued that any worthy aesthetic criticism needed to be mindful of political issues while refusing to submit to any political test or criterion. So-called socialist realism was a formula for the destruction of art. It was derived from a false philosophy—Marxism—that presented "an order of values not acceptable to man nor in keeping with man's nature." Because Marxism undermined the basis of aesthetic judgment and offered an "inhuman" moral perspective, Burnham would not invest his hopes in any aesthetic that Marxism might produce. [11]

Nine months later he called for a revolutionary seizure of power and announced that he accepted the dictatorship of the proletariat "as the indispensable instrument of the revolution." It would not be his last dramatic reversal. A summer tour of the country had brought Burnham, for the first time, into direct contact with the misery and desperation of auto workers, coal miners, farmers, and the unemployed. The impact of these encounters was reinforced by his friendship with Hook and his reading of *Towards the Understanding of Karl Marx*. Burnham's conversion to communism was decisively influenced, however, by Adolf A. Berle and Gardiner C. Means's classic 1933 study of corporate capitalism, *The Modern Corporation and Private Property*. [12]

The book was a revelation to him. It charted not only the massive maldistribution of wealth in the United States, but also the making of a revolution within corporate capitalism itself. With the advent of the modern corporation, Berle and Means argued, effective control over the use of corporate capital had passed from its owners to a managerial class of administrators. The authors regarded this development as a boon to their own liberalism, but for Burnham it confirmed the accuracy of Hook's Marxism. Berle and Means argued that managerial capitalism represented a revolution in the social relations of production, transferring effective control over the process of investment to a more enlightened class of educated and public-minded administrators. To Burnham, however, managerial capitalism was merely a more sophisticated—and thus more deadly—form of capitalism. The separation of ownership from control did not change class and property relations, or question the profit motive, or equalize the existing maldistribution of wealth. Burnham would later return to the same theme when he was finished with communism. In 1933, however, the evidence that modern capitalism was generating unacceptable disparities of wealth and mutating into more slippery and sophisticated forms of organization drove him into the arms of the communists. John Diggins later observed that Burnham became a communist less from philosophical conviction than from a sense of desperation. He was skeptical from the beginning about dialectical materialism, the withering away of the state, the classless society, and the slogan of "to each according to his needs." "Need" is an impulse limited only by imagination, he noted. For the remainder of the decade, he would defend a Trotskyist variant of Marxism, not because he was convinced that Marxism was true, but because it was "our only hope."[13]

Burnham's apologetic strategy sought to strip Marxism of its Hegelian ethos and to emphasize the concrete proletarian struggle for power. The theory of dialectical materialism was "only a disguised form of monistic objective idealism," he wrote, conceding to Max Eastman that Marxism had taken on the characteristics of a religion. Authentic Marxism was a scientific instrument, or rather, a revolutionary strategy "which insolubly combines scientific objectivity with the intransigent struggle for power." The mission of a revitalized communist movement was to build a Fourth International committed to Lenin's original conception of proletarian dictatorship. Burnham was the chief spokesman for this cause throughout the 1930s, and he was repeatedly called upon by Trotsky to rationalize or implement his tactical maneuvers. It was Burnham who orchestrated the Trotskyists' entry into the Socialist party in 1936 and Burnham again, the following year, who reluctantly carried out Trotsky's order to split the party and form the Socialist Workers party.[14] These intrigues earned the Trotskyists a host of enemies on the Left.

The year after they carried out their deceitful manipulation of the Socialists and were expelled by the Socialist party, a series of revelations about Trotsky's role in the suppression of the Kronstadt rebellion raised deeper questions about his moral character and the morality of his politics. In 1921, a group of sailors from the Kronstadt soviet had announced the liberation of their workers' council from the dictatorship of the Communist party. After their rebellion was crushed by Bolshevik troops, the captured sailors were executed on Trotsky's order. The belated revelations about Trotsky's practice of shooting hostages and his role in the massacre of the captured Kronstadt sailors ignited a firestorm of moral criticism from American progressives. Hook, Dewey, Eastman, Dwight Macdonald, Bertram Wolfe, and Trotsky entered an impassioned discussion over the political morality of means and ends. Their debate extended to the equally troublesome question of whether Leninism led to Stalinism.[15]

By then, most of these American radicals were prepared to concede that the violence and tyranny of Lenin's dictatorship had laid the foundations for Stalinism. For many, the recent revelations about Trotsky's past suggested that the essential difference between Trotsky and Stalin was that Trotsky lost. The poet Selden Rodman spoke for these disillusioned leftists when he questioned whether a Trotskyist regime in the Soviet Union would have been any less murderous than the existing Stalinist regime. Did not Trotsky and Stalin both share a "common grounding in Marxist absolutism and its dependency on violence?" he asked.[16] The question drove many leftists in the late thirties, including Hook, to disavow their earlier support for any variant of real or imagined Leninism.

The question left Burnham unmoved, however. He had little patience with the moral qualms of liberals or wavering leftists. The so-called moral issues, he explained, like the liberal cries for "freedom" and "truth," were either meaningless abstractions (if invoked as absolutes) or were relativized by their embodiment in specific historical contexts. For communists, the moral question was always relativized in the realm of means by the revolutionary goal—the achievement of socialism. Burnham found nothing in Trotsky's past to give him pause.

In their 1939 roundup of what they called "intellectuals in retreat," he and Shachtman castigated those supposed revolutionaries who had lost their stomachs for the real thing. The list included Eastman, Hook, Dewey, Edmund Wilson, Philip Rahv, Eugene Lyons, and nine others. Burnham and Shachtman attacked these backsliders for their "negative, irresponsible, and unprincipled" deviations from revolutionary communism. Having begun with criticisms of Stalinism that were usually justified, the authors noted, these purported revolutionaries were now impugning the principles of Marxism-Leninism itself. They were casting doubt on the theory of dialectical materialism, criticizing the doctrine of one-party dictatorship, insinuating that Leninism was the source of Stalinism, and even making sniveling complaints about "the harsh tone of revolutionary polemics."[17] For Burnham and Shachtman, Hook's recent critique of the Bolshevik revolution exemplified the cowardice and bad faith of the backsliders.[18]

Hook had broken with Stalinism in the mid-thirties over the theory of "social fascism"—the Stalinist doctrine that social democracy and fascism were twins. The vulgarity of this formulation had been too much even for a defender of communist terror like Hook. The Moscow Trials of 1936–37 drove him shortly afterward to adopt the opposite thesis—that it was Stalinism that deserved to be linked with fascism.

Despite their contempt for Stalin, Hook's argument made the Trotskyists nervous from the outset. Like Hook, the Trotskyists were enraged by the frame-ups of Trotsky and others at the Moscow Trials, but Hook's linkage between Stalinism and fascism threatened to impugn communism itself. Their fears were confirmed in the later thirties, when Hook, Lyons, and others began to advance the "incredibly vulgar conclusion" that the evils of Stalinism could be traced to the Leninist doctrine of one-party dictatorship. [19] This argument implicated the Trotskyists. "Since Trotskyism is also the child of Leninism, communism in its Leninist and Trotskyist form as well as in its Stalinist perversion is shown to be the twin of fascism," Burnham and Shachtman observed. [20]

Their furious response epitomized the movement's rhetorical style. What Hook now seemed to hold against the Bolsheviks, they incredulously observed, was that the Bolsheviks hadn't relinquished state power to the only possible alternative. If the Bolsheviks had abandoned the revolution, they could have kept themselves morally pure and escaped the accusations of later progressive moralists that they paved the way for Stalinism. The accusation itself was disproved, however, by the fact that Stalin found it necessary to murder Lenin's colleagues and abolish Lenin's policies "on the hundred and one questions of colonial revolt, trade unions, united front, war, the soviet organization of society." Since Hook and the others knew these things (Hook, after all, had taught them to Burnham only a few years before), their heresies could only be attributed to inner weakness and "pathetic self-deception." [21]

Hook's backsliding had done some good for the movement. His disgust with the Moscow Trials had moved him to organize the Commission on Inquiry, chaired by Dewey, which exposed the hypocrisy and injustice of the Soviet frame-ups. The Trotskyists were therefore indebted to him. Nonetheless, he was at the same time becoming a peculiarly troublesome critic of communism itself. As a result of his "overreaction" to the Moscow Trials, the doctrine of social fascism, and the worsening tyranny of the Soviet state, he was undermining revolutionary Marxism while claiming to be saving it.

Hook further confirmed this interpretation of his position the following spring, when he enlisted ten of the "backsliders" to sign the manifesto of a new organization called the Committee for Cultural Freedom. The document, written chiefly by Lyons, was signed by 142 intellectuals, including Dewey, Eastman, and Norman Thomas. It warned that the "tide of totalitarianism" was rising throughout the world. "Through subsidized propaganda, through energetic agents, through political pressure, the totalitarian states succeed in infecting other countries with their false doctrines, in intimidating independent artists and scholars, and in spreading panic among intellectuals. . . . Unless totalitarianism is combated wherever and in whatever form it manifests itself, it will spread in America."[22] The statement explicitly placed Soviet communism under the same category as German and Japanese fascism. Just as "Culture and Crisis" had lined up American intellectuals to support communism in 1932, Hook was now organizing intellectual opposition to communism in the name of opposing totalitarianism of all kinds.

Hook's efforts were rewarded with an enraged counterattack from the fellow-traveling and procommunist Left. Macdonald announced the formation of the Committee for Cultural Freedom and Socialism, which denounced the "currently fashionable catchword: 'neither communism nor fascism.' " The group included Burnham, Rahv, James Farrell, and William Phillips. They explained that their concept of cultural freedom was more substantive and inclusive than the bourgeois formalism of Hook's group. True cultural freedom required socialism, or as they put it, the liberation of culture was "inseparable from the liberation of the working classes and of all humanity." A more hysterical reaction was orchestrated by Corliss Lamont's procommunist American–Soviet Friendship Committee, which published a group letter in The Daily Worker that condemned the Committee for Cultural Freedom's manifesto as a reactionary smear. Since the reactionaries in Hook's group couldn't get far with a straightforwardly fascist appeal, the letter explained, they had promoted the "fantastic falsehood" that the Soviet and totalitarian states were basically alike. This was the kind of smear that only "fascists and their allies" made in order to rupture the united front of progressive forces. Most of the letter's signatories were party hacks and fellow-travelers, but the fellow-travelers included Harry F. Ward, Max Lerner, F. O. Matthiessen, Dashiell Hammett, Carey McWilliams, and Waldo Frank. It was also signed by a handful of communist intellectuals, including Clifford Odets, John Howard Lawson, and Richard Wright. Thus the line was drawn between the democratic and procommunist sides of the American Left, only a few days before the signing of the Nazi–Soviet pact.[23]

The announcement of the non-aggression agreement between Hitler and Stalin on August 24, 1939, was traumatizing for the procommunist Left—excepting the Trotskyists. Trotsky's hatred for Stalin and his shrewd reading of Stalin's foreign policy goals had prepared his followers for a Soviet agreement with Hitler. When the pact was announced, it confirmed their realism. Burnham had long regarded a Nazi–Soviet alliance as likely. The convulsions it caused among the fellow-travelers and Communist party members confirmed, as well, his sense of superiority.

The shocker came a week later, when Trotsky reversed course and declared his support for the Soviet troops invading Poland. The announcement was a bombshell for Burnham and many of his comrades. Nothing in their devious tradition had prepared them for (what seemed to them) this final betrayal of principle. Trotsky's declaration ignited an intense debate among his followers—and reminded Burnham and Shachtman of Eastman's earlier warning to them, that Trotsky was above all a Russian nationalist and a man of state. The debate within the Socialist Workers party heated to a climax when Stalin declared war on Finland. Trotsky incredibly argued that Stalin's expropriation of Polish and Ukrainian estates and his military advance into the eastern front were "progressive." A "degenerated workers' state" was still a workers' state. The gains of October were not to be renounced. Since public ownership was the defining feature of Soviet society, the Soviet Union at war was a deformed but nonetheless objectively progressive nation that all Marxist-Leninists were obliged to defend. [24]

This was too much even for Burnham, and after six months of ferocious factional fighting over the issue, he resigned from the Socialist Workers party in 1940. He confessed to Trotsky in February that he had apparently been seduced into socialism by the power of Marxist imagery and by the "sudden, witty, flashing metaphors" that sparkled through Trotsky's pages. "Here, I believe, is the heart of the mystery of the dialectic, as it appears in your books and articles," he wrote. "The dialectic, for you, is a *device of style*—the contrasting epithets, the flowing rhythms, the verbal paradoxes which characterize your way of writing." Trotsky's artful use of dialectic made him think he could rationalize anything—including Soviet attacks on Poland and Finland. His "bewildering shifts in position," always justified by dialectical reasoning, had finally led him "to defend a false theory and a wrong policy; and to stand as attorney for a cynical group of small-time bureaucrats," Burnham concluded. [25]

Burnham and Shachtman both gave up on Leninism. They gave in to the arguments of the backsliders, which they had only recently denounced. The doubts they entertained all along came roaring out. Burnham and Shachtman left the party at the same time with the same borrowed theory of "bureaucratic collectivism" ringing in their heads.

THE NEW CLASS AND THE QUESTION OF BUREAUCRATIZATION

The idea of the New Class is a product of anarchist and Trotskyist history. As early as the mid-1920s, the notion of the Soviet Union as a workers' state was disputed by Marxists and anarchists—some of them in Stalin's concentration camps—who referred to the Soviet regime as a state capitalist order run by a "New Class" of professional bureaucrats.

From his internal Soviet exile in 1929, Christian Rakovsky characterized the Soviet leadership as a new "class of rulers" whose power was based on "a type (also new) of private property: the possession of the state power."[26] This contention drew upon a tradition of pre-Bolshevik anarchist criticism represented by Michael Bakunin, Peter Kropotkin, and Jan Waclaw Machajski. Bakunin had warned in his debates with Marx in the 1870s that state socialism would produce a new managerial class that ruled over the workers in the name of their revolution. Machajski applied this critique specifically to the Russian social democratic intellectuals, arguing that intellectuals were scheming to replace the capitalist class by riding a proletarian revolution to power.[27] These arguments were later popularized in Max Nomad's accounts of the revolutionary tradition in the 1930s.[28] The theory of the New Class was revived and significantly reworked, however, in the factional Trotskyist debates of the later 1930s—to Trotsky's disapproval.

Trotskyism was based on the premise that the Soviet regime would either move forward to socialism or backward to capitalism. This assumption was challenged by Burnham and Joseph Carter in 1937, however, at the founding congress of the Socialist Workers party. The Trotskyists had just been expelled from the Socialist party. Seeking to revise their movement's position on the Soviet Union, Burnham and Carter questioned Trotsky's either/or formulation. The degenerated workers' state was taking on a viable structure of its own, they argued. Burnham and Carter did not (yet) question the duty of revolutionists to defend the Soviet regime "from imperialist attacks." The gains of October remained basically unchanged in the Soviet economic structure, though even here the bureaucracy was "actively sabotaging the plan." In the past year, they claimed, the Soviet bureaucracy had decisively committed itself to destroying its nationalized economy. What was less clear was the revolution's direction. The Soviet Union wasn't degenerating into capitalism, but it wasn't moving toward socialism either. A third alternative, not accounted for in Marxist theory, appeared to be taking shape. The Soviet Union was apparently turning into neither a workers' state nor a bourgeois state, but a bureaucratic deformation of a workers' state. If this was the case, the Trotskyist movement needed to account for what had happened. [29]

Trotsky swiftly informed his (unidentified) American disciples that there was no third alternative, and therefore no need to account for one. His article "Not a Workers' and Not a Bourgeois State?" reproved "B. and C." for obscuring the crucial issue. Their error was the kind of thing that one expected from anarchists and radical dandies, he snapped, "who are used to hopping carelessly from twig to twig." He expected more from revolutionary Marxists. Trotsky conceded that the Soviet Union was not a workers' state in the Marxist sense of the term. "This simply means that the USSR does not correspond to the norms of a workers' state as set forth in our program," he argued. "Our program has counted upon a progressive development of the workers' state and by that token upon its gradual withering away. But history, which does not always act 'according to a program,' has confronted us with the process of a degenerating workers' state." History had its own lessons, as Marx had warned. "A workers' state does not create a new society in one day," Trotsky lectured. "Marx wrote that in the first period of a workers' state the *bourgeois* norms of distribution are still preserved. One has to weigh well and think this thought out to the end. The workers' state itself, as a *state*, is necessary exactly because the bourgeois norms of distribution still remain in force." [30]

Trotsky tried to assure the Americans that he wasn't clinging to Marxist dogmas. "We are not, it goes without saying, fetishists; should new historical facts demand a revision of the theory, we would not stop at doing so," he claimed. The facts trumpeted by "B. and C." were not new, he reminded them. Lenin had conceded fifteen years earlier that the Soviet regime was riddled with "bureaucratic deformations." For Trotsky, the crucial point was that, with all of its deformations, the Soviet state had not reverted to capitalism. A liver poisoned by malaria didn't cease to be a liver, he reasoned. The nationalized Soviet economy made the Soviet Union a workers' state worth defending—albeit a "partial and mutilated expression of a backward and isolated workers' state." [31]

Burnham was not reassured, however. Trotsky's reply struck him as a model of fetishism. Italian Trotskyist fellow-traveler Bruno Rizzi, who read the exchange in the French Trotskyist press, had the same reaction. Rizzi's response to this debate would raise the argument over bureaucratic collectivism to a new level of intensity. His book, *La Bureaucratisation du Monde*, was published in 1939 and was immediately seized upon by Trotsky as an example of what came from denying that the Soviet Union was a workers' state. *La Bureaucratisation du Monde* developed a sustained argument, in the movement's polemical-factional mode, for the theory of

bureaucratic collectivism. Building on the fragmented tradition of anarchist criticism, Rizzi argued that the Bolshevik revolution had created a
new ruling class that converted the means of production into a new form
of property. "Possession of the state gives the bureaucracy possession of all
those goods which, despite being socialized, do not belong any the less to
the new ruling class," he observed. "The Soviet state, rather than becoming socialized, is becoming bureaucratized; instead of gradually dissolving
into a society without classes, it is growing immeasurably."[32]

Rizzi reproached Trotsky for fetishizing Marx's predictions. Taking
his argument from Marx, Trotsky had lectured Burnham and Carter that
the bourgeois state would be abolished by the proletarian revolution and
replaced by the workers' state. There was no middle way for history to
take. Rizzi charged that it was "the lazy answer of a Marxist content to
echo literally the thoughts of the master." Trotsky had become like the
Jesuits, he claimed, "who, when short of arguments, drown you with
quotations from this or that saint, to thwart one's argument." Good
Marxists examined contemporary events in the light of Marxist method,
Rizzi argued. They didn't try to make contemporary events fit the schematism of the master's forecasts. Marx didn't foresee the rise of a bureaucratic
class that would own the state in a nationalized class form. This was the
reality that confronted his followers, however.[33]

Trotsky never replied directly to Rizzi, but he used Rizzi's book in his
factional disputes with Burnham, Carter, and Shachtman. The crucial
issue, he argued, was whether the Soviet bureaucracy was to be categorized as a caste (which was based on functions of control) or as a class
(which was based on ownership). He called the Stalinist bureaucracy a
"caste" and argued that no bureaucratic establishment could rightly be
called a class, because a class was defined by its independent role in the
structure of an economy. Each class worked out its own special forms of
property, which was not true of bureaucracies. To call the Soviet regime
a class was to obliterate the either/or. Trotsky refused to take that fateful
step. "Bruno R. has caught on to the fact that the tendencies of collectivization assume, as a result of the political prostration of the working class,
the form of 'bureaucratic collectivism,' " he observed. "The phenomenon
in itself is incontestable. But what are its limits, and what is its historical
weight?"[34] He answered that the phenomenon was a passing aberration.
Trotsky held out for the degenerated workers' state. The socialist mission
of the proletariat had not changed, he argued; the existing Soviet order
was not a sustainable alternative to socialism, but a perversion of socialism
that had to be overthrown.

For Burnham and Shachtman, however, the theory of bureaucratic collectivism explained more than the recent history of Soviet communism. Following Rizzi's lead, they argued that the traditional definition of a class did not cover the new form of social organization invented in the Soviet Union. "What we have called the consummated usurpation of power by the Stalinist bureaucracy was, in reality, nothing but the self-realization of the bureaucracy as a class and its seizure of state power from the proletariat, the establishment of its own state power and its own rule," Shachtman asserted. He noted that before the Bolshevik revolution, Trotsky and Lenin had repeatedly observed that socialism would never succeed in Russia without the aid of the international proletariat. A workers' state could never be achieved in an economically backward country merely by socializing poverty. What Trotsky now failed to consider, Shachtman explained, was that his own prediction had come true. The Bolsheviks were left on their own and the workers' state *was* overthrown, though not by a bourgeois restoration, but by a new kind of counterrevolutionary class. "The old crap was revived," Shachtman wrote, "in a new, unprecedented, hitherto unknown form, the rule of a new bureaucratic class."[35]

When the state owned the means of production, the crucial question became, Who owns the state? This question eventually drove Shachtman, after a prolonged bout with quasi-Trotskyism, to a form of democratic state socialism. The only true workers' state, he would argue, would be a state that was democratically owned and controlled by workers. The history of Soviet communism was not part of the history of socialism at all, because democracy was the essence of socialism. Just as the defining feature of capitalism was private ownership and the defining feature of communism was totalitarian ownership, the defining feature of socialism was democratic ownership and control. Having co-founded American Trotskyism in 1929, Shachtman was forced by the first gleanings of this conclusion to start over again, a decade later, this time in one of the smaller sects of American radicalism.

In April 1940, Shachtman left the Socialist Workers party to form the new Workers party. (Originality in nomenclature, as Macdonald observed, was not a strong point in these circles.) Macdonald, Irving Howe, and young Irving Kristol followed Shachtman into this new "Third Camp" revolutionary socialist party. Shachtman would later become the chief theorist of "democratic Marxism" and mentor of the Young Socialist League grouplet in which Michael Harrington received his political education. He would later move to the far Right of the Socialist party, after maneuvering his Independent Socialist League into the party of Debs and Thomas. His winding sectarian journey eventually led him to Hook's right-wing social democratic politics. Their disciples would become the first neoconservatives. Like Hook, Shachtman combined a militant anti-communism with a democratic reading of Marx. Shachtman took longer than Hook to find his political home, however. He spent most of the 1940s and 1950s trying to build a post-Trotskyist movement among the tiny coteries of leftists who spoke his language. [36]

MANAGERS AND MACHIAVELLIANS:
BURNHAM'S RIGHT TURN

Burnham gave this option only a few weeks. He followed Shachtman into the Workers party, but resigned shortly afterward, in May 1940, explaining that he no longer accepted the Leninist theory of the party and had never accepted the theory of dialectical materialism. "Marxist economics seems to me for the most part either false or obsolete or meaningless in application to contemporary economic phenomena," he wrote. [37] He was finished with radicalism. The lesson he took from the emergence of bureaucratic collectivism was not the need for democratic socialism, but the need to understand the dynamics of what he called the "worldwide managerial revolution."

The argument of Burnham's monumental bestseller, *The Managerial Revolution*, took shape in his mind during his final months of debate with Trotsky. The book was published less than a year after his break from the Trotskyists. "During the past twenty years many elements of the theory have been included in various articles and books, to which I must acknowledge a general indebtedness without being able to name any particular one by which I have been especially influenced," he declared at the outset. It would be his only acknowledgment. [38] For many years afterward his critics, including Rizzi, would claim that he plagiarized Rizzi's book. None of Burnham's accusers ever proved, however, that he stole Rizzi's formulations—some of which elaborated Burnham's own arguments with Trotsky. The concept of the New Class was original to neither of them. Whether Burnham directly borrowed from Rizzi's book, or even saw the book before writing *The Managerial Revolution*, would remain unknown. [39] His version of New Class theory turned the notion of bureaucratic collectivism into a planetary explanation of (as the subtitle put it) "What Is Happening in the World."

What was happening was the emergence of a new social system in which control over the means of production—the basis of capitalist power—was passing not to the working class, but to a new class of managers. It was not merely a Soviet phenomenon. Burnham explained that the ongoing war in Europe was itself an important but secondary episode in the working out of the managerial revolution. The book owed most of its enormous commercial success to its timing and to its strangely commanding tone and assurances. Burnham's chief assurance was that the seemingly chaotic whirl of current events could be explained rationally. Inexorable social forces were at work. The former Trotskyist still knew the story behind the newspaper stories. The newspapers were filled with accounts of the German invasion of the Balkans and the Nazi subjugation of France and Scandinavia, but Burnham explained that the war was merely a phase in the managerial revolution. The hegemonic power of the capitalist class was shifting not to the workers, but to a managerial class of administrators, finance-executives, finance-capitalists, and major stock-holders. The emerging new world order would be shaped by the struggles of this nationally diverse New Class for domestic and international power.

The theory did not require any awareness by the managers of what they were doing. "Nor will the bulk of those who have done, and will do, the fighting in the struggle be recruited from the ranks of the managers themselves," Burnham argued. "Most of the fighters will be workers and youths who will doubtless, many of them, believe that they are fighting for ends of their own." The fact that neither the beneficiaries nor the servants of the revolution understood what they were doing proved the inexorability of the social forces at work. In Burnham's account, even the intellectuals were unaware that all their theorizing in the name of truth and the common good was contributing "to the power and privilege of the managers and to the building of a new structure of class rule."[40]

The Nazi–Soviet pact was an important example of a world event that could only be explained by managerialist theory. "Faced with an ultimate challenge, with the first great opening war of managerial society, Hitler and Stalin acted altogether correctly, from their point of view," Burnham explained. Both sides needed first to "drive death wounds into capitalism" before they could consolidate their strategic bases for the next round of the managerial war. There was no other plausible explanation of the pact.

The inexorable logic of managerialism could be seen in the replacement of representative institutions in the Soviet Union, Germany, and the United States by centralized managerial systems. In the Soviet Union, the workers' councils had given way to Stalinism; in Germany, the Weimar Republic was replaced by Nazi fascism; in the United States, a republican system was being overtaken by the steadily expanding statism of the New Deal. An inner drive toward hierarchy and centralization was inherent in modern industrialized societies. Neither capital nor labor could match the partly unconscious but nonetheless self-aggrandizing drive for power of —

the New Class. All of the industrial world's revolutions were managerial revolutions. [41]

To comprehend the social forces at work was to foresee the outcome of the war. Writing in 1940, Burnham took a German victory for granted and predicted that three competing "superstates" would control the world after the war. The war itself was relatively insignificant, since the structure of the coming world order was already evident. Burnham made no attempt to conceal his admiration for the imperial ambitions and efficiency of the Nazis. He argued that German control over Europe was assured whether the Germans won or, somehow, lost the war. By virtue of their comparative managerial superiority, the Germans would control most of Europe, the Japanese would control Manchuria and eastern China, and the Americans would control the western remains of the British Empire. [42] These superstates would prevail as world powers because only they possessed the means to refuel their war economies by exploiting new capital markets and expanding their markets for industrial goods. All economies were war economies, Burnham insisted, since war was a "normal and integral part" of human life. The Germans took this truism more seriously than their neighbors, and were therefore bound to rule over them.

"The day of a Europe carved into a little score of sovereign states is over," Burnham pronounced. [43] The most advanced managerial society in the world was destined to rule over its weaker and decadent neighbors. Burnham assumed that democratic England would not resist the Nazis for long, if at all, since England displayed "all the characteristics which have distinguished decadent cultures in past historical transitions." He further assumed that the Germans would not attack the Soviet Union until they conquered Europe. Despite the strength of the Soviets' own managerial class, Burnham thought that their economic and technological backwardness would make them no match for the Germans. The Soviet Union would split apart under the strain of the war, he predicted. The nation's eastern half would fall under Asian control and the western half under German control. As late as the summer of 1944, after the Soviets failed to crack, Burnham predicted that they would soon form an alliance with Japan to prevent a Japanese defeat. [44]

Managerialism assumed—like the ideologies it purportedly surpassed—that possession of the means of production was all-determinative. All power derived from economic power. Burnham had dropped most of his Marxist language, but his mode of analysis remained a variant of vulgar Marxism. Stalinism, Nazism, and the New Deal were ideological rationalizations or superstructures of determinative economic interests. Economics inevitably swallowed politics.

and yet, they're all wrong!

It was important to Burnham to avoid any value judgments on the emergence of managerialism. His function was merely to explain what was happening in the world. He had no patience with moral arguments of any kind; as he would soon explain in *The Machiavellians*, he believed that those who called for more democracy in the face of the managerial onslaught were fools. *The Managerial Revolution* tipped its hand, however, in a closing aside on the future of capitalism: "In truth, the bourgeoisie itself has in large measure lost confidence in its own ideologies. What was Munich and the whole policy of appeasement but a recognition of bourgeois impotence? The head of the British government's traveling to the feet of the Austrian housepainter was the fitting symbol of the capitalists' loss of faith in themselves."[45] Neoconservatives would later amplify Burnham's disgust with bourgeois impotence and appeasement.

Burnham's view of democracy was vengefully unillusioned. He did not pass through liberalism on his way to the Right. He regarded democracy principally as a ruse to control the masses. "A certain measure of democracy is an excellent way to enable opponents and the masses to let off steam without endangering the foundations of the social fabric," he allowed in *The Managerial Revolution*. Politics was about the struggle between elites for power. "If we put the question in the popular form, 'Will democracy win?', there can be little doubt that the answer must be, No," he announced in 1941. "Democracy can never win. Democracy always loses, because the forces of democracy in winning, cease to be democratic. Those who want democracy, therefore, must be willing to lose."[46] This was not an argument against going to war. Burnham was not traumatized—like Norman Thomas—by the fear that American intervention would destroy America's democratic gains at home. His admonition was a sign that the move from Trotskyism to right-wing elitism would leave much of his political philosophy intact.

For Burnham, democratic rhetoric was a sometimes useful device by which one elite sought mass support for its drive to displace another elite. *The Machiavellians* belabored this opinion with didactic persistence. In 1943, while most Americans thought they were fighting for democracy, Burnham argued that democracy was a fraud. He called upon the Machiavellian sociological tradition of Gaetano Mosca, Roberto Michels, and Vilfredo Pareto to amplify his case, with supporting arguments from the revolutionary syndicalist turned fascist, Georges Sorel. *The Machiavellians* argued that democracy was, at best, a useful deception employed by elites to secure their power over the masses. Mosca's theory of the ruling class was called upon to demonstrate the emptiness of representative government and the inevitability of elite rule; Sorel's disquisitions on the necessity of violence for political change were invoked to ridicule the idealistic pieties of liberal democracy; Michels's famous "iron law of oligarchy" added ballast to Burnham's insistence on the autocratic nature of all large social organizations; and Pareto's theory of the "circulation of elites" sealed the argument about the myth of democratic self-government. As Burnham explained, the character of any society was always, above all, the character of its elite. "Its accomplishments are the accomplishments of its elite; its history is properly understood as the history of its elite; successful predictions about its future are based upon evidence drawn from the study of the composition and structure of its elite."[47]

The latter-day Machiavellians exposed the essential deceits of democratic thought and rhetoric. If revolutions were occasionally possible without violence, they never occurred without massive fraud. From the English Puritans to the Jacobins to the Bolsheviks, revolutionaries invoked the will of the people only to secure their support for a new order—ruled by the revolutionaries. Historical and political science therefore properly studied, above all, the composition and structure of the ruling elite, whose primary object "is to maintain its own power and privilege." The rule of any elite, Burnham instructed, was inevitably based upon force and fraud.[48]

The Machiavellians scratched for a bit of moral consolation. Any intelligent elite protected its own interests by looking out for the larger interests of society, Burnham observed. A society degenerated into decadence (and thus became ripe for revolution) when its ruling elite paid more attention to culture, philosophy, or pleasure than to the business of ruling; or when it failed to assimilate new members from the lower classes; or when it lost confidence in itself and the legitimacy of its rule; or when it failed to use force "in a firm and determined way" and was thus forced to rely entirely on manipulation and fraud.[49] Burnham denied that his argument abandoned the cause of freedom. For him, as for Machiavelli, freedom was a product of social conflict, emerging from the struggle between rival interest groups. The Machiavellians were defenders of freedom because they defended the preconditions of social conflict. In the service of freedom, they opposed the emerging "Bonapartist" alliances in the industrialized societies that increased the power of centralized governments.

The New Deal was a harbinger of the trend, which Burnham called "democratic totalitarianism." It was a trend currently promoted by "pathological newspapers like New York's *PM*, frustrated poets like Archibald MacLeish, choleric bureaucrats like Harold Ickes, gutter-columnists like Walter Winchell, trying to crawl out of the gutter," and other liberal statists.[50] The efforts of such democratic totalitarians to seduce mass support for big government were inimical to the survival of liberty. The march to collective serfdom could only be turned back, Burnham insisted, by cunning elites that aggressively used their own methods to pacify the masses. Pareto's theory of elites explicated the essential task. To keep itself in power, Pareto explained, any ruling elite must continually co-opt and recruit to its ranks the most able members of the underclass. Burnham argued that this strategy stood its best chance of succeeding in a society that retained such rights as freedom of the press and the right to collective bargaining. The most stable and efficient examples of elite rule traded on democratic habits that were themselves sustained by limited institutional forms of democratic entitlement.

This posed the central dilemma. The elites were too sophisticated to believe in actual democracy. By virtue of their superior education and realism, they did not believe in the political pieties about self-government embraced by the masses. They were thus alienated from the masses. But the myth of democratic self-government served the interests of freedom, as well as the interests of the ruling elites. The scientifically informed elites thus found themselves in a bind. "A dilemma confronts any section of the elite that tries to act scientifically," Burnham explained. "The political life of the masses and the cohesion of society demand the acceptance of myths. A scientific attitude toward society does not permit the belief in the truth of the myths. But the leaders must profess, indeed foster, belief in the myths, or the fabric of society will crack and they will be overthrown. In short, the leaders, if they themselves are scientific, must lie."[51] To keep the peace and maintain their own power, the elites needed to promote religious and democratic pieties they knew to be false. Burnham was righteous in his advocacy of deceit. He was pure; only his critics—who knew better—were corrupt.

Burnham's claims to science meshed oddly with his apocalyptic rhetoric. Machiavelli's "new science of politics" conceived politics in the ironical mode. His scientific claims were not made to announce iron laws of history, as with Burnham, but to limit the unintended consequences and contingencies of political action. Burnham's mechanistic explanations of recent history exaggerated not only his connection to Machiavelli, but the extent of the managerial revolution.[52] The disjunction between ownership and control posited by managerial theory did not apply to the Soviet Union, where the state owned the means of production. Burnham failed to prove that a managerial Soviet class had attained any authority over or apart from the ruling Soviet political bureaucracy. In Nazi Germany, the capitalist class and the Junkers maintained most of their control over investment and production decisions. In America, control over investment and production decisions continued to be held by large stockholders. The managerial class in a managerial society could give advice and make decisions about how businesses should be run, as Diggins later observed, but they still took orders on what should be done. [53]

The struggle to defeat America's new liberalism would require greater cunning and tougher minds than the traditional elites had demonstrated. Burnham's attraction to Machiavellianism was based, in part, upon this tradition's moral cynicism—which cut against the American grain. The "permanence of oligarchical rule" was not a theme of traditional American conservatism. American conservatives had long decried the purported decline of the elites under the pressures of mass democracy. To bring the Machiavellian tradition to America was to call for a new kind of American conservatism. A generation later, most neoconservatives would renounce Burnham's cynicism about democracy, but they would embrace his conception of American politics as a war for position between rival elites. Neoconservatives would use the language of democracy to fight the New Class's democratic totalitarianism. Whether the fight against the New Class should be more ideological than Machiavellian was a question that Burnham never completely settled for himself, and this question later divided neoconservatives. But all of the neoconservatives, like Burnham, would define their domestic mission as that of a counter-elite struggling (with the corporate sector) against the New Class of statist intellectuals and government officials.

The neoconservatives' international mission would be to wage an ideological war against communism. Here again, the key conceptual categories of neoconservatism were formulated by Burnham. It was Burnham who theoretically generalized the symmetry between Nazi and communist forms of totalitarianism. It was Burnham who first applied the antifascist term "fifth columnist" to communist fellow-travelers in the United States. And when the war turned out rather differently than he expected, it was Burnham who provided the ideological apparatus for fighting what he called the Third World War.

He began with a send-up of his forsaken Trotskyist faith. The ostensible argument of "Lenin's Heir," published in 1945 in *Partisan Review,* was that Stalin was Lenin's rightful heir. The Trotskyists and other anti-Stalinist communists were kidding themselves. They derided Stalin as an uncultured hack who betrayed the revolution, but Burnham countered that, literary snobbery aside, Stalin was a "great man" who used his "creative political imagination" to fulfill the promises of the revolution. Though his powers of rhetoric were no match for Trotsky's, Stalin was the great master in the real "historical world of Becoming" whose bold collec-

tivizations and purges saved the revolution. Stalin's genius was demonstrated by his consolidation of power, which included a long-term campaign to liquidate his various opponents, primarily by getting them to kill
each other and themselves. By comparison, Trotsky was crude and unimaginative. Stalin's "boldness and dash," his military brilliance, his mas-
tery of political techniques, and his unrivaled geopolitical vision made him
"a great man in the grand style." Unlike Trotsky, Stalin rejected a priori
conceptions of revolution and accepted the one that history delivered.[54]
To this inheritance, he added a crucial appeal to national pride and
devised a grand geopolitical strategy for Soviet domination of the world.
Every move he made was shrewdly calculated to advance this geopolitical
vision, which Burnham described with a torrent of Neo-Platonist metaphors:

> Starting from the magnetic core of the Eurasian heartland, the Soviet power,
> like the reality of the One of Neo-Platonism overflowing in the descending
> series of the emanative progression, flows outward, west into Europe,
> south into the Near East, east into China, already lapping the shores of the
> Atlantic, the Yellow and China Seas, the Mediterranean, and the Persian
> Gulf. As the undifferentiated One, in its progression, descends through
> the stages of Mind, Soul and Matter, and then through its fatal Return back
> to Itself; so does the Soviet power, emanating from the integrally totalitarian
> center, proceed outward by Absorption (the Baltics, Bessarabia, Bukovina,
> East Poland), Domination (Finland, the Balkans, Mongolia, North China,
> and tomorrow Germany), Orienting Influence (Italy, France, Turkey, Iran,
> central and south China . . .), until it is dissipated in MH ON, the outer
> material sphere, beyond the Eurasian boundaries, of momentary Appease-
> ment and Infiltration (England, the United States).[55]

The praise for Stalin was a put-on, but Burnham's geopolitical Neo-
Platonism was deadly serious. He warned that the Soviet Union—which
was destined so recently to fall apart—was already on the verge of
conquering "Eurasia." (In Burnhamese, Eurasia was principally the Soviet
Union, Europe, the Middle East, China, and India.) It was because Stalin
was already pursuing a grand strategy for world domination that Burnham
lauded him in January 1945 as a towering superman. The patronizing
leftist image of the "triumphant Babbitt of the revolution" needed to be
exploded, as did the wartime American image of "Uncle Joe." Stalin was
far from the mere cipher described by Trotsky—the crude, ignorant,
provincial personification of bureaucracy who triumphed only because the
revolution had fallen.[56] Burnham might have contented himself with
arguing that Stalin's totalitarian terror was prefigured in the dictatorship

erected by Lenin and Trotsky. However, this unoriginal thesis would not have made the impact he was seeking. The war was ending, and the succeeding war for the world had already begun. In the guise of a tribute to the Soviet leader, Burnham tried to prepare the intellectuals for the struggle to come, while concealing his intention.

The intellectuals fell for it. Burnham's admiration for Stalin's purported geopolitical strategy was taken as admiration for Stalinism. One by one, in the early months of 1945, Lionel Abel, Macdonald, and others lined up to condemn Burnham's perverse apologies for Stalinism.[57] Like all of Burnham's recent writings, Macdonald justly complained, "Lenin's Heir" could be read in contradictory ways. The author's political convictions were concealed by his scientific pretensions and his deliberately ambiguous formulations. Macdonald thought, however, that Burnham's comments on the question of Stalin's legitimacy contained the chief clue to his position. Burnham had written that "as Stalin expands before us, we can more readily grant his legitimate succession."[58] This disturbing announcement seemed, to Macdonald, the key to Burnham's otherwise carefully hidden purpose. Burnham's "restless quest for a Father, for authority" was leading him to Stalin. This was the single theme that linked all of his writings.[59] *The Managerial Revolution* had praised even Hitler's greatness. Now his search for a Father had taken him to Stalin—an attitude that repelled Macdonald, who was moving at the time from Marxism to anarcho-pacifism.[60] His power-worshiping might-makes-rightism was symptomatic, for Macdonald, of the modern totalitarian sickness.

The following year, George Orwell took up the same argument in an essay titled "Second Thoughts on James Burnham." Orwell had long been fascinated and revolted by Burnham's work. The geopolitical order depicted in 1984, with its three competing superstates of Eastasia, Eurasia, and Oceania, was taken directly from *The Managerial Revolution*. Burnham's theory of managerialism was reproduced in the novel as "The Theory of Oligarchical Collectivism." Orwell's intellectual debt to Burnham was thus considerable. His novel was, nonetheless, a polemic against the totalizing world-historical trend that Burnham described and apparently embraced. In "Second Thoughts," Orwell rounded up Burnham's impressive list of wrong predictions and observed that in each case, Burnham had simply predicted the continuation of something that was presently occurring. This was not simply a bad habit, Orwell argued. The fault ran deeper. "It is a major mental disease, and its roots lie partly in cowardice and partly in the worship of power, which is not fully separable from cowardice," he charged.[61]

Burnham's power-worship led him time and again to "bow down before the conqueror of the moment" and to "accept the existing trend as irreversible," Orwell observed. His recent homage to Stalin offered a striking example, which Orwell read as an act of piety and self-abasement. The same power-worship showed up in Burnham's other writings, however, including the "almost open admiration for Nazi methods" that filled *The Managerial Revolution*. Orwell conceded that Burnham's general thesis about the trend toward managerial statism in the industrialized countries was correct. Although each national case falsified specific aspects of the theory of managerialism, the theory was plausible as a high-ground generalization.

The chief problem with Burnham's presentation of the theory was that he couldn't account for the failure of an advanced managerial power to achieve its goals. Neither could he account for a democratic political system not based on fraud and repression. "Although he reiterates that he is merely setting forth the facts and not stating his own preferences, it is clear that Burnham is fascinated by the spectacle of power, and that his sympathies were with Germany so long as Germany appeared to be winning the war," Orwell observed. He noted that Burnham's books contained an "unmistakable relish over the cruelty and wickedness" of the processes they described. In Orwell's reading, it was this thinly veiled admiration for the Nazi regime that made Burnham so unprepared for the resistance of the decadent democracies to German rule. The actual experience of German rule had aroused such disgust that, by 1941, the Allies hadn't needed any motivating objective other than getting rid of the Germans. By any quantifiable measure, including the amount of quislingism or the proportion of prisoners to casualties, the democracies had come out of the war ahead of the fascist countries. This was not an outcome for which Burnham could account. [62]

Now, Orwell thought, Burnham was on his knees again. "His own power-instinct leads him to brush aside any suggestion that the Machiavellian world of force, fraud, and tyranny may somehow come to an end," Orwell wrote. Burnham was thus to be seen abasing himself before Stalin, panting about the brilliance of Stalin's vision, the greatness of his leadership, the magnificence of his banquets, and so forth.

Orwell countered that the Soviet regime would either democratize itself or perish. "The huge, invincible, everlasting slave empire of which Burnham appears to dream will not be established, or, if established, will not endure, because slavery is no longer a stable basis for human society," he declared. Orwell's own view was that the Soviet Union would destroy itself. As for Burnham, he remarked, it should not have required an enormous intellectual effort for someone to keep from admiring Hitler or

Stalin. "That a man of Burnham's gifts should have been able for a while to think of Nazism as something rather admirable, something that could and probably would build up a workable and durable social order, shows what damage is done to the sense of reality by the cultivation of what is now called 'realism,' " he concluded. [63]

Orwell missed the target only on Burnham's new political position. He missed the conservative implications of *The Machiavellians* and, while conceding that "Lenin's Heir" might contain a tinge of irony, he was inclined to take the essay's Stalin-worship at face value. It was more plausible to him that Burnham was converting to Stalinism than that he was becoming some kind of American conservative. In fact, Burnham had already secretly worked for the Office of Strategic Services (the forerunner of the Central Intelligence Agency) in 1944, preparing a study of the coming American war with the Soviets. In 1947, the publication of an expanded form of this study (under the title *The Struggle for the World*) would end the arguments about how to interpret Burnham's politics. Managerial-ism posited that the Soviet Union was neither capitalist nor socialist, but a strange hybrid that defied conventional ideological categorizations. It therefore provided a poor basis for an ideological crusade. By 1947, however, the Cold War had taken over Burnham's life. He discarded—at least in the foreign policy area—his Machiavellian ambiguities. The imperatives of the Cold War would leave no room for the luxuries of ambiguity, objectivity, or realpolitik.

THE WAR FOR THE WORLD

The Struggle for the World declared in its opening sentence: "The Third World War began in April, 1944." Burnham's reference was to a failed mutiny of communist-led Greek sailors in the harbor at Alexandria. A few shots were fired before the mutineers were captured, and the story barely made the newspapers. It was not understood at the time, but needed to be under-stood now, he instructed, that a new war for the world began that day under the cover of the Second World War. Through their affiliated Greek party, the Soviets had made their first attempt to turn the antifascist resistance against the West. Since that day, they had unrelentingly plotted to destroy the United States and expand their own empire to the ends of the earth. The United States, meanwhile, had elected at the end of the war against fascism "to go home, to Mother, the Best Girl, a local job, and the corner drugstore or saloon."[64] For Burnham, the present threat to the survival of civilization was capsulized in this pathetic reaction.

The Struggle for the World ridiculed the culture and democratic ethos of America. Burnham argued that the United States was a mature nation in only one respect: American methods of mass production were unequaled in the world. The enormity of the American war effort had left no doubts on this score. But supremacy in the technique of production was like a wild artistic talent, "irrational, only half-conscious, uncontrolled, out of balance with intelligence and other impulses." This facility reinforced a peculiarly American image of the world as a market for American goods. Americans loved commerce more than they hated communism. If only the world's generals and politicians would get out of the way and let commerce run its course!

But the generals and politicians remained, Burnham observed, to the evident confusion and dismay of America's frivolous elites. What the civilized world needed at this late hour, above all, was for Americans to grow up. "It is the nation, not the soldiers alone, that is unprepared," he thundered. "It was the members of Congress, not the soldiers, who showed real cowardice and blindness when they responded to the complaints of the soldiers not by pointing out to them the responsibilities of world power but by yielding to the homesickness, and seeking demagogically to gain a few cheap votes by joining in the clamor to bring the boys home at whatever cost to the interest of the nation—and of the world."[65] The United States was supposed to be a world power, but America's leaders were shirking the responsibilities that world power imposed. "The young men of a world power must be ready to act in the world, to seek their career and its fruition in far places." Burnham argued. But the American government, while intervening all over the world—"from Argentina to Spain to Iran to Manchuria"—didn't have the stomach to keep a draft going.

American political culture had been corrupted chiefly by two influences, he claimed. The first was the "abstract, empty, sentimental rhetoric of democratic radicalism" unfortunately bequeathed to the nation by Thomas Jefferson. The second was the small-minded provincialism of American machine politics. Burnham wasted no further commentary on the former influence, since "Jeffersonian rhetoric has no connection with reality." The second influence was a more serious matter. Burnham conceded that the ward-heeling, spoils-system practices of American machine politics were remarkably effective in their own sphere. The problem was that this kind of politics produced a political culture that didn't comprehend world history or geopolitics. "Great nations, with a tradition and a culture, do not operate in terms of quashed parking tickets, building contracts, and soft jobs in the local courthouse," he wrote. The level of political knowledge in the United States was the lowest of any nation in the world. The country's political leaders were ignorant hacks and demagogues, learned only in the arts of flattery, self-promotion, and appeasement. The country's journalists considered themselves political analysts because they socialized with famous hack politicians in fashionable bars. The country's few men of learning, "blocked from contact with the springs of power," had become pedantic and sterile. It was a theme that neoconservatives would later pursue with equal foreboding. While the enemy produced manly, disciplined warriors dedicated to the greatness of their nation, America was turning out soft, emasculated little men with pathetically domesticated dreams. [66]

The Communists, by contrast, were committed to nothing less than world domination. Burnham's definition of communism only implicitly referred to economic nationalization. Communism, he wrote, was "a world-wide, conspiratorial movement for the conquest of a monopoly of power in the era of capitalist decline." [67] The theorist of managerialism would never doubt that capitalism was passing away. The struggle for the world was not a struggle between capitalism and socialism, but a struggle for literal domination over the entire world by a single state. Burnham argued that the existence of atomic weapons made world domination by one or another world power a necessary goal. To allow two or more countries to possess atomic weapons "would be equal to a grenade with the pin already pulled," he observed. He conceded that by inventing atomic weapons, it was possible that the West had already committed suicide. Burnham was sensitive to the dangers inherent in any strategy to deal with the problem. It was nonetheless obvious to him that the only solution to the problem posed by the existence of atomic weapons was for a single world empire to secure and maintain monopoly control over nuclear technology.

This would not be the world government called for by liberal internationalists and fuzzy-minded idealists. A freely and deliberately chosen world government with true international sovereignty would be the best solution to the atomic crisis, he averred, but this would require a world political unity that did not remotely exist. A world government was thus an impossibility for the foreseeable future. What was possible was a world empire or superstate, "not necessarily world-wide in literal extent but world-dominating in political power, set up at least in part through coercion (quite probably including war, but certainly the threat of war), in which one group of peoples (its nucleus being one of the existing nations) would hold more than its share of power." [68] This was Burnham's ambition for his country, since the only other candidate was the Soviet Union.

His description of the nature of the communist threat was utterly monolithic. His depiction of its advance centered on a spherical diagram of the world as it purportedly existed in August 1939. It was the terrifying geopolitical image attributed to Stalin in "Lenin's Heir." A fourfold series of concentric rings was drawn around a dark circle representing the Soviet Union. Each ring demarcated the extent of Soviet authority or influence in the world. Closest to the dark center were those countries in the Absorption ring, which included the Baltic states, East Poland, Moldavia, Mongolia, and other nations. The Domination ring included Finland, Scandinavia, Poland, Germany, Austria, the Balkans, the entire Middle East, northern China, Manchuria, and Korea. Burnham explained that the Soviet regime was pushing only to dominate these nations rather than literally to absorb them into itself. The Orienting Influence sphere consisted of those nations that the Soviets were in no position to absorb or dominate, but that they were pushing to win over to a pro-Soviet foreign policy. These included France, Italy, all of Latin America, southern China, and the lesser Western European states. That left only the United States and Great Britain in the fourth ring (Canada didn't make the chart), against whom the Soviets were said to be waging a "very extensive" campaign of Infiltration and Demoralization. [69]

The strategy in the fourth ring was to isolate the United States from the rest of the world (a task already largely accomplished, as the diagram showed) and internally weaken, divide, and demoralize American society. Burnham drew on his extensive experience in the communist movement to describe how Communists infiltrated and manipulated civic, commercial, and political organizations. In his estimation, the Communists had already thoroughly penetrated the trade unions and the public opinion industry. They were presently working with some success to infiltrate the intelligence services and scientific organizations. Most importantly, they were "actively penetrating" every political, cultural, religious, commercial, governmental, and educational sector of American society. The infiltrated divisions of American society would then be in a position to sabotage America's industrial and military machine. The communist world empire would begin with the downfall of the United States.

This was not merely a warning to the uninitiated about the realities of communist infiltration or the sinister purposes of communist political activism. It was, for Burnham, a description of the inevitable outcome of the Third World War if the United States did not soon accept the mission and responsibilities of a world empire. He noted that an American empire already existed throughout the Americas and in far-flung parts of the world dominated by American military power. American imperial policy toward

Latin America was "vague and irresolute," he admitted, and thus inspired Latin American complaints about Yankee imperialism. He argued that Latin Americans would complain less about their situation if the United States took its imperial responsibilities more seriously. It was America's unease with its imperial role, and its hypocrisy in denying responsibility for this role, that engendered most of the complaining. The United States maintained classic imperialist relationships with the nations of Latin America while denying it was an imperial power at all. "Nevertheless, for the issues that decide, the Empire is real," Burnham observed, as the long history of American military interventions in Latin America demonstrated.[70]

Burnham reasoned that if he could get American leaders to acknowledge their responsibilities over the already-existing American empire in the Americas, Japan, the Philippines, parts of Africa and Europe, and elsewhere, he might begin to challenge the deeply ingrained, though absurd, American myth that imperial strategies were un-American or necessarily undemocratic. The two most democratic governments in the history of the world, he noted—Athens and England—were also two of history's greatest imperial powers. Burnham's fear was that the dominant trends in postwar American popular and intellectual culture were reinforcing antimilitarist sentiments among both the elites and the masses. He denounced the "renunciation of power" and the attack on military values that filled contemporary literature. The same revulsion against war was fueling a renewal of interest in mysticism, he noted, which showed up in the work of writers such as Gerald Heard, Aldous Huxley, Ignazio Silone, and Evelyn Waugh. The recent interest in existentialism was a related phenomenon. All of these trends were testimonies to the sickness of the postwar Western soul. The literature of the modern West was preoccupied with guilt, alienation, redemption, and the immorality of power. It was a sickness deeply rooted in Western culture and continually reproduced by the world-renouncing teachings of Christianity. Burnham was less openly hostile to religion than Hook, but he decried the influence of the "winged words" of Christ, Buddha, and St. Francis on the immorality of violence. The world-renouncing mysticism of the various modern secular and spiritual religions was an indulgence that Americans could no longer afford. The first war to be fought was therefore against the culture of appeasement.[71]

The second would be the war for the world, waged against a disciplined enemy that rejoiced in power and force. *The Struggle for the World* was a call to arms. "If the communists are not to win, there must be presented to the governments and the peoples of the world a positive alternative to the communist plan, which will meet, at least as well as the communist plan, the demands of the crisis," he asserted. Burnham conceded that the American empire would have to be called something else. Some euphemism for the imperial superstate would have to be found. Americans were too pious and hypocritical to give the correct name to what they were doing, or needed to do, in the world. "Whatever the words, it is well also to know the reality," he declared. "The reality is that the only alternative to the communist World Empire is an American Empire which will be, if not literally world-wide in formal boundaries, capable of exercising decisive world control."[72] The need for an American empire was predicated on the existence of a monolithic Soviet conspiracy, as well as the existence of atomic weapons. Neutrality in the struggle for the world was impossible. Though most of the neoconservatives would not repeat his explicit call for an American empire, they would later repeat, with equal vehemence, Burnham's strictures against the possibility of neutralism. The term itself would be used only as an epithet.

Burnham's battle plan was grimly specific. The British dominions and all the countries in the Western Hemisphere would be immediately required to accept subservient roles in the American empire. Faced with the existing Soviet threat, the United States had no choice but to reinstate the draft, fight anticommunist wars all over the world, and make the world choose sides. Faced with the immaturity, softness, weakness, and provincialism of American culture, Burnham was doubtful that his country was capable of carrying out what he called "a long, difficult and perhaps most terrible process." But there was no alternative—except extinction—to making Americans face up to their historical task. The lesson was drawn from Arnold Toynbee. "History offers each of its great challenges only once," Burnham concluded. "After only one failure, or one refusal, the offer is withdrawn. Babylon, Athens, Thebes, Alexandria, Madrid, Vienna sink back, and do not rise again."[73]

The Struggle for the World was published the same week that President Truman announced both his commitment to defend Greece and Turkey and his larger commitment to prevent communist expansion elsewhere in the world. The book and the Truman Doctrine became linked in the public mind—an association that Burnham encouraged by speaking out in favor of Truman's new policy. His book was loudly trumpeted in *Time* and *Life* magazines and quickly became a best seller. Within a year of its publication, however, he began to argue that the Truman Doctrine had no conception of the struggle in which America was engaged. The Truman Doctrine, Burnham insisted, lacked a comprehensive foreign policy vision, lacked a consistent military strategy, took a merely defensive posture toward the Soviet threat, implicitly conceded earlier communist gains, and failed to bring about an economically unified Europe. This critique was detailed in Burnham's subsequent book, *The Coming Defeat of Communism*. "Eternal containment of communism cannot be an objective; it is both empty and impossible," he claimed. "Containment can make sense only as a temporary device for the sake of some genuine objective to be gained later on."[74] The Truman Doctrine had alerted the country to the danger; what was needed now was a vision of an American empire and a strategy to attain it. A hopeful note was tactically appropriate. The American century was still within reach. Burnham therefore rejected Hook's plea to give the book a different title. For the moment, he would strike an optimistic chord. Americans needed to believe that communism could be defeated. Burnham believed, however, that the Truman administration was making only half-hearted responses to the communist threat—a situation that left him with the tiresome task of making the same arguments over and again.

At the same time, despite the far-right lurch of his foreign policy views, Burnham remained on good terms with the anticommunist liberals and social democrats in the American Committee for Cultural Freedom (ACCF), the American affiliate of the international Congress for Cultural Freedom. In the early 1950s, the founders of neoconservatism were ACCF members. Their later desire to revive the ACCF anticommunism of the 1950s would give rise to neoconservatism. They would argue that liberal anticommunism had lost its nerve. The first to make this argument, however, was Burnham, whose role in the ACCF marked a turning point in his career.

The ACCF was essentially Hook's former Committee for Cultural Freedom resuscitated. It was revived by Hook in response to a series of procommunist "peace conferences" held between 1947 and 1949 in East Berlin, Wroclaw, New York, and Paris—the most famous of which was the 1949 Cultural and Scientific Conference for World Peace at the Waldorf-Astoria Hotel in New York. When the National Council of the Arts, Sciences and Professions announced in 1949 that it would sponsor a peace conference at the Waldorf-Astoria, Hook submitted a lecture proposal on the communist notions of racial, national, and class truth to the program committee. His proposal was rejected. After making a few inquiries, Hook learned that the conference was endorsed by such fellow-traveling luminaries as Albert Einstein, Aaron Copland, Paul Robeson, Charlie Chaplin, Leonard Bernstein, Clifford Odets, Lillian Hellman, and others. The peace conference was, in fact, another procommunist spectacle in the making. Hook responded by enlisting the veterans of his dormant

Committee for Cultural Freedom to organize an anticommunist counter-conference.

Though he could not match the star power of the Waldorf-Astoria conference, Hook assembled more than two hundred sponsors for a conference of his own that included Burnham, Phillips, Rahv, Daniel Bell, Norman Thomas, Arthur Schlesinger, Jr., Clement Greenberg, Mary McCarthy, and Lionel Trilling. With financial assistance from the president of the International Ladies Garment Workers Union, David Dubinsky, Hook's group rented a room at the Waldorf-Astoria and organized a rally at Freedom House. Their attempts to challenge the speakers at the conference were effectively turned aside, but at Freedom House an overflow crowd gathered in Bryant Park to hear Hook, Schlesinger, Eastman, and others denounce the persecution of Soviet intellectuals. Afterward, the speakers agreed that an international organization was needed to counteract procommunist propaganda and make the case for cultural freedom.[75]

The idea was brought to fruition the following year, when a group of American intellectuals led by Hook and Burnham traveled to Berlin for what became the founding convention of the Congress for Cultural Freedom. The conference was organized principally by Melvin Lasky and Michael Josselson under circumstances to be described in the next chapter. It featured an attack by Burnham on neutralism, pacifism, and the "pious litany of the Left," as well as several dramatic presentations by Arthur Koestler. Burnham's acidly written paper, "The Rhetoric of Peace," informed the delegates that he was not "against atomic bombs" but was rather "for those bombs made in Los Angeles, Hanford, and Oak Ridge," which constituted the sole defense of Western European freedom. On the final day of the five-day conference, Koestler spoke to a large public gathering in the summer garden of the Funkturm and declared that freedom had seized the initiative. His enthusiasm was fired by the delegates' decision to establish an international anticommunist organization with national affiliates and a headquarters in Paris. When Hook and Burnham returned home, they formally organized the ACCF as an affiliated member of the Congress for Cultural Freedom.[76]

The Congress would be an open community of mostly liberal and social democratic intellectuals united by their opposition to totalitarianism. Though the ACCF was more narrowly and militantly anticommunist than the Congress's other affiliates, even the ACCF was comprised mostly of liberals and social democrats. This fact made Burnham's relationship to the organization increasingly uneasy during the early 1950s, until the controversy over McCarthyism broke their differences into the open. At an ACCF conference at the Waldorf-Astoria in March 1952, the first major Communist-turned-conservative, Max Eastman, gave a blistering speech that implicitly defended Joseph McCarthy's anticommunist tactics. As a veteran of the Palmer raids and the persecution of radicals during the First World War, Eastman ridiculed the belief that a second Red Scare was in progress. The only genuine threat to cultural freedom in their time, he announced, came from the international communist conspiracy. The audience included Macdonald. "Standing in all his white-maned splendor, speaking in a voice trembling with emotion and/or dramaturgy, the Grand Old Man of Ex-Radicalism poured it on," Macdonald recorded. In the postlecture discussion, after two members of the audience criticized the tactics of E. S. Harnett's McCarthyite publication, *Red Channels*, Eastman praised *Red Channels* "for cleaning the Commie termites out of radio." He loudly announced that McCarthy's only faults were his excessive honesty and his overdelicate sense of fair play.[77]

This performance forced the ACCF to take a position on McCarthyism. Macdonald, Schlesinger, and Diana Trilling made the case for an outright repudiation, arguing that any group calling itself the American Committee for Cultural Freedom was compelled to take a stand against McCarthyism. Bell and Irving Kristol led a centrist faction that tried to mollify Burnham and the committee's other conservatives while expressing their disapproval of "certain kinds of anticommunism." They sponsored a resolution stating that "communism and demagogic anti-communism nourish each other." Few of the committee's members actually disagreed with this statement, but Burnham denounced it, claiming that a condemnation of McCarthyism in particular (rather than of political lying in general) would split the organization. Besides Burnham and Eastman, the committee included such conservatives as Henry Hazlitt and George Schuyler.

Burnham's warning stopped the liberals in their tracks. Though several of them (including Hook) issued individual condemnations of McCarthyism, and though the ACCF subsequently criticized several of McCarthy's specific accusations, the campaign against McCarthyism itself demanded by Macdonald and Schlesinger never materialized. The failure of the ACCF to mount a serious campaign against McCarthyism allowed Burnham to remain in the organization and eventually drove several of its members to resign in disgust. Schlesinger and Trilling resigned from the ACCF in 1955—the same year that Whittaker Chambers was elected to the organization's executive committee. They were soon joined by John Kenneth Galbraith, Richard Rovere, James Wechsler, and David Riesman. The ACCF tirelessly condemned violations of cultural freedom in the Soviet Union—where it had no leverage—but couldn't bring itself to campaign against cultural tyranny at home. Schlesinger's explanation for this failure was that the ACCF—partly due to Burnham's influence—retained its obsession with communist infiltration long after the threat had passed. The author of the liberal anticommunist manifesto, *The Vital Center*, would reluctantly conclude that liberal anticommunism was becoming more anticommunist than liberal. Michael Harrington went further, charging that the most indiscriminate kind of anticommunism had become "the only essential requirement for membership." The ACCF had become little more than a public relations bureau of the State Department, "an agency propagandizing the American party line." Commenting on the same development, Irving Howe argued that liberal anticommunism had degenerated into a "cheap and illiberal" ideology that advanced "as a strategy for adapting to the American status quo."[78]

For Burnham, however, the ACCF was never illiberal enough, and in 1954 he resigned from the organization. His last controversy in the organization featured a campaign for his expulsion by the editor of the *Bulletin of the Atomic Scientists*, Eugene Rabinovitch, who resented Burnham's accusation that American scientists were relaying atomic secrets to Soviet agents. Burnham's endorsement of Medford Evans's book on the subject sparked a fierce controversy in the ACCF and led Robert Oppenheimer, Harold Urey, Rabinovitch, and other members to insist that Burnham be expelled from the organization.[79] At the height of the controversy, Burnham was asked to resign from the advisory board of *Partisan Review* on account of his anti-anti-McCarthyism. When it became clear that Hook would not press for Burnham's expulsion from the ACCF and that Burnham would therefore not be expelled, Burnham resigned from the ACCF, explaining that the so-called anticommunist opponents of McCarthyism had fallen into a trap. "They have failed so far to realize that they are, in political reality, in a united front with the Communists, in the broadest, most imposing united front that has ever been constructed in this country," he declared. "As in all united fronts, only the Communists can benefit from it. Politics has an objective logic of its own."[80] To oppose McCarthyism in whatever manner, for whatever reason, was objectively to join forces with the Communists. As Bell observed, the argument was a striking specimen of Burnham's inverted Leninism. Many years later, Burnham would argue that the anticommunism of the Congress was fundamentally compromised by the organization's openness to liberal and social democratic currents.[81]

It was not immediately apparent that these events would diminish Burnham's political influence. Though Rahv pronounced that Burnham had committed suicide in the intellectual community by breaking ranks over McCarthyism, it was in Burnham's work during the same period that the case for rolling back the Soviet empire was most importantly argued. [82] A generation later, neoconservatives would argue that George Kennan's containment strategy was designed not merely to thwart the spread of communism, but to reverse earlier communist gains. They would claim that containment's original proponents (such as Kennan and Schlesinger) had once committed themselves to *defeating* communism—and then lost their will to maintain the struggle. [83] Neoconservatives viewed themselves as redeemers of an abandoned foreign policy commitment. In the early 1950s, however, when containment strategy was at the height of its influence, it was vigorously criticized and rejected by Burnham for its timidity on this very point. *Containment or Liberation?*, published in 1953, explained why Kennan's containment strategy would never defeat or even impede Soviet communism.

Kennan's interpretation of the Soviet system and his strategy for containing the existing Soviet threat were presented in his famous "X" article of 1947. He portrayed the Soviet Union as a crude imperial power with a grossly inefficient economy and a war-weary population. Though Soviet leaders continued to blather Marxspeak about the uneven development of capitalism, he observed, they were unable to build even a highway system. Though they blustered about the coming world triumph of communism, their own people were physically and spiritually exhausted, and the bankruptcy of their ideology was increasingly evident to the masses. Given these circumstances, and given the fact that Marxism assured Soviet leaders of their eventual victory, these men were not likely to pursue adventuresome or dangerous operations abroad, Kennan argued. Soviet foreign policy was "fortified by the lessons of Russian history," which taught the value of circumspection, flexibility, and deception. In Kennan's estimation, the Soviets could be counted upon to retreat in the face of superior force.

Kennan's strategy was to keep American power in their faces. American diplomatic and military policy would be devoted to making the Soviets pay for any further foreign adventures. "The main element of any United States policy toward the Soviet Union must be that of a long-term, patient but firm and vigilant containment of Russian expansive tendencies," he wrote. What was needed was an "adroit and vigilant application of counter-force at a series of constantly shifting geographical and political points, corresponding to the shifts and manoeuvres of Soviet policy." [84] Kennan believed that such an application of diplomatic and military counterforce not only would impede Soviet adventurism, but could very well accelerate the self-destruction of Soviet communism. He noted that the remaining power of Soviet ideology was strongest in those parts of the world "beyond the reach of its police power." No one could know for sure, he conceded, but it was quite possible that if the United States merely kept the pressure on for ten to fifteen years and showed itself to be a more attractive alternative, the monolithic discipline of the governing Soviet party could be undermined. "And if disunity were ever to seize and paralyze the Party, the chaos and weakness of Russian society would be revealed in forms beyond description," he asserted. "Soviet Russia might be changed overnight from one of the strongest to one of the weakest and most pitiable of national societies."[85]

These eerily prophetic words struck Burnham, at the time, as so much wishful fantasizing. Kennan believed that Soviet economic and foreign policy failures would bring about a "gradual mellowing of Soviet power," if not the utter collapse of Soviet legitimacy. He apparently assumed, as Burnham showed, that communism was a natural reaction to desperate social and economic problems. The failure to solve these problems would presumably engender a crisis of faith among the younger generation of Soviet leaders. The former Leninist set him straight. Communism was not a natural product of anything, but rather, as Lenin repeatedly explained, a political apparatus imposed by revolutionaries. To think that Soviet leaders would turn inward, self-destruct, or mellow in response to their own inevitable failures, or to the failures of their system, was to misunderstand the nature of communism. "Orthodox communist movements neither wither nor fade away," Burnham instructed. "They must be smashed." The theorists of containment were not out to smash anything, but were merely attempting to prevent communism from expanding beyond the present Soviet sphere.[86]

Was Soviet foreign policy driven more by ideological or geopolitical factors? Kennan's position on the question was too complex and equivocal for Burnham, as it proved to be for numerous interpreters afterward. He could be quoted either way, and often was. While he regarded Soviet ideology as an important explanatory factor, Kennan generally emphasized geopolitics and the importance of Russian history and cultural traits in his explanations of Soviet behavior. His famous Long Telegram of 1946 interpreted Soviet foreign policy as essentially a product of historic Russian insecurity and brutality. The role of Marxism for Soviet leaders, he explained, was to cover these traits with a "fig leaf of their moral and intellectual respectability."[87] Soviet ideology was an important, but secondary, instrument by which Soviet leaders rationalized their imperialism to themselves and the world.

For Burnham, this interpretive framework was the problem. Though his "X" article paid greater attention to the ideological factor, Kennan's failure to take Soviet ideological claims seriously permitted his self-deception that Soviet communism would mellow or self-destruct. Kennan was able to conjure visions of an unraveling Soviet state because he viewed the Soviet Union as an imperial power not unlike other imperial powers of the past. He failed to take the self-rationalizing power of Soviet ideology seriously enough, even refusing to believe that the Soviets were determined to conquer the world. His reading of Soviet intentions owed more to the Machiavellian realpolitik tradition of Burnham's middle phase than to the ideological determinism of Burnham's maturity. For example, Kennan's geopolitical reading of Soviet policy interpreted Stalin's recent foreign advances as attempts to consolidate Soviet domination over Eastern Europe and the Balkans, rather than as steps toward some ideologically commanded drive to rule the world.

To repudiate this reading, as Burnham did in *Containment or Liberation?*, was to discard the basic argument of *The Machiavellians*. Machiavellianism viewed the Cold War as essentially a conflict among nation-states for contiguous spheres of imperial influence or domination. It was conservative in a bad sense of the term, and therefore appealed to theorists like Kennan and Walter Lippmann because its geopolitical perspective led to a status quo politics. It emphasized the struggle for power rather than the power of ideas. The imperatives of the Cold War forced Burnham to drop his Machiavellianism—at least with regard to the Cold War.[88] Realpolitik theory was unable to comprehend the Cold War for the same reason that containment strategy was too weak and defensive to win it. The same author who once instructed his readers never to take political ideas at face value—which he called the fallacy of formalism—now cited texts from Lenin and Marx to substantiate his claims about Stalin's foreign policy. Burnham argued that the Soviet Union was not a nation or state in the traditional sense at all, but rather "the main base of an unprecedented enterprise which fuses the characteristics of a secular religion, a new kind of army, and a world conspiracy."[89]

A serious American policy would therefore recognize the primacy of the ideological factor in contemporary world politics and prescribe a goal that addressed it: the overthrow of communist regimes throughout the Soviet bloc. "For a man to endure resolutely, he must believe that he is pursuing a goal—he must believe so even if the goal is in reality an illusion or a lie," Burnham instructed. But containment strategy prescribed no concrete goal at all. Containment was an "absurd" notion representing nothing more than "the bureaucratic verbalization of a policy of drift." It traded on Kennan's wishful reading of the lessons of Russian history and his vague premonitions of Soviet self-destruction. Containment strategy absolved the Free World from having to take the offensive in the struggle for the world, leaving the outcome of the struggle to history. "Its inner law is: let history do it," Burnham explained. "We haven't got the intelligence, courage and determination to grapple with the Soviet problem head on. Let's duck the responsibility, then, and slip the ball to old mother history. Maybe she will do our work for us."[90]

The former Machiavellian was driven to call for a revival of "honor" and "spirit" in American politics. "Spirit must direct matter toward a goal," he announced, without explaining where this most un-Machiavellian notion had come from or on what it was based. "It is perhaps the crucial defect of the policy of containment that it is incapable of meeting this moral and spiritual demand," Burnham contended. "Who will willingly suffer, sacrifice and die for containment? The very notion is ridiculous. The average man cannot even understand the policy of containment, much less become willing to die for it."[91] The point was effectively made. The problem was that Burnham's alternative was more ridiculous. *Containment or Liberation?* called for an American war to liberate the Soviet bloc. Burnham wanted to recognize European governments in exile, organize domestic opposition movements, and train national armies backed by American forces to prepare for an invasion of Eastern Europe. He claimed to believe that a war to *defeat* communism would be inspiriting to average Americans. The notion that Americans would willingly die for a rollback of the Soviet bloc conveniently overlooked, among other things, the fact that the same Americans silently observed the destruction of East European governments in 1939.

The point would not be lost on most neoconservatives, who later adopted an aggressive containment strategy that split the differences between Burnham and Kennan. While they embraced Burnham's Cold War imagery, his insistence on the centrality of ideological conflict, his doctrine of totalitarianism, and his belief that Soviet communism was conquering the world, neoconservatives eschewed his conclusion that containment was therefore futile. They distinguished between a solidified communist core that could not be overthrown and peripheral communist regimes where rollback was achievable. They rejected much of Kennan's analysis of Soviet behavior, but adopted a militarized version of his containment prescription.

Burnham went too far. He believed, in 1953, that the Soviets had already won the decisive victories they required to conquer the world. He claimed that the struggle for the world was already lost if America did not reverse these victories. "If the communists succeed in consolidating what they have *already* conquered, then their complete world victory is certain," he declared. "The threat does not come only from what the communists may do, but from what they have done. We do not have to bring in speculation about Soviet 'intentions.' The simple terrible fact is that if things go on as they now are, if for the time being they merely stabilize, then we have already lost. That is why the policy of containment, even if 100 percent successful, is a formula for Soviet victory."[92] Containment strategy certified a Soviet world victory. Since the Soviet Union was a totalitarian power driven by its ideological animus to achieve world domination, it could not be contained at all. Since the Soviets had already conquered the geopolitical base they needed to launch their conquest of the world, American leaders were presented with a starkly brutal either/or: smash the Soviet empire or perish. It was the either/or of inverted Leninism, which viewed the world, as Schlesinger remarked, in permanent apocalypse. For Schlesinger, *Containment or Liberation?* marked the end of taking Burnham seriously. "He is the Bix Beiderbecke of our political journalism, only he has hit that high note once or twice too often," Schlesinger wrote.[93] He would find much company in the judgment.

Burnham was thus driven by his commitment to "logic" to the outer fringe of American politics. His subsequent career would have diminishing significance for neoconservatism, except as a cautionary example. Though he originated much of the intellectual firepower that neoconservatives later employed, his career would also confirm to neoconservatives the need for a new conservatism. In 1955, he joined William F. Buckley, Jr., in launching *National Review*. Burnham had recruited Buckley to the CIA in 1951. The former Leninist and Machiavellian who never warmed up to religion or capitalism found his home at the magazine that mixed conservative Catholicism with free enterprise ideology. For the next twenty-three years, he wrote a biweekly column, "The Third World War" (later retitled "Protracted Conflict"), which excoriated every president from Truman to Carter for appeasing the Soviets. Neoconservatives would later praise Truman for his exemplary anticommunism. In the second issue of *National Review*, however, Burnham argued that the "man of decision" spent most of his presidency appeasing the Soviets: Truman prevented General Patton from marching into Czechoslovakia, he allowed the Soviets to enter Berlin first, and he lost China.[94]

Burnham was slow to come to terms with the Chinese revolution. Throughout the 1950s and early 1960s, he insisted that the so-called Sino-Soviet split was merely a verbal dispute over the best way to bury the United States. He finally conceded in 1964 that a conflict of some significance did appear to exist between the Soviet and Chinese rulers.

However, the conflict had nothing to do with competing conceptions of communism; it was rather "a struggle for control of the international Communist enterprise, of 'the Party,' 'the movement,' 'the apparatus.' "[95] Those who did not comprehend the nature of communism, such as Kennan, failed to understand that for a Communist, control over the organization was the crucial factor. "Without 'the Party,' the Communist enterprise is nothing—verbal wind, utopian fantasy," Burnham explained. "But if the Communist has the Party, then shall all else be given to him. A Communist state is a Party state; a Communist empire, a Party empire; a Communist world, a Party world." This was Lenin's great invention. The putative political, socioeconomic, and cultural differences between Soviet and Chinese communism were negligible factors; the only question at issue between these two communist giants was simply, "Who shall be master in the house?" Fortunately for both parties, he concluded, the enemy was sitting on the sidelines "as if waiting passively to learn which set of undertakers will handle the job of burying him."[96]

The acid test for Burnham's liberationism occurred in 1956 with the Hungarian uprising. To the shock of many of his followers and associates, Burnham fell silent for more than a month during the crisis—and then rediscovered his Machiavellianism. The Hungarian crisis shook Burnham's faith in rollback as a serious foreign policy. The nuclear threat was undeniable in the Hungarian case. Burnham couldn't dismiss the threat, even if it meant abandoning the liberationist cause. He lectured his associates that anticommunism was not a substitute for realism. Those who called for rescuing the Hungarians were utopians who refused to accept "the reality of our time," he asserted. Rollback failed the test of realism. For the first (and last) time, Burnham argued that America needed to work out a satisfactory coexistence with the Soviets. He proposed an "Austrian solution" in which a withdrawal of NATO forces from Western Europe would be exchanged for a Soviet military withdrawal from Eastern Europe.[97]

The name later given to this proposal, after it was promoted by Kennan, was mutual disengagement. Burnham's response to the Hungarian crisis enraged many of his closest associates, however, especially Frank Meyer and William Schlamm. They charged that he was abandoning his earlier strategy of "aggressive pressure" for a strategy of gradual surrender. At the hour of its greatest need, he was betraying the cause in which he had led them. The charges evidently stung Burnham—and stiffened his resolve. He soon reverted to form, urging Eisenhower to "knock Albania out of the Soviet empire." He returned to using "coexistence" only as an epithet. He later criticized Eisenhower for failing to back the Hungarian

Freedom Fighters, while failing to note that at the moment of truth he had defended Eisenhower's policy. [98]

Kennedy's inaugural pledge to "pay any price, bear any burden" briefly stirred Burnham's hopes that America might yet take up the struggle for the world. He pleaded with Kennedy to "*somewhere*, in *some* theater or on *some* vital issue . . . strike a blow against the enemy." He nominated Cuba as the place to begin, arguing that America should overthrow Castro's government "with overwhelming power, maximum speed, and total success." When Kennedy subsequently botched the job by failing to provide air support for the Bay of Pigs invaders, Burnham scolded him for his loss of nerve and his "Boy Scoutist" leadership style. "Now he must find his nerve again," he instructed. The presidency was no place for a Boy Scout and the liberation of Cuba was not a job for amateurs. This was a job for the American Air Force, Navy, and Marines. "Our own central power has got to be brought to bear directly, this time: preferably—and it would be more humane so—in a concentration so massive that prolonged resistance would be out of the question," he wrote. [99]

The following year, Burnham urged that Vietnam should be dealt with in the same way. "What if Hanoi were wiped out, as it could easily be by a single raid—a single plane, for that matter?" he excitedly asked. "What if the incredible chemical and biological weapons now available to Americans were turned against the Viet Cong and the North Vietnamese? If really massive combined forces were assembled from the U.S., Philippines, Free China and Australia? If Chinese north–south communications were cut, as they can be without too much difficulty? If operations into the Chinese mainland were launched?" [100]

Burnham later conceded that many Americans feared that invading China and using biological weapons might provoke a nuclear war with the Soviets. As usual, American policy was calculated primarily to avoid confronting the Soviet Union. Neoconservatives would later repeat Burnham's bitter complaint that American foreign policy was based on a paralyzing fear of Soviet power. American policymakers disguised their fear of Soviet power by claiming to work for peace. In the cases at hand, Burnham assured, the fear was groundless. Vietnam was not Hungary. The Soviets would never sacrifice Russia to save Vietnam, much less to save Cuba or China. [101]

While Cuba was more important to the United States than Vietnam, the stakes in Vietnam were nonetheless apocalyptic. Burnham explained the ABC's of domino theory in 1964, arguing that the fall of Indochina would "inevitably lead to the toppling of one after another of the row of dominoes—Thailand, Burma, Malaya, and in the end Indonesia and the

Philippine Republic also, right up to New Zealand and Australia." He recalled that General Bill Donovan, chief of the wartime Office of Strategic Services (OSS), had proposed for this reason that America should regard the entire region as a single combat theater requiring a single theater command.

Burnham was aware that taking over the entire Asian-Pacific theater would raise a fuss about American imperialism. But the dominoes were already falling. Vietnam was the crucial test of whether or not the United States would "begin the long retreat to San Diego." America's "major historic drive" had always moved westward, he noted. At the moment, America's western strategic frontier was the great arc that ran from Alaska to Japan to Southeast Asia to the Philippines to Australia. Burnham claimed that giving up Vietnam would surrender the entire arc to neutralism and communism. "Through that vast strategic retreat we will have been reduced from a global to a parochial power; we will enter the eastern Pacific only at the will of another; we will be under seige within our own inner bastion," he warned. [102]

Burnham cited several factors over the years to explain why America was doing so little to avoid this fate. Chief among them were American provincialism and moralism. Americans couldn't bring themselves to fight communism and stabilize their own receding empire even in the Caribbean. These character failings were compounded by weak-willed policymakers who claimed that the issues at stake were complex. The argument over Vietnam amply demonstrated the "perils of under-simplification," Burnham argued, which had led to "insurmountable chaos" in America's Vietnam policy. "What is or ever has been complicated about policy in Vietnam?" he implored. Though policy implementation was sometimes complicated, he allowed, the policy question itself was very simple: "either move in with enough force to smash the Vietcong or get out." The policy question was no more complicated than that clarifying slogan, "Better Dead than Red." [103] Burnham understood from the outset that victory over a fanatically determined enemy in Vietnam might well require genocidal force. He was the first to propound the lesson of Vietnam later embraced by neoconservatives, that America should use whatever force is necessary, at the outset, to smash the enemy—or not go in. America's unwillingness to exterminate the Vietnamese proved to Burnham not only that Americans were overly fearful of Soviet power, but also that the United States was not worthy of its own power.

Faced with the advancing communist tidal wave, Burnham charged that American policymakers were responding by attacking their most reliable allies. His longstanding disgust with American moralism reached its apogee with the Ford and Carter administrations. Burnham repeatedly decried American criticism of the South African and Rhodesian regimes, complaining that for American policymakers and intellectuals "white racism is the one unforgiveable sin."[104] A nation's foreign policy was determined fundamentally by its choice of an enemy, he lectured in 1976. The Soviet Union had made its choice entirely clear. Faced with the relentless aggression of the Soviets, the Ford administration chose Rhodesia.[105] After America sold out Rhodesia, he bitterly commented that there were times when a nation had to betray its friends, "but you don't have to do it with all this garbage about peace and democracy."[106] Burnham reviled the invocation of "human rights" as a serious foreign policy concern. He complained that American acquiescence to human rights ideology was consigning America's most faithful allies to a "Whipping Boys Club."[107] America's surrender to communism meanwhile was going unannounced, he claimed, because "hardly anyone except J. Edgar Hoover and the John Birch Society takes communism seriously any longer."[108] The complaint was, by then, a fair measure of his location on the political spectrum.

He died in 1987 at the age of eighty-two, eight years after a stroke took away his memory. The ascension of one of his most ardent admirers, Ronald Reagan, considerably boosted Burnham's reputation during the last years of his life. Burnham was lionized by the conservative Right throughout the Reagan era. Buckley lauded him in 1980 as "the dominant intellectual influence" on the development of *National Review*, and in 1983 Reagan awarded him the nation's highest civilian award, the Medal of Freedom. The citation proclaimed that Burnham's influence "profoundly affected the way America views itself and the world." Reagan added that he owed Burnham a personal debt, "because throughout the years traveling the mashed-potato circuit I have quoted you widely." Burnham was the first conservative intellectual ever to receive the award.[109] Having allied himself with an American Right that traditionally was protectionist and isolationist, he was praised throughout the 1980s as the figure who had done the most to rescue the American Right from its provincialism.

 He would never receive the recognition he deserved, however, from neoconservatives. Having crossed to the farther shores of the American Right, Burnham was not the figure whom neoconservatives would quote when they held forth on the New Class, the role of elites, the primacy of ideology, the nature of Soviet totalitarianism, the struggle for the world, or the culture of appeasement. They were not eager to affirm their association with Burnham when they appropriated his ideas—even after they took over the foreign policy division of the Reagan administration. In each of these cases and others, however, a defining feature of what became the neoconservative movement was first or most importantly formulated by Burnham.

Though they had little direct contact with him, the neoconservatives' debt to Burnham was immense. His rapid transition from Trotskyism to conservatism set an often-followed example; like those neoconservatives who followed it, his later writings bore the marks of his sectarian training and his ambivalence toward democracy. A larger number of neoconservatives would share, in more palatable forms, his emphasis on elite rule, his Machiavellian cynicism, his rejection of human rights as a foreign policy concern, and his strictures against the culture of appeasement. Many of them would repeat his charge that American foreign policy was shaped principally by an unacknowledged and cowardly fear of Soviet power. Most of them would eventually repeat his opinion that the American war effort in Vietnam was mistaken only in its failure to use sufficient military force. Nearly all of them would recycle his images of the Soviet threat and his denigrations of neutralism, as well as repeat his calls to take the offensive in the war against communism. All of them would invest great significance in a mutation of his theory of the New Class. Neoconservatives would pay their respects to Bazelon, Djilas, Shachtman, and occasionally even Rizzi for their concept of the New Class, but it was Burnham who first turned the theory of bureaucratic collectivism into an explanation of what was happening throughout the world.

But Burnham had gone too far. His alliances with reactionaries and his nearly unremitting extremism made him a cautionary figure for those who came after him. Though his writings prefigured much of what was later called neoconservatism, he was not the one who formed a personal link with the new conservatism when it emerged in the late 1960s. He was not the one who would be lauded by neoconservatives as their link to an earlier generation. This mantle would fall on his longtime friend and colleague, with whom he maintained cordial relations after renouncing his last remaining ties to the anticommunist Left.

KEEPING THE FAITH:
HOOK'S ANTICOMMUNIST CRUSADE

Sidney Hook never explicitly renounced his ties to the Left, but rather charged that the anticommunist liberalism of the ACCF was abandoned by intellectuals who couldn't stomach the demands of the Cold War. He saw himself as the embattled defender of freedom who kept the faith, nearly alone, until the rise of neoconservatism. Near the end of his life he observed, "Almost always I found myself in a minority. . . . I have always been somewhat premature in relation to dominant currents of public opinion. I was prematurely antiwar in 1917–1921, prematurely antifascist, prematurely a Communist fellow-traveler, prematurely an anticommunist, prematurely, in radical circles, a supporter of the war against Hitler, prematurely a cold warrior against Stalin's effort to extend the Gulag Archipelago, prematurely against the policy of detente and appeasement, prematurely for a national civil rights program and against all forms of invidious discrimination, including reverse discrimination."[110]

The personal link between neoconservatism and the New York Intellectuals would be embodied by Hook, who directly influenced Kristol, Podhoretz, and even Novak, and who was a member of the right-wing socialist group on which Harrington first pinned the neoconservative label. The first neoconservatives all shared Hook's militant anticommunism, his leftist past, and his contempt for the liberal intelligentsia. Though many of them were Shachtman's disciples, it was Hook who showed them how to translate their politics into an American idiom. Shachtman never found an audience beyond his sectarian base. For those who subsequently identified with neoconservatism, Hook represented the aggressive, self-affirming, militantly anticommunist Americanism that modern liberals had abandoned.

The parallels between his career and Burnham's were telling. Like Burnham, Hook allowed the fight against communism to take over his life after his break with communism; like Burnham, he fought liberals with the same factional tactics he learned as a Communist; like Burnham, he justified his politics in the name of logic and science; like Burnham, his view of the Soviet threat eliminated neutralism as a possibility for any nation; and like Burnham, he often grossly exaggerated the power of the Communist party in the United States between 1930 and 1960. Burnham's volume on the latter subject was later republished, with his approval, by the John Birch Society.[111] Hook's imagination on the topic was less febrile, but he nonetheless repeatedly claimed that communist propaganda and communist Popular Front organizations "dominated" American culture throughout the 1930s. These assertions undoubtedly applied to the factionalized world of the New York Intellectuals in which Hook lived. That America was not an extension of this world was a point that Hook, for the rest of his life, would have difficulty absorbing.

 What saved Hook from his friend's extremism was his commitment to democratic values and institutions. He did not share Burnham's elitist disdain for the masses or the contempt for liberal democracy that Burnham brought over, virtually unchanged, from his Trotskyist past. When he left the communist movement, Hook identified himself (in his own way) with the social democratic tradition of Eduard Bernstein and Norman Thomas. He supported the establishment of the welfare state, the socialization of certain major means of production, the principle of progressive taxation, the passage of the civil rights bills, and the goals of American trade unionism. He explained in his memoirs that he could never accept free enterprise ideology because a free enterprise system left the masses unprotected from massive suffering and deprivation during economic downturns. Free enterprise inevitably eroded the allegiance of the masses to freedom. Having condemned the New Deal during its implementation as a desperate attempt to save capitalism, Hook made his peace with the New Deal during the early 1940s and thereafter supported its extension. "I no longer believe that the central problem of our time is the choice between capitalism and socialism but the defense and enrichment of a free and open society against totalitarianism," he later explained.[112]

Like the trade unionists and ACCF intellectuals with whom he was aligned, he regarded trade unionism as a bulwark of democracy (though he had doubts about the Smith Act) and democracy as the undergirding of his anticommunism. For his continuing association with liberal organizations, he was chided by Burnham in the sixties as a "fellow traveler of liberalism . . . guilty of liberalism, we might say, by association."[113] Though he accepted Burnham's bipolar image of the struggle for the world, Hook shunned Burnham's inverted-Leninist arguments for an American empire. He championed an aggressive form of containment strategy that sought not merely to contain communism, but to defeat it. In his view, Burnham never extricated himself from the trenches of his factional past, where he fought Stalinism by promoting Trotsky's Fourth International. The worldwide struggle against communism would have to be waged, Hook believed, in the American grain, as a crusade for democracy. Most neoconservatives would adopt Hook's view of the struggle for the world.

But Hook remained in the same trenches in his own way. His numerous books nearly always returned to the same points about the evils of communism, the communist threat to the West, and the mistakes of communist sympathizers. None of his writings after 1939 matched the sustained power or intellectual energy of his early books on Marxism. Most of his later books were collections of essays and reviews. Though he wrote voluminously about America's problems and enemies, he made few original contributions to the debates that absorbed his life, nor did he ever reach the mass audience that Burnham repeatedly reached. His 600-page memoir fairly seethed with accounts of his long-running battles with liberals, dupes, fellow-travelers, and Communists. Upon his retirement from New York University in 1973, Hook planned to turn his attention to philosophy, but his preoccupation with America's internal and external enemies prevented him from making the transition. He wanted to write a systematic exposition and defense of Deweyan pragmatism, but the call to fight the culture of appeasement repeatedly overcame him. He spent his final years at the Hoover Institution, inveighing against multiculturalism and the "irresolute" anticommunism of Ronald Reagan. Though Reagan awarded him the Medal of Freedom in 1985, Hook later reported that he had refused to vote in the 1984 election because Reagan was soft on communism.[114] He claimed merely to be taking containment strategy seriously, but he could never find an American leader who took it seriously enough. His neoconservative followers would experience the same difficulty.

As a veteran of the anticommunist battles of the 1940s, Schlesinger tried to explain Hook's political exodus. "I was at Hook's side in some of those battles after the war, and I rejoiced with him as he struck down the infidel," Schlesinger recalled in 1987. "But he has been wrong, I believe, in letting anti-communism consume his life to the point that, like Aaron's rod, it has swallowed up nearly everything else." Schlesinger argued that it was this obsession that explained Hook's continual drift to the Right. His last years were spent as a one-man socialist caucus in the Republican party, where he criticized Reagan for appeasing the Soviets. "He finds more security and vindication in the indiscriminate anticommunism of Ronald Reagan than in what seem to him the dangerous vacillations of liberals who detect changes in the Soviet Union or who worry about nuclear war," Schlesinger observed. The dogma of totalitarianism assured Hook that America was never fighting communism seriously enough. Schlesinger concluded that intellectual refugees from communism appeared to fall into two categories. There were those, like Hook and Burnham, who were transfixed by the communist issue for the rest of their lives. And there were others, like Koestler, Richard Rovere, James Wechsler, and Theodore Draper, who kept their balance and became liberals rather than reactionaries, "concluding that there were more things in heaven and earth than were dreamed of in the anticommunist philosophy."[115]

Neoconservatism would come to represent more than an anticommunist philosophy. The movement was born, however, as a reaction to the anti-anticommunism of the sixties. The American antiwar movement would revive the spirit of the ACCF in a further-right form. Though he was never a vigorous proponent of America's war in Vietnam, Hook was much less ambivalent in his attitude toward the American antiwar movement. The protesters repulsed him. He was quick to draw parallels between the fellow-travelers and dupes of the 1930s and the antiwar activists of the 1960s. He later saw the McGovern presidential candidacy as a throwback to the politics of Henry Wallace. Hook's exertions against the revival of anti-anticommunism absorbed the rest of his life. He found surprising company in the effort. Just as the radicalism of the 1930s produced the conservative intellectuals of the succeeding generation, so, too, would the radical movements of the 1960s drive another herd of independent minds to search for a new conservatism.

3

The War of Ideology: Irving Kristol

The first self-described neoconservative has aptly described the connection between neoconservatism and his former Trotskyism. "The neoconservatives are the political intellectuals, and that's what the Trotskyists were," Irving Kristol explains. "The Trotskyist movement produced political intellectuals, which is why so many went into sociology and achieved distinction. It was much more rigorous intellectual training than you could get in college. If someone came up with some matter on which you were not well read, my God, you were humiliated. It was jesuitical. The Republican Party, meanwhile, produced antipolitical intellectuals. Those people are not in my tradition."[1] His tradition is the stream of New York Intellectuals who found their way to neoconservatism, following Kristol's lead.

Daniel Bell has noted Kristol's influence on neoconservatives. "Whenever I read about neoconservatism," he once remarked, "I think, 'That isn't neoconservatism; it's just Irving.'"[2] If Kristol's stature among neoconservatives has been somewhat exaggerated by David Stockman, who once called him "a secular incarnation of the Lord himself," it is perhaps more fittingly signified by their customary reference to him as "The Godfather."[3] While it would be a mistake to identify neoconservatism with all of Kristol's opinions, as Bell suggests, it is Kristol who has most influenced the movement's character and style.

He was born in Brooklyn in 1920, the son of Eastern European Jews who immigrated to the United States in the 1890s. Kristol's father went to work as a garment worker at the age of twelve and later became a clothing subcontractor. Though Kristol was not religious as a youth, his family was observantly Orthodox. He attended the local Hebrew school in addition to Brooklyn public schools, and graduated from Boys High School in

1936. The following autumn he entered City College of New York in uptown Manhattan, where his classmates included Bell, Kenneth Arrow, Nathan Glazer, Irving Howe, Alfred Kazin, Melvin Lasky, Seymour Martin Lipset, Bernard Malamud, Seymour Melman, Philip Selznick, and Albert Wohlstetter. Like many of his subsequently celebrated classmates, Kristol chose City College not so much for the strength of its academic program (which was undistinguished), but because it was tuition-free and reachable from Brooklyn by subway. Like those of his classmates who eventually turned against liberalism, Kristol's later pilgrimage to the Right was at least slowed by his awareness that he was the beneficiary of a government-subsidized education. [4]

Kristol was indifferent to the official curriculum, but he was quickly politicized by the radical political atmosphere at City College. Unlike Sidney Hook and Irving Howe, who were greatly influenced during their City College years by the eminent philosopher Morris Cohen, Kristol paid little attention to his courses, his grades, or his professors. His actual undergraduate education took place in a horseshoe-shaped stall adjoining the college cafeteria, called Alcove No. 1, where the finer points of Marxism were fiercely debated by Bell, Glazer, Howe, Lasky, Lipset, Melman, Selznick, and numerous others. These deracinated Jews dealt with their Jewishness by leaving it behind. They joined a world-embracing radical movement that made ethnicity irrelevant. Howe later recalled, "The movement eased my loneliness, gave me a feeling of place, indulged me in the belief that I had scaled peaks of comprehension." The movement's breadth was reflected in Alcove No. 1, which housed City College's various Trotskyists, social democrats, anarcho-syndicalists, and other anti-Stalinist Marxists. They found common ground only in their anti-Stalinism. Under the circumstances, it was enough. [5]

The Stalinists in Alcove No. 2, who included Julius Rosenberg, heavily outnumbered Kristol's group and were supported by a sizable faculty contingent. Since the Young Communist League cadre was forbidden by party discipline from speaking to anyone in Kristol's group, the anti-Stalinists (as they called themselves) were forced to dispute each other's revolutionary credentials. Kristol found the Trotskyists most persuasive. He joined a dozen-member grouplet led by Howe that was part of the Young People's Socialist League. The Trotskyists were fearsomely aggressive debaters, skilled at cross-examining their opponents. Kristol's intellectual style was shaped in this earnestly sectarian environment, which tended to produce, as Howe recalled, not the most thoughtful kind of thought. [6] It was Howe who recruited Kristol to the movement, an act he later regarded as one of the larger mistakes in his life. "But the experience served him well," Howe recalled. "He learned to theorize and conceptualize. He learned the uses of the appearance of a coherent argument."[7]

Kristol's education was drawn mainly from *The New International*. His undergraduate years matched the high-water mark of American Trotskyism. By his account, he learned how to construct an argument by reading the high-powered polemics of James Burnham, Max Shachtman, Leon Trotsky, and C. L. R. James that filled *The New International*. Kristol supplemented this intellectual diet by struggling with the leftist, culturally modernist *Partisan Review*—"even simply to understand it seemed a goal beyond reach"—but it was the Trotskyist theoretical organ that provided the formative influence on his development.[8] As Howe recalled, the young Trotskyists learned in the factional tournaments of the 1930s that politics could be "deep knowledge, high-wire virtuosity, opera, circus, all brimming with passion and assault."[9] Kristol later recounted that on one occasion, many of his comrades questioned Burnham's seriousness after Burnham gave a presentation lasting only two hours. If he thus gained a better education at City College than many students attained at supposedly better colleges, Kristol explained, it was because the Trotskyists forced him to study, think and argue—like themselves—with furious energy.[10] Along the way he met his future wife, Gertrude Himmelfarb, who was a member of the Young People's Socialist League.

Kristol graduated in 1940, just after Burnham and Shachtman split the Socialist Workers party. He followed Shachtman into the new Workers party and took the name "William Ferry." In a factional Trotskyist debate between Shachtman and his chief rival, James P. Cannon, the latter, whose English was tenuous, had once referred to the City College Trotskyists as "these students on the *peri-feri* of the movement." Kristol thus took the name Ferry, and his friend Earl Raab became Perry. His career as a grown-up Trotskyist proved short-lived, however. Less than a year after he entered the Workers party, Kristol followed the "Shermanites" (a small group led by Selznick) into the Socialist party. The Shermanites rebelled against what they justifiably called the "Bolshevik spirit" of the Workers party. Kristol returned his party card to Howe, but the chief characteristics of his sectarian training would survive his disaffection from the far Left.

The Shermanites launched a magazine called *Enquiry* in 1942. The same year, Kristol happily relinquished his job as a machinist's apprentice in the Brooklyn Navy Yard to accompany Himmelfarb to Chicago. While Himmelfarb pursued graduate studies at the University of Chicago, Kristol worked part-time as a railroad freight handler, hung around the university, and waited to be drafted. He also edited and wrote for *Enquiry* (at first under the name William Ferry), supplementing the magazine's conventional Marxist fare with reflective pieces on W. H. Auden, Ignazio Silone, Lionel Trilling, and a lengthy assessment of *Partisan Review's* celebrated "Failure of Nerve" symposium on the conformism of modern intellectuals.[11]

He was surprised to encounter intellectual communities at the university that were not preoccupied with radical politics. Chicago had its own community of anticommunist leftists, including Saul Bellow, Leslie Fiedler, H. J. Kaplan, Isaac Rosenfeld, and Oscar Tarcov, but even this group seemed more interested in literature than in politics. Undergraduates at Chicago discussed the Great Books with the same passion that Kristol and his friends reserved for Marxism. Kristol's discovery that serious intellectual inquiry could exist outside New York's hothouse sectarian environment gave him a new perspective on his own education and weakened his identification with leftist politics in general. "Joining a radical movement when one is young is very much like falling in love when one is young," he later concluded. "The girl may turn out to be rotten, but the experience of love is so valuable it can never be entirely outdone by ultimate disenchantment."[12]

The reasons for Kristol's disaffection from the Left would be presented directly nowhere and indirectly everywhere in his subsequent work. He never specifically examined the process by which he rejected Marxism and then democratic socialism in the early 1940s. In scattered references to the issue, and when pressed on the topic in conversation, he waved the question aside with dismissive comments about finally deciding to grow up after college. "By the time I got to Chicago, I had drifted away from Marxist radicalism into some kind of Norman Thomas socialism," he explained. "Then the army shook that out of me. They convinced me that they knew more about people than I did."[13]

Kristol joined the army in 1944 and entered combat in France and Germany with the Twelfth Armored Division. He was discharged in 1946 as a staff sergeant, and later recalled that his military experience was important for him primarily because it revealed to him the parochialism of his world view. He had declined officer training in order to join a Midwest regiment of enlisted commoners. Midwestern Americans turned out to be rather different than he expected, however. "It turned out that most of the guys there came from a town called Cicero, a town I had never heard of," he recalled. "I said to myself, 'I can't build socialism with these people. They'll probably take it over and make a racket out of it.'" He was not greatly affected by the loss of his leftist faith, he later explained, because he "was always rather snotty about radical movements."[14]

He came out of the army, in his description, as a neoliberal of the Lionel Trilling/Reinhold Niebuhr variety—"I have never been a liberal"—and joined his wife at Cambridge University, where she was conducting research for her dissertation on Lord Acton. Himmelfarb's dissertation on the eminent Catholic historian and political philosopher confirmed Kristol's own drift toward what he later called a "right-wing liberal politics."[15] He served as a staff correspondent for *The New Leader* during his year in England and wrote a bad novel that ended up in the fireplace. He also began, more fortuitously, to write for the newly founded *Commentary* magazine. [16]

The American Jewish Committee had founded *Commentary* in 1945 and installed the former editor of *The Menorah Journal*, Elliott Cohen, as its editor. Kristol's brother-in-law, Milton Himmelfarb, was director of information and research for the American Jewish Committee. Two years later, when Cohen needed an assistant editor, Kristol got the job. He made his early mark in political journalism over the next five years, eventually becoming managing editor and helping Cohen create one of the country's most culturally sophisticated, vigorously anticommunist, and unabashedly Jewish magazines. A former radical, Cohen at first included anti-Stalinist communists such as Howe and Sherry Mangan in the magazine's intellectual orbit, but his line narrowed in the late 1940s with the beginning of the Cold War. Cohen drew the line over support for the West. His magazine defined postwar liberal anticommunism, becoming the chief outlet for the urbane anticommunism of the American Committee for Cultural Freedom.

This formula found a ready market. *Commentary*'s cosmopolitan style appealed to a wider readership than *The Menorah Journal* had ever attracted. However, unlike the journal it more closely resembled, *Partisan Review*, *Commentary* made no effort to conceal its Jewish character. Cohen often expained that the chief difference between *Commentary* and *Partisan Review* was that *Commentary* admitted to being Jewish and *Partisan Review* didn't. From the outset, the magazine's chief writers were drawn from the group that Norman Podhoretz later called the "Family" of New York Intellectuals, including Harold Rosenberg, Mary McCarthy, Paul Goodman, Alfred Kazin, Hannah Arendt, Saul Bellow, William Barrett, Sidney Hook, Bell, and Howe. These early contributors and the superb editing of Cohen, Kristol, Robert Warshow, and Nathan Glazer quickly made *Commentary* one of the country's premier political and cultural journals. Within five years of its founding, the magazine's circulation climbed to twenty thousand, and those associated with it found themselves at the center of America's postwar intellectual life.

Near the end of his term at *Commentary*, Kristol agreed—at Hook's urging—to serve as the first executive secretary of the newly founded ACCF. It was during this period that Kristol made his early notoriety as a liberal-baiter and less-than-vigorous critic of McCarthyism. He acquainted himself during the same period with the classics of Western political philosophy, after hearing a lecture by conservative political philosopher Leo Strauss. Kristol had bypassed Aristotle at college. Under Strauss's influence, he was introduced to the possibility of a nonutopian politics and provided with a language for expressing it. Aristotle's prudential approach to politics conceived the political task not as an effort to shape society according to some moral or political ideal, but to cope with the world as it was. Prudence did not begin with moral principles, but took its principles from the existing world. The possibility of a nonideological approach to politics was a revelation to Kristol in the early 1950s. His later work would be marked by a never-resolved tension between his invocations of Aristotelian prudence and his ideological preoccupations. He would occasionally lament that the ideologized politics of modernity made it difficult or futile for him to write about politics in the mode he would have preferred.

ATTACKS ON LIBERALISM

Kristol's early writings showed little trace of this inner tension, however. He made his early mark as an ideologue. "When Irving Kristol was executive secretary of the ACCF," Michael Harrington recalled, "one learned to expect from him silence on those issues that were agitating the whole intellectual and academic world, and enraged communiqués on the outrages performed by people like Arthur Miller and Bertrand Russell in exaggerating the dangers to civil liberties in the U.S."[17] Kristol's idea of safeguarding cultural freedom, Harrington observed, even at the height of the McCarthyist hysteria, was to focus his attention on those remaining fellow-travelers who tried to exploit the civil liberties issue raised by McCarthyism.

As an ACCF insider, however, Kristol saw the issue differently. McCarthyism presented the ACCF with a wrenching organizational dilemma in which Kristol viewed himself as a mediator. While most ACCF members disapproved of McCarthy's demagoguery and his scattershot tactics, most were also unwilling to press the issue because of Burnham's and Max Eastman's tacit support for McCarthy. Between those who wanted the ACCF to campaign against McCarthyism and those who supported

Burnham's anti-anti-McCarthyism, Kristol later explained, he led a larger group that chose to focus only on "specific cases of violations of cultural freedom." The ACCF issued statements that vaguely criticized "certain kinds of demagogic anticommunism" and occasionally criticized abuses against the rights of specific individuals. To campaign against McCarthyism itself, however, proved to be too much to ask of liberal anticommunism. Kristol explained that, for him, "McCarthy himself was never really an issue." The question was whether America's guardians of cultural freedom in the early 1950s should not have fought against McCarthyism with the same passion they reserved for foreign struggles over which they had no influence.[18]

Kristol's response to the question was amply displayed in his legendary polemic against anti-anticommunism, " 'Civil Liberties': 1952—A Study in Confusion," published in *Commentary*. The article was written primarily as an attack on the liberal anti-anticommunism of Henry Steele Commager and Alan Barth. Holding to his centrist approach, Kristol dismissed McCarthy at the outset as a "vulgar demagogue" before taking aim, in the same paragraph, at his own target. If McCarthy was the wrong kind of anticommunist, Kristol suggested, he was at least preferable to American liberals on America's crucial political issue. "For there is one thing that the American people know about Senator McCarthy: he, like them, is unequivocally anti-Communist," Kristol wrote. "About the spokesmen for American liberalism, they know no such thing. And with some justification."

He swiftly reviewed the recent sins of American liberalism, rolling widely disparate cases ranging from Commager to the National Lawyers Guild into a single indictment, before moving to his breathless conclusion. It was a fact of modern American history, Kristol announced, that until recently "the major segment of American liberalism" had denied the existence of Soviet concentration camps, "blessed" the liquidation of millions of Soviet kulaks, "apologized" for the Soviet purges of 1936–38, "solemnly approved" the trials of the Old Bolsheviks, and "applauded" the massacre of the noncommunist Left by Communists during the Spanish Civil War. American liberals routinely claimed to be anticommunist, "but their rejection of Communism has all the semblance of a preliminary gesture, a repudiation aiming to linger in the memory as a floating credential." It was this betrayal of authentic liberalism that McCarthyism fed upon. Kristol posed as the true liberal. By failing to distinguish between its genuine achievements and its sins, he argued, American liberalism was disarming itself before McCarthy, "who is eager to have it appear that its achievements *are* its sins."[19]

Kristol then reasserted his centrist pose, contending that as long as liberals and McCarthyites insisted that the right of Communists to teach or work in government was a matter of principle, "we shall remain distant from that intelligent discrimination between one case and another, and one situation and another, which alone can give us our true bearings."[20] The underlying source of liberal confusion over the civil liberties issue, he claimed, was that liberals assumed that defending liberalism required protecting the "right" to be a Communist.

It was an extraordinary polemic, filled, as R. M. MacIver and Joseph Rauh observed, with Kristol's considerable powers of sarcasm and demeaning characterization as well as his penchant for sweeping generalizations based on quotations ripped out of context. It was a spectacular falsehood to claim that "the main segment of American liberalism" had denied the existence of Soviet concentration camps, blessed the liquidation of the kulaks, apologized for the mass purges, approved the trials of the Old Bolsheviks, and applauded the Soviet secret police (GPU/NKVD) massacres of the noncommunist Left during the Spanish Civil War. Applied to the fellow-traveling procommunism purveyed by *The Nation*, Kristol's polemic was devastating. Applied to the main segment of American liberalism, it was something else.[21] The attack foreshadowed his later career. While he deftly ridiculed those who exaggerated the ravages of McCarthyism, his own attacks on current American liberalism were equally exaggerated. In his descriptions, liberals were fellow-travelers like Owen Lattimore, who "followed the Communist line as if magnetized by it, including a docile zig-zag during the Stalin–Hitler pact." Or more commonly, they were dupes like Barth, who defended the civil liberties of Communists with arguments that amounted to "arrant nonsense . . . uttered in all sincerity."[22]

Two polemical misrepresentations were combined. The first was that fellow-traveling pro-Communists were categorized as liberals. Procommunist intellectuals such as James Aronson, Cedric Belfrage, and Hewlett Johnson were quite forthcoming about their contempt for liberal democracy. As Kristol observed, their politics was amply represented in the National Lawyers Guild. During the same period, Norman Thomas tirelessly explained why liberalism and procommunism were antithetical: The wellspring of any liberalism worthy of the name was a commitment to individual freedom; to associate Soviet apologists with liberalism was to trash the liberal democratic tradition. But while Thomas continued to regard communism as an evil perversion of socialism, he became alarmed after the war that the causes of freedom and anticommunism—which he regarded as liberal and democratic socialist causes—were being exploited by reactionaries.[23] Kristol's essay gave him an occasion to press the point. After Kristol's essay appeared, Thomas generously complimented *Commentary* for publishing several articles on what he called certain "sentimental professional 'liberals' " (the quotation marks made his first point), and then proposed that *Commentary* should next address the resurgent antiliberalism of the Right. "Our cultural war for freedom cannot be won by tactics as nearly imitative of Communism as those of Senator McCarthy and others of his ilk," Thomas warned. It was not advice that Kristol or *Commentary* acted upon.[24]

Kristol's second basic misrepresentation lay in his characterizations of liberal scholars such as Barth, who defended the constitutional rights of Communists. Those who upheld the civil liberties of Communists practiced a crafty rhetoric, he observed. While their writings were not explicitly pro-Communist, their arguments were "compelled by the logic of disingenuousness and special pleading to become so in effect." Barth's appeal to the indivisibility of freedom was a sham. When he and others claimed to defend "our" liberties while defending the liberties of Communists, Kristol claimed, they deserved to be taken *as* Communists.[25]

At the end of his indictment of what he called the main segment of American liberalism, Kristol announced that the existence of Soviet concentration camps, the liquidation of the kulaks, and other communist crimes carried no weight at all with a liberal like Barth, "who knows that, though a man repeat the Big Lie, so long as he is of a liberal intention he is saved."[26] This characterization was easily falsified by Barth's writings. However, when Rauh refuted Kristol's accusation by quoting extensive passages from Barth's *The Loyalty of Free Men*, Kristol replied only that he couldn't take the space to make a textual analysis. Barth had expressed personal sympathies for those non-Communists who joined the Loyalist cause in Spain and the Popular Front in the United States during the 1930s. His writings had nonetheless fully recounted and condemned the crimes of the Soviet state and the guilt of American pro-Communists in closing their eyes to "the suffering and degradation of millions of human beings" in the Soviet Union. He further reproached the naivete and poor judgment of noncommunist progressives who joined the various front organizations in the 1930s. He asserted without equivocation that American Communists were "enemies of the United States because they are enemies of American values, no less than because they are tools of a foreign government."[27]

Kristol brushed these arguments aside. His article closed with the announcement that Barth, like former attorney general Francis Biddle, was refusing to admit "what is now apparent: that a generation of earnest

reformers who helped give this country a New Deal should find themselves in retrospect stained with the guilt of having lent aid and comfort to
Stalinist tyranny."[28] This rendering of the legacy of Franklin Roosevelt
drew apoplectic replies from some of those stained by their association
with the New Deal. Rauh indignantly recalled that the New Dealers had,
in fact, spent their time "drafting, administering, and enforcing progressive legislation to make this country safe from Stalinist tyranny—or any
other kind of tyranny for that matter."[29]

Kristol struck back. "I am charged with a flagrant misreading of the
history of the '30s when I assert that the major segment of American
liberalism allowed itself to be used as an echo for the Communist Big Lie,"
he observed. He countered that New Dealers like Rauh were spinning a
"pure myth" about the supposed anticommunist record of modern American liberalism. "There are still enough people whose memories are good
enough to recall the imposing list of 400 names signed to a public letter
vigorously defending the Soviet regime—published in the *Nation* in the
very same issue that announced the Stalin–Hitler pact!" he wrote. "American liberalism was grievously infected by Communism during that period;
to deny it serves only to encourage a suspicion that the infection has not
been eliminated."[30]

Though he claimed to support the New Deal heritage in certain
undefined respects, Kristol's polemical strategy again equated New Deal
liberalism with procommunist Popular Frontism. The public letter to
which he referred was the 1939 group letter (described in the preceding
chapter) organized by Corliss Lamont's procommunist American–Soviet
Friendship Committee and co-sponsored by *The Daily Worker*. It actually
contained only 165 names and was signed mostly by little-known party
hacks and fellow-travelers. In his outraged response to Kristol, Arthur
Schlesinger noted that only one of the letter's signatories, Robert Morss
Lovett, could be classified as a New Deal liberal. This fact, he asserted,
"amply suggests the character of Mr. Kristol's argument."[31] Schlesinger
reeled off a list of actual New Dealers to substantiate his claim that the
New Deal was engineered by practical, anticommunist reformers who
were now being defamed by Kristol's "disingenuous" and "symptomatic"
attacks.

Schlesinger didn't deny that a handful of Communists had wormed
their way into the New Deal government by concealing their political
views. For Schlesinger, however, what was finally at issue between liberals
and critics like Kristol marked the difference between the New Deal
reformers and the New York Intellectuals. During the 1930s and 1940s, he
observed, while the New Dealers saved and extended democratic gains in

America's existing system, the New York Intellectuals ranted that liberal democracy was about to be overthrown by a proletarian revolution. The same traits marked the New York Intellectuals after they gave up Trotskyism. The New York Intellectuals were displaying "the same vision and the same hysteria today," he argued, though now from the Right. "And they are not the slightest bit more reliable in their views of American politics than they were in the days of the *Modern Quarterly*."[32] It was an observation that anticipated the emergence of neoconservatism.

Schlesinger's rejoinder went to the heart of Kristol's characterization of existing American liberalism. In Kristol's portrayal, American liberalism had been and continued to be dominated by fellow-travelers and dupes who effectively conspired, as he put it, to defend communism as "merely another form of 'dissent' or 'noncomformity.' "[33] This claim was made after the Americans for Democratic Action (ADA) had decisively outstripped the fellow-traveling Progressive Citizens of America (PCA) as American liberalism's predominant organizational vehicle. Founded in 1947 by such anticommunist liberals as Reinhold Niebuhr, Chester Bowles, David Dubinsky, Marquis Childs, Eleanor Roosevelt, Walter Ruether, Leon Henderson, James Loeb, Wilson Wyatt, and Joseph Rauh, the ADA had grown out of Niebuhr's Union for Democratic Action (UDA) and had continued the UDA policy of excluding Communists from membership. Kristol rightly observed that the latter policy had been unpopular among liberals while the United States and Soviet Union were wartime allies, but the swift demise of the PCA after the war and the humiliating defeat suffered by Henry Wallace in his 1948 presidential campaign had reduced the fellow-traveling movement to fragments by the time that Kristol bemoaned its hegemony over American liberalism. The Wallace campaign was derailed by the overwhelmingly negative counter-campaigns waged by ADA liberals and others, including Norman Thomas, who exposed the communist influence in Wallace's Progressive party and forcefully condemned Wallace's blindness toward it.[34] By the end of that campaign, the death of what remained of procommunist "liberalism" was certified, and the triumph of the anticommunism of Niebuhr, Ruether, Rauh, and Schlesinger within American liberalism was unarguable. Most American liberals, for example, supported their country's intervention in Korea. As Schlesinger suggested, what was finally interesting about Kristol's writings in the early 1950s was the enduring influence of his sectarian leftist background, not only upon his polemical style, but also upon his attitude toward modern liberalism.

Though most of his writings during this period attacked American liberalism, Kristol continued to think of himself as a neoliberal of some kind, if only because he accepted Lionel Trilling's often-cited remark that liberalism was America's only intellectual tradition. Working out one's own form of liberalism was an intellectual necessity in a country where no conservative intellectual tradition existed. This assumption was strengthened by Kristol's awareness as a Jew that the struggles to attain equal rights for religious and racial minorities in America had been advanced by left-liberal movements. Against this background, conservatism did not exist as a serious alternative.

But Kristol's liberalism never extended far beyond his reflections on these particular factors. Not only was he not a liberal, as he made emphatically clear, in the sense of the term represented by Barth, Commager, or Eleanor Roosevelt, but he was not a liberal of the militantly anticommunist kind represented by Niebuhr, Ruether, Schlesinger, or Thomas. These figures retained an energizing sympathy for the poor and a commitment to further democratic gains toward equality that Kristol lacked. For them, liberalism stood for more than individual freedom. As Stephen Spender would soon complain, however, Kristol did not share their sympathy with the condition of victims or their commitments to greater equality. Spender's assessment would be drawn from his acquaintance with Kristol as co-editor of *Encounter*, the journal founded in 1952 by the Congress for Cultural Freedom. Though he later claimed with believable incredulity to have been oblivious to the Congress's inner workings, the trajectory of Kristol's life was significantly affected by his employer's association with the Central Intelligence Agency.

THE CULTURAL FRONT: CCF, *ENCOUNTER*, AND THE COLD WAR

The Congress for Cultural Freedom was principally forged through the efforts of Kristol's former sparring partner in Alcove No. 1, Melvin Lasky. After the war, which he spent as a combat historian with the U.S. Seventh Army in France and Germany, Lasky remained in Germany to serve as the poorly remunerated American correspondent for the *New Leader* and *Partisan Review*. Living under the government of the Allied Four-Power Kommandatura, he cut a flamboyant figure, as Peter Coleman has recounted, "with his short, stocky figure, his oriental eyes, his Lenin-like spade beard, his cosmopolitan culture, his easy-going New York manner, and his histrionic delivery, alternately whispering and thundering."[35] In October 1947, at the height of the Zhdanovist purges of Soviet intellectuals, Lasky gave a blistering speech at the German Writers Conference in East Berlin condemning the purges. It was a courageous act in a city not yet divided but threatened by Soviet forces. Under pressure from Soviet protests, the U.S. commander, General Lucius D. Clay, briefly considered expelling Lasky from Berlin. But Lasky's speech also caught the attention of more sympathetic officials in the American government, who sought his advice on how to influence the cultural politics of postwar Europe. Lasky recommended an editorial venture which in 1948 became the U.S.-sponsored German cultural magazine, *Der Monat*: Melvin Lasky, editor.

The following year, after the Berlin blockade, Lasky met with Michael Josselson to organize an international conference of anticommunist liberals and social democrats to be held in Berlin. They received crucial assistance from the city's newly elected anticommunist mayor, Ernst Reuter, and were funded by the German and U.S. governments. This conference, which convened in June 1950, became the founding convention of the CCF. [36]

Like Lasky, Josselson was a former OSS officer who remained in Europe after the war. Independently from Lasky's efforts in Germany, Josselson organized a branch of the CCF in Paris, with assistance from Arthur Koestler, Raymond Aron, and American unionist Irving Brown. The Congress's organizing convention was thus launched principally through the efforts of Lasky and Josselson, both of whom, it was later revealed, were working through the cultural affairs program of the CIA. [37] Josselson, who became the executive director of the CCF, clearly knew the source of the Congress's funding, since he was a CIA agent. Whether Lasky knew would remain a matter of dispute.

The CCF was meant by most of its members to be an open community of mostly left-leaning, anticommunist intellectuals who opposed totalitarianism without waving national or narrowly ideological flags. [38] It campaigned for the rights of persecuted intellectuals and organized international conferences on such topics as the politics of science, the future of ideology, and strategies of economic development. Congress events ranged widely over these subjects, featuring a rich mixture of liberal, social democratic, and conservative anticommunist opinion. The difference in spirit between the liberal anticommunism of the CCF and the neoconservative anticommunism that succeeded it would be measurable by the wider range of arguments entertained at Congress events of the 1950s. [39]

But the crowning legacy of the CCF was its network of periodicals. These journals, which were strongly anticommunist and generally pro-American in their editorial lines, included Lasky's *Der Monat* in Germany, Ignazio Silone and Nicola Chiaromonte's *Tempo Presente* in Italy, François

Bondy's *Preuves* in France, Friedrich Torberg's *Forum* in Austria, James McAuley's *Quadrant* in Australia, Nissim Ezekiel's *Quest* in India, Julian Gorkin's *Cuadernos* in Latin America (published in Paris), and, among others, *Encounter* in England. In the 1960s, the Congress would add to this list Tawfig Sayigh's *Hiwar* in Lebanon, Hoki Ishihara's *Jiyu* in Japan, Rajat Neogy's *Transition* in Uganda, and Rodriguez Monegal's *Mundo Nuevo* in Latin America.[40]

Encounter, the organization's flagship journal, resulted from the merger of two separate proposals. Hook proposed an English-language journal with Kristol as editor, an idea that was endorsed by CCF officers in Paris. The Congress's newly formed British affiliate wanted to launch a journal with the eminent poet Spender as editor. The two proposals were eventually conflated. Needing to get away from the overbearing and increasingly unstable Cohen, Kristol resigned from *Commentary* and moved to England to become co-editor of *Encounter* with Spender.

Their journal quickly became one of the premier cultural and political periodicals in the English language. From the outset, the dividing line of editorial labor was drawn between the literary and political areas. Spender filled the literary sections of the October 1953 inaugural issue with pieces by Christopher Isherwood, C. Day Lewis, Albert Camus, Virginia Woolf, and himself. Kristol's political section ran articles by Leslie Fiedler and Nathan Glazer and covered the Congress's institutional interests with articles by Nicholas Nabokov (the Russian-born CCF secretary general) and Denis de Rougemont (president of the CCF executive committee). Kristol also wrote the opening editorial, "After the Apocalypse," which declared that with the deaths of Mussolini, Hitler, and Stalin, the mythologies of an epoch had also finally been extinguished. *Encounter* would not promote a political line, he promised, "though its editors have opinions they will not hesitate to express."

A liberal note was sounded. In the wake of the destruction of the Marxist-Leninist creed, Kristol wrote, the task of the current generation was to reconcile equality with liberty and confront "the intolerableness of hunger and degradation in a world that seems to have the resources to remove them." These problems had survived the pernicious solutions they provoked. What united such otherwise disparate intellectuals as John Dewey, Karl Jaspers, Jacques Maritain, and Bertrand Russell in the Congress's work, he explained, were love of liberty and respect for culture. Kristol promised that *Encounter* would explore differences of interpretation and opinion rather than slur them.[41]

Robert Nisbet later remarked that even during this transitional phase, Kristol was a conservative without realizing it. Kristol's inaugural editorial for *Encounter* nonetheless gave a reasonably accurate and liberal-leaning description of the magazine's outlook. *Encounter* mixed a vigorously anti-communist and generally pro-American perspective with otherwise wide-ranging coverage of political and cultural topics.

The extent of Kristol's editorial independence at *Encounter* would later be fiercely disputed, however. Kristol and his editorial successor at the magazine, Melvin Lasky, repeatedly insisted that the CCF did not exercise any control over the magazine's editorial policies. Though there was little direct evidence to the contrary, Kristol's assurances on the matter were clearly exaggerated; for in the early years of the magazine's existence, he was repeatedly forced to defend his editorial independence from Jossel-son's and Nabokov's attempted encroachments. This conflict reached its peak in 1955, when Josselson and Nabokov joined in an unlikely coalition with Spender, merging different complaints about Kristol, to press for his removal as co-editor. Because the CIA refused to divulge information about its dealings with the CCF, it would remain unclear afterward whether Josselson acted on his own or under orders from his superiors in the agency. In any case, as his exchange of letters with Kristol in February 1955 made clear, Josselson believed that Kristol was pitching the maga-zine too narrowly toward the provincial interests of its intellectual British readership. Josselson wanted more attention given to Central Europe, the United States, the Third World, and the errors of the British Labour party. At Josselson's insistence, Kristol agreed to run an article criticizing the Labour party's policy toward China. However, he begged Josselson for time and independence to prove that his own editorial mix was the best prescription for the magazine. "I believe I know the kind of magazine that you and the Congress want, and I shall do my best to deliver," he pleaded. "Let's wait and see. . . . Your suggestions are always welcome—but, basically, I have to do things my way, because I don't know how to do it any other. If my way turns out to be inadequate, there's always a 'final solution.' "42

But Josselson decided the solution couldn't wait. The same month, Nabokov asked Schlesinger to inquire whether Dwight Macdonald would care to replace Kristol as co-editor of *Encounter*. The former editor of *Politics* was definitely interested. For his own reasons, Spender eagerly supported the idea and wrote to Josselson that getting Macdonald would be "the most amazing piece of good luck and should be seized."43 His public reason was that Kristol lacked the stature and experience for his position. At the time, Kristol's writings amounted to a few articles and book reviews. "I think Stephen, understandably, rather resented being coeditor with me," he later recalled. "He was a very distinguished poet and writer, and I was not particularly distinguished, certainly not in England."[44] Spender therefore urged the CCF to offer Kristol's position to Macdonald.

There was a further reason to offer the job to Macdonald, which Spender explained in a letter to Hook. The political editor of *Encounter* "should be concerned not just with the wickedness of communists but also with the condition of victims, and with victimization everywhere," he argued. "The concept of the defence of freedom has surely to be based on a concept of the rights of humanity and not just on a 'case' held by anticommunists against communists."[45] Spender was uncomfortable with the spirit of the ACCF's anticommunism, which Kristol exemplified. Most of the Americans seemed obsessed with what Hook called "taking the fight to the enemy." Their consuming passion was anticommunism. Kristol's few substantive articles and his conception of the magazine's purpose revolved around this axis. What was needed to advance the magazine's mission of reconciling equality with liberty, however, was a driving concern with the condition of victims and an interest in constructing the most emancipatory social alternatives to communism. These were qualities that Kristol lacked. For the same reasons, Spender urged (apparently not realizing where the money was coming from) that Macdonald would make an ideal editor for the magazine.[46]

Kristol's supporters in the ACCF viewed this development with alarm not only because it demeaned Kristol, but also because they viewed Macdonald as the wrong kind of anticommunist. Macdonald had a "plague-on-both-your-houses attitude toward the Kremlin and the West," Hook later explained. "I admired his editorial independence, but I regarded Macdonald as irresponsible." Taking the offensive against Josselson's maneuvers, Hook ominously threatened to resign from the CCF board and "blow the Congress out of the water" if Kristol was dismissed.[47] That stemmed the tide. Macdonald subsequently accepted an invitation to join the *Encounter* staff for one year as an associate editor working under Spender and Kristol.

The incident would be revealing for the light it cast upon the question of CIA control over the magazine. Though it was rumored throughout the 1950s that such foundations as the J. M. Kaplan Fund (which funded Norman Thomas's Institute for International Labor Research) and the Farfield Foundation (which funded the CCF) were CIA fronts, the rumors were always indignantly denied by officers affiliated with these organizations. The rumors themselves were generated, in part, by ACCF officers who had figured out how the CCF was financed. Diana Trilling once recalled that as an officer in the ACCF, she was aware, "and it was my clear impression that everyone else on the board was aware, that the international body with which we were associated was probably funded by the government." They strongly suspected that the Farfield Foundation was fronting for the CIA or the State Department. Because the American committee was the only national committee that did not receive Farfield subsidies, and because it was known that the CIA was prohibited from subsidizing organizations within the United States, it was widely believed among ACCF officers that the CCF's funds came from the CIA. "And this was often a subject of discussion between myself and my friends," Trilling explained. "The editors of *Partisan Review*, for instance, felt handicapped in terms of foreign circulation by lack of a subsidy such as was given *Encounter*, the intellectual journal which the Congress supported in England."

Their suspicions were confirmed in the early 1950s at an ACCF Executive Board meeting that Trilling attended, when Norman Thomas (the board chairman) announced that the chronically insolvent organization was too broke to pay the next month's rent. "Mr. Thomas could see but a single solution," Trilling recalled. "He would 'phone Allen'; he returned from the telephone to tell us that a check for a thousand dollars would be in the mail the next morning. None of us could fail to know that the 'Allen' who tided us over was Allen Dulles, head of the CIA, and that in the strictest sense it was even a breach of legality for him to give us help. But none of us, myself included, protested."[48] By then, the ACCF's link with the CIA was apparently well enough known or assumed that phoning Allen Dulles for money (in this case, an illegal subsidy) was a task casually performed and reported.

Yet when *The New York Times* finally revealed, in 1966, that the CIA had funded the CCF through a system of dummy foundations, Spender, Kristol, and Lasky tried to discredit the story without explicitly denying it. (Lasky had succeeded Kristol as editor of *Encounter* in 1959.) They wrote to the *Times* that the CCF's funds were "derived from various recognized foundations—all of them (from such institutions as the Ford and Rockefeller Foundations to the smaller ones) publicly listed in the official directories." This evasion and others like it from their supporters, including Schlesinger, successfully deflected public attention to the CCF's more reputable sponsors. The *Times* meekly editorialized in response that *Encounter* was "a distinguished international journal of independent opinion."[49] But it was through the smaller institutions, as *Ramparts* revealed the following year, that the CIA subsidies were passed along.

Encouraged by the timid response of *The New York Times*, *Encounter*'s editors moved to restore their reputations by going on the offensive. Shortly after the articles in the *Times* appeared, Conor Cruise O'Brien made an inviting target of himself by tweaking the *Encounter* editors for their connections to the CIA. O'Brien had a theory about how the magazine had operated. The most shameful aspect of the *Encounter* affair, he knowingly argued, was that for more than a decade, the magazine's editors had induced major writers unwittingly to serve the CIA's purposes. Their contributions provided respectable cover for the magazine's actual mission, which was to produce CIA propaganda. The propaganda interest was served by lesser writers, O'Brien explained—people who were, "as the Belgians used to say about Moise Tshombe, *comprehensifs,* that is, they could take a hint."

O'Brien's accusation presumed greater complicity by *Encounter's* editors than anyone had admitted or proved, and in its subsequent issue, the magazine's monthly columnist responded with calculated vengeance. Goronwy Rees bitterly accused O'Brien of McCarthyist tactics in his attack on *Encounter* and concluded that O'Brien had become "the Joe McCarthy of politico-cultural criticism, hunting for CIA agents beneath the beds of Stephen Spender, Irving Kristol, Melvin Lasky, and Frank Kermode." This table-turning cry of "McCarthyism" soon backfired, however, when O'Brien sued *Encounter* for libel and won a judgment in Ireland.[50] Shortly afterward, *Ramparts* revealed that CIA infiltrators had manipulated the National Students Association since the early 1950s. The story disclosed numerous details about the workings of the CIA's elaborate front system. "They're out for the kill this time," Josselson wrote to Macdonald. Subsequent investigations revealed that *Encounter* was established with a $30,000 grant from the CIA and sustained until 1964 with CIA subsidies. These disclosures forced *Encounter* off the attack mode. Faced with overwhelming evidence and the prospect of heavy legal damages, the magazine apologized to O'Brien and agreed to pay his legal expenses.[51]

But Spender, Kristol, and Lasky continued to deny that they had ever known anything about the relationship between the CIA and the CCF. Spender angrily resigned his position as a corresponding editor for *Encounter,* claiming that he had been deceived. His English replacement as co-editor, Frank Kermode, who had only recently threatened to sue the *New Statesman* over a prospective article by O'Brien, also resigned in protest. The most elementary facts about the origins and financing of the CCF, which were understood among the officers of its American affiliate, were somehow completely unknown to the American and English editors of its chief periodical. Kristol maintained that he remained ignorant of the CIA role in the CCF after he returned to the United States.

The issue became more uncomfortable for *Encounter* editors in May 1967, when the former CIA official responsible for CCF affairs took the offensive in an article titled "I'm Glad the CIA Is 'Immoral.'" "Writing in the

Saturday Evening Post, Thomas Braden (later of television *Crossfire* fame) defended the CIA's covert operations record and revealed a secret in the process. He explained that the CIA's International Organization Division was organized to disguise operations that advanced America's national interest. In Europe, the CIA had concentrated on manipulating social democrats because, in the CIA's estimation, the social democrats were "the only people who gave a damn about fighting Communism." Agents placed in the field by the CIA were made aware that CIA-financed foundations would be "quite generous" toward foreign magazines that advanced America's interests. For example, Braden wrote, there was *Encounter,* "the magazine published in England and dedicated to the proposition that cultural achievement and political freedom were interdependent. . . . We had placed one agent in a Europe-based organization of intellectuals called the Congress for Cultural Freedom. Another agent became an editor of *Encounter.* The agents could not only propose anti-Communist programs to the official leaders of the organizations but they could also solve the inevitable budgetary problems. Why not see if the needed money could be obtained from 'American foundations'?"[52]

Braden's article was a bombshell for those associated with *Encounter.* It had been bad enough when Spender, Kristol, and Lasky were forced to claim that they hadn't known about the CIA's role in their work. Now one of them was identified as a CIA agent. The agent on the CCF staff was Josselson. The unanswered question was, Who was the agent editor?

Spender was ruled out because, as Steinfels later remarked, he somehow seemed to everyone the natural dupe. Among insiders, opinions varied over Spender's professed ignorance about the CIA's role in CCF affairs. Some ACCF veterans, including Arnold Beichman, were convinced that Spender couldn't possibly have worked so closely for so many years with the group without learning about the CIA connection. Kristol, on the other hand, insisted that he believed his former colleague's denials. On at least one occasion, Spender had questioned a contributing foundation about the CIA rumors and had received an indignant denial. Spender was justifiably angered, Kristol said, when the rumors turned out to be true.[53]

Diana Trilling offered a helpful assessment of the matter. "While it seems hard to believe," she conceded, "I think it is possible for Stephen to have done as much work as he did for the Congress for Cultural Freedom without realizing it was being funded by some department or agency of the United States government and reporting back to it." She observed that Spender was a poet—"and poets can be pretty vague characters"—but from personal experience with Spender she also knew him to be an extraordinarily trusting person. This was the natural dupe defense, but

Trilling didn't leave it there. "Still, when he and Nicky Nabokov were sent by the Congress to India to see Nehru," she noted, "I should think that even a poet would begin to ask questions about the purpose of the visit."[54]

Between the two remaining possibilities, the evidence seemed to weigh most heavily against Lasky, especially after Lasky belatedly admitted in 1967 that he had, in fact, known about the CIA connection since 1963. Spender was particularly bitter that Lasky had deceived him for at least the succeeding four years. He complained that Lasky's mendacity on the matter had misled several people, including himself, into making false statements about it.[55] These deceptions damaged Lasky's reputation and confirmed the suspicions of many observers that he was the agent identified by Braden. Along with Josselson, Lasky had organized the CCF's founding conference. His professional attainments were directly attributable to his government contacts. Despite his continued denials, many observers concluded that, assuming the credibility of Braden's report, the agent to whom he referred was Lasky.

The problem with this conclusion was that the duties described cynically by Braden—solving "the inevitable budget problems" by seeing "if the needed money could be obtained from 'American foundations' "— were those of a founding editor. If Kristol wasn't the agent referred to by Braden, his subsequent threat to sue Braden was justified, since Braden's remarks clearly pointed toward him.[56] Kristol later explained that although he heard the rumors about CIA funding over the years, he routinely dismissed them as leftist propaganda. He was assured on several occasions by the president of the Farfield Foundation, Julius Fleischmann, that there was no truth to them.[57] Apparently, he was easily assured on the matter, even though many of his American colleagues believed the rumors and had evidence to support them. Kristol could only have sustained his belief about the CIA stories by choosing to ignore the evidence his own friends had gathered.

In his account, he dismissed their conclusions on the basis of his personal experience, having never been censored by anyone representing the CIA, the Farfield Foundation, or the CCF. As he acknowledged, however, censorship would have been unnecessary in an operation run with some sophistication by agents who had the right people in place. Kristol conceded, "Perhaps it will be said that my own frequently expressed opinions were so clearly 'safe,' from the CIA's point of view, that censorship was superfluous. Maybe so."[58]

Kristol disputed this reading of the episode by noting that he was nearly replaced in 1955 by Macdonald. "Could the CIA really have 'endorsed' him?" he asked. "Dwight has spent a fruitful life and distinguished career purposefully being a security risk to just about everyone and everything within reach of his typewriter."[59] As Kristol suggested, it was certainly true that if Macdonald *had* become the uncensored political editor of *Encounter*, the CIA would have found itself with a bad investment problem. The problem with Kristol's argument was that Macdonald didn't get the job. Though his nomination was strongly supported by those in the CCF who apparently didn't understand the nature of their organization, the proposal was derailed by Kristol's American supporters, who were more in tune with the sponsor's agenda. The political section of *Encounter* remained in Kristol's hands until 1958, when, from the CIA's perspective, the position was passed to someone at least equally reliable. Steinfels later remarked that if it was difficult to imagine how Kristol could have been so deeply involved in this affair without ever realizing what it was about, it was also true that no one could prove he had dissembled on the matter.[60] Kristol's account was not unbelievable, since it would not have marked the first or last time that he dismissed a substantive challenge to his beliefs on ad hominem grounds. What bothered Steinfels was that, unlike Spender, Kristol never reacted to the episode like a man who had been wrongfully deceived.

Kristol left *Encounter* in 1959 to become editor of Max Ascoli's biweekly liberal anticommunist magazine, *The Reporter*. The following year he was appointed senior editor and executive vice president of Basic Books, the small but prestigious publishing firm. A highly accomplished editor, Kristol played a key role in turning Basic Books into one of the country's premier social science publishers. His position also opened opportunities for him to become the chief publicist and rainmaker for an emergent intellectual Right.

THE 1960S: A NEW CONSERVATISM EMERGES

Using the editorial facilities of Basic Books, a gift from Warren Manshel, and a sponsorship arrangement with Freedom House, Kristol and Bell launched their scholarly, right-leaning social policy journal, *The Public Interest*, in 1965. Bell had recently completed an unsatisfactory project with the Commission for the Study of Automation and was disturbed that the social policy field was producing "a lot of sloppy thinking."[61] Kristol concurred that most government policymakers were working with a shortage of hard information. The most potentially valuable information generated by the universities was not getting filtered to policymakers or the public, they thought. This problem was especially troublesome in the mid-sixties, when public disputes were generating inflamed declarations of moral certitude on both sides.[62] The field's most celebrated work at the time—Michael Harrington's *The Other America*—typified the problem. With few hard numbers to cite, the book used anecdotal information, the few quantitative studies that existed, and a powerful moral argument to make he case for massive government efforts to alleviate poverty in the United States. *The Other America* called for a response of national outrage "at a monstrous example of needless suffering in the most advanced society in the world."[63]

The Public Interest would be written in a more dispassionate spirit. Bell and Kristol announced in their inaugural issue that the aim of the journal would be simultaneously modest and presumptuous. "It is to help all of us, when we discuss issues of public policy, to know a little better what we are talking about—and preferably in time to make such knowledge effective," they wrote. Their journal would run the risk of seeming a "middle-aged magazine for middle-aged readers." It would resist the passions of the time and their ideological progeny. The editors explained that it was the nature of ideology to preconceive reality, but that their magazine would eschew such prefabrications. Ideological writing was often interesting, but was always subjective, unbalanced, and distorted. *The Public Interest* would pursue objectivity, making room "for the occasional 'dull' article that merely reports the truth about a matter under public discussion." Bell and Kristol cautioned that the truth in social science was often no more intellectually or emotionally exciting than the truth about mathematics.[64] Their strictures against ideology were undoubtedly inspired by Bell, author of *The End of Ideology*, but the closing analogy and the casual claims to "the truth" bore the marks of Kristol.

The Public Interest gave the first notice that a new conservatism was brewing in America. Bell and Kristol filled the journal with cautionary warnings about the limits and unintended consequences of social policy. Nathan Glazer, Edward C. Banfield, Roger Starr, and Aaron Wildavsky catalogued the failures of the Great Society's housing and welfare policies. James Q. Wilson highlighted the problems of government bureaucracy and criticized liberal approaches to America's racial dilemmas.[65] Daniel P. Moynihan gave an early warning, in 1967, that America's war on poverty was faring as badly as its war in Vietnam. The following year, John H. Bunzel gave an early verdict against black studies a generation before multiculturalism had a name.[66]

Kristol later explained that the purpose of *The Public Interest* was to promote good social science, which he defined as empirical analysis that corrected the illusions of bad social science and dampened all liberal enthusiasms.[67] In the name of promoting equal opportunity, his journal tirelessly argued, modern liberalism was breeding dependency in the welfare class, impeding America's economic growth, and overexpanding America's New Class of public sector functionaries. American policy-makers needed hard information to combat the fantasies and interests of America's intellectual class.

Steinfels aptly observed in the late 1970s that there were three Irving Kristols. The first was the amateur philosophical essayist who pondered such questions as the lessons of history, the social functions of religion, and human nature. The second was the figure who, while never writing this way himself, promoted the hard-minded, quantitative, putatively nonideological work of the think-tank economists and policy analysts. The third was the political polemicist who was "less concerned with large truths or precise facts than with skewering particular political opponents; or rather concerned about wielding large truths or precise facts *in order* to skewer particular political opponents."[68] Kristol's editorial tasks satisfied his second self, but during the early 1960s the pundit and ideological polemicist in him found their chief outlet in *The New Leader*.

His distinctive polemical style was perfected during his term as a *New Leader* columnist. Unlike the articles that he approved for *The Public Interest*, which often proved as dull as he predicted, Kristol's magazine columns were unfailingly provocative, opinionated, and sometimes inflammatory. Whether his topic was the politics of book reviewing, the failures of the Kennedy administration, the stakes in Vietnam, or the poverty of equal-ity, his columns featured attention-grabbing, exaggerated assertions de-fended with an air of utter certainty.[69] Before his own turn to neoconserva-tism, Joseph Epstein characterized Kristol's style as "commanding in tone, supremely confident about subjects that are elsewhere held to be still in the flux of controversy, assuming always that anyone who thinks differ-ently is perverse or inept." An essay by Kristol, Epstein observed, "is scarcely designed to incite reasoned discussion."[70] This characterization was itself a polemical exaggeration—the kind often incited by Kristol's polemical thrusts. As his columns on Kennedy's economic and Vietnam policies exemplified, Kristol was unafraid to admit his lack of expertise on various topics. These admissions didn't prevent him, however, from pronouncing on the basic faults of Kennedy's economic policy or the plain truth about Vietnam's cultural backwardness. The frequently noted smug-ness of Kristol's writing style was affected, in part, by his penchant for announcing "the plain truth," "the simple truth," or "the obvious truth" about his subjects, which was always identical with his verdict on them.

The plain truth about Vietnam was that this pathetic country was "barely capable of decent self-government under the very best of conditions." Kristol's position on Vietnam was advanced with his customary acerbic wit. "While I am prepared to give credence to most of the criticisms directed against the Diem Administration," he wrote two months before Diem was murdered, "I cannot place my hope in political-religious leaders whose mode of protest is to make funeral pyres of themselves. Such men doubtless have great virtues, but it is unlikely that a capacity for effective government can be reckoned among them." The most that could be hoped for in Vietnam, he argued, was "to remove this little, backward nation from the front lines of the cold war so that it can stew quietly in its own political juice."[71]

Kristol's few writings about the war, which were uncharacteristically tentative, leaned toward a doubtful view that serious American national interests were at stake. The war posed a larger question for Kristol: Could America's vision of world order, which had gone largely unquestioned (at least at home) since 1942, be sustained in the face of its evident new costs? Kristol celebrated the achievements of the Pax Americana, under which the world's nations had been "persuaded, shamed, coerced, and bribed to observe the civilities essential to a decent international community." He conceded that the world order imposed by American power was parochial and nonhistorical, and that there was "more than a little hypocrisy involved, as the United States found itself of necessity engaging in traditional imperialist maneuvers while rejecting the imperialist ethos and proclaiming the inviolable rights of nations."[72] But because the Pax Americana promoted democracy and served America's interests, he submitted that the moral, political, and economic costs of what he called America's "welfare state imperialism" had proved, until recently, to be worth bearing. The question in 1966 was whether America's war in Vietnam was also worth the costs.

It was an open question for Kristol. He fretted that the responsibilities of empire were difficult to bear in democracies, because empires required anti-egalitarian ideologies, large professional armies, and landed ruling classes driven by visions of imperial glory. An empire's sense of purpose, he cautioned, could only be sustained by self-confident ruling elites. These prerequisites were lacking in the United States. Moreover, Vietnam was not Guatemala or the Philippines. America wasn't in Vietnam to help the Vietnamese. The United States was faced in Vietnam not merely with a challenge to its welfare-state imperialism, but with "the naked responsibilities of world power, the assumption of which has too close a resemblance to imperialism of an older and more classic variety."[73]

The resemblance to classic imperialism was magnified by the fact that, unlike in the Korean War, the United States was fighting in Vietnam without any legitimating support from the United Nations. The United States was on its own in Vietnam, fighting an ugly war that increasingly required an imperial rationale. Though America's intervention in Vietnam was still widely supported at home, Kristol warned that this support would rapidly erode when the war's imperial nature became more widely recognized. Modern Americans had been trained to think of their country as the world's admired and benevolent champion of democracy, he observed. Even if America finally won the war in Vietnam, most Americans wouldn't like what they saw. Win or lose in Vietnam, Kristol asked, "are we not in the future going to be facing exactly the same kinds of situations in Asia, and in Africa and South America too? Are we really going to fight, on our own, an endless series of 'dirty little wars'? Is this a reasonable or tolerable prospect?" Though he rejected the appeals for military withdrawal from Vietnam that were beginning to draw media attention, Kristol admitted that he couldn't defend America's present policy without resorting to an imperialist rationale. What was needed was a new international order "that is more than a convenient cover for national self-centredness." But as long as America was forced to defend the existing order on its own, without any legitimating support from other Western nations, he warned that the increasing burden was likely to become heavier than America's democratic public would be willing to sustain.[74] Though he commended the Pax Americana for promoting world democracy, Kristol couldn't bring himself to repeat his government's claims about fighting for democracy in Vietnam. He would later reject the notion that exporting democracy was a proper aim of American foreign policy.

Kristol was generally more concerned, however, with America's antiwar movement than with the war itself. He saw the antiwar reaction coming in the mid-sixties, but felt no sympathy for it when it arrived. Though he recognized the problematic nature of America's intervention from the outset and doubted that vital American interests were at stake, and though he had predicted that Americans would not support such a war for long, he granted the protesters no legitimacy when they appeared. The war at home drew most of Kristol's attention during the later 1960s. He drifted further to the Right during this period not because he strongly supported America's intervention in Vietnam, but because he was repulsed by the opposition to it.

His idea of worthy opposition to the war was epitomized by Walter Lippmann. Kristol admired Lippmann's intelligence and especially his independence. Lippmann owed nothing to any political interest and spoke for no party faction; he was therefore regarded, Kristol confessed, with "suspicious awe" by partisans like himself. By 1965, Lippmann had emerged as the most formidable proponent of the view that Vietnam was, as the saying went, the wrong war in the wrong place at the wrong time. He was not, however, a bleeding-heart anti-imperialist like the professors in the streets. Kristol noted that when the Marines invaded the Dominican Republic in 1965, the same Walter Lippmann defended Lyndon Johnson's intervention. "One can imagine how *that* went down with the anti-war crowd," Kristol chortled. Johnson's Dominican adventure had given rise "to very few demonstrations and, so far as I know, to not a single 'teach-in'," he observed. "Americans are still reluctant to argue with the U.S. Marines, so long as they have the situation under control."[75]

Kristol was equally unprepared to argue with successful American invasions. The only problem in Vietnam was that the situation was not under control, which provided a serious reason for figures such as Lippmann to oppose American policy there. Lippmann's position was based entirely on his calculation of the national interest. He opposed America's intervention in Vietnam because, in his estimation, a non-nuclear war on the Asian mainland was unwinnable for the United States, because Southeast Asia was historically and geopolitically part of the Chinese sphere of influence, and because America's presence in Vietnam was forestalling an open break between the Chinese and Soviet governments. Kristol found these arguments unconvincing but worthy of respect. What made Lippmann a serious opponent of U.S. policy in Vietnam was that he had no hidden political agenda. Unlike the organizers of the so-called teach-ins, Lippmann didn't use the Vietnam situation as a pretext for opposing American imperialism elsewhere in the world. Unlike the alienated students and junior faculty in the streets, "Mr. Lippmann engages in no presumptuous suppositions as to 'what the Vietnamese people really want'—he obviously doesn't much care—or in legalistic exegesis as to whether, or to what extent, there is 'aggression' or 'revolution' in South Viet Nam."[76] That Lippmann didn't care what the Vietnamese people might want for themselves was, for Kristol, the key to his exemplary realism.

While not accepting this position for himself, Kristol accorded it his respect. He granted no credibility to what he called "the radical movement in search of a radical cause" that finally settled on the war in Vietnam. His reading of the antiwar movement characteristically focused on the difficulties of growing up. "One of the unforeseen consequences of the Welfare State is that it leaves little room for militant idealism," he mused in 1965. "Which is to say, it satisfies the middle-aged while stifling the young." By the 1960s, he explained, American youth had become bored with their parents' dreams of professional and material success. They were looking for something more outward-looking and exciting than their parents' banal suburban lives. Their fleeting taste of this excitement had come through the now-triumphant civil rights movement, which provided the standard. "It is the Civil Rights movement which instructed them in the tactics of 'civil disobedience' that are now resorted to at the drop of a hat," Kristol wrote. But because the Civil Rights movement had already achieved its key legislative goals, it was now too deeply enfranchised to serve as the basis for a radical movement. This explained why the movement's younger militants were pushing for such absurdities as equality of condition. But even this temporarily satisfying gambit, he noted, had become rather boring in recent times.[77] America's alienated white youth and their junior faculty professors were thus forced to look for a redeeming cause of their own. They floundered about with Castro beards and Che posters and Little Red Books, Kristol explained, until someone noticed that the government's war in Vietnam, "already under some criticism, and patently not working out as the government desired, was conveniently at hand."[78] Thus was the antiwar movement founded.

Though he had anticipated its arrival, Kristol was not prepared to respect a movement led by students and junior professors. The movement's adolescent immaturity clashed with his own chastened wisdom, which was that "we are stuck with South Vietnam."[79] As he explained in 1967, the truth for grown-ups was that "the United States is not going to cease being an imperial power, no matter what happens in Vietnam or elsewhere. It is the world situation—and the history which created this situation—that appoints imperial powers, not anyone's decision or even anyone's overweening ambition."[80]

These truisms had recently become the objects of controversy, Kristol claimed, only because New Class intellectuals were undermining the moral authority of America's government by asserting their own will to power. "What is at stake is that species of power we call moral authority," he explained. The war's intellectual critics undoubtedly believed that their arguments were right, but their more important belief was in themselves. Like the sermonizing clerics of a dimly remembered past, modern intellectuals routinely made pronouncements on subjects over which they held no technical or professional competence. The crucial distinction for Kristol was between the intellectual and the expert. When a linguist wrote about linguistics, he or she wrote as an expert, not as an intellectual. When the same linguist criticized American foreign policy, he or she wrote as an intellectual.

It was the intellectuals who were causing the problems. "It has been interesting to observe the kinds of faculty men and women who have been active in 'teach-ins'," Kristol reported. "Not only are they junior in rank; they are also usually in professions that have precious little to do with Viet Nam. The psychologists have been especially keen. . . . The mathematicians, chemists, and philosophers have also been highly visible, I can't imagine why." Notably absent from the protest movement, he claimed, were those who knew more about Asian politics or American foreign policy than could be gleaned from reading *The New York Times*. The experts were missing from the antiwar movement not only because they knew more about Vietnam, but also because they knew their good ideas could always get "a prompt and respectful hearing" at the Pentagon. Thus, unlike the intellectuals in the streets, those who knew what they were talking about had no reason to feel alienated from the political and military establishments. [81]

The analogy with premodern clericalism broke down on one count. Unlike their clerical forebears, Kristol argued, modern intellectuals were consumed by their lust for political power. "There is this critical difference between the intellectual of today and the average cleric of yesteryear," he explained. "The intellectual, lacking in other-worldly interests, is committed to the pursuit of temporal status, temporal influence, and temporal power with a single-minded passion that used to be found only in the highest reaches of the Catholic Church."[82] With the eclipse of the aristocratic prestige of rank under modernity, intellectuals were promoting themselves as the rightful claimants to political power. For Kristol, the transition marked a cultural decline.

"It is simply not possible to comprehend what is happening in the United States today unless one keeps the sociological condition and political ambitions of the intellectual class very much in the forefront of one's mind," he declared in 1967. The intellectual class was different from the Silent Majority. Though most Americans were indifferent to politics, their patriotism generally moved them to support their government's foreign ventures. Intellectuals, by contrast, nearly always arrogated their own moral authority over their government's authority. Kristol argued that they unfailingly rationalized this conceit with ideological claims. Intellectuals based their self-importance on their ability to manipulate ideologies, which furnished their interpretive keys to history and constituted "the essence of their rationality." It was through their manipulation of ideologies that intellectuals understood historical events and conferred meaning upon them.

Ideological skills thus provided the means by which intellectuals sought to gain power. In the foreign policy field, however, this facility had no appropriate use. Kristol explained that foreign policy was a pragmatic art that required complex contextual judgments about economic, political, and military relationships with various nations. Foreign policy was therefore the area of politics least reducible to ideological reason. Unlike the classic texts of political economics, Kristol noted, Western foreign policy classics from Machiavelli to Hans Morgenthau emphasized circumstantial and prudential arguments. This comparative irrelevance of ideology threatened the interests of the intellectual class and explained why they were stirring up so much trouble over American policy in Vietnam. The antiwar professors were motivated not by their moral revulsion against Vietnam's devastation nor by the planeloads of corpses returning to the United States, but by their own desire for power. Given their sociological condition and political ambitions, Kristol argued, the intellectual class could not abide the plain truth that foreign policy was a field best left to professional experts. [83] He did not ponder the irony that this assertion of faith in the wisdom of America's experts was written at a time when these experts had committed more than 500,000 troops to Vietnam and had convinced themselves that victory was attainable without committing genocide.

The notion that intellectuals comprised a power-seeking "adversary culture" remained in the forefront of Kristol's mind after the war. [84] Throughout the 1950s, Lionel Trilling had claimed that modern literature's "bitter line of hostility to civilization" was spreading throughout America's intellectual class. To an increasingly alienated intelligentsia, Trilling warned, Matthew Arnold's ideals of order, convenience, decorum, and rationality pointed only to "the small advantages and excessive limitations of the middle-class life of a few prosperous nations of the nineteenth century." [85] Trilling feared that the intellectuals' disenchantment with bourgeois culture would eventually filter down to the newly educated middle class. The adversary culture would expand through massification as the New Class learned to be alienated. Kristol viewed his work as an antidote to this cultural virus. In 1969, he was named Henry Luce Professor of Urban Values at New York University; three years later, he became a Board of Contributors columnist for the *Wall Street Journal*. His early columns warned the *Journal*'s readers about the pathologies of the New Class and clarified his conception of his intellectual vocation. Kristol's writings in the mid-seventies increasingly advised American corporate executives, with diminishing subtlety, on how to defeat their New Class opponents.

His critique differed from populist criticisms of the New Class. [86] For Kristol, the problem with the New Class was not that government bureaucrats, academics, psychologists, and public sector lawyers had usurped control over American institutions such as the media. The populist focus on control was misleading and self-defeating. The problem with the New Class was that "they *are* the media—just as they *are* our educational system, our public health and welfare system, and much else." The New Class was fighting to attain the power to shape America's civilization, "a power which, in a capitalist system, is supposed to reside in the free market."[87]

He conceded that so-called free enterprise typically produced and rewarded mediocrity, vulgarity, and banality in the cultural realm. This truism suggested a useful function for the New Class. The newly educated intellectuals and public servants could have devoted themselves to elevating the tastes of less-educated consumers, Kristol observed. "But it is so much easier to mobilize the active layers of public opinion behind such issues as environmentalism, ecology, consumer protection, and economic planning, to give the government bureaucracy the power to regulate and coerce, and eventually to 'politicize' the economic decision-making process. . . . And this is, of course, exactly what has been happening."[88]

New Class intellectuals and bureaucrats usually claimed to serve the public good. This was their idealism, which Kristol conceded was often sincerely expressed. But the motivating factor underlying even the most sincere expression of New Class idealism, he insisted, was "almost embarrassingly vulgar in its substance." Under the banner of equality, in the language of democratic idealism, the New Class was waging a class war. "The simple truth is that the professional classes of our modern bureaucratized societies are engaged in a class struggle with the business community for status and power," Kristol explained.[89] His Trotskyist training had taught him about the ruses of class war. The true agenda of American liberalism was camouflaged by the appeals of liberal class warriors to morality and fairness.

Kristol exposed their self-deceits in an essay he later reprinted in three different books. Though the New Class spoke the language of progressive reform, he argued, it was actually scheming to transform America's patchwork welfare state into state socialism. This agenda was concealed by the New Class's libertarian face. The New Class was more libertarian than liberal in most areas—except in economics. New Class liberalism defended individual freedom of speech and expression "to an unprecedented degree," but not in the economic realm. Modern liberalism was founded on a contradictory commitment to maximized individual freedom and economic planning. The contradiction ran even deeper when the hypocrisy factor was taken into account. "It is instructive to note that these same people, who are irked and inflamed by the slightest noneconomic restriction in the United States, can be admiring of Maoist China and not in the least appalled by the total collectivization of life—and the total destruction of liberty—there."[90] Kristol had once accused the New Dealers of promoting Stalinism. Time had not improved America's liberals. They had switched to Maoism, but were still hypocrites. They supported economic planning and social libertarianism, but their libertarianism was only for themselves. Kristol claimed that they were infatuated with Maoist totalitarianism. He warned that this infatuation "tells us much about their deepest fantasies and the natural basis of their political imagination."[91]

The seeds of an instructive critique of modern liberalism were there. Having identified the tensions between modern liberalism's statist and libertarian impulses, however, Kristol settled for name-calling. His sinister allusions to the deepest fantasies of American liberals, like his attacks on the New Class, carried Trotskyist echoes. Vosol Rogat claimed that Kristol rarely cared about his ostensible subjects, but only used them as emblems of the putative conflict between the Silent Majority and the New Class. If this assessment exaggerated the extent of Kristol's cynicism, it was nonetheless evident, as Steinfels later observed, that Kristol often used the great issues merely as stalking horses for his polemical assaults.[92] His attacks on the New Class exemplified this strategy. For example, Kristol claimed that the totalitarian fantasies of liberals were revealed by their campaigns against air and water pollution. The effect of most New Class campaigning against pollution, he observed, was to transfer basic economic decisions from the marketplace to New Class operatives in the public sector. The New Class's purported concern for the environment merely rationalized its drive for power.

His chief example, however, was the putative liberal concern for equality, which illustrated Kristol's "simple truth" that intellectuals, public sector bureaucrats, and other professional class liberals were waging a class war with the business community for status and power. The new class war was invariably waged under the banner of equality, just as the bourgeoisie's revolutions had been. Kristol disputed the notion that modern liberalism was energized by a moral concern for fairness. Those who pushed for greater equality were merely persuaded that "they can do a better job of running our society and feel entitled to have the opportunity," he argued. "This is what *they* mean by 'equality'."[93] The effort to promote greater equality of condition was doubly perverse, in his accounting. It was politically perverse because it was only pursued by power-seeking hypocrites. It was perverse on a deeper level, however, because the effort itself defied the laws of nature. Kristol proposed a novel variant of natural law reasoning. He claimed it was a demonstrable fact that "human talents and abilities, as measured, do tend to distribute themselves along a bell-shaped curve, with most people clustered around the middle, and with much smaller percentages at the lower and higher ends." It was also demonstrable, he said, that "in all modern, bourgeois societies, the distribution of income is also roughly along a bell-shaped curve, indicating that in such an 'open' society the inequalities that do emerge are not inconsistent with the bourgeois notion of equality."[94] America's apparent maldistribution of wealth was thus in accordance with nature and the natural bell-shaped distribution of human talents. To promote greater equality in the United States—where nature was triumphant—was to assault the laws of nature. Since people in bourgeois countries generally got what they deserved, according to their abilities, Kristol argued that worrying about inequalities of wealth in these countries was both inappropriate and self-defeating.

His argument assumed that human talents and abilities were distributed along a single curve. Kristol claimed that human talents and abilities broke down in the pattern of a bell-shaped curve that was "naturally" replicated in the economic system and later replicated in the political system. His implication was that bourgeois democracy unfolded in accordance with an inner law or *telos* of nature. The triumph of bourgeois democracy represented the consolidation of the most advanced form of the good society attainable within history.[95] Kristol was not moved by the objection that this argument rationalized a complacent attitude toward America's remaining injustices. His purpose was to stifle moral criticism of the existing system's maldistribution of wealth.

The argument itself, however, presupposed a one-dimensional conception of distributive justice. While personal income is indeed distributed along a single curve, the curves for intelligence, courage, creativity, athletic ability, mechanical skill, vocational dedication, and insight are all different for each individual and do not necessarily correlate with the existing income curve. Responding to Kristol, Michael Walzer observed that equality was a complex notion that required that many "bells" should ring.[96] Just as there were many different kinds of goods to be distributed, he noted, there were also many different rationales by which the distribution of goods could be justified for different people. What made the question of distributive justice a complicated matter was that, contrary to Kristol, there was no single talent—such as the ability to make money—or even any combination of abilities that entitled any individual to all of the available social goods.

Kristol claimed that equality remained an issue in American politics only because "we have an intelligentsia which so despises the ethos of bourgeois society, and which is so guilt-ridden at being implicated in the life of this society, that it is inclined to find even collective suicide preferable to the status quo." But rather than kill themselves, he complained, intellectuals had chosen to "pursue power in the name of equality" and thus aspired to a tyranny of their own.[97] But were intellectuals any more power-hungry than lawyers, investment bankers, politicians, or corporate executives? In each case, the critical need in a democracy was to observe the boundaries that inhered in each vocational sphere. Walzer replied that the task of distributive justice was to promote freedom from every form of tyranny, including the tyranny of money. Domination was always mediated by some set of social goods, such as birthright, family inheritance, religious sanction, capital, education, or state power. To hold in mind and heart the vision of a society free from domination, he argued, was not to act out of envy or resentment, but to make a conscious effort to escape the conditions that produced these feelings.[98]

SHAKING THE TREE: CORPORATE ADVOCACY AND INTELLECTUALS

Kristol worried less about the motives of corporate functionaries and consultants than he did about those of the New Class. In the early 1970s, after switching to the Republican party, he became an unofficial advisor to the Nixon administration and, on one occasion, assured Nixon that the student protesters "don't know what country this is. They think it's Bolivia."[99] His advice was increasingly sought during the same period by corporate executives. Kristol repeatedly informed them that they needed to "defund" the New Class and recruit their own intellectuals. If the corporate sector was to mount a serious offensive against the New Class, he argued, corporations needed to pay closer attention to the politics of the institutions and individuals they subsidized. As he explained in his widely reprinted essay on corporate philanthropy, any university that asked for money from corporations was required to court the corporate sector's good opinion. If America's colleges and universities remained indifferent to corporate opinion, he declared, "they will just have to learn to be indifferent to the money too."[100]

His prescription for dealing with news organizations went a step further. America's corporate sector needed to take the offensive against the media, he declared. When faced with media criticism, corporations needed to respond with public rebuttals that were "detailed, polemical, and sharply phrased so as to challenge the reporter's (or newscaster's) professional integrity." Kristol insisted that these rebuttals had to impugn the motives of journalists, who "have to be hit over the head a few times before they pay attention." Since the New Class was a permanent fact of life, attacking the media needed to become a permanent part of doing business. Kristol advised his clients to run aggressive ads in national magazines and newspapers. "I should make it clear that I am not talking about 'issue-oriented advertising,' which sometimes has its uses but suffers from many of the limitations of 'economic education'," he explained. He was talking about fighting like an aggressive trial lawyer, who always assumed that the best defense was to undermine the personal credibility of the prosecution's witnesses.[101]

He later took the same fight to academe, arguing that university trustees demonstrated "the impotence of non-ideological pragmatism." Kristol complained that at colleges and universities across the country, business executives raised money to finance "left-wing humanities and social science departments, 'women's studies' programs that are candid proselytizers for lesbianism, programs in 'safe sex' that promote homosexuality, 'environmental studies' that are, at bottom, anti-capitalist propaganda, and other such activities of which they surely disapprove." The trustees' desire to avoid conflict thus contributed to America's subversion. Kristol reported that when he pointed this out to trustees, they usually mumbled an evasively embarrassed reply. "The sad truth is that they would prefer not to know what is going on within the institutions they supposedly govern," he argued. "Such willful ignorance protects them from thinking about issues that are ideological (they don't know how to do it) or getting involved in an argument with highly ideological types on the faculty (they don't know how to do this, either)."[102]

What they needed were intellectuals to argue ideology for them. Kristol made an impressive career in this field, recommending the right kind of intellectuals, including himself, to his corporate acquaintances. He straightforwardly insisted that corporations needed to defend their interests by subsidizing the work and careers of ideologically sympathetic intellectuals. To defend their own prerogatives and also make an impact on academe, he argued, corporations needed "to give support to those elements of the New Class—and they exist, if not in large numbers—which do believe in the preservation of a strong private sector."[103] These were the people qualified to write attack-ads, advise executives, and organize seminars and think tanks. Kristol's first published solicitation of this kind appeared in 1977—when his own corporate network was already legendary. He had shown how a counterintellectual could gain national influence and power in the political and corporate arenas.

In 1978 Kristol joined the American Enterprise Institute as a senior fellow. He and William Simon also founded the Institute for Educational Affairs, which poured corporate-donated millions into the war against the New Class. "I raise money for conservative think tanks," Kristol explained. "I am a liaison to some degree between intellectuals and the business community."[104] In 1981, when queried about his influence in the Reagan administration, he replied, "I don't pick up the phone and tell them how to run the country, but I will occasionally pick up the phone, and some people return my calls."[105] More than a few of them owed their positions to his influence. Kristol's "Godfather" title was, among insiders, a tribute to his considerable rainmaking talents. One of the chief publicists of supply-side economics, Jude Wanniski, was a primary beneficiary. Wanniski's modestly titled supply-side primer, *The Way the World Works*, was financed by grants that Kristol secured from the Smith Richardson Foundation. Kristol also obtained an academic fellowship for Wanniski at the American Enterprise Institute. When asked to describe Kristol's influence on his career and the careers of his friends, Wanniski replied, "Irving is the invisible hand." George Weigel explained that neoconservatism's infrastructure of policy institutes and magazines, which included his Ethics and Public Policy Center, was made possible, in part, by the fact that "Irving understood historically how philanthropy and ideas and politics went together."[106]

The benefits of Kristol's money-shaking did not fall only on others. In 1985, the Olin Foundation gave him $600,000 to start a magazine, *The National Interest*, and made payments on his John M. Olin Distinguished Professorship at New York University. Kristol became an Olin Fellow at the American Enterprise Institute in 1988 and collected $376,000 from the Olin Foundation that year alone. The supreme irony of his attacks on the self-promoting opportunism of New Class intellectuals was that they were most convincing as descriptions of the career he knew best.[107]

He conceded the obvious when pressed on the point. "I am, admittedly, part of the same New Class," Kristol remarked. He acknowledged that neoconservatives wanted power no less than their liberal enemies and that neoconservatives enjoyed considerable advantages over them in applying for corporate funding. The crucial difference was that neoconservatives were dissidents within the New Class. "We are dissidents from the New Class liberal ideology, which was a new development in American politics," he argued. "The liberalism of the New Class was nothing but a vehicle for gaining power for themselves. That is the strategem we have unmasked, while admittedly being part of the New Class ourselves."[108]

For a brief time, in the late 1970s, Kristol called himself the only self-confessed neoconservative.[109] He was also the first neoconservative to join the Republican party. "Slowly, slowly, the rest of them are accepting the term neoconservative," he noted in 1980. "And they are becoming Republicans. The question of becoming a Republican, to put it bluntly, is often a matter of class. Neoconservative intellectuals are too snobbish to join the Republicans and the country club. They identify the Republican Party, not without some reason, with businessmen playing golf. You join the party in which you feel at home."[110]

Most of Kristol's subsequent work attempted to define neoconservatism, which he described as the self-imposed assignment of explaining to the American people "why they are right, and to the intellectuals why they are wrong."[111] The counterintellectual vocation was thus precisely described. It was not, unlike neoconservatism itself, a persuasion of recent vintage. The counterintellectual tradition included Edmund Burke and Alexis de Tocqueville, as well as such modern forerunners of neoconservatism as Joseph Schumpeter and Raymond Aron. The link that connected these figures, as Steinfels observed, was their rejection of the critical attitude toward Western culture adopted by most intellectuals.[112] Like Burke and Tocqueville, Kristol argued that the heralded independence of Western intellectuals was an alienated conceit; like Schumpeter and Aron, he claimed that most intellectuals were ungrateful for their privileges and frustrated by their unrequited ambition. Though America's intellectuals were apparently alienated from the American way of life, Kristol observed, most Americans did not share their homeless feelings.[113] For Kristol, neoconservatism was fundamentally an ideological expression of common American sense. He offered a schematic explanation for the difference between the alienated anticapitalism of most intellectuals and the pro-American capitalism of neoconservatives: While most modern intellectuals were descendants of the French-Continental Enlightenment, neoconservatives identified with the Anglo-Scottish Enlightenment.

THE OTHER ENLIGHTENMENT: KRISTOL'S IDEOLOGY

By his own account, Kristol was a reluctant ideologue. It was an unfortunate fact of modern political life, he argued, that politics had become inescapably ideological. He was tempted by Michael Oakeshott's purportedly nonideological conservatism, in which the purpose of politics was to tend to society's arrangements, keeping the existing social fabric in good repair through prudential practices rooted in long-established traditions.

Kristol's fondness for this Aristotelian conception of politics showed up in scattered asides throughout his work. He would have preferred to write about politics in the style of Oakeshott or Leo Strauss,[114] whose premodern understanding of the political vocation would have been ideal for a static society. But in a world driven by the need for ever-increasing economic growth and technological innovation, "with all its transformations of economic and social reality as well as the accompanying changes of values and habits, politics must of necessity assume another guise." Modernity imposed ideological requirements on anyone seeking political effectiveness. Conservatives and neoconservatives needed to be as committed to shaping the future as they were to preserving the traditions of the past, Kristol argued, for in the modern world "a non-ideological politics is a politics disarmed."[115]

An armed politics would accept modernity and offer a progressive vision of a better world. "But there are different modes of progressiveness with radically different political implications," Kristol instructed. In modern Western societies, two modes were dominant. The first was the mode of the French-Continental Enlightenment, symbolized by the French Revolution, which Kristol viewed as the source of modernity's most pervasive and destructive political myths. He condemned the French Revolution for promoting the notion that freedom and equality were compatible and equally important. The central error of the French Revolution, however, was not its sloganeering for liberty, equality, and fraternity, but its pursuit of happiness. Kristol conceded that the same phrase wormed its way into the American Declaration of Independence. The difference, he contended, was that this notion took on a peculiarly destructive meaning in the French-Continental Enlightenment. The central conceit of the French-Continental tradition was the belief that the state was ultimately responsible for the well-being of its citizens. Given this utopian commitment, it was only logical that the nineteenth-century heirs of this tradition "should affirm that the state, in the hands of the 'right men,' and following the 'correct' policies, could solve, through central planning, the economic problems of society."[116] It was a faith, in Kristol's schematization, that linked Robespierre, Saint-Simon, Marx, Lenin, European social democrats, and modern American liberals.

The Anglo-Scottish Enlightenment represented by John Locke, David Hume, Adam Smith, Adam Ferguson, Burke, and James Madison was a more prosaic affair. The aim of this tradition was not to deprecate economic self-interest or replace economic incentives with incipiently totalitarian social incentives, he explained, but to channel self-interest into the disciplinary contexts of the economic marketplace and representative government. In contrast to the ambitious utopianism of the French-Continental theorists, whose revolutions required unknown revolutions of consciousness, the Anglo-Scottish theorists sought only to promote greater civility. Their operative assumption was that people would become more civil and enlightened in their relations with each other as they became more prosperous and gained experience in representative government.

This notion was joined, in Kristol's reading, by a further assumption that "the increase of affluence would bring with it a strengthening of those traditional moral values hitherto associated with church and synagogue."[117] Unlike the antireligious ideologues of the French-Continental tradition, with their deracinated calls to transvalue all values, the Anglo-Scottish theorists sought to reinforce Western civilization's traditional moral values. Kristol observed that it was possible for Burke and Smith to be friends because they shared a respectful attitude toward traditional morality. Having adopted a realistic estimate of human nature, a modest conception of the ends of politics, and a deep concern for the preservation of Western moral values, the Anglo-Scottish theorists constructed a mode of progressive politics that stood, in Kristol's assessment, as the chief alternative to the various collectivisms deriving from the French-Continental Enlightenment.

The problem, for Kristol, was that the French-Continental tradition dominated modern political discourse. The egalitarian-utopian conception of politics had been advanced throughout the world with brutality (as under communism), with hesitation (as under social democratic regimes), and insidiously (as in modern American liberalism, which "has moved decidedly leftward in the past fifty years").[118] The classical liberalism of the Whigs no longer existed as an ideological alternative. Kristol lamented that modern liberalism was actually a form of socialism, "that is to say, it has become far more interested in equality than in liberty."[119] He recalled that when the neoconservatives first lost their faith in socialism, there was no apparent alternative for them to embrace—until they rediscovered the Whiggish liberalism of the Anglo-Scottish tradition.

Kristol's appeal to social limits and to the importance of traditional moral wisdom offered a compelling corrective to much of the inheritance of Western radicalism. He effectively contrasted the modesty and humanity of the Anglo-Scottish tradition to the ravages of radical utopianism. His idea of an "Anglo-Scottish Enlightenment" made an effective polemical construct. The problem with this construct, on its own terms, was that it was drawn from a rather bowdlerized account of the tradition he embraced. In his scattered remarks on the moral inheritance of the

Anglo-Scottish tradition, Kristol assumed that traditional moral values pertaining to family life, sexuality, and the role of religion were sustainable in commercial societies. In a dismissive aside, he conceded that under modernity the moral values previously associated with church and synagogue were inevitably secularized. The chasm between Locke and Smith was thus implicitly acknowledged, but was dismissed as insignificant for his argument. Though Smith and Hume discarded Locke's theological underpinnings, Kristol contended that they nonetheless retained Locke's moral philosophy and demonstrated that traditional moral values could be sustained in the transition to commercial society.

Kristol occasionally suggested that Smith and Hume were silent about religion only because they took its existence for granted. He argued that Smith and the tradition's other founders "were able to take for granted a *coherence* in the private sector achieved through the influence of organized religion, traditional moral values, and the family." While acknowledging that Smith's hostility for religion eventually consumed even his earlier pale deism, Kristol contended that Smith nonetheless assumed that organized religion would perdure as a cultural restraint on egotism. Smith's confidence in the ability of men and women "to live together socially and civilly under capitalism" was not a fantasy in his own time, Kristol argued. [120] As he elsewhere explained, the Anglo-Scottish theorists believed that Western moral values previously founded on religion could subsist on their own and would play a civilizing role in socializing individuals into the new society. [121] They further assumed that greater affluence would strengthen the force of traditional Christian moral teaching.

Kristol claimed that these were realistic expectations for Smith and Hume in their time. "But that was before the modern world was touched by the breezes of nineteenth-century rationalist doctrine, and devastated by the hurricanes of twentieth-century nihilism," he explained. Nihilism was inconceivable to Smith. The twentieth century would witness apocalyptic evils unimaginable to the founders of Anglo-Scottish liberalism. If Americans no longer believed in their notion of natural human sociability, this was not because the founders were utopian, Kristol argued, "but rather because the preconditions of social life, which they imagined to be immutable, have turned out to be fragile." [122]

Kristol liked to quote the remark by George Fitzhugh, a Southern apologist for slavery, that "virtue loses all of her loveliness, because of her selfish aims." Kristol interpreted American history as a dramatization of this lament. "From having been a *capitalist, republican community*, with shared values and a quite unambiguous claim to the title of a just order, the United States became a *free, democratic society* where the will to success and privilege was severed from its moral moorings," Kristol argued.[123] The social order of slaveholding America was unambiguously just? America became increasingly unjust as it became more free and democratic? To dissociate the social vision of the founders from modern commercialized democracy, Kristol was prepared to romanticize America's early past, slavery and all. The Whigs were not to be blamed for the ravages of modernity.

Kristol's disdain for bourgeois culture gave a Tory cast to his Whiggery. His cultural criticism made him closer to the eighteenth-century Whigs than to the revisionist "democratic capitalism" of nineteenth-century American Whiggery. He complained that happiness in bourgeois society meant "little more than the sovereignty of self-centered hedonism." Bourgeois society emphasized the pleasures of consumption over the virtues of work. The constant manipulation of consumer appetites in bourgeois society undermined the values and loyalties on which this order was founded, he argued. The same debasement of the founders' vision extended to politics, where the political vocation had been reduced to pandering to electoral interests. "I do not think that the United States today is an altogether admirable place," he remarked. "I am not particularly happy with it. I think this society is vulgar, debased, and crassly materialistic. I think the United States has lost its sense of moral purpose and is fast losing its authentic religious values." Reformist attempts to arrest the corruption of America's political process were useless, he argued, since "the bourgeois-democratic state can rely only on the self-discipline of the individual, which affluent capitalism itself subverts."[124]

This situation was not foreseen by the Anglo-Scottish founders, nor was it caused by the system of political economy they defended. Kristol contended, rather, that any attempt to halt the erosion of American moral values or to impede the debasement of American politics needed to recover, in new form, the bourgeois ethic of the Anglo-Scottish Enlightenment. "The 'economic man' of modern economics is not quite the same creature as the 'bourgeois man' of The Theory of Moral Sentiments or even The Wealth of Nations," he explained. "They do overlap, to be sure, but less than completely. Smith never did reduce man, as modern economic thought does, to the status of a naked individual who was the sum of his individual appetites."[125]

Kristol conceded that the founders made one error: They assumed that "the bonds of social solidarity in a bourgeois community were too strong to be disrupted by the acquisitive instincts." As a Scotsman living in the latter half of the eighteenth century, Smith took for granted the perdurance of such institutions as organized religion and the family. While

Smith admittedly took no personal interest in these institutions, Kristol argued that he ascribed an important role to religion as a restraint on consumer egotism and assumed that organized religion would withstand the acids of modernity. Smith's single misjudgment was that he took for granted those cultural institutions later undermined by capitalism. "Bourgeois affluence has liberated men (and women) from these wholesome influences and has thereby reopened all the large questions of moral and political philosophy that Adam Smith and the Founding Fathers thought had been definitively answered by 'modernity' itself," Kristol concluded. [126] This was not a minor oversight, however. As Kristol acknowledged, Smith ignored religion in his description of the emerging commercial society. His only discussion of religion in *The Wealth of Nations* was a brief excursus on the history of religious instruction. [127] Smith ignored religion, however, not primarily because he took its durability for granted or even because he disliked Christianity. His exhaustive account of the rise of commercial society gave short shrift to religion because religion was losing its social importance. Commercial society pushed religion to the margins. What remained important in this society was not any theological memory, but the memory and practice of moral values rooted only in habit.

Kristol justifiably insisted that the textbook image of Smith as an amoral economistic libertarian was exaggerated. The reductionistic notion that human beings are, by nature, antisocial animals driven entirely by their egotistical interests was not Smith's axiom, but rather that of his predecessor, Bernard de Mandeville. "What we call Evil in this World, Moral as well as Natural, is the grand Principle that makes us sociable Creatures," Mandeville claimed. He and his followers claimed without equivocation that all social progress was fueled by egotism. [128] Smith was not completely with them. Though his fulsome praise for self-interest resembled Mandeville's celebration of egotism in the *Fable of the Bees*, Smith assumed, as a follower of the eighteenth-century Sentimental School of moral philosophy, that egotism was properly restricted by limitations grounded in nature. Though he famously celebrated the pursuit of self-interest as the driving force of a productive economy, he never claimed that self-regarding virtues were superior to other-regarding virtues. [129] In his early treatise on the nature of human sympathy, *The Theory of Moral Sentiments*, Smith inquired how self-interested human beings could form moral judgments elevating other-regarding virtues over the self's immediate interests. His answer was that an "impartial spectator" within each individual internalized moral judgments rendered by the surrounding community. By imaginatively projecting one's self into the position of a third person, Smith argued, the impartial observer was able to present to the self an objective (rather than egotistical) perspective on particular situations. The individual imagined what he or she would feel (or should feel) as a spectator of the situation. This interpretation of the function of the moral imagination stood at the center of what was otherwise, excepting Smith's apologies for the new commercial society, a traditionally Stoic account of the ethics of propriety, merit, justice, duty, utility, and virtue.

Having taken his distance from Mandeville (whom he accused of sophistry for insisting that all self-interested passions were both personally vain and socially beneficial), Smith nonetheless concluded that Mandeville's work had "made so much noise in the world" because its fundamental claims "bordered upon the truth."[130] Unlike Mandeville, Smith believed that the new consumer society needed ethical restraints; but like Mandeville, he otherwise celebrated the transformations in social relationships wrought by what was later called capitalism. The upshot of this kinship for Kristol's argument was missing in his belabored defense of Smith. Just as he assumed that commercial society would diminish the social importance of religion, Smith also viewed capitalism as an emancipation from what he called "the force of blood." As he explained in *The Theory of Moral Sentiments:*

> In commercial countries, where the authority of law is always sufficient to protect the meanest man in the state, the descendants of the same family, having no such motive for keeping together, naturally separate and disperse, as interest or inclination may direct. They soon cease to be of importance to one another; and, in a few generations, not only lose all care about one another, but all remembrance of their common origin, and of the connection which took place among their ancestors. Regard for remote relations becomes, in every country, less and less, according as this state of civilization has been longer and more completely established.[131]

In Smith's work, as in the writings of other founders, indifference to the unraveling of family relationships under capitalism was plainly expressed. The founders believed that new habits would replace those practices eclipsed by the commodification of social values. Smith gave short shrift to those who criticized the uprooting and disintegration of family ties under the emerging order. These ties, he claimed, were mere products of precommercial history and practice. "What is called affection is in reality nothing but habitual sympathy," he instructed.[132] The new society would create practices appropriate to itself and would thus engender its own associative habits.

Kristol's account of the Anglo-Scottish tradition disregarded this theme. Kristol allowed that Smith overestimated the staying power of Western moral traditions under the pressure of commercial society. But Smith not only failed to protect the cultural inheritance treasured by Kristol. He rationalized the onslaught against this inheritance. While his writings contained withering asides about the mendacity and greed of business leaders, the overall effect of his work, as Harold Laski observed, was to elevate the pecuniary longings of the capitalist class to the status of natural law. [133] Kristol nearly conceded the point in his asides. He observed that *The Wealth of Nations* regarded human beings as by nature "little more than self-seeking, acquisitive creatures." It also introduced the concept of the economic sphere as an autonomous realm. [134] These were the very claims that rationalized the consumer culture that Kristol decried. Nicholas Xenos remarked that Kristol's attempt to blame the degradation of the work ethic on the heirs of the French Enlightenment amounted to shooting the messengers. [135] If the French tradition was not as innocent as this exaggeration implied, neither was Kristol's Anglo-Scottish Enlightenment.

Kristol repeatedly complained that equality had become an important concern even for comparatively nonideological economists. For Kristol, this concern reflected the degree to which socialist conceptions of justice had permeated American political and intellectual culture. [136] One of his most compelling arguments was joined to this complaint. Kristol observed that the architects of welfare-state socialism did not regard themselves as socialists. Their vision was technocratic. Modern social scientists eschewed the moral question about the nature of a good society. They asked themselves only how society's mechanical arrangements should be managed. Their essentially managerial conception of democracy filled modern textbooks in sociology, political science, economics, and journalism. [137]

Managerial democracy conceived democracy as a political system in which the mechanical arrangements of society were managed with maximally attainable fairness. "Democracy is then seen as a set of rules and procedures, whereby majority rule and minority rights are reconciled into a state of equilibrium," Kristol observed. "If everyone follows these rules and procedures, then a democracy is in working order." He reported in the early 1970s that he couldn't help feeling that there was something ridiculous about this conception of democracy. He confessed that he felt "a sneaking sympathy for those of our young radicals who also find it ridiculous." The absurdity of modern liberal democracy was the absurdity of idolatry, he argued, "of taking the symbolic for the real, the means for the end." [138] Managerialism offered no purpose for democracy, only the perpetuation of democracy's political machinery. But the purpose of any worthy political regime, Kristol insisted, was to strive toward some conception of the good life and the good society. To attain the kind of democracy described in the textbooks, on the other hand, would be to construct a procedurally fair and well-functioning system that failed to explain why anyone should care about it.

Kristol's alternative was early America's premanagerial republicanism, in which democracy bore a self-legitimating moral purpose. Republican democracy conceived democracy not as a system of arrangements, but as a form of self-government promoting a particular quality of public life. Republicanism emphasized the qualitative responsibilities of self-government rather than entitlement rights or the fairness of institutional arrangements. It therefore ascribed greater importance, Kristol explained, to the character of those who governed. The right to self-government was contingent upon the moral worthiness of those who proposed to govern themselves, since only an "idolator of democratic machinery" would endorse a debased democracy. Certain forms of authoritarianism were superior to degraded democracies. Though Kristol rarely noted the patronage, this was a Straussian theme. Kristol shared the Aristotelian sentiment of his mentor, Leo Strauss, that the state was responsible for shaping and reinforcing moral virtue in its citizens. Because self-government was only desirable when those who would govern were morally worthy of the task, republican democracy needed to be concerned, above all, with the moral character of its citizens.

Because republican democracy was directly solicitous of the individual, it attempted to socialize individuals into republican virtue. Because public opinion held final authority in a democracy, republicanism also needed to be solicitous of the collective self. Kristol conceded that American republicans in the past had been known to make overly zealous attempts to shape American moral character into a particular mold. He countered that the more important point, however, was that republicans had "cared not merely about the machinery of democracy but about the quality of life that this machinery might generate."[139] This argument showed up in Kristol's case for censorship of pornography and obscenity, but similar arguments appeared in his laments over the decline of religion, the moral bankruptcy of liberal democracy, the eclipse of republicanism, and the moral ravages of nihilism. His critique of managerial democracy and his advocacy of republican virtue shared much of the spirit of modern communitarian theory. Kristol's laments for a forsaken moral sensibility fit rather uneasily, however, with his political rhetoric. "Moralism" was one of his stock epithets. He repeatedly ridiculed the "moralistic" character of modern liberalism, human rights theory, civil rights, feminism, the mainline

churches, and environmentalism. He found most reform legislation moralistic. In 1976, after a series of corporate bribery cases made the news,
Kristol's response in *The New York Times Magazine* posed the question,
"Post-Watergate Morality: Too Good for Our Good?" Faced with a genuine moral issue affecting the corporate sector, the advocate of republican
virtue argued that public moral standards in the wake of Watergate had
become "self-righteous" and, indeed, too good for our own good.[140]

His reflections on political strategy bore the same tone. Kristol
regularly urged his partisan advisees to use greater cunning and deceit, or
what he called "a dose of Machiavellian shrewdness," in their campaigns.[141] He repeatedly chastized the Republican party establishment for
its supposed overemphasis on managerial skills and efficiency. As he
explained in *The Wall Street Journal*, the real political talents were "quick-
wittedness, articulateness, a clear sense of one's ideological agenda and the
devious routes necessary for its enactment."[142] Though he preferred to
invoke Machiavelli, Kristol's emphasis on the ideological uses of deceit—
like Burnham's—carried the imprint of his Marxist background. When
asked about the proper role of morality in politics, Marx reportedly burst
out laughing. The same bemusement was amply displayed in Kristol's
writings on politics.

This did not mean, as was often claimed, that Kristol's moral pronouncements were therefore insincere. It meant that he defended a highly
truncated conception of the moral realm. Kristol's notion of moral reason,
like his view of religion, was circumscribed by his commitment to shore up
what he called the bourgeois order. He frequently commended conservative theologies for others, though he was religiously nonobservant. For
Kristol, the proper function of religion was to serve as a moral anchor for
bourgeois society. He conceded that biblical Christianity made a poor
candidate for the task. Whenever he lectured to clergy, he reported, "I
always say the same thing. I tell them to stop being so interested in
politics, and I ask them why they don't take an interest in religion instead.
Invariably, they are disinclined to take my advice."[143] His explanation was
that modern clerics embraced a politicized form of early Christian gnosticism.

GNOSTIC VERSUS ORTHODOX FAITH

Following Eric Voegelin, Kristol divided religions into two types, distinguishing between "orthodox" and "gnostic" faiths.[144] Orthodox Judaism
was his example of the former. Orthodox Judaism was orthodox because

it emphasized the primacy of the Law and was unapologetically institutionalized. The distinguishing mark of an institutionalized orthodoxy was
that it made peace with the world as it was. This was what made Orthodox
Judaism different, Kristol argued, from the peculiar form of Jewish gnosticism that became Christianity. As a product of the "gnostic millenarian
bubblings" of first-century Judaism, he explained, Christianity was born
alienated from the world. The early church attracted a following because
it appealed to Jews who resented the Law and to others who were already
alienated from the world. The central claim of the New Testament was the
gnostic promise "to achieve a radical reconstruction of reality, and a
redemption of human beings from a condition that they perceived to be
inhuman." Kristol allowed that Christianity's disaffection from the existing
world was the source of its immense spiritual energy. Christianity's
dethronement of the Law gave it spiritual advantages over such institutionalized religions of the Law as Orthodox Judaism and Islam. But in the
practical world, he asserted, where institutionalized religions were most
valuable, it was Christian teaching that "creates enormous problems."[145]
Kristol's chief example of such problems was Christianity's denigration of
materialism. While Judaism and Islam both regarded the demands of
commerce as morally unobjectionable, the opposite assumption was
plainly evident in the New Testament. "The act of commerce, the existence of a commercial society, has always been a problem for Christians,"
he noted. Kristol argued that Jesus and the early church revived the spirit
of gnostic millenarianism, which asserted "that this hell in which we live,
this 'unfair' world, can be radically corrected."[146]

Orthodoxies were more realistic and conservative. Kristol explained
that orthodoxies engendered a Stoic attitude toward the evils of the world.
They offered spiritual consolation for afflictions that could not be explained or alleviated. Orthodoxies helped people cope with a world they
couldn't change. When Kristol urged the clergy to become more interested
in religion than politics, it was this kind of religion that he had in mind.
He thus retained the Marxist view of religion, though not to Marx's
purpose.

Kristol readily conceded that the New Testament did not endorse this
kind of religion, but he regarded the objection as irrelevant. Though he
allowed that biblical Christianity provided a possible warrant for progressive politics, Kristol contended that Christianity itself only survived the
second century by shedding its original prophetic character. Faced with
the destructive logic of its own gnosticism, the Christian church transmuted its teachings into an institutionalized orthodoxy. The church
fathers turned the alienated perfectionism of early Christianity into a

priestly religion. Since the spirit of the New Testament could never be completely extinguished by the church, this spirit had always created "tremendous problems" for the church in the real world. The overriding achievement of the church fathers, however, was to save the Christian faith (or some version of it) by tempering the prophetic utopianism of its founders.

Kristol rightly observed that the inclusion of the Old Testament in the Christian Bible preserved a vital religious heritage for the church and enabled it to turn away from the dualistic gnosticism of the Marcionites. His admiration for the achievement of the antenicene church, however, went well beyond his respect for the church's decision to temper its gnostic tendency and reaffirm its Jewish roots. Kristol admired premodern Catholicism because it effectively transmuted a prophetic faith into an institutionalized guardian of existing arrangements. It was this very achievement, in his reading, that modern Catholicism was throwing away.

The problem with modern Catholicism was that it was becoming "much more gnostic in its lack of calm acceptance of the world."[147] The church was failing to be faithful to its own tradition. Instead of repeating that the evils of the world somehow contributed "to the glory of the world," Kristol observed, modern bishops offered pastoral letters on nuclear deterrence and the "trivial moral issue" of distributive economic justice. "It is ironic to watch the churches, including large sections of my own religion, surrendering to the spirit of modernity at the very moment when modernity itself is undergoing a kind of spiritual collapse," he remarked. "If I may speak bluntly about the Catholic church, for which I have enormous respect, it is traumatic for someone who wishes that church well to see it modernize itself at this moment."[148] His view of the Second Vatican Council was not complex. "Pope John XXIII was a disaster," Kristol asserted. "We needed the Catholic church to remain the Catholic church, not to reconcile itself to modernity."[149]

The modern church's preoccupation with fairness distressed him. This preoccupation followed the trend in modern liberalism, he observed, in which the term " 'unfair'. . . has recently entered political discourse."[150] Kristol rarely used the term "unfair" without mock quotation marks. He complained that modern clergy and church officials were translating the otherworldly language of orthodoxy into a characteristically modern concern for social, political, and economic fairness. This preoccupation with the presumed social mission of the church undermined the historic achievement of Christian orthodoxy. "Religion is about transcendence, the eternal, not trying to change the world," he insisted. "Liberation theology has nothing to do with theology."[151] The modern liberal churches and Third World liberationist movements had reverted to gnosticism and, thus, reverted politically to utopianism.

His compelling implication was that the church's spiritual integrity was threatened whenever the church entered the public arena. To politicize religion was to violate the sacred mystery it represented. Kristol had more difficulty dealing with the fact that the opposite is also true. To accept the world as it is and turn away from the struggle for justice is not only alien to the spirit of Christianity, as he conceded, but also alien to Judaism. The Hebrew Scriptures call believers to pour themselves out for the hungry and meet the needs of the afflicted (Isaiah 58:10). Unlike the prophetic Jewish and Christian faiths that he eschewed, Kristol's orthodoxy was as enervated as Adam Smith's deism. It reduced the church's social mission to the cultivation of "a stoical temper toward the evils of the world." Kristol regarded as nonsense the New Testament conviction "that there is something especially good about poor people, that they are holy in a sense."[152] He lamented that Christian teaching contradicted his rather less sympathetic attitude toward the poor. The cultural influence of Christianity made neoconservatism, in this respect, the common sense of the few. With perverse determination, America's mainline churches had returned to their prophetic enthusiasms of old, railing in the name of moral fairness against America's military budgets and its maldistribution of wealth. "It is all very sad," he concluded.[153]

NATIONAL SELF-INTEREST AS FOREIGN POLICY

Kristol turned his attention during the 1980s toward foreign policy. In 1985 he turned an Olin check into a new journal, *The National Interest*. The name was an echo of his other journal, but this time Kristol made no pretense of avoiding ideology. He no longer claimed that foreign policy should be left to the experts or that ideology and foreign policy made a bad mix. The premier issue of *The National Interest* proclaimed that a nonideological politics in foreign affairs was a disarmed politics. Though his positions on international issues often differed from those of other neoconservatives, Kristol insisted—like most neoconservatives—that foreign policy needed to be defined and driven by ideological claims. For him, as long as the Soviet threat existed, the war of ideology had no boundaries.[154]

His basic foreign policy argument replicated his critique of managerial democracy. Kristol argued that every administration quickly lost its sense of direction in the foreign policy area. The reason this happened, he claimed, was that every administration inherited a cesspool of treaties, conventions, and alliances that the foreign policy establishment piously accumulated through its quest for a "world community." These commitments prevented American governments from pursuing America's national interests. America's foreign policy establishment claimed to believe in something called international law, which, Kristol contended, was a fiction that subverted the purpose of foreign policy itself. The foreign policy establishment assumed that pursuing the national interest was to be subordinated to the "rule of law" in international relations. Instead of promoting America's national interests, American diplomats thus devoted themselves to building mechanisms that bound all nations under the code of so-called international law.

The Rio Treaty of 1947 was one of Kristol's favorite examples of this problem. It stipulated that no country in the Americas could use military force against another North or Latin American nation without the unanimous consent of the other signatories. Kristol observed that this "absurd" treaty thus formally committed the United States to pursue nonexisting common interests with nations "whose chronic instability is matched only by their economic irresponsibility." In 1948, the United States compounded this absurdity by helping to establish the Organization of American States, "a kind of mini–United Nations where we can be voted down in only three languages, thereby saving translators fees."[155] The same absurdity rationalized the existence of the United Nations, which to Kristol was not merely offensive, but seriously detrimental to American security. He complained that the United Nations had created the Third World—a coalition of nations with no common interests "except the political capital to be gained domestically by striking anti-American, anti-Western, anti-'colonialist' postures."[156] He argued that the United Nations should be abolished, or at least moved to Lagos or Kuala Lumpur. The United Nations would more likely stay where it was, he lamented, because America's foreign policy establishment was not interested in foreign policy, but only in its own version of diplomacy. A utopian piety about the desirability of a world community had become, like managerial democracy, an idol that impeded the true practice of politics.

A self-respecting America would not have lowered itself to look for common ground with Third World nations. Kristol was incredulous at the notion that Americans should feel guilty about world poverty. [157] He was equally forthright about his main reason for wanting to abolish the United Nations: Getting rid of the United Nations would primarily benefit the "large, powerful and affluent nations" in their relationships with poor countries. In direct negotiations, the dominant nations nearly always could pursue other options when confronted by demands from uncompliant poor countries.[158] He suggested that abolishing the United Nations would also benefit poor countries, since it would force them to solve their own problems rather than devoting their energies to manipulating world opinion. Like spoiled children, Third World leaders needed the corrective discipline of self-respecting parents. Kristol claimed that their behavior would improve under stronger American leadership. "We are a strong nation, and they will respect our strength, as well as our loyalty to our own political and social ideals, when we behave in a self-respecting way," he declared. "In forum after forum, we speak in placatory or apologetic accents, in response to their absurd or venemous accusations."[159] A self-respecting America would shut them up. The echoes of Burnham were strong whenever Kristol warmed to the theme of national self-respect. If Third World leaders had abused the forums that America stupidly provided for them, he observed, the reason could be traced to America's lack of a self-confident ideological vision, as well as to its record of compromising national interests in return for nothing.[160]

Kristol's major writings during the 1980s developed this ideological construct, which he alternately called "global unilateralism" or "nationalist unilateralism." His first version offered a different way to fight the Cold War. Kristol argued in the mid-eighties that America's basic foreign policy problem was that "we are an imperial power with no imperial self-definition." Like the Soviet Union, America had acquired a vast network of imperial responsibilities, but unlike the Soviets, America lacked an ideology that rationalized its right to intervene in the internal affairs of other nations.[161] His rather schematic reading of the Cold War emphasized this putative ideological disadvantage.

He reasoned that the twentieth century was fundamentally defined by the struggle between two ideologies, which he defined as "political ideas that breathe quasi-religious aspirations and involve quasi-religious commitments." These conflicting ideologies were incarnated by the United States and the Soviet Union, "the only two large nations in the world today that were born out of a self-conscious creed, and whose very existence as nations is justified and defined in creedal terms." Ideology was as constitutive to the identities of these nations as Catholic doctrine was constitutive of Catholicism. The twentieth century had, of course, witnessed the rise of other ideologies, over which wars had been fought. Yet there was "always something 'unreal' about them, and while they are capable of enormous destruction they also seem destined to self-destruction," he remarked.[162] While the possibility could not be excluded that some form of reactionary barbarism would yet prevail over the world, he conceded in 1985, the struggle for the world was currently being waged between the ideologies of liberal internationalism and Marxism-Leninism.

He defined liberal internationalism as a strategy to eliminate national conflicts "by granting 'self-determination' to all viable national entities and then constructing a 'world community' that would peacefully abide—or be constrained to abide—by the rules of international law as established by a written charter." Marxism-Leninism countered that world peace could only be achieved "by a world communist order that would abolish the 'contradictions of capitalism' that were the 'real' causes of national conflict."[163] On this level, the struggle for the world was no contest. America's creed prevented America from fighting at all, he charged. America's ideology was a legalistic utopia. The goal of American liberal internationalism was for the United States to have no foreign policy at all. The American creed subordinated American interests to the supposed interest of a phony world community.

The Soviet situation, though anomalous, was entirely different. The Soviets brandished a highly effective ideology that nobody within the country believed. Though Leninism was completely discredited among the Soviet people, this "self-conscious and fully articulated secular-messianic religion" nonetheless provided Soviet leaders with a potent foreign policy weapon. Because it made a powerful appeal to alienated elites in the West and the Third World, Kristol argued, Marxism-Leninism did real work in the international arena—a "fact" he noted with evident envy.

If the authority of the Soviet regime was only legitimated by its ideology, and if this ideology was already discredited throughout the Soviet Union, it was tempting to think that Soviet leaders were operating from a weak position. Kristol inveighed against this illusion. It was the same illusion that Burnham condemned in Kennan's foreign policy prescriptions. The "messianic" power of Soviet ideology was so great that Soviet communism, backed by its military power, enjoyed towering advantages over the United States in the international arena. Kristol warned that it was therefore futile to strive for a "live and let live" relationship with the Soviet Union. "No nation under the dictatorship of a Marxist-Leninist party can explicitly accept that idea, and no communist nation ever has," he asserted. Even Yugoslavia and China had never renounced their strategic Leninist goal of a communist world. To abandon this goal would undermine the legitimacy of communist governments. Kristol implicitly acknowledged that America was not actually threatened by Yugoslavia or China. American coexistence with these governments was therefore possible. "The United States would not be much troubled by a 'Titoist' Cuba or Nicaragua—*i.e.*, one that is not a military and political ally of the Soviet Union—just as it is not much troubled by the current regimes in Yugoslavia or China," he wrote.[164] The crucial factor was whether the messianic vision of world communism still functioned to sanction state power and define foreign policy goals.

Kristol conceded that most Americans apparently wanted coexistence with the Soviets. It was this desire for a "live and let live" policy that needed to be counteracted. Liberal internationalism rationalized appeasement. The needed alternative to it would be a fighting, "self-consciously ideological" creed, he argued. The new conservatism would be "the appropriate response of the American 'public philosophy' and the American 'national interest' to the condition of democratic capitalism in the last part of the twentieth century." Unlike most neoconservatives, Kristol wasn't proposing to make the world safe for democracy. Nationalist unilateralism was not out to redeem Wilson's fantasies about remaking the world in America's image. It was liberal internationalism that promoted the religion of democracy. America's rhetorical devotion to liberal internationalism shackled American power. Kristol repeatedly complained that even America's foreign military bases weren't *American* bases at all, since America could only use them with the permission of the host countries.[165] The United States was impeded from pursuing its interests in the world because it was entangled in the separate interests of its supposed allies.

His "new conservative nationalism" countered that the purpose of American foreign policy was not to contain the Communists, but to defeat them. Neoconservatism was uniquely suited to provide the foreign policy vision that a risk-aversive American society needed, precisely because neoconservatism was unapologetically ideological. "The spirit of this new conservatism is enterprising, not at all risk-averse, which is why there is so much friction between it and the spirit of traditional conservatism," he declared.[166] The first task of the new conservatism would be to unmask America's reigning, self-weakening ideology of human rights.

Contemporary liberal internationalism was fueled partly by its appeal to the seemingly irreproachable notion of human rights. Kristol argued that human rights was actually not a legitimate foreign policy concern at all. It was only in the United States, he argued, that the human rights crusade against unjust imprisonment, police brutality, torture, and political executions had been enshrined as an aim of national foreign policy. This distortion of the foreign policy process had occurred only in America because it was only in America that liberals were forced to disguise their political objectives.

The chief purpose of American human rights organizations, according to Kristol, was to provide ideological cover for progressive activism. He ominously noted that most human rights activists were also members of environmentalist, feminist, antiwar, and antinuclear organizations. The reason these people gave so much energy to publicizing human rights abuses in foreign countries, he claimed, was that they couldn't openly advocate democratic socialism in antisocialist America. American democratic socialists had been forced to concoct the human rights movement because, unlike their European counterparts, they had no meaningful role to play in their country's political process. "The result is that those Americans who, in Europe, would belong to socialist or social-democratic parties are forced to channel their political energies into 'causes' which, in sum, approximate as closely as possible to those parties' programs," he argued. European social democrats thus had little interest in human rights, Kristol claimed, since they felt no need to hide their ideological convictions. But in the United States, "where it is imprudent to avow a socialist ideology, these convictions go underground and then emerge in 'causes' such as 'human rights' or 'arms control' or 'unilateral nuclear disarmament,' which present themselves as apolitical or transpolitical."[167]

This explained the campaigns against torture by organizations such as Amnesty International and Americas Watch. Kristol argued that the real purpose of these campaigns was to promote democratic socialism under the cover of a seemingly transpolitical moral concern. Because human rights leaders were well aware that torture was repulsive to bourgeois-liberal sensibilities, he explained, "a focus on torture is a brilliant bit of public relations."[168] In their campaigns these organizations even broadened the definition of torture to include mere police brutality. Kristol was sure that most Americans, if they understood the difference, would disapprove of police brutality in distant lands, but would not be outraged by it. As it was, however, they recoiled in revulsion from reports of torture in other countries. It was instructive for Kristol that torture had become an important political issue only in the past generation, whereas "in years past it never even entered any discussion of international relations." Kristol professed nostalgia for the unsentimental realism of the past. He claimed that Americans had been manipulated by leftists into caring more about the sufferings of foreign victims than about their own national interests. He thus dismissed the moral appeals made by human rights organizations. Though he admitted ("lest I seem paranoid") that "many of the people involved in these organizations are naive innocents," he insisted that their efforts were discredited by the social democratic politics of the human rights movement.

Kristol argued that the supposed moral concern over the practice of torture by governments around the world could be taken seriously only if torture had increased in recent years. Lacking such evidence, he denied that torture should be an American foreign policy concern. A certain amount of torture was inevitable in the world. American policy needed to be realistic about these things. This was especially the case because, as he observed, some of America's best military allies had longstanding records of torturing their domestic opponents. He noted that in Turkey, for example, "there has always been a thin line between sheer brutality and outright torture in its prisons." But Turkey was a military ally of the United States. "Are we really willing to help destabilize its government in the interest of prison reform?" he asked. [169] To put the question this way was to highlight the stakes in the disingenuous politics of human rights. America's military pact with Turkey was a serious matter. To threaten this relationship by pressing Turkish leaders on human rights abuses would be ridiculous. Foreign policy pursued the national interest, not moral reform. Kristol assumed without argument that these concerns did not fit together. America had no serious national interest in promoting human rights in countries such as Turkey.

While regretfully conceding that most Americans apparently believed their country should promote democracy and human rights in its foreign policy, he replied that getting rid of the human rights test was actually a precondition for recovering a self-respecting American foreign policy. What needed to be recovered was the self-respecting assumption that America possesses "a proprietary claim to the world's future." [170] National-ist unilateralism was a self-respecting alternative to what he called "liberal antinationalist isolationism." Kristol emphasized that liberal anti-interven-tionism bore little resemblance to America's traditional isolationism. "Whereas traditionalist isolationism wished to avoid 'foreign entangle-ments' lest the United States be corrupted by such involvement and its role as shining exemplar be sullied," he explained, "the new isolationism believes that the United States is simply unworthy of any such involve-ment because it is 'out of step' with the march of history, which it perceives in very simplified quasi-Marxist terms." [171]

So-called "antinationalist isolationism" proposed that America's inter-ests were best served through a general policy of nonintervention, cooper-ation with other nations, and respect for the rights of national self-determination. For Kristol, this was, at best, the politics of guilt. Liberals generally opposed force not because they held a serious alternative conception of the national interest, but because their guilt feelings led them to regard their country as unworthy of pursuing its interests.

Kristol claimed that his nationalist unilateralism was a more powerful current in American political culture than either the Old Right or New Left isolationisms. The new conservatism was activist, interventionist, and stridently ideological. It asserted that America held a "proprietary right" to pursue its interests unilaterally in the world. In its original form, it asserted that the fundamental mission of American foreign policy was not to contain communism, but to defeat it. The neoconservative approach to the Cold War was that "we should aim to win this war, instead of pursuing a defensive policy that sees stalemate as the goal." America needed to face the responsibilities of its global mission. "In the years ahead, the United States will be far less inhibited in its use of military power, with or without the approval of its allies," he predicted. "But no American president will be able to commit American troops to battle without a commitment to 'victory,' as this is defined by American public opinion." What Americans meant by victory, he explained, was the "healthily unsophisticated" view that winning meant defeating your opponent. [172]

This neoconservative foreign policy was to be a decidedly unilateralist project. Kristol's opposition to entangling alliances extended to the North Atlantic Treaty Organization (NATO) and the Organization of American States (OAS). He argued that American commitments to NATO were too expensive and confining to serve American interests. If it was the burden of the United States to fight and win the Cold War, he did not assume that this burden should continue to include a disproportionate share of the cost of defending Europe. He further insisted—to the discomfort of American officials—that it was absurd to believe that America would ever launch a nuclear strike to defend Europe from a Soviet attack. Thus, NATO's deterrence strategy was an expensive bluff. It was also a corrupting self-deception. The only way that European democracies might be frightened into paying for their own defense, he argued, was for America to call the bluff on itself and withdraw its troops from Europe. [173] The only credible deterrent would come from a build-up of conventional European forces. America's foreign burden did not include defending Europe in perpetuity. Nationalist unilateralism would not be played for a sucker.

At the same time, Kristol assured that as long as the world was menaced by communism, nationalist unilateralism would be outward-looking, aggressive, and fiercely ideological. [174] This was the caveat. Kristol later acknowledged that he never seriously considered the implications of this aside for his position. Nationalist unilateralism was more than a strategy to defeat communism. Yet in the middle of his manifesto for a nationalist unilateralist ideology, he conceded that "live and let live" would make an "appropriate and desirable" policy if the Soviets ever relinquished their messianic mission. [175] If the Soviets ever abandoned their goal of dominating the world, America could revert to a hands-off foreign policy.

America could return to nationalist isolationism. For Kristol, it was a throwaway assurance about a fantasized world.

He was quicker than most neoconservatives, however, to assimilate the implausible events of the late 1980s. Kristol did not cling to his preconceptions about the efficacy of communist totalitarianism. He was not impervious to the early evidence that communism was unraveling, nor did he insist on believing, like many neoconservatives, that Gorbachev's reforms were cunning Leninist plots to entrap the West. Throughout the later 1980s, he cautiously admonished his friends, to the contrary, that there were times when one had to take "yes" for an answer. [176]

His apostasy on NATO enabled his early openness to new evidence. Having already concluded that America's European allies were corrupted by their dependence on American defense spending, Kristol had little sympathy for the allies' anxieties when Gorbachev suddenly embraced their longstanding proposal to eliminate medium-range missiles on both sides. It was their proposal, he reminded them, and now they would have to accept it. The same lesson applied to American conservatives and neoconservatives. Like America's European allies, they were screaming about Soviet military advantages over a denuclearized NATO. Soviet conventional strength would no longer be counterbalanced by NATO's nuclear arsenal if NATO removed its medium-range missiles. "Unfortunately, after publicly insisting for a decade that we had to install those medium-range missiles in order to get the Soviets to remove theirs, they cannot suddenly insist that, in retrospect, the installation of those missiles was a good idea in its own right," Kristol declared. The American Right would have to take yes for an answer. The crisis in NATO over the looming disarmament agreements did not result from Gorbachev's cunning, he argued, but rather from NATO's failure to devise a serious or believable defense policy. Kristol maintained that the Soviets would never reduce their conventional forces in Europe, since they lacked any reason to do so. The German demand to this effect was a non-starter. If the allies wanted security, they would have to summon the will to rebuild their own conventional forces. [177]

In December 1987, while Podhoretz and others insisted that *glasnost* was a Leninist ruse, Kristol announced that he was prepared to take *glasnost* seriously. He noted that Gorbachev was liberalizing not only Soviet foreign policy, but also, incredibly, Soviet domestic politics. Even totalitarian regimes apparently were not exempt from the rules of change. The Soviet economy was a shambles, the Soviet intelligentsia was sullen and restless, and Soviet foreign policy was seriously overstretched. Though he assumed that Soviet hostility toward the West would remain the "fundamental theme of Soviet foreign policy," Kristol acknowledged that Gorbachev's reforms were opening genuine opportunities for better relations between the dominant imperial powers. The object of American statecraft was not to change Soviet politics, but to limit Soviet options and encourage Soviet leaders to take the Yugoslavian road. This was a modest agenda, barely in step with the changes in Soviet politics that were effective by the end of 1987, but by neoconservative standards Kristol's outlook was dangerously idealistic. [178]

By the following summer, *glasnost* had clearly outstripped Kristol's agenda. He was thus emboldened to speculate about the prospects for Eastern Europe. No one seriously expected the Soviets to withdraw from Eastern Europe because the region was "just too important for Soviet national security, providing as it does a protective barrier against another invasion from the West." Eastern Europe was destined to remain a defensive barrier. But could it become more than that? Kristol believed that a Finlandized solution was attainable and that America held some leverage to make it come about. He noted that Soviet officials were dropping hints about renegotiating the terms of their rule over Eastern Europe. None of them defended Soviet hegemony over Eastern Europe in anything but strategic terms. The ideological rationale was only a memory. Eastern Europe had become an albatross to the Soviets; it was valuable to them only as a defensive barrier. The seeds of a renegotiated settlement were thus already evident on the Soviet side. [179]

The problem was that the European democracies were "horrified" by the prospect of a Finlandized solution. The rot had penetrated too deeply for that. "For despite the routine expressions of concern, even of solidarity, the sad truth is that the governments of Western Europe don't give a damn about Eastern Europe," Kristol argued. "In their small-minded addiction to the status quo, with which they are basically comfortable, they privately pray that the peoples of Eastern Europe will remain passive and quiescent—indefinitely." The addiction metaphor was carefully chosen. The Western allies were corrupted by their dependence on the United States. The moment had therefore come to remove at least part of their security blanket. "If the Soviets are going to move toward some version of 'Finlandization' in Eastern Europe, which is the most one can expect, they will demand a price," he observed. "Perhaps it will be too high a price for the nations of NATO to contemplate. But we shall never know until we start negotiating the issue." [180] He assumed that American budget restraints would eventually reduce America's commitment to NATO in any case. It was therefore crucial to begin negotiations over Eastern Europe as soon as possible, he argued, before the United States lost its remaining leverage over the Soviets and the Western allies.[181]

Kristol did not join the Cold War holdouts when the Soviet bloc collapsed in the final weeks of 1989. He immediately exulted that the world's map would be transformed by the imminent collapse of communism.[182] He predicted that the end of the Cold War would allow the United States to calculate its national interests with fewer complications. In a substantially deideologized world, for example, Africa and Latin America would become less important to the United States. Kristol allowed that America would still be forced to pay attention to Mexico, "since Americans do fear being inundated by millions of refugees fleeing chaos." America was stuck with this geographical misfortune. Aside from Mexico, however, Kristol predicted that U.S. interest in Latin America would decrease precipitously as the economic gap between the Northern and Southern Hemispheres increased. This he regarded as a welcome prospect. What was needed, he announced, was "some new, imaginative thinking about America's role in this world," though his own thinking was curiously oblivious to the importance of relieving Latin American foreign debts or of reopening Latin American markets for U.S. goods.[183]

He did not seek a new American crusade to make the world safe for democracy. The death of communism prompted many neoconservatives to discover the positive side of anticommunism. Kristol rejected their claim, however, that the United States had "an original commitment to act unilaterally so as to make the world safe for 'democratic capitalism.' " The notion that America had a mission to promote world democracy was, to him, a presumptuous conceit. "In the entire history of the U.S., we have successfully 'exported' our democratic institutions to only two nations— Japan and Germany, after war and an occupation." The United States had failed to establish viable democracies in the Philippines, South Korea, El Salvador, Haiti, Panama, and elsewhere. "Why should anyone think we can do so in Eastern Europe or Southeast Asia?" he asked. He argued that with the eclipse of the Soviet threat, the United States was no longer compelled by an adversary to be concerned with every part of the world. America didn't need to replace its anticommunist crusade with a crusade for global democracy.[184] What America needed was to redefine the American interest on American terms. "We should be seriously concerned only about events abroad that affect us seriously, less seriously concerned by what affects us only indirectly or obliquely or remotely, and not at all concerned by what is likely to have no appreciable effect at all," Kristol contended.[185]

He offered a personal illustration of this point. After the Second World War, *The New York Times* had resolved to devote the opening pages of its front section primarily to international news. Kristol recalled that this was a bold decision at the time, which cut against the well-founded belief that most Americans would rather read about their own country than about foreign affairs. The editors at the *Times* reasoned that with the advent of the Cold War and the rise of the United States as a world power, international news had become more important to America—if not to Americans—than most domestic news. The *Times* would make educated Americans deal with the world beyond their shores. Kristol admired this attitude while communism menaced the world. With the end of the Cold War, however, he found himself skimming the articles on foreign affairs, "irritated by what I now feel to be their obtrusiveness." With the collapse of the communist threat, he explained in 1990, he couldn't stir up any interest in the fortunes of little countries far away, and couldn't see why he should care about them. Liberia was a current example. In Liberia a dissident military faction led by someone named Taylor was leading a rebellion against the apparently dictatorial and corrupt government of a tyrant called Doe. No one knew whether the rebels stood for anything except replacing someone named Doe with someone named Taylor. "I read the accounts of this situation with a sense of numbness," Kristol confessed. "What am I supposed to feel and think? If the Soviets (or the Chinese or even the Cubans) were involved, I would know what to think, since we would then be confronting a challenge." But this was a purely Liberian matter in a world no longer threatened by communist subversion. Kristol could no longer see why Liberia "should even be within the purview of American foreign policy—or why the *Times* should be devoting so much space to it."

Ethiopia was another current case in point. A brutal Marxist government was being challenged by an apparently equally barbaric army of Marxist guerrillas. The Marxist factor might have drawn some interest in the past; lacking any Soviet involvement, however, the sad fate of the Ethiopian people had now "slipped off the spectrum of American foreign policy." It was also slipping out of mind. "We have no national interest there," Kristol concluded, "and my own interest in reading about events there is minimal." The collapse of communism had sucked all the excitement out of foreign affairs. [186]

Most neoconservatives were trying to create some excitement by enlisting America in a new moral crusade for democracy. Kristol countered that boredom was preferable. Speaking to a Committee for the Free World conference in 1990—which turned out to be the committee's last hurrah—Kristol told the assembled neoconservatives to give up their quest for a defining moral cause. American military force would be required often enough in the future to protect American interests. The time had come, however, to stop imposing American moral visions on unappreciative foreigners. The basis for American foreign policy in the future would be America's national interest, he argued, and not a moral purpose.

Whether Kristol could entirely sustain this position for himself was open to question. The stiffest test for his realpolitik was America's relationship to Israel. Against those who implored the United States to support the "peace process" in the Middle East, Kristol argued that there was no peace process to support because no Arab nation had a national interest in solving the region's dilemmas. The often-invoked concept of a Middle East peace process was a misnomer, since the only model for such a process—the Camp David agreement—was a singular, nonreplicable event. Kristol observed that the Camp David negotiations succeeded because each side was in a position to concede something that the other side desperately wanted. But this precondition didn't exist between Israel and any other Arab country.

Though he conceded that Israel's conflict with the Palestinians would be worth settling on its own merits, Kristol insisted that there was nothing for Israel to gain in its relations with Arab nations by attempting to do so. His proof was that no Arab government had any interest in the Palestinians themselves and no national interest in seeing the Palestinian issue resolved. Since Israel's Arab neighbors had all refused to absorb the Palestinians, Kristol argued that their pronouncements on the Palestinian issue were disingenuous. Egypt had governed Gaza for twenty years prior to 1967 and refused to annex the territory or even permit the Palestinians to visit Egypt. Nobody wanted them. Kristol noted that even the ruse was usually scorned by Syria, Iraq, and Iran, which routinely called for the destruction of Israel while showing no interest in the Palestinians or the creation of a Palestinian state. Syria's ambition was to incorporate the West Bank and Israel into itself—"a permanent Syrian dream, reflected in its official maps."[187]

He allowed that the Palestinians themselves wanted a Palestinian state. The 500,000 Palestinians in the Gaza Strip thought that their state should begin with Gaza. "But a Palestinian state in Gaza would be nothing more than an armed camp for intransigent irredentists who would be at permanent war with Israel," Kristol argued. "Why should Israel agree to any such scenario? It won't, since it would only end up having to occupy Gaza all over again." He found the West Bank even less hopeful, since Jordan wanted no part of it. The Hashemite regime in Jordan ritualistically called for Israeli withdrawal from the West Bank in the name of Palestinian self-determination. In truth, Kristol observed, the prospect of a Palestinian state in the West Bank terrified King Hussein. During the two decades that it occupied the territory, Jordan refused to annex the West Bank because annexation would have created an overwhelmingly anti-Hashemite Palestinian majority. For the same reason, the Hashemite regime feared an autonomous Palestinian state on the West Bank. Hussein preferred Israeli occupation, but needed not to say so. "So Jordan has nothing to give and nothing to ask for in any negotiations with Israel," Kristol remarked. "That is why, quite sensibly, it doesn't negotiate." He thus disbelieved Jordan's official claim that it hoped for a confederated state between a future Palestine and Jordan. Though he was right that the Hashemite monarchy never granted Palestinians the right to vote, Kristol overlooked the fact that the West Bank was, nonetheless, part of the Kingdom of Jordan from 1948 to 1967. Until the late 1980s, the salaries of West Bank civil servants employed before 1967 were paid by Jordan. More importantly, West Bank residents still carried Jordanian passports.

Kristol's pessimism about the "peace process" did not drive him to desperate Zionist visions of a Greater Israel. He gave short shrift to Israelis who favored annexing "Judea and Samaria," since there were 700,000 Arabs in the West Bank. On the other hand, the steadily mounting population of Israelis in the West Bank made it difficult to imagine an Israeli withdrawal. In his view, every solution to the Palestinian problem was a dead end; the irredentist dynamic was built into the situation. "The million or so Palestinian refugees—by now mainly children and grandchildren of the original refugees—did not come from the West Bank, have no family connections on the West Bank, have no memories of the West Bank," Kristol observed. "During the twenty years that Jordan occupied the West Bank, prior to the 1967 war, it never occurred to anyone that this area might be a suitable homeland for the Palestinians, or the site of a Palestinian state." Most Israelis thus appropriately assumed that a Palestinian state on the West Bank would not represent a peace settlement, but rather a new stage in the Arab war against Israel. [188]

He did not conclude, however, that the best course for Israel was therefore to defend the status quo. Kristol favored Yigal Yadin's largely ignored proposal for Israel to withdraw from part of the West Bank. Under Yadin's proposal, Israel would unilaterally annex the Israeli-settled and strategic areas of the West Bank—comprising approximately 25 percent of the West Bank—and withdraw its troops from the rest of the area. "Israel would then cope with West Bank turmoil as it copes with the turmoil in Lebanon," Kristol explained. He speculated that Jordan would probably seize the territory, but if a Palestinian state were formed instead, Israel's military forces would be forced to keep it in check. In either case, Kristol argued, this solution would be more tolerable for Israel than its current futile attempt to police the occupied West Bank. [189]

Kristol occasionally asserted, without pressing the point, that American interests were best served in the Middle East by siding with Israel against its various Arab enemies. It was not necessary to question his sincerity in believing this, however, to see that the question of Israel posed special problems for his foreign policy realism. American interests unarguably differed at times from those of Israel. More importantly, there were plausible scenarios under which America's interests in the Middle East could force America to cut its special ties to Israel. Kristol would undoubtedly oppose such a change to the bitter end, arguing that the interests of a reliable democratic ally in the region outweighed the material benefits to be gained by cutting a deal, for example, with a revolutionary Saudi government. But there were plausible scenarios under which a bare American national interest criterion would dictate a policy shift undercutting Israeli interests. That is, there were conceivable circumstances under which Kristol's realpolitik would become unconvincing even to himself. In that event, he would surely reclaim moral arguments that he presently eschewed. His exclusion of moral considerations from his foreign policy calculus was clearly reinforced, on the Palestinian issue, by his lack of sympathy for the Palestinians. He did not sustain the same attitude, however, toward the interests of the Middle East nation he cared about. The "new thinking" he called for excluded overriding moral commitments, but his own passionate commitment to the survival and well-being of Israel revealed a concern for something more than American national interests.

Kristol was adamant that the new thinking must exclude any role for the United Nations. "The whole business of the United Nations is absurd," he insisted. "The United States should deal with other nations by advancing its own interests on a case-by-case basis." Five months before the beginning of the Persian Gulf crisis in 1990, I pressed him on this position. The role of the United Nations as a force for peace had significantly increased in recent years and seemed likely to become even greater in a post–Cold War world, I observed. The United Nations had recently supervised military withdrawals or elections in Afghanistan, Angola, Nicaragua, and the Persian Gulf. (Later that year, the United Nations Security Council would pass twelve resolutions supporting American-initiated sanctions and force against Iraq.) Given that longstanding military alliances and ideological barriers were collapsing around the world, wouldn't it make sense to support the United Nations in its efforts to deal with the problems of the 1990s: with environmental destruction, the drug trade, AIDS and other diseases, refugee settlements, famine relief, collective security, election supervision, peacekeeping missions, and so forth? Kristol paused only for a moment. "No, no," he persisted. "The United Nations is a ridiculous institution. It was stupid to begin with and it's still stupid."[190]

He reaffirmed, as well, his desire to abolish NATO and the OAS, "which only hinder our capacity to act in our own interests." When asked for a single example in which the United Nations, NATO, or OAS had ever prevented the United States from intervening on behalf of its interests in the world, he paused with apparent irritation. I suggested that he certainly couldn't have in mind America's interventions in Korea, Guatemala, Cuba, Vietnam, the Dominican Republic, Chile, El Salvador, Grenada, Nicaragua, when he interjected that the OAS had "killed us on Nicaragua." But hadn't the OAS's insistence on negotiations leading to elections helped to break the Nicaraguan stalemate? Kristol waved his hand. The real point, he said, was that liberal internationalism's established pieties impeded America from pursuing its foreign interests long before, in any particular case, military intervention became necessary.[191]

He held firm when Saddam Hussein invaded Kuwait. Kristol wanted no part of the New World Order trumpeted by the Bush administration, especially if it meant working with the United Nations. Though he supported Bush's military response to the invasion, he repudiated Bush's decision to secure step-by-step approval for American initiatives from the U.N. Security Council. The last thing America needed was to entangle itself in the snares of another New World Order. America needed a nationalist, not an internationalist policy. Rather than set his own course of action, Kristol complained, Bush allowed the State Department "to swaddle his action in a complex set of multilateral arrangements, under the aegis of the U.N." It deserved to be a fundamental axiom of Republican politics, he declared, never to allow the State Department to guide American foreign policy.[192] Neither was he moved to reconsider the United Nations' usefulness. "The U.N.'s decisiveness in responding to the Gulf crisis was an exceptional case provoked by exceptional circumstances, and the odds are overwhelming that its members will now quickly revert to the self-interested maneuvering that is its normal state," he declared. The State Department's dreamers and social engineers, likewise, would undoubtedly go back to solving "problems" in the Middle East. Kristol would have saved them the trouble. "There are no 'problems' to be solved in the Middle East, only deeply rooted conditions to be coped with indefinitely," he wrote.[193]

Much of Kristol's neoconservatism was conservative in the traditional sense of the term. His nationalistic rhetoric, his disdain for the Third World, his contempt for the human rights organizations, his opposition to "exporting democracy," his wistfulness about the decline of moral authority, and his opposition to environmentalism, feminism, and egalitarian politics were longstanding conservative positions. His support for the welfare state was characteristically neoconservative. Throughout the 1980s, Kristol periodically scored the Reagan administration for its miserly domestic policies and specifically urged higher benefits for the elderly and those living below the poverty line. [194]

His distinctive contribution to neoconservative thought, however, was his concoction of isolationism and interventionism. Though originally formulated as an alternative to communism, nationalist unilateralism later stood on its own, merging two contradictory schools of foreign policy thought. Theodore Draper once observed that various kinds of isolationism and interventionism had become familiar before the advent of neoconservatism. What had never been seen before the rise of neoconservatism were isolationists who were also interventionists. [195] Nationalist unilateralism claimed the right to intervene unilaterally in the affairs of other nations without accepting responsibility for otherwise maintaining any particular form of world order in cooperation with others. As long as the Soviet threat loomed over all discussions of American foreign policy, it was possible for Kristol to maintain that his peculiar form of nationalism was the only effective strategy for fighting communism. Nothing less would suffice in the age of "quasi-religious aspirations." [196]

This argument turned out to be untrue. Like nearly everyone else, Kristol underestimated the extent to which Soviet communism had already inwardly collapsed by the mid-eighties. The more telling point was that the eclipse of the Soviet threat turned out not to matter anyway. The collapse of the messianic threat that supposedly necessitated Kristol's counter-ideology left him saying virtually the same things as before about America's "proprietary claim" over the world. The dissolution of the ostensible enemy did not rescue America from its imperial burdens. Kristol's previous assurances about returning to "live and let live" were not to be taken seriously. The proprietary claim was still to be invoked over a world that had otherwise lost most of its interest. Kristol adopted the language of foreign policy realism after the death of communism dismantled his ideological framework. The purpose of American foreign policy, he claimed, was only to protect and advance America's national interests. His conception of America's interests and his prescriptions for their advancement, however, preserved nationalist unilaterialism in all but name. His foreign policy prescriptions were offered not only as a self-respecting alternative to liberal internationalism, but also as an alternative to the moralistic internationalisms of other neoconservatives.

The war at home took priority for Kristol. He believed that neoconservatism's battle against the alienated, feminized, guilt-ridden anti-Americanism of the New Class would be enough to keep the fires burning. Neoconservatism didn't need a foreign demon to stay alive. Just as he had been more prepared than most neoconservatives to take *glasnost* seriously, he was later disinclined to join their crusade for world democracy. Defending America's interests in the world would be enough. Having staked so much in the Burnhamian struggle for the world, Kristol's neoconservative critics questioned whether his peculiar form of nationalism and his polemics against the New Class could sustain their movement. It was a fair question.

4

The Culture of Appeasement: Norman Podhoretz

In the summer of 1989, Norman Podhoretz and U.S. Senator Bob Kasten led a delegation of American neoconservatives to the Soviet Union for a conference with Soviet intellectuals at the Kinocenter. The Soviets endured the senator's "class in Civics 101" on the concept of checks and balances before asking him rather more advanced questions about how to deideologize American–Soviet relations, control runaway bureaucracies, and tone down the self-righteous tone of American politics. A vivid example of the latter was provided by Podhoretz, who unleashed a blistering seventy-minute tirade on the Soviet Union's "absolutely evil" role in world politics. "Norman Podhoretz travels to Moscow in search of enemies," sighed a Soviet participant. When his hosts questioned whether their history wasn't somewhat more complex morally than he claimed, Podhoretz assured them it was not. He would not indulge their self-deceiving nuances, just as he would not be deceived by Gorbachev's cunning plot to disarm the Western alliance. He told them he was alarmed at the ease with which Gorbachev's scheme was succeeding. He claimed to believe that the West was being suckered into Finlandization. By negotiating arms reductions with Gorbachev, the West was surrendering to the evil empire in the name of peace.

These articles of faith were beginning to ring false even to Podhoretz, however. In Moscow, he could no longer deny the reality of *glasnost*. The seriousness of Gorbachev's reforms confronted him in the streets, in the media, and at the Kinocenter. Near the end of his remarks, he conceded the obvious, noting that remarkable changes did appear to be taking place in the Soviet Union. Having assumed for so long that Soviet society was irredeemably evil, he wondered aloud whether he, too, was now becoming beguiled by Gorbachev's smile. For Podhoretz, much more than for

Irving Kristol, the loss of a defining foreign demon would prove difficult to absorb. [1]

Like most neoconservatives, Podhoretz moved to the Right after a brief fling with radicalism and a longer career as a Cold War liberal, though in his case, the radical detour occurred in the middle. He was born in Brooklyn in 1930 and grew up in Brooklyn's racially mixed, working-class Brownsville section. His father was a milkman. Like many Jewish immigrants of his generation, Julius Podhoretz retained an emotional identification with Orthodox Judaism and insisted that his son undertake religious instruction long after he himself gave up regular religious observance. His children were to be Americanized Jews. Young Norman Podhoretz therefore attended public schools and a Hebrew high school, and was vigorously pressed by his parents and teachers to excel in school. His educational prowess, he was told, would free him from Brooklyn. This theme was reinforced by a patrician high school teacher who assiduously corrected his Brownsville manners and exhorted him to strive for a Harvard scholarship. At the age of sixteen, Podhoretz won a Pulitzer scholarship, instead, to Columbia, where he doubled as a seminarian.

The Seminary College next to Columbia was the undergraduate liberal arts division of Jewish Theological Seminary. Since he was not religious, Podhoretz was later unable to explain his presence at the seminary beyond his desire to please his father, who was then seriously ill. To him, the seminary was stifling, parochial, even morbid; Columbia represented universality, enlightenment, and cultural sophistication. The contrasts were overwhelming. Podhoretz disliked the rabbinical students, whom he suspected of seeking an easy life. The seminary offered a familiar link with his past, but his unfashionably unabashed desire was to break from his past and join the ranks of his senior professors at Columbia.

His attempts to ingratiate himself with F. W. Dupee, Richard Chase, Moses Hadas, Mark Van Doren, and Lionel Trilling were not subtle. Podhoretz's classmates despised his brazen efforts to win their professors' favor. He later recalled that the "supercilious" homosexuals and the "prissily bred middle-class Jews," in particular, found his aggressive classroom behavior unbearable. Jason Epstein was among them. Their reaction hurt Podhoretz's feelings, but not enough to chasten his hyperactive ambition. He told himself that his classmates were jealous. They were bound by some code of manners he couldn't fathom. Whatever it was, the code didn't work. He was the one who won their professors' attention and affection. Trilling and his colleagues rewarded Podhoretz's enthusiasm, his unfailing eagerness to please, and his "great gift for intellectual mimicry." Through their acceptance he was desperately determined to become a major writer in a culture not known—until that approximate historical moment—for its openness to Jews.

Podhoretz was able to withstand the contradiction because he couldn't bear the thought of not becoming a great literary figure. One of his professors later recalled, "Most of Norman's friends were the sons of New Jersey dentists; at least they looked like the sons of dentists. They had crew cuts, and they talked about 'breaking Keats' and were all terribly aggressive and got very good grades. I believe Norman wore two-toned shoes, brown and white, and he brought his lunch in a spattered brown paper bag."[2] He made a striking contrast to Epstein, who wore Brooks Brothers suits, frequented high-class restaurants and concerts downtown, and carefully concealed his own considerable ambitions under an air of boredom. He and Podhoretz became friends only after their college careers were behind them.

CRITICISM AND CULTURE: PODHORETZ'S EARLY CAREER

Upon realizing that he lacked poetic talent, Podhoretz turned to criticism, following the examples of his teachers, who became his guides not only to literature but also to theology, philosophy, and politics.

Randall Jarrell would later call this moment the Age of Criticism. While American philosophy departments reduced the scope of philosophy to logic and language analysis, literary theorists such as Dupee and Trilling took up philosophy's abandoned metaphysical questions. This enterprise extended the boundaries of literary criticism and stirred intense intellectual excitement in Podhoretz. He embraced Trilling's dictum that the literary mind was "the best kind of critical and constructive mind that we have, better than the philosophic, better than the theological, better than the scientific and the social-scientific." Upon graduating from Columbia, Podhoretz won a Kellett fellowship at Cambridge University and took to Cambridge a "veritably gnostic sense" of the power and importance of the New Criticism.[3]

This outlook was reinforced by two years of further undergraduate study at Cambridge, where Podhoretz arrived "burning to learn, burning to impress, burning to succeed." He calmed down somewhat at ancient Clare College—"the most complacently English of all the Cambridge colleges"—but eventually found his way to Downing College, where the eminent critic F. R. Leavis held forth. Podhoretz became an ardent Leavisian. Leavis's analytical brilliance reminded Podhoretz of Trilling, but Podhoretz found Leavis a more challenging teacher. Trilling and Leavis both regarded literature as an act of moral imagination. Both taught that the function of criticism was to be a cultural guardian of worthy literary standards. Leavis upheld the preeminent cultural importance of criticism with a fervor, however, that Trilling lacked. For Leavis, the literary vocation was the supreme calling. His faith in the importance of literature explained his disgust with nearly everything he read. As Podhoretz recalled, "Trilling's eyes did not blaze with a fierce Calvinist light upon the written word; he did not erect the capacity for 'true judgement' into the very principle of being; he did not conceive of criticism as the rod of the Lord's wrath." Leavis's ferocious prophesying made him an inspiring figure to Podhoretz, as well as Podhoretz's most influential teacher.[4]

Leavis was prodigiously opinionated, fearsomely dogmatic in his literary judgments, and more than a bit paranoid about his intellectual reputation. His opening sentence in *The Great Tradition* characteristically announced that "the great English novelists are Jane Austen, George Eliot, Henry James, and Joseph Conrad—to stop for the moment at that comparatively safe point in history." He tirelessly complained that none of his contemporaries could meet his standard for great writing. Leavis saved his most abusive polemics, however, not for bad novelists, but for those who disputed his critical opinions. He tried to temper his ferocity with his students, seeking to encourage "independent critical judgement" in them. But even Leavis's students trembled at the prospect of disagreeing with him. Podhoretz recalled, "To express the view, say, that Wordsworth's 'Immortality Ode' was a great poem, would elicit from Leavis a look of such long-suffering, such pain, such weary and hopeless resignation that one might have refrained from speaking up out of compassion for him, even if one were not already terrorized into silence by the fear of convicting oneself of an incapacity for 'independent critical judgement.' "[5] The example was drawn from personal experience. Podhoretz's first published article—which compared Trilling and Matthew Arnold—appeared in Leavis's journal, *Scrutiny*, only after Leavis eliminated the offending paean to Wordsworth. No one with independent critical judgement could possibly admire the "Immortality Ode," Leavis informed him. Podhoretz was twenty-one years old and burning, as he put it, not only for the "word" about literature, but also for the word about himself.

A year later, with a Cambridge B.A. and a First in hand, he returned to New York for the summer to seek advice on his career. Returning to Cambridge was a strong possibility, partly because he didn't think of himself as an American. "I came from Brooklyn, and in Brooklyn there were no Americans," he later explained. "There were Jews and Negroes and Italians and Poles and Irishmen. Americans lived in New England, in the South, in the Midwest: alien people in alien places."[6] At the end of the summer, he returned to Cambridge to begin his doctorate after Diana Trilling recommended law school (which he took as an insult) and after he visited the offices of *Commentary* magazine for the first time.

Podhoretz's visit to *Commentary* changed his life. Lionel Trilling had told Elliott Cohen about his protégé. Arriving for his meeting with Cohen, Podhoretz was greeted by eminent art critic Clement Greenberg, who shared an office with Robert Warshow, Nathan Glazer, and Irving Kristol. It was the summer of 1952, when the controversy over Kristol's attack on liberal anti-anticommunism was still raging. Cohen took Podhoretz aside and, after establishing that he knew enough about baseball, asked him to review Bernard Malamud's first novel, *The Natural*. By the time he left the office, Podhoretz later recalled, he would have given anything to be a *Commentary* editor.

He returned to Cambridge in that mood, "my heart lusting for publication and for very little else." The ancient serenity of Cambridge now drove him nearly insane. He groused about the comparative stupidity and dullness of English academic life compared to *Commentary*, which discussed and often fiercely debated the problems of popular culture, the significance of existentialism, the nature of totalitarianism, the prospects for economic expansion, and the future of democracy. Did Cambridge understand the implications of totalitarianism or the meaning of suburbanization? Had Cambridge ever heard of Elliott Cohen or Robert Warshow? The questions answered themselves. Although Podhoretz didn't feel like an American, his alienation from English academe confirmed his desire to become a New York Intellectual.

He returned to New York in 1953 and wrote several reviews while waiting to be drafted. Podhoretz's early writings were driven not so much by his desire to say anything in particular as by his desire to have written. What he sought "was to see my name in print, to be praised, and above all to attract attention."[7] Specifically, he strove for the attention of Phillip Rahv, William Phillips, Mary McCarthy, and other elders in what he later called the "Family" of New York Intellectuals. He later recalled that there was nothing he loved more than to hear Family gossip, and there was nothing he wanted more than to be able to call Phillips and Rahv and Macdonald by their first names.[8] Podhoretz made a bid for their attention with a series of aggressively written Leavisian-style reviews that appeared in five successive issues of *Commentary* in 1953.

His first was an attack on the notion that poetry and literature were somehow affected by the fate of religion. The article marked a rite of passage for Podhoretz. His own anticlericalism was reinforced by Warshow, who despised all clerics of all faiths.[9] Podhoretz shared his friend's Voltairean prejudices. With a recent symposium titled *Spiritual Problems in Contemporary Literature* as his foil, he made his own assault on what he called the "overstrained myth-mongering tendency" in contemporary literature.[10] Many otherwise intelligent people had apparently come to believe that poetry was in some way dependent on religious or spiritual experience, he observed. Podhoretz traced this absurd notion to T. S. Eliot, who argued that poetry was torn from its religious roots by the dissociation of sensibility wrought by modern science. For the past thirty years, Podhoretz lamented, poets such as Eliot, W. H. Auden, Allen Tate, and uncountable lesser talents had tried to recover this lost religious world view. Their efforts had engendered such asinine ventures as the volume under review. Podhoretz was incredulous that anyone might draw religious meaning from modern theologies, which he said reduced the conception of religious truth to metaphor. He offered an alternative explanation for the recent renewal of interest in spirituality, symbolism, and myth. The explanation was that religion offered "not so much a way of salvation as a means of writing."[11] That was writing in the Family style.

If Podhoretz had already captured the highbrow polemical style of Family writing, however, his outspoken contempt for religious "overconsciousness" presented a potential problem for the flagstaff publication of the American Jewish Committee. He was sensitive to the problem. The magazine's biographical blurb identified him as a former student at Jewish Theological Seminary. Near the end of his article, Podhoretz asked what it meant for Jewish writers to think of themselves as Jews if they refused to accept any religious creed. He answered that the crucial task for Jewish writers was to come to terms with the Jew *in* themselves while eschewing creedal attachments. "If Jewish writers now understand that they must come to terms with the Jew in them," he wrote, "why must it have anything to do with Judaism as a *faith* or a way of life, or with the superior or inferior cogency of Judaism as compared with other systems?"[12] Affirming one's Jewishness did not require one to accept any form of Judaism.

The same theme was brought forward in Podhoretz's subsequent reflections on the work of Sholom Aleichem. In Aleichem's writings, he observed, Jewishness did not consist of particular values or racial or national characteristics or any particular religion. Jewishness did not depend on the existence of Judaism or the survival of Jewish moral values. Jewishness inhered simply in the activities of Jews themselves, rather than any theology, ideology, or ethos that might be offered to define them.

Podhoretz thus adeptly cut his ties to Judaism while affirming his own Jewishness in the urbane Family style.[13]

His breakthrough occurred the following month, September 1953, with the publication of his withering attack on Saul Bellow's *The Adventures of Augie March*. The book was already a smashing critical success when Podhoretz read it. Trilling and numerous others had praised it for its energy and originality. Podhoretz took them all on. He conceded that *Augie March* was a more interesting failure than Bellow's previous novels. Bellow's earlier works had been ruined by their "non-dramatic subjectivity" and by their failure to relate the inner feelings of his characters to the outside world. *Augie March* marked an improvement over *Dangling Man* and *The Victim*. For all of its vivid external descriptions and its nearly overwhelming pace, however, *Augie March* was riddled with the same nondramatic solipsism that marred Bellow's previous novels. The most successfully drawn character in the book was "not a human being but an ego."[14] Podhoretz commended Bellow's attempt to create an ambitious, self-made, willful Jewish character representing the American dream—"the inviolable individual who has the courage to resist his culture." He could see himself in the portrait. The problem was that this character was not finally a human being at all, but a device. Augie was like the animals in the cartoons "who get burned to cinders, flattened out like pancakes, exploded, and generally made a mess of, yet who turn up intact after every catastrophe, as if nothing had happened. Though he goes through everything, he undergoes nothing. He doesn't change in the course of the novel; he doesn't even learn, for all his great show of having learned." Like his chief character, Bellow was resisting the lessons of his own experience. His overly celebrated book was filled with one-dimensional figures exhibiting mere peculiarity.[15]

That got their attention. The Family regarded Bellow as their most promising novelist. He was a contributor to *Commentary* and was greatly admired by the magazine's editors. His efforts to create a postwar Jewish sensibility were congruent with their own. They were concerned not to offend him, and therefore sent him the galley proofs of Podhoretz's review.

Bellow was enraged by the review. His Cromwellian response begged Warshow not to publish it. "In the bowels of Christ, think it possible you may be mistaken," he pleaded. Copies of his petition were sent to more than a dozen Family members, but Warshow published the review. For Podhoretz, whom Bellow could only bring himself to call "your young Mr. P.," Bellow's reaction marked a breakthrough. The review ignited a literary furor. While nearly everyone in the Family disagreed with Podhoretz's arguments, his aggressive style won their notice.

He was summoned at the height of the affair for an evening of libations and gossip at Rahv's apartment. Podhoretz later compared the occasion to a bar mitzvah. Rahv told him that he didn't like *Augie March* either—because it didn't have a plot—and then regaled his guest with malicious tales that left Podhoretz babbling, "You mean Dwight *Macdonald?*" and "You mean Mary *McCarthy?*" Shortly before Podhoretz became too drunk to remember anything else, Rahv informed him, "Today you are a man." He meant that he wanted Podhoretz to write for *Partisan Review.*[16]

Podhoretz's euphoria proved to be short-lived. He received his draft notice shortly after *The New Yorker* also asked him to write for them. A few weeks earlier, the prospect of military service had intrigued him. To get drafted at the very moment when the Family was talking about him, however, was devastating. His interest in the military had evaporated. He worried that his career was ruined. He asked Cohen if he would have to make a name for himself all over again when he returned from the army. Cohen assured him that he wouldn't, and offered to hold Kristol's recently vacated position for him until he returned. Podhoretz accepted the offer, as he later put it, as a man embraces his destiny.

The army sent Podhoretz to Germany to run a compulsory lecture program on "Democracy vs. Communism," which left him plenty of time to keep his name in print. His slashing attack on William Faulkner's *A Fable* was accepted by Warshow after *The New Yorker* turned it down. The opening paragraph set the tone. *A Fable* was perhaps not Faulkner's worst book, he began—"one would have to re-read *Pylon* to make a definitive judgement, and I personally could not face the ordeal."[17] But if it was not necessarily his worst book, *A Fable* was nonetheless "so dull, so tortured, and so pretentious" that it forced the reviewer to reassess Faulkner's entire literary corpus. Having thus reread *Light in August, The Sound and the Fury,* and the others, Podhoretz reported, he could only now conclude that Faulkner was a minor talent who had written several masterful but very narrowly conceived novels. Even his best work focused on only one kind of person—"possessed, fated, doomed"—acting in one kind of situation. The question was always whether the protagonist would bear his burden with beauty and grace. Faulkner at his best was like Faulkner at his worst—the difference was the difference between simplistic religious anthropocentrism artfully fashioned or crudely preached.

A Fable was the latter. It was Faulkner's version of the Passion of Christ, which, for Podhoretz, represented a final proof "that an artist must accept the religious view of the universe as a literal truth or leave its myths alone."

If an artist doubted that Christ walked on water, he had no business trying to appropriate the moral meaning of the Gospels. The attempts of modern novelists to dig some meaning out of a demythologized narrative invariably produced the kind of insipid paean to human striving that Faulkner had written. A *Fable* was "one of those disembodied, religiose affirmations that we have learned to regard as the typical literary symptom of a failure of nerve in difficult times," Podhoretz declared. Rather than face up to the ultimate meaninglessness of life and the moral necessity of struggling with the concrete complexities of politics, Faulkner had become "bamboozled by irrelevant religiosity." His turn to liberal Christianity was cutting him off from the real-world drama of salvation, which was occurring in the world of politics and culture. Podhoretz conceded that his own generation, "living now in a limbo that is neither war nor peace," had not yet found its voice. What was certain was that Faulkner's pieties were archaic. This overrated novelist had copped out altogether. His depoliticized appeal to the power of faith sounded "like a chill echo from a dead world."[18]

The drive for power, by contrast, was life-affirming and real. Nietzsche trumped any religious appeal. The echoes of faith were sickly and hypocritical. The "way of Christ" echo was especially nauseating to Podhoretz, since he embraced Trilling's assurance that everybody was out to gain as much power as they could through fame or money or achievement.[19] Faulkner's Christian pieties were literally unbelievable. Those who appealed to them were hypocrites, in Podhoretz's view. His own unabashed lust for fame was more genuine than the drivelings of nervous pietists like Faulkner. When Warshow informed him that his attack on Faulkner offended several Family members, Podhoretz rejoiced that they were still talking about him.[20]

He joined what remained of the magazine's staff the following year, in 1955, which was a calamatous year for *Commentary*. Warshow died of a heart attack at the age of 37; Glazer became an editor at Anchor Books; and Cohen fell into a severe depression that left him virtually paralyzed. After months of staring vacantly at his desk, Cohen was sent to a psychiatric clinic for treatment. His departure left Martin and Clement Greenberg (the former as managing editor) in sole editorial control of the magazine when Podhoretz arrived in December.

He was not welcomed with open arms. The Greenbergs had been thrust into a difficult position. Their editorial authority was undercut by Cohen's shadow as well as by their own apparently interim status. They felt threatened by Podhoretz and made no secret of their judgment that he was a self-promoting opportunist. He had made a name for himself too quickly for his own good or for theirs. Their disdain for him deeply injured Podhoretz. A decade later, when he recounted the experience in his memoirs, he refused to utter their names, but only referred to them jointly as "The Boss." In his account, The Boss unceasingly ridiculed his efforts and was overly anxious about the presumed wishes of the American Jewish Committee. This anxiety drove The Boss to defend editorial positions that he personally rejected. Martin Greenberg in particular needed his job at Commentary and was fearful of disappointing or alienating any members of the committee. As Podhoretz insightfully recalled, Greenberg thus placed himself "in that special condition of unfreedom which is the fate of any employee who tries to second-guess the boss, who spends so much time and energy in figuring out what his immediate superior will or will not like that he becomes a slave to an unrealistically rigid notion of what is required of him."[21]

The experience taught Podhoretz that good editors acted on their own convictions rather than the presumed desires of owners or the market. The conclusion was especially apt in this case, since the committee was too heterogeneous to uphold an editorial line. Rather than use their power to shape the magazine's character, the Greenbergs settled for bullying their subordinates. The experience was humiliating but instructive for Podhoretz. Through the Greenbergs' failure to risk their power, he saw that power was not only position, but freedom. Freedom without empowerment was meaningless, but power itself was useless if one failed to risk losing it.

Podhoretz felt not only that the Greenbergs were abusing him, but that they were ruining the magazine. Less than two years after joining the magazine's staff, he took these feelings to the committee's personnel office and offered his resignation. The Greenbergs were turning Commentary into a stale imitation of what it had been under Cohen's editorship, he charged. Podhoretz also charged that if Cohen ever returned, the Greenbergs were plotting to make life so miserable for him that he "would last only long enough to induce a relapse and set the stage for a coup." This incredible accusation got the committee's immediate attention and triggered a different kind of coup. After six weeks of hearings and deliberations, the committee fired Clement Greenberg, demoted Martin Greenberg to associate editor, and promoted Podhoretz to equal rank. A third associate editor, Theodore Frankel (later replaced by George Lichtheim) was hired to serve as a buffer between Greenberg and Podhoretz.

Podhoretz later recalled that he conducted this struggle for power "with just the right combination of diffidence and fervor" while denying that he was struggling for power at all. "The one charge that everyone was actually hurling against me—the charge of ruthless ambition—I indignantly repudiated and could not tolerate," he recounted. He denounced the accusation that he was scheming for power, but as he later conceded, the truth was evident to everyone but himself.[22]

His editorial criticisms were justified, however. *Commentary* became boringly predictable in the mid-fifties. Its best articles were written by ACCF stalwarts such as Sidney Hook and J. L. Talmon, who rehashed ACCF positions for a dwindling readership. Its worst articles were written by their imitators. Liberal anticommunism was losing its liberalism. Those like Schlesinger and Galbraith who resisted the trend resigned from the ACCF and didn't write for *Commentary*. The decline of liberal anticommunism matched the decline of *Commentary*, which went stale on a handful of overworked themes. Greenberg declined to publish even commissioned articles by major writers that questioned the magazine's decaying orthodoxy. This was what the committee purportedly wanted.

After the committee demoted Greenberg to associate editor, Podhoretz worked successively with Frankel and Lichtheim to restore the magazine's spirit. Their efforts were stymied, however, when Cohen returned to the office, severely debilitated by his uncured illness. His physical and emotional exhaustion prevented him from taking command of the magazine. At the same time, despite Greenberg's alleged intrigues against him, Cohen felt indebted to Greenberg for keeping the magazine alive during his absence. He repeatedly sided with Greenberg's editorial judgments. The balance of power shifted again. When Cohen and Greenberg rejected commissioned articles by Hannah Arendt and Robert Graves because the articles were too controversial for *Commentary*, Podhoretz conceded defeat and resigned his position.

It seemed a risky move on the surface. Two years earlier, Podhoretz had married Midge Decter, a writer who had two young children from a previous marriage. Now, with a third child at home and a corpus consisting mostly of book reviews, he set out to see if he could make a living as a writer. Podhoretz was confident that he could do it, mainly because his reviews had rarely failed to attract attention. He could get along without *Commentary* and was relieved to leave behind the abuse he had taken there.

There was a method to his success. As Podhoretz later explained, his reviews were written in the Family style as vehicles for his own ideas. Book reviewing offered the opportunity to do some writing of one's own, usually by relating some aesthetic aspect of the book ostensibly under review to a cultural or literary issue outside the book. This method allowed Podhoretz "to show off, in short, how much I knew about this, that, and the other thing."[23] It also allowed him to show up his peers and the country's leading novelists in the country's most prestigious journals.

The role of the cultural guardian had its drawbacks, however. Shortly after he left *Commentary*, an encounter with a young novelist he had just attacked made Podhoretz face the main drawback. The writer pulled him aside at a party and asked why he, unlike Edmund Wilson, was refusing to support the writers of his generation. Wilson had encouraged the best writers of his time, "whereas I was for some reason choosing to act as an enemy of the writers of mine."[24] The query drove him to question his critical purpose. Did he really want to end up like Leavis, condemning every novelist since D. H. Lawrence in the name of the great tradition? What was the point of upholding Leavis's standards if they required cutting up one's peers? The question was particularly haunting for Podhoretz because he lacked Leavis's missionary sense of himself as a guardian of Western literature. The standards he had taken from Leavis were not his own. He observed in a semiautobiographical essay that the writers of his generation were earnest, sober, career-minded types with no collective identity whatsoever. They had married early and adopted the manner of civilized adults, while writing books that projected an air of maturity "almost wholly divorced from experience." This air of unearned maturity was their only identifying trait. They had no beliefs and no identity. They were, rather, a non-generation, "a collection of people who, for all their apparent command of themselves, for all the dispatch with which they have taken their places in society, for all their sophistication, for all their 'maturity,' know nothing, stand for nothing, believe in nothing."[25] Podhoretz was describing himself, but not only himself. His point would soon prove to be telling. Having confessed that he had no beliefs, he couldn't justify the kind of criticism he was writing.

His inner struggle over the issue reached the breaking point after he reviewed Jack Kerouac's *On the Road*. Podhoretz gave Kerouac's book a thorough Leavisian pounding, complaining that it was unimaginative, shallow, and badly written. These failings undoubtedly explained the book's spectacular commercial success, Podhoretz observed. He blasted Kerouac's primitivism and anti-intellectualism, and he despaired that Kerouac's "pathetic poverty of feeling" actually contributed to the book's popularity.[26] Podhoretz's pulverizing review was a routine exercise for him—but one which he was no longer prepared to defend. When Kerouac and Allen Ginsberg personally complained to him about the severity of his criticisms and questioned the appropriateness of his literary standards, he took their objections to heart. He admitted to himself that he didn't really care whether a "bunch of idiot kids" thought Kerouac's book was great literature. He wasn't sure he believed "all that Leavisian stuff" about criticism as the guardian of culture and civilization.[27] The Leavisian stuff was only appropriate for an age that produced great literature. But current American literature was far from great by any standard. It compared poorly to the literature of the 1920s. Contemporary criticism therefore had no important work to do. All it could do was repeatedly explain why celebrated works by writers such as Bellow, who had no beliefs of their own, were actually second-rate.

For Podhoretz, the choice was between cutting down his peers or indulging in patronizing sentimentality toward them. For a brief period, he tried to split the difference. He wrote a lengthy celebration of Wilson's career (which Kristol published in two installments in *The Reporter*) and followed with an admiring portrait of the one current novelist he respected, Norman Mailer.[28] Kristol had returned to New York in 1959 and asked Podhoretz to write for him. The invitation was propitious for Podhoretz, since *The New Yorker* had recently stopped assigning books to him. Podhoretz never learned whether the *New Yorker's* editors had grown tired of his negativism or disliked his recent attempts to find a different voice. Whatever the case, their decision to drop him hurt his finances and his self-confidence. His reviews for Kristol kept him going through a difficult period.

Podhoretz dealt with his financial problems by securing an advance for a book on the role of intellectuals in twentieth-century America. This project produced his essay on Wilson but nothing else. His inability to complete the book threw him into a panic. He switched to a book on postwar American fiction, producing the essay on Mailer and a shorter piece on Bellow before hitting the wall again.[29] This time he couldn't kid himself about what was happening. The uncertainty that had begun in him with the comparison to Wilson had become a paralyzing writer's block. He told himself he was being punished for his power lust. "Because of this lust," he later recalled, "I was doomed to unhappiness in the world of jobs, unable to rest content with powerlessness and yet unable to satisfy my disgusting need for power." Retiring from the power struggle at *Commentary* hadn't freed him from the obsession; instead, it turned on his instrument for attaining power—his writing. Podhoretz fantasized about taking a job that held no possibility for advancement or competitive achievement, one that wouldn't ensnare him again in the vicious cycle of ambition. He decided that working as a factory floorsweeper would fill the requirements.

He tried to picture himself as a floorsweeper until Epstein offered him a position as a part-time editor at Anchor Books. Epstein was already a publishing prodigy at Doubleday, having launched the paperback revolution with his idea to publish classics and other high-quality texts in inexpensive paperback editions. Podhoretz gratefully took the job and was promptly forced to decide whether he wanted Epstein's job. Epstein's long-running conflict with the Doubleday system ended less than a month after Podhoretz began working there, and Podhoretz's new employers offered him Epstein's position as editor of Anchor Books—for considerably more money than he, or even Epstein, had been making. Podhoretz turned them down, partly out of friendship and partly because he didn't like the work.

He followed Epstein to Random House, where Epstein launched Looking Glass Library. The idea of Looking Glass Library was to apply the lesson of Anchor Books to children, publishing high-quality children's books in relatively inexpensive editions. Podhoretz became the company's first editor-in-chief, and later recalled that the experience taught him that children's literature was for children. Looking Glass Library published a few titles, but never got off the ground. The experience solved Podhoretz's immediate financial problems, but it didn't cure his blocked ambition. He had not wanted to be a commercial editor in the first place, much less an editor of children's literature.

The remedy for Podhoretz's career problem was evident to his friends, though Podhoretz spent several weeks denying that he was interested in it. Cohen had committed suicide in May 1959, and Martin Greenberg kept *Commentary* going while its governors looked for a new editor. They finally offered the position to Kristol, who turned it down, and followed with offers to Daniel Bell and Alfred Kazin that were also rejected. They approached Podhoretz next, ostensibly to ask him what qualities he felt the next editor should possess. Podhoretz described himself while claiming not to want the position. At their next meeting, he told them he would take the job only if they offered him a high salary and complete editorial freedom.

He settled for the latter. Diana Trilling warned him that becoming an editor at his age would ruin him as a critic, but Podhoretz considered himself already ruined as a critic. His first issue was published in 1960, two weeks after his thirtieth birthday. He observed at the outset that no editor ever hid from his readers more insistently than Elliott Cohen.[30] During its best years, he implied, *Commentary* had benefited from Cohen's quiet, classic, and chaste editorial style. But the magazine had become less interesting in recent years, partly because it was dominated by professional celebrants of all things American.

Commentary had never been adventurous. It was launched in 1945, as Cohen put it, "as an act of faith in our possibilities in America." Though the magazine pledged to keep a vigil with history—because historical events "have so often marched over us"—it rarely criticized America in any way. Cohen's hardcore anticommunism and his celebrative attitude toward America defined the magazine's content and, especially, its tone. *Commentary's* liberalism consisted mostly in its sympathetic view toward blacks and Jews. As Podhoretz later recalled, the magazine otherwise attributed all of America's problems to the human condition itself, "against which it was of course 'childish' or 'foolish' or 'infantile leftist' or pathological to struggle." American society defined reality.[31]

This was Cohen's legacy. His faith had been carried on, with diminishing imagination, by Martin Greenberg. For his part, Podhoretz shared the hard anticommunism of his mentors. The critic in him had always choked, however, at the magazine's America-worship and its Jewish parochialism. Articles by anti-anticommunist writers were forbidden; articles critical of American society were nearly always rejected. The magazine was overloaded with boring articles by second-rate writers who shared Cohen's world view. Podhoretz swept them out—and broke all of Cohen's rules. He brought the magazine back to the Family—but with a twist. The first issue sent the message.

He needed a Family-style feature that broke the *Commentary* mold by criticizing American politics and culture. He found it in Paul Goodman's unpublished book, *Growing Up Absurd,* which had already been rejected by nineteen publishers. The veteran anarcho-pacifist represented nearly everything that Cohen abhorred. His extraordinary indictment of American society finally made it into print in an unlikely forum. More than half of Goodman's landmark oracle was published in Podhoretz's first three issues, creating a sensation that helped reverse the magazine's declining fortunes.

Podhoretz overhauled nearly every aspect of *Commentary's* appearance and content, but it was his publication of Goodman's manifesto for a new generation that transformed the magazine's long-cultivated image. Goodman's articles generated a windfall of publicity for what was then called "the new *Commentary.*" At Podhoretz's urging, Epstein published the book, which immediately became a best seller. The new *Commentary* became the first journal to pay serious attention to the New Left. In six years, its circulation grew from 20,000 to 60,000. During the early 1960s, the magazine's coverage of the New Left was surpassed only by a new journal, *The New York Review of Books,* which Epstein founded during the newspaper strike of 1962–63. For several years, Podhoretz and Epstein published many of the same writers and shared the same politics. By the end of the 1960s, Goodman was still writing for both publications, but most others were forced to take sides between them.

The chronically blocked Cohen had used his position to get others to do his writing for him. Upon taking Cohen's position, Podhoretz was presented with the same solution. His breakthrough had occurred while he was incapable of writing. Now, having given up on writing a book, he reasoned that he was paying the price for turning his writing into an instrument for attaining fame. Podhoretz tried to get around his block—and maintain appearances—with an editor's column introducing each issue. His inaugural column introduced the new magazine and hailed Goodman's contribution to it.

For Goodman, Podhoretz explained, modern America was a nation of unfulfilled revolutions. Modernity's revolutions had failed to replace the customs and social arrangements that they overturned. The democratic revolution had been fulfilled in America only in truncated forms. Though industrial workers had won the right to organize and engage in collective bargaining for better wages and conditions, they had failed to push for gains toward production for use. They were therefore alienated from their labor and were often personally degraded in it. Their failure to attain production for use was creating an economy devoted to the production of junk, Podhoretz explained, "and this in turn has bred a huge class of promoters and salesmen whose job is to stimulate artificial needs in a consumer already badgered beyond endurance, and whose advertising methods have contributed immeasurably to the debasement of language and the wild growth of a general public cynicism." America was devoting its energies "to holding a defensive line not only against the very real threat of Soviet power but against the promise of our own future potentialities."[32]

A new utopianism was needed. American society was driven by the desire for status and money, Podhoretz observed, but this very drive for success "encourages the development of the worst human qualities and strangles the best."[33] The new *Commentary* would offer a passionate effort of will and consciousness to speak "not on behalf of what man happens at the moment to be, but on behalf of what he has it within him to become."[34] The 1950s were over, and the new editor was reclaiming his right to a youthful idealism.

His earlier article, "The Young Generation," presented an essential clue to this rediscovered idealism. If his peers had no beliefs or character of their own, he had reported, there was at least some evidence that they realized something was missing. His prematurely serious generation was beginning to feel cheated of its youth. They tried to skip adolescence by willing themselves from childhood directly into adulthood. But the attempt was self-defeating, "for a man can never skip adolescence, he can only postpone it." Podhoretz forecast that at the moment his generation

finally reclaimed its adolescence, "something very wonderful" would oc-
cur. The moment would be signaled, he said, when his generation broke
loose and took a swim in the Plaza fountain in the middle of the night. [35]

Podhoretz jumped in the fountain with his first issue. His flirtation
with Goodman's utopianism restored his adolescence and revived Cohen's
tired magazine. His success also lifted him from his own premature
malaise. [36] The column, however, didn't work. Podhoretz struggled to
produce a page of introductory comments for each issue, but when people
started asking if he would ever write for the magazine, he realized he
wasn't fooling anyone. The columns grew shorter and, after eight issues,
he gave up. He stopped writing altogether for two years, taking the
Cohen solution of communicating through others.

Since his utopian phase coincided with what he called his period of
literary impotence, the depth of Podhoretz's commitment to the ideas he
published during this period would prove difficult to measure. Some critics
later implied that his commitment to radicalism was never deep. [37] Along
with Nathan Glazer and David Riesman, however, Podhoretz was active
in the National Committee for a Sane Nuclear Policy, and he vigorously
defended his utopian turn at Family gatherings. In a rather disjointed piece
for a *Partisan Review* symposium in 1962, he defended his utopianism and
repeated Goodman's arguments about America's truncated democracy.
The most effective American challenge to communism, he suggested,
would be to commit the United States to "a humanitarian and idealistic
policy" that fulfilled the democratic commitments of its own revolution. [38]
Though he continued to publish hard anticommunist articles by Hook and
other ACCF veterans, Podhoretz opened the magazine to various currents
of anarchist, progressive, and democratic socialist thought represented
by, among others, Goodman, Michael Harrington, Staughton Lynd, H.
Stuart Hughes, and Edgar Friedenberg.

Meanwhile, he drank enough each night to drown his literary temptations. This ritual stopped only after Podhoretz was asked to write a
monthly book review for *Show* magazine, the glossy arts periodical
founded on Huntington Hartford's millions. He dismissed the proposal
until Hartford's editors offered him $750 per review. In 1962, this sum was
too staggering to refuse. Podhoretz willed himself through several reviews, driven by the image of the check that awaited each completed
effort, and in the fall he was invited to Hartford's private island off the
coast of Nassau to attend a writer's conference organized by the magazine.

His transfiguration occurred during his stay on Paradise Island.
Throughout this exhilarating week, he later recalled, "I was in total
command of my energies at every moment, uninhibited in the use of them,

unwearying in their exercise. I could drink all night without getting drunk and still wake up after only two or three hours of sleep without being in the least bit tired. My senses had never been so alert, my brain so alive, my spirits never so high." He was surrounded by celebrities whom he categorized as generals, majors, and lieutenants according to their degree of fame. He looked out from his Caribbean resort deck and enthused that "*this* was what success looked like, all its various components brought together in one dazzling display." The sight was intoxicating. "This was what it meant to be rich: to sleep in a huge bright room with a terrace overlooking an incredibly translucent green sea, to stretch one's arms out idly by the side of a swimming pool and have two white-coated servants vie for the privilege of depositing a Bloody Mary into one's hand, to sign checks (which we had to do, though of course we would never have to pay them) without giving money a second thought." He looked upon those who possessed the kind of fame that directly converted into wealth, "and I liked what I saw; I measured myself against them, and I did not fall short." Podhoretz's disaffection from alienated intellectualism and the culture of the Left began that week. He left Paradise Island with the words of a Clifford Odets character ringing in his head: "From now on, the best of everything is good enough for me."[39]

THE POLITICS OF GUILT:
PODHORETZ'S "NEGRO PROBLEM"

He found an outlet for his rejuvenated energies within days of his return to New York. Podhoretz had commissioned an article on the Black Muslim movement from James Baldwin and had periodically reminded Baldwin, when the article failed to appear, of its importance to the magazine. Upon returning from Paradise Island, he learned that Baldwin had sold the article to *The New Yorker* for $12,000—more than twenty times the fee offered by *Commentary*. Podhoretz was livid. Like the Ancient Mariner, he later recalled, "only even more demented," he ranted against Baldwin all over town, condemning "the unspeakable thing Baldwin had done," until he realized that his friends were inclined to overlook Baldwin's indiscretion because of his race. The apparent double standard made Podhoretz even more furious. His anger exploded when *The Fire Next Time* became a national sensation. Baldwin's success was hard to take. His hypocrisy was infuriating, and the acclaim he received proved that American liberals were afraid to criticize blacks.

Podhoretz's response was titled "My Negro Problem—And Ours." He

explained that he didn't share the guilt feelings toward blacks that were
common among his patronizing liberal friends, because as a youth he had
feared blacks and was victimized by their violence against him. He was
terrorized throughout his childhood by Brownsville's tougher, ruthless,
and more athletic black youths. Podhoretz recounted several incidents in
which he was persecuted by blacks. He recalled that when his older,
left-wing sister tried to explain to him that blacks were uniquely oppressed
in America, he believed her but still feared them. "And I still hated them
with all my heart."[40]

His experience was arguably unrepresentative. For Podhoretz, however, this anticipated objection was exactly the point. Writers such as
Baldwin graphically described the sense of entrapment that made blacks
hate their white jailers. On the other side, the hostility of whites toward
blacks was often similarly attributed to their unacknowledged guilt feelings. These feelings converted into hatred, it was said, because whites
failed to accept their guilt. In both cases, racial hatred was primarily
attributed to the pathology of white domination over blacks.

Podhoretz conceded that these explanations were not altogether implausible. They probably accounted, to some degree, for the racial
feelings of people in clearly defined oppressed and oppressor groups. The
problem was that they couldn't explain his own experience. In his neighborhood, the jailers were black and the victims white. Far from feeling
guilty toward blacks, his friends were afraid of them and envious of their
"free, independent, reckless, brave, masculine, erotic" demeanor. The
white youths could only fantasize about living like their black enemies.

> We all went home every day for a lunch of spinach-and-potatoes; they roamed
> around during lunch hour, munching on candy bars. In winter we had to wear
> itchy woolen hats and mittens and cumbersome galoshes; they were bare-
> headed and loose as they pleased. We rarely played hookey, or got into
> serious trouble in school, for all our street-corner bravado; they were defiant,
> forever staying out (to do what delicious things?), forever making distur-
> bances in class and in the halls, forever being sent to the principal and
> returning uncowed. But most important of all, they were tough; beautifully,
> enviably tough, not giving a damn for anyone or anything.[41]

He therefore despised them and felt no guilt toward them whatsoever. He
had nothing to feel guilty for, he explained, just as they had nothing
to be resentful about. He was not an oppressor and they were not
oppressed.

Yet they still hated each other. This was the point. "If we managed the
job of hating each other so well without benefit of the aids to hatred that

are supposedly at the root of this madness everywhere else," he observed, "it must mean that the madness is not yet properly understood."[42] He didn't claim to understand it, either, but as he wrote elsewhere, he believed there was a psychotic dimension in American race relations that prevailing theories didn't grasp. The typical dialectics of master and slave were part of the problem.[43] They drove white liberals to romanticize blacks and pander to them. They also drove whites to assume "a guilt that is not properly theirs." Liberal pandering granted blacks, in turn, a moral license to be deceitful and cunning. Podhoretz knowingly fumed that liberals were allowing themselves to be exploited by blacks whom they employed or tried to befriend.

He confessed that he continued to "fear them and envy them and hate them still," though not in the same way that he had hated them as a youth. The difference was that he now felt guilty about his racial feelings, "like the good liberal I have grown up to be." Just as he envied blacks during his youth for their superior masculinity, he now envied their superior physical grace in dancing and playing basketball. The hatred he felt for blacks was painfully difficult to explain. It was "the hardest of all the old feelings to face or admit, and it is the most hidden and the most overlarded by the conscious attitudes into which I have succeeded in willing myself." He was reminded of his hatred for blacks by "the disgusting prurience that can stir in me at the sight of a mixed couple," and especially by "the violence that can stir in me whenever I encounter that special brand of paranoid touchiness to which many Negroes are prone."[44]

These experiences made Podhoretz despair of the current push for racial integration in America. He argued that the civil rights movement was miscalculating the depth of the problem. The integrationist strategy of the movement was therefore disastrously mistaken. Podhoretz claimed that there was a better strategy. The Jews had survived centuries of oppression because they were tied to a theological memory of past glory. Their religious dream of redemption had given them no choice but to carry on. But a black person in America had nothing to compare to this memory. "His past is a stigma, his color is a stigma, and his vision of the future is the hope of erasing the stigma by making color irrelevant, by making it disappear as a fact of consciousness," Podhoretz declared. The only way this goal could ever be attained was to push far beyond the integrationist pieties of the civil rights movement. Color could only be made irrelevant by making color itself disappear. "And that means not integration," he concluded, "it means assimilation, it means—let the brutal word come out—miscegenation."[45] The only solution to racism was to make blacks and whites themselves disappear.

Podhoretz later exulted that "My Negro Problem" was not only the best thing he had ever written, but the first piece he wrote in his own voice. He published it in *Commentary* because he knew the value of sensation. The article sparked a sensation beyond even Podhoretz's fantasies, however. It provoked hundreds of letters—many of which commended his presumed courage in writing it. Podhoretz corrected this presumption. Having grown up in Brownsville, he explained, it had taken no courage for him to express his feelings for blacks.

Courageous or not, his article was searingly honest as a description of one man's racial hostility and confusion. Podhoretz justifiably regarded his honesty as more honorable than the liberal hypocrisies he criticized. As a challenge to liberals to acknowledge their own racism before sounding off on the solution to America's racial dilemma, his article marked an advance over much of the literature he described. His argument was offensive, however, for reasons he never acknowledged. "My Negro Problem" was widely attacked for its apparent bigotry. Podhoretz bitterly rejected this accusation, but it was more than his confession of racial hatred that gave his article such an ugly tone.

His insistence that all people held racial prejudices was potentially constructive. His further insistence that the civil rights movement failed to grasp the psychotic dimension of racism in America was equally merited. To insist that the blacks he knew in Brownsville had no reason to feel oppressed, however, was absurd. "My Negro Problem" resurrected childhood memories. As a child would, Podhoretz ignored the formative social history behind the events he described. In Podhoretz's account, the black youths he feared had no reason to feel oppressed by white society. His descriptions of their alienation from white America gave evidence of *their* awareness of this larger social context, however, even if he was not aware of it.

Moreover, to characterize blacks by the stereotype of the libidinal bad boy was grotesque. When Podhoretz tried to express what he, as a liberal adult, admired in blacks (before getting to the various things he hated in them), all he could come up with was their "superior physical grace" in dancing and playing sports. The same distorted perception appeared in his conclusion, where he characterized the color of African-Americans as a stigma and insultingly announced that American blacks had no legacy worth preserving. The stigmas he assigned to African-American color and history belonged to the history of white America. It was white Americans who enslaved and degraded blacks and thereby stigmatized their own history. The mere existence of African-Americans reminded white America of its racist history. Miscegenation would erase *this* stigma by eliminating blacks themselves. If only they would eliminate themselves, the memory of their persecution could be erased. Morton Weitzner caught the spirit of this proposal and brought it home: "Thus a new school of thought is born. . . . To eliminate persecution, bigotry, prejudice and the like we just remove the victim. . . . If this is a proposed solution, then *Commentary* should start looking for a new editor. Or, better still, no editor will be necessary since the very reason for the existence of *Commentary* will have disappeared."[46]

Podhoretz emphasized throughout the ensuing controversy that he was a liberal. His racial attitude was not far, he claimed, from that of other white liberals. The claim was disputed by many, but his article owed its considerable notoriety to its liberal pedigree. Had the same article appeared in *National Review*—which opposed the civil rights movement—it would not have created the sensation that "My Negro Problem" ignited. Podhoretz's identification with liberalism was crucial to his article's effect. It was an identification that he was already describing, however, with less-than-convincing assurances. What liberalism meant to him, he explained, was guilt. Upon moving from Brooklyn to the upper west side of Manhattan, he realized that the police were working for him and not for blacks. This realization introduced him to the experience of liberal guilt—the basis of liberalism itself. Liberalism expressed the guilty conscience of the intellectual class to which he had ascended. But his chief point was that integration was "sentimental nonsense" promoted by white liberals who had never lived among blacks. Podhoretz had taken on enough of the anxieties of his liberal friends to recognize the social type, but the lessons of his childhood inoculated him from internalizing liberal attitudes on race. He dismissed the integrationist liberalism of his friends as a pathetic product of middle-class guilt. If it took no courage for him to reveal his negative feelings toward blacks, his identification with liberalism—by his own definition—was already tenuous.

The significance of this disaffection was concealed at the time by Podhoretz's radical pose. Liberalism in the early 1960s promoted economic growth, expansion of federal power over the states, and, relatedly, racial integration. During this period, *Commentary* regularly criticized the politics of the Kennedy administration and its intellectual apologists. Liberalism rationalized the economic interests of the military-industrial complex. For the young editor steeped in William Blake, Charles Dickens, John Ruskin, D. H. Lawrence, and T. S. Eliot, the New Left struck deeper chords. He found the anti-industrialism of Goodman and the then-unknown E. F. Schumacher intuitively appealing.[47] At the height of the struggle for the civil rights bills, Goodman argued that centralized power was always inimical to freedom. For Podhoretz, Goodman conferred a leftist respectability on arguments with tainted associations. The segregationists had a point. *Commentary* published several New Left critiques of liberal statism and economic developmentalism, but Podhoretz saved the civil rights movement for himself. Having revived the magazine by attacking the liberal establishment, he insisted that "My Negro Problem" was a similarly radical assault on current "liberal ideas and pieties." Though he positioned himself to the left of liberalism, however, the article unwittingly prefigured his lurch to the Right.

It also provoked Stokely Carmichael to charge that Podhoretz was a racist—an accusation that nearly brought Carmichael a libel suit. At the time, the term retained the precise meaning that some races were genetically inferior to others. Having expressed his repugnance for racism, Podhoretz was deeply angered when so many readers found his article racist. In his bitterness toward this exaggerated misreading, however, he deceived himself about the kind of article he had written. Two years later, after Daniel Patrick Moynihan was unfairly attacked for his government report on the condition of black American families, Podhoretz claimed that Moynihan was victimized by the same liberal hypocrisy that had been inflicted on him.

But the analogy wasn't close. Moynihan observed that a disproportionate number of black children were being raised without fathers. Notwithstanding the chorus of accusations to this effect, he did not blame the victims for the crisis of African-American families. He traced the causes of the crisis to American slavery and discrimination, rapid urbanization after World War II, a welfare system that gave incentives to fathers to abandon their children, and high rates of unemployment among black American males.[48] Moynihan did not recycle stereotypes about blacks, minimize black oppression, express hatred for blacks, chastise the civil rights movement, or ridicule the historical legacy of American blacks. Claiming not to comprehend why his statements on these subjects were considered offensive, Podhoretz bitterly contended that his critics were guilty of "stupidity or incomprehension or straightforward ill will."[49] The controversy over his attitude toward race thus foreshadowed his later intellectual career.

DISAFFECTION WITH THE NEW LEFT

His first misgivings about the New Left occurred during this period and were strenuously reinforced by his mentors. Podhoretz was keenly aware throughout the early 1960s that Trilling and Hook, among others, felt betrayed by his radical turn. Just as Trilling had carried on the cultural and ideological legacy of his mentor, Elliot Cohen, he expected his own student to carry on this tradition as Cohen's successor. Various attempts to discuss the matter produced ugly scenes between Podhoretz and Trilling, Podhoretz and Hook, and Podhoretz and Bell. Friends of Podhoretz recalled that at three successive dinners where he and Trilling were both present, Podhoretz loudly insulted Trilling, calling him a coward and hypocrite. At a fourth dinner, when Podhoretz attacked Hook for similar failings, Trilling politely excused himself and walked out, unable to stand any more of it. Arnold Beichman later explained, "There are a lot of people you have to kill when you are young and you've made your mark early." In Podhoretz's case, he observed, the list included Trilling, Hook, Bell, and Cohen.[50]

The metaphor was somewhat exaggerated. For all of the bitter words that crossed between them, Podhoretz continued to socialize with the Family's right-leaning elders and listened to their complaints. Under the pressure of their disgust with his conversion to radicalism, he was careful to publish articles expressing their politics as well. The result was an extraordinarily interesting magazine—especially when it took up issues on which the editor's mind was undecided. Commentary's debates on nuclear deterrence and the origins of the Cold War provided the best examples. These debates featured sharp disagreements between Hughes and Hook on deterrence policy and between (among others) Lynd and Moshe Decter on the Cold War.[51]

Though he pulled for his New Left acquaintances, Podhoretz was troubled by their inability to respond to substantive criticism. Hughes's article on "The Strategy of Deterrence" was a key example. Hughes eloquently described the dangers of deterrence and argued that existing deterrence policy was not a credible or tolerable solution for America's security needs. The article provoked a Commentary symposium called "Western Values and Total War." At the outset of the discussion, Hughes reported that he was not a pacifist. He believed that the enemy should be met with force, "but real force on a human scale which would give men the old alternative of making a personal choice as to whether they wanted to die." Faced with a communist invasion, he explained, he would willingly take up arms, "but that would be my personal choice. It wouldn't involve all sorts of neutrals, the animal world, unborn generations. . . ." Hook summarized this position with characteristic tartness: "Mr. Hughes maintains that he'd rather be red than dead, but then tells us that of course he's prepared to die fighting against Communism." For Hook, the problem with Hughes's argument was that it overlooked the disproportion between the two posited alternatives of surrender and willingness to resist. "The main thing I want to stress, however, is that it is a mistake to make an easy equation of the alternatives between surrender on the one hand and the cost of resistance on the other," Hook explained. "For if we are prepared to take the risk of fighting for freedom, then we must prepare ourselves in such a way that the costs are diminished." As for himself, he was not willing to sacrifice the safety of the free world, and was therefore opposed to giving up the nuclear deterrent.[52]

This debate proved unsettling to Podhoretz. Though it seemed to him that Hook demolished Hughes's argument for nuclear disarmament, it was equally clear that Hook had no response to Hughes's critique of the terrible dangers of nuclear deterrence. Though he couldn't support Hughes's argument for nuclear disarmament, he accepted Hughes's critique of the deterrence system. Given the apparent lack of a solution to the problem, it seemed to Podhoretz that a vigorous all-sides-included debate on the issue was needed. Throughout the 1960s, his magazine admirably succeeded in the task.

It was one thing to promote utopian progressivism within intellectual circles, however, and quite another to watch these ideas become the slogans of a student-based political movement. The latter development repelled Podhoretz from the outset. In 1962, he received an early draft of a manifesto for a new radical movement, several months before the document was endorsed by the founding convention of Students for a Democratic Society. The Port Huron Statement was written chiefly by Tom Hayden and endorsed by SDS in June. By the end of the summer, the new organization had to struggle to fulfill an enormous demand for copies at universities throughout the country. Though it quickly became one of the epochal documents of modern American politics, Podhoretz insisted throughout the 1960s that he had been right not to publish it. In his judgment, the Port Huron Statement was a self-aggrandizing mish-mash of themes borrowed from Goodman, Riesman, and C. Wright Mills, "stripped of all complexity, qualification, and nuance." At every point, the statement counterposed its own self-attributed values of selflessness, generosity, creativity, and fraternity to the supposed power-seeking and possessive values of most Americans. Podhoretz later recalled that seeing his own politics reduced to such callow, derivative, and self-righteous language made him wonder whether he believed in the causes he was promoting.[53]

That piercing question stopped him from writing about politics. Podhoretz wrote very little during the mid-sixties. While he continued to publish New Left criticism, he quietly nursed a growing revulsion for the pretentiousness and hypocrisy of the movement with which he was associated. Though his right to self-righteousness would often be questioned, the steadiest refrain running throughout Podhoretz's work was that people kept failing his tests for honesty, courage, and seriousness. In the mid-sixties, he and Epstein journeyed to Mexico City on behalf of the Farfield Foundation and later flew (along with Decter) to Acapulco to engage in anticommunist cultural activities on the beach. The Farfield Foundation was well known for its extraordinarily generous junkets and widely believed to be a CIA front. Podhoretz later insisted that he had no idea it was, in fact, one of the CIA's dummy foundations. In Acapulco, however, Epstein walked up and down the beach introducing himself as an American spy.[54]

Epstein later criticized those who frolicked for anticommunism at the taxpayers' expense. Though it was "the allrightniks" who took most of the expensive junkets, he recounted, he had taken two of them himself.[55] Podhoretz was more indulgent toward his own mistakes, however. At the same time, he became increasingly intolerant of those he judged to be less genuine than himself. A campaign fundraiser for Eugene McCarthy in 1968 brought these feelings to the surface. Before a well-heeled crowd of partygoers and hangers-on, he was supposed to moderate a political discussion between Irving Howe and Dwight Macdonald. But by the time Podhoretz staggered to the microphone, he was too drunk to perform the task upright. He later explained that he needed to get drunk to get through the assignment, not only because he couldn't stand the kind of people who came to political fundraisers, but also because he was still pretending not to hold such feelings.[56]

His uniquely bizarre memoir was published during this period, against the advice of his friends. Upon reading the manuscript for *Making It*, Podhoretz's agent forfeited her commission and his first publisher forfeited a sizable advance to dissociate themselves from it. His publisher's reaction was especially striking. "It was as if I had handed him something obscene," Podhoretz later recalled. When he insisted on finding another publisher, Trilling and Epstein told him it could only be published if he added a final chapter taking back everything he had written. It was not just that the book incessantly boasted about his school grades, his attainment of power as a magazine editor, and the parties to which he was invited, they explained. There was also the unseemliness of his bragging about a literary career that, to that point, had produced only a collection of youthful articles and reviews.

For Podhoretz, these reactions only confirmed the "dirty little secret" of American life: Americans lusted for power and success but were too hypocritical to admit it. This vice was particularly acute, he felt, among intellectuals. Though Epstein's firm eventually published the book, Epstein's attempt to dissuade Podhoretz from publishing it confirmed his long-established hypocrisy on the subject. "My Negro Problem" had bared the truth about American racism and ridiculed the reigning liberal pieties on race. *Making It* revealed even deeper and more disingenuously obscured truths about Americans. The hypocrisy of humility was a prime example. Until then, only Norman Mailer had been courageous enough to expose the self-deceits in America's pieties about humility and ambition. *Making It* ended with a tribute to Mailer, who assumed "in the most straightforward way that everyone was out for all the power he could get every minute of the day." He was thus the only (other) living American "who was capable of perfect honesty on the subject of success," Podhoretz declared.[57] Trilling was not in their company. Though he was the one who first assured Podhoretz that everyone was out for all the power they could get, Trilling was now appalled that Podhoretz would proclaim his power lust at book length. His reaction proved to Podhoretz, not for the last time, that Trilling had no courage.

Trilling did perceive, however, what Podhoretz was in for. *Making It* took a distinctive pounding. Wilfrid Sheed wrote in *The Atlantic Monthly* that Podhoretz "has written a book of no literary distinction whatever, pockmarked by clichés and little mock modesties and a woefully pedestrian tone." The book had one gear and one track "and rolls down it like a *Daily News* van," Sheed claimed. It chronicled a career "founded largely on showing off for the grown-ups," and therefore not unsurprisingly presented "a fairly infantile version of success: comfort, admiration, power, for their own sakes, the baby's triumvirate." The long-time editor of *Partisan Review*, William Phillips, similarly criticized the book's consuming preoccupation with fame and material success. The Family was driven "more by literary and intellectual ambitions than by the desire to 'make it,' " he lectured. He didn't want the Family's reputation to be besmirched by Podhoretz's conceits. *The New York Review of Books* went further. Epstein gave the book to Edgar Z. Friedenberg, a New Left writer whom Podhoretz had discovered and frequently published. "What Podhoretz takes seriously, it seems to me, is not his career but his quest for fame, power, and money," Friedenberg observed. Podhoretz misunderstood what ambition was. The way he constantly checked upon his progress by attending literary parties was not ambition, "but a perversion of it." The book was so impersonal that it could have been titled *Manhole in the Promised Land;* its strongest emotion was frozen hatred. Friedenberg looked forward to sequels, however. "In 'Podhoretz Returns' and 'Son of Podhoretz,' the monster may turn out to have a heart of gold," he speculated. The crowning insult was delivered by the author of *Advertisements for Myself.* Despite Podhoretz's glowing praise for Mailer and his reference to their close friendship, Mailer added to the book's critical pummeling by calling it "a blunder of self-assertion, self-exposure, and self-denigration." The book combined autobiographical exhibitionism with shameless flattery of the Family, he charged. Podhoretz was still performing for the grown-ups. *Making It* was not a major work, Mailer concluded, but for all of its embarrassing poses was rather "a restrained muted limited account of a young provincial, a modest example when all is said of a Julian Sorel who is making his way up in the world."[58]

The Mailer and Friedenberg reviews hurt the most. Podhoretz was infuriated that both Mailer and Epstein betrayed him. He reasoned that Mailer had joined the herd lest the herd trample him as well. The book was too honest, too brave, and too supportive of middle-class American values for Mailer to risk any association with it, Podhoretz told himself. A friendly review would have jeopardized Mailer's standing in the cultural vanguard. The fact that he was singularly praised in the book compelled his dissociation from it. Having grasped the meaning of the outcry against the book, Podhoretz explained, Mailer chose "to turn his back on a friend, now convicted of treason to the cultural ruling class." Though he adopted the pretense of being even more treasonable in his own way, Mailer carefully submitted to the code of the cultural ruling class. He criticized the New Class intelligentsia while repeating its strictures against Podhoretz. His performance demonstrated the "terrible power" of the cultural ruling class, Podhoretz claimed.[59]

It was a deeply alienating experience that ended Podhoretz's friendships with Mailer and Epstein. Epstein had urged him not to publish the book—and then commissioned Friedenberg's devastating review of it. His journal set the standard for numerous imitators. The terrible power of America's cultural ruling class was epitomized by *The New York Review of Books.* Though Podhoretz and Epstein later pointed to their increasing political differences as the cause of their broken friendship, most observers traced the beginning of their feud to Podhoretz's feelings of betrayal over Friedenberg's review. "Norman feels that he performed the ultimate act of friendship by refusing Jason's job," Harold Steinberg explained. "A few years later, when he'd finished his book, he felt that Jason should reciprocate by giving his wholehearted endorsement to the book. Jason didn't, and Norman felt that he had been betrayed."[60] The feeling deepened as Epstein's journal continued to promote the Movement and Podhoretz began to attack it.

Podhoretz came early to the debate over Vietnam, having published Hans Morgenthau's warnings against an "American Algeria" in Asia in 1961. Throughout the 1960s, his undeclared opposition to America's intervention in Vietnam was based on Morgenthau's realpolitik objections to it. [61] Though he believed that Morgenthau generally underestimated the significance of ideological factors, Podhoretz cited Morgenthau's prudential objections to the war whenever he was pressed, in private, for his personal position on it. Vietnam was the wrong war in the wrong place at the wrong time. Podhoretz repeated the slogan while explaining that "wrong" meant the war was unwinnable, not that it was morally wrong. Though Morgenthau never put it this way himself, his approach allowed Podhoretz to oppose America's intervention in Vietnam while reaffirming his anticommunism.

The problem was that the New Left had turned against anticommunism altogether. In the early 1960s, Podhoretz published Lynd's revisionist perspective on the Cold War and defended its integrity from attacks by Hook, Moshe Decter, and others. [62] But by 1965, Lynd was marching under Vietcong flags and rhapsodizing about the poetry and song at the heart of Vietnamese communism. [63] As Podhoretz later recalled, by the mid-sixties "there was no way I could blind myself any longer to the fact that Lynd and his friends and allies in the peace movement were not interested in creating a new radicalism that would be free of the old illusions about Communism." The leaders of the antiwar movement were not against the war at all, but only against one of the sides fighting it. [64] As Norman Thomas sadly put it, the chief organizers of the antiwar demonstrations loved the Vietcong more than they loved peace. During the later years of the decade, Podhoretz became increasingly appalled that he had ever been associated with them. He still opposed the war but felt greater revulsion for the antiwar movement.

A 1967 symposium on "Liberal Anti-Communism Revisited" helped him clarify these feelings. The CIA's sponsorship of the Congress for Cultural Freedom, the Farfield Foundation, and its various front organizations had recently been exposed. These revelations had moved Epstein to publish a blistering attack on the corruption of the intellectuals, in which he acknowledged his own junketeering for cultural freedom. Epstein recalled that it was evident to him throughout the 1950s that the government was running "an underground gravy train whose first-class compartments were not always occupied by first-class passengers." Though he disapproved of his government's efforts to set up "an apparatus of intellectuals selected for their correct cold-war positions," he had taken the junkets offered to him. He noted that certain anticommunists with greater moral character—such as Irving Howe—never went anywhere. He argued that the CIA cultivated a deeper corruption in America's intellectual community, however, through its routinization of deceit. The project's insiders were forced to lie continually to their colleagues. "Organizations ostensibly devoted to cultural freedom and the pursuit of truth were thus based upon lies," Epstein observed. He added that by the 1960s, most of the CIA's beneficiaries understood that its numerous conferences, organizations, and magazines were funded not to promote cultural freedom, but to protect and extend American power. [65]

Podhoretz's symposium responded to Epstein. With token exceptions, the questions were addressed to liberal anticommunists. "As someone whose name has been associated with the anti-Communist Left, do you feel in any way responsible for American policies in Vietnam?" Podhoretz asked. "Would you call yourself an anti-Communist today?" Moreover, did the recent revelations about CIA fronts "prove that liberal anti-Communism has been a dupe of, or a slave to, the darker impulses of American foreign policy?" Though the replies from Bell, Lewis Coser, Harrington, Hook, Howe, Schlesinger, the Trillings, and most others held few surprises, their insistent defenses of liberal anticommunism bolstered Podhoretz's own hesitant return to the faith. He would soon leave most of them behind in his move to the Right. The respondents split on the final question. Harrington and Howe condemned the CIA program and its corrupting influence on American intellectuals, while Bell, Hook, Schlesinger, and the Trillings variously characterized the program as regrettable but justified. The first two questions brought wider agreement. The liberal anticommunists explained why their opposition to America's involvement in Vietnam (or at least to the way the war was being fought) was consistent with their abiding anticommunism. Podhoretz was particularly impressed by their willingness to criticize not only the American war, but also America's antiwar movement. Having stacked his symposium with liberal anticommunist veterans, he used the occasion to make amends with old mentors and friends. The magazine increasingly reflected their politics, as Commentary began to devote as much attention to the wrongs of the Movement as to the wrongs of the war.

The opening shot had been fired by Tom Kahn in 1966, in an article sharply criticizing the politics and character of the New Left. Over the next two years, Commentary's attacks on the Movement included Bayard Rustin's critique of the Black Power movement, Nathan Glazer's indictment of the New Left, Diana Trilling's scathing account of the student uprisings at Columbia University, and Kahn's obituary for the Great

Society Poor People's Campaign.[66] These articles were balanced by critiques of American imperialism and inequality by Robert Heilbroner, Harrington, Howe, and Noam Chomsky, as well as by Mailer's famous account of the Vietnam Moritorium.[67] Though the balance increasingly tipped to the Right during the later 1960s, *Commentary* swung both ways, reflecting the exotic turbulence of the times and the editor's struggle to define his politics. Podhoretz wrote very little during this period, but he interrogated his friends intensely about their political choices. How could they justify making alliances with the rabble in the streets? How could they call themselves liberals and then abide the anti-Americanism of the Movement? How could they indulge the idiocies of the Black Power and feminist movements? How could *The New York Review of Books* glorify the Movement and condemn America's admittedly mistaken war as evil?

The two sides of liberal anticommunism were being pulled apart. Podhoretz's alienation from the civil rights movement, the antiwar movement, the liberal wing of the Democratic party, and the emerging feminist movement were driving him from any kind of progressive politics. He complained that liberalism was becoming radicalized. He tried to return to liberal anticommunism, but found that it wasn't there. Those who tried to hold liberalism and anticommunism together—like Schlesinger and Galbraith—were reducing the faith to meaninglessness. Liberalism was accommodating feminism and Black Power and other radicalisms that the ACCF never imagined. The fiasco in Vietnam was creating a "liberalism" that refused to fight communism at all. The new liberalism was forsaking America's imperial responsibilities. People like Schlesinger were kidding themselves. The Vital Center had collapsed, and liberalism was moving Left. In reaction, Podhoretz lurched to the Right, into uncharted territory. One step remained to be taken, however, before he could make any announcements on the matter.

He had never publicly called for American withdrawal from Vietnam. Podhoretz finally made such a declaration in 1969, during a speech in New York City. Two years later, he published his position in a column accompanying Glazer's argument for immediate withdrawal. "As one who has never believed anything good would ever come for us or for the world from an unambiguous American defeat, I now find myself . . . moving to the side of those who would prefer just such a defeat to a 'Vietnamization' of the war, which calls for the indefinite and unlimited bombardment by American pilots in American planes of every country in that already devastated region," he announced.[68] After nearly ten years of groundbreaking analysis and debate, *Commentary* finally took a clear position—in

1971—on the central issue of the 1960s. By the time this position was announced, however, Podhoretz was embarked on a campaign that would transform his magazine again.

FIGHTING APPEASEMENT:
COMMENTARY AND THE NEW CONSERVATISM

The turning point was 1970. Having welcomed the 1960s with a call for utopian experiments, Podhoretz opened the 1970s with a series of vehement disavowals. The 1960s were a disaster. His role in promoting the early counterculture was now deeply embarrassing to him. The radical enthusiasms of the decade lay in ruins. The expectations they generated among women, blacks, and New Class whites were poisoning the country's politics. Having stifled his growing revulsion for the antiwar movement, feminism, environmentalism, and liberalism itself, Podhoretz resolved to denounce them all. He announced his conversion and immediately refashioned the magazine in his new image. *Commentary* stopped covering both sides. An editorial line was established on issues that the magazine had debated freely for years. Liberals and social democrats who had written for *Commentary* for more than a decade suddenly found themselves excluded from it. Criticizing the Movement would no longer be enough. In the late 1960s, Howe and Harrington had sharply criticized the Movement's anti-intellectualism, its procommunist sympathies, its liberal-bashing, and its cultural nihilism. The new *Commentary* would have no place for social democrats like Howe or Harrington, however. What began as an attack on the illusions of the Movement was now expanding into a project outstripping the ACCF anticommunism in which it was rooted. A new conservatism was taking shape. The new conservatism wanted no part of the Vietnam fiasco on its back, which explained Podhoretz's belated endorsement of military withdrawal. The line would be drawn at that point, however. Nothing else was to be conceded to the Left in the new war for ideological position.

Having written very little during the late 1960s, Podhoretz was energized by his conversion. He reinstated his column and took his opening shot at the emerging environmentalist movement. The central conceit of Earth Day, he announced, was the notion that the imperative to protect the earth transcended conventional interest-group politics. Podhoretz explained the genesis of this confusion: "Some of the idiot young and those of their elders who, seeing their own idiocy so handsomely reflected in these healthy and supple bodies, narcissistically praise it as wisdom and idealism, think that in pollution we have an issue at last transcending politics."[69]

That set the tone. From this point forward, *Commentary* ridiculed virtually every aspect of contemporary American liberalism. In Podhoretz's characterization, the magazine took on a "harsh" and "defiantly provocative" style that specialized in personal attacks on former associates.[70] Early entries included Samuel McCracken's "Quackery in the Classroom," Dorothy Rabinowitz's two-part offensive against activist professors and clerics, Midge Decter's polemic against the "liberated woman," and Arlene Croce's report on the cultural ravages of feminism. Epstein and Friedenberg came in for an especially vigorous drubbing in Dennis Wrong's "The Case of the 'New York Review.'"[71] Subsequent issues featured Kristol's critique of "the religion of democracy" and Glazer's report on how he overcame the temptations of radicalism.[72] Later entries included Michael Novak's ruminations on the moralistic hypocrisy of the New Class and Jeane Kirkpatrick's denunciation of McGovernism.[73]

The new conservatism attracted the immediate attention of its targets. Podhoretz later recalled that *Commentary* created a sensation in the early 1970s because its polemical thrusts were able to draw blood. Unlike *The Public Interest, Commentary* was written in a contentious and often wildly accusatory style. Unlike *National Review*, however—which it otherwise increasingly resembled—*Commentary* featured writers who knew about the Left from personal experience. "There was usually something off-center in the way *National Review* talked about the New Left or the counterculture," Podhoretz explained. "It could get the doctrines right and could sometimes analyze them accurately, but it was so remote from the actualities of the Movement and so little in touch with the people involved that its criticisms were unable to draw blood." His own writers enjoyed a crucial advantage over conservatives in their polemics against the Left. "We knew what they really thought and felt, which did not always coincide with what they considered it expedient to say in public; and we knew how to penetrate their self-protective rhetoric," he explained.[74] The new conservatives demystified Movement-speak and denounced its penetration into the mainstream of the Democratic party.

Podhoretz's turn to the Right broke numerous friendships, several of which were terminated at his insistence. His attacks on former friends forced them to decide whether to respond in kind. Some of those who chose not to respond to Podhoretz's attacks assured themselves that he had lost his mind. The experience was exhilarating for Podhoretz, however. Rather than fret over his broken friendships, he later recalled, "I experienced the special happiness that comes from breaking out of a false position and giving free reign to previously inhibited sentiments and ideas."[75]

The floodgates opened. After fifteen years of periodic writer's blocks and failing to write a substantive book, his literary energies were liberated by his conversion. Though it would take him until 1975 to find his distinctive voice, Podhoretz's neoconservatism took shape in the ferociously opinionated columns he wrote during the early 1970s. It was in these columns that he first explained his disaffection from liberalism, identified the New Class as the enemy of American interests, and declared that the formative question for his politics would heretofore be, "Is it good for the Jews?"[76]

His chief theme was disgust. He explained in 1973 that the reason New Class liberals were inept at winning elections—as distinguished from their success at taking over the Democratic party—was that they misunderstood the disgust of ordinary Americans. Most Americans were disgusted not by America's role in the war, but by the movement that opposed it. They were further disgusted by "the bureaucrats, the lawyers, and the judges who in the name of what they considered racial justice were taking it upon themselves to order the busing of children from one school to another, the building of public-housing projects in middle-class neighborhoods, and the institution of job quotas for accredited 'minorities'."[77] A new conservatism was needed to express the common sense of this disgusted majority. Liberalism had run amok. If the old conservatism was discredited by its opposition to the welfare state and the civil rights bills, American liberalism was discredited by its near-pacifism, its failure to defend middle-class values, and its support for affirmative action. American disgust with the degradation of liberalism was shrewdly exploited by Richard Nixon's 1972 campaign, which "exhibited something close to perfect pitch in its ear for the national mood."[78]

The 1972 campaign proved to be a watershed for the neoconservatives. For them, the McGovern candidacy epitomized the degeneration of American liberalism. McGovern's world view, like his slogan—"Come Home, America"—was defeatist, isolationist, and guilt-driven. The neoconservatives would untiringly denounce McGovernism for many years afterward. A few of them—notably Glazer—reluctantly voted for him anyway, but most voted Republican for the first time in their lives. The neoconservatives openly admired the message and tone of Nixon's campaign. The later fuss over Watergate struck most of them as New Class revenge. Nixon's landslide appeal to the Silent Majority confirmed their warnings. The Silent Majority perceived the anti-Americanism in the New Class's moralistic rhetoric. Neoconservatives argued that this perception was giving the Democratic party the beating it deserved.

Most of them were not prepared to stomach the electoral alternative, however. Though they voted for Nixon, most neoconservatives were not ready in the early 1970s to follow Kristol into the party of the banks and the country club. The defining struggle was for control of the Democratic party. Along with such ACCF-style Democrats as Henry Jackson, Hubert Humphrey, Max Kampelman, Ben Wattenberg, Jeane Kirkpatrick, Evron Kirkpatrick, and Daniel Patrick Moynihan, Podhoretz therefore co-founded the Coalition for a Democratic Majority, whose objective was to wrest control of the party from the younger generation of McGovern-ites. Neoconservatives posed as true Democrats fighting to save the party from the New Class's feminized anti-Americanism. Right-leaning liberals such as Humphrey, Bell, and Moynihan associated themselves during this period with the neoconservative reaction, believing that neoconservatives were providing the chastening tonic that the party needed in the wake of its colossal defeat. Podhoretz and his colleagues repeatedly claimed that they were defending the party's mainstream from its liberal leaders. Liberals had overreacted to Vietnam. Their "New Politics" was based on guilt. Neoconservatism was merely a self-respecting, pro-American cor-rective to liberal guilt-mongering. Neoconservatives only wanted to re-place the party's McGovernite leaders and operatives with moderates such as Humphrey and Jackson.

The neoconservatives were changing more than even they seemed to realize, however. In the early 1970s, they hotly rejected their label and indignantly defended their conception of themselves as moderates or "real liberals." Having come from the Left, it was difficult for them to accept that they had become conservatives of any kind. The matter became clarified for most others, however, during the party's electoral debates of the mid-seventies. Neoconservatives supported Jackson in the 1976 primary campaign, mostly on account of his militant anticommunism. They took an early disliking to the moderate Southern Democrat who defeated Jackson in the primaries. Neoconservatives quickly perceived that Jimmy Carter wanted America to atone for Vietnam. His otherwise moderate politics was corrupted by guilt. Neoconservatives like Pod-horetz were repulsed by Carter's moralism. They ridiculed his presidency nearly from the outset, making "Carterism" a term to be invoked only in a sneering way. Jeane Kirkpatrick characterized Carter's foreign policy as "McGovernism without McGovern." As Podhoretz explained, the chief reason for the neoconservatives' repugnance for Carter was that under his presidency, the United States "continued and even accelerated the strategic retreat begun under the Republicans."[79] That is, the Carter administration failed to base its foreign policy on the apocalyptic warnings issued by Podhoretz in his 1975 pronouncement, "Making the World Safe for Communism."

This was the article in which the former literary critic found his voice. It was a blockbuster essay in the Burnhamian mold. "Making the World Safe for Communism" offered a sweeping account of the current struggle for the world and a stinging indictment of America's recent "failure of will" in advancing this struggle. The Soviet enemy was winning without having to fight. Kristol's premature warnings about the collapse of liberal anti-communism were coming true. Until quite recently, Podhoretz observed, most of the actual fighting against communism had been led by liberals. While conservatives generally talked tougher than liberal Democrats, it was under liberal Democratic administrations that America intervened in Korea and Vietnam. Throughout the 1950s, Eisenhower backed away from intervening in Vietnam; in the early 1970s, Nixon terminated America's commitments there. Between those two points, two Democratic administrations pressed the implications of anticommunist rhetoric into action. The difference was instructive. Succeeding a passive Republican administration, it was a liberal Democrat who vowed to "pay any price, bear any burden, meet any hardship . . . to assure the survival and the success of liberty"—and then acted on his pledge.

This was the voice of authentic American liberalism. Podhoretz contrasted John Kennedy's Cold War idealism to McGovern's dovish neo-isolationism to make his chief point. What was now called liberalism was a castrated faith. McGovern's call for America to come home again and reorder its priorities was a craven abandonment of the historic liberal mission. Podhoretz defined this mission, without irony, as the crusade "to use American power to make the world safe for democracy."[80] This was a noble creed. Unlike the new, deformed liberalism, it did not shrink from projecting American military power throughout the world. The new liberalism didn't disdain foreign affairs altogether, but it stupidly assumed that foreign policy should "be based on cooperation rather than power and conflict and competition." It further assumed that the world was becoming more interdependent—"a favorite liberal phrase"—and that the superpowers were unavoidably losing their power "to impose their will on other countries." These anti-American notions were products of a "spiritual surrender" that Podhoretz named "Finlandization from within." American liberals were making the world safe for communism because they considered their country morally unworthy of defending its foreign interests.

Podhoretz had long since left the guilt-ridden liberals behind. The more interesting question was whether conservatives offered a better alternative. It was here that he discovered the ultimate ravages of the

Vietnam syndrome. Conservative rhetoric sounded healthier and more aggressive than the accommodating self-abasement of American liberalism, he conceded. To judge from the records of the Nixon and Ford administrations, however, the conservatives were isolationists at heart. The central actor in this sorry narrative was, of course, Henry Kissinger, whom Podhoretz characterized as "a reluctant and heavy-hearted isolationist."

Podhoretz painted Kissinger as a tragic figure. He explained that Kissinger was the kind of isolationist "who would no doubt much rather be presiding over the growth of an empire, but who finds no realistic alternative to the withdrawal of the United States from the role it has played since the end of World War II in checking the expansion of Communist power."[81] It was Kissinger who orchestrated America's withdrawal from Vietnam, promoted the Strategic Arms Limitation Treaties, questioned the value of attaining strategic nuclear superiority, and declared that America was entering the first stage of a Spenglerian decline. Though Kissinger made occasional Churchillian pronouncements out of the other side of his mouth and urged anticommunist interventions in Portugal and Angola, his record was otherwise indistinguishable from the Finlandized policy actually advocated by the liberals: "that is, of withdrawal from anti-Communist intervention."

A new conservatism was therefore needed that would take up the old liberal mission of winning the world for democracy. The United States was morally worthy of playing the dominant role in the world, Podhoretz insisted, because America was the least repressive nation in the world. This was not to assume that America was always morally required to repel communist advances wherever they occurred. America's national interests didn't extend to every corner of the world. Vietnam was a good example. The prudential arguments against intervention in Vietnam were eventually vindicated, Podhoretz observed. He cited *Commentary*'s early articles on Vietnam as a reminder that he had opposed the war from the beginning. The pernicious legacy of the Vietnam War, however, was that the wrong lesson was constantly being drawn from the failure of America's intervention there. America's war in Vietnam was wrong only for practical reasons. The war hadn't served any national interest large enough to justify the enormous loss of blood and treasure it required. The purpose was honorable, but the price was too high.

This was not the lesson constantly invoked by the pundits, however. The lesson of Vietnam monotonously repeated in the media was "the isolationist lesson that we can no longer do anything to make the world safe for democracy."[82] Podhoretz warned that if America's elites ever *if* Dorrien is attempting to illustrate any intellectual power in neoconsrv., he is failing.

170   The Culture of Appeasement: Norman Podhoretz

accepted this verdict, American military withdrawal from the Middle East, Western Europe, and Japan would become an "ineluctable necessity." It was a Burnhamian warning. Podhoretz was more selective than Burnham in choosing where America needed to commit military force, but his geopolitical assumptions and his view of America's spirit and culture were in the Burnhamian mold. The country was going soft. Though McGovern was defeated, McGovernism was infecting the country's politics at the highest levels. America was withdrawing from the struggle for the world, and thereby betraying the American heritage of liberty.

This was the situation inherited by Carter. It did not take long for Podhoretz to conclude that Carter was determined to make things worse. Podhoretz wrote "The Culture of Appeasement" during Carter's first year in office. He claimed that a rising tide of pacifist sentiment was making America not only unwilling, but literally incapable of fighting the Soviet enemy. He noted that many of the same liberals who ran the Vietnam War under Kennedy and Johnson were now perched in the upper levels of the Carter administration. But this time they were determined to keep America at home. Having resorted to force in Vietnam, they were now earnestly making amends for their earlier mistakes and were minimizing the threat to America posed by Soviet conventional and nuclear strength. They were wrong again, "this time in their dovishness toward the Soviet Union—not because they want to reach an accommodation with the Russians, but because they fail to see that the Russians are after something larger and more ambitious than an accommodation with us."[83]

This rather early conclusion about Carter's team had a background. Shortly after Carter's election, the Coalition for a Democratic Majority and the Committee on the Present Danger had presented Carter with a list of sixty prominent neoconservatives seeking appointments, including Jeane Kirkpatrick, Max Kampelman, Nathan Glazer, and Richard Perle. Carter was put off by the neoconservatives, however, and his team included only one of their nominees—Peter Rosenblatt—who was appointed to a special-representative post. "We were completely frozen out," Elliott Abrams later recalled. "We got one unbelievably minor job. It was a special-negotiator position. Not for Polynesia. Not Macronesia. But Micronesia. The Carter Administration turned out to be ideological, a New Left administration."[84]

Neoconservatives failed to convince the new president that the Soviets were winning the arms race. Even more than Kissinger before him, Carter didn't understand the value of attaining strategic superiority. But the purpose of attaining superiority was not that complicated, Podhoretz argued. It was to "intimidate other nuclear powers who might wish to stand in your way when you start to move ahead."[85] He warned that the Soviets were outstripping the United States in conventional forces as well as strategic nuclear weapons. The Soviet navy was being redesigned for offensive purposes, placing warships in distant waters, while Soviet interventions in Africa (through Cuban surrogates) were paving the way for Soviet control over vital commercial sea-lanes. As long as America failed to massively rearm and to project its power abroad, Podhoretz claimed, Soviet leaders could be expected to extend their empire "as far as their ideological and imperial ambitions, and the absence of effective resistance, will carry them." He assumed that they were determined to conquer the world.

Carter failed to grasp the nature of the Soviet threat because he was a product of the culture of appeasement. He was eager to accept the "elaborate exercises in statistical manipulation and sophistical rationalization" produced by the CIA and Department of Defense. These reports willfully underestimated the depth of the Soviet desire for world domination and the scope of Soviet military power because, except for the neoconservatives, nearly everyone was unwilling to face up to the cost of fighting the Soviet enemy. Current intelligence reports were fatuous. Podhoretz saw an analogy to the Vietnam War. Kennedy, Johnson, and Nixon had wanted to hear that the war was going well and were thus continually assured that America was winning in Vietnam. Carter now wanted to hear that defense spending could be cut without endangering the nation's security. In both cases, the CIA and the Pentagon proved obliging. Their latest exercises in make-believe were the CIA's 1977 Team A Report and the Defense Department's Review Memorandum 10—both of which described American and Soviet military strength as functionally equivalent. Armed with such assurances, Carter was congratulating himself and his fellow Americans for overcoming their "inordinate fear of communism." For Podhoretz, this declaration exemplified not only the naiveté of a man out of his depth, but the corruption of spirit affecting his entire culture. "The Culture of Appeasement" reproduced not only Burnham's chief theme, but his explanation for it. What lay behind the claim that we no longer inordinately feared communism, Podhoretz argued, was a deep fear of Soviet power that paralyzed America's capacity to resist it.[86]

The primary sowers of this fear, as it happened, were homosexual writers. The spirit of appeasement infecting America could only be compared, Podhoretz declared, to England's corrupting homosexual decadence after the First World War. The British had suffered so many casualties during the war that they experienced their victory as a defeat. Like the

United States after Vietnam, they were traumatized by the horror of the war. Like the Americans, they were left in a state of numbness by the loss of their ideals in fighting it. Podhoretz conceded that British revulsion toward the war was widespread, a reaction that was understandable and even sympathetic. The problem was that England's intellectuals preyed on their country's postwar disillusionment, using it to justify their alienation from their country, martial values, and liberal democracy. The poetry of W. H. Auden, Wilfred Owen, Brian Howard, and others used the nation's sadness as a warrant for their own sick resentment. Podhoretz argued that the deep revulsion toward war and militarism they expressed could only be explained by the fact that most of them were homosexuals. "In war poem after war poem and in memoir after memoir, the emphasis was on the youthful, masculine beauty so wantonly wasted by the war, their bodies meant for embrace by their own kind that were consigned so early to the grave," he explained. [87] It was an explanation that even Burnham had shied away from. What made war so horrible to the intellectuals was the loss of those "helpless, good-looking boys" for whom they lusted. According to Podhoretz, the intellectuals' homosexuality distinguished their antimilitarism from the "natural" postwar disillusionment of ordinary people. It also, unfortunately, influenced the culture and attitudes of ordinary people.

Homosexuality also engendered intellectual hostility for bourgeois society. Podhoretz traced this hostility to their refusal to procreate. Intellectuals were alienated from bourgeois society—then as now—because they refused to be fathers. To refuse fatherhood, he explained, was to reject "all that fatherhood entailed: responsibility for a family and therefore an inescapable implication in the destiny of society as a whole." [88] British intellectuals repudiated their duties to their country when they forsook the responsibilities of fatherhood. Through the writings of Auden, Howard, Harold Acton, Christopher Isherwood, and numerous others, a "generalized contempt for middle-class or indeed any kind of heterosexual adult life" was inculcated in British students.

The legacy of British antiwar homosexuality was important to recall for two reasons. The first was that it convinced Hitler that England would never fight. Homosexuality tempted one's enemies. The second was that the same virus was currently debilitating American society. "Anyone familiar with homosexual apologetics in America today will recognize these attitudes," Podhoretz wrote. "Suitably updated and altered to fit contemporary American realities, they are purveyed by such openly homosexual writers as Allen Ginsberg, James Baldwin, and Gore Vidal—not to mention a host of less distinguished publicists—in whose work we find the same combination of pacifism (with Vietnam naturally standing in for World War I), hostility to one's own country and its putatively middle-class way of life, and derision of the idea that it stands for anything worth defending or that it is threatened by anything but its own stupidity or wickedness." America's culture of appeasement featured the same "sluttish antinomianism" that George Orwell famously attacked in his polemic against the "so-called artists who spend on sodomy what they have gained by sponging." Homosexuality spawned a diseased politics. To defend the American way of life therefore required that one repudiate the perverted sensibilities of homosexual apologists. [89]

The larger task was to reverse the insidious Finlandization of America, "this new species of surrender" that was accommodating the Soviet drive for world conquest. In the wake of Brezhnev's invasion of Afghanistan, Podhoretz warned that Carter's huge military increases could be too late to stop the Soviets from invading the Persian Gulf region. Those who claimed that Soviet leaders were constrained by Arab nationalism and Muslim religious feeling were now refuted. These obstacles in Afghanistan had "not exactly proved effective as a powerful force against Soviet ambition," Podhoretz observed. He assumed throughout the early 1980s that the Soviets would conquer Afghanistan. The notion that the Soviets were already overstretched in Afghanistan was, to him, a liberal fantasy. The Finlandizers downplayed Soviet might because they secretly feared it. The present danger was that the Soviets were driving to conquer the oil states under the assumption that America would never fight to stop them. [90]

America's danger also transcended this particular scenario, however. If the Soviet Union invaded the Persian Gulf, even American liberals would recognize that vital national interests were at stake. The equally threatening possibility was that the Soviets would not invade. A Soviet peace offensive would damage American interests worse than a war. If Soviet leaders chose not to invade the Persian Gulf or foment insurrections in the region, Podhoretz worried, "the finally aroused American giant" would probably go back to sleep. [91] The extra billions for the Pentagon recently ordered by Carter would be canceled and Finlandization would proceed.

Finlandization was the much-used neoconservative term for the trend toward "a new era of 'peace' and 'friendship' and 'cooperation' between the Soviet Union and the United States." America was becoming Finlandized as a consequence of its unacknowledged fear of Soviet power, Podhoretz argued. Without a revolution in American consciousness and policy, the United States would continue to appease its stronger enemy while celebrating a new era of cooperation. Trade and arms control agreements would be hailed as signs of progress toward peace. The new theater nuclear weapons would not be deployed in Western Europe. Plans to build the MX missile would be voted down. "A world in which the Soviet Union had the military power to seize control of the oil fields would be a world shaped by the will and tailored to the convenience of the Soviet Union," he claimed. [92] He believed that the Soviets were winning their struggle for world domination. The Americans, by contrast, refused to recognize what was happening in the world or to acknowledge the role of their own fearfulness in Finlandizing the West. Though Carter increased defense spending in real terms by 5 percent, Podhoretz despaired of Carter's moralism, his human rights policy, and his unwillingness to *use* American power. In 1980, however, the neoconservatives did not despair for their country, Podhoretz explained, "because in Ronald Reagan we thought we had found a political force capable of turning things around."[93] It was only after Reagan took office that Podhoretz despaired for his country.

The problem wasn't the military budget. Building on Carter's 5 percent increase in military spending and the additional 4 percent authorized by Congress for 1981, the incoming Reagan administration immediately added another 3 percent of real growth for the same year. To this 12 percent increase in real growth, another 15 percent was added the following year. The results were staggering even to the Pentagon. As David Stockman recalled, the early Reagan military budgets were not based on cost projections for needed weapons, readiness, or force structure, but upon a "gigantic fiscal syllogism" that increased real defense spending by 10 percent per year for six years.[94] The base figures were based on rhetoric, and the syllogism quickly blew the numbers far beyond Reagan's campaign trail projections. Actual military expenditures between 1980 and 1986 more than doubled Reagan's 1980 campaign promises. Neoconservatives nodded their approval while the same administration slashed federal spending for job training, infant nutrition, education, and welfare.

Reagan's early military budgets evoked squeals of delight from the military-industrial complex. Neoconservatives, however, proved more exacting in their demands. The point for them was not only to build up the military, but to use it. Podhoretz complained in 1982 that instead of stationing American ground forces in the Persian Gulf, the Reagan administration was resurrecting Nixon's strategy of relying on surrogates to protect American interests. The chief surrogate this time was Saudi Arabia, which was being armed with American-made AWAC attack aircraft. Robert Tucker hung *Commentary*'s most insulting epithet on this policy, calling it "Carterism Without Carter."[95] In his own condemnation of what he called the "habit of appeasing Saudi Arabia," Podhoretz repeated

Tucker's complaints and argued that American interests in the Middle East could only be served by defending Israel from its various enemies.[96]

His anguish over the new administration was not caused primarily by Reagan's Middle East policy, however. A year after Reagan took office, Podhoretz published "The Neo-Conservative Anguish over Reagan's Foreign Policy" in *The New York Times Magazine*, in which he explained his despair over Reagan's defeatism. Notwithstanding his militant rhetoric, his skyrocketing military expenditures, and his appointments of neoconservatives, Reagan was practicing the politics of détente. It was not, Podhoretz granted, the corrupt form of détente "so often indistinguishable from appeasement" practiced by Carter. Reagan was reviving the more sophisticated Nixon–Kissinger version, in which the purpose of American policy was to help the Soviet Union stabilize its empire. Though Reagan gave better speeches, he was, incredibly, turning out to be no better than Nixon.

Part of the problem was that Reagan was more solicitous toward commerce than determined to defeat communism. Shortly after martial law was declared in Poland, America paid the interest due on Poland's debt. "The Administration seemed more worried about hurting a few bankers than about hurting the Soviet empire," Podhoretz bitterly observed. This solicitude for the banks and multinationals was preempting any serious effort to fight communism. As Burnham had complained, America's struggle for the world was undercut by its devotion to commerce. Podhoretz decried the Reagan administration's inordinate love of commerce, which produced a foreign policy more concerned with the balance of payments than with the balance of world power.

But the deeper problem was a failure of will. Though he talked about breaking up the Soviet empire, Reagan was unwilling to pursue the task. What was needed was a massive shipment of arms to the anticommunist guerrillas in Afghanistan and Angola, equally massive support for the Salvadoran government, severe economic sanctions against the Soviet bloc, and a steadfast commitment to build the next generation of nuclear missiles. Nuclear parity with the Soviets was not desirable—it was a prescription for disaster. America needed enough superiority over the Soviets to ensure a margin of safety from them. Reagan had flunked every test thus far. He offered meager support to the Afghan and Angolan resistance, allowed himself to be thrown on the defensive in Central America, accommodated Soviet imperialism in Eastern Europe, and endorsed the Jackson-Warner version of a nuclear freeze. The ironies were galling. The neoconservatives had placed all their hopes on a Reagan presidency. Many of them held high posts in his administration. But the president himself was actively pacifying the Soviets at every turn.

This time, however, there was no alternative. "For those who see the world as I and so many of my neo-conservative friends do, there is no one else in sight," Podhoretz reported. They would keep working on Reagan. He was surrounded by neoconservatives like Kirkpatrick, Perle, Abrams, and Kenneth Adelman. Perhaps they could turn him around. "The objective has to be clear, the determination to pursue it has to be unrelenting and there has to be a willingness to pay the necessary political price," Podhoretz argued. Reagan had shown these qualities in the domestic sphere. His tax cuts and his attacks on the welfare state showed Podhoretz that he had the guts for a political fight. The same resolve was failing him, however, where it mattered most. With each day, the precious opportunity he represented to neoconservatives was thus slipping away. [97]

The opportunity was America's chance to break up the Soviet empire and defeat Soviet communism. In Podhoretz's reading, this was the ultimate objective of George Kennan's 1947 containment strategy. Though Kennan never believed (as Podhoretz failed to acknowledge) that Soviet leaders were determined to conquer the world, he did believe that they were culturally and ideologically driven to expand their sphere of domination. A finely calibrated strategy of containment, prioritized according to America's geopolitical interests, was therefore required to hold them in check. To those—such as Walter Lippmann—who objected that containment would be too expensive and unwieldy, Kennan had contended that the costs would not be prohibitive. He further argued that America's economic and moral advantages over the Soviets would make the decisive difference in the coming struggle for the world.

The latter point distinguished Kennan's concept of containment from the version later promoted by followers such as Podhoretz. For Kennan, the crucial factors in the Cold War were America's moral legitimacy and its superior economic system. He emphasized the importance of preserving and using these advantages. In his view, the Soviet Union was severely limited by its suffocating ideological and cultural traditions. The purpose of containment was not merely to hold Soviet imperialism in check, but to hasten the internal collapse of the Soviet state. He believed that a determined resistance to Soviet advances would eventually force the Soviets to turn inward and deal with the failures of their system. The Cold War would be a protracted but winnable struggle against an enemy trapped in what he called a "cruel and wasteful" political tradition. "It is difficult to see how these deficiencies can be corrected at any early date by a tired and dispirited population working largely under the shadow of fear and compulsion," Kennan argued. "And as long as they are not overcome, Russia will remain economically a vulnerable, and in a certain sense an impotent, nation, capable of exporting its enthusiasms and of radiating the strange charm of its primitive political vitality but unable to back up those articles of export by the real evidences of material power and prosperity."[98]

Podhoretz embraced Kennan's words, but not their meaning. His own position mixed Kennan's vision with Burnham's critique of containment strategy. Kennan did not believe that Soviet rulers were out to conquer the world, he did not believe that they were driven primarily by their ideology, and he did not support worldwide American military efforts to enforce containment. He objected throughout the 1950s that many of his "followers" were appealing to an overly militarized, ideological, and expansive interpretation of containment. His conception of counterforce was primarily political. In the 1960s, while Burnham called for genocidal force in Vietnam, Kennan opposed American intervention in Vietnam. He further disputed that America's drive for nuclear superiority could be justified by containment theory. In the early 1980s, he forcefully argued that adding to America's nuclear overkill capacity added nothing to American security, while placing the world in greater danger of incineration.[99]

On every point, Podhoretz was closer to Burnham than to Kennan, though he insisted that his militaristic anticommunism simply carried on Kennan's "forsaken" containment strategy. Like Burnham, Podhoretz believed that America needed nuclear superiority. Like Burnham, he despaired over America's culture of appeasement. Like Burnham, he believed that Soviet leaders were ideologically driven to conquer the world. Like Burnham, he increasingly argued that America was therefore compelled to fight the Soviets wherever they made advances.

Vietnam was the acid test. The memory of Vietnam was a curse on Podhoretz's notion of containment. It poisoned nearly every discussion of America's role in the world. Throughout the war, Podhoretz had repeated the Morgenthau-Kennan-Lippmann objections to American intervention. Vietnam flunked the pragmatic tests. In the late 1970s, however, he was driven by the logic of his foreign policy position to reconsider the debate. *Why We Were in Vietnam*, published in 1982, was the result. The book never explicitly repudiated his earlier position. In a carefully hedged formulation, Podhoretz concluded that America's effort to save Vietnam from communism "was indeed beyond our intellectual and moral capabilities."[100]

The question was whether it should have been. The book's answer was vehemently negative. Podhoretz rounded up the most idiotic pronouncements of the Vietcong sympathizers and Amerika-haters. He also pointedly recalled and condemned the moral objections to the war offered by

Howe and Michael Walzer. Moral responsibility required moral choice, Podhoretz lectured. The moral critics failed to choose sides. He recalled the pragmatic skepticism of the realpolitikers more respectfully, but finally rebuked them as well. He argued that the war had been a noble cause inspired by American idealism. It deserved to be supported by the intellectual class. Though on a political level America's intervention in Vietnam shared all of the typical defects of idealism, it was undertaken with the very spirit and ideological conviction that now needed to be recovered. *Commentary* made the same argument without equivocation in subsequent years.

The implications of Kennan's containment strategy were faced, not by Kennan, but by those who fought communism in Vietnam. The same implications were now being faced, not by Kennan, but by those who called for a massive nuclear rearmament. Podhoretz repeatedly insisted that his own politics, rather than Kennan's realpolitik, fulfilled Kennan's prescription for containment of communism. What had changed since 1947 was not the necessity of fighting anticommunist wars, but America's willingness to pay the price. He grieved that the architect of containment strategy had incredibly become a symbol of the new culture of appeasement—"perhaps the most dramatic single case of the loss of faith in containment caused by the experience of Vietnam." What was needed was a militarily and ideologically aggressive "new nationalism" that would take up the struggle Kennan and others like him had sadly abandoned. [101]

At a time when the argument seemed quixotic to most, Podhoretz rightly insisted that the Soviet empire should not be regarded as a permanent fact of life. The empire was threatened by internal and external forces. Its economy was disintegrating. The implacable hostility of captive populations made the empire increasingly difficult to manage—and to bear. Podhoretz nonetheless had no patience with those, such as Kennan and Stephen Cohen, who argued that the Soviet bloc's reform and dissident movements were gaining strength as a consequence of these conditions. For neoconservatives, there were axiomatic implications that followed from the "fact" that Soviet bloc regimes were totalitarian dictatorships. There was not "the slightest possibility that even the most minimal degree of civil or political liberty will ever be allowed under Communism," Podhoretz insisted. [102] Armed with this certainty, his magazine knowingly dismissed those who invested significance in the Soviet bloc's dissident stirrings. Certain things were not to be questioned. Soviet rulers had already consolidated a totalitarian domestic order and were out to conquer the rest of the world. All serious observers began with these presuppositions. Soviet totalitarianism had destroyed the political and cultural preconditions for reform, democracy, or even meaningful dissent. It was the same lesson that Burnham tried to teach Kennan. The Soviet state would never endorse or permit any expansion of rights to civil or political freedom. Those who entertained such fantasies failed to grasp that Soviet communism was a conspiratorial machine bent on world conquest.

In the early 1980s, Podhoretz repeatedly warned that a grave danger faced the United States. An unnecessary surrender to an implacable Soviet enemy was being peddled to the American people "in the language of realism, national maturity, and survival."[103] Foreign policy intellectuals like Kennan, Cohen, and Jerry Hough were portraying the Soviet Union as a competing superpower, wracked by its own internal problems, with which the United States could negotiate cooperative accommodations on specific issues.[104] In this version of containment, America's underlying ideological war with the Soviet Union was assigned less significance than such factors as geopolitics, material interests, and mutual security. For Podhoretz, as for Burnham, this approach obscured the issue. To portray the Soviet Union as a competing superpower was to undermine America's will and capacity to fight communism. This was the tragedy of the Nixon, Ford, and Carter administrations. America's will to fight the Soviets could only be summoned if the Soviet Union was viewed as "a Communist state hostile in its very nature to us and trying to extend its rule and its political culture over a wider and wider area of the world."[105] Anything less than this call to arms would further dissipate America's will to save the world for democracy. Even with Reagan as president, the struggle for the world was being lost. It would be irrevocably lost if America didn't begin to fight its totalitarian enemy.[106]

Though he rightly argued that America shouldn't take the permanence of Soviet communism or the Soviet bloc for granted, Podhoretz dismissed the significance of the very events that produced the implausible outcome he called for. During the early and mid-eighties, he was aware that the Soviet economy was in a shambles. He occasionally noted that the Soviet command-model system was not well suited to compete in a postindustrial international economy. He was also aware that the utter failure of the Soviet system to keep pace with economic and technological developments in the world was regenerating various dissident, nationalist, and reformist currents in the Soviet republics. What he could not recognize, partly as a consequence of having demonized Soviet society, was that these dissenting currents were capable of bringing about changes in the Soviet system. He could not believe that the Soviet system was vulnerable from within. Like most of *Commentary*'s chief contributors on the subject, Podhoretz regarded Soviet totalitarianism as a uniquely demonic and effectively repressive system.[107] Though he knew that Soviet leaders confronted immense economic and political problems, he continued to write about them—as Kennan complained—as though they were ten feet tall.[108] The neoconservatives were the last true believers in the efficacy of totalitarianism.

In his scorching 1983 indictment, "Appeasement by Any Other Name," Podhoretz thus pictured the Soviet enemy as a fearsome totalitarian monolith towering over the United States. The article cast a wide net. Podhoretz thumped his usual targets, including Reagan's appeasement of the bankers, and warned that the appeasers were multiplying. Even Kristol was calling for no-first-use of nuclear weapons and American military withdrawal from Europe. In Kristol's case, withdrawal was justified on nationalist grounds. Kristol believed that America's European allies were addicted to American assistance and protection. Podhoretz shared Kristol's concern about the Europeans' feeble efforts to defend themselves, but he feared that the shock treatment of withdrawing American troops would backfire on America, leading to the Finlandization of the European democracies. Kristol's unwillingness to bear the burdens of empire, though defended with a nationalistic twist, further confirmed the sickness of America's spirit.

This new "mighty wave of appeasement" was the product of pacifist and isolationist currents. Podhoretz rehashed the evils of homosexual pacifism and the Vietnam syndrome to explain why most Americans apparently were opposed to intervening in Central America. The same antiwar sentiment was behind the current spectacle of nuclear pacifism. The nuclear freeze movement, the arguments for no-first-use, and the Catholic bishops' recent pastoral letter on nuclear deterrence were variations on an old moralism, Podhoretz argued. He allowed that few Americans embraced absolute pacifism. However, a looser variant of pacifism had become pervasive in American society. The recent hysteria over the nuclear threat conveyed its character. Antinuclearism, like all pacifist movements, was fueled by fear. The fear underlying the current antinuclear movement was that the evils of war would always outweigh the worth of any objective for which a war might be fought.

The same fear accounted for what Podhoretz called "the incredible perversity of the new isolationists."[109] The old isolationists, in his account, were mostly leftists. They promoted appeasement and rationalized Soviet imperialism because they were sympathetic to communism. The new isolationists were a different breed. Their liberalism was perverse because it was rooted in fear rather than political conviction. Liberal writers such as Anthony Lewis and Tom Wicker minimized the Soviet threat not because they admired communism, but because their unacknowledged fear of Soviet power drove them "to persuade themselves and others that safety can be found in negotiations with the Soviet Union."[110]

Burnham had sniffed out this fear three decades earlier. Podhoretz charged that its increasingly paralyzing effects were evident in America's failure to face up to the communist insurgency in El Salvador. He complained that all of the old isolationist slogans about Yankee imperialism were being resurrected by liberals and church leaders, who used gruesome stories about Salvadoran army massacres to manipulate American guilt and demand termination of American military aid to El Salvador. The new isolationists denounced America's alliance with the Duarte-led Salvadoran government, even though this regime enjoyed "vast popular support" and was seriously attempting "with some success both to carry social reform forward and to cut down on the murders and other horrors that always and everywhere accompany guerrilla war."[111] The genocidal rampages of the Salvadoran army and death squads were thus written off as inevitable by-products of counterinsurgency warfare.

For Podhoretz, the issue was not America's support for a savagely brutal army or its complicity in maintaining the social system that produced El Salvador's death squads. The overriding issue was whether America would do whatever was necessary, "up to and including the dispatch of American troops," to defeat the Salvadoran insurgency. If the United States could not prevent a communist victory in El Salvador, he warned, "it will stand revealed as a spent and impotent force." There was no alternative between massive military aid to the Salvadoran government and conceding defeat to the FMLN insurgents. Those who insisted on looking for a third way, he declared, were guilty of appeasement, the "stench" of which "now pervades the American political atmosphere."[112]

Podhoretz's son-in-law, Elliott Abrams, directed the Reagan administration's policy toward Central America with the same disgust for America's political atmosphere. As a Harvard Law School student, Abrams had rented an attic room from Nathan Glazer, who introduced him to Podhoretz. At the age of 33, he became the youngest assistant secretary of state in the twentieth century. Abrams and Podhoretz bitterly criticized congressional ambivalence toward America's interventions in El Salvador and Nicaragua throughout the 1980s and pushed hard for military solutions in both countries. Calling himself the "Gladiator for the Reagan Doctrine," Abrams repeatedly condemned congressional "vipers" who, he charged, would have blood on their hands for blocking American aid to the Nicaraguan contras. After congressional funding for the contras was terminated by the Boland Amendment in the mid-eighties, Abrams solicited congressionally proscribed private donations to keep the Nicaraguan war going. During a walk through Hyde Park in London in 1986, he strong-armed an official of the Brunei government for off-the-books funding. His $10 million windfall from the Sultan of Brunei and his dissembling appearances before congressional committees later provided some of the Iran–contra scandal's most bizarre material. Abrams subsequently pleaded guilty to two counts of a plea-bargained federal indictment for his attempts to deceive congressional committees. *Commentary*, for its part, claimed throughout Reagan's second term that the Boland Amendment's sponsors were making Central America safe for communism. [113]

Central America was important to Podhoretz, however, primarily as an extension of the Cold War. His magazine's principal attention was devoted to the Soviet threat. Throughout the 1980s, *Commentary* fought off America's "stench of appeasement" with Burnhamian articles bearing titles like "Why the Soviet Union Thinks It Could Fight and Win a Nuclear War" and "Why We Need More 'Waste, Fraud, and Mismanagement' in the Pentagon." [114] Richard Pipes, Edward Luttwak and—more judiciously— Walter Laqueur repeatedly warned that Soviet military strength was superior to America's and that Soviet communism was winning the struggle for the world. New *Commentary* writers such as Robert Jastrow, Patrick Glynn, and Angelo Codevilla amplified these arguments, making the case for a massive nuclear rearmament leading to strategic superiority. [115]

The key figure was Pipes. Baird Professor of History at Harvard and former director of Harvard's Russian Research Center, Pipes was appointed chairman of "Team B" in 1976—the group commissioned by the President's Foreign Intelligence Advisory Board to prepare an independent estimate of Soviet military strength. The following year he began writing for *Commentary* and established the magazine's line on the Soviet threat. According to Pipes, Soviet leaders were developing the capacity to fight and win a protracted nuclear war. Unlike the United States, which relied on its counter-population ("countervalue") arsenal to deter nuclear war, the Soviets were in the process of building enough land-based counterforce missiles to launch a successful attack on America's counterforce arsenal. Soviet nuclear doctrine was primarily offensive, he explained. The American attitude toward nuclear weapons had no counterpart in Soviet military thinking. It was a "middle-class, commercial, essentially Protestant" notion that nuclear weapons were primarily useful for their deterrent value. This American notion did not exist in Soviet doctrine. America's Protestantized ruling elites generally assumed that resorting to force was a sign of weakness or failure. Soviet leaders, by contrast, reflected the Russian attitude toward force. For a Russian, Pipes explained, failing to use force revealed a fatal inner weakness. [116]

American and Soviet nuclear doctrines differed accordingly. Soviet rulers didn't place nuclear weapons in a separate category or assume that the main reason to possess them was to prevent nuclear war. They were building a superior counterforce arsenal because they believed that they could fight and win a protracted nuclear war, beginning with a surprise counterforce attack. They were seeking "not deterrence but victory, not sufficiency in weapons but superiority, not retaliation but offensive action." Since their enemy didn't accept the principle of mutual deterrence, American officials were foolish to subscribe to it. American defense strategists were reluctant to adopt the Soviet view, or even to accept that the Soviets subscribed to it, because it was alien "to their experience and view of human nature." For Pipes, the chief threat to American security lay in this reluctance. [117]

He did not deny that even a fantastically successful Soviet attack would leave part of America's counterforce arsenal intact, as well as thousands of submarine-based countervalue missiles. America would need to use less than three hundred of its ten thousand countervalue missiles to obliterate every city in the Soviet Union. Assuming even the most horrible attack imaginable, the United States would retain enough nuclear overkill capacity to incinerate the Soviet population more than thirty times over.

For the neoconservatives, however, this wasn't enough. Pipes argued that American strategists placed too much emphasis on the retaliatory capacity of their countervalue arsenal. America's reliance on the deterrence value of its countervalue missiles was creating a situation in which Soviet leaders were tempted to make a surprise attack. They were seriously tempted, Pipes claimed, because they were fully prepared to accept tens of millions of casualties to win a nuclear war. Having lost tens of millions in World War II, the loss of forty million more in World War III was a tolerable prospect. They did not, after all, place the same high value on life as America's Protestantized elites. American squeamishness about committing nuclear genocide was precisely what made a Soviet nuclear attack conceivable. American officials would have approximately thirty minutes to retaliate with their own counterforce missiles. The Soviets would therefore have to assume that millions of citizens living near the silos along the trans-Siberian railway would be killed.

Their next assumption was the crucial one. They would count on the unwillingness of America's leadership to take the next step and initiate countervalue warfare. Though they were prepared to sustain massive losses, the Soviets knew that an all-out countervalue war would incinerate both countries. Their wager, Pipes explained, was that nuclear war would never go that far. A successful Soviet attack would leave America with the choice of launching its countervalue missiles or submitting to a Soviet dictat.[118]

This ultimate "present danger" rested on Pipes's highly dubious claims about the feasibility of a successful first strike—an attack covering thousands of miles in the teeth of winds, rough weather, and gravitational fields. *Commentary* argued for the MX missile and, later, the Strategic Defense Initiative on the basis of this supposed danger.[119] The deeper issue raised by this discussion, however, concerned the character of the enemy. In Pipes's portrait, Soviet leaders were so utterly depraved that the deaths of tens of millions of Soviet citizens counted for virtually nothing to them and the prospect of fighting an all-out counterforce war was a serious temptation.

This portrait raised several unanswered questions. Neoconservatives failed to explain why Soviet leaders would not become more likely to start a nuclear war if they saw America building toward strategic superiority. The legendary insecurity of Soviet leaders presumably would have heightened at the spectacle of an American government that didn't believe in deterrence. Neoconservatives also failed to explain why a Soviet counterforce strike would leave the United States and its allies with only two (suicidal) options. Even with forty million dead and the loss of most of its counterforce arsenal, America would have retained thousands of countervalue missiles, its military forces, its superior industrial capacity, its remaining counterforce arsenal, and its network of highly armed and technologically advanced allies. A Soviet attack would have provoked the combined force of this economically and technologically superior alliance in a protracted conventional war, backed by the threat of countervalue nuclear strikes. Neoconservatives insisted that Soviet leaders regarded this as a tempting prospect. A window of vulnerability was inviting Soviet leaders to launch a suicidal attack. What neoconservatives ultimately failed to explain was why *any* rational defense strategy would work if Soviet leaders were truly as depraved as they were portrayed.

ISRAEL AND ZIONISM

Virtually all of Podhoretz's writings during the 1980s dealt with the struggle for the world. Nearly half of them focused on the dangers to Israel posed by regional and superpower conflicts. Podhoretz's Zionism was a faith to which he had come late. Through most of the 1960s, his magazine handled the Jewish question with articles on Jewish culture and history that were, like himself, "neither especially religious nor much Zionist." *Commentary* filled a critical need for students and intellectuals, like the young Bernard Avishai, who wanted to claim their Jewish identity without turning to Judaism. "We keenly awaited *Commentary* every month as if it were a public realm in which Jews were permitted to live on the questions," Avishai recalled. "*Commentary* established itself as our mail-order polity; one could, it seemed, be actively Jewish just by reading about the Jews' history, debating the place in culture of Jewish ritual law, or discerning the American 'emancipation' in the elegance of the magazine's prose. And one could hope to be a good Jew by writing with virtuosity about issues that were on our minds."[120]

The magazine's highly sophisticated coverage of Jewish culture, history, and religion was undertaken by writers as ideologically and theologically diverse as George Steiner, Irving Howe, Robert Alter, Elie Wiesel, Alfred Kazin, Norman Mailer, Saul Bellow, Richard Rubenstein, Leo Strauss, Milton Himmelfarb, and Emil Fackenheim. Its coverage of Israeli affairs was similarly urbane, pluralistic, and generally moderate in its politics. *Commentary's* outstanding issue on the 1967 Arab–Israeli War set the standard. Laqueur and Theodore Draper contributed carefully reasoned and meticulously detailed accounts of the war. These articles, while sympathetic to Israel and its security concerns, were also distinguished by their lack of chauvinism toward the defeated Arab enemy. Though Israel had defeated its Arab aggressors, this was no time for triumphalism, they warned. New dangers were posed by the Middle East's superpower proxy conflicts. It was important not to indulge the temptation to propagandize, Draper added, because the worst victim of one's propaganda was often oneself.[121]

Amos Elon went further. His first article for *Commentary* was a report from the Sinai front. Israeli forces had defeated three Arab armies and suddenly found themselves, in less than a week, in possession of huge territories that included Jerusalem and the West Bank. Elon observed that some Israeli leaders wanted to set up a semiautonomous Arab state under Israeli tutelage on the West Bank. The Herut party and some others favored outright annexation. He feared the latter attitude. This was the moment to solve the Palestinian refugee problem, he argued, and such a moment was not likely to reoccur. A generous victory could lay the groundwork for peace. The Palestinian issue could finally be settled if Israel summoned the necessary imagination and "farsighted statesmanship." But without the "generosity of wise victors," Elon warned, the fruits of this victory would be lost just as they were in 1948 and 1956.[122]

This sentiment could still be published in *Commentary* in 1967. The magazine's approach to Israeli affairs would soon flatten to a hard line, however. The Six Day War awakened Podhoretz's Zionism—at the same moment that his politics were turning Right. [123] His Jewish awakening was a common phenomenon, as Arthur Hertzberg explained in his account of the American Jewish reaction to the Six Day War. "As soon as the Arab armies began to mass on the borders of Israel during the third week in May," Hertzberg wrote, "the mood of the American Jewish community underwent an abrupt, radical, and possibly permanent change."[124] The response of American Jews to the Israeli crisis was "far more intense and widespread" than anyone could have expected. Except for certain Jewish New Leftists—whose identification with their Jewishness was undermined by their Third-Worldist politics—virtually all American Jews reacted to the Arab attack as an attack on themselves. The war immediately galvanized deep feelings of solidarity among Jews who lacked any religious reason whatsoever to identify with their Jewishness.

This was what needed to be explained. One contributing factor was the largely unspoken revulsion felt by American Jews toward the passivity of the Holocaust's victims. Faced with a serious threat to Israel's existence, Hertzberg explained, most American Jews felt that if Israel was going to go down, it had better go down fighting. The memory of the Holocaust commanded active resistance. This command was reinforced by a closely related memory. During the Holocaust, American Jews failed to urge their government to provide refuge for persecuted European Jews. The American Jewish response to the outbreak of the Six Day War was, among other things, a way of saying "never again."

"But Israel evoked more in American Jews than a sense of moral reparation for the memory of the passive victims of mass murder," Hertzberg argued. The "more" was what needed to be explained. Hertzberg ventured a guess. "The sense of belonging to a worldwide Jewish people, of which Israel is the center, is a religious sentiment, but it seems to persist even among Jews who regard themselves as secularists or atheists," he observed. "There are no conventional Western theological terms with which to explain this, and most contemporary Jews experience these emotions without knowing how to define them." One possible explanation was that the war occurred "at precisely that moment in the history of American Jews when an ascending curve of nearly complete outer and inner emancipation intersected with a descending curve of Jewish commitment."[125] American Jews were now so securely assimilated that they felt free to speak up for Jewish interests, even though they cared less and less about Judaism. If this was the case, Hertzberg reasoned, the new Jewish consciousness would undoubtedly soon dissipate as Judaism itself disappeared.

There was another explanation, however, which took the emergence of a nonreligious Jewish consciousness more seriously. What might have occurred was that one variant of nineteenth-century Zionism had come true. The distinguishing theme of "neo-messianic" Zionism was that a Jewish state in Palestine would re-energize Jewish loyalties throughout the world. Neo-messianism had taken two predominant forms, represented by the secular Zionism of Ahad Ha-Am and the Marxist Zionism of Ber Borochov. Both forms agreed, however, that a reconstituted Israel would provide a focal point for Jewish loyalty and thereby provide the vehicle by which Jewish identity could be sustained, with or without religion. Hertzberg had given short shrift to neo-messianism in his important book on the history and varieties of Zionist thought. As he explained, secularized Zionism failed to solve the riddle of how to reject religion while affirming chosenness. Ahad Ha-Am was an instructive example. His neo-messianism had failed to explain "how to be a nineteenth-century liberal in practice and yet find support for the unique life and self-image of the Jew," Hertzberg argued. [126] He concluded that secular Zionism was too deracinated to support or sustain the Jewish sense of chosenness.

The Six Day War moved Hertzberg to reconsider this claim, however. He observed that a vital Jewish consciousness appeared to be surviving the acids of modernity. If Jewishness was, indeed, surviving the disappearance of Judaism, the phenomenon could only be explained as a vindication of the neo-messianic vision. For Jews, Israel itself might substitute for the lost object of religious faith.

Hertzberg's account of this phenomenon was descriptive. His own Zionism was rooted in his Jewish faith. Despite his ambivalence in advancing it, however, his argument proved to be prophetic—as the transmutation of *Commentary* magazine would illustrate. Hertzberg claimed that the Six Day War marked a transforming moment in the lives of American Jews, bringing them into contact with their Jewishness while redefining what it meant to be Jewish. Shortly afterward, Podhoretz confirmed that this was exactly what happened to him.

He had confessed in 1963 that in thinking about the Jews, he often wondered "whether their survival as a distinct group was worth one hair on the head of a single infant." He knew why the Jews had previously insisted on surviving as a distinct group, but with the loss of that earlier theological memory, he remarked, "I am less certain as to why we still do." [127] This situation was unsettling for him, partly because he found himself unable to explain why modern Jews should preserve their cultural tradition. Liberalism countenanced the religious feelings of individuals, but it was far more problematic to sustain a collective Jewish consciousness divorced from religion. Though *Commentary's* religion section occasionally mentioned the neo-messianic tradition, secular Zionism seemed no more fruitful to Podhoretz than to Hertzberg—until the war. Now Hertzberg was suggesting that the focal point for a renewed Jewish consciousness already existed in the apparent triumph of Zionism.

The following year, Emil Fackenheim substantiated this claim with an appeal for Jewish solidarity. What did it mean to be a Jew in the modern world? Fackenheim argued that it meant, above all, to be a witness to the Holocaust. To be a Jew was to bear witness to Auschwitz's "unique descent into hell" and be faithful to its victims. It was not that the Holocaust provided a new purpose for Jewish life. "A good Jewish secularist will connect the Holocaust with the rise of the state of Israel," he conceded, "but while to see a causal connection here is possible and necessary, to see a purpose is intolerable." To ascribe a purpose to Auschwitz, religious or not, was blasphemous. But if it was forbidden to ascribe a purpose to Auschwitz, it was utterly necessary to make a response to it. The Voice of Auschwitz called religious and nonreligious Jews alike. It was not a redemptive, but a commanding Voice, which declared: "Jews are forbidden to grant posthumous victories to Hitler." In ancient times, the most heinous sin for a Jew had been to commit idolatry. After Auschwitz, Fackenheim argued, the most heinous sin for a Jew was to be an accomplice to the further destruction of the Jewish people. [128]

The crucial difference between being a Jew and being a Christian was that, while one became a true Christian only through voluntary commitment, a Jew was anyone who became or was born a Jew. Fackenheim's purpose was not only to remind lapsed and nonbelieving Jews of their irrevocable Jewishness, but to drive home the meaning of the "new and perverse reality" that Hitler had bequeathed. For a Christian to be murdered at Auschwitz, he noted, required being a saint; for a Jew to be murdered, nothing beyond being a Jew was necessary. Through his cunning and terror, Hitler led most Christians into temptation. He manipulated Christians into the self-assurance that the fate of the Jews had nothing to do with them. He thus created an abyss between Jews and Christians that outlived Nazism. Because the Jews at Auschwitz were abandoned, Jews after Auschwitz lived with the knowledge of abandonment. Because most Christians abandoned the Jews, Christians could not bear their responsibility for the Holocaust. "He knows that, as a Christian, he should voluntarily have gone to Auschwitz, where his own Master would have been dragged, voluntarily or involuntarily, and he is wracked by a sense of guilt the deeper the less he has cause to feel it," Fackenheim explained. "Hence the Christian failure to face Auschwitz. Hence Christian recourse to innocuous generalities. Hence, too, Christian silence in May 1967."[129]

The last was Hitler's most recent victory. The key events were recounted by Hertzberg. Except for a few prominent individuals—including Reinhold Niebuhr and Martin Luther King, Jr.—the Christian churches were silent when the Israeli crisis broke in May 1967. America's churches failed to proclaim their support for Israel's right to defend itself. But as soon as the war ended, the same Christian denominations held meetings with Jewish ecumenists to express their concerns about the Arab refugees. It was an ugly message, and it was taken as such. As Hertzberg wrote shortly afterward, "Many Christians, the Pope among them, are being very precise in their concern about the Old City and the Arab refugees, and very vague in their concern for Israel's safety and peace."[130]

Hertzberg was not unsympathetic toward the Arab refugees or the Palestinians. He conceded that Christian concern for displaced and disenfranchised Arabs had a strong moral and political basis. He argued, however, that no matter how legitimate these concerns might be, Christian preoccupation with these issues deserved to be taken by Jews as an evasion, or worse, because "the effect of such talk, if it was not linked to Israel's right of existence, would be to encourage the Arabs to remain obdurate."[131] The churches needed to understand that the existence of Israel, as an issue, was as important to American Jews as the Christian roots of anti-Semitism or the theological status of Judaism. If the churches were not willing to begin their moral calculations by assuming Israel's right to exist and defend itself, then American Jews were prepared to forego ecumenical relations with Christian churches. Hertzberg thus set the terms for future Jewish–Christian relations.

Fackenheim went further. The churches failed to speak against a "second Auschwitz" in 1967, he charged, not because they were indifferent to the cries for help from Damascus, but because they did not hear them. The churches failed to recognize a second holocaust in the making, because they still hadn't recognized "the fact of the first."[132] Having failed to come to terms with their part in the Nazi Holocaust, they were incapable of making a moral response to the threat of a second holocaust. This was Hitler's posthumous victory. To be a Jew after 1967 was to live with the knowledge of being twice abandoned; to be a Christian was to bear the unbearable responsibility for this abandonment.

This argument had a powerful effect on Podhoretz. More than twenty years later, while pleading a weak memory on much that he published during the same period, he could quote parts of Fackenheim's article verbatim. [133] His first entry on the subject was published in 1971, in a column that picked up Fackenheim's argument and tied it to *Commentary*'s current vendetta against the New Class. He recalled that the Six Day War engendered a passion of solidarity among American Jews that transcended their previous commitments to Zionism or Jewish survivalism or Judaism. The experience was far more profound than any political or moral or religious commitment, he claimed. It was an ontological phenomenon, an ineffable feeling of literal identification in which Jews were made aware that each of them was part of every other. Their victory in the war marked a recovery from the nearly fatal wounds the Nazis had inflicted on the Jewish spirit.

"But others, we soon found, did not celebrate at all," he recalled. "The churches of the world, most of them, lamented it with an unction whose oily odor lingers in the air and still has the power to sicken any healthy stomach." Numerous governments similarly reproved the Jewish victory with high-sounding laments about the plight of the Palestinians. These sentiments were rationalized by "the intellectuals of the world," Podhoretz noted, whose sympathies for Jews only extended to dead Jews. Most intellectuals couldn't bring themselves to defend Jews who defended themselves. "And so a wave of what pleased to call itself 'anti-Zionism' swept through the intellectual communities of the world, including the intellectual community of America, despite the fact—but of course in some sense also because of the fact—that so many members of that community in America are Jews," he wrote. [134]

This wave of "so-called anti-Zionist feeling" in America was motivated primarily by the spectacle of the Jew as victor, Podhoretz argued, but it was also fueled by the intellectuals' alienation from middle America. The anti-Zionism of the intellectuals was part of a larger hostility toward the values of America's middle class and the industrial system that created the middle class. It was a murky argument, filled with debatable premises and loose connections. Rather than develop the argument, however, Pod-horetz cut to the moral: The greatest threat to Jews in America no longer came from the Right, but from the New Class clerics and intellectuals. It was not a coincidence that most of America's so-called anti-Zionist intellectuals were also known for their anti-Americanism. Those who disdained the Jewish drive for acceptance and success in America were alienated from America in the first place.

Podhoretz did not conceal his suspicion that so-called anti-Zionism was usually a cover for anti-Semitism. While conceding that it was possible for someone to oppose Zionism while not being anti-Semitic, he argued that most anti-Zionist positioning was a cover for anti-Semitic prejudice. The need for a cover was dissipating, however. Anti-Semitism in America was no longer censored by a powerful cultural taboo. The force of the post-Holocaust taboo on anti-Semitism had been weakened in America by the Six Day War and by the anti-Semitic pronouncements of certain Black Power advocates. In this context, Podhoretz asserted, any expression of so-called anti-Zionism merited careful scrutiny.[135]

It was not enough to try to restore the force of the earlier taboo. He argued that a specifically Jewish collective interest needed to be defined and promoted. Having shed the role of the victim, Jews could no longer depend on a diminishing taboo against anti-Semitism. They were compelled to learn the lessons of their abandonment. They could no longer afford not to promote their own interests. In the political arena, Podhoretz declared, they needed to revive the old and wrongly neglected question, Is it good for the Jews? "That is to say, I think that Jews must once again begin to look at proposals and policies from the point of view of the Jewish interest, and must once again begin to ask what the consequences, if any, of any proposal or policy are likely to be so far as the Jewish position is concerned," he argued.[136] It was not that Jews should care only about the Jewish interest, but that they should always begin with the question of the Jewish interest.

Affirmative action was an important example. Since Jews constituted only 3 percent of the population and were "commonly said to be over-represented almost everywhere they are represented at all," Podhoretz opposed affirmative action. His magazine later amplified the case against affirmative action, but the fundamental test was the Jewish interest. Affirmative action schemes to employ or promote racial minorities failed the crucial test because Jews would not benefit from them.[137] Podhoretz applied the same test to electoral politics. The problem with Jews, he complained, was that they kept voting for liberal politicians who no longer served Jewish interests. Having ascended to the upper regions of the middle class, many Jews continued to support the same liberal politicians as blacks. Podhoretz and Kristol explained that part of the problem was that Jews were overrepresented in the New Class. Many of them voted liberal because liberalism did serve their New Class interests. The problem was more complicated than the New Class angle, however. Jews voted liberal because, more than any other upwardly mobile group, they felt guilty about those they surpassed. They were especially prone to feel guilty about poor blacks. Jewish liberalism was a function of lingering Jewish guilt. Throughout the 1980s, Podhoretz and Kristol periodically speculated (usually just before an election) that the guilt factor was finally wearing down. The claim revealed more about their politics than about American Jews. *Commentary* repeatedly argued that America would be better off when Jews became like everyone else and voted their own interests.[138]

This conception of the putative Jewish interest and *Commentary*'s general turn to the Right cost the magazine many of its best writers on Jewish affairs. In the late 1970s, Podhoretz began to fill the vacuum with his own entries. His articles carried titles like "The Abandonment of Israel," "J'Accuse," and "The Hate that Dare Not Speak Its Name," sometimes in screaming bold type. Their accusatory style rarely invited rational discussion of the politics of Jewish interests. Podhoretz inspired more than a few of his targets to respond in kind. The bitterness of his polemicizing was often attributable, however, to his critics' antipathy for Israel and to their disrespect for his devotion to it. As he tirelessly repeated, Israel was a tiny democracy surrounded by hostile dictatorships pledged to its destruction. Podhoretz was enraged by anti-Zionists who regarded this truism as a mere debating point or as a cover for Israel's mistreatment of the Palestinians. His position on the question of trading land for peace, he often explained, was that it would be presumptuous for anyone not living in Israel—and therefore not physically threatened by its Arab enemies—to make declarations on the subject. Though he later found it impossible to follow his own counsel on the matter, Podhoretz tried harder than most.

He did not attribute all criticism of Israel to anti-Semitism, as was often charged. Though he believed that *The New York Times* was routinely unfair to Israel, Podhoretz conceded that the *Times* employed a consistent moral standard toward Israel and its Arab neighbors. He explained that anti-Semitic criticism was distinguished by its invocation of a double standard for Jews. Traditional anti-Semitism attributed certain universal human frailties particularly to Jews: Jews were greedy, ambitious, conniving, obnoxious, clannish. They deserved condemnation for pursuing the same goods pursued by others.[139] Podhoretz argued that the same tradition produced a double standard for judging the Jewish state. The United Nations resolution condemning Zionism as a form of racism was a case in point. According to the logic of this resolution, "all other people are entitled to national self-determination, but when the Jews exercise this right, they are committing the crimes of racism and imperialism. Similarly, all other nations have a right to insure the security of their borders; when Israel exercises this right, it is committing the crime of aggression. So too, only Israel of all the states in the world is required to prove that its very existence—not merely its interests or the security of its borders, but its very existence—is in immediate peril before it can justify the resort to force."[140] He might have added that for many of Israel's critics, even threats to Israel's existence would have made no difference, since they disputed Israel's right to exist.

Gore Vidal was among Israel's most volatile critics. In 1986, Vidal made it abundantly clear that he also therefore regarded Podhoretz as a racist interloper. His attack on Podhoretz and Decter, "The Empire Lovers Strike Back," made the case for deporting the Podhoretzes—or at least making them register as foreign agents. According to Vidal, modern Zionists were "predators . . . busy stealing other people's land in the name of an alien theocracy." While alien Jews in Palestine consolidated their conquests over the natives, he charged, their alien cohorts in America were manipulating the government of "the host country" to secure U.S. Treasury funds for Israel. These "Israeli fifth columnists" were choosing to "stay on among us," Vidal explained, only to raise money and make propaganda for Israel. They were not Americans at all. They called themselves neoconservatives to show "that their hearts are in the far-right place," but the nonsense about conservatism was merely a cover for their Zionist maneuverings.

Vidal claimed that neoconservatives ranted about communism mainly to attain protective camouflage for their predatory Israeli brethren. This explained why they were making common cause "with every sort of reactionary and anti-Semitic group in the United States, from the corridors of the Pentagon to the TV studios of the evangelical Jesus-Christers." People like Podhoretz had figured out how to keep the Zionist gravy train rolling. They were foreign lobbyists of a distinctive kind, Vidal explained. They weren't registered with the Justice Department, and they had no tact. A bit of tact would have prescribed "a certain forbearance when it comes to the politics of the host country," he observed. "But tact is unknown to the Podhoretzes." The Podhoretzes preferred the politics of fear and hate. Their scheme was to frighten Americans "into spending enormous sums for 'defense,' which also means the support of Israel in its never-ending wars against just about everyone."[141]

"The Empire Lovers Strike Back" thus managed to resurrect not only the "dual loyalty" bigotries of American nativism, but also the classic anti-Semitic image of the Jew as conspirator. It was not so much an argument as a retaliatory smear. In her Committee for the Free World newsletter, *Contentions*, Decter had recently tweaked Vidal's politics and declared that he obviously didn't like his country very much. Her attack echoed Podhoretz's broadsides against alienated homosexual intellectuals. Vidal replied that of course he liked his country; he was writing all these historical novels about it. "But now that we're really leveling with each other," he told her, "I've got to tell you I don't much like your country, which is Israel." Nor did he care for the "politics of hate" practiced by Decter and her husband, with its "plangent attacks on blacks and/or fags and/or liberals, trying, always, to outdo those moral majoritarians who will, as Armageddon draws near, either convert all the Jews, just as the Good Book says, or kill them."

This was the nerve center. Podhoretz had enraged Vidal with his attacks on homosexual writers. "The Culture of Appeasement" identified Vidal as a chief purveyor of America's moral corruption. Alienated homosexuals were sapping America's resolve to defend democracy. Decter had similarly demeaned homosexuals in her *Commentary* article, "The Boys on the Beach." Podhoretz later recalled that he could hardly believe his eyes when he read Vidal's diatribe, but many readers of "The Boys on the Beach" were equally stunned by the harshness of Decter's gay-baiting. Her article recycled the entire stock of stereotypes about homosexuals with a blistering mean-spiritedness, presenting gay men as self-loathing, self-obsessed, self-abusing neurotics bound only by a "common and mutual loathing of the flesh."[142]

The AIDS epidemic inspired Podhoretz to add to this literature of abuse. He complained that AIDS victims were getting overly sympathetic treatment in the media. Because the media constantly pandered to the AIDS lobby, he declared, it was important to remember that AIDS was "almost entirely a disease caught by men who bugger and are buggered by dozens or even hundreds of other men every year." America's politicians and health care officials, he claimed, were snared in their own twisted sense of compassion, which made them easy prey for the AIDS lobby. They were caving in to the demand for an AIDS vaccine and were thus "giving social sanction to what can only be described as brutish degradation."[143] Podhoretz and Decter did not explain how gay men and lesbians were supposed to develop healthier self-images in a society that depicted them as perverse and subjected them to repeated ridicule, harassment, blackmail, and entrapment. If gay men appeared to have special difficulties building monogamous relationships, this phenomenon was presumably no fault of a culture that ridiculed their efforts to sustain them. When the New York City Council passed a bill that proscribed discrimination against lesbians and gay men, Podhoretz denounced the measure as proof that America's body politic was "suffering from the spiritual equivalent" of the AIDS plague. [144]

This was the background noise to Vidal's assault on Zionism. The noise explained the Left's initially muted reaction to his incendiary accusations. Though *The New Republic* condemned Vidal's "brazen racist hate" and *Dissent* denounced his article as a "racist diatribe," much of the left-liberal press let the article pass in silence. Many observers apparently assured themselves that Vidal's anti-Semitic screed was not really about anti-Semitism at all. It was, rather, an outrageous rejoinder to Podhoretz's and Decter's gay-bashing and their related attacks on minorities and liberals. Hertzberg's endorsement of this reading was instructive for many. While criticizing Vidal's "screaming rhetoric of American nativism," Hertzberg argued that the affair was essentially a personal quarrel that should have been conducted as a private shouting match. [145]

Hertzberg had performed the Podhoretz–Decter wedding ceremony. His pronouncement on the controversy deeply wounded Podhoretz, who angrily replied that Hertzberg and others were trivializing the issue. The episode was not about himself or Decter at all, he claimed; it was an attack on Jews in general. He explained that he had hoped "not that others would spring to my defense, but that a protest would be mounted by people sympathetic to The Nation's left-wing political position who would say that while they detested everything Norman Podhoretz, Midge Decter, and all the other neoconservatives stood for, and while nothing made them happier than seeing neoconservatives raked over the coals, they were outraged by the reintroduction of anti-Semitism into American political discourse in general and their own political community in particular." He argued elsewhere that the lack of a liberal outcry against Vidal created "a silence as deep as the moral pit into which The Nation itself has fallen." [146]

The affair was instructive as a measure of Podhoretz's notoriety. The same attack on nearly anyone else would have generated a firestorm. Against Podhoretz and Decter, it brought mostly silence and a tendency to personalize the issue. Podhoretz once recalled that Lionel Trilling regarded Hook as the cautionary figure of his generation. Hook was the one who had gone too far in his attacks on the liberal intelligentsia. For the generation after Hook, the cautionary figure was Kristol. Podhoretz recalled this assessment to underscore his disappointment over Trilling's purported lack of courage. But the Vidal affair confirmed that he had outdistanced Hook and Kristol in going too far. His succeeding volume of memoirs recounted the trail of friendships he left behind in the 1970s. [147] Breaking Ranks explained why Podhoretz broke friendships with all of his previous political allies, excepting the right-wing social democrats. In the 1980s, he left behind his social democratic friends, as well. Neoconservatism lost its social democratic wing in the eighties, partly because the movement's leaders kept moving further Right. "It took me a long time to do it," Podhoretz later explained, "but I finally decided to join my own side. Many of us [neoconservatives] went through the same thing. I kept getting pulled into reconsiderations after I wrote *Breaking Ranks,* and I finally decided—like a lot of neoconservatives—to join the people who agreed with me. We joined forces with those in the *other* party who wanted to be our friends."[148]

He was thus driven to the right wing of the Republican party, partly because he found his previous friends to be insufficient friends of Israel. As he observed with increasing sarcasm throughout the 1980s, his ex-friends unfailingly defended their pro-Israeli credentials. Daniel Patrick Moynihan was a prominent example. Moynihan had once accused the Carter administration of "joining the jackals" when it supported a U.N. resolution censuring Israel.[149] He was now to be found, however, among the signatories of a Senate statement criticizing the Shamir government for failing to support a particular negotiating formula. Like all of the politicians, professors, and pundits who signed such statements, Moynihan claimed to be Israel's friend. "Indeed," Podhoretz bitterly remarked, "to judge by the protestations that invariably accompany chastisements of Israel nowadays, never has a nation been blessed with so many loving friends."[150]

He allowed that some of these people did mean well for Israel. But in calling for Israeli withdrawal from the occupied territories and the establishment of a Palestinian state, these friends invariably reminded him of the pragmatists who justified Nazi aggression against Czechoslovakia in 1938. Just as the Czechs were accused of mistreating the German minority in the Sudeten regions under Czechoslovakian control, Podhoretz noted, the Israelis were constantly accused of mistreating the Palestinians in the occupied territories. And just as the Czechs were forced at Munich to cede the Sudetenland to Germany, so the Israelis were constantly exhorted to trade land for peace. This time, the "friends" assured, appeasement would work.

There was no reason, however, to believe that the Palestinians could be appeased. There was no reason to believe that creating a Palestinian state would accomplish anything except to create a new staging ground "for a new round of aggression against a more vulnerable military target."[151] The language of compromise and negotiation spoken by the politicians, academics, and diplomats was the language of appeasement. Those who sincerely advanced proposals for a peaceful settlement, Podhoretz declared, deserved to be called fools. "As for those who should know better but still propagate it, fool is too kind a word."[152] Podhoretz made alliances for this position where he could find them, and spent much of the 1980s explaining why Jews should not feel anxious about the politicization of Protestant fundamentalism.

GORBACHEV AND THE COLLAPSE
OF THE COLD WAR

He was equally convinced that Reagan was selling out the country to the Communists. Podhoretz's early frustration with Reagan's foreign policy hardened into something close to contempt during Reagan's second term. He bitterly complained in 1985 that Reagan was repeating the worst mistakes of his predecessors. The emerging arms control agreement was a throwback to Kissinger's Basic Principles of Détente of 1972; the Reagan approach to Central America increasingly resembled the purportedly ill-fated resolution of the 1962 Cuban missile crisis; the approach to Nicaragua, in particular, recycled the disastrous 1962 Declaration on the Neutrality of Laos, which called for the withdrawal of all foreign troops from the area. To continue down this road, he observed at the outset of Reagan's second term, would be a cruel disappointment to those who once believed in Reagan's intention to fight communism. [153]

Reagan's second term proved savagely disappointing to Podhoretz. Under such disgusted titles as "Reagan: A Case of Mistaken Identity," "How Reagan Succeeds as a Carter Clone," and the plaintively disbelieving "What If Reagan Were President?" he repeatedly charged that Reagan was betraying the cause of anticommunism. To Podhoretz, the "single greatest lie of our time" was that arms control served the ends of peace and security. He was thus incredulous during the mid-eighties when Reagan approved the groundwork for a substantial arms agreement with Gorbachev. In 1986, after Reagan traded a Soviet spy for the release of an American journalist, Podhoretz thundered that Reagan "shamed himself and the country" because of his "craven eagerness" for an arms agreement with Gorbachev. [154] The culture of appeasement was winning. By playing on the fear of war, Podhoretz claimed, the culture of appeasement was turning even Ronald Reagan into a servant of the Big Lie.

This verdict was resisted by many of Podhoretz's friends. As he observed, the Reaganites gamely tried to relieve Reagan of responsibility for the foreign policies of his administration. Under the slogan "let Reagan be Reagan," they blamed a series of Reagan officials—Alexander Haig, James Baker, Michael Deaver, and finally George Schultz—for his Finlandizing record. But Podhoretz spurned these pious evasions, claiming that the craven character of the Reagan administration had been established by Reagan himself. The Reagan of the Reaganites existed only as a speechmaker. The real Reagan was not the courageous anticommunist that his supporters imagined, but rather a politician whose insatiable greed for popularity was driving him into the arms of the Soviets. Reaching for the ultimate insult, Podhoretz desperately announced in 1986 that Reagan had become a Carter clone. But while poor Carter could never get away with being Carter, he complained, it seemed that Reagan would get away with it. [155] The only remaining hope for his administration was that his supporters would stop ganging up on scapegoats like Shultz and vent their rage at Reagan himself. "Maybe if they did," he wrote, "the President would think twice before betraying them and his own ideas again."[156]

Betrayal now became Podhoretz's dominant theme, with occasional exceptions. As the American delegate to the Conference on Security and Cooperation in Europe in 1986, Michael Novak refused to certify Soviet compliance with the Helsinki human rights provisions of 1975. Reagan supported Novak's judgment, and for a moment Podhoretz was able to celebrate the reappearance of the pre-elected Reagan. These moments proved fleeting, however, for behind the spectacle of Reagan's massive betrayal of his country stood the cunning figure who had softened up Western opinion and thereby seduced America into lowering its guard. [157]

For Podhoretz, Gorbachev was a nightmare come to life. His success at lowering Western fear of the Soviet Union convinced Podhoretz in the late 1980s that the danger was greater than ever. [158] Step by humiliating step, he wrote in 1987, the Reagan administration was falling into full retreat from its earlier anticommunist mission. Among the intellectuals, only Podhoretz, Kissinger, and a few neoconservatives understood Gorbachev's real agenda. Everyone else had been duped, in step with a president who was making cuts in defense spending, "even though we have not yet made up for the neglect of the '70s."[159]

Gorbachev's agenda was a two-step process, Podhoretz explained. Gorbachev's immediate objective was to get the West to bail his country out of its current economic crisis. His second objective was to preserve his military advantages over the West. Podhoretz warned that Gorbachev was attaining both objectives through his deceitfully calculated show of good will. America's recent cuts in military spending perfectly accommodated this scheme. [160] The sky was falling. America was surrendering and calling it peace. Podhoretz incredulously observed that even some Committee on the Present Danger (CPD) veterans were being duped. They were endorsing the ban on medium-range missiles and the strategic arms reduction agenda. The very people who had founded CPD in the late 1970s to oppose SALT II were now committing themselves to a far more radical arms control agenda. This process had been given a new name—START I instead of SALT III—purportedly because it promoted arms reduction rather than arms limitation. Podhoretz saw a more telling reason for the name change, however: "It relieves the President himself and some of his advisers of the burden of reconciling their past criticisms of the arms control process with their enthusiasm for the latest and most dangerous trap this process has managed to set for us yet."[161]

The cause for which CPD was created was being betrayed by people he had trusted and whose advancement he had promoted. On the eve of the watershed betrayal—the signing of the INF treaty banning medium-range missiles—Podhoretz therefore called for a new committee to replace the Committee on the Present Danger. The new committee he envisioned would resume CPD's abandoned crusade against the SALT process and condemn START as a radical offspring of the SALT process. This "politically adulterous embrace of arms control and détente" was throwing away America's last chance to neutralize the Soviet advantage in offensive weaponry, Podhoretz warned. He argued that SALT III would deprive America from gaining the strategic advantage it had spent so much to attain. It would thus forsake the proper goal of American military policy— which was to regain the superior power to intimidate rival nations. [162]

He was convinced that the seemingly diminished Soviet threat was actually greater than ever. Gorbachev had suckered the West. In mid-1989, Podhoretz was still claiming that Gorbachev was a crafty Leninist who had figured out how to strengthen the Soviet empire and disarm the West. [163] His touchstone was the theory of totalitarianism. The twin pillars of communist totalitarianism were the absolute domestic power of the Communist party and the duty to create a communist international order. Soviet power was rationalized by this creed. Just as Lenin had loosened economic restraints during the 1920s to impede an economic collapse, Gorbachev was opening the Soviet system just enough to entice Western aid and thereby save his totalitarian structure. For Podhoretz, it was axiomatic that totalitarian systems were fundamentally unlike all other political structures. The rulers of totalitarian regimes had no room or capacity to seriously reassess the national interest, Podhoretz claimed. It was ludicrous to think that Gorbachev would undermine the basis of his rule by opening the Soviet system or dismantling the Soviet empire. [164] (Podhoretz inveighed against the Arias Peace Plan for Central America on the same grounds, arguing that it was "naive to the point of dementia" to believe that the Nicaraguan Sandinistas would ever permit a legitimate election.)[165]

Gorbachev's strategy was therefore transparent. The question for Podhoretz was not why Gorbachev had embarked on a peace offensive, but why the West was falling for it. He darkly suggested that the answer lay in the warning he had issued ten years earlier. Unless America committed itself to attaining strategic superiority, he had warned, the West would become Finlandized in the name of peace. An unspoken fear of Soviet power would lead the West to sign trade agreements with the Soviets involving the transfer of technology, grain, "and anything else the Soviets might want or need . . . negotiated on terms amounting to the payment of tribute."[166] While others stupidly celebrated the approaching end of the Cold War, Podhoretz carried on with the grim disgust of a man who knew what was coming. Reagan's military build-up was too little and too late. This explained why Reagan and the other "outgunned" Western leaders were kowtowing to Gorbachev and rushing to Moscow "with bags of tributary gold." Having lost the Cold War, the West was now frantically negotiating the terms of its Finlandization. It was a species of surrender. Burnham's outer rings were being sucked into the Soviet dungeon. Podhoretz bitterly complained that those who told the truth about America's surrender were being castigated as warmongers—even by the Reagan administration.[167]

His first glimmer that the West hadn't lost the Cold War occurred during his visit to Moscow in June 1989. Podhoretz and his friends were stunned by the freedom of expression and criticism they witnessed in Russia. *Glasnost* was apparently more than a ruse. A greater shock awaited them, however, when they met with Gorbachev's chief strategist, Aleksandr Yakovlev. Many of them had had a particularly difficult time coming to terms with the reputed father of *glasnost*. Yakovlev's 1985 book, *On the Edge of the Abyss*, had strenuously criticized American egotism, selfishness, "and the cult of money and property" in traditional Marxist language. The neoconservatives had bitterly resented what Jeane Kirkpatrick called his "implacable, unrelieved, splenetic" hostility toward American politics and culture. In 1988, Kirkpatrick was still warning that Yakovlev's posture toward America was "about as benign as Joseph Stalin's," and Podhoretz agreed that Yakovlev was simply an especially cunning Leninist. By the following summer, however, it was no longer possible even for them to deny that Gorbachev and Yakovlev were opening up Soviet politics. The neoconservatives came to their meeting with Yakovlev a bit off-guard, determined to press him on the limits of his political vision, but already taken aback by the apparent seriousness of his reforms.[168]

They were determined to press hardest on Soviet policy toward Eastern Europe and the Baltic republics. How did Soviet leaders plan to handle Eastern Europe's growing political unrest? they asked him. Yakovlev matter-of-factly informed them that the Eastern European governments were on their own. He quickly cautioned that the Baltic republics were in a different category, since Baltic dissidents were threatening the

Union. It was therefore imperative for the Soviets to control or, if necessary, suppress dissident movements in the Baltic states. He calmly returned to the bombshell. As for the Eastern Europeans, he repeated, Soviet leaders were much less concerned. These were other peoples' countries. The future of Eastern Europe would be determined by Eastern Europeans.

Podhoretz and Decter repeated these impossible words to each other and asked why Gorbachev's principal adviser would lie to them. Nothing made sense, especially since Yakovlev seemed equally forthcoming about prospects for the Baltic states. The meeting was staggering, bewildering. Was this really happening? Five months before the rest of the world learned that the Soviets were, indeed, prepared to relinquish their control over Eastern Europe, Podhoretz puzzled over how such a transformation could be possible and what it would mean for the West. He stopped writing. The major articles he had planned to write upon terminating his newspaper column in February went unwritten. In the closing weeks of 1989, Gorbachev forced the issue in East Germany and watched his European satellites fall in chain reaction. [169]

The certainties that had fueled Podhoretz's writing for the past twenty years were swept away. The "totalitarian" regimes of Eastern Europe collapsed overnight, most of them without violence. The theory of totalitarianism collapsed with them. The experience was exhilarating, confounding, and deflating all at once. Asked in June 1990 why he had stopped writing, Podhoretz explained that he no longer knew what to think. He still wasn't convinced that the Cold War was over or that Gorbachev was serious about trying to democratize Soviet politics, but he wasn't prepared to make anything of these suspicions, either. He had lost his compass. He found current policy debates perplexing. In certain cases, he knew what should be done, even if he didn't know what to think. He was "ashamed" of the Bush administration's reckless policy toward Lithuania and "disgusted" with Kristol's defense of it. ("Lithuania is not a lucky country," Kristol had explained). Otherwise, Podhoretz didn't know what to think about the Soviet Union. He wondered aloud whether Gorbachev was the Soviet Jimmy Carter or the Soviet Franklin Roosevelt. It was obvious that Gorbachev was trying to split the United States from Europe, but he doubted Gorbachev's capacity to shape the post-totalitarian world. Gorbachev was trying to convert weakness into strength, but was too weak to pull it off. He had an illusion about "his power to calibrate reality," but, stopping in mid-sentence, Podhoretz paused, shrugged, and said, "Who knows?"

The moment for politics, in any case, had clearly passed. Podhoretz observed that the recent historical phase of politicization had run its course; even he was losing interest in politics. He laughed at the fact that Kristol had moved to Washington just before the spirit blew out of the Beltway. The battleground for neoconservatism was shifting to the cultural realm. "I am pro-American to the point of chauvinism," he exclaimed, but immediately explained that he was only chauvinistic about America's political and economic systems. He took no pride in American culture. "American culture is spiritually illiterate," he said, borrowing a phrase from his friend, Huw Wheldon. [170] "Americans don't know what spiritual literacy is. There is a vocabulary of the spirit which is different from the languages of politics or economics or morality which most Americans know nothing about . . ."—a long pause followed—"and which I have a great deal of difficulty trying to express, also."[171]

He had been trying for months to get started on a third volume of memoirs. *Making It* was about career, *Breaking Ranks* about politics, and the third volume would be about culture, especially religion. "The one thing I really want to write about is the one subject I've never been able to write about," he observed. Podhoretz had always been interested in religion as a cultural force, and in recent years he had developed a stronger personal interest in religion. "I'm getting older," he shrugged. And as a political force? "Well, yes," he said. He had been criticized for making alliances with Protestant fundamentalists, and he was aware that fundamentalists had their own reasons for supporting Israel. "The main thing, however, is that they've continued to fight against communism and moral relativism after the liberal churches moved to the Left. And of course, for whatever reasons, the fundamentalists are strong supporters of Israel."

His deepest interest now was Zionism—especially the connection between Jewish religion and Jewish survival. I suggested that the survivalist perspective he took from Fackenheim was theologically problematic. Survivalism commanded that all Jews, whether religious or not, stand at Auschwitz and defend some conception of the Jewish interest. Contrary to Fackenheim's implication, however, this command was not analogous to the ancient injunction that Jews must act as though they stood at Sinai. The traditional command significantly differed from Fackenheim's reformulation. The traditional command was inherently theological, and therefore presented comprehensive moral teachings about how Jews were to live in the world. The Torah spelled out the theological and moral meaning of faithfulness, which was not reducible to the claim that Jewish survival was the ultimate commandment. Survivalism reduced Jewish moral teachings to the claim that Jewish survival was an end in itself, transcending—and if necessary, replacing—all other claims.

Podhoretz accepted the thrust of this critique and explained that his theological position was "unabashedly heretical." From his perspective, the secular Jew in Detroit who occasionally contributed money to Zionist organizations was a better Jew than the pious rabbi in Brooklyn who believed that David Ben-Gurion should have waited for the messiah. If one cared about the well-being of the Jewish people, he argued, then heresy was unavoidable, since the theologically correct choice often failed to serve the more important cause of survival. His survivalist Zionism was linked with Orthodox Judaism, however, in its emphasis on the primacy of "peoplehood" for Jewish existence. Survivalism took the theme further than Orthodox Judaism, but for both there was no Judaism without Jews. "The concept of a distinction between the people and the faith is a Christian notion, not a Jewish one," he argued. "It is possible to conceive a Protestant theology without a Protestant community, but not a Jewish religion without Jews." His variant of Zionism took a further step, insisting that the interests of the people must take priority over the moral and theological claims of Jewish tradition. [172] When informed that this outlook bore a striking resemblance to the most radically politicized forms of liberation theology, Podhoretz unsurprisingly disliked the analogy without finding any way to refute it. Except for his antipathy toward the leftist politics of liberation theology, he lacked any basis to criticize even its most politicized variants, since his own argument operated by the same logic. [173]

He took his longest pause when asked how he viewed the intensifying debate about "global democracy" as a foreign policy doctrine. The globalist crusade was his own. He was its rightful champion. For twenty years, he had proclaimed that America needed an ideological mission transcending any particular calculation of its national interest. The American mission was to defend and promote democracy throughout the world. With the end of the Cold War, neoconservatives such as Ben Wattenberg, Charles Krauthammer, Joshua Muravchik, and Gregory Fossedal were now claiming that this mission represented the positive side of anticommunism. This was no time to come home. Having won the Cold War, the United States needed to do something with its victory. America could use its moral authority and its power to export democracy and establish a new Pax Americana. Democratic globalism was the worthy ideological successor to anticommunism. [174]

Podhoretz nodded. Yes, this was his theme. He had rung this bell the loudest during the closing generation of the Cold War. He noted that Decter was speaking out on the subject. She was urging the Committee for the Free World to make the transition from anticommunism to democratic globalism. He counted himself among the new Wilsonians, but his heart wasn't in it. Someone else would have to be the lightning rod for democratic globalism. Someone else would have to write the manifestos, draw the ideological fault lines, and, especially, defend the movement from its critics. "I don't have any writing projects in mind on this," he reported. His silence in 1990 was broken only by Melvin Lasky's request for a puff piece on "who was right about communism" and by Patrick Buchanan's seemingly anti-Semitic rumblings during the early days of the Persian Gulf crisis. [175]

The war against Iraq briefly threatened to revive his old enthusiasms. Shortly before America's air strikes began, Podhoretz reminded the wavering realpolitikers that "oil *is* the lifeblood of our civilization and any threat to the supply of it *is* a threat to our way of life." This was a war to defend vital American interests. It was inevitable, he warned, that a new peace party would emerge, "with its constant harpings on body bags."[176] Every war brought them out, and this war would be no different. Now that the Soviet threat had subsided, the only question was whether America would be "permanently debellicized and forever unmanned" by the dovish sentiments of feminized intellectuals and activists. Podhoretz appealed to Nietzsche for moral authority. The notion that nothing was worth killing and dying for was the mark of a slave, he recited. He delicately refrained from recalling that this was Nietzsche's reason for condemning Christian morality. [177]

Podhoretz journeyed to Israel for the first week of the war. On the night the bombing began, he wrote in his journal: "I can't remember when I last tasted such exhilaration." He enthused that an American victory would bring

> a new surge of confidence in America—in American technology, so trium-
> phantly on display in our planes and their smart munitions; in American
> wisdom and courage, so vividly manifest in the very act of going to war; in
> American leadership, so brilliantly exhibited in the coalition politics
> through which George Bush has brought us to this point. Goodbye to the
> decline-of-America theories; goodbye to the idea that Japan and Germany are
> outstripping us; goodbye to the isolationists of the Left and Right who
> have come out of the woodwork since the end of the cold war: goodbye to all
> that. And goodbye, at long last, to Vietnam. [178]

His magazine, like the president, would celebrate the war for the next several months—though in Podhoretz's case, the celebration was chastened by his awareness that the war brought new pressures on Israel to accommodate the Palestinians.[179] The rout of Iraq lifted Podhoretz's spirits, but it didn't breathe new life into politics. Iraq was not Vietnam. The recent phase of politicization was still over, and Podhoretz went back to his cultural memoirs.

William Phillips once remarked that it often seemed as though Podhoretz had been created by the Left. He claimed that Podhoretz would have nothing to write about "if left-liberals did not feed him with their illusions about Soviet communism, the Third World, or the P. L. O."[180] At the outset of a new era, Podhoretz insisted that Phillips was wrong. He welcomed the end of ideology. "I started out as a literary critic, and maybe I'll end up as one," he mused. His writings in the early 1990s tried to make this transition.[181] His chief difficulty in making the shift, however, was that even his literary imagination had long been consumed by his ideological preoccupations. Podhoretz's literary writings during the 1980s typically weighed the anticommunist credentials of modern novelists. This preoccupation worked with certain topics. His insightful essay on Aleksandr Solzhenitsyn made a compelling case for the superiority of Solzhenitsyn's nonfiction works over his novels.[182] More often, however, Podhoretz reduced his subjects to position-taking. His treatment of George Orwell focused on the burning question whether Orwell would have been a neoconservative in the 1980s. Though Orwell was unfortunately a democratic socialist in his own time, Podhoretz was certain that he would have been a *Commentary* writer in the 1980s because only the neoconservatives were serious anticommunists.[183] Albert Camus, on the other hand, would not have made a good neoconservative. "The truths of *The Rebel* were on the whole the truths of the Right," Podhoretz judged, but Camus unfortunately failed to defend these truths because of his "cowardice and hypocrisy." Camus' fatal conceit was his cowardly insistence that literature transcended political lines. He therefore failed to join the struggle against political radicalism.[184]

The same mistake marred the otherwise promising work of Milan Kundera. "I am appalled that you have been cooperating with your own kidnappers," Podhoretz wrote to Kundera in 1984, referring to liberal book reviewers. Kundera was filling his implicitly anticommunist novels with sex scenes and abstract discussions of being. He was adding to the damage by making "irritable" remarks to interviewers that scorned politicized writing. Podhoretz could understand why Kundera would want to eschew politics, but to actually do it was an act of cowardice. The New Class was already celebrating Kundera's work as literature that "transcended political and ideological differences." Podhoretz implored him to stir up his courage. "I beg you to stop giving aid and encouragement to the cultural powers who are using some of your own words to prevent your work from helping to alert a demoralized West to the dangers it faces from a self-imposed Yalta of its own," he pleaded. [185] Like Camus, Kundera was forsaking the one mission worthy of his efforts in the name of literature. It was the same fault that Podhoretz had scorned in his teacher, Lionel Trilling.

Sidney Blumenthal captured the aesthetic. Taken as a whole, he observed, Podhoretz's literary writings represented "a tremendous, though narrow, feat of literary imagination." They reproduced, with impressive exactitude, the faded literary sensibility of American Stalinism. [186] Just as the American Stalinists of the 1930s judged every work of literature by its politics, and especially by its position toward the Soviet Union, so also, with few exceptions, did Podhoretz. The prospect of writing literary criticism or anything else without the devouring Soviet threat to confer seriousness on his work was a deflating turn. Podhoretz's later writings resumed his remaining themes, but with diminishing energy and influence. [187] The ravages of feminism and gay rights would make poor substitutes for the communist threat.

5

The Renewal of Whiggery:
Michael Novak

Neoconservativism has roots other than the New York Intellectual milieu. For one of the movement's chief theorists, neoconservatism represents a return—after a radical detour—to the values of an upwardly mobile working-class Pennsylvania family. In one of his periodic attempts to explain his transformation from New Left to neoconservative critic, Michael Novak has written, "If I had been knocked from a horse by a blinding light on a single memorable day, it would be easier to say. Instead, it was quite gradual, through examining my own left-wing presuppositions one by one. Underneath this questioning, perhaps, lay a pursuit of self-knowledge, a drive to be faithful to my family and roots, to be myself."[1] His prolonged process of self-discovery was characteristically disclosed, at every stage, in print. His most important discovery along the way was that his friends in progressive church circles "were simply not my people."[2] As a youth, his father had told him never to bet against Notre Dame or the United States. He would later make his distinctive mark on neoconservativism as a celebrant of the American idea. It was as a refugee from what he called the progressive "tyranny of acceptable moral lines" that Novak would come to promote a Whiggish philosophy of democratic capitalism.[3]

He was born into an ethnic, working-class neighborhood in the downtown section of Johnstown, Pennsylvania, in 1933. His grandparents came to the United States from villages in the Tatra Mountains in Slovakia, not far from the southern Polish border. Novak's father worked for an insurance company, and in 1940 the family moved up the hill to Southmont, "where the Americans lived." Three moves later—following the elder Novak's promotions—they resettled in Johnstown, shortly after Michael Novak went off to seminary. Against the opposition of his father, who didn't want Michael to become a priest, he entered the junior seminary program at Notre Dame's Holy Cross Seminary. Novak was uncertain of his call to the priesthood, but determined to put his religious vocation to the test. He was fourteen years old.

He gave twelve years to the question, studying at Stonehill College, the Gregorian University, and Catholic University of America before finally deciding against ordination in 1960. Two factors were determinative for him. Novak's prolonged struggle with the prospect of committing himself to lifelong celibacy eventually drove him to accept, six months before his scheduled ordination, that his desire to be married and have children was stronger than his desire for ordination. During the closing years of the pre–Vatican II era, he also reflected on his prospects for an intellectual career if he became a priest. "Chastity was difficult for me; obedience even more so," he later explained. "I've always believed that a priest should teach and defend church doctrine. The problem for me was that I also wanted to be a writer, which required a degree of intellectual independence I couldn't have as a priest."[4] He chose independence, and shortly afterward wrote to the editors at Commonweal magazine, telling them he hoped to be "introduced to the world" when he visited their offices. James Finn recalled that before they could decide how they would respond to this unusual overture, Novak showed up, "young, quietly energetic, openly inquiring, interested—it seemed—in everything."[5] The books started coming the following year, beginning with a novel about the ordination of a young seminarian, published shortly after Novak enrolled in Harvard University's graduate program in philosophy.[6]

He had it in mind to become a socially engaged philosopher/novelist in the tradition of François Mauriac, Jean-Paul Sartre, and Albert Camus, though he was aware that Harvard's philosophy curriculum emphasized logic and language analysis. Novak assumed that Harvard's positivism could not be more narrow or lifeless than the Thomistic scholasticism he had learned in Catholic universities, but this assumption was soon corrected by his professors. Harvard's conception of philosophy was disillusioning to him. In reaction, Novak sought refuge at Harvard Divinity School, where he continued his studies and began to write for Commonweal, The New Republic, and other journals on the need to rescue the Catholic church from the Vatican's "nonhistorical orthodoxy." His proposals prefigured many of the reforms of Vatican Council II. Shortly after his marriage to an artist, Karen Laub, in 1963, Novak went to Rome to report on the second session of Vatican Council II. His honeymoon and subsequent trip to Rome produced articles for Commonweal, The National Catholic Reporter, and Time magazines, as well as an influential book on the council's significance.

The Open Church observed that Roman Catholicism was finally opening its windows to the modern world. Novak claimed the Church had been stuck in a nonhistorical memory of its past. Catholic doctrine recycled a frozen Roman theology that was impervious to developments in modern science, history, and philosophy. Catholic social doctrine failed to grasp or appreciate the achievements of modern industrialism, democracy, and pluralism, largely because the church itself had been ghettoized by the overweening influence of its Italian and Spanish traditions. Roman Catholicism needed to learn from the experiences of Catholics who knew the blessings of modernity. Having opened itself to the modern world, Novak argued, the church now needed to learn, especially, from the American experience. America was the first modern country, the harbinger of the world's future. Not for the last time, he insisted that the success of the American Experiment necessitated corrections in Catholic teaching.[7]

Novak became friends with ecumenical Protestant theologian Robert McAfee Brown at the council, which Brown attended as a Protestant observer. With Brown's assistance, Novak was offered a position in the Special Program in Humanities (later called the Religion Department) at Stanford University. Despite his lack of a doctorate, he thus became the first Roman Catholic to secure a teaching position in Stanford's Religion Department, as he had earlier become the first Catholic to serve on the editorial boards of the country's leading liberal Protestant journals, *The Christian Century* and *Christianity and Crisis*.

In 1964, Novak's younger brother Dick, a twenty-seven-year-old priest, was murdered in Dacca, East Pakistan. Father Richard was stabbed to death by a gang of teen-aged river pirates as he departed from a ferry, joining thousands of others killed in the Moslem–Hindu riots. "Something in me died with him, a certain unreality of sorts," Novak later wrote. "The absurdity, the unfairness, the harshness of reality ceased being theoretical." His brother had specialized in Arabic and Islam, reasoning that Islam was the major religion least understood by Christians. His death taught his older brother "that death has its own hour, plans are futile, one must do what one must—and, in a way, quite as coldly as reality itself is cold."[8]

Novak was writing *Belief and Unbelief* at the time of his brother's death. His grief did not produce the book, but it intensified its meaning to him. *Belief and Unbelief* reflected Novak's personal crisis of faith, which had begun during his seminary career. The book contended that belief in God could be sustained through a philosophy of self-knowledge. Belief, Novak argued, was in part the search for personal identity. To believe in God was to "accept the universe as radically personal." He suggested that those who could not construe the universe as personal were often not as different from believers as they assumed. Believers and nonbelievers were both voyagers in the darkness. "Among us thrives a brotherhood of inquiry and concern, even of those who disagree in interpreting the meaning of inquiry—the meaning of human spirit—in the darkness in which we live.[9]

Belief and Unbelief was published in 1965. Novak's conversion to political radicalism began the same year at Stanford. His first articles on Vietnam tentatively supported America's intervention. He was disinclined to bet against America. Novak observed that most middle-class Christians were impervious to the massive violence that was required to maintain their way of life. But while they scarcely noticed the violence upon which their privileges depended, he noted, they were often, at the same time, quite fearful about the use of violence by others. Novak based his Niebuhrian case for military intervention on this irony. Since force was "the inevitable base of international life," he reasoned, America's military escalation in Vietnam could be justified so long as political methods serving American national interests took precedence over military objectives.[10]

The following year, however, after the United States bombed the oil fields of Hanoi and Haiphong, he began to fear that the nature of the war itself was changing. Though most of his students at Stanford were conservative, Novak was surrounded by friends who, as he then put it, "abhor the war and oppose it vociferously." He struggled with the question whether, in order to avert an immense evil, America was not committing a greater evil through the way it was fighting the war. The question drove him into the antiwar movement. Novak announced his opposition to the war in January 1967, arguing that America's intervention had become an exercise in mechanized terror. America's central political objective was becoming obscured by its massive use of napalm, B-52 strato-fortresses, and other instruments of mass destruction "so out of proportion with the political problem . . . that it appears to be self-defeating." The same year, he denounced the notion that one could "rebuild a country by pounding it with bombs, defoliating it, razing its villages, scarring its people with napalm." The course that America had chosen, he argued, "a course of total militarization, destroys everything: the landscape, the people, the hopes for the future, the possibilities of any but a craven capitulation from others, and all pride in ourselves. When one has chosen a wrong course, whether by accident or by lack of foresight or by inertia, the only remedy is to change one's course."[11] On those moral grounds, Novak joined the antiwar movement, and then swiftly moved to the movement's radical wing.

He lost his remaining link with liberal reformism when Robert Kennedy was assassinated. Novak worked for Eugene McCarthy in the 1968 Democratic primary campaign, but switched to Kennedy after the Ne-

braska primary. He disliked the effete liberal style of McCarthy's campaign and was attracted to Kennedy's emphasis on building a coalition of
working-class whites and blacks. With the death of the last mainstream
political figure who could speak the language of his ethnic/Catholic/
increasingly radical style, Novak moved further left. For the next two
years, when such attitudes were most fashionable, he epitomized the
social type of the liberal-bashing New Leftist. His writings repeated the
kind of abuse for "corporate liberalism" that Stokely Carmichael and Tom
Hayden had recently popularized. Novak's first attacks on the New Class
came from the Left. His major work of this period, A Theology for Radical
Politics, was littered with antiliberal sneers borrowed from Carmichael and
Hayden, including Hayden's declaration that "it is the liberal way of life
and mind that represents the evil of America."

Novak upped the ante on this pronouncement, declaiming that "the
enemy in America, then, is the tyrannical and indifferent majority: the
good people, the churchgoers, the typical Americans."[12] He skewered the
alienated mediocrity and hollowness of Americans, which was reflected in
"the vacant eyes watching television and drinking beer; the tired eyes of
the men on the commuter train; the efficient eyes of the professor and the
manager; the sincere eyes of the television politician." He insisted that
Americans were bored, apathetic, manipulated, and violent, knowing not
what they were but only what they were useful for. "One could cry out in
anguish that the suffering and sacrifices of past generations have come to
this," he wailed. "A grown man with a can of beer finds his chief fulfillment
in a televised game, watched by thirty million others, and believes our
land free, brave, and just."[13] Having announced at the outset that he
wanted "to bring a radical Christian theology to the support of the student
movement," Novak titillated his readers with near-summonses to revolutionary violence. "Against armed ranks of policemen, a grenade is more
serious and effective than calling names," he observed. Though the
moment for armed revolution in America had not yet arrived, he counseled, "those who serve now in the Army may one day be grateful to have
learned military skills."[14] That must have quickened the heartbeats of
alienated sophomores.

For all of its posturing, however, A Theology for Radical Politics was
driven by Novak's genuine moral opposition to "the slow advance of the
United States, its military bases, its economic interests, and its political
policies into the inner lives of other nations."[15] His trip to Vietnam in 1967
informed the book's moral passion against America's imperial maneuvers.
Novak argued that America's basic foreign policy values had become
distorted over the past generation. Rather than assume the priority of

national self-determination, the United States in recent years had subordinated this principle to the interest of stabilizing its own dominant position in the world order. If this argument was naive about America's earlier foreign policy record, it was nonetheless significant for its emphasis on the primacy of national self-determination and for its claim that America had become "the world's foremost counterrevolutionary power."[16] The irony of America's intervention in Vietnam, Novak asserted, was that America was ostensibly defending freedom and justice in Vietnam without any conception of what these terms meant or could mean in a Vietnamese context.

America was "defending" Vietnam while massively disregarding "the psychic tissue of Vietnamese culture." Because it was so certain of its self-designated role as Defender of the Free World, America projected its power throughout the world without any regard for the ways that other nations viewed their own pasts or the role of the United States. "With the confidence of having universalist principles on our side, we ruthlessly disrupted homes, villages, and provinces in the name of our ideals, our conceptions, our methods," Novak observed. America's intervention in Vietnam was immoral because it combined American ignorance of Vietnamese culture with a strategy that ensured massive destruction and death. "We cannot be in Vietnam for the sake of the Vietnamese, but for our own version of righteousness," he concluded.[17]

In 1968, Harris Wofford launched an experimental branch of the State University of New York. Wofford was a co-founder of the Peace Corps and would later represent Pennsylvania in the U.S. Senate. His college made an unlikely staging ground for a Senate career, however. SUNY–Old Westbury was conceived in the spirit of the times. It was meant to be an experimental college in the vanguard of educational reform and innovation. Wofford invited Novak to join Old Westbury's faculty. For Novak, moving to Old Westbury was an act of committment to the Movement. It also marked the beginning of the end of his radical phase. Novak later recalled that the first hundred students admitted to Old Westbury were so radical that, in one survey, all but one agreed that electoral politics was a bourgeois fraud. The exception planned to vote for Eugene McCarthy. Novak confirmed their prejudices, claiming that Hubert Humphrey was not worth voting for, even if Richard Nixon thereby won the upcoming election. His students and colleagues soon gave him second thoughts, however, about his radical turn.

The demonstrations against Wofford began shortly after classes opened. Novak was shocked when a faculty member smashed the door of the bourgeois bookstore and permitted students to steal from it. Another professor proved his thoroughgoing egalitarianism by holding his seminar about itself. The "what" of religious faith, however, was never quite there. The author's myth was obscured. His own theological position was shrouded in a haze of quotes and vague ruminations about faith-as-mystery. *Ascent of the Mountain* ended with a long list of recommended guides to the horizon of modern Christian theology. Before long, he would find himself attacking nearly every theologian on the list.

THE UNMELTABLE ETHNIC

The pivotal book of his early career was published the same year, in 1971. *The Rise of the Unmeltable Ethnics* contained the lessons of Novak's campaign experiences. It also reflected his feelings about being an alien in an academic culture dominated by WASPs and Jews. Novak argued that the myth of the American melting pot was imposed by a dominant WASP culture to reinforce its own values and social position. Homogeneity was not a reality in America, or even a worthy goal, he claimed. It was a mythical instrument of domination that required a "reconstruction of the self" for ethnics.

Novak demythologized this ruling mythology. The melting pot image not only denied the reality of ethnic diversity in America, it also rationalized cultural chauvinism. Having written several books on finding one's identity, Novak discovered his ethnicity. The notion of homogeneity taught in American schools and proclaimed by America's dominant institutions, he argued, was a Northern European construct that sacralized the values of WASP elites, whose culture was repressed, rationalistic, moralistic, reformist, obsessed with cleanliness, and above all, individualistic. It loosened the bonds of family ties to enable individuals to become successful. It was devoted to material success and to controlling self and society through reason. "In all God's world, is there anything as cool as a Yale lawyer across the carpeted office of a major philanthropic fund?" Novak wrote. "How could any other race ever fashion its psyche to that style?" He complained that the WASPs universalized their cultural eccentricities and their Lockean politics. They were "the soap and water experts of the world" who self-righteously imposed their antiseptic sterility and individualism on America's ethnic immigrants.

The imposition was resented. For ethnics, to be Americanized was to be humiliated. It was to fashion their psyche to a suffocating style. "Immigrants from southern and eastern Europe had to learn order, discipline, neatness, cleanliness, reserve," Novak explained. "They had to learn to modulate emotion, to control passion, to hold their hands still, to hold classes underneath a classroom table. "Think of this as childish vulgar Marxism," Novak later recalled. "The grown-up version has uncannily repeated itself in every Communist Party victory."[18] Finding himself outflanked on the far Left, he eventually rebelled against students who demanded no standards or authorities or requirements. He became provost of an intra-college disciplines college, trying to redirect the moral energies of his students away from the anti-intellectualism and lewdness of their New Left culture. It was a deeply alienating experience. Novak's five years at Old Westbury tamed his passion for a revolution of consciousness.

A friend described him, during this period, as someone whose temperament was conservative but who thought himself into left-wing positions. By 1970, Novak's distaste for most of the antiwar movement moved him to temper his positions as well. Two years after he had repeated the New Left's most obnoxious rhetoric in his "theology" for radical politics, he began to look for a way to become involved again in mainstream liberal politics. His answer came in a call from Wofford's former Peace Corps mate, Sargent Shriver, who asked Novak to be his speechwriter in a national campaign for Democratic congressional candidates. Novak thus spent the summer of 1970 traveling with Shriver, meeting thousands of the vacant-eyed Americans he had ridiculed in his writings. He later recalled that the humanity and generosity of the people he met across the country made him ashamed of the literary snobbery that filled his writings about them. "Comparing the actual American people to the vision of America cherished in the literary culture I then took part in, I was subverted," he wrote. "I came to think there was more health in the people than in their literary elites, including me."[19] The experience was subversive for him, since the kind of progressivism he had adopted assumed that most Americans were backward and stupid, if not morally corrupt.

The same year he published a novel about the spiritual and sexual odyssey of a Slavic ex-seminarian from a Pennsylvania steel town. *Naked I Leave* chronicled Jon Svoboda's sexual adventures and his loss of faith while sojourning from Greenwich Village to a nudist island on the Riviera to journalistic duty at Vatican Council II. The book's rather graphic preoccupation with sex moved Novak to caution that it was fiction masked as autobiography, and not, "as enemies will suggest," autobiography masked as fiction.[20] *The Experience of Nothingness*, published the same year, covered the same confessional turf at a higher level of abstraction. This richly perceptive meditation was ostensibly concerned with the destructive power of America's myths of "rationality" and "realism," but between the lines, Novak's own disillusionment with the New Left and his crisis of moral and religious faith showed through. The book scrounged for consolation. "Granted that I am empty, alone, without guides, direction, will, or obligations, how shall I live?" Novak asked. He answered that the experience of nothingness provided the opportunity to create oneself. The subjective experience of nothingness was a primal experience—like St. John of the Cross's dark night of the soul—which one could survive by creating an edifying mythology out of personal commitments to honesty, freedom, courage, and community. "The experience of nothingness liberates persons from conventional institutional demands; it desacralizes the status quo," Novak explained. "Thus it is extraordinarily capable of breeding revolutionaries. . . . The revolutionary who has learned in the night to cherish reflective choice and the drive to question, and to regard institutions as myths, will not expect more of them than they can provide."[21] His books were still pushing the revolution, though his political convictions were plainly in doubt, as was his faith.

Novak's most powerful works were written during this period, when he was most confused about his own moral, political, and religious beliefs. His reflection on religious experience, *Ascent of the Mountain, Flight of the Dove*, offered a highly imaginative approach to religious studies, anticipating the distinctive themes of what was later called narrative theology. The book took an existential approach to theology in a strikingly personal, though often rambling and elusive, voice. "There is a new, odd form of 'alienation' spreading throughout modern society," Novak observed. "Insofar as the ideal of personal autonomy is realized, the social system itself seems to elude the capacity of individual persons (or even associations of persons) to make the system 'congruent' with their own sense of reality, stories, symbols. The more autonomy they pursue, the less their hold upon their culture, their society, and its institutions. The more their culture, their society, and their institutions are brought into 'congruence' with their own sense of reality, stories, symbols, the less freedom seems to be allowed to those whose sense of reality, stories, and symbols diverge from their own."

Modernity was seen as an emptying, deracinating force. *Belief and Unbelief* had conceived religion as a search for personal identity in the face of modernity. *Ascent of the Mountain* leaned heavily on the slippery notions of myth, symbol, and story to defend religious forms of story-making. Religious story-making made greater sense than its rival discourses did of "the still darkness of the night and the pure dark desire: the drive to live, the longing to become, the fierce will to be." This was the natural territory of religion, Novak argued. The more that one penetrated the depths of one's identity, "the more reverential one becomes."[22] This explained why religious myths were deeper and more profound than America's myths the muscles of their face placid, to find food and body odors offensive, to quieten their voices, to present themselves as coolly reasonable." America assaulted their natural earthiness, their passion, and their blood-rich culture. Ethnic immigrants, he observed, retained thicker family and kinship ties than WASP Americans. The thickness of ethnic culture was a bulwark against utopianism and other deracinated WASP enthusiasms. The blood-thick family-style politics of American ethnics was usually called machine politics, he noted, "but if anything in America is a 'machine,' it is reform politics: impersonal, procedural, moralistic, abstract, constructed by rules." He warned that the conceits of America's dominant WASP elites were stirring a backlash. The value systems of Southern and Eastern European immigrants were as complex and as worthy of respect as the WASP values imposed upon them. America's ethnics weren't buying the melting pot anymore.[23]

A new cultural pluralism was therefore needed. "In the country clubs, as city executives, established families, industrialists, owners, lawyers, masters of etiquette, college presidents, dominators of the military, fund-raisers, members of blue ribbon communities, realtors, brokers, deans, sheriffs—it is the cumulative power and distinctive styles of WASPs that the rest of us have had to learn in order to survive," Novak declared. "WASPs have never had to celebrate Columbus Day or march down Fifth Avenue wearing green. Every day has been their day in America. No more." A new radicalism was brewing. A new coalition between ethnics and blacks threatened to expose the conceits of American liberalism. Most liberals were far more concerned about prejudice against blacks than against ethnics, Novak observed. This fact was consistent with liberalism's rootage in WASP culture. America's "elite Protestant politics" pitted blacks and Catholic ethnics against each other in a struggle for economic survival. The resentments of blacks and ethnics toward each other were therefore understandable, but wrongly focused. A different kind of politics would refocus their resentments. "Ethnics can understand the strategic interests of blacks," he assured. "Hence, to place costs and needs on a frank trading basis would no doubt constitute a step forward."[24]

Novak proposed that blacks and ethnics establish "a decent quid pro quo" between each other. They could then become allies in a struggle against their common enemy. "The enemy is educated, wealthy, power-ful—and sometimes wears liberal, sometimes radical, sometimes conserva-tive disguise," he asserted. "The enemy is concentrated power." An Ameri-can progressivism worthy of the name would include the ethnic working class constituencies spurned by the Democratic party's overeducated New Class operatives. It would forge a progressive alternative to the mean-spirited ethnic politics that was emerging in many American cities and epitomized by Frank Rizzo's candidacy in Philadelphia. It would attack the real enemy by affirming the new cultural pluralism.

Though he worked the following year on George McGovern's presidential campaign staff, Novak worried throughout the campaign that the party's cultural liberalism was alienating its traditional working-class constituencies. One incident on the 1972 campaign trail was symptomatic. The incident occurred at the Joliet Steel mill in Illinois. While campaigning for the McGovern–Shriver ticket, Novak noticed that Shriver was getting a frosty reception from the steelworkers—who looked like Novak's relatives. He looked around to see why the familiar-looking Slavics were treating Shriver so coldly, and discovered that Shriver's local advance person was "a young woman wearing a miniskirt, high white boots, and a see-through blouse, with a large proabortion button on her collar."[25] For him, the scene confirmed everything he had warned about in his by-then controversial book.

The Rise of the Unmeltable Ethnics refashioned Novak's radicalism, focusing on the "hegemony of economic power" wielded by the WASP establishment. He excoriated America's "monstrous" pursuit of economic growth, which required "thinking of the earth as a planet to be conquered and despoiled." The existing system subjected the working person "to poor and dispirited educational systems, a horizonless income peak, [and] a constant stream of silent contempt."[26] The first task for a worthy progressive movement was therefore to unmask the ideology of modernization that rationalized the ruling class's disproportionate power. The second was to forge an alliance with the movement's natural allies in the working class.

The book offered a suggestive, albeit highly literary vision of a decentralized social order in which economic institutions and processes would be reintegrated into the more humane patterns of community and family life. It also contained interesting and often wildly opinionated discussions of ethnic sensibilities. Explaining that most white ethnics, like most blacks, did not share the WASP preoccupation with guilt, Novak wrote, "White ethnics refuse to feel guilty. Guilt is not their style. They react to guilt feelings with anger. They do not imagine life as an effort to live up to abstract ideals like justice, equality, fairness, reasonableness, etc.; but as a struggle to survive. The virtues of survival have most appeal to them: compassion, forgiveness, mutual help. They tend to be cynical about the language of high ideals, but open to the argument that someone else needs help."[27] The book's strategic argument called the Democratic party to broaden its political base beyond the New Politics emphasis on blacks, women, students, and the New Class. The following year, he founded the Ethnic Millions Political Action Committee (EMPAC) to mobilize ethnics into a progressive political force. He later served for several years as editor of *Slovakia,* the annual publication of the Slovak League of America.

Much of *The Rise of the Unmeltable Ethnics* tried to explain the sensibilities of ethnics to its New Class and student readership. But while it was offered as in-house progressive criticism, the book's celebratory attitude toward America's ethnic communities struck many of its readers as a veiled attack on McGovern-style liberalism (which, in fact, it was). While it retained much of the New Left's critique of the personal and social ravages of modernization, the book was criticized in the liberal press for its implicit antifeminism, its electoral opportunism, its appeals to envy and resentment, and its cultural conservatism, as well as its occasionally sweeping generalizations about blacks and ethnics. Observing that ethnics were increasingly alienated from the Democratic party, Novak offered himself as the model of "an intellectual who tries to give voice to their instincts."

The reply by Garry Wills in *The New York Times Book Review* was piercing: "So quickly does listening to one's blood become a matter of sniffing around after loose votes." Wills blasted the book. He found it dismaying that a moral man could write such an "immoral book," and charged that Novak's "bright aphorisms and seductive phrases" were being used to demonstrate the "social uses of hatred." The apparent purpose of the book, Wills argued, was to teach Archie Bunker new hatreds and thus "extend the already vast repertoire of American resentments." His prime example was a typical Novakism: "There is nothing that so infuriates me as the disguised aggressions of a Quaker." Novak's crowning achievement was to prove that civility was an Anglo-Saxon deceit. Like other volumes in its rapidly growing field, his book invented new hatreds and resentments as he went along, "working his gentle soul into Zorba-the-Greek exhibitionism."[28]

That set the tone. The reviews that followed Wills's review were so insulting that Novak took to his bed. He was repulsed by the vulgar radicalism of the New Left; he disliked the effete liberalism of the New Class; his experiences in the Shriver campaign had reawakened his identification with middle America; he had offered a strategy for the Democratic party to reclaim its working-class constituencies—and now the guardians of American progressivism were assuring him that these sentiments had no place in their ranks. He later described the experience as an excommunication. Novak protested his expulsion for several months, until the 1972 election. The McGovern debacle helped him accept it. The enormity of McGovern's defeat confirmed his warnings about the alienating conceits of the New Class. Middle America was wiser than the intellectuals. Novak reasoned that the Democrats could be saved only if their humiliation drove them to repent. He therefore joined forces with Norman Podhoretz and others to form the Coalition for a Democratic Majority. The neoconservatives would try to recapture the party from the coalition of liberals, feminists, blacks, neopacifists, and intellectuals who had ruined it.

COMING HOME: NOVAK'S TRANSITION TO CONSERVATISM

Novak accepted his excommunication and came home. He aligned himself with the neoconservatives at the moment that neoconservatism was emerging as a phenomenon worth naming. His identification with the neoconservatives posed immediate problems for him, however, since he was intellectually unprepared for the transition. He later recalled, "Though I slowly was becoming deradicalized, the information in my head during these years was very often exclusively derived from writers of the far left."[29] *Ascent of the Mountain* had argued that America's political institutions were frequently overpowered by its economic system, which "in fact, seems to govern the political system." American foreign policy, Novak claimed, was governed by corporate interests and by the Pentagon's own bureaucratic interests, which largely determined "what 'the realities' of American life are."[30] Three years later, Novak was still denouncing "the rush of money and celebrity and conglomerated industries" that dominated American life.[31] *Choosing Our King* replayed the 1972 election in an ironical mode, but Novak repeated his earlier broadsides against corporate capitalism. He complained that capitalist America was making room for racial minorities, but not for ethnics. He opposed affirmative action mainly because it discriminated against ethnics. He still opposed capitalism ostensibly for the same reason—but really because anticapitalism was the only political faith he knew. Though he had turned away from leftist politics, Novak's writings in the early 1970s repeated leftist socioeconomic arguments because, as he later explained, his mind was stuffed with them and he couldn't find an alternative mentor or tradition that satisfied him.[32]

The first figure he considered was Reinhold Niebuhr. Novak remarked in 1972 that although Niebuhr had died only the year before, it seemed like ten. The social enthusiasms of the past decade made Niebuhr's once-towering work seem remote and irrelevant. But Niebuhr's message was as relevant as ever. "The new moralism we see all around us is all too like the old moralism, against which Niebuhr directed the central energies of his life," he observed. "In many ways it is as if he had lived and worked in vain."[33]

The old and new moralism both looked forward to the greening of America. It was America's "most ineradicable national fantasy," Novak declared, to believe that gains toward the common good could be attained through greater rationality or the growth of religiously inspired goodwill. This was the idealistic faith that Niebuhr had spent his career trying to destroy. The same faith was now being revived as though he had never lived. Then as now, the moralists failed to comprehend "the brutal character of the behavior of all human collectives and the power of self-interest and collective egoism in all inter-group relations."[34] This theme connected all of Niebuhr's writings, ranging from his Christian Marxism in the 1920s and 1930s to his Cold War liberalism of the 1950s and 1960s. Niebuhr's contempt for liberal idealism linked his early Marxism and his later liberal anticommunism. Progressivism was a form of bad faith. For Niebuhr, the common good was to be sought not through appeals to reason or goodwill, but by restraining human egotism. For Novak, this was a reorienting maxim.

The McGovern campaign epitomized everything Novak was turning against. Novak worked for McGovern after his first choice—Edmund Muskie—dropped out of the race. Two months before the election, however, he was already lambasting the "sentimental effusions of a peculiarly American idealism" that McGovern proclaimed. The old moralism condemned by Niebuhr was taking over the Democratic party in the form of a new, feminized, guilt-ridden liberalism. Novak especially disliked the new liberalism's emphasis on racial politics. "White racism" was outstripping "McCarthyism" as the favorite liberal smear term, he complained. Under the pressure of this moralistic revival, even veteran Niebuhrians such as John Bennett were caving in, urging *Christianity and Crisis* to give a platform "to those who push the white man hardest, for we see that white racism is a deeper cultural sickness than we realized in the early 60's." Novak argued that this was the old moralistic sickness, fueled by an unsupportable sense of guilt. The new moralism was more potent than the moralism of Niebuhr's time, however, because the new moralism was not confined to mainline Protestants. This time Jews and Catholics were equally afflicted. Novak turned to the concept of the New Class for an explanation.

The notion of the New Class had recently been revived by David Bazelon and appropriated, for different purposes, in Michael Harrington's

Toward a Democratic Left.[35] Harrington observed that by virtue of its education and work experience, the New Class was predisposed toward social planning. It was therefore in a position to forge alliances with working-class, unionized, and poor people—or to become their sophisticated enemy.[36] The New Class could use its education to create a good society or to protect its own new privileges. Harrington pushed for the former choice. He argued that instead of opting for a narrowly self-interested politics, the New Class could become the "conscience constituency" of American society. His argument echoed James MacGregor Burns's hope that the New Class would create an American politics that emphasized "issues of the mind and the heart, and not just of the stomach."[37] To regard education merely as a means for personal advancement, Harrington said, was to overlook the possibility that education could also expose students to ideas, broaden their horizons, and inspire feelings of solidarity with people less fortunate than themselves. The liberalism of the future needed to build upon such experiences.[38]

This was exactly the kind of idealism that had begun to turn Novak's stomach. "There is something beguilingly deceptive in this self-flattery of educated professionals," he wrote. The notion of a conscience constituency was repulsive to a Niebuhrian. Harrington's vision was coming true, but not for the reasons he thought. The liberalism of the New Class was cloaked with a suffocatingly moralistic aura. Novak conceded that the new liberalism's chief concerns—civil rights, poverty, and the Vietnam War—were morally justified. The problem was that the moral righteousness of the new liberals concealed their class interests. The moral legitimacy of its causes permitted the New Class "to conceal its own lust for power and its own class interests, at least from itself." The deepest interests of the New Class were less than moral.[39]

The New Class endlessly complained about its alienation from the present system, Novak observed, without acknowledging that its own advancement and prestige required an expanding federal government committed to social change. The local patronage jobs of machine politics were being nationalized by social engineers eager to do something meaningful with their degrees. Their interests were further revealed by the kind of good they performed, which was usually done at the expense of others. The New Class supported school busing, for example, "but its own children will not suffer loss of status, or quality education, or wealth, or safety by being bused." The New Class would run busing programs for the sake of racial integration and equality, but it would not lose what the lower classes lost along the way. The New Class was likewise managing to keep its own sons out of Vietnam.

The New Class also had special psychic interests. "It somehow feels it must exorcise its complicity in various social evils: white racism, militarism, imperialism, male chauvinism, consumerism, affluence," Novak reported. The rest of the country was paying the price for the New Class's need to escape the moral ambiguities of life "and to be thoroughly good." The New Class dismissed Niebuhr's realism as dated and was therefore able to ignore his chief theme, "that claims on the part of groups to represent 'conscience,' 'morality,' and 'principle' must be exposed for what they are: disguises for naked power and raw interest."[40] Conscience was an individual phenomenon; the moralities it produced were therefore for individuals. Groups only appealed to morality to cover their collective interests. This categorical schematism was not entirely fair to Niebuhr, but it perfectly expressed Novak's emerging "realism." Liberal moralism produced unhealthy individuals and even worse politics.

Novak spent the early 1970s trying to overcome his own moralism and idealistic yearnings. He discovered that his idealism was shaped by intertwining religious, moral, and ideological roots. These were the influences that had driven him to compare capitalism to an unrealized socialist ideal. "It wasn't until the mid-'70s that I became able to think of the issue in empirical terms at all," he later recalled. "My religious background and my lack of background in economics made it difficult for me to keep the actual comparative factors in focus."[41] He was thus led to frame the central political issue as a choice between rival moral visions. On that level, democratic socialism always won. His religious background had filled his imagination with solidaristic, communal images of the good society. This predisposition was reinforced by his study of liberal theory, which offered images of atomized individuals forming contracts and compacts. The narrowly empirical, pragmatic, individualistic ethos of capitalism seemed to him "not only foreign but spiritually *wrong*."[42]

Novak's inner struggle was to purge himself of this moralistic framework. His idealism was fixated on moral visions, but realism compared existing systems. Democratic socialism existed only as an unrealized moral ideal, which raised the question whether a democratized social order was actually achievable. In his determination to rid himself of his religiously inculcated idealism, Novak reasoned that the lack of a historical example of democratic socialism revealed something about the worthiness of socialism even as an ideal. Democratic socialism didn't exist, and the existing socialisms were totalitarian prisons. If the struggle to attain the ideal always failed, the arguments for democratic socialism were refuted historically. Novak later recalled that as this conclusion first took hold of him in the mid-seventies, he was afraid to write about it or even to discuss it with his wife and friends. He avoided the subject, writing a book on sports and another on the 1897 Slavic miners strike in Lattimer, Pennsylvania.

The Joy of Sports retreated from Novak's earlier WASP-bashing. He confessed his special affection for baseball—that perfectly Lockean game of straight lines, individualism, and self-control. In baseball, he noted, cooperation among teammates was necessary, but limited. Baseball lacked the organic, flowing qualities of football or basketball. It was not thick with body contact and flowing interchanges, but featured confrontations between individuals bound together by a legalistic social contract. Baseball reproduced the mythos of WASP culture. Like Anglo-Saxon culture, however, baseball could also be played and enjoyed by non-WASPs. "*Anyone* can learn to operate within the Anglo-Saxon mythic world; humans everywhere can, and do, imitate and assimilate a mythos not entirely their own," Novak wrote. "While the spiritual world of baseball, acted out in a public arena, exhibits almost perfectly the myths of the white Anglo-Saxon population that settled the towns, prairies, and southlands of America, all Americans can share in this 'national pastime.'" The joys of baseball, like the joys of America, were open to all Americans. Enjoying baseball was "a form of Americanization" that provided access to the Anglo-Saxon world.[43] The Los Angeles Dodgers helped Novak feel less alienated. *The Joy of Sports* signaled that he was ready to give up his ethnic resentments and reclaim his Americanism.

The hard part was making a complete break from the Left. Novak tried to talk himself into a social democratic compromise during the mid-seventies. He resolved that his ideology would be liberal-democratic in politics, mildly socialist in economics, and a blend of conservatism and modernism in culture. "But even when I held up to myself pictures of Sweden, it didn't help," he later recounted. He couldn't stand the complexities or inherent tensions of a social democratic politics, and he no longer believed that the social democratic vision of worker- and community-controlled enterprises was viable. Even social democracy was too utopian. In 1976, he finally stirred up his courage and announced that he was a "closet capitalist." If the ideal of a democratized socioeconomic order was actually unattainable, then the moral claims on which social democracy was based were also unworthy.[44]

Novak conceded that social democracy seemed to hold moral advantages over its rivals. The language of democratic socialism—the language of freedom, equality, community, and the common good—seemed more consistent with Christian and Jewish moral values than did the rhetoric of capitalism. The first task for the religious opponent of social democracy was therefore to undermine socialism's moral appeal.

DEMOCRATIC CAPITALISM AND THE WHIG TRADITION

Novak turned to Ludwig von Mises and F. A. Hayek in the mid-seventies for economic instruction. Because these figures had so little to offer on a moral level, however, he was forced to struggle with the moral question on his own. Niebuhr's writings were equally unhelpful in this area, since the early Niebuhr was a Marxist and the later Niebuhr rarely addressed the capitalism–socialism debate at all. For Novak, the crucial need was to reformulate Hayek's perspective "in highly moral terms," presenting a morally grounded realism that could replace the socialist faith he had discarded. [45] The only way to rid oneself of a powerful idea, as John Henry Newman famously observed, is to replace it with an even more powerful idea. Novak later recalled that he felt a profound inner emptiness over the loss of his socialist vision, until "fortunately, there fell into my hands, among other writings, some of the essays of Irving Kristol, recalling me to an intellectual tradition I had hitherto avoided: that of the American Framers and that of the British and French liberals of the early nineteenth century." [46] Kristol's defense of Anglo-Scottish Whiggery offered Novak an alternative intellectual tradition. Novak's more powerful idea was already forming in his mind. His identification with the Whig tradition would strengthen the idea's hold over him. The idea was democratic capitalism.

Novak served as director of humanities at the Rockefeller Foundation in the early 1970s, after leaving Old Westbury. In 1975, Jimmy Carter asked for a meeting with him. Novak was supporting Shriver's presidential candidacy at the time—out of friendship more than politics—but he assured Carter of his support if Shriver failed. By the following spring, however, Carter was no longer a political unknown, and Novak greatly disliked what he had learned about him. "I began to believe that Jimmy Carter didn't have any vision of what he wanted to do, was naive, and might prove to be both incompetent and a fraud," he later explained. He flew to Pennsylvania "in a certain desperation" to help Scoop Jackson's campaign, but Carter won the Pennsylvania primary and later the nomination. Novak couldn't bring himself to support Carter in the fall, and therefore sat out the election, privately rooting for Gerald Ford. After the election, the Republican Party Chair, William Brock, presented the Republicans' Favorite Democrat Award to Novak.[47]

He taught at Syracuse University for three semesters during 1977 and 1978, and became a resident scholar at the American Enterprise Institute in 1978. The first fruit of what Novak called his "new and stronger set of ideas" was offered the same year in a book published by his new employer. *The American Vision* introduced the idea of democratic capitalism in its opening sentence. The problem with most discussions of American capitalism, he argued, was that they focused too narrowly on the economic system as a mechanism for exchange and failed to place the economic system in its larger context as part of a political, cultural, and economic system. Because most specialists in these areas typically restricted themselves to their specific areas of expertise, they usually missed the essence of the system. The dynamism of democratic capitalism originated in the conviction "(1) that both elites and those at the economic bottom will circulate; and (2) that there is equality for all, whatever their starting place, not only to better their positions but also to go as far as imagination, work, and luck will take them."[48] *The American Vision* thus implicitly denied that actual equality of opportunity required any particular degree of equality of condition. The significance of one's starting place could be dismissed in an aside. The book's appropriation of Daniel Bell's theory of the tripartite society and its celebration of American capitalism laid the groundwork for Novak's subsequent writings.

The Republicans' Favorite Democrat announced in October 1980 that he was going all the way over to Ronald Reagan. Novak explained, "I cannot tolerate the thought of another four years of Jimmy Carter." His reasons were a neoconservative hit list. "Carter is forever looking into the mirror of his own vanity, trying to strike a profile in courage for someone or other," he claimed. "He is in love with his own 'integrity'—and will do anything he needs to make it prevail, you can depend on it." Novak was indignant that Carter had questioned Reagan's racial views and record. He was contemptuous of Carter's presidency. Carter's policies were an incoherent mixture of economic conservatism and foreign policy radicalism, he observed. "With one foot in Georgia and one foot in Massachusetts, he feels pain right about Washington." This pain-in-the-crotch president had so weakened the United States that "danger spots are multiplying, wars are breaking out like hives, and the great climax Solzhenitsyn predicts draws nearer." The present danger left Americans with no choice. Carter's weakness was making the world safe for communism. "Reagan understands the present danger; Carter is at sea," Novak concluded. "While Carter fiddles songs of peace, the structure of peace is collapsing. . . . I stand with those who want to redress the errors of the last eight years (including the strategic retreat engineered by Nixon and Kissinger). Reagan is the only candidate we have."[49]

Though he regarded the Soviet threat as America's chief political challenge, Novak generally left the subject to Podhoretz and others. His own work focused on the case for democratic capitalism. His major work, *The Spirit of Democratic Capitalism*, was published in 1982. He later reported that it was only with the writing of this book that he was able to rid himself completely of his idealism.[50] *The Spirit of Democratic Capitalism* offered extended critiques of democratic socialism, economic dependency theory, and liberation theology, but the book's chief argument reformulated Bell's theory of the tripartite society. The argument was taken from Bell's *Cultural Contradictions of Capitalism*. Bell had rejected all interpretive frameworks—including the Hegelian-Marxist and Durkheimian-functionalist models—that conceived modern societies as structurally interrelated unitary wholes. He developed a pluralistic alternative to the unitary models of classical sociological theory, distinguishing among modern society's techno-economic structure, polity, and culture.[51] A distinctive axial principle and structure established the foundation for institutions that belonged to each realm. Bell argued that America's three realms were not congruent with each other and that each of them contained its own distinctive norms, types of behavior, and dynamics of change. The contradictions of capitalism were produced by the discordances between America's political, economic, and cultural spheres.

Bell explored these discordances, emphasizing the personally and socially destructive effects of commercial advertising, credit cards, and economic growth. He observed that modern bourgeois societies needed cultural systems that encouraged and affirmed hard work, prudence, thrift, deferred gratification, familial loyalty, and a sense of the sacred. The problem was that commercial societies undermined these virtues by manipulating their consumers to crave unnecessary goods and services and demand immediate gratification. Capitalism subverted the very ties of family, community, religion, and moral habit on which modernity's cultural realm was based.

The concept of American society as a threefold system was thus presented as a descriptive framework for Bell's argument about the cultural ravages of capitalism. His point was not that the three realms were mutually supportive; the contradictions of capitalism were caused by the contradictions between the realms. But it was in the former sense that Novak adopted Bell's model of American society. Throughout *The Spirit of*

Democratic Capitalism and his subsequent writings, Novak described the three realms, acknowledged his debt to Bell, and then claimed that only democratic capitalism could generate and secure a pluralistic coexistence among them.[52] Bell's critique of modern capitalism was turned, in Novak's hands, into a normative ideal identified with it.

"In the conventional view, the link between a democratic political system and a market economy is merely an accident of history," Novak asserted. "My argument is that the link is stronger: political democracy is compatible in practice only with a market economy." His extreme position was thus compared to a "conventional" view rarely defended by anyone. The more complex views that fell between Novak's "compatible only" claim and the "accident of history" reading were disregarded. Novak argued that both political democracy and capitalism "nourish and are best nourished by a pluralistic culture."[53] He traced the origins of modern democracy and capitalism to "identical historical impulses" that "had moral form before institutions were invented to realize them." These impulses limited the state's power and thus liberated the energies of individuals and independent communities.

Two revolutions were linked in theory and historical practice. The linkage between the political and economic revolutions of modernity were enshrined in Marx's phrase, bourgeois democracy. For Novak, the phrase was apt, regardless of Marx's attitude toward it. Novak argued that the coherence of democratic capitalism derived from the "fact" that modern democracy and modern capitalism sprang "from the same logic, the same moral principles, the same nest of cultural values, institutions, and presuppositions."[54] The link between political democracy and the market society was not only historical, but logical. "While bastard forms of capitalism do seem for a time to endure without democracy," he conceded, "the natural logic of capitalism leads to democracy."[55] Market societies created middle-class constituencies, which eventually demanded political rights for themselves.

In the process of turning Bell's descriptive framework into a normative model called democratic capitalism, Novak failed to address Bell's fundamental argument that capitalism subverted the very habits of community, tradition, and religious practice that sustained healthy societies. Novak claimed that the alternatives to capitalism were inherently unitary or "monistic." Pluralism could only be sustained by a capitalist economy. But this was precisely what Bell denied. As Bell documented, the problem was that America's political and cultural realms were overmatched by the power of its organized economic interests. Though Novak sprinkled his writings with supporting quotes from *The Cultural Contradictions of Capitalism,* his misuse of the book's argument was signaled by Bell's explanation that he was a socialist in economics, a liberal in politics, and a conservative in culture.

Bell did not claim that democracy or democratic pluralism could be sustained only by a capitalist economy. He argued, rather, that although capitalism and democracy "historically have arisen together, and have been commonly justified by philosophical liberalism, there is nothing which makes it either theoretically or practically necessary for the two to be yoked." For Bell, pluralism was politically safeguarded by liberalism— that is, by subordinating the needs of the community to the rights of the individual. In the economic realm, however, pluralism was best protected by democratic socialism, in which "the community takes precedence over the individual in the values that legitimate economic policy."[56] Bell specifically rejected Novak's assurance that only capitalism nourished a pluralism of realms. For Bell, social democratic gains in the economic realm were needed to preserve the pluralism of realms otherwise undermined by commercial society.

Though he evaded the force of Bell's critique, Novak did acknowledge that the spirit of Bell's work was different from his own. For Bell, the capitalist principle was empty. Bell wrote in *The Winding Passage* that, having lost its original justifications, "capitalism has taken over the legitimations of an anti-bourgeois culture to maintain the continuity of its own economic institutions." Citing Kristol and Joseph Schumpeter on capitalism's lack of a transcendental justification, Bell argued that capitalism "is simply instrumental and rational, and creates no values of its own." For Novak, however, this was exactly the problem. Nearly all intellectuals thought capitalism had no spiritual basis. This mistake prevented them from grasping the essence of capitalism. "It is simply not true that capitalism 'creates no values of its own,'" he argued. "Capitalism is intrinsically related to some core values—to liberty in the sense of self-discipline; to invention, creativity, and cooperation, the root of the corporation; to work, savings, investment in the future; to self-reliance, etc." Like most intellectuals, including the conservatives, Bell misunderstood capitalism because he missed its spiritual basis. "He misses the underlying spiritual power of democratic capitalism and its capacities for self-renewal," Novak explained. "He conceives of it in too purely instrumental terms, neglecting to note the disciplines it teaches, the moral abuses it is designed to prevent, and the virtues it uniquely elicits." The crucial dimension was the realm of spirit. Even most apologists for capitalism missed its "powerfully self-transforming, creative, and inventive" spirit.[57] *The Spirit of Democratic Capitalism* would correct this mistake.

Novak's structural argument was taken from Bell, but the spirit of his project had other roots. One intellectual tradition validated much of his capitalist faith. Kristol led him to it; Hayek explained it to him. In his essay "Why I Am Not a Conservative," Hayek dissociated himself from both conservative traditionalism and liberal individualism, identifying himself with the Whig tradition of Macaulay, Tocqueville, Acton, Burke, and Madison.[58] Novak recalled that reading this essay marked a turning point in his intellectual pilgrimage.[59] He recognized himself in Hayek's description of the Whig sensibility. His subsequent books repeatedly offered lists of Whig intellectual heroes, some of which added Aquinas, Bellarmine, Hooker, the Jesuits of Salamanca, Montaigne, Smith, Montesquieu, Mill, Cobden, Jefferson, Hamilton, and Lincoln to the roll, as well as, among other moderns, Mises, Don Luigi Sturzo, Yves Simon, William Roepke, Konrad Adenauer, John Courtney Murray, Paul Johnson, Kristol, Robert Nisbet, John Paul II, and Jacques Maritain.[60] It was an extraordinarily malleable "tradition," making room for Novak's favorite Thomists, humanists, deists, utilitarians, Jews, monarchists, republicans, and neo-Tories. The list included one figure whose approval Novak had never failed to invoke over every stage of his career. If Maritain fit rather oddly in a tradition with Smith, Jefferson, and Mises, the enrollment was perhaps no more implausible than Novak's assurances during his radical phase that Maritain was "more New Left than liberal."[61]

Despite his attempts to pad the roll, however, there was a serious meaning in Novak's identification with the Whig tradition. "One of the great achievements of the Whig tradition was its new world experiment, *Novus Ordo Seclorum*," he explained. "Its American progenitors called that experiment the commercial republic. The Whigs were the first philosophers in history to grasp the importance of basing government of the people upon the foundation of commerce. They underpinned democracy with a capitalist, growing economy."[62] That is, the Whigs invented democratic capitalism. If his increasingly overloaded roster of Whig heroes threatened to reduce Whiggery to meaninglessness, there was, nonetheless, a direct connection between Novak's neoconservatism and the historic Whig tradition.

Whiggery derived from the twin revolutions behind bourgeois democracy. The key to the Whigs' strategy in eighteenth-century Europe was to play their aristocratic and working-class enemies off against each other. The English Whigs and French Liberals opposed the ruling aristocracies of their time and thus won the support of workers and small property owners. When the same workers and petit-bourgeois demanded the right to vote through the Reform Act and the July Charter, however, the Whigs and

Liberals opposed them. Faced with the despotism of the aristocrats and the presumedly insatiable demands of the working class, the Whigs split (or "trimmed") the differences between their traditionalist and democratic opponents, advocating constitutional monarchy and limited suffrage.

The problem with this strategy in America, however, as Louis Hartz famously recounted, was that America's lack of aristocratic and proletarian forces deprived the Whigs of their needed enemies. In *The Liberal Tradition in America* Hartz explained, "Here there are no aristocracies to fight, and the Federalists and the Whigs are denied the chance of dominating the people in a campaign against them. Here there are no aristocracies to ally with, and they cannot use their help to exclude the people from political power. Here there are no genuine proletarian outbursts to meet, and they cannot frighten people into fleeing from them." The American Whigs were therefore isolated, "put at the mercy of a strange new giant" they couldn't control. Until they discovered "democratic capitalism" in the 1840s, the American Whigs were thus deprived of their liberal veneer. Their haughty diatribes against "the mob" not only were politically suicidal, but in an American context were absurd, since the commoners were as liberal as they were.[63]

Novak screened out this antidemocratic heritage. Though he frequently appealed to the wisdom of such Whig trimmers as Smith, Burke, Macaulay, and Montesquieu, he characterized the Whig tradition itself in American terms. The Whigs were the party of liberty, he explained, believers in republican government who created "in accord with nature and nature's God, a system of natural liberty."[64] His highly compressed accounts of American history ignored the considerable differences among America's founding fathers, placing all of them—from Jefferson to Hamilton—in the Whig column. The American Whigs were distinguished not by any particular ideology or political philosophy, he claimed, but by their sensibility, which was cautious, chastened, and empirical. The Whigs were forward-looking, but respectful of the wisdom of the past. They respected the negative view toward commerce espoused by moralists of the past, but perceived that commerce itself had changed with the rise of capitalism. Their prudential, antirationalistic spirit created a politics that was preoccupied with checks and balances. The Whig tradition would thus be "more suited to the middle-aged mind than to the youthful mind."[65]

Novak was slow to historicize democratic capitalism. *The American Vision* defended democratic capitalism without any appeal to a supporting Whig tradition. *The Spirit of Democratic Capitalism* noted only that Hayek was probably correct in tracing democratic capitalism to the Whig tradition.[66] The following year, while fretting that the term bore "the faint sense of the attic about it," he finally embraced Whiggery.[67] He had found his alternative tradition. His intuitive attraction to what he called the Whig temperament was crucial. The most important factor, however, was the link between Whig politics and Novak's central concept, the idea of democratic capitalism.

Though he never traced the American rootage of democratic capitalism, the idea was rooted in the history of American Whiggery—that is, in the history of America's Whig party. The Whigs began to accept the realities of American politics in 1840. Moved by their party's repeatedly impressive defeats, politicians such as Thurlow Weed and Daniel Webster finally recognized the inanity of disdaining the common people in a democracy. Their alternative was a Jeffersonian form of capitalism. "Giving up the false aristocratic frustrations of the past, and giving up as well its false proletarian fears, they embraced America's liberal unity with a vengeance, and developed a philosophy of democratic capitalism," Hartz recounted. Calvin Colton took this theme to the campaign trail and declared that "every American laborer can stand up proudly, and say, I AM THE AMERICAN CAPITALIST."[68] It was a novel strategem. Hartz remarked,

> We think of the Whigs in the age of Harrison as stealing the egalitarian thunder of the Democrats, but actually they did more than that. They transformed it. For if they gave up Hamilton's hatred of the people, they retained his grandiose capitalist dream, and this they combined with the Jeffersonian concept of equal opportunity. The result was to electrify the democratic individual with a passion for great achievement and to produce a personality type that was neither Hamiltonian nor Jeffersonian but a strange mixture of both: the hero of Horatio Alger.[69]

Though critics such as Henry Adams taunted them for their purported intellectual feebleness, it was the Whigs who concocted America's triumphant ideology.[70] The Whigs uncovered the peculiar ethos of American society, as Hartz put it, when they gave up their aristocratic yearnings and "catered openly to the acquisitive dreams of the American democrat."[71] From these materials they fashioned the myth of Americanism. America's vision of the good society would be defined by the myth of a classless melting pot of self-made individualists. It would also delegitimize any form of class-conscious opposition. Though the Whigs failed to survive the nineteenth century as an electoral force, their ideology prevailed. With the triumph of their conception of Americanism, even the mildest progressivism could be stigmatized as un-American. Hartz characterized this legacy as a form of ideological terrorism. The myth of democratic capitalism "tried to frighten the American democrat with his own absolute liberalism," he observed. The myth denigrated the state and stigmatized those who turned to the state to gain or protect their rights. "And the best way of doing this was to call him a 'socialist' which, of course, was to make him perfectly 'un-American.' "[72]

During his transitional phase, Novak had condemned the myth of the melting pot as an instrument of WASP domination. WASP ideology rationalized cultural imperialism, while WASP economic power reduced all racial and ethnic minorities to second-class citizenship. The enemy was America's concentration of economic power. Upon turning to the Right, however, Novak made his peace with Americanism. The Anglo-Saxon apologists he had denounced as imperialists became his heroes. The once unmeltable ethnic denied that his harsh attacks on WASP America were meant to be taken literally. *The Rise of the Unmeltable Ethnics* was a pitch for status recognition, he explained. He had merely meant to speak for Burke's little platoons of (ethnic) families and neighborhoods. He had harbored no desire to see the WASP establishment pulled down. "I can still recall the astonishment I felt at the time when a fortress I thought both admirable and impregnable was suddenly surrendered without a fight," he recalled. [73] The spectacle reinforced his resolve to defend the Whig vision against the ravages of the New Class.

Novak's philosophy mixed Catholic and early American Whiggery, but his capitalist enthusiasms echoed a more recent American tradition. Like the nineteenth-century American Whigs, he insisted that capitalism was the only economic system that promoted political democracy or individual achievement. Like the Whigs, he celebrated the productive power of capitalism and claimed that most of its critics compared capitalism to an unattainable moral ideal. [74]

The Whigs celebrated the material achievements of capitalism and the moral virtues that entrepreneurialism engendered. Novak shared these enthusiasms—and surpassed them. His "theology" of the corporation considerably surpassed Whig standards for boosterism. *Toward a Theology of the Corporation* defended the record of multinationals in the Third World and announced that corporations "mirror the presence of God" in seven sacramental ways. The crucial feature of modern capitalism was not entrepreneurship, Novak argued, but "the communal focus of the new ethos: the rise of communal risk taking, the pooling of resources, the sense of communal religious vocation in economic activism." He asserted that by virtue of their communal-religious character and their liberty (meaning their independence from the state), corporations "offer metaphors for grace, a kind of insight into God's ways in history."[75] However, modern corporations could only flourish—and thus mirror God's presence—when the state's power to control rights and goods was strictly limited. Fortu-nately, he observed, this attitude toward the state was "the distinctively American way of thinking about private property."[76]

The Whigs insisted that capitalism not only required virtue, but engendered it. "For them, the enabling agent and protector of liberty is virtue—indeed, a full quiver of virtues, one against each of the vices that commonly deprive human persons of their liberty," Novak observed.[77] If Kristol gave two cheers for capitalism, Novak gave four. Democratic capitalism was not only productive and tolerant, but virtue-producing.[78] "With the invention of democratic capitalism in America, new demands were made upon the citizens, for which new virtues were required," he explained.[79]

The first new virtue created by American capitalism was civic responsi-bility. The colonists turned to a regime of private property after their experiments with communal ownership failed. The result was a distinctive political culture that blended individual initiative and community coopera-tion in equal parts. Novak gave short shrift to the critics of American individualism. He denied that C. B. Macpherson's critique of possessive individualism had anything to do with American culture. He argued that American self-reliance, community-building, and self-government had produced, rather, a "new kind of human being"—the communitarian individual.[80] Under American capitalism, the ambitions of free individu-als—especially the "most imaginative and able members"—were chan-neled to build new communities and lay the groundwork for new enter-prises.

These enterprises required and continually reproduced the second new virtue, the "peculiarly capitalist virtue" of enterprise itself. Novak allowed that the spirit of enterprise was not unknown in precapitalist history. Under capitalism, however, this spirit became "so to speak, the red-hot center, the dynamo, the ignition system, of development. It is the very principle of economic progress." The spirit of enterprise discovered new needs of communities, or at least new markets for consumption. The "moral moment" of enterprise consisted, he explained, "in the effort, ingenuity, and persistence required to bring that insight into reality."[81]

The third virtue was entrepreneurial creativity. For Novak this was capitalism's central virtue. Though it was true, as Marx observed, that capitalism used private property, markets, and profit incentives in a distinctive way, Novak argued that capitalism was not properly defined by these institutions. Capitalism was, rather, an economic system "legally and institutionally organized around mind."[82] Capitalism was defined by its promotion of invention, discovery, and enterprise—that is, by the activities of the creative mind. It was the economic system "designed to nourish the creativity of the human subject or to nourish, in Smith's phrase, 'skill, dexterity, and judgment.' "[83] This redefinition was crucial to Novak because it permitted him to distinguish capitalism from the precapitalist economies of biblical times, eighteenth-century British mercantilism, and, especially, modern Latin American mercantilism. Novak contended that the recognition of intellectual property in the U.S. Constitution's patent and copyright clause was thus a crucial moment in modern capitalism's development.[84] America's economy was more capitalist than Third World regimes featuring private property, markets, and profit incentives, he argued, because American capitalism promoted intellectual creativity. "Capitalism is a new order in history precisely because it is centered more than any other system on the creativity of the human mind," he explained. "Therein lies its historical fertility."[85] The material world itself became "more and more mind" when capitalism took root and flourished.

The fourth virtue was "a special kind of communitarian living." Capitalist societies abounded "in many varieties of frank and friendly association, in a great deal of teamwork, in habits of openness and easy companionship that are marvelous to see and to experience." Novak conceded that capitalism broke down longstanding communal, family, ethnic, and religious ties, and he acknowledged that there was "said to be much loneliness" in commercial societies. He responded that overall, however, with all of its committees and meetings and consultations, most economic activities under modern capitalism were nothing if not associational.[86]

The last virtue was competitiveness. Novak observed that competitiveness was usually mistaken for a vice. This prejudice was a hangover from Christian morality and the moralism of English literature. He argued that competitiveness should be viewed as a virtue, however, not only because it was a "sentinel of economic fairness," but also because it protected societies from monopolistic collusion. Competition impeded the concentration and abuse of economic power. Novak contended that competitiveness was a specifically capitalist virtue, though social democratic regimes in Europe had also promoted it. Social democracy mixed competitiveness and greater democratization to prevent economic concentration. For Novak, however, this was the chief problem with social democratic alternatives—social democracy tried to prevent economic concentration by politicizing the economic sector.

Novak acknowledged that "bastard forms of capitalism" had flourished under various kinds of dictatorships, but he insisted that the "natural logic of capitalism" leads to democracy.[87] He was prepared to mean, "leads in the very long run." The European democracies were capitalist long before they permitted universal suffrage, but this fact did not complicate Novak's attribution of a democratizing logic to capitalism. Democratic rights were finally gained in the West primarily through the struggles of working-class and reformist movements, which were invariably treated by the capitalist class as enemies of the existing system. Novak avoided this point and its implications. Though democratic ideas derived remotely from ancient Athens and, more directly, from the English, American, and French revolutions of the seventeenth and eighteenth centuries, political democracy itself existed virtually nowhere outside America before 1850. The struggle to attain merely the right to vote—a right not universally secured in most European nations or the United States until the twentieth century—was not a natural product of what Novak called the "dynamic balance of emergent democratic capitalism." Democratic gains were attained, rather, by the very movements stigmatized as "un-American" for their challenges to private economic power.

The link between capitalism and democracy first appeared in eighteenth-century England in the form of the liberal state. As Macpherson observed, it was the liberal state that upheld the competitive market system "by keeping the government responsive to the shifting majority interests of those who were running the market society."[88] There was nothing democratic about the liberal state, but it *was* liberal insofar as it protected the freedoms of speech, association, and enterprise. The ideological guardians of predemocratic liberalism were the Whigs. The Whigs needed the commoners to break the aristocracy's grip on political power, but at the same time, they were determined to prevent actual rule by the common people. Novak rightly asserted that the capitalist economic system they defended eventually created pressures for democratization among the newly created middle class. It was another matter, however, to claim that the achievement of democratic gains revealed the natural logic of capitalism.

By attributing democratic gains in the West to the genius of the "dynamic balance" of modern capitalism, Novak attempted to claim the democratic mantle for his neoconservatism, even as he denigrated virtually all liberal and progressive movements that actually promoted further democratic gains in the political and economic spheres. But the struggles for universal suffrage, the progressive income tax, the rights of collective bargaining, social insurance, and civil rights for minorities and women were actually waged, against the opposition of business interests, by the very reformist, unionist, and social democratic movements that Novak opposed. Like other neoconservatives, he opposed further gains toward a democratized social order while attributing to democratic capitalism the

inheritance of democratic entitlements historically resisted by the capitalist class. That democracy advanced in the West partly as a consequence of
pressures from middle-class and working-class constituencies created by
capitalism was a justifiable claim. That democracy emerged from the
natural logic of capitalism and was compatible only with capitalism was a
rather more problematic set of claims. These claims could only be sustained if one categorized economic and social democracy—as Novak
did—as left-wing variants of capitalism. His neoconservatism, however,
opposed these democratizing forces.

The coherence of his organizing idea, "democratic capitalism," was
questioned by various critics of his work. As an adjective, "democratic" did
not modify, describe, or define the noun to which it was joined. Since
Novak acknowledged that the essential structure and practice of capitalism
were undemocratic, he was challenged by Steinfels, John Cort, Russell
Kirk, and others to justify his continued use of the phrase.[89] He replied
that democratic capitalism was a system of political economy "arising from
the conjunction of a democratic polity and a capitalist economy." Democratic capitalism arose "when a polity constituted as a democratic republic,
with inbuilt checks and balances, and with auxiliary precautions to protect
personal and minority rights against their usurpation by majorities, is
added to a capitalist economy," he explained. "The latter is constituted by
laws, customs and institutions that promote the creation of new wealth
through invention, discovery and enterprise."[90]

Novak thus used the phrase "democratic capitalism" to refer to a social
system featuring a democratic-republican polity and a capitalist economy.
The fact that two words could be put together, however, didn't mean that
they represented anything in reality. Steinfels observed that while Novak
was both tall and balding, this didn't establish "tall baldingism" as a
meaningful concept. Neither did the existence of societies like the United
States and Canada necessarily establish the existence of "democratic
capitalism." Cort extended the point. The idea of "democratic capitalism"
made no more sense than "the democratic Mafia," he argued, if one was
only referring to capitalist economies or Mafia syndicates that existed in
politically democratic societies.

These analogies were exaggerated. There was no significant connection between being tall and balding, or between democracy and the Mafia,
but there was an important connection between the historical emergence
of capitalism and the rise of modern democracy. The question was, What
kind of connection? Was capitalism the cause of democracy? Was it a
necessary cause? Did capitalism and democracy maintain the same relationship through all stages of their development? As Steinfels observed,

these were questions that Novak simply bowled over by the force of his rhetoric.[91] By sheer repetition, "democratic capitalism" took on a life of its own in his work, becoming the subject of active verbs and even being personified. Novak explained that democratic capitalism was merely a "parallel to democratic socialism," but this explanation confirmed the problem with the concept. The phrase "democratic socialism" was grammatically coherent for the very reason that "democratic capitalism" was not. The goal of democratic socialism was to democratize society's political and economic realms. In the case of "democratic socialism," the adjective did describe and define the noun. Novak explained that his purpose in speaking of democratic capitalism was to save the language of democratic socialism for his own ends.[92] The sentiment was compelling, as was the need to find a shorthand term for the model he celebrated. The phrase he embraced for this was adopted by many journalists and political writers in the late 1980s. The phrase remained literally an oxymoron, however.

QUESTIONING LIBERATION THEOLOGY

The Spirit of Democratic Capitalism devoted much of its analysis to a refutation of Latin American liberation theology. Much of Novak's subsequent work elaborated the same arguments, expecially his book *Will It Liberate? Questions about Liberation Theology.*[93] That he would be forced to devote so much attention to this movement came as a surprise to him. In 1975, Novak declared that liberation theology was a "cheap Marxist," semi-Christian fad. "We can expect liberation theology to become popular for a while, until a new and equally simple version comes along," he argued.[94] The stunning failure of this prediction forced him, in succeeding years, to explain repeatedly why Latin American liberationism should not have flourished. "The Case Against Liberation Theology," published in *The New York Times Magazine,* offered a typical account. Liberation theology was essentially a popular front phenomenon, he argued, that "gains its excitement from flirting with Marxist thought and speech, and from its hostility to the North."[95] Liberationism used Marxist slogans to exploit Latin American resentment—and especially envy—toward the United States. The chief faults of liberation theology, he argued elsewhere, were traceable to its reliance on neo-Marxist dependency theory and to the fact that Latin Americans "do not value the same moral qualities North Americans do."[96]

Novak's critique of liberation theology focused on the purported errors of economic dependency theory. This theory took several forms, ranging from the unicausal neo-Marxism of Andre Gunder Frank and Samir Amin to the multicausal, social democratic analyses of Raul Prebisch and Fernando Henrique Cardoso. The fundamental argument shared by all dependency theorists, however, was that developed nations create "centers" that dominate more vulnerable nations in their "periphery," causing the latter to become disproportionately dependent upon external economic decisions. Dependency theorists cited unfavorable trade agreements, the promotion of cash crops for export, exploitative policies of transnational corporations, aid to corrupt and repressive governments, and large external debts contracted with these governments as examples of these dependent relationships.[97] The Peruvian Roman Catholic bishops offered a striking formulation, in 1969, of the dependency perspective. Like other nations of the Third World, they wrote, "we are the victims of systems that exploit our natural resources, control our political decisions, and impose on us the cultural domination of their values and consumer civilization. . . . Foreign interests increase their repressive measures by means of economic sanctions in the international markets and by control of loans and other types of aid."[98]

Novak's rejoinder attacked the bishops' tone of grievance. The bishops and their theoretical mentors had cultivated the attitudes and habits of victims. "They accept no responsibility for three centuries of hostility to trade, commerce, and industry," he charged. "They seem to imagine that loans and aid should be tendered them independently of economic laws." He argued that the bishops claimed to be aggrieved "because others, once equally poor, have succeeded as they have not."[99] In the early 1950s, Latin Americans could have chosen the same path as Japan, Singapore, and Taiwan. "They did not, in part because of the influence of Raul Prebisch, tradition, culture, and well-meaning Americans," he asserted. "They have reaped what they have sown." The chief cause of Latin America's problems was that "Latin America has been a continent with a dependent frame of mind."[100] The only sense in which dependency theory was true, therefore, was as a reflection of the victimization complex of Latin Americans themselves. Latin American programs for economic modernization had failed because Latin Americans were culturally backward and were always looking for outsiders to blame for their problems.

Though the defining purpose of the liberationist movement was to become liberated from dependency, Novak argued, liberationist rhetoric reinforced a victimization complex among Latin Americans that was itself disempowering. Novak's critique of liberationist arguments extended well beyond this arguable point, however. He disputed the basic historical and economic claims of dependency analysis, denying that the bishops' grievances were justified in the first place. Noting that the total investments made by U.S.-based corporations in Latin America between 1950 and 1965 averaged $253 million per year, and that the total value of U.S. investments in 1965 was still only $11 billion, he remarked that it was ridiculous to believe that such small sums were responsible for Latin America's poverty or dependence. The claim that Third World economic development was impeded by the power and influence of the dominant nations, he concluded, "is merely a clever restatement of the proposition that the poverty of the poor is explained by the wealth of the wealthy. For this there is not a shred of evidence."[101]

He perhaps had in mind the strand of dependency theory that attributed Third World underdevelopment primarily to the ravages of First World political and economic imperialism. The most influential examples of this idea were the writings of Frank and Amin, in which Third World poverty was indeed explained primarily as the consequence of structural First World domination. Even in this form, dependency theory explained more about the worsening immiseration of the Third World than Novak acknowledged. Novak rightly contended, however, that base-periphery models were too one-dimensional to explain the dynamics of modern international trade. Frank's emphasis on the determinative impact of economic neocolonialism overlooked the fact that some of the world's most desperately impoverished nations have had little or no commercial contact with the outside world.

Dependency theory included more complex variants than the unicausal explanations offered by Frank and Amin, however. Prebisch and Cardoso used dependency theory as a method of analysis to focus on the relative extent of national control over specific social and economic variables. The forms of dependency theory adopted by such liberation theologians as Leonardo Boff and Gustavo Gutierrez fit this type. Boff and Gutierrez endorsed Cardoso's rejection of the notion of dependence "as a way of 'explaining' internal processes of the dependent societies by a purely 'external' variable."[102] These theorists nonetheless insisted that Latin American societies were exploited by First World interests. In the past generation, networks of modernized airports, hotels, and telecommunications systems had been financed with enormous loans for Latin American nations where most people had never driven a car or used a telephone. This process of economic distortion was reinforced by the arms trade, as in Venezuela and Honduras, which had used their military credits to purchase F-16A and F5-E jet fighters from U.S. defense contractors eager to expand their markets. The high-tech militarization of a desperately poor country like Honduras plainly made that country dependent on external economic and political decisions.

Novak ignored the role of military sales and aid in promoting economic dependency. [103] For him, the socioeconomic and political factors discussed by dependency theorists were epiphenomena of a more basic cultural choice that, unlike East Asia's business class, Latin Americans were unable to face up to. He argued that Latin Americans could achieve the same economic growth as the East Asian rim nations if they developed the East Asian work ethic and promoted commerce and transnational investments as aggressively as the South Koreans and Taiwanese. "In 1950 the East Asian countries were desperately poor, but under capitalism they are becoming rich," he observed. "Were Latin American nations to become as well organized and successful as East Asia, they too would enrich the entire planet."[104]

Novak assumed that further modernization eventually would make East Asian societies more democratic. [105] Though he emphasized the importance of spurring economic development "from the bottom up," the East Asian countries he chose as models were marked by high levels of state-directed economic planning and dictatorial political systems. [106] These points will be elaborated in Chapter 6. More pertinent to the present discussion was Latin America's already-considerable acquaintance with modernization strategies. The factors highlighted by dependency theory were derived from this experience. By selling multimillion-dollar technologies to Latin America's often-corrupt governing elites, First World financial and business corporations saddled these countries with unpayable debts and stripped them of their capacity to invest in their own future. Foreign debts exceeding $400 billion in Latin America created debt service obligations outstripping incoming credits. Most of this debt was structured like variable-rate mortgages, with interest percentages tied to fluctuations in the U.S. prime rate. Loans taken out at 4-percent interest in the early 1970s became repayable at 15- to 20-percent rates after the inflation later in the decade. More than half of Latin America's external debt thus reflected the compounding of inflated interest rates rather than original principal. The debt burden debased Latin American currencies, deprived the United States of Latin American markets, undermined prospects for new investment, and, in some cases, reinforced the need for Latin American military and paramilitary repression to enforce conformity. [107] By assuming increasing control over Latin American finance capital, natural resources, production, and marketing, multinational firms skewed the investment priorities of undeveloped nations and undermined their prospects for economic self-determination.

Faced with the historical fact that Latin America's large foreign-owned banana and mining companies, banks, and various agribusinesses typically controlled their markets and opposed democratic reforms in the name of capitalism, Novak alternated between two responses. The first was that multinationals stimulated economic growth through their investments in the Third World. Regardless of the possible misdeeds of multinational firms, Novak argued, multinational investments played a progressive role in promoting Third World economic growth. This claim was made in the face of considerable disconfirming evidence, however. In his exhaustive study for the United Nations, *Estrategia Industrial y Empresas Internacionales*, Fernando Fajnzylber revealed that multinational enterprises in Latin America had taken, on average, approximately 75 percent of their net profits out of Latin America, and had traditionally financed the same percentage of their investments from local capital. Between 1957 and 1965, for example, only 17 percent of the capital investments of U.S.-based multinationals were brought in from outside the periphery countries themselves. [108] Studies by Peter Evans, Aldo Ferrer, E.V.K. FitzGerald, and Richard Newfarmer confirmed this pattern. [109]

Novak's more important rejoinder was that Latin America's modernization experience had nothing to do with capitalism in the first place. This explained his insistence on redefining capitalism. He rejected dictionary definitions of capitalism primarily to dissociate it from the histories of the peripheral countries. For Novak, a system was capitalist only if it featured "a predominantly market economy; a polity respectful of the rights of the individual to life, liberty, and the pursuit of happiness; and a system of cultural institutions moved by ideals of liberty and justice for all." [110] The upshot was that there were no capitalist nations in Latin America. Referring to the eleven Latin American dictatorships that moved toward democracy in the 1980s, Novak claimed that none of them was capitalist—which absolved capitalism's apologists from having to deal with the legacy of capitalist modernization in Latin America. [111]

Novak claimed that his conversion to neoconservatism was the result of his effort to think empirically in a sustained way, but his insertion of cultural variables into his definition of capitalism eliminated the possibility of subjecting his statements about capitalism to comparative empirical tests. His discussion of Third World alternatives resorted to a culturally based definition of capitalism that reproduced the very apologetic he derisively attributed to the democratic Left. Multinational-based modernization schemes had produced crushing debts, legacies of environmental and economic exploitation, military repression, and economies based on export dependence throughout Latin America. In Novak's account of Latin

America's economic history, however, capitalism existed only as a promise; it had no history. He argued that structures of middle-class democracy could be built up in Latin America if Latin Americans opened up their markets and encouraged greater multinational investment.

His writings eloquently described some of the obstacles to this solution. Latin American societies were not free, he observed, but statist, "not mind-centered but privilege-centered, not open to the poor but protective of the rich. Large majorities of the poor are propertyless. The poor are prevented by law from founding and incorporating their own enterprises. They are denied access to credit. They are held back by an ancient legal structure, designed to protect the ancient privileges of a pre-capitalist elite."[112] Though he failed to assess or even mention the ruling elite's sponsorship of military terror to enforce conformity, Novak aptly described its parasitic character. "This elite invents virtually nothing, risks virtually nothing, takes virtually no new initiatives," he observed. "It is parasitic upon and distributes the goods and services of foreign enterprises, whose inventiveness and dynamism it does not emulate. Thus do the Latin American elites sit behind a thick wall of law, whose purpose is to prevent capitalism from arising. These elites fear economic competition. Their greatest preoccupation is the protection of ancient privilege."[113] He argued that Latin America needed to promote grassroots economic development and dismantle the neofeudal structures that impeded economic growth from the bottom up.

He specifically urged that Latin Americans needed to maximize popular ownership (especially home ownership and ownership of small businesses), "change legal structures" to permit cheap incorporation of small businesses, "change laws and restructure banking institutions" to permit universal availability of credit to the poor, "change laws to protect patents and copyrights" to foster economic creativity, establish private school systems, and invest in universal education. "All these recommendations spring from one central core," he explained. "The cause of the wealth of nations lies within citizens themselves, in their native capacities for creativity, in their propensities for improving their condition, and in the insights, habits, and skills they acquire as they prepare themselves for economic activism."[114]

The sentiments were commendable; the recommendations in this particular list were unassailable. Novak envisioned an entrepreneurial culture for Latin America in which "commerce" was not a dirty word to Latin America's entrepreneurs, workers, intellectuals, or elites. He frequently observed that Latin America needed to enact its own versions of the Homestead Act. His arguments echoed the prescriptions of eminent Mexican writer Octavio Paz, who once stated that liberation theologians wanted to rescue the poor from their poverty while rejecting the preconditions for a productive economy.[115] Liberationists often wrote as though commerce itself was the enemy. Novak argued convincingly that this prejudice was hostile to the interests of the poor. His vigorous criticism of liberationism helped to engender among liberation theologians a growing recognition of the importance of fostering economic development from the bottom up.[116] His constructive role in the liberationist debate was repeatedly overwhelmed, however, by his overgeneralized attacks on the movement as a whole, by his failure to offer a strategy to overcome the "thick wall of law" that protected the elites, and by his insensitivity to the contextual differences between his experience and the experiences of Latin American liberationists.

His book on liberation theology asserted that Latin America's ruling elites needed "to yield place to the talented millions among the poor who show greater imagination, initiative, inventiveness, and creativity."[117] This sentiment sidestepped the strategic problem, however, and recycled the very kind of idealism that Niebuhr ridiculed. Novak asserted that Latin America's ruling class needed to forsake its cozy contacts with First World multinationals, its protection by the U.S. government, and its alliances with Latin America's military forces to "yield place" to the poor. He offered no consideration of what would be required to force them to "yield place," nor did he criticize the American government and the American-based corporations that had subsidized, reinforced, and supported the rule of Latin America's elites. His energies were devoted, rather, to condemning the one mass-based, decentralized, nonviolent movement in Latin America that actually challenged the rule of the elites. Novak wrote off the liberationist movement as any part of Latin America's solution because, he claimed, the movement was infected with Marxism.

His strategy in *Will It Liberate?* exemplified his approach. In a book ostensibly devoted to liberation theology, Novak disregarded theology and the Christian base communities altogether, concentrating instead on the socioeconomic pronouncements of the movement's most politicized theorists. He gave detailed attention, for example, to José Miranda's arguments for communism and his vulgar-Marxist rendering of Marx's labor theory of value.[118] Novak carefully examined these arguments, offered an effective critique of state collectivism, criticized the liberationist dependency on Marxism, and then—encouraged by his success at deflating liberationist utopianism—delivered a highly generalized attack on the entire liberationist movement. He argued that liberation theologies were theoretically and praxiologically distorted because virtually all of them were based on economic dependency theory.

But dependency theory explained more than Novak acknowledged. Dependency theory emphasized political and economic variables that clearly have played determinative roles in Latin America's economic history. Novak devoted much of his work to discrediting liberation theology while passing over its theological and communitarian roots. He scored numerous points against liberationists, offering arguments about economic culture and incentives that liberationists could ignore only at their peril. Many of his criticisms of liberationist political and economic arguments were justified. Yet his attacks on what he called liberationist "rubbish" were ultimately chauvinistic and unfair.[119] In its most representative forms, and in the common experience of those who had been changed by it, liberation theology was a rejection of the cultural legacy of Latin American authoritarianism and a call for community self-determination, economic democracy, and political freedom. Theologically, the movement's mainstream was deeply rooted in scriptural teaching and the spiritual traditions of the church.[120] Politically, the movement was characterized mainly by a democratic, cooperative, community-oriented praxis that Novak entirely overlooked. His criticisms of the movement's early Marxist pronouncements were sound and effectively presented; his attacks on the movement as a whole were not. Throughout the 1980s, liberation theology increasingly discarded its Marxist overtones and began to reflect the concrete experiences of the base communities themselves.[121]

Liberationists wrote so much about oppression, not to score points for Marxism, as Novak constantly implied, but because they were moved by the immense suffering of the poor. Novak claimed that liberation theology existed "much more powerfully in books than in reality."[122] The claim was disputed, however, by those who came into direct contact with the movement's hundreds of thousands of base communities. These communities worked together to dig community wells, build roads to inaccessible villages, create small businesses, establish community health care services and schools, organize trade unions, and found producer and consumer cooperatives—often at the risk of their lives. Liberationism was essentially their vision of emancipation, as well as their struggle for it. When Novak lectured in São Paulo in 1985, a protester held up a sign that read "Liberation theology is ours."[123]

Novak misread the grassroots nature of the movement because he viewed Latin American liberationism as a replay of his personal struggle over socialism versus capitalism. He believed the base communities were merely repeating his old mistakes. He got some of the arguments right and effectively criticized the movement's Marxist pronouncements, but he missed the cultural differences. More reliable than his characterization of liberationism was his confession that he often had difficulty comprehending the writings of liberation theologians because their framework of experience was so different from his own. [124]

This acknowledgment, in an earlier period, would have moved Novak to question the universal import of his experience. He once powerfully argued, drawing on the works of Claude Lévi-Strauss, that the myths of so-called "primitive" and other Third World cultures were no less logical than the dominant myths of Western civilization. "Our myth happens to be aimed at acquiring power over nature and of controlling our environment efficiently," he observed. "It is a moot point whether our myth is morally superior to myths aimed primarily at reconciling men both to the irrationalities of existence and to one another."[125] The universalistic dictums in his "theology" of the corporation later repudiated these culturally sensitive words with a revealing vengeance. Novak repeatedly charged those who remained in progressive politics with bad faith. [126] The charge was, in part, a projection of his own experience of defending positions he once disbelieved or deceived himself into accepting. To make the transition to the universally binding ideology he had apparently sought all along, he was forced to drop a wide range of discourses from his intellectual horizon. [127] His previous references to Lévi-Strauss, Paul Tillich, Rollo May, John Mbiti, and Jürgen Moltmann were replaced by quotes from Mises and Hayek. His lists of Whig theorists attempted to compensate for the loss.

ECONOMIC RIGHTS VERSUS POLITICAL RIGHTS

Novak turned to the Whig tradition after he lost his faith in socialism. Much of his work after his turn to the Right chronicled the death of socialism. In *The Spirit of Democratic Capitalism*, he acknowledged that nationalization was no longer an important feature of democratic socialism in Europe or North America. He further observed that modern democratic socialism was characterized by its commitment to political and cultural pluralism and by its defense of the market system. Modern democratic socialism emphasized decentralized forms of socialization, especially cooperative ownership, as well as the necessity of economic incentives and market discipline. But when social democrats rejected nationalization and promoted decentralized economic democracy, he asked, what was left of socialism? When socialists defended private property and personal owner-ship, as well as "a pluralistic political system, an open and tolerant moral-cultural system, and even economic techniques like the market and personal incentives, it is difficult to distinguish their fundamental ideals from those of democratic capitalism."[128]

Novak concluded that democratic socialism had died the death of a thousand qualifications. Socialism was an endlessly redefined moral vision that, having lost its ideological coherence, had become merely a symbol for grand ideals. "Insofar as democratic socialism has given up the classic positions of Marxism and the collectivized state, it may now be no more than a left-wing variant of democratic capitalism," he asserted. [129] Because cooperatives were still private forms of ownership, he argued, there was no difference in principle between democratic capitalism and modern democratic socialism. And what of those politicians and theorists who continued to call themselves socialists? Novak quoted Mises: "If anyone likes to call a social idea which retains private ownership of the means of production socialistic, why, let him! A man may call a cat a dog and the sun the moon if it pleases him."[130]

Novak allowed that there were significant differences remaining be-tween democratic capitalism and democratic socialism. Because socialists desired "more caring and compassion, more cooperativeness and practices of brotherhood," he observed, they promoted too much political control over the economy. So-called "democratic socialism" therefore needed to be rejected. [131] The difference was in degree rather than principle, how-ever, for "most democratic socialists are, in principle, democratic capital-ists."[132]

He assumed that socialism meant state ownership, though Western social democrats had eschewed this definition for the past half century. It was explicitly rejected in the Frankfurt Declaration of the Socialist Interna-tional in 1951. To Novak, this meant that Western social democrats were no longer socialist. Having rejected so much of its Marxist and Fabian heritage, modern democratic socialism had moved in the direction of becoming a variant of democratic capitalism. The difference between a social democratic and a liberal capitalist politics, however, was the differ-ence of economic democracy. It was a serious difference, as attested by the fact that when the U.S. Roman Catholic bishops endorsed economic democracy in the first draft of their pastoral letter on political economy, it was Novak who successfully campaigned for its removal.

He observed that strategies for economic democracy promoted worker- and community-controlled forms of ownership, establishing greater democratic accountability over the economy (especially the process of investment) in the context of political freedom.[133] American progressivism was presently reassimilating liberal themes "into its own new beginnings," extending the logic of liberal democracy into the economic sphere.[134] "Some call the new socialist ideal 'economic democracy,' by which they mean the submission of the economic system (or at least the large corporations and financial institutions) to political controls," he explained. "They may accept some limits upon government action over markets, especially for farmers, cooperatives, and small businesses, and some institutions of the liberal polity. But they do not accept the separation of the political system from the economic system." He opposed social democratic strategies because they blurred the distinction between politics and economics. Strategies to expand the cooperative sector and attain greater worker control over investment inevitably politicized the economic system. "In the name of the moral-cultural values of socialism, they desire to subordinate the economic system to the political system, thus collapsing the triune order of democratic capitalism into the unitary order of socialism."[135]

Novak did not prove or even try to demonstrate that social democratic governments had undermined pluralism in the European democracies. He effectively criticized old-style state socialism for politicizing the economic system and thus "collapsing the triune order" into some variable form of bureaucratic collectivism. He was less sensitive to similar outcomes when they occurred under democratic capitalism.[136] Novak repeatedly characterized social democratic planning as politicized and bureaucratic, but his writings skirted the deeply politicized and bureaucratic character of American capitalism, whose economic planning featured a colossal patchwork of government loans, import quotas, tax breaks, bailouts, price supports, subsidies, marketing restrictions, and research grants that profoundly shaped American life. Since the large corporations possessed the economic and political means to influence legislation, they were also the chief beneficiaries of government economic planning.[137]

Novak's most direct engagement with this issue occurred in his debate with Charles Lindblom, who argued in his influential *Politics and Markets* that corporate enterprises possessed the means to outstrip democratic gains within America's economic and political realms. It was a curious feature of modern democratic thought, Lindblom observed, "that it has not faced up to the private corporation as a peculiar organization in an ostensible democracy." He argued that the disproportionate power of large corporations prevented popularly elected governments from serving the interests of the public good.[138] The integrity of the political realm was undermined by the power of the corporate sector to dominate activities outside its own realm. Where Bell emphasized the cultural contradictions of modern capitalism, Lindblom emphasized the threat to political democracy posed by concentrated economic power.

Novak replied to Lindblom that government agencies such as the Pentagon and the Health and Human Services Administration employed more people than any single corporation. Most corporations were not large, and even the largest firms were smaller than some government agencies. Furthermore, large firms often needed to be large to make missiles for the Pentagon, to pass on retail savings to consumers, or to compete with large competitors in world markets. [139] Lindblom's point, however, was not that large enterprises were inherently unjustifiable. He questioned whether the far-reaching power and undemocratic structure of large corporations could be justified in a democracy. The problem was not that large firms were large, but that they were unaccountable to their workers and the communities in which they existed.

Novak rejected Lindblom's implicit call to democratize the economic system. "To organize industry democratically would be a grave and costly error, since democratic procedures are not designed for productivity and efficiency," he declared. [140] This abruptly dismissive judgment was rendered without any reference to the literature on mutual fund ownership or to the records of America's worker-owned enterprises. [141] The failure of Yugoslavian worker ownership was conclusive for Novak. He correctly implied that democratically managed capital was less mobile than corporate capital, and that the return on cooperative capital was often lower than that in corporations, because cooperative workers were more committed to keeping low-return firms in operation. Whether these disadvantages could be offset by gains in productivity and efficiency caused by worker control, however, was not a question he pursued. [142]

"To be a progressive is to be ennobled by an inner vision of a superior truth," Novak admonished. He reported that he had been able to resist the lure of "Irving Howe visions" of democratic socialism because his inner life was sustained by Roman Catholicism—"a much tougher faith." Those who didn't need socialism as a religion were in the best position to evaluate socialism and capitalism by their historical records. Though he embraced the phrase "democratic capitalism" as a parallel to democratic socialism, Novak elsewhere claimed that capitalism was actually asymmetrical with democratic socialism. Since democratic capitalism offered no vision of a democratized social order, he asserted, it was easier to subject capitalism to empirical tests. It followed for him that the free market capitalism of Adam Smith was more consistent with Roman Catholic faith than modern social democracy, because capitalism was more productive and because capitalism left it to other parties—such as the church—to define morality. [143]

Most of Novak's subsequent writings would be devoted to teaching the church about democratic capitalism. In 1982, he and Ralph McInerny founded the monthly magazine *Catholicism in Crisis* (later shortened to *Crisis*) as a vehicle for neoconservative criticism of modern Catholicism. The inaugural issue tried to instruct the American Catholic bishops on the ethics of nuclear deterrence. [144] The following year, Novak's impassioned defense of nuclear deterrence was published in his magazine and reprinted as a special issue of *National Review*. [145] "Moral Clarity in the Nuclear Age" was written in response to the first draft of the American bishops' pastoral letter on deterrence, *The Challenge of Peace*, and against what Novak called the "widespread, well-organized, and well-financed 'peace movement' " that was Finlandizing the West. [146]

Novak pleaded with the bishops not to encourage the appeasers, but was not surprised when they did. Dealing with the bishops was like dealing with the Moonies, he warned. Like the Moonies, there was no point in arguing with the bishops, because they were impervious to factual evidence. Novak labored to deradicalize the bishops' letter. He campaigned against their moralism and, after two years of debate, drew some consolation from the softer tone of their final draft. The first two drafts had nearly rejected the moral legitimacy of nuclear deterrence. Novak alternated between ridicule and reason in his efforts to dissuade the bishops from calling for unilateral disarmament initiatives. He accepted the bishops' condemnation of the nuclear targeting of cities and successfully implored them to defend the moral legitimacy of nuclear deterrence. In their final draft, the bishops accepted the moral legitimacy of the deterrence system as long as serious negotiations leading to disarmament were taking place. [147] *The Challenge of Peace* nonetheless considerably worsened the crisis in Catholicism. The letter was filled with peace language, and it insistently called for a halt to the arms race. Novak's early warning explained this outcome. The bishops' "positively Gnostic" and irresponsible "glorification" of the peace movement was inevitable, he had argued, given the spell under which they had fallen. [148] "One can only hope for them to be deconverted, as once they were converted," he wrote. [149]

From there he turned to the bishops' forthcoming letter on the political economy of capitalism. "Judging by my own education in American Catholic seminaries and in Rome, and judging by the current political climate, I think they may be tempted to emphasize the negative," he warned. "That, certainly, is the Catholic reflex on this subject." [150] The bishops needed to keep their reflexes in check by facing the overwhelming historical facts: "In the world of fact, the American social system is morally superior to any historical Catholic social system, whether of the Vatican or of any Catholic state," he subsequently wrote. "In the world of theory, American social teaching, in all its rich pluralism and radical depth, is both morally superior and far more highly developed than Catholic social teaching."[151]

In 1983, Novak and former U.S. Treasury Secretary William Simon organized a corporate-dominated lay commission to instruct the bishops. The following year, fearing that the bishops were composing another morally inferior pronouncement, the group issued its own manifesto on the superiority of American social teaching. *Toward the Future* celebrated the material blessings of modern capitalism and declared, against all advocates of strategic planning, that "the condition of inventiveness is liberty."[152] The statement was written principally by Novak and published shortly before the bishops' first draft was released in November 1984. The bishops, in turn, did not disappoint their critics. Their long-awaited draft vigorously criticized America's maldistribution of wealth, endorsed steps toward economic democracy, and called for the recognition of basic economic rights for all American citizens. They argued that providing justice for the poor was the "single most urgent claim on the conscience of the nation" and asserted that the nation's investment process should be directed specifically toward meeting the economic needs of the poor. Basic economic rights, they contended, were "as essential to human dignity as are the political and civil freedoms granted pride of place in the Bill of Rights of the U.S. Constitution." The bishops cited America's long struggle to secure civil and political rights for all Americans and declared, "We believe the time has come for a similar experiment in securing economic rights: the creation of an order that guarantees the minimum conditions of human dignity in the economic sphere for every person."[153]

The shadow-boxing was over. The publication of this "whiney and ungenerous" letter confirmed Novak's worst suspicions about the direction of American Catholic social teaching. The bishops were proposing not only to reaffirm, but to extend the logic of earlier Catholic teaching on economic rights and the moral duties of the state. Novak strenuously attacked these perceived errors, especially the bishops' affirmation of the doctrine of economic rights. He argued that this doctrine undermined the American idea of the limited state, since economic rights inevitably engendered greater state power. The doctrine also undermined the social structure of economic incentives, since it seemed to shift basic moral obligations to provide for one's family from the individual to the state. Novak helpfully noted that the bishops needed to define their conception of economic rights more carefully, distinguishing the notion as a claim in justice from possible constitutional or legal claims. It was unclear from their text whether they were advocating a constitutional amendment or sanctioning a new class of legal entitlements.[154] In either case, the doctrine was unnecessary and dangerous. It was unnecessary, Novak claimed, because the existing American alternative of equal opportunity for individuals already met the practical objectives of the 1948 United Nations Declaration of Human Rights. It was dangerous because, joined with the bishops' endorsement of economic democracy—which Novak characterized as "a democratic socialist battlecry"—it sanctioned greater state power. He later recalled, "After I explained to the bishops that 'economic democracy' was a wedge for democratic socialism, they stopped using the phrase."[155]

In October 1985, shortly before the bishops dropped their explicit references to economic democracy, Novak renewed his attack on the concept of economic rights. The essential strategy of the concept's proponents, he argued, was to include economic rights within the concept of human rights, "in order to gain for the former the prestige won by the latter through the horrors of World War II." Their first move was "to weaken the concept of political rights (e.g., by reducing 'rights' to 'claims'), in order to make them seem analogous to economic rights." Their second move was "to invest economic goals with moral content, and to describe them in at least a loose sense as 'rights.' " Their final move was to endorse what amounted to a preferential option for the state "as the final and normally the chief bearer of responsibility."[156] The most instructive example was David Hollenbach's *Claims in Conflict: Retrieving and Renewing the Catholic Human Rights Tradition*.[157] A Jesuit moral theologian, Hollenbach was, as Novak noted more than once, the chief theological consultant for the bishops' letter on economic policy. Under the banner of his interpretation of human rights theory, the bishops were marching to a new Constantinianism. "The extensive effort underway to commit the church to 'economic rights' has the potential to become an error of classic magnitude," Novak insisted. "It might well position the Catholic Church in a 'preferential option for the state' that will more than rival that of the Constantinian period."[158]

He charged that under the influence of theologians like Hollenbach, the bishops were misusing Pope John XXIII's endorsement of economic rights. In *Pacem in Terris*, John XXIII asserted that human beings possessed a right to sustainable income, food, shelter, medical care, and social services. These essential needs were listed under the category of "rights to life." "But he did not make these rights universal," Novak observed. "He confined them explicitly to the person who cannot meet his own responsibilities to provide for these basic needs 'through no fault of his own.' "[159] The new development in Catholic social thought was to turn John XXIII's endorsement of limited welfare rights into a doctrine of universal economic rights. Catholic social doctrine was already too socialistic. It sanctioned anticapitalist sentiments and overemphasized the value of community and solidarity. The bitter irony was that the claims of Catholic natural law theory were now being extended by *American* bishops. Their letter revealed an utter failure "to grasp the full power of the American legacy."[160]

Novak admonished the bishops that in the vocabulary of American politics, "solidarity" was a dangerous notion. The term didn't carry the moral glow for most Americans that it obviously held for the bishops. Solidarity was "a more proper term for the hive, the herd, or for the flock than for the democratic community."[161] The bishops were trying to impose "the Marxist definition of 'economic rights' upon the Western tradition of civil and political rights." They were therefore drawing upon such un-American concepts as solidarity, participation, marginalization, and economic democracy. These words were foreign to the American experience. Under the influence of their New Class theological consultants, the bishops were also using "horrible words" to describe the American system, Novak claimed. His example was the following: "The concentration of privilege that exists today results far more from institutional arrangements that distribute power and wealth inequitably than from differences of talent or lack of desire to work."[162] This statement capsulized the tragedy of the entire pastoral letter. It used phrases such as "concentration of privilege" that had nothing to do with America. "Where is this 'concentration'?" Novak indignantly asked. "Which American inherits 'privilege'? . . . This sentence is an outrage. It is wholly unsupported by evidence, because it cannot be. It is a species of 'blaming America first.' "[163]

It could not be that America had concentrations of wealth or privilege. This was a literary convention, perversely repeated by the New Class, which had no basis in fact. America showed why economic rights were unneccesary. America offered equal opportunity to everyone. The American alternative was superior to the statist conceptions of economic rights promulgated in social democratic and American Catholic social theory. Novak reserved his most bitter polemicizing for those who questioned the reality of this alternative. His argument presupposed, however, that equal opportunity existed in America. He denied that actual equality of opportunity required any base-line degree of equality of condition. What was needed to become successful in America, he later argued, was not any particular condition, but a particular spirit. The determinative inequity was not that some people were born into economic poverty or destitution, but that some people were born into poor cultures. Asian Americans and black Americans were presently confirming the point in contrasting ways. [164] Novak thus denied that the necessary preconditions for equal opportunity were lacking in the United States.

The American bishops nonetheless persisted in their determination to retain the language of economic rights. Though he argued that economic rights should be interpreted as a moral and not a political obligation, Novak later conceded that the moral obligation in question was a matter not only of charity, but of justice. He thus affirmed that such goods as food, housing, employment, and medical care were, according to Catholic natural law theory, "goods indispensable to a full human life." The "true conceptual force of the argument in favor of economic rights" was not that such goods were actually rights inhering in the nature of persons, he contended. This interpretation would only aggrandize the powers of the state and diminish human dignity. The goods posited by Catholic economic rights theory were, rather, indispensable goods that at present levels of American economic development "ought in justice to be provided." [165]

In succeeding years, Novak would insist that he won his arguments with the bishops over economic policy. On several points, his claims were justified. His concessions to Hollenbach over distributive justice, however, lost the crucial argument on which the bishops' letter was based. If economic security was a morally obligatory question of justice, it followed that state power should be used, when necessary, to obtain it. If basic economic goods were indispensable to a full human life, as Novak conceded, then economic needs were as important as civil and political rights. Hollenbach replied to Novak that since the provision of economic goods was indispensable to a full human life, it followed that these needs qualified as rights inhering in the nature of human beings. They were not to be regarded merely as worthy goals of the individual moral life. [166]

This was not to assume that economic goods were more important or morally significant than freedom. The bishops argued that rights to security and freedom were equally important. After the final draft of *Economic Justice for All* reaffirmed this principle, Novak objected that the "same so-called economic 'rights' whose aim is to 'empower' the poor would also greatly empower the state." To extend rights to the economic sphere would undermine the notion of rights itself, since the function of civil and political rights was to limit state power. The poor could be helped within liberal democratic societies "without involving this second-ary, and largely mischievous, use of the precious term 'rights,'" he argued. [167] His argument pressed a distinction where no material difference obtained, however. State power was required to uphold any entitlement in any sphere. The civil rights bills, most environmental legislation, and the various entitlement laws underlying the welfare state already used state power in ways that the bishops believed should be extended to employ-ment planning and comprehensive health coverage.

As Hollenbach explained, the bishops' approach built upon traditional Catholic natural law theory by incorporating aspects of modern liberal and communitarian moral theory. From modern liberal theory, which presup-posed that the right is prior to the good, they appropriated the language of individual rights and freedoms. [168] From communitarian theory, which presupposed that the good is prior to the right, they appropriated the language of virtue and the common good. [169] Liberal theory lacked the corrective Aristotelian and Thomist emphasis on the morally constitutive roles of communities in shaping individual sensibilities. On its own terms, liberalism was incoherent. It neglected the constitutive role of community in shaping the individual self—the "self" on which liberalism was ostensi-bly based. On the other hand, the communitarian emphasis on the cultivation of virtue and the common good needed the corrective liberal insistence on individual rights. Communitarianism without liberalism was suffocating. The moral theory behind contemporary Catholic teaching was thus, in Hollenbach's characterization, "a liberalism of a strongly revisionist kind" that blended the languages of rights and the common good. The task for Catholic social ethics, in this reading, was to synthe-size the Aristotelian–Thomist notion of covenanted community with liberalism's commitment to the freedom and equality of all individuals before the law. [170]

Novak disputed this formulation because it appropriated only modern egalitarian liberalism, while ignoring the classical liberalism of Smith, Mises, and Hayek. Hollenbach's blend of liberalism and communitarian-ism produced a social democratic politics. Its constitutive liberal element was statist and egalitarian, Novak argued. Much of the communitarian concern for the common good was already built into this kind of liberal-ism. But it was the classical liberalism of the Whigs, Novak insisted, that had been "crucial to the American experiment"—an experiment he consid-ered morally superior to Catholic moral theory. [171]

The Whigs taught the virtue of enterprise. "But when was the last time we heard in church, or learned from a text of moral theology, that personal economic enterprise is a necessary moral virtue?" he implored.

"Or received instruction in how to practice it? Or learned to criticize social systems in the light of how well, or how badly, they nourish and promote personal economic enterprise? Does our catechism teach us even so much as the basic conceptual definition of this virtue?"[172]

Novak told a story to illustrate the legacy of Catholic teaching. A group of Latin American priests traveled to an American university for a seminar on economics. They listened to lectures by North American economists for nearly a week, and learned a good deal. At the last session, the group's spokesman made a statement on their behalf. The priests had enjoyed the seminar and greatly appreciated the information it brought them, he said. They could see that U.S. capitalism was more productive and efficient than Latin American economic systems. "But we still think that capitalism is an immoral system," the priest reported. Novak observed,

> No doubt these priests were thinking that capitalism is based upon self-interest; but in their view, self-interest is an immoral motive. They believe that capitalism depends upon an ethic of "having," but they favor an ethic of "being." They hold that capitalism depends upon, and encourages, human tendencies toward selfishness, acquisitiveness, and even greed, whereas, in their eyes, a truly moral system would encourage habits of unselfishness, cooperation, and concern for the common good. After a full week of study, therefore, these priests were prepared to conclude that, although capitalism more effectively produces material goods than other systems, it does not nourish the moral and spiritual side of human life. In their view, capitalism is a system based on cynicism, corrupting the very springs of moral development.

For Novak, the story dramatized Catholicism's economic backwardness. Modern Catholicism had become modernized in the wrong ways. Novak was cheered by John Paul II's favorable words for market economies in *Centesimus Annus* and encouraged by the pontiff's apparent attention to his work. With ample warrant, he insisted that the Vatican did not approve of the American bishops' pastoral letters on nuclear deterrence or, especially, economic policy. He nonetheless repeatedly complained, however, that the church largely held to traditional ways of thinking about human nature, wealth, and materialism.[173]

The church needed an infusion of Whig realism, which taught a different set of virtues. The major Whig theorist of this century was Hayek, whom Novak cited as an instructive theorist for Catholic social doctrine. As Novak observed, Hayek stood in the mainstream of Whig theory.[174] His focus on social order, law, legislation, and tradition distinguished him from Whig libertarians such as Milton Friedman and John Hospers.[175] Novak complained that Catholic ethicists typically confused libertarianism with the wider Whig tradition. Their critiques of classical liberalism usually assumed that all Whigs endorsed the egotistical notion of the self posited by libertarians. The assumption was unjustified. Hayek, like the Smith of *The Theory of Moral Sentiments*, did not reduce self and society to economistic interchanges. Novak's belabored insistence on the point, however, bore witness to the narcissism of small differences. Like Friedman, Hayek repudiated the very idea of social justice. His major work, *The Mirage of Social Justice*, contended that "the common good" was an atavistic concept inherited from the collectivistic consciousness of tribal societies, in which hunters derived emotional benefits from providing food for their tribal dependents. Hayek derided the notions of "social justice" and "the common good" as tribal hangovers. These infantile sentiments attempted to compensate, he argued, for the loss of fellowship experienced within tribal societies.[176]

This was not Novak's position. His proposed merger of Catholic and Whig social thought remained Catholic enough to oppose the Whig denigration of the common good. The distinctive characteristic of the "Catholic Whig tradition," he averred, was its attempt to build the good society by giving equal primacy to the individual person and the community.[177] His conception of the common good blended Catholic and Whig themes. "The essence of the common good is to secure in social life the benefits of voluntary cooperation," he argued.[178] This blend was a Whiggish reduction, however, of a rich theological heritage. Unlike Whig theory, Novak's formulation preserved the language of the common good; unlike Catholic moral theory, it denigrated and minimized the role of the state. Novak tried to wring as much of a social conscience as he could out of classical liberalism. The problem was that the "benefits of voluntary cooperation" remained the benefits of charity, not of social justice. Justice required state power and action. When pressed on the point, Novak protested that he supported the existence of a limited welfare state. He was quick to accuse others, such as Hollenbach, of taking cheap shots at him when they questioned his support for the welfare state.[179] His denunciations of liberalism, welfare, employment planning, progressive tax policy, environmentalism, and the state itself raised the question, however, on nearly every page of his work. For Novak, the crucial test of the economic system was whether it created wealth; for most Catholic moral theory, the test was how the system produced and distributed wealth. Despite his considerable efforts to narrow the gap, Novak's emphasis on the independence of the economic sphere was finally irreconcilable with modern Catholicism's emphasis on the organic connections between the political, economic, and cultural spheres.

THE MORAL-CULTURAL REALM: NOVAK'S LATER WRITINGS

Novak's work presented a curious reversal. It was, perhaps, fitting that the same person who wrote a theology of radical politics at the height of the student rebellion in the 1960s later wrote a theology of the corporation and a catechism of capitalist virtues during the Reagan–Bush era. The differences between his early and later writings, however, transcended the changes in his political outlook. The depth and sophistication of Novak's political writings after his conversion to neoconservatism far surpassed his earlier work. His neoconservative writings on politics were unfailingly interesting, insightful, probing, and solidly researched. His work was enriched by his passion to claim the language of democracy for the Right. Novak's political writings continually explored new lines of inquiry as well as the implications of contemporary theoretical debates for his position.

This project unfortunately eclipsed his theological interests.[180] Though his early writings were riddled with poorly informed political judgments, his deep and critically engaged interest in modern theology compensated for these failings. Such works as *Belief and Unbelief, All the Catholic People,* and *The Experience of Nothingness* were inspired not by political debates, but primarily by Novak's religious imagination. As he explained in *The Rise of the Unmeltable Ethnics,* his writings were driven by a single overriding concern, which was "to attend to the imaginative, perceptual, and affective sides of human consciousness, to what I have called 'intelligent subjectivity.' " [181] *Ascent of the Mountain, Flight of the Dove* significantly advanced this project. Novak's early work was typically concerned, sometimes profoundly, with the human search for meaning through myth, symbol, and community. His early writings contained a religious message that outweighed the worth of his political opinions or purposes.

His early writings also contained extensive discussions of developments in systematic and philosophical theology. In his 1967 collection, *A Time to Build,* he wrestled with subjects that later dropped from his intellectual horizon. The obligatory section on the Vietnam War was outweighed considerably by his theological reflections on Niebuhr, Bernard Lonergan, Paul Tillich, Dietrich Bonhoeffer, and others.[182] Though he later complained about the tyranny of progressive moral style, Novak's mind was most open to various theological, philosophical, sociological, and anthropological currents before he turned to neoconservatism. His work afterward was saturated with his ideological preoccupations.

After his neoconservative turn, Novak no longer contributed to Catholic systematic theology. His earlier interests in the theologies of Lonergan, Karl Rahner, and Johannes Metz disappeared. In his later writings he handled theological questions by invoking Jacques Maritain, explaining that he wanted to revivify Maritain's work. "You may assume that his philosophy and his theology are mine," he declared. [183] But to wave aside the questions of theological method, hermeneutics, language, and authority in this way was to drop out of contemporary theological discussion. The theologies of Lonergan, Rahner, and Metz were crucial for modern Catholic thought, as Novak once understood, precisely because Maritain's neo-Thomist apologetics were too disengaged from developments in modern philosophy and the sciences to address the epistemological, methodological, and hermeneutical issues that contemporary theologies are required to address. Robert McAfee Brown bitterly complained that Novak's writings about liberation theology were not about liberation theology at all, but were really about Novak's own politics. [184] The same point obtained for most of Novak's ostensibly theological writings. Though he criticized the liberationists for overly politicizing Christian theology (a charge that was merited in certain cases), Novak had become as politicized, in his own way, as the most fervent liberationist.

His main theological work after his conversion to neoconservatism confirmed this judgment. *Confession of a Catholic* was an often moving account of Novak's personal faith, structured as a gloss on the Nicene Creed. The narrative was driven not by a theological argument, however, but by Novak's animus against feminism and modern liberalism. He noted at the outset that he no longer felt at home with magazines he used to write for, such as *Commonweal*, *The National Catholic Reporter*, and *Christianity and Crisis*. "A drift to the Left, both in theology and in politics, has taken these magazines out of the orbit of what used to be called liberal Catholicism or biblical realism," he contended. [185] He attributed much of the reason to the rise of feminism, which he charged had infected modern Christianity with the ancient virus of gnosticism. Novak condemned modern feminism's egalitarian character, claiming that feminism was a dehumanizing ideology fueled by an irrational rage against the embodied realities of sexual difference. Echoing Gerhart Niemeyer, he argued that feminism raged not only against the abuse of difference, but against difference itself. [186] Novak therefore deprecated feminist criticisms of traditional patriarchal language and ecclesiology. Feminism was driven not by a moral concern for justice and human dignity, he argued, but by an irrational gnostic rage against the natural order.

He elaborated the argument elswhere. "The gnostic spirit, asserting in part that sexual differentiation entailed no essential difference in the ordering of natural or supernatural life (and, consequently, none in ecclesiastical life), also asserted that, in a sense, the ultimate force in nature is the mothering force of spiritual inclusiveness," he explained. The "female principle" was oceanic, blurring crucial differences, while the "male principle" insisted upon necessary distinctions. The feminist virus had infected modern Catholicism because church leaders no longer taught why God had to be conceived in masculine images, why the Messiah needed to be a son rather than a daughter, and why it was important "that the sacraments of Catholicism should not be imagined as inclusive and oceanic, but fenced in by male images." The church needed a reassertion of discriminating and authoritative male teaching. The church's problems with feminist criticism were largely attributable to the meekness of church leaders, he argued. "If men and non-feminist women were to respond as feminists allege that they do—with decisiveness, competitiveness, and repression—these [feminist] absurdities would long since have been laughed out of currency," Novak declared. "But in the presence of feminists, most men are meek, humble, and submissive. They scrutinize feminism seriously, seeking some possible way, absurd as it seems, in which the will of God might actually be expressed in it."[187]

The church's problems with modern feminism were traceable to this strategy of appeasement, he argued. The church was plagued with vengeful feminists because it tried to appease their absurd anger. "The rage of feminists is partly to be explained by the weakness of the males they encounter," he instructed. "Men find it more difficult to stand up to the fury of a woman than to any other thing on earth; nothing so tests their manhood." Church leaders were flunking the test. The result was that the church found itself besieged by self-hating feminists demanding a world made over. Novak claimed that feminism was finally a declaration of war against nature, experience, and tradition. The revolution called for by feminists was not progressive, humane, or even radical, but total. "That is why the hatred they manifest is so unbelievably intense," he explained. The early church fathers finally figured this out in the third century, he noted, when they reversed the church's earlier openness toward women taking prophetic, priestly, and episcopal roles.[188] The wisdom of Catholic orthodoxy, for him, was exemplified by the church's tradition of suppressing female voices. Though he wrote comparatively little on the subject,

Novak's antipathy for feminism was an important element of his neoconservatism. His admiration for the tradition of Catholic orthodoxy, like Kristol's, was linked to the antenicene church's delegitimization of female leadership and its suppression of early Christianity's prophetic spirit.

If church leaders had not yet reverted to the preorthodox practices of early Christianity, he conceded, they had nonetheless already made a mockery of the church's ancient liturgical tradition. "I normally leave the contemporary liturgy in a state of numbness," Novak reported. "I think of the progressive Church as 'progressive bourgeois Christianity,' and its sentiments of peace, love, community, solidarity and the like remind me of the saccharine holy cards of an earlier form of bourgeois Christianity, which I also did not like." Modern liturgies were trashing the church's sacramental tradition. The ancient liturgy of the church was being turned into "a celebration of our being together," he moaned. "It's awful."[189]

Modern liberal theology was ripe for feminism because it had long operated within what Novak called the horizon of democratic socialism. He noted ruefully that nearly every major Christian theologian of the twentieth century had been a democratic socialist.[190] The list included Walter Rauschenbusch, Karl Barth, Tillich, Charles Gore, William Temple, Charles Raven, the early Niebuhr, Moltmann, Rahner, Gutierrez, James Cone, and Rosemary Ruether. The influence of this intellectual legacy was evident in the American Academy of Religion, the Society of Christian Ethics, and in most of the prestigious theological journals, which imparted "a democratic socialist vision of reality." The vision of a democratized social order held a virtual monopoly on permissible views within modern theology. He observed that even such an irenic and comparatively unpoliticized theologian as David Tracy assumed that some form of democratic socialism was needed as an alternative to state socialism and late capitalism. The "tacit favoritism toward the Left" in modern theology was thus demonstrated both by those who were outspokenly politicized and by those who were not.[191]

This situation left Novak with much work to do. His chief response to it was that modern theology mistakenly appropriated feminist, communitarian, liberal, and neo-Marxist social theories while disregarding the Whig tradition.[192] Novak argued that a full-scale theological project in the Whig mold was needed. His work did not meet this need, however, for reasons that were arguably telling.

Novak frequently called his position "biblical realism," explaining that his approach to politics was always informed by a biblical sense of the limitations and sinfulness of human nature.[193] "It is a rather humbling insight about human nature that we must accept human beings in their sinfulness rather than in their grandeur," he explained. "At the heart of capitalist creativity lies self interest."[194] He never developed the biblical meaning of biblical realism, however, beyond this passing invocation of the term. Novak tried to cover his position with the glow of religious authority by calling it "biblical," but he otherwise made no attempt to relate actual biblical texts or themes to his arguments. His vague references to biblical realism made no reference to scriptural texts or modern biblical scholarship. The question thus arose whether his "biblical realism" had any scriptural basis.

His critique of Latin American liberation theology provided the answer. As Novak conceded, most liberation theology was deeply biblical. Liberationists typically appealed to scriptural passages and themes, usually in conversation with modern biblical scholarship. Novak coped with this fact by dismissing the relevance of the Bible's social teachings. His attack on the easiest liberationist target—José Miranda—was typical. "It never occurs to Miranda that in its economic views the Bible is a pre-capitalist document," he declared. "The secrets of economic development were not discovered until the end of the eighteenth century."[195]

The Bible's numerous injunctions against accumulating wealth therefore could be dismissed, he claimed, on account of the Bible's economic context. The New Testament's condemnations of materialism could be written off as precapitalist. "In the premodern world, wealth played a rather different and far simpler role than it plays today," Novak reasoned. "Correspondingly, the moral judgment passed on it was simpler."[196] Novak explained that the Pauline injunction against loving money needed to be understood as the moral perspective of a precapitalist observer. Capitalism changed the moral equation, because under capitalism it was no longer necessary to conquer others to attain wealth. What the New Testament meant to condemn (as distinguished from what it unfortunately proclaimed) was not pursuing material self-interest, but domination. The pursuit of self-interest, as Novak observed, lay at the heart of capitalism. He conceded that the New Testament repeatedly condemned this very preoccupation. He tried to bridge the contradiction by claiming that the early Christians would have felt differently if they had lived under capitalism.[197]

"The rage for equality is a wicked project," he asserted, quoting Madison. "I'm afraid that under the influence of the Latin Americans, the church has gotten hooked into this project." It was a destructive development, because the church had a crucial role to play in shaping the moral culture in which capitalism operated. "Neoconservatism is not just an argument about capitalism, but an argument about the whole," he explained. "A key feature of neoconservatism is the priority of culture over economics."[198] Novak argued that most of America's social ills were cultural rather than political or economic. Like the problem he described, however, his characterization of America's moral culture was not so much integrated into his defense of capitalism as overwhelmed by it.

He claimed that the relative autonomy of the political and economic realms under modern capitalism could be secured by a vigorous moral-cultural realm, which he described as a system that paralleled the political and economic realms. The moral-cultural realm, though often neglected in social and political theory, was "the chief dynamic force behind the rise both of a democratic political system and of a liberal economic system."[199] The primary function of the moral-cultural realm was to shape and control the forces unleashed in other realms. A vital moral-cultural realm was needed to restrain commercial society's assaults on the ties of family, community, and tradition. The moral-cultural realm needed to counteract the egotism and materialism promoted by capitalist economies and to reinforce the moral habits engendered by entrepreneurialism. Novak's rejoinder to Bell, therefore, was that modern democratic societies could remain productive and pluralistic only if they remained capitalist and preserved a moral-cultural order that restrained the worst effects of commercialism.[200]

But this was exactly the problem. It was the alcohol and entertainment industries, and not the churches, that spent billions of dollars manipulating the desires and sensibilities of young consumers. It was chiefly the commodification of personal and social values under modern capitalism that undermined the force of the moral-cultural realm. Moreover, most "cultural" institutions operated within the economic and political systems. Most of America's major cultural institutions were either profit-making firms or government agencies. As Steinfels observed, these included the television networks, the film and music industries, the pornography trade, and the advertising industry, as well as such nonprofit entities as think tanks funded by the Pentagon and vast sectors of the government itself.[201] The attractive notion that democratic capitalism ensured pluralism ignored the predominance of economic power over the rest of society. It also overlooked the fact that most of the cultural system was part of the economic system.

Novak worked both sides of the cultural issue. He frequently enthused about the popularity and influence of American culture around the world—and elsewhere condemned its vulgarity. Reflecting on the power of commercial advertising and the dominant values of the commercial media, he lamented that "we are beseiged by ideas, ideals, and solicitations that on reflection we find morally repulsive."[202] He reported that he and his wife had long felt "that the world of the media was a tidal wave, which we could hardly hold back by ourselves. We have long felt under seige, even in our own home. . . . Our own public moral culture, formed preeminently by television, cinema, and music, is a disgrace to the human race."[203]

Novak claimed, however, that the shortcomings of America's moral culture had nothing to do with modern capitalism. He declared that if America's moral-cultural realm ever attempted to fulfill its proper role, and then failed in the effort, he would concede that the country's economic system might bear some responsibility for the problem. Lacking such an effort in the moral-cultural realm, he refused to blame America's social ills on the corrupting effects of its economic system, but instead blamed those who shaped American culture.[204] He insisted that the distinction was clear. The cultural issue had become paramount for neoconservatives because "the Left still owns the heights of American culture." The problem was that the New Class controlled the media, the educational system, and the churches, he argued, resulting in "the lagging scholastic competence of American students; the widespread use of drugs; violence in and near our schools; the rising incidence of suicide; the pointlessness that so many experience and express; the vacuity of the music they listen to and the moral heedlessness of the rock videos they watch." America needed a countercultural offensive to overturn and regenerate its corrupt liberal culture.[205]

In 1990, he recalled,

> For several years, it was all going our way. Reagan was president, defense spending increased, the rate of social spending was reduced, a tax cut was reviving the economy, people felt good again about their country. We got used to winning—and then the Bork hearings brought us back to reality. We underestimated the power of the Left, and we paid for it. The campaign against Robert Bork's nomination [to the Supreme Court] was a rude surprise for us. It shocked us into realizing how much power the Left still holds over our country, and what we need to do about it.[206]

Novak belonged to neoconservatism's democratic globalist wing. He believed that with the demise of the Soviet threat, American foreign policy should be devoted to exporting American democracy around the world. His writings mainly focused, however, on neoconservatism's other remaining battleground: the fight against New Class liberalism.

In 1987, *The Christian Century* asked him to assess the legacy of Reinhold Niebuhr. Novak did not claim, as the article's title ("Reinhold Niebuhr:

Model for Neoconservatives") implied, that Niebuhr was a neoconservative or a model for neoconservatives. He acknowledged that Niebuhr was
a man of the Left who undoubtedly would have criticized neoconservatism. In his view, however, Niebuhr would have been a fatherly critic who
looked upon the neoconservatives as independent children to whom he
"had taught a thing or two." The main thing was that so-called American
progressives were members of a New Class that cloaked its drive for power
in the language of moral idealism. [207]

Novak recycled the debating points from his 1972 essay on Niebuhr.
The same books were cited; the same incriminating quotes from Michael
Harrington, James MacGregor Burns, and Christopher Lasch were resurrected. The implication was that nothing had changed in the meantime.
The New Class had changed, however. It had spawned one movement
that featured the chief characteristics attributed to it by neoconservatives.
This was neoconservatism itself. Novak condemned political liberalism for
its "redistributionism," while the Reagan administration carried out a
massive redistribution of wealth to the rich. [208] He accused liberation
theologians of sacralizing their own politics, while claiming that corporations mirrored the presence of God. He claimed that his turn to neoconservatism marked a return to his working-class roots, while ridiculing
those who opposed cutting the capital gains tax to 15 percent. (Opposition to the proposal was based, he explained, on "childish calls to class
warfare." For Novak, "class warfare" was an epithet reserved not for those
who made the tax system more regressive, but for those who complained
about it.)[209] He chided the tenured prophets of academe for their worldli-
ness, while attaching himself to the American Enterprise Institute and
accepting grants from the Olin Foundation. [210]

In the late 1980s, Novak's celebrations of American capitalism began
to be featured regularly in *Forbes* magazine, sandwiched between its
massive advertising sections and its updates on leveraged buy-outs, greenmail, junk bonds, and executive salaries. He rejoiced in America's economic and military power. He enthused that American power and the
power of the American idea were remaking the world. In the next breath,
he eloquently castigated the cultural ravages and failures of America's
cities, schools, media, churches, and governments. He denied that America's social problems were partly attributable to what he once called
"America's concentration of social and economic power." Had he conceded the point, this once unmeltable ethnic might have been forced to
reconsider whether he really had found his way home.

6

Facing Up to Modernity: Peter Berger

A more chastened neoconservatism is conceivable. If neoconservatives are typically the Trotskyists of American conservatism, as Irving Kristol says, it is at least possible to imagine a neoconservatism that would be less preoccupied with culture wars, unilateralist presumptions, and foreign crusades. This neoconservatism would be less concerned with ideological wars for position than with attempting to defend existing arrangements in the name of realism. It would be less concerned with the responsibilities of empire than with America's economic decay. To face up to modernity, it could be argued, is to accept the logic and consequences of capitalist modernization. Neoconservatism is amply represented in academe, but few of its chief theorists have functioned primarily as academics. It is from academe, however, that the movement's most moderate and empirically minded major publicists have come, including Nathan Glazer and Peter Berger. Due to the greater range and influence of his writings, the possibility of a more chastened neoconservatism is best exemplified by Berger's work.

He has never been a leftist of any kind. Berger was born in Vienna in 1929 and lived in Austria until mid-adolescence. He once recalled that his conservatism was nurtured as a youth not by Burkean pastoral visions, but by the stories he heard of the vanished glories of Habsburg Austria. "Perhaps the last *really* worthwhile political enterprise in the twentieth century would have been to try and preserve the Austro-Hungarian monarchy," he mused. "The cause, alas, is lost, and in any case I was born a quarter-century too late for joining its banners."[1] The downfall of the Austro-Hungarian empire would inoculate him from later neoconservative crusades for world democracy, since the empire was dismembered, in part, by Woodrow Wilson's imperial democratism. Berger was compensated during his youth by the deeply conservative Lutheranism of his parents, which he accepted for himself.

Except for an occasional aside about his memories of the rise of fascism, he did not discuss his childhood and declined to answer any questions about it. His father, a businessman, brought the family to New York in 1946. Berger enrolled at Wagner College at the age of seventeen and graduated in 1949. He completed a master's degree in sociology the following year at the New School for Social Research and entered Lutheran Theological Seminary in Philadelphia shortly afterward, intending to become a Lutheran pastor. He lasted one year. Berger later recalled that throughout his enjoyable but ultimately unsettling introduction to modern theology and biblical scholarship, he repeatedly asked himself, "Could I preach that?" The question finally answered itself. Berger's theological conservatism was shaken at seminary. At the same time, he found prevailing liberal theologies to be poor substitutes for his earlier faith. He decided that he would not seek ordination if he couldn't espouse the creedal affirmations that his seminary education caused him to doubt. It would take him nearly fifteen years to assimilate the experience.[2]

Berger returned to the New School to earn his doctorate in sociology, where he studied under Carl Mayer, Albert Salomon, and Alfred Schutz, and completed his degree in 1954. He became an American citizen in 1952 and entered the army the following year. While serving in the army, he taught at the University of Georgia and later taught at the Evangelical Academy in Bad Boll, Germany, where he became friends with the father of the German academies, Eberhard Müller. He subsequently taught for two years at the Women's College of the University of North Carolina before moving to the Hartford Seminary Foundation in 1958.

He thus came early to the New Class world of institutes, foundations, and consulting. As director of Hartford Seminary's Institute of Church and Community, Berger organized conferences on medical ethics and worked with the University of Connecticut to teach professional sociologists how to become church consultants.

FAITH AND BAD FAITH

It was during Berger's term at Hartford Seminary that his first, widely debated books on America's religious establishment were published. *The Noise of Solemn Assemblies* and *The Precarious Vision* were both published in 1961. The former was a Kierkegaardian attack on the triumph of the therapeutic in the churches. "When I started writing, I was interested in criticizing the church from within, as an avowed Christian," he later recalled. *The Noise of Solemn Assemblies* argued that America's mainline Protestant churches were not preaching the transcendent gospel of Christ, but a therapeutic form of culture-religion. The mission of the modern churches was not to save souls, but to socialize middle-class individuals into what Berger called "the O.K. world." The churches baptized the existing social order and integrated its members into that order. "Our psychologists tell us that the mentally healthy individual is one who is capable of coping with reality," he observed. "What they commonly overlook is that reality itself is socially constructed. The values and cognitive beliefs of a society construct the world in which its members live. The place of religion in this socially constructed world will determine the way in which it will help or hinder the individual in adjusting to reality."[3]

In Berger's view, the mainline churches were protecting their role in American society by swallowing a bourgeois form of the Durkheimian bargain. The institutional interests of the churches were served by reducing the otherworldly claims of Christian faith to a therapeutic endorsement of middle-class American life. The churches emphasized "the 'O.K.' character of typical middle-class family life" and thus implicitly censured those outside it. The result was an especially insidious form of bad faith in which religion shielded individuals from the truth about themselves and their world. The faith of the churches engendered and reinforced inauthenticity. "It ratifies the routines, sanctifies the values by which the social roles are rationalized, comforts the individual if personal crises threaten his social adjustment," Berger argued. "The 'O.K. world' is the world of inauthenticity." The churches were protecting their privileged place in American society by refusing to adopt a critical or even an independent perspective toward it. In sociological terms, the religious establishment's functionality was obtained through its social irrelevance. The churches were functional in American society to the exact degree that they were passive within it.[4]

Berger allowed that this strategy was achieving its ostensible purpose. From a sociological standpoint, the churches' therapeutic turn was enabling them to attain optimal functionality in a middle-class consumer society. The former seminarian observed that it also trivialized and debased authentic Christianity. Berger's conception of that faith was a page torn from Karl Barth. The church existed not to fill emotional needs for meaning or society's need for order, but to witness to Christ. The business of the church was to confront the world with truth claims about the divinity of Christ and salvation in Christ's name. "We must decide whether to believe in the truth of this message and whether to accept the demands it makes on our existence," Berger asserted. "The Christian faith is not a mystical path into the mysterious depths of our own being. Indeed, the Christian faith might seriously question whether we possess any such depths. The mystery to which it points is an external one. It lies in history, not in psychology."[5]

In their pronouncements about spirituality, spiritual nurture, and the religious needs of the self, America's mainline churches were reducing the muscular Christianity of the Reformers to a sentimental consumer good. Instead of preaching salvation through Christ, they were selling the experience of being well churched. "There occurs a process of religious inoculation, by which small doses of Christianoid concepts and terminology are injected into consciousness," Berger explained. "By the time the process is completed, the individual is effectively immunized against any real encounter with the Christian message." Since the entire process actually paraded under Christian flags, most of those subjected to it and even most of those who professionally administered it were impervious to its faith-killing consequences. "The ideology under whose auspices this travesty occurs is very fond of organic analogies to the religious life," Berger observed. "It likes to speak of 'nurture,' 'growth,' 'maturation.' " In a sociological sense, the maturation metaphor was well-chosen; the churches' rhetoric reflected their function in American society, which was to produce well-adjusted middle-class conformists. Religion thus became a "sentimental accompaniment" to the socialization process.[6]

The triumph of the therapeutic thus inoculated American churchgoers from ever hearing the gospel. "To say the least, it is difficult to imagine how the religiously mature, socially respectable, and psychologically adjusted church member in our situation can come to terms with the naked horror of Calvary or the blazing glory of Easter morning," Berger concluded. "Both his religion and his culture compel him to sentimentalize, neutralize, assimilate these Christian images. If he did not do so, they would challenge his religiosity and his respectability and might even threaten his so-called mental health."[7]

It was not the proper function of Christian faith to provide the basis for morality, social order, respectability, or even a good way of life. The Precarious Vision catalogued the ways in which America's churches were reducing Christianity to such inferior ends by reducing Christianity to a spiritual religion. Berger drew on Dietrich Bonhoeffer's call for a secularized or "religionless" Christianity to describe how the churches might recover their biblical heritage.[8] Following Bonhoeffer, he argued that the historical roots of secularization were in the biblical tradition. "By denuding the cosmos of its divinity and placing God totally beyond its confines, the biblical tradition prepared the way for the process we now call secularization," Berger explained. "It was Protestantism even more than Renaissance humanism which inaugurated the great process which Weber called 'disenchantment.' "9

Not for the last time, Berger called on Americans to face up to modernity. The challenge for the churches was to face up to modernity's desacralizing logic, which brought the secularizing thrust of the Bible to its ultimate conclusion. The concept of a "religious self" bearing "spiritual needs" was a throwback to the age of magic. Any church that based its existence on ministering to these purported needs was dooming itself to inevitable extinction as the secularization process continued. The prophetic church would break free from religion. It would call for an exodus from the illusion-breeding bad faith of the modern churches, "an exodus out of the Egypt of deceptive social safety, but also out of the Zion of deceptive religious security."10

Restrained by his relative lack of theological training, Berger did not elaborate a constructive theological rationale for his position. This task was taken up by Harvey Cox.11 Not for the last time, Berger's ideas were later sharpened and developed by someone considerably to his Left. Like Norman Podhoretz and Michael Novak, however, Berger spent the early 1960s tweaking America's religious and political establishments for their conformism. His call for alienation struck a responsive chord among college students. The 1950s were over. *The Noise of Solemn Assemblies* and *The Precarious Vision* were read in college chapels across the country. The popularity of Berger's early books owed more to his sarcastic criticisms of the churches than to any constructive purpose he had in mind. To judge from the reviews, many of his readers found this purpose rather opaque. By the time he returned to the subject, at the end of the decade, Berger had discarded the theological position on which his early books were based. What remained from his early writings was his emphasis on freedom and bad faith.

These themes were brought forward in his classic introduction to sociological reasoning, *Invitation to Sociology*, which became an academic best seller. Traditional sociology presented a highly deterministic perspective on society, he observed. From a traditional sociological perspective, the human subject was viewed largely as a product and victim of his or her social environment. Human beings were the prisoners of society, which "encompasses our life on all sides . . . and confronts us especially in the form of coercion." Our specific location in the social system "predetermines and predefines almost everything we do, from language to etiquette, from the religious beliefs we hold to the probability that we will commit suicide." An impressive variety of punitive social sanctions awaited those who failed to accept their assignments. From this perspective, Berger observed, "society is the walls of our imprisonment in history."[12]

He knew his audience. The sixties generation craved alienation. Turning to the culturally vaunted virtue of maturity, Berger asked his student readers to consider the example of the middle-aged Joe Blow. Having reached middle age, Mr. Blow accepted the fact that his wife would never become more attractive and that his job as an assistant advertising manager would never become more interesting or rewarding. He looked back on his life and decided that his earlier dreams to fornicate with many beautiful women and write the great American novel had been immature. This was what society called maturity. Maturity was the state of mind in which one relinquished one's dreams of adventure, achievement, and fulfillment. "It is not difficult to see that such a notion of maturity is psychologically functional in giving the individual a rationalization for having lowered his sights," Berger commented. "Nor is it difficult to imagine how the young Joe, assuming the gift of augury, would have recoiled from his later self as from an image of defeat and desperation."[13] The rationalization that society venerated as maturity was one of the most powerful control mechanisms by which society imprisoned its inmates, he argued.

In the face of this rather grim sociological account, Berger appealed to the existential notions of freedom and bad faith. The problem with traditional sociology's account of the human predicament was that, like the modern churches, it reinforced bad faith. An oversocialized account of the human subject reinforced human tendencies to evade personal responsibility for important decisions. People often said, "I must do this," when they were actually making a voluntary choice. " 'I must' is a deceptive explanation in nearly every social situation," Berger claimed. The essence of bad faith was to pretend that something voluntarily chosen was necessary. "Bad faith is thus a flight from freedom, a dishonest evasion of the 'agony of choice,' " he declared. The alienated waiter who shuffled through his rounds, the woman who pretended not to notice that she was being seduced, the terrorist who excused his crimes in the name of following orders from his superiors—all were examples of bad faith. Bad faith covered society "like a film of lies."

The same social fact, however, revealed the possibility of freedom. People could choose to be in bad faith only because they were, in fact, free not to accept their freedom. Bad faith was the "shadow of human liberty." Berger explained that every social role carried with it the possibility of bad faith. The complex of roles within which the human subject existed in society amounted to an immense apparatus of bad faith. "Every man who says 'I have no choice' in referring to what his social role demands of him is engaged in bad faith," he argued. This was not to say that the excuse-maker's explanation was always untrue within the context of a given role, but rather that the role itself was nearly always chosen. In bourgeois societies, people chose to be business executives, lawyers, farm workers, soldiers, friends, parents, and the like. "They are in bad faith when they attribute to iron necessity what they themselves are choosing to do," Berger explained. [14]

Anti-Semitism offered a classic example. Following Jean-Paul Sartre's analysis, Berger observed that the anti-Semite identified with a mythological nation or race and thus attempted to relinquish responsibility for his or her own freedom. [15] Like any form of racism, anti-Semitism was a pernicious type of bad faith because it identified people "in their human totality with their social character." Berger assigned persecution of homosexuals to the same category. "In both cases, one's own shaky identity is guaranteed by the counterimage of the despised group," he observed. The racist and the homophobe both legitimated themselves by despising those supposedly most unlike themselves. Their identities were confirmed by the establishment of their right to hate others in the despised group. Humanity itself thus became "a facticity devoid of freedom." The participant in bad faith lived in a mythological world in which all people were identified with their social designations. It did not require much insight, Berger noted, to perceive the cold panic that lurked behind the hateful fulminations of the bigot. [16]

"Since society exists as a network of social roles, each one of which becomes a chronic or a momentary alibi from taking responsibility for its bearer, we can say that deception and self-deception are at the very heart of social reality," Berger argued. "Society provides for the individual a gigantic mechanism by which he can hide from himself his own freedom. Yet this character of society as an immense conspiracy in bad faith is, just as in the case of the individual, but an expression of the possibility of freedom that exists by virtue of society." [17] He would later argue that bad faith was engendered and reinforced in American culture by leftist politics even more than by the churches.

Invitation to Sociology thus ended on a prescriptive note, correcting the cold determinism of sociological description with an existentialist insistence on the reality of freedom. The human subject was a prisoner of society only to the extent that he or she failed or refused to recognize the influence of society upon the self, as well as upon the choices that each situation presented. Sociological analysis could reinforce bad faith if it reconciled the reader to a fatalistic attitude toward personal or public choices. To begin to understand the complex social and psychological causes of racism or poverty or war was, for many, to be driven to hopelessness. Anyone who took sociological analysis only this far would use it in bad faith. Berger insisted that sociological analysis could be liberating, however, when it was used to inform and empower one's growth in freedom. "Sociology is justified by the belief that it is better to be conscious than unconscious and that consciousness is a condition of freedom," he concluded. "Even those who do not find in this intellectual pursuit their own particular demon, as Weber put it, will by this contact have become a little less stolid in their prejudices, ·a little more careful in their own commitments and a little more skeptical about the commitments of others—and perhaps a little more compassionate in their journeys through society."[18]

CONSTRUCTING THE SOCIAL WORLD

Sociology deconstructed the social fictions that rationalized most human behavior. More positively, sociological analysis provided the means to understand the constructive character of human behavior. Human behavior was not determined completely by nature or social circumstances or some conflation of these factors. Human behavior was a construction shaped by natural and social forces open to human modification. This conception of social reality as a human construction was further developed in Berger's systematic treatise in the sociology of knowledge, *The Social Construction of Reality*, written with Thomas Luckmann.

In 1963, Berger joined the Graduate Faculty of the New School as an associate professor of sociology, a position he held for three years before moving to Brooklyn College. The same year, he and Luckmann drew up the first plan for *The Social Construction of Reality*. This book elaborated Alfred Schutz's pioneering phenomenological investigations into the notion of society as a subjective reality, with supportive borrowings from Emile Durkheim, Karl Marx, Max Weber, and George Herbert Mead. *The Social Construction of Reality* brought forward the dialectic of "man in society" and "society in man" that Berger introduced in *Invitation to Sociology*, taking up such classic philosophical questions as whether knowledge was rooted in rationality or historical existence. These questions had fallen to the sociologists, they explained, having been abandoned by a positivist-leaning philosophy profession. The sociology of knowledge studied the means by which society shaped or determined people's beliefs, as well as the means by which society convinced its subjects that these beliefs were objectively true. Berger and Luckmann argued for an understanding of human reality itself as a social construction, contending that sociology's reigning functionalist and structuralist theories were ahistorical and manipulative. What was needed, they asserted, was a sociological account of the "total social fact" that avoided the "theoretical legerdemain" of functionalism and the "distortive reifications" of structuralism. [19] Berger and Luckmann thus leaned toward the social-historical view of the nature of knowledge. The principal subject matter of the sociology of knowledge, they declared, should be "that of the commonsense knowledge of everyday life." Reconstituting the sociology of knowledge along these lines would make it possible to pursue Weber's ideal of sociology as a value-free mode of inquiry. Sociological inquiry could become the descriptive, empirical, synthetic, nonideological mode of analysis prescribed by Weber, in which the single value embraced by the sociologist was that of scientific integrity. [20]

On the level of theory, they argued, what was needed was to use a dialectical perspective in the social sciences. [21] The truth would not be attained by resorting to one-dimensional methodologies immune from empirical falsification, but by bringing together from various disciplines all of the relevant facts that comprised the total social fact. The dialectic of humanity and society was constitutive of the entire process. Society was entirely a human product, yet society also profoundly influenced and shaped its own producer.

The implications of this dialectic for religion were developed in Berger's subsequent book, *The Sacred Canopy*. "The two statements, that society is the product of man and that man is the product of society, are not contradictory," he asserted. "They rather reflect the inherently dialectic character of the societal phenomenon. Only if this character is recognized will society be understood in terms that are adequate to its empirical reality." [22] *The Sacred Canopy* thus applied the theoretical perspective of *The Social Construction of Reality* to the social and historical phenomenon of religion.

The fundamental dialectic of the social world, in this perspective, was a three-step process that Berger called externalization, objectivation, and internalization. Externalization was the outpouring of human physical and mental energies into the world. Objectivation occurred when the products of human physical and mental efforts attained a reality that confronted its creators as a "facticity" outside themselves. Internalization occurred when this objectivized reality was subjectively reappropriated by human agents, "transforming it once again from structures of the objective world into structures of the subjective consciousness."[23] Berger argued that society was created through externalization and became an apprehended reality through objectivation. The producing human subject became a product of society, in turn, through internalization. Through the reabsorption of the objectivized world into consciousness, he explained, the social world became determinative for the structures of the subjective self. The social product of human imagination and energy—society—itself became the formative means by which individual consciousness was shaped.

Berger defined socialization as the process by which society transmitted its objectivized customs and ideas from one generation to the next. He noted that the transmission of the meanings of a culture typically was described in psychological theory as a learning process. He observed that from the perspective of the sociology of knowledge, however, the socialization process was more than a learning process. Socialization not only taught the objectivized cultural meanings of a society to the individual, but also brought the individual to identify with these meanings and become shaped by them. The meanings of a society became one's own meanings through the process of internalization, in which the self no longer merely possessed meanings, but also represented and expressed them. The success of the process of socialization was measured by the extent to which the self's subjective world reflected and corresponded to the objective world of society.

The socialization process was natural, necessary, and, by implication, worthy of respect and protection. In his earlier books, Berger's theological Barthianism cast a derisive pall over his discussions of socialization. Since normal human development was defective, the proper business of religion (or at least, the mission of the Christian church) was not to sacralize existing social structures, but to challenge them. Normal human socialization reconciled a sinful individual to a corrupt social order. The church was called not to promote or enable successful socialization, but to make a prophetic challenge to the existing order. By reconciling the sinful individual to a corrupt society, normal socialization reinforced humanity's inheritance of original sin. The church was called not to sacralize this process, but to proclaim salvation from it. "Socialization" was thus a term that the early Berger pronounced only with a sarcastic edge.

But now the edge was gone. *The Sacred Canopy* was written out of Berger's reawakened awareness that order is the first need of all. Having turned during the late 1960s to an examination of the sociological significance of religion, Berger was led to a new appreciation of the value and fragility of the socialization process. The chief cultural meanings of a society could only be sustained, he observed, if these meanings were internalized by most of that society's members. While he opposed America's intervention in Vietnam, Berger worried that the social fabric of his adopted country was being ripped apart by the war. The antiwar movement in the United States was generating a cultural politics that opposed not only America's war in Vietnam, but the American way of life. Berger's abhorrence of the war was matched by his revulsion for the counterculture. *The Sacred Canopy* abjured politics, but its subtext presented a response to America's current political situation.

If order was the first need of all, the crucial function of religion was its ordering or "nomizing" capacity. The socially constructed world was most importantly an "ordering of experience" in which a meaningful order (or nomos) was imposed upon the experiences and meanings of human agents. "To say that society is a world-building enterprise is to say that it is ordering, or nomizing, activity," Berger explained. "The ordering of experience is endemic to any kind of social interaction." When the nomos of any society acquired the status of appearing self-evident to the members of that society, these socially constructed meanings merged with that society's teachings about the nature of the cosmic order. Nomos and cosmos became co-extensive. "Whatever the historical variations," Berger noted, "the tendency is for the meanings of the humanly constructed order to be projected into the universe as such." The historical tendency was that securely established nomoi were generally placed within larger frameworks of meaning. Communities proclaimed that their socially constructed "natural order" reflected the nature of the cosmic order.[24]

From a sociological standpoint, this was where religion entered the picture. The purpose of religion was to construct a sacred cosmos. "Put differently, religion is cosmization in a sacred mode," Berger wrote. Religion dichotomized reality into sacred and profane spheres, attributing a quality of mysterious and transcendent power to certain objects of human experience. Sacred power was nearly always constitutive of human experience while also transcending it. The sacred character of particular objects of experience was enshrined in ritual, "the loss of which is tantamount to secularization, that is, to a conception of the events in question as *nothing but* profane."[25]

Berger argued that the deepest antonym to the sacred, however, was not the profane, but chaos. The great cosmogonic myths depicted the sacred cosmos as emerging from chaos and continuing to struggle with chaos. The ultimate danger for the self was to lose all connection with the sacred and thus become swallowed up by chaos. Religious fear was rooted in the fear of returning to chaos. "All the nomic constructions, as we have seen, are designed to keep this terror at bay," Berger observed. "In the

sacred cosmos, however, these constructions achieve their ultimate culmi-
nation—literally, their apotheosis."[26]

While it was the burden of every society to construct a humanly
meaningful world, it was religion that waged society's ultimate struggle
against incoherence, anomie, and the dissolution into nothingness. Religion was not, of course, the only possible form of cosmization. Berger
noted that several thoroughly secular versions of cosmization had appeared in modern times, of which modern science was the most important.
Modern science also identified its constructed meanings with the nature of
reality. The most far-reaching and arguably most sustainable attempts to
infuse reality with human self-externalized meanings, however, occurred
in religion. Religion offered a protective canopy of transcendent legitimacy, meaning, and order to the precarious constructions that society
called "reality." The fate of any social order was therefore inevitably bound
up with the fate of religion.

The Sacred Canopy was carefully noncommital in its assessment of the
future of religion under modernity. Berger identified the sociological
processes of secularization and pluralization as closely related historical
phenomena that undermined the credibility of traditional Western religions. "Any particular religious world will present itself to consciousness as
reality only to the extent that its appropriate plausibility structure is kept
in existence," he observed. "If the plausibility structure is massive and
durable, the religious world maintained thereby will be massively and
durably real in consciousness." In the optimal case, as in medieval Catholicism, the credibility of the received religious world view was regarded as
self-evident. "However, as the plausibility structure is weakened, so will
the subjective reality of the religious world in question." The challenges to
religion brought by modern science, historical criticism, and, especially,
the increased awareness of alternative world views undermined the assumed credibility of any particular religion. An act of "faith" was then
required to overcome doubts engendered by modernization. "In a further
disintegration of the plausibility structure, the old religious contents can
only be maintained in consciousness as 'opinions' or 'feelings'—or, as the
American phrase aptly puts it, as a 'religious preference,' " Berger noted.[27]
Modernity ultimately reduced religion to a commodity.

Berger's closing chapter traced the history of liberal Protestantism's
attempts to cope with this inheritance. More than any other Western
theological tradition, he noted, it was mainline Protestantism that had
long and seriously struggled to face up to modernity. If modernity's
historical drama was fated to bring about the decline of religion, "then
Protestantism can aptly be described as its dress rehearsal."[28] Berger

described the features of Friedrich Schleiermacher's revisionist theological method, captured the spirit of Barth's neo-orthodox alternative—in which the "subjectivizing, compromising, mediating efforts of liberal theology are passionately rejected"—and aptly characterized the theologies of Rudolf Bultmann and Paul Tillich as reconstructions of the liberal revisionist strategy. The neo-orthodox alternative in which Berger had invested his own earlier hope now appeared to him as a "more or less 'accidental' interruption of the over-all process of secularization."[29] The accident was the First World War, which destroyed the liberal belief in progress on which liberal Protestantism had based its revisionist apologetics. The neoliberal theologies of Bultmann and Tillich had taken up where the earlier liberalism left off, and now the next generation of theologians was going beyond even Tillich's revisionism and radicalism.

Berger gave short shrift to current "death of God" theologies. The highly publicized atheologies of Thomas Altizer, William Hamilton, and other radical secularists would not carry the field, he predicted, "for the simple reason that they would undermine the very existence of the religious institutions they are intended to legitimate." As strategies to re-legitimize the theological enterprise, atheological systems were self-defeating. The strategy more likely to carry the field, he argued—barring the interruption of another cataclysmic world event—was the subjectivizing revisionism pioneered by Schleiermacher. This forecast was presented as a "value-free" judgment. Berger was not offering a theological prescription. *The Sacred Canopy* was sociology. It argued that theological liberalism offered the best legitimizing strategy for theology. Though he denied any prescriptive intent in making the argument, this was not the conclusion—sociological or otherwise—that one might have expected from the author of *The Noise of Solemn Assemblies*. *The Sacred Canopy* appeared to represent a major shift in Berger's theological perspective.

His next book confirmed this suspicion. As Berger conceded, *The Sacred Canopy* could be read as a requiem for Western religion. It was not his purpose to proclaim the death of religion, however—if only because his perspective on religion was "not exhausted by the fact that I am a sociologist." As a Christian, he was offended by the arrogance of the relativizers. As a Christian and as a sociologist, he knew that relativism refuted itself. *A Rumor of Angels* would relativize the relativizers. The often-repeated announcement of the death of the supernatural was exposed as merely one relative construction among other possibilities.[30]

This was not to deny, he cautioned, that "sensate" perspectives prevailed in academe and, increasingly, in popular consciousness. Sensate world views were "empirical, this-worldly, secular, humanistic, pragmatic, utilitarian, contractual, epicurean or hedonistic, and the like."[31] Berger granted that the modern preeminence of sensate world views increasingly made the theologian look like a witch doctor stranded among logical positivists—or like a logical positivist stranded among witch doctors. As a sociologist, he appreciated the strain under which theologians tried to maintain their cognitive deviance. The theologian was constantly exposed to the exorcisms of his or her cognitive antagonists. "Sooner or later these exorcisms will have their effect in undermining the old certainties in his own mind," he remarked. The only way to maintain even a highly subjectivized form of religious belief under modernity was to "huddle together with like-minded fellow deviants—and huddle very closely indeed."[32] Those who defied the spirit and culture of modernity, such as the neo-orthodox theologians, were likely to find themselves huddled in ever-shrinking ghettos. But those who tried to bargain with modernity, like the Tillichian liberals, were likely to find themselves making unending concessions to an overpowering aggressor. In either case, modernity was the stronger party.

But if the logic of secularization was prevailing on a sociological level, it did not necessarily follow that secularism was philosophically stronger or more worthy of acceptance than theism. Might did not establish truth. The primary threat to religious belief in the modern world was not the inexorable logic of science, Berger argued, but the "pluralization of socially available worlds." To construct reality under the conditions of pluralism was a very different matter than to do so under the conditions of consensus. "It is relatively easy, sociologically speaking, to be a Catholic in a social situation where one can readily limit one's significant others to fellow Catholics, where indeed one has little choice in the matter, and where all the major institutional forces are geared to support and confirm a Catholic world," he observed. "The story is quite different in a situation where one is compelled to rub shoulders day by day with every conceivable variety of 'those others,' is bombarded with communications that deny or ignore one's Catholic ideas, and where one has a terrible time even finding some quiet Catholic corners to withdraw into."[33]

This sociological truism accounted primarily for the crisis of religious belief under modernity. Modernity was a great leveling process in which every community's distinctive beliefs and characteristics were reduced to common banalities. Under the conditions of modernity, religious people were pressured relentlessly to accept the sensate world view of "a slightly drowsy, middle-aged businessman right after lunch."[34] The fact that this was a powerful social process did not mean that it could not be challenged. What was needed, Berger argued, was to relativize the logic of relativism.

He observed that the same uncritical attitude toward the present was displayed by academics and nonacademics alike. Under the pressure of modernity's secular presuppositions, people learned to reject the traditions or beliefs of the past in the name of a contemporary world view that remained unaccountably immune from criticism. Sociological analysis and historical criticism were used to reveal the relative, historical, socially constructed character of all beliefs from the past. The beliefs of the New Testament writers, for example, were routinely explained away by biblical scholars as reflections of a precritical or false consciousness. Bultmann argued that modern people could not use electric lights and radios and simultaneously believe in the spirit world and miracle stories of the New Testament.[35] As Berger noted, this construction placed all radio listeners intellectually above St. Paul. The same scholars who dismissed the world views and accounts of the New Testament writers, however, virtually never questioned the social and historical determinants of their own consciousness. But this was the only constructive way to deal with the relativity monster. What was needed, Berger asserted, was "to see the relativity business through to its very end," to reveal the relativism of the skeptics, the debunkers, the believers, and all others. Only then could the critical pursuit of truth move forward.

Berger acknowledged that such an approach would preclude any resort to neo-orthodox theology's a priori immunity claims. Barth's contention that Christianity was not a socially constructed religion was an important example. The credibility of Christianity could not be protected by claiming that Christianity was a divinely revealed faith immune from the kind of scrutiny applied to mere religions. Like any other belief system, Christianity was open to criticism. To open all forms of consciousness to criticism, however, including those of modern rationalism, was to reopen the possibility of an "inductive" or experiential faith.

Berger proposed that a theology liberated from the tyranny of the present could begin to look again for "signals of transcendence" within, but pointing beyond, the natural world. He offered five examples. The first was the evidently universal human impulse to impose order on reality and relate this construction to an ultimate or transcendent order. He drew a metaphysical argument from this phenomenon. The natural world was not the only world, Berger argued, but merely the foreground of a supernatural world "in which love is not annihilated in death, and in which, therefore, the trust in the power of love to banish chaos is justified."[36] The universal human propensity to create order implied a transcendent order, "and each ordering gesture is a signal of this transcendence." A mother's reassurance to a child frightened and confused by a nightmare was such a gesture. Her assurance that "everything is all right" ultimately meant, "Have trust in being." Berger hastened to explain that he was not describing Jungian archetypal symbols buried in the unconscious mind (he had little use for psychological arguments of any kind), but was describing experiences that belonged to everyday awareness.

His other examples followed the same pattern. The second was the act of play, in which time collapsed into the movements of a game and the outside world ceased to exist. The suspension of time in play, and the joy that it brought, represented "an affirmation of the ultimate triumph of all human gestures of creative beauty over the gestures of destruction, and even over the ugliness of war and death." This signal of transcendence was closely related to the third example, the phenomenon of hope in the face of suffering or death. Through hope, men and women found meaning and were given courage in the face of suffering or death. Hope acknowledged the omnipresence of death in nature, but also inspired the various gestures of faith and courage that signaled a life beyond nature.

Berger's fourth example also began with experience, though with a somewhat different kind of experience. This was the "argument from damnation," the human sense that certain evils were so hideous that they cried out for supernatural punishment. The monstrous deeds of the Nazis were an outrage not only to human moral sensibilities, he argued, but to something deeper than morality. They violated "a fundamental awareness of the constitution of our humanity." The monstrosity of the Holocaust transcended any calculus of (relative) moral standards or judgment. It therefore also made any possible human punishment inadequate.

The final example was an argument from humor. Berger observed that all humor was rooted in the awareness of discrepancy. Nearly any discrepancy could make people laugh, including the "comic discrepancy in the human condition." The essence of the comic was to reflect and laugh at "the imprisonment of the human spirit in the world." From a serious perspective, the victim was always to be pitied over an oppressor, even if the victim laughed at his or her oppressor. But from the standpoint of the comic, more pitiable was the figure who harbored self-delusions. Power was the final illusion, "while laughter reveals the final truth." To be able to laugh at the imprisonment of the human spirit in the world was to signal that such imprisonment was not final, but would be overcome. Humor was an intimation of redemption. Like play, it was a signal of transcendence because it was ultimately a "religious vindication of joy."[37]

To refashion theology in this mode would require paying greater attention to the religious implications of ordinary experience. Beginning with experience did not mean focusing on somebody's mystical encounters, but focusing rather on the religious implications of the experiences of

loving, caring, ordering, playing, laughing, encountering evil, and finding hope. Berger explained that it also required giving up the protected
deductionism of traditional and neo-orthodox theologies, which began
with certain ideas preceding and untested by experience.

Among these ideas was the often-repeated claim that Christian theology should begin with the figure of Christ. Berger observed that at its
worst, the Christocentric approach "systematizes the rape of the historical
materials," as when Christian beliefs were read back into the Hebrew
Scriptures. Even at their Barthian best, however, Christocentric approaches crammed the plurality of historical materials and interpretations
into a single focal point. Berger was bluntly forthcoming about how much
his theological position had changed. "I repudiate such a procedure," he
announced. "I would take the historical materials concerning Christ, both
the New Testament itself and the subsequent literature, as a record of a
specific complex of human experience." The New Testament as such had
no special status compared to the scriptures of other religions. The same
questions needed to be brought to any such account: "What is being said
here? What is the human experience out of which these statements come?
And then, to what extent, and in what way, may we see here genuine
discoveries of transcendent truth?"[38]

Theologically, Berger had moved considerably to the Left. To face up
to modernity in theology required that one give up neo-orthodoxy's
immunity claims and face the implications of historical and cultural
relativism. All theologies were first the products of historically condi-
tioned and constructed human experience, whether they posited a divine
Revealer or not. What was needed in theology was to acknowledge and
affirm the authority of experience. A reformulated Christian theology that
proceeded inductively would undoubtedly reaffirm certain aspects of
classical Christianity over against modern secular consciousness, Berger
observed. Other aspects would be discarded or reinterpreted. "My approach would thus be 'heretical' in the strict sense of the word," he
remarked.[39] To face up to the relativity of theological knowledge required
that one affirm certain elements of the tradition and reject others. He later
called this selective task the "heretical imperative."

BERGER'S CONSERVATIVE HUMANISM

Though his writings throughout the 1960s were sprinkled with criticisms
of America's intervention in Vietnam, Berger only began to write seriously
about politics in the early 1970s, after he had worked out his views on

religion and social theory. He moved to Brooklyn College in 1966, where he taught sociology for four years and became friends with Richard John Neuhaus, who was then a prominent antiwar activist and a pastor at St. John the Evangelist Lutheran Church on the border of Bedford-Stuyvesant. It was his involvement in the antiwar movement and his friendship with Neuhaus that belatedly politicized Berger's interests. In the late 1960s he joined Clergy and Laymen Concerned About Vietnam, the national antiwar organization co-founded by Neuhaus, and served for one uncomfortable year on its national steering committee. The experience confirmed his distaste for liberals and leftists, but strengthened his friendship with Neuhaus. "Neuhaus and I shared the same concern about the secularizing thrust in the church," he later recalled. "Aside from that, and our opposition to the war, we didn't have much in common at first. Theologically, he has always been an 'evangelical Catholic,' so we argued about theology from the beginning."[40] Neuhaus would later become a prominent neoconservative and a Roman Catholic convert. His first editorial venture with Berger was conceived in 1969 while they vacationed together at Ivan Illich's educational institute in Cuernavaca.

Berger's trip to Mexico marked a turning point in his life. In 1969, shortly after he returned to New York from a Vatican conference on secularization, he received an unexpected phone call from Illich. "I hear you're coming to Mexico," Illich told him. "Come to my center—we need you!" Berger was intrigued and flattered. Why would a radical like Illich need him? He went to Cuernavaca and became convinced, while a new world opened up to him, that Illich had figured out what he should be doing.[41]

Berger was fascinated by Mexican culture and deeply shaken by the country's immense poverty. Illich worked on these reactions, imploring him to apply his expertise in the sociology of knowledge to the problems of Third World modernization and economic development. The invitation proved arresting to Berger. The idea of turning his attention to the Third World was personally and intellectually appealing. He resolved to expand the scope of his analysis of modernization. While struggling to imagine what his turn to Third World studies would mean, he and Neuhaus resolved to write a book on the political situation in the United States. The book would discuss not only the Vietnam War and the antiwar movement, but also the relationships between American power and the Third World.

The following year—the same year that Berger accepted a teaching position at Rutgers University—he and Neuhaus published *Movement and Revolution*, a volume of essays on the Movement. "Between System and

Horde" was Berger's first major political statement. It was offered as advice to reluctant activists who fit his own profile. The fire-breathing proclamations were left to Neuhaus, who was still declaiming in the revolutionary apocalyptic mode. Neuhaus's essay, "The Thorough Revolutionary," defended the Movement from various criticisms and announced that a revolutionary struggle to bring down the American empire was a moral and political necessity. In the clipped cadences of Movement-speak for which he was noted, Neuhaus announced that the Movement was fundamentally revolutionary: "A revolution of consciousness, no doubt. A cultural revolution, certainly. A non-violent revolution, perhaps. An armed overthrow of the existing order, it may be necessary. Revolution for the hell of it or revolution for a new world, but revolution, Yes."[42]

This would be a grimly serious project. Neuhaus explained that he was writing only for those who no longer laughed. These were the only people he took seriously. Too many of them were already agitating for a violent revolution, he noted, without having calculated the chances for success. The Movement needed to become more serious in its calculations, which would include an accounting of the extent to which the use of torture and terrorism would be necessary in a revolutionary struggle. In his accounting, even Che Guevara had not been a serious revolutionary, since Guevara was unwilling to intimidate the Bolivian peasants he tried to recruit to the revolution. What was needed in America was a rigorous calculation of the costs of revolutionary violence by those "in whose minds there has formed the awesome thought of revolution." Neuhaus was uncertain whether revolutionary violence would be necessary or could succeed in the United States. He was certain, however, that only those who counted and exacted the costs of revolution deserved to be called revolutionaries. "The Thorough Revolutionary" was an admiring description of himself.[43]

Berger was no revolutionary. He wasn't even a liberal. His contribution to *Movement and Revolution* was to demonstrate that one could oppose the war without buying any of the conceits of the Movement. One could seriously oppose the war without shrieking. To be outraged by the "atrocious" American war in Vietnam and offer one's voice against it did not require that one take sides with the New Left, he argued. To anyone who aggressively asked, "Which side are you on?" he quickly replied, "Not yours, Mac!" Most activists had bad motives, he argued, which usually brought bad consequences. Most activists were driven to politics by a pathological hunger for power or redemption or, in the case of middle-aged intellectuals, to "find their orgasms where they can."

Berger expressed sympathy only for the latter. He otherwise found virtually all political activists to be humorless and "thoroughly uncongenial." The Brechtian admonition against laughter that Neuhaus invoked ("He who laughs has not yet received the terrible news") perfectly captured the moral ugliness of the ideologue. Berger perceived that there was more to Neuhaus than ideological righteousness, however; Neuhaus shared Berger's humanistic concerns. For Berger, there was one motive for intense political commitment that commanded respect. This was the motive of compassion. The only political commitments worth making were those which sought to reduce human suffering. Most political problems were too mundane to require or evoke compassion, Berger argued. But among those problems that did evoke it, only the motive of compassion was worthy of moral respect. When dealing with revolutionaries, he counseled, one should never trust the enthusiasts because they were either pretenders or oppressors. "Listen to their voices," he advised. "Watch for the signals of compassion. Watch how they laugh." It was in the name of promoting a "community of the compassionate" that Berger put forth his own "conservative humanism."[44]

He distinguished his politics from traditional American conservatism. Berger supported what remained of the pre-1968 civil rights movement, declaring that "any society that institutionalizes racial oppression in any form *ipso facto* declares its lack of humanity."[45] He felt no affinity with the kind of conservatism that defended racial discrimination or opposed the civil rights bills. His variant of conservatism differed from traditional conservatism, he explained, in its lack of piety toward the status quo. Traditional conservatives opposed social change in the name of tradition or nature or divine law. They defended the status quo with arguments based on faith.

Berger's conservatism was a more skeptical brew that owed more to sociology than to reverence or nostalgia. "There is a powerful debunking, disenchanting element about the perspective sociology," he explained. His sociological understanding of the ways that individuals and organizations attained and institutionalized power made it impossible for him to revere existing institutions. But the same sociological perspective made him skeptical toward most efforts to change society. "Needless to say, such efforts must often be undertaken," he allowed. "But the sociologist will always be aware of what Max Weber called the unintended consequences of social action and others have called the irony of history." The chief lesson of history was that social crusades of any kind, no matter how well-meaning, nearly always produced a greater mess than the one they addressed.[46]

Unlike progressive enthusiasms of every period, his conservatism accepted history's messiness and was skeptical toward the notion of progress. Conservative humanists, he explained, rejected the temptation to impose a new order on history's mess. Most of the time, they contented themselves with learning how to cope with it. They were skeptical toward innovation and "doubly skeptical" toward causes that required violence. They were skeptical toward all movements, ideologies, and strategies for social change and attributed great importance to order, continuity, and the freedom to be trivial. Above all, they accepted human beings as they were. Conservative humanism put no stock in strategies to transform human consciousness or create a new humanity. It respected people as they were and left them alone.

This was the key to the sickness of the Movement. The New Leftists masked their dislike for ordinary people by claiming to love humankind. They would have been less preoccupied with radically transforming ordinary Americans, Berger observed, if they had liked Americans in the first place. This alienation from ordinary people guaranteed that the Movement would not go far in American politics. It also produced such "grotesque" spectacles as the New Left enthusiasm for participatory democracy.

For Berger, the idea of participatory democracy epitomized the depravity of the Movement. For all of its railing against authority and centralized power, the Movement was driven by its contempt for ordinary people to embrace an incipiently totalitarian conception of politics. The participatory ideal of the New Left violated the fundamental precept of any humane politics, which was to leave people alone. "It is of fundamental importance to reiterate, in the face of these ideological aberrations, that human life is infinitely richer in its possibilities of fulfillment than in its political expressions, and that it is indeed a basic human right to live apolitically—a right that may be denied only for the most urgent reasons," Berger argued. "For most of human history, politics has been left to the few whose vocation it was supposed to be, leaving the many to go about their own (possibly much more interesting) business." There was nothing wrong with leaving politics to the politicians and government bureaucrats, especially if they managed things reasonably well and left people alone. In the United States, it was only in recent years that they had screwed up so badly that people like himself were forced to become politicized.[47]

Berger resented the intrusion and blasted America's recent administrations for their failures. He was a reluctant pundit. Like all of the neoconservatives, however, he resented the Movement more. Though he agreed with the New Leftists about the immorality of the war, he was repelled by their manners and their ideology. His opposition to the war was based on his moral revulsion toward the way it was being fought. It was not the imperialist nature of America's intervention that disturbed him, he explained, since he believed that the American empire was largely a force for good in the world. What disturbed him about the Vietnam War was the indiscriminate killing of civilians and the devastation of the country that American policy rationalized. Distinguishing his antiwar position from the antiwar movement, he explained, "My opposition was based on such simple (to them, of course, simplistic) convictions that it is wrong to drop napalm on villages inhabited by children. Their opposition was not to napalm-dropping at all—it was to 'American imperialism.' Indeed, they had no objection at all to acts of violence that killed children, even with deliberation—as long as it was the 'right people,' from their viewpoint, that did the killing."[48]

The new American radicalism, he claimed, was essentially a variant of European fascism. Like the Nazi ideologists, the New Leftists were anti-intellectual and contemptuous toward the idea of value-free sociology. The same combination of antibourgeois, anticapitalist, and antiliberal negations characterized the Nazi and New Left movements. This fact was "an evil itself," he wrote. The angry proclamation of these negations and the Movement's cultivation of the mystique of the street stirred up memories of the Nazi anthems he heard during his youth. The Movement's emphasis on organizing students reminded him of Mussolini's cult of youth. The New Leftist evocation of Rousseau's doctrine of the general will reminded him of the mystical elitism of Nazi ideology. "If one adds up these themes, one is confronted by an ideological constellation that strikingly resembles the common core of Italian and German fascism," he concluded. "Indeed, one is drawn to the conclusion that the concepts and interpretations drawn by many contemporary radicals from Marxism are grafted upon a body of motives and perspectives on the world that have nothing to do with Marxism."

This conclusion confirmed his earliest intuitions about the Movement. When he first observed the language and gestures of the new radicals, he reported, "I was repeatedly reminded of the stormtroopers that marched through my childhood in Europe." He first dismissed the significance of this association, thinking it was subjective or that perhaps all political activism bore the same traits. "But when, for example, I thought of Communist (Old Left) activists I have had occasion to observe, I realized that, although I had no affection for them either, they did not arouse these particular associations." Though Communists had no use for liberal democracy, either, it was not from them that the New Leftists took their anti-intellectualism, their anger, their street theater, their glorification of youth, or their mysticism. The New Leftists were goose-steppers in bell-bottoms.[49]

This was an odd way to call for a more humanistic antiwar movement. The infantile vulgarity of the Movement's most publicized leaders disabled Berger's capacity for distinctions. Most of America's antiwar activists abhorred racism, opposed militarism of any kind, and were repulsed by the incineration of Vietnam. To call them Nazis in disguise was not to make a call for political dialogue. In Berger's reading, the antiwar movement consisted mostly of fascist New Left idealogues and their bored suburbanite followers. The suburbanites were not motivated by compassion for "yellow people in rice paddies," he claimed. They were merely ridiculous. They were bored with Connecticut. He appealed to the supposed few that remained—those who opposed the war purely out of compassion for its victims—to act "with sober confidence in their values and their reason." America, he remarked, had already had its fill of politics as psychodrama.[50]

His relation to American conservatism was more complex. Berger observed that most people were conservative in the sense that they took society's structures for granted and worked out their problems within these structures. As Alfred Schutz put it, their social world was "taken for granted until further notice." This type of conservatism was unreflective and self-assured, as in Edmund Burke's image of contented cows grazing under ancient trees. Intellectual conservatism was more reflective and defensive than this. It produced theories that were "typically aggressive rather than self-assured," defending the status quo against various intellectual, moral, and practical challenges. Intellectual conservatism was therefore typically a defensive response to the ideas of others. It spoke in the voice of dissent.

Berger regarded himself as a conservative of both kinds. He was temperamentally predisposed to work within existing social structures rather than challenge them. This predisposition was reinforced by his admiration for his adopted country. The paradox of what was ordinarily called conservatism in America, however, was that American conservatives didn't defend the existing social order. This was because America was a liberal society. American institutions were largely the products of liberal ideology and practice. "Thus the intellectual conservative in America, deeply critical of liberal ideology as he is, finds himself in the position of standing for the preservation of an order based on all those principles which offend him," Berger observed.

Classical conservatism was a quixotic position in America, "comparable to that of, say, running for Senator from Kansas on a monarchist platform." But even the more common conservatism of America's contemporary Right faced the same dilemma. American conservatism typically defined itself by its opposition to New Deal liberalism. The existing social order, however, had been decisively shaped by New Deal liberalism. The American conservative opponent of liberalism thus "still finds himself in the position of being for a status quo founded on the institutional and ideological products of precisely this liberalism."[51]

Berger offered a solution to the dilemma, while conceding in advance that most conservatives would never buy it. He counseled that American conservatives should accept and preserve "the basic status quo of American society as a practical political goal" while refusing to glorify these structures or embrace liberal ideology. "Middle-class values are not the apex of man's moral history, capitalism is not the final marvel of economic ingenuity, and neither the national state nor mass democracy represents the ultimate political redemption," he argued.[52] Conservatism should not sacralize the inheritance of a liberal past. To preserve present arrangements, however, would be a conservative project. It was the burden of American conservatism to protect a liberal order from liberal enthusiasms. American conservatism could only rid itself of its air of negativism and petulance, he argued, if it reconciled itself to the task of conserving the gains of American liberalism.

Berger was especially troubled by American conservatism's selective moral perspective, which he characterized as a reverse image of the Left's selective humanism. In America, the Right kept watch over the ongoing horrors of communist tyranny. Berger observed that only conservatives seemed to recognize or care that hundreds of millions of people were being humiliated and oppressed in the world's totalitarian prisons. The suffocating degradation of Soviet totalitarianism and the "moral monstrosity" of Maoism were regularly condemned only in conservative publications. While America's mass media celebrated the social achievements of a genocidal Chinese regime, only the hard Right seemed to share his own moral revulsion at the human cost of Chinese modernization.

What he could not abide in American conservatism was its preoccupation with the evils of communism, which produced a double standard of moral judgment. In the international arena, the moral concerns of the American Right were circumscribed and apparently exhausted by its ideological opposition to communism. Unlike his treatment of the New Left, Berger carefully avoided the question whether right-wing anticommunism deserved to be called a moral concern at all. He did not subject the Right's coincidence of moral and ideological concerns to the same ridicule he poured on this coincidence in the New Left. But Berger did forcefully criticize the Right's evident lack of moral concern for the human ravages of dictatorships aligned with the United States. American conservatives failed the test of consistent moral engagement. In recent years, he noted, governments in Indonesia and Brazil had waged vicious campaigns of torture, repression, and mass murder to enforce civilian conformity and eliminate opposition movements. Faced with the evidence of state terror by these regimes, American conservatives routinely looked the other way or, when pressed on the subject, replied that right-wing dictatorships were preferable to communism. Berger conceded the latter point while insisting that this was not, by itself, an acceptable response to the issue.

The war in Vietnam was a case in point. "The devastation of large areas of the country designated as 'free fire zones,' the merciless bombing and shelling of inhabited villages vaguely suspected of sheltering the enemy, the routine torture of prisoners, the deliberate 'generation' of vast masses of refugees—all these have been part and parcel of the human reality of this war," he observed. Most conservatives defended these otherwise hideous methods of warfare in the name of realism. "Fine," Berger replied. "I too have heard of *Realpolitik*. But one cannot have it both ways. Either 'everything goes' in the struggle for power in the real world, or there are limits beyond which moral outrage has a right to be heard."[53] Conservatives undermined their right to make moral judgments of any kind when they defended America's savage conduct of the war, he argued. A new conservatism was needed. The kind that Berger had in mind was not the ideological neoconservatism of Kristol and Podhoretz, but his own conception of humanism. What was needed was a conservative humanism that pragmatically sought to minimize the amount of suffering in the world and consistently refused to reduce morality to ideology.

CAPITALISM AND DEVELOPMENT

Berger's major work of the 1970s was written in this spirit. *Pyramids of Sacrifice* brought his humanistic conservatism to bear on the problems of Third World development. It redeemed Illich's challenge to him. The book focused on the two predominant ideologies of development, which Berger called the theory of modernization and the theory of imperialism. Modernization theory was rationalized by the capitalist myth of growth; anti-imperialist theory was rationalized by the socialist myth of revolution. Each theory contained what sociologists called clue concepts. Modernization theory was, of course, about "modernity" as well as "development," "economic growth," "institutional differentiation," and "nation-building." Anti-imperialist theories employed such clue concepts as "dependency," "exploitation," "neocolonialism," and "liberation." "Each camp also has a pejorative vocabulary for the respective rival, and a conceptual apparatus designed to liquidate intellectually whatever definitions of the situation emerge from that tainted source," Berger observed. "Basically, each camp understands the other as a workshop of ideological smoke-screens for conflicting political strategies."[54]

Berger attempted to cut through the mystifications of reality and anathematizing on both sides, pointing out the inadquacies of both models. He argued that the deepest fault with both approaches was that they assumed the necessity of sacrificing one or more generations for the sake of foundational social and economic gains. Neither theory could justify the sacrifices it called for, he insisted, because neither theory could predict the outcome of its prescriptions. The starting point for any morally acceptable strategy of development was to rule out the imposition of hunger or terror as an instrument of development. Brazil was his chief example of the modernization and hunger strategy; China exemplified the strategy of socialism and terror. Though he had never visited China, Berger made effective use of the literature on Chinese communism to enumerate the most obvious costs of "development" through totalitarian terror. It was not a difficult argument to assemble. The more interesting section of the book made extensive use of his travels in Latin America, especially Brazil.

Latin America: The Cost of Modernization

At the heart of the capitalist myth of growth, he noted, was the vision of the cargo cult—the arrival of abundant goods and services as the gifts of economic modernization. Modernization theory traded heavily on this vision. But throughout Latin America, he reported from experience, the cargo ships on which so much had been invested had still not arrived. And in places where parts of the cargo had arrived, people were left wondering whether it was worth the staggering debts, economic maldistribution, and social and cultural upheaval it had cost. The glittering business districts of Brazil were filled with skyscrapers and well-dressed consumers. The residential areas nearby featured quiet streets, luxurious homes, and plenty of deferential servants. These zones were invariably surrounded, however, "by huge rings of human misery and degradation, endless miles of slums, slums, and more slums."[55]

Modernization theorists insisted that the benefits of growth would eventually trickle down to Latin America's poor majorities. Countries like

Brazil had not yet reached the take-off stage at which a sufficient level of accumulation could trigger a more equitable distribution of wealth in a continually expanding economy. It was difficult to refute such an argument, Berger noted, "which depends for verification on an empirically inaccessible future." But the present evidence offered no encouragement. Even though these countries had made massive investments in economic modernization over the past two generations, he noted, "there is *more* hunger and *more* disease today than there was some decades ago, not just in terms of absolute figures but even when the increase in population is taken into account." By all available evidence, capitalist development strategies were increasing unemployment and underemployment in the Third World and further polarizing the maldistribution of income and wealth in these nations. There was not even any evidence that the number of people in the affluent minority was increasing. "Thus, the situation is marked by what Brazilian economist Celso Furtado has aptly called 'growth without development,' " Berger commented. "The growth is real enough, in terms of conventional economic indicators, but it has brought about a possibly permanent coexistence of a relatively well-off and dynamic modern sector and a sector of stagnant or even deepening misery." To sacrifice further generations in the name of the myth of growth was therefore morally unacceptable. [56]

This conclusion led Berger to take up the claims of economic dependency theory. He gave short shrift to the more ideological variants of dependency analysis. He quickly dismissed the Leninist proposition that early Western economic development was based primarily on neocolonial exploitation. He similarly denied that the West's present affluence was significantly sustained by its exploitation of the Third World. By comparison to markets within the advanced industrial societies, the Third World was not an expanding market for capital growth, and its raw materials (except for oil) were no longer crucial for further Western development. Berger had little patience with any argument that attributed First World prosperity to exploitation. He rejected any variant of dependency theory that used the failures of capitalist strategies in the Third World to impugn the success of capitalism in the advanced industrial world. "Contrary to the Leninist theory, the affluence of the West is largely due to the superior productive system it has created, a system which by now is mainly autonomous," he contended. Dependency theory exaggerated the extent and effects of imperialism, clinging to the outmoded Leninist assumption that expanding capital investments required vulnerable foreign markets to exploit.

He conceded, however, that there was more to dependency theory than the Leninist misuses of it. Berger distinguished the empirical findings of dependency analysis from dependency theory, arguing that it was possible to accept dependency theory's empirical basis while rejecting its theoretical elaborations. Dependency theory was founded on well-established facts, he allowed. The empirical realities identified by dependency theory were not matters of faith or ideology, but of evidence.

> Polarization between rich and poor nations, polarization within the latter between relatively affluent factors and sectors of massive misery, growth in the major indicators of this misery (from downright starvation to pervasive unemployment), growing economic dependency of poor nations upon the rich (as reflected in mounting debts, deteriorating terms of trade and balances of payment, vulnerability to decisions made by governments and nongovernmental bodies in the rich nations)—all these are not inventions of Marxist ideologists, but empirical facts readily available to any objective observer. It is, therefore, of the greatest importance that the *no* to various theoretical affirmations of the Marxist critique be balanced by an emphatic *yes* to many of its specific empirical assessments. [57]

If dependency theory exaggerated the crippling effects of economic exploitation in the Third World by the industrial powers, it nonetheless identified certain empirical factors that refuted the capitalist myth of growth.

Pyramids of Sacrifice pointed to the necessity of a pragmatic, morally grounded Third Way. The necessity of such an alternative was asserted with deep conviction; the features of the alternative itself were only vaguely suggested. Berger did not call it democratic socialism. In his vocabulary, "socialism" meant state economic planning and state ownership of the means of production. His operative conception of democratic socialism was the faded state collectivism of the Fabians. In the real world, "socialism" was the alternative exemplified by communist China and the Soviet bloc. It bore no relation to liberal democracy except opposition.

The Third Way he had in mind, as he later explained, would be "some sort of a so-called mixed model" that borrowed from the methods and analyses of modernization and dependency theory. [58] His only certainty in calling for a more humane form of capitalism was that no morally acceptable strategy for development could impose starvation or terror on its subjects. His starting point in assessing the remaining policy options was that Third World societies would never overcome their poverty if they were not liberated from dependency on the advanced industrial societies. This did not imply that the misery of the Third World was mainly attributable to Western imperial penetration, nor that the present wealth of the West was sustained by imperial exploitation, nor that socialist revolutions represented the only effective way to break free from dependency. It did imply that Third World societies were negatively affected by most of their socioeconomic dealings with the rich countries.

"Put simply, in most bargains between the poor and the rich, the rich get richer and the former, at best, don't gain very much," Berger remarked. "It is also clear, in that case, that development, if it means anything at all, must mean a change in this relationship."[59] Third World officials needed to make more pragmatic bargains or stop bargaining altogether. They needed to measure the moral worthiness of their policy decisions according to a "calculus of pain" that avoided undue human suffering and a "calculus of meaning" that took a respectful attitude toward the cultural values of those subjected to modernization. Anticipating a theme from his later work on mediating structures, Berger briefly suggested that the key to any worthy development strategy might be to engender and support intermediate social structures between the state and the mass of individuals uprooted by modernization.

Commerce and Communism: America's Role

On the American side, he was uncertain whether the United States could do very much for the Third World. What was important was that America stop doing certain things to the Third World. Vietnam was his chief example. The most important thing the United States could do for the Third World was to restrain its worldwide projection of political and military power. Such a shift in policy would need to be accompanied "by a deescalation of ideological rhetoric and evangelistic fervor," he argued. It would eschew American conceits about needing to save the world for democracy.[60]

That was in 1974, the year before the United States finally pulled out of Vietnam. Two years later, Berger was already having second thoughts about restraining American power. He worried that America's defeat in Vietnam was creating strange affinities in American politics, especially the increasing convergence between the perceptions and interests of the New Class and the business class. Berger took Kristol's arguments about the New Class for granted. The interesting development for him was that the knowledge industry's basically dovish perspective was beginning to take hold among America's financial elite. A new "intellectual-industrial complex" was taking shape, Berger argued, in which American military and political power was being eclipsed by the moral rhetoric of the New Class and the commercial interests of the business class. "The agenda is the dismantling of the American empire," he warned.[61]

He did not claim or imply that this new convergence of interests was the result of a conspiracy. In Weberian terms, this phenomenon was an elective affinity. The New Class's dovish anti-imperialism increasingly fit the interests of the business class more than the defense establishment's military commitments. That the knowledge-and-policy industry was politically leftist did not require demonstration. America's intellectual elite was socialistic, Berger argued, not only because it benefited from expansions in state power, but also because most of its members sincerely subscribed to the socialist myth. "Socialism is the only good myth going in the world today, and intellectuals are its most important protagonists," he explained. "Everywhere it is a vision of a society in which the alienations of modernity are overcome, in which there is not only a high degree of equality but also a new ethic of human community."[62] In the United States, he observed, this faith was generally softer and more open than among its European and Third World counterparts and was therefore generally more pacifist than militant. American progressives mixed an egalitarian domestic politics with a disinclination to project American power abroad. They wanted a strong American government with a weak American military.

All of this was well known. The interesting question was why America's corporate elite was increasingly mouthing the dovish sentiments of the New Class. It was not because the business class had suddenly converted to McGovernism, Berger assured. The greening of the corporate elite was attributable to the fact that "the American empire, previously perceived as an economic asset, is now coming to be perceived as an economic liability in many parts of the world." The economic costs of maintaining the American empire were increasingly viewed as prohibitive. America's war in Vietnam had been enormously wasteful, inflationary, and destabilizing. It had also antagonized important trading partners and affected the attitude of America's business class toward the struggle against communism. Berger was most concerned about the latter development.

He observed that the primary concern of any economic elite was naturally with political stability. Successful commerce required political stability. This requirement had forced numerous American administrations to support "all sorts of morally distasteful regimes" to protect America's foreign investments. The United States generally preferred to support stable dictatorships over unstable democracies, which made bad business risks. "There is no need to repeat here the uninspiring record of American corporations meddling in the internal affairs of foreign countries to insure a profitably stable political environment," Berger remarked.[63]

The problem was that America's business class was beginning to look at communist regimes in the same way. In recent years, Berger observed, several Soviet bloc countries had demonstrated that they could be reliable trade partners with the West. The notion was thus spreading among American business leaders that they could do business with the Communists. As Soviet bloc nations proved themselves to be good business partners, their (purported) stability made them especially attractive to American investors. "In these countries there are no problems with a volatile public opinion, with anti-American intellectuals and political movements, with coups or terrorism, with aggressive labor unions," Berger explained. The business class increasingly saw no reason to fight communism, since communists made perfect trading partners. [64]

America's corporate elite had always loved commerce more than it hated communism. Berger feared that it was now forsaking its anticommunism altogether. His early warnings against the emerging symbiosis of New Class and business class attitudes toward communism raised what soon became a major neoconservative theme. "If the proposition is to dismantle the American empire, the intellectuals make it seem morally right and the businessmen make it appear realistic," he remarked. "A combination of self-righteousness and hard-nosed realism is hard to beat in American politics." [65] It was a dangerous trend. Whatever evils American militarism may have committed in the past, he observed, American power was nonetheless "the only significant shield of free societies in different parts of the world." Now the shield was down. The communist enemy, to whom America's business class lusted to sell its goods and technology, stood to make enormous gains. An early plank in the "window of vulnerability" thesis was thus established.

East Asian Capitalism: A Model for Development?

The crucial turn in Berger's politics began the following year, in 1977, when he visited East Asia for the first time. "When I wrote *Pyramids of Sacrifice*, my perspective on dependency theory was based on my studies of Latin America and my experiences there," he later explained. [66] The empirical claims of dependency theory had been confirmed, for him, by his encounters with Latin American modernization, and his criticisms of the economic and social ravages of capitalist modernization were drawn from evidence he had gathered there. If he held onto the hope that a liberalized, pragmatic capitalism could still engender Third World modernization, his acquaintance with Latin America's modernization record made this a chastened and highly qualified hope. Dependency analysis seemed to explain too much about the failures of modernization strategies in Latin America for anyone to sustain much enthusiasm for the same strategies elsewhere in the Third World. Berger disliked this conclusion, but he couldn't muster a case against it, since it was based not on ideological claims but on "empirical facts readily available to any objective observer."[67] The facts about the prospects for Third World development were prohibitive so long as one focused on the Latin American experience.

This was a dead end. In the later 1970s, Berger therefore began to look for more promising terrain. It was one thing to establish that the empirical facts identified by dependency theory were relevant, and even determinative, in Latin American contexts. It did not follow, however, that the existence of comparative disadvantages elsewhere would necessarily produce the same results. Japan offered an arresting example of an underdeveloped country that had overcome its dependent inferiority to become a highly advanced industrial power. If Japan could succeed, Berger reasoned, it was apparent that the comparative disadvantages emphasized by dependency theorists could be overcome and that the import of these factors was relativized by other political, cultural, and economic variables. Berger turned his attention in the late 1970s to Japan and the "Four Little Dragons" of the East Asian Rim—South Korea, Taiwan, Hong Kong, and Singapore. His reflections on the economic success of these nations eventually moved him to reject dependency analysis altogether. As he observed, East Asian capitalism was as structurally dependent on the West as Latin America's failed modernization experiments were. What needed to be explained in the field of development economics was why East Asian capitalism was succeeding.

Berger taught at Boston College for two years and then moved to Boston University in 1981, where he was named University Professor of Sociology. The same year he used a grant from the SmithKline Corporation to launch his Seminar on Modern Capitalism, which became a key project of Kristol's Institute for Educational Affairs.[68] Berger made several trips to East Asia in the early 1980s under the auspices of the Council on Religion and International Affairs and the Asia and World Institute. In 1985, he founded the Institute for the Study of Economic Culture at Boston University. As he later put it, the purpose of this institute was not simply to conduct and sponsor research on the dynamics of successful modernization, but to develop an approach to modernization theory and disseminate this new approach among academics and business leaders.[69] "Not to put too fine a point on it," he explained at the time of the institute's founding, "I have become much more emphatically pro-capitalist."[70] He made few concessions thereafter to critics of capitalist modernization.

A new approach was needed because most of the literature on economic modernization confirmed the imperialist thesis, either by prescribing the necessity of replicating American or European models or by criticizing the destructive effects of such strategies. What was needed was a body of developmentalist literature that analyzed the relationships between culture and socioeconomic change and specifically examined the lessons of successful modernization outside the United States and Europe. The Asian crescent stretching from Japan to the Malay Peninsula provided the showcase examples.

Berger's new approach defined successful economic development by three criteria: sustained and self-generating growth, the achievement of a minimally decent standard of living for the underclass, and the establishment of at least minimal standards of human rights.[71] Successful development required more than economic growth, since growth could take place in the midst of massive hunger and destitution (as in Brazil) or under regimes that terrorized their own citizens (as in China). In the early 1980s, Berger began to argue that the achievement of these goals in Japan and the Four Little Dragons represented a second case of modernization in the making. A new type of industrial capitalism was being constructed in societies that lacked Western individualistic traditions.[72] East Asian capitalism was casting a new light on modernization theory and dependency theory. In Berger's revised estimation, it refuted dependency theory. The success of East Asian capitalism revealed which characteristics were essential to the nature of industrial capitalism and which characteristics were culturally relative. As Berger recounted in his major work, *The Capitalist Revolution*, the success of East Asian capitalism could be measured by the fact that within a single generation, Japan and the Four Little Dragons had constructed systems that featured self-generating economic growth, substantial improvements in the standards of life for the poor, and no massive violations of human rights.

He allowed that Japan was an exceptional case. Between 1868 and 1912, the Meiji Dynasty virtually abolished feudalism and created a free labor market. Japan's aristocratic class was compensated for its loss of fiefdoms and other feudal privileges with cash and government bonds, which it was required to invest in new industry. A capitalist class was thus created overnight. This arrangement secured the loyalty of the ousted aristocrats and built an indigenous supply of investment capital on the feudal gentry's divested holdings. Japanese capitalism was the product of this late-nineteenth-century social transformation. Berger observed that the Meiji revolution apparently confirmed Simon Kuznets's thesis about the causal connection between growth and inequality in the early stages of economic modernization. Japan's early development was forged on the backs of the poor. This situation of worsening poverty in the midst of high economic productivity and growth obtained until the late 1920s, when the Great Depression and the militarization of Japan's economy reduced consumption levels across the entire society. [73]

Japan's enormous economic growth in the generation following World War II reconfirmed the Kuznets thesis. Between 1956 and 1971, Berger observed, the income share of the population's poorest 20 percent significantly decreased while the share of the wealthiest 20 percent substantially increased. "Put bluntly, the rich benefited from growth at the expense of the poor." However, the maldistribution of Japanese income began to level off in the early 1970s—as the Kuznets thesis predicted. Income distribution in Japan became more equitable in the 1980s than in most Western welfare states. [74]

Though he claimed that the Japanese case alone refuted the causal claims of dependency theory, Berger was well aware that Japan presented a highly peculiar and problematic model for Third World economic development. The political history and economic culture of Japan were too obviously remote from Latin American or African experience to serve as instructive examples to these regions. For this reason, Berger turned his attention to the more recent and seemingly relevant examples of successful modernization in South Korea, Taiwan, Hong Kong, and Singapore. As he observed, South Korea and Taiwan were nation-sized economies; Hong Kong and Singapore were essentially city-states. South Korea and Taiwan were ruled by Japan until 1945. Given this fact, and the fact that the economic transformation of the Four Little Dragons occurred during the same period that Japan became a world economic power, Berger allowed that their economic histories could be viewed as extensions of the Japanese experience.

More relevant for Berger, however, was the fact that since 1960 these previously impoverished nations had compiled economic records that were "almost monotonous in their relentless onward-and-upward thrust." Gross national product (GNP) tripled in South Korea between 1963 and 1974, growing at an annual rate of 10 percent, while per capita GNP doubled. Annual exports grew from less than $10 million to more than $4 billion in the same period. Aggregate output between the early 1960s and the mid-1980s grew by a factor of seven. These stunning figures were matched proportionally by Taiwan, Hong Kong, and Singapore. The economies of the Four Little Dragons were marked by rising wages, low unemployment, and little evidence of Kuznets-type maldistribution. Economic modernization in East Asia had lifted four dependent countries in one generation from grinding poverty to decent standards of living. "East Asia, to put it bluntly, is bad news for Marxists," Berger remarked. [75]

He viewed the success of East Asian capitalism not so much as a tribute to the determination of East Asians to overcome the structural obstacles identified by dependency theory, but as a refutation of dependency theory itself. The economic record of Japan and the Four Little Dragons "is the most important empirical falsification of dependency theory," he asserted, because the achievements of East Asian capitalism were inexplicable within the terms or categories of dependency theory. East Asia's capitalist dynamos suffered all the ravages of colonial and neocolonial domination catalogued by dependency theorists, yet succeeded in their modernization projects. Japan's modern history began in 1853 with an act of old-style American imperialism, when Commodore Perry forced Japanese rulers at gunpoint to open their society to Western commercial trade. Japan's more recent resurgence began under American military occupation, after the United States dropped atomic bombs on two Japanese cities.[76] Berger noted that from a dependency perspective, British and American neocolonial domination over the Four Little Dragons should have undermined their modernization efforts. "One cannot go on doing dependency theory while ignoring this region of the world, but its development cannot be explained from within the theory," he argued.[77]

To Berger, successful modernization in these countries proved that dependency was an irrelevant factor in economic development. He conceded that high degrees of external dependency could inflict serious nondevelopmental costs on developing societies in the political and cultural realms; in some cases, these costs could even prove to be decisive. They had nothing to do, however, with economic development or capitalism. "Thus, for example, the question here is not whether United States economic power in Latin America makes this or that country in the region a pawn of foreign power politics or whether it seeks to subvert Hispanic culture or whether it is just a great annoyance to have all those *gringos* marching about the place," he explained. "The question is, very sharply, whether this capitalist economic power, in the aggregate if not in all individual instances, tends to improve the material lot of most of the people."[78]

His economic focus thus eliminated most political and cultural variables in order to permit empirical assessments of alternative economic models. Berger occasionally invoked Novak's notion of "democratic capitalism" in the early 1980s before rejecting it because it introduced political and cultural variables that precluded empirical comparisons.[79] Berger defined capitalism as an economic system featuring private ownership of the means of production and a predominance of market forces in making production decisions. Though it often did not succeed, he argued, and

thus provided grist for the dependency mill, the capitalist road to economic modernization constituted the best development strategy for poor
nations. The vague "Third Way" prescriptions of *Pyramids of Sacrifice* were
seriously mistaken precisely on this point. The starting point for a Third
World economic strategy was not to become liberated from dependency,
as *Pyramids of Sacrifice* asserted, but to become dependently integrated into
the international capitalist system. The Four Little Dragons had shown the
way.

Berger allowed that the development of East Asian capitalism did not
conform to Western free-enterprise prescriptions. The negative view toward government espoused by Western capitalism's ideologists had no
place in the rhetoric or practice of East Asian capitalism. For example, it
was the Meiji government in Japan that abolished feudalism and established a highly corporatist form of political economy in the nineteenth
century. The Meiji government instituted a massive agrarian reform
program, heavily subsidized a universal system of education, and established a system of close cooperation between the state and the newly
created capitalist class. Japan maintained essentially the same system of
elite symbiotic planning and intervention thereafter, notwithstanding the
fact that after World War II, the United States imposed a Western-style
system of political democracy upon its defeated enemy. [80]

This imposed political system was itself superimposed on Japan's
traditional elite social structure, which, as Berger noted, included the
country's most prominent politicians. Government agencies in Japan—
especially the Ministry of International Trade and Industry—worked
closely with Japanese business executives to develop and finance national
industrial policies to secure competitive advantages for Japan in international markets. [81] As Berger observed, essentially the same symbiotic
relationship between government and business marked the "synarchic"
economic systems of the Four Little Dragons. In South Korea, for example, an elite group of heavily subsidized conglomerates called the *chaebol*
worked closely with the state to guide the country's industrial strategy. By
one estimate, sales of the top ten *chaebol* in 1984 accounted for 67 percent
of South Korea's gross national product. Sales figures included inputs
produced by other firms, of course, but as Alice Amsden noted, most
suppliers to South Korea's large business groups were satellite subcontrac-
tors. This figure was thus, by all available evidence, an accurate measure
of the country's aggregate economic concentration. [82]

The volumes, types, and prices of exports under East Asian capitalism
were highly political matters. During the 1960s, South Korea's drive for
foreign markets was organized and funded by an authoritarian govern-

ment, headed by Park Chung Hee, which nationalized the banks in 1961. By nationalizing the country's banking system, the South Korean state acquired the means to organize its industrial policy and control the process of foreign loan allocation. South Korea's "free-market" society organized its economic development with seven consecutive five-year plans; Taiwan began operating on four-year plans in 1953. Berger observed that the success of East Asian corporatism thus falsified the Western capitalist dogma "that a high degree of state intervention in the economy is incompatible with successful capitalist development."[83] Though the point was already well-established, in significantly contrasting ways, by various fascist and social democratic governments, Berger carefully avoided any comment on the similarities between fascist and East Asian corporatist models. He further rejected any association between East Asian capitalism and European welfare-state economies. His argument about the efficacy of East Asian capitalism was not to be construed "as an argument for a 'mixed economy' as advocated and to some degree practiced by Western social democrats," he emphasized. "The East Asian economies under consideration are much more unambiguously capitalist."[84] East Asian state intervention was more selective and economistic than Western social democracy. It concentrated on industrial policy and education while abjuring government efforts to equalize wealth or provide social insurance.

Japanese social policies were, to be sure, more generous in the social sphere than any of the Four Little Dragons, not only because the Four Little Dragons had modernized more recently, but more importantly because they were not democracies. Berger treaded lightly on this subject, taking care not to repeat Novak's claims about the inexorable logic of capitalism. Though he suggested that successful capitalist development in the Third World should generate pressures toward democracy, Berger did not exaggerate existing evidence for this belief. Japan remained undemocratic, to put it mildly, through the entire period of its initial modernization. Moreover, Japan's postwar democracy was not the product of any internal democratizing force, but was imposed as a consequence of its military defeat.

The dramatic expansion of the middle-class sector in the Four Little Dragons seemed to provide the necessary groundwork for democratic gains in these nations. During the 1980s, some progress toward greater political openness was achieved. South Korea and Taiwan permitted participatory institutions to develop in carefully selected (mostly economic and nonpolitical) areas, and in 1988 a voluntary transfer of presidential authority took place in South Korea for the first time in the country's history. Nonpolitical participatory organizing was permitted on a lesser scale in Singapore and Hong Kong. Berger took care throughout the 1980s not to overstate the evidence for a democratic trend, however.[85]

The evidence for such a trend was thin at best. Neoconservative political scientist Nicholas Eberstadt observed in 1989 that there was virtually no evidence that East Asian modernization had overturned entrenched cultural barriers to the recognition of individual rights or the rule of law. East Asian political cultures were generally sustained by nationalistic ideologies of racial rule, he noted, which valorized the individual by virtue of race or ethnicity. Moreover, South Korea and Japan featured the worst patterns of wage discrimination against women in the world. Singapore had been ruled for more than thirty years by the People's Action Party of Lee Kuan Yew as a Leninist-style right-wing dictatorship based on secretive party cells. Berger acknowledged that East Asian modernization was apparently compatible with racialism, nationalism, patriarchal domination, and dictatorial politics.[86]

"I think it is important to assume, however, that in the long run there *is* a democratizing trend inherent in capitalism," he asserted. "The key is that capitalist development must first become successful; the democratic pressures only get released after that point."[87] Since the long run was not yet evident in East Asia, it was too soon to see capitalism's democratizing effects in the region. Berger's criterion of success thus performed the same function for his argument that Novak's redefinition of capitalism performed for his claim about the democratizing logic of capitalism. For Novak, the ravages of economic modernization in Latin America were explained away on the grounds that true capitalism didn't exist in Latin America. Modernization had failed throughout Latin America because capitalism's political and cultural dimensions were missing.[88]

Berger proceeded much more cautiously, declining to use Novak's subjectively loaded terminology and generally refraining from making categorical judgments about Latin American culture. "Very cautiously, I would say that Latin American culture is apparently not conducive to modernization, but whether this is the major factor that has undercut Latin American development projects is something I'm not prepared to say," he explained.[89] In his case, the definition of success kept the question open. Latin America's experience of modernization added nothing to the debate over the democratizing logic of capitalism, since no Latin American nation had successfully modernized. Berger noted that from the standpoint of the economic-growth criterion, Brazil once appeared to be on the road to successful modernization. Why it failed to raise the condition of the underclass and then lost its economic momentum, he remarked, was the kind of question that needed to be answered.

Researchers using the more analytical and multidimensional variants of dependency theory identified several factors that might have begun to answer this question. When pressed with the kind of evidence presented by Fernando Fajnzylber, Aldo Ferrer, Fernando Henrique Cardoso, and Peter Evans on the exploitative policies of transnational companies, the effects of foreign control over domestic finance capital, the consequences of protected markets in the developed countries, and the legacy of American military aid to repressive Latin American governments, Berger typically responded by changing the subject to East Asia.[90] Dependency did not have to be crippling, he asserted, pointing to the success of East Asian capitalism. His later writings described dependency theory only in general terms before claiming that East Asian modernization refuted dependency claims. "Each of the Four Little Dragons can easily be described as 'dependent'—South Korea and Taiwan overwhelmingly so upon the United States (economically as well as politically and militarily), Hong Kong as a British colony, and Singapore as a very small actor in the international capitalist system that thoroughly penetrates its economy," he observed. "To call the situation of these societies 'dependent development' is a verbal legerdemain that only serves to underline their disconfirming weight upon dependency theory."[91] Dependency theory's apologists needed to reflect on the success of East Asian capitalism, which offered a model of Third World modernization.

Berger did not dispute that certain critical aspects of East Asian culture and experience were not replicable in other parts of the Third World. The high rates of literacy and the influence of the Confucian moral tradition in East Asia were factors not found or paralleled in much of the Third World. The Confucian emphasis on family loyalty, education, cooperation, honesty, and hard work have, by all accounts, contributed greatly to the success of East Asian economic development. If this moral-cultural factor or some variant of it was indeed crucial to any modernizing project, as Weber argued in a different context, the possibility of appropriating the East Asian experience in an African or Latin American context was, to say the least, highly problematic.

Neither did he dispute—when pressed on the point—that the peculiarities of East Asia's modernization experience extended beyond the cultural domain. The modernization projects of the Four Little Dragons were aided during the 1950s and 1960s by massive infusions of American foreign aid, by the economic stimulus provided by the Vietnam War, and especially by the Japanese influence. The Four Little Dragons were the beneficiaries (indirectly, in the cases of Singapore and Hong Kong) of what amounted to an East Asian version of the Marshall Plan. Between

1951 and 1965, the United States gave approximately $1.5 billion in economic aid to Taiwan and several billion more in military aid, financing more than 90 percent of Taiwan's trade deficit. South Korea received nearly $6 billion in economic aid between 1945 and 1978, which nearly equaled the amount of economic aid given to all African countries combined over the same period. During the critical period of the 1950s, when the foundations of South Korea's export-based economy were built, more than 80 percent of the country's imports were financed by American economic assistance. While the rest of the Third World was lectured by the American government, the International Monetary Fund, and the World Bank on the necessity of maintaining free trade and capital mobility, the United States looked the other way when Taiwan and South Korea placed tight restrictions on foreign investment and protected their own markets. These protected domestic markets provided the base on which subsidized Taiwanese and Korean conglomerates launched their successful drives for foreign markets. [92]

The war in Vietnam aided these efforts. Just as America's intervention in Korea boosted the Japanese economy in the early 1950s, America's intervention in Vietnam created huge markets for agricultural and industrial commodities and recreational services that the Four Little Dragons amply provided. Korean firms like Hyundai and Daewoo grew into powerful enterprises by signing construction contracts with the United States to assist the war effort.

The Japanese influence was decisive. Berger acknowledged that the modernization of the Four Little Dragons could be viewed as extensions of the Japanese experience. [93] Taiwan and Korea were Japanese colonies in the first half of the twentieth century. When Japanese firms began to look for cheaper labor markets on a large scale in the 1960s, they looked first to their former colonies. Taiwan and Korea built their manufacturing bases partly on the basis of the cheap labor they offered to Japanese firms. Japan, in turn, provided much of the technology and machinery that the Four Little Dragons needed to build their export businesses in toys, radios, television sets, and computer monitors. While devoting very little of their budgets to their own research and development, the Four Little Dragons remained dependent on Japan for technology and new machinery. The export successes of these nations in consumer electronics, automobiles, and semiconductors during the 1970s and 1980s were made possible by Japan's provision of these technologies to its dependent partners. During the same period, the Japanese kept their high technology secrets to themselves. A system of "triangular trade" in manufacturing goods thus developed in the 1970s, in which the markets for Newly Industrialized

Country (NIC) goods were provided by the United States while Japan provided selected NICs with necessary (and dispensable) technology and machinery. Walden Bello and Stephanie Rosenfeld summarized the shape of this arrangement: "By the mid-1980s, while the NICs were running multibillion-dollar trade surpluses with the United States, they were running multibillion-dollar trade deficits with Japan," they observed. "In 1988, Taiwan enjoyed a $10.4 billion surplus with the United States but suffered a $6 billion deficit with Japan. In the case of Korea, the surplus with the United States in 1988 came to $8.6 billion while the deficit with Japan amounted to nearly $4 billion." The export successes of the NICs were thus highly remunerative, as Berger claimed, but at the price of extreme economic dependence on Japan for technology and capital goods.[94]

Though he dismissed the concept as a verbal legerdemain, "dependent development" thus exactly described the structural characteristics of East Asian capitalism. The East Asian model that Berger promoted was a form of calculated dependence in which the export-based economies of vulnerable nations were tied to the economies of the great powers. To accept this bargain was to accept the risks associated with structural dependence. That Taiwan and South Korea had instituted economic modernization strategies in cultures particularly well suited for economic modernization was evident. That they had established a development model for other nations or refuted the empirical claims of dependency analysis was a more problematic pair of assertions.

Though the differences between East Asian and Latin American cultures were undoubtedly highly determinative factors, as Berger carefully suggested, the differences between the economic modernization strategies of the Four Little Dragons and most Latin American countries were also significant. In the 1960s and early 1970s, most Latin American nations adopted "import substitution" strategies aimed at developing their own internal production and markets. Brazil later epitomized the monumental failures of this strategy. The East Asian decision to opt for a strategy of export-based integration paid vastly higher dividends. The parallels between the strategies of the Four Little Dragons and the most advanced Latin American economies were also instructive, however. Like Brazil in the early 1970s, the Four Little Dragons achieved massive economic growth while developing very little capacity for self-sustaining technological innovation. Like Brazil, they established top-down models of elite economic management. Like Brazil, they built their economies partly on their capacity to offer cheap labor to corporate enterprises. And like Brazil, their goal was to make the transition to higher value-added, high-technology production. The Four Little Dragons failed to make this transition, however, and they were increasingly squeezed by cheaper labor competition from less-industrialized countries such as Malaysia and Indonesia. At the same time, the agricultural and environmental ravages of their extended hyperindustrialization were becoming vividly evident by the late 1980s. Four decades of heavy pesticide use and largely unregulated waste dumping had produced high levels of agricultural contamination and air and water pollution. [95]

The argument that East Asian capitalism offered a replicable model of economic modernization was therefore problematic on several counts. The economic development of the Four Little Dragons was built on massive American economic aid, American military spending, American preferential treatment, Japanese technological assistance, cheap labor, export-oriented production, an undervalued currency, the distinctive cultural ethos of Confucianism, and economic planning by authoritarian government/business elites. The extreme dependency and vulnerability of NIC capitalism raised serious questions about the capacity of this model to attain economically and environmentally sustainable development. The Four Little Dragons modernized while retaining severely repressive political systems. Berger himself described East Asian capitalism as extremely materialistic, obsessively hierarchical, and "diabolically meritocratic." [96] The argument that these societies offered a replicable model of economic modernization for the Third World assumed that the world economy could absorb and reward an ever-increasing number of national economies based on manufacturing exports. It further assumed that the world's ecosystem could tolerate many Taiwans.

THE ROLE OF MEDIATING STRUCTURES

Since the East Asian model was the only example of successful modernization in the underdeveloped world, Berger's focus on East Asia as the symbol of what it meant to face up to modernity was well chosen. In the face of overwhelming military defeat and the shattering of their dreams of imperial rule and racial destiny, the Japanese (like the Germans) belatedly embraced modernity at mid-century with instructive enthusiasm. Having lost the right to waste their resources on military spending, the Japanese and Germans rebuilt their devastated economies by modernizing their industrial infrastructures, developing technologies geared to production for specialized markets, and investing heavily in education. Both nations drew on premodern traditions of collective discipline to attain secularized goals of peace, prosperity, and social welfare. This presumably enlightened project would bear significant spiritual, cultural, and political costs, in the view of recent communitarian and civic republican theorists. Christopher Lasch observed that these costs included not only the spiritual shallowness of modern commercial societies, but also a shallow concept of democracy. Modernization promoted an ever-widening split between the private spheres of uprooted individuals and the managerial functions of the state and other large institutions. Like other communitarian, populist, and civic republican theorists, Lasch argued that commercial societies thus eviscerated the republican notion of the public sphere as a realm of participatory citizenship. Under the pressure of business civilization, politics was reduced to the technocratic management of society's best-organized and most powerful interests. The function of the political realm in this conception of democracy, as Kristol complained, was not to inculcate the character-forming virtues of citizenship, but merely to manage the distribution of external social goods. [97]

If Kristol was neoconservatism's most significant proponent of this argument (in its conservative form), Berger was the movement's most influential dissenter from it. The "moral bankruptcy of liberalism" was not one of his themes. He was forced to defend his dissenting position with increasing frequency in the early 1990s, after the Soviet collapse prompted most neoconservatives to embark on new crusades for world democracy and a transformed American culture. Berger was particularly caustic toward any call for a more participatory politics, since the first rule of any desirable politics was to leave people alone. He was content to leave politics to the professional and special-interest elites. Those who moaned about the loss of citizenship under modern democracy failed to appreciate that most people were commendably disinterested in politics.

Some of Berger's most compelling and potentially valuable work implicitly addressed this subject, however, under the rubric of what he called "mediating structures." In 1975, he and Neuhaus initiated a research project funded by the American Enterprise Institute that explored the role of mediating structures in American politics and society. Their conclusions were published by the Institute two years later in a highly suggestive monograph that prefigured the revival of communitarian theory. *To Empower People: The Role of Mediating Structures in Public Policy* defined "mediating structures" as institutions that stood between the private life of the individual and the large institutions of public life. The latter included such "megastructures" as the state, business and financial corporations, trade unions, and the professional bureaucracies. The megastructures were typically hard and alienating, they noted, driving most people to look for personal meaning in the softer (though notoriously unreliable) private sphere of the self.

Modernity's double crisis was a product of this dichotomy between the public and private spheres. For the individual who struggled to meet the widely differing demands of the two spheres, Berger and Neuhaus observed, modern society presented a lonely and often bewildering challenge to keep one's balance. The size and remoteness of the megastructures produced a second crisis for modern societies in which the state and other large institutions appeared to individuals as unreal, alien, threatening, and sometimes malignant. Berger and Neuhaus bypassed conventional reformist/therapeutic prescriptions for humanizing society's megastructures or helping individuals adjust to them. They observed that those who coped most effectively with modernity's alienating dualisms usually participated in such mediating structures as neighborhoods, families, churches, and voluntary associations. To Empower People argued that the survival of these primary mediating structures was crucial to America's vitality.

Two programmatic arguments were advanced. The first was that public policy should stop undermining America's mediating structures and attempt, instead, to strengthen them. This was the minimalist proposition. The maximalist argument was that "wherever possible, public policy should utilize mediating structures for the realization of social purposes."[98] The second argument was advanced cautiously. Berger and Neuhaus emphasized the qualifying "wherever possible." Government efforts to co-opt or control America's mediating structures would only accelerate their disintegration. The test was pragmatic. The purpose of public policy should be to protect the mediating structures, to promote their well-being, and to utilize their benefits wherever such action did not undermine the functioning of these institutions. The goal was not to decentralize government functions, but to strengthen those institutions that mediated between government and the individual.

To support local neighborhoods, for example, required a shift away from America's existing synthesis of individualism and government collectivism. Berger and Neuhaus argued that an unbalanced emphasis on individual rights in the nation's courts and policy agencies was destroying the power of local communities to determine or sustain their own values in the public sphere. In the name of protecting individual rights, the legal fiction of a "unitary national community" was being imposed on America's widely diverse communities by federal agencies. They noted that the right of communities to prohibit pornography, for example, was being undermined by precedents established in Berkeley and Times Square.

For Berger and Neuhaus, this onslaught against community standards was the inheritance of a civil rights movement run amok. They charged that policies deriving from America's belated effort to prohibit racial discrimination were being extended to other areas "where they are neither practicable nor just." The government was effectively sanctioning new forms of discrimination, including reverse discrimination, in the name of civil rights. American public policy needed to become more discriminating in its efforts to prohibit discrimination. It needed to distinguish between proscription and prescription. The original purpose of the civil rights movement, Berger and Neuhaus recalled, was to spur American society to proscribe racial discrimination in the public realm. The achievement of this end in the mid-1960s was a monumental achievement. The proper business of the state was to enforce the proscriptions against discrimination contained in the civil rights bills.

But instead of limiting state intervention to this area, they observed, the federal government was pushing prescriptive schemes for racial integration and equality. Berger and Neuhaus warned that government support for affirmative action and school busing was risking a revolutionary backlash from the Right. The effects of these policies on local communities were already evident, they claimed. The prescriptive federal effort to promote racial integration and equality was "eroding community power, distracting from the tasks of neighborhood development, and alienating many Americans from the general direction of domestic public policy."[99] What was needed was a federal policy that withdrew from the prescriptive area, enforced the proscriptive civil rights laws, and supported existing communities with more generous assistance and tax breaks for housing and home improvements.

Existing federal policies also undermined the rights of families. Berger and Neuhaus made a passing rejoinder to the rights-of-children literature, arguing that much of it rationalized the ideological and pecuniary interests of child-care professionals and academics. Their main focus was on educational policy, however, where the state had already expropriated power from families. The disenfranchisement of the family was nearly an absolute fact of life in American education, they observed. The state's rhetoric of human rights and national norms had reduced the family to the status of an auxiliary agency. The state controlled the educational process for all children except the privileged, exercising coercive powers over all families except those wealthy enough to buy out of the system. This disenfranchisement violated "perhaps the most fundamental right—the right to make a world for one's children."[100] What was needed in education was a strategy to break up the state's monopoly. Empowerment was the issue. To give real choices to families in the area of education—as with any area affecting a mediating institution—was to promote the empowerment of the disenfranchised working and middle classes.

Berger and Neuhaus thus endorsed the concept of educational vouchers. They argued that a voucher policy would treat parents like adults. Educational vouchers could be disbursed to families to make their own decisions about which schools to attend. The schools would then be reimbursed by the state for the number of vouchers they turned in. "This proposal would break the coercive monopoly of the present education system and empower individuals in relating to the megastructures of bureaucracy and professionalism, with special benefits going to lower-income people," they argued. "In addition, it would enhance the diversity of American life by fostering particularist communities of value—whether of lifestyle, ideology, religion, or ethnicity."[101] Berger and Neuhaus conceded that the literature on voucher policy was empirically thin; several key voucher experiments were still too new to have generated meaningful data. The unintended consequences of making all certified schools public schools were still largely unknown. In their reading, however, it was an instructive fact that virtually none of the objections typically raised against the voucher idea were about education. Most objections to voucher policy focused on the politics of certification or the opposition of teachers' unions. But it was on the educational merits of the idea that this policy deserved to be judged, they contended. The educational merits of voucher policy outweighed interest-group objections.

Wherever the state undermined mediating institutions, they argued, poor and middle-class people were disempowered in the name of their ostensible rights. In each case, the New Class expropriated powers of citizenship from ordinary people. What was needed at the political level was a chastened recognition that ordinary people nearly always understood their needs better than anyone else. Berger and Neuhaus granted that their call for a public policy that protected and supported mediating institutions might appear quixotic. "A strong argument can be made that the dynamics of modernity, operating through the megastructures and especially through the modern state, are like a great leviathan or steamroller, inexorably destroying every obstacle that gets in the way of creating mass society," they conceded.[102] They countered that most Americans took a skeptical view toward the megastructures, however, and thus resisted massification. The cultural ravages of modernity were mitigated, they claimed, by the humanizing, community-sustaining work of the mediating institutions.

This was a fruitful departure. Berger's turn to the concept of mediating structures implicitly cut across conventional Right and Left positions, taking its distance from both the "old faith in the market" and the "new faith in government" without claiming to represent a new vital center. Big business and big government were both viewed as massifying, freedom-crushing social forces. Berger and Neuhaus uncovered a common feature of contemporary conservatism and liberalism—both ideologies were products of the Enlightenment faith in abstract reason. *To Empower People* was a call for a return to human-scale, community-oriented politics. To be liberated was not to escape from particularity, as Enlightenment ideologies assumed, but to discover the particularity that fit one's circumstances.[103]

It was not the neoconservatives, however, who would go on to develop the implications of these ideas. Berger's implicit critique of the collectivizing logic of modern capitalism was ideologically problematic for neoconservatism and its corporate sponsors. When Novak and his American Enterprise Institute (AEI) colleagues organized a symposium on the policy implications of Berger and Neuhaus's book, they expanded the definition of mediating structures to include business and financial corporations and (to even the score) trade unions. The AEI's conference on "Democracy and Mediating Structures" treated such "human-scale" enterprises as General Dynamics and Exxon as mediating institutions. A former executive of Mobil Oil defended AEI's definitional revisionism and argued that multinational corporations practiced an ethic of "altruistic egoism" that was first expressed "some two thousand years ago, by Jesus of Nazareth."[104] Tom Kahn explained why the AFL-CIO's corporatist business-unionism also constituted mediating action, emphasizing that the AFL-CIO rejected European codeterminist strategies.[105] The conference's outcome was foreordained. The communitarian character of the mediating structures idea was sacrificed to protect corporate capitalism from criticism. The only megastructure worth worrying about, it turned out, was the state.

Berger's subsequent writings contributed to this trivialization of his thesis. As he became increasingly convinced that East Asian capitalism refuted dependency theory, his writings became more one-sided in their advocacy of capitalist modernization. He relinquished his earlier tendency to look for a Third Way within a capitalist framework; to face up to modernity was to stop carping about modernization's drawbacks. It was therefore left to such Left-communitarian theorists as Lasch, Michael Sandel, Michael Walzer, Robert Bellah, Benjamin Barber, and Harry Boyte to elaborate the politics of mediating structures.[106] *To Empower People* challenged too much of Berger's neoconservatism for him to develop the politics implicit within it. Those who carried this task forward unsurprisingly did not share many of his specific policy positions.

THE ROLE OF THE MARKET

Having witnessed and abetted the trivialization of his thesis, Berger made only passing references to it in his subsequent writings. *The Capitalist Revolution* mentioned mediating structures only once. [107] The real business of modernization, as he emphasized at another AEI conference, was not to promote grassroots democracy or citizenship, but to maximize the opportunities for capitalist investment and growth. In modern societies, Berger argued, the crucial socioeconomic tasks were the responsibilities of elites. The crucial factor in any modernization project was therefore the nature of the elite in that country. "My hypothesis is that it is very important to have a clearly defined elite that overlaps economic and political spheres and is capable of engaging in a continuing communication process that makes such decisions possible," he explained. "Whether that elite has to sell itself to the electorate as it does in Japan or can do things in a more authoritarian manner as it does in the Four Little Dragons may be an important question for other reasons, but I doubt if it is the crucial variable." [108] Berger wagered that successful modernization would eventually generate pressures for democratic change in East Asia, but he cautioned that democracy was not necessarily related to modernization at any stage of its development. Facing up to modernity required that one abjure Novakian enthusiasms. Modernization was not about democracy, but about elite-dominated development.

Was a capitalist-driven liberal democracy therefore the most humane and desirable system attainable? Berger asserted that the evidence strongly supported this conclusion without producing an absolutely conclusive verdict. He argued that social democratic rhetoric obfuscated the real-world, either/or alternatives, and that social democratic theories of economic democracy were utopian. Both capitalism and socialism were systems of production under which various kinds of distribution systems were possible, he explained. Social democracy was not a third way between capitalist and socialist models, but an approach to distribution. Berger claimed that social democratic rhetoric about democratizing the economy therefore confused the issue. "Market socialism is a contradiction in terms," he asserted. "At critical points, any so-called 'mixed model' is going to be driven either toward the market or the plan." Social democracy was only coherent as a welfare-state distributional system. It lost this coherence—and confused the debate over capitalism—whenever it posed as an alternative mode of production. [109]

Like Novak, Berger liked to quote Mises on this point. In his major work on socialism, Mises argued in 1932 that the market was the essence of capitalism. He effectively criticized the variant of market socialism promulgated by Oskar Lange, the Polish economist, who tried to show that market mechanisms and incentives could be integrated into socialist theory. Lange argued that a large state sector could coexist with and simulate the pricing system of a private sector of small enterprises. Though Lange's variant of socialism allowed greater room for the market than traditional state socialism, his model was still essentially statist, featuring state-owned firms run by managers hired on profit-bonus arrangements. [110] As Mises observed, the chief problem with this scheme was that people did not risk their own capital in making investment decisions. The basic dynamic of a productive economy was thus arrested at the outset, because capital was controlled by a state planning board that lacked the competence or knowledge to replicate the market's enormously complex pricing decisions.

Mises gave short shrift to syndicalist alternatives. Under any form of worker ownership, he observed, workers either lost their shares in an enterprise upon leaving it or were allowed to keep them. In the former case, the productive and adaptive capacities of the enterprise were undermined by the workers' vested interest in making no changes in production. In the latter case, a reversion to capitalism effectively took place. [111] Berger remarked, "One may sum up von Mises's judgment on the two types of 'market socialism' by saying that just as managers cannot be made to play at being capitalists, workers cannot play at being shareholders—or, rather, both 'artifacts' are not possible as long as a system remains socialist." In his reading, the failures of market socialist experiments in Hungary and Yugoslavia provided powerful confirming evidence for Mises's arguments. Berger therefore claimed that "there can be no effective market economy without private ownership of the means of production."

He allowed that Hungary's and Yugoslavia's experiments in "market socialism" were hampered by Soviet domination of Eastern Europe and by Yugoslavia's bitter ethnic strife. He failed to note that in both cases, as in the case of what he called Chinese "market socialism," the economic system in question functioned under the conditions of a state dictatorship. It was not a negligible consideration, though Berger's rather bloodless discussion of market socialism proceeded as though the questions of democracy, legitimacy, and dictatorship were irrelevent to the issue. His contention that an effective market economy could only be sustained under capitalist modes of production and management was subject to stronger challenges in the Western democracies. Berger conceded in a one-sentence aside that his argument altogether avoided "the question of so-called mixed economies." Like Mises, he assumed that mixed systems could not endure and that Western Europe's mixed economies were being driven toward either purer capitalism or suffocation. [112]

Given these assumptions, I asked him in 1990 for his view on the trend toward worker and community ownership in the United States and Europe. I noted that more than 5,000 worker cooperatives had been organized in the United States during the 1980s. There were presently more than 8,000 worker-owned companies in America, including the United Parcel Service, Chicago Northwestern Railroad, Northwestern Steel and Wire, Vermont Asbestos, Weirton Steel, South Bend Lathe, Farmland Industries, Agway, Ocean Spray Cranberries, and the sixteen plywood cooperatives of the Pacific Northwest. Though some of these firms featured share owning without worker control, many others featured outright worker and community control. [113] On a larger scale, the Mondragon cooperatives in the Basque region of Spain employed over 90,000 workers in an integrated network of more than 125 financial, industrial, and service companies. These highly successful enterprises were owned by their own workers and were managed democratically on the basis of cooperative membership. The Mondragon network included more than seventy industrial firms, an agricultural cooperative, five schools, a technical college, and a central bank, the Caja Laboral Popular. Twenty percent of each enterprise's capital was provided by workers, another 20 percent came from a government grant, and the remaining 60 percent came from the bank, which was half-owned by its employees and half-owned by other cooperatives. In three decades, the Mondragon cooperatives had witnessed only two closings. [114]

On a more expansive scale, the Meidner Plan for Economic Democracy in Sweden presented a nationwide experiment in decentralized worker and community ownership and control. Berger had not heard of the program when I asked for his view of it. A modified form of the Meidner Plan had been enacted by Sweden's social democratic government in 1982. The plan called for an annual 20 percent tax on major company profits to be paid in the form of stock to eight regional mutual funds controlled by worker, consumer, and government representatives. As their proportion of stock ownership grew, workers and public representatives were collectively entitled to representation on company boards. The Meidner Plan was not a program promoting worker ownership of specific firms, but a program for social ownership. In the compromised form of the Meidner Plan passed by the Swedish government, the eight funds combined could not own more than 40 percent of any single firm. The plan nonetheless made a substantial national move toward effective democratic control over the process of investment. Since the worker funds represented part of workers' compensation, the plan contained a built-in system of wage restraints and also facilitated a new form of capital formation. The Meidner Plan signified a possible shift in social democratic politics away from the traditional emphasis on continually expanding the welfare state.[115]

What did Berger make of these developments? He quickly replied that only the Meidner Plan was potentially significant. "If they go ahead with it, and it works, this would falsify my argument," he observed. "These other examples of worker ownership that you describe—they can't prove anything. They're cooperative enterprises in a capitalist system. This Swedish thing is different. It's really a type of syndicalism." He paused briefly. "Of course, I don't think this would work, either. I expect that worker ownership would replicate the same economic problems as state socialism," he continued. "But it sounds like a fascinating empirical case to me."[116] He warned that any effort to democratize the process of investment would inevitably paralyze any nation's capacity to compete in international markets. If Sweden's intelligentsia was trying to further democratize their already overly democratized society, this only confirmed for him that intellectuals found it desperately difficult to give up the socialist myth. As he observed elsewhere, intellectuals were especially capable of adhering to myths "in the teeth of mountains of empirical counterevidence."[117] He regarded his own neoconservatism not as an ideological position, but as a prudential reflection of available evidence.

THE HERETICAL IMPERATIVE:
CONFRONTING PLURALISM

In their article "Our Conservatism and Theirs," Berger and his wife, noted sociologist Brigitte Berger, explained the empirical spirit of their outlook. The Bergers eschewed ideological enthusiasms. Two cheers for capitalism were enough for them. They argued that the litmus test for any worthy conservatism, however, was whether it faced up to modernity. Neoconservatives were compelled to dissociate themselves from other conservatisms on this count. The crucial issue was "the area of modern consciousness, and specifically the experience of relativity—the awareness that all world views and value systems are contingent upon specific historical and social circumstances." The Bergers' own awareness of the constructed nature of social reality compelled a pragmatic outlook. Since the social world was relative and "makeable," the test of a worthy social doctrine or practice was whether it worked. They observed that it was primarily in the modern social sciences that the experience of relativity and the necessity of a pragmatic outlook had been theoretically elaborated. It was thus no accident that most neoconservatives were social scientists, while most conservatives were "generally hostile to all the social sciences and especially to sociology."[118] Most conservatives regarded their beliefs as given, but it was precisely this faith in the givenness of moral and social values that the experience of relativity negated.

The Bergers cautioned that their argument did not preclude making truth claims. The plurality of world views and the constructed character of social knowledge did not preclude the possibility that one world view was true. The difference was that one became aware of having chosen certain beliefs. The experience of modernization was fundamentally a "movement of the mind from destiny to choice," they explained. To comprehend the reality of pluralism and relativity was to lose the intellectual innocence plaintively claimed by most conservatives. "We cannot participate in the alleged certainties of the other conservative groupings," they declared. "We are, if you will, conservatives not by faith but by skepticism."[119]

Their faith was a theologically liberal form of Lutheranism. They noted that Lutheranism was the most socially and politically conservative of the major Christian traditions. While recognizing that the church was required to involve itself in the public realm, the Lutheran tradition was characterized by a deep mistrust of perfectionism and utopianism of any kind. The Bergers shared this attitude. Lutheranism opposed not only the utopianism of the political Left, but also the perfectionistic absolutism of Protestant fundamentalism. In Luther's doctrine of the two kingdoms, they found a compelling analogue to Weber's distinction between the ethic of absolute ends and the ethic of responsibility. For Luther, as for Weber, the political realm was the sphere of the law and the sword, which required a pragmatic ethic of responsibility. The Bergers claimed that modern mainline Christianity was distorted by its introjection of the absolute moral ends of the gospel into the public realm. Modern churches blurred the distinction between the realm of the gospel and the Spirit and realm of the law and the sword.[120]

Berger thus found himself doubly alienated from modern American Christianity. His theological liberalism was anathema to conservatives and his political neoconservatism was rejected by America's mainline denominations. His participation in the formulation of the Hartford Appeal intensified these contradictions. In 1974, he met with seventeen theologians at the Hartford Seminary Foundation to discuss what they called "pervasive, false, and debilitating notions undermining contemporary Christianity and its influence in society." Berger was theologically the group's most liberal participant. The following January, they published the "Hartford Appeal for Theological Affirmation," a sharply worded attack on modern Christianity's purported reduction of religion to psychological and political categories. [121] The statement ignited a fire storm of protests from pastors and denominational officials who disputed the Hartford group's characterization of their churches. The Hartford Appeal was generally read as an exaggerated and rather mean-spirited assault on the mainline churches—an interpretation that Berger tried to correct. "As I put it then to one such inquirer," he later recalled, "I was not concerned with a return to the tradition but with a return to the *struggle* with the tradition; such struggling, I thought then and think now, is made meaningless if the tradition itself is secularized."[122] He was not aligning himself with the religious Right, but joining them in a critique of mainline secularization. He signed the Hartford Appeal to distinguish himself "from those to the 'left' of the liberal position I espoused."[123]

The Hartford Appeal was not nearly as subtle as Berger's purpose, however. His association with it and the controversy it provoked moved him to clarify his theological position in *The Heretical Imperative*. Building on the revisionist method he sketched in *A Rumor of Angels*, he argued in *The Heretical Imperative* that modernization compelled individuals to make heretical engagements with pluralism. The bare fact that modern individuals were constantly confronted with alternative world views and traditions made it necessary for them to piece together their own world views, he explained. Exposure to the plurality of world views and traditions undermined the possibility of uncritically living out an assumed or given world view. Modernization dethroned fate and universalized the necessity of choosing among alternative beliefs. This compulsion to make choices was what Berger called the heretical imperative.

He rejected all deductive refusals to ignore the challenges of modernity. He also rejected all reductive strategies to reduce religious doctrines to psychological, political, or other secular categories. Berger defended the inductive, experiential approach to theology pioneered by Friedrich Schleiermacher, which took the individual's experience of divine reality as the starting point for theology. Experience preceded all theories about it. "The essence of religion is neither theoretical knowledge nor practical activity (such as moral actions) but a particular kind of experience," he contended. Religious consciousness was not reducible to human self-consciousness, but was rightly consciousness of something beyond itself. "In other words, to start with human consciousness does not mean that one must also end there," he argued. "On the contrary, in Schleiermacher's case, human consciousness is of interest to the theologian only insofar as it bears the marks, the 'imitations,' of a God who is utterly beyond human measure."[124] Berger claimed that it was only by adopting Schleiermacher's experiential method that modern Christian theology could remain authentically Christian while also coming to terms with the existence of other world religions.[125]

"Reductionism" is a slippery accusation. From a more traditional standpoint, Berger's theological position was extremely reductionistic. Most of his writings on religion nonetheless reserved their sharpest criticism for what he called the reductionism of modern Protestant and Catholic churches. "When I go to church or read church publications, I'm irritated when confronted with statements that I consider to be empirically flawed," he reported. "I don't go to church in order to hear vulgarized, 'pop' versions of my own field. The irritation deepens when these terrible simplifications are proclaimed to me in tones of utter certitude and moral urgency. Bad analysis obviously makes for bad policy, and here I'm not just intellectually irritated but morally offended."[126] He complained that even when the churches refrained from reducing the transcendent claims of the gospel to leftist politics, they typically gave undeserved sanction to leftist views in their moral and social teachings. "Put simply, I fail to see the moral superiority of an ideology committed to unilateral disarmament, a vague socialism, and an assault on the family," he explained.[127]

Berger admitted that he probably would have felt less offended if the churches endorsed his political views. He did not propose, however, that the churches replace their dovish progressivism with his politics. Neither agenda belonged in the church's liturgy or literature. "Would I have wanted the Roman Catholic bishops to issue the Novak document, *Toward the Future: Catholic Social Thought and the U.S. Economy?*" he asked. "No, I would not have wanted the bishops to issue the Novak document, even though I think it is much closer than the bishops' pastoral on economics to what I think empirical reality to be."[128] To embellish any social agenda with such authority, in his view, was to commit what Luther called the sin of "works-righteousness," which was an act of apostasy.

Berger conceded that the church's theological and moral teachings compelled some kind of social mission. But if every issue tainted with ideological implications was to be excluded from the discussion, how were the church's social teachings and mission to be construed? His answer centered on the concept of mediating action. The church should neither withdraw from the political arena nor become a partisan participant within it, he argued. Since the church had no answers to any social or political problem, the church had no business formulating social or political policies. The social function of the church was to mediate between contending social and political forces. The church should become an open forum or "zone of freedom" in which current moral and social concerns were freely discussed from a variety of perspectives.

Berger allowed that the church was obligated to condemn certain extraordinarily clear examples of social evil—such as racial segregation or totalitarian rule—where such evils existed. But beyond this carefully circumscribed function, he argued, the church's only social mission was to serve as a social mediator. He did not attempt to offer biblical support for this ecclesiology. "I'm firmly convinced that there are no 'Christian answers' to any social or political problem," he explained. "Yet a Christian will approach the socio-political world in a different spirit. Not the least important part of this spirit is an acceptance of one's ignorance, of the moral ambiguities of all human action, and therefore of the need for forgiveness." The church should mediate its own equivocal moral perspective to all contending parties, Berger argued, which should be "profoundly relativizing" on all levels. The church had no answers and had no right to have any answers. Secular organizations had no answers, either, but they could be encouraged to look for them in dialogues mediated by the church. "Even if the mediating action of the church does nothing else than to make the contestants less sure of themselves, it will have rendered an important service to society," he claimed. [129]

Berger contrasted this modest mission with the "moral arrogance" that prevailed in modern churches. He cited the Barmen Declaration of 1934 as an example of the church fulfilling its limited social mission. The Barmen Declaration—which was authored principally by Karl Barth— condemned the encroachments of the Nazi state upon the church's theological and social identity. For Berger, the Barmen Declaration represented the proper form and special circumstances under which the church's prophetic social witness was appropriate. The example arguably highlighted the chief problem with Berger's ecclesiology, however. By the time that a dissident faction of the German Protestant churches finally overcame its deeply ingrained ghettoization to denounce the blasphemies and terror of German fascism, the Nazis were in power. The brave words of the Barmen Declaration were too little, too late. They were heeded only by a small number of the well-churched German faithful, who were long-accustomed to an ecclesiology in which the church stayed out of social affairs. The acquiescence of the German churches under Hitler was part of the legacy of "two kingdoms" ecclesiology.

Berger's neoconservatism rejected not only the moral idealism of the churches, but the moral campaigns of other neoconservatives. "There's no question that the end of the Cold War has produced a crisis for many neoconservatives," he observed in 1990. "And some of them are offering bad substitutes." The crusade for world democracy was a primary example. Most neoconservatives applauded President Reagan's call for a "global campaign for democracy" during the middle and late 1980s. Berger's early response to this summons was carefully measured. While affirming the superiority of political democracy, he cautioned against a "missionary-like" crusade for global democracy. "The day of the missionary is past," he argued. It would be enough for America to defend and uphold the humane achievements of Western civilization, which included the achievements of political democracy. This wasn't nearly enough for most neoconservatives, however. Berger cringed while they replaced the Cold War with a new foreign mission. The globalists' arguments for "exporting democracy" and "fulfilling the American mission" made him fear that neoconservatism couldn't survive without foreign crusades. "I find this doctrine frankly offensive," Berger declared. "It doesn't take much insight to see what is wrong with this new Wilsonianism. It's another politicized religion. The idea that the United States has some obligation to export democracy in the world is an extremely dangerous doctrine. The last thing that we need, or that the world needs, is for the United States to become the world's policeman. I want no part of that campaign."[130]

He also begged off from neoconservatism's culture wars. "I'm very uneasy with this argument that the culture is our remaining problem," he explained. "In the first place, we have serious economic problems to deal with. We've hardly begun to deal with certain economic issues, especially the Japanese challenge. As to the alleged sickness of American culture, I disagree with those who go on about our 'disgusting, vulgar, left-wing culture.'" He noted that friends such as Neuhaus, Novak, Podhoretz, Midge Decter, and other neoconservatives were determined to bring the Cold War home. He reported that he was having "ugly arguments" with some of them, especially Hilton Kramer, about the purported evils of American culture. "This business that American culture is vulgar and perverted isn't my theme," he remarked. "Kramer and others go for this. The issue looks very different from a world perspective, however." Berger observed that "the whole world" was wearing American blue jeans, listening to American music, watching American movies, and learning to speak English. "I don't see American culture going down the sewer," he explained. "By and large, the culture is our strong suit. American cultural values are triumphant throughout the world." His exception was American higher education. "This is the cultural depravity we need to go after," he asserted. "This campaign for multiculturalism in the curriculum is appalling. It's making a mockery of education. If you want to assign Shakespeare under the new rules, you have to find a black lesbian writer to match up with him."[131]

His own teaching career had come to a halt with the growth of his Institute for the Study of Economic Culture. "Running this institute takes all of my time now," he reported. "I don't have any time for teaching or writing. I don't even read very much!" Like most neoconservative projects, Berger's institute was funded by the Olin Foundation and the Sarah Scaife Foundation. It sponsored research on the sociology of corporate culture, the psychology of the New Class, the culture of entrepreneurship, the economics of East Asian capitalism, and the prospects for capitalism in Latin America. With more justification than most neoconservatives, Berger insisted that his work as a scholar and program director was shaped by empirical evidence. That he often exaggerated the "value-freeness" of his work was a point that his critics justifiably pressed, sometimes rather indignantly.[132] *The Capitalist Revolution* was filled with purportedly value-free arguments that only a neoconservative would make.

Notwithstanding his exaggerations on the point, Berger's polemics generally heeded his own strictures against moral arrogance and presumption. His critiques of mainline Christianity made good examples of this attitude—until he warmed to his ravages-of-feminism theme. "The model of development which I, after some fifteen years of thinking about this, have concluded is the most promising and the most morally acceptable is a Taiwan-type development," he explained. "That is not an unmitigated good. There are costs to it. There is the issue of dictatorship. I want to be questioned on that. The ruthless meritocracy. I would want the church to question people like me on the real moral costs of the policies and strategies that we recommend, that we advocate." He didn't want the church to make statements on political issues or development strategies, he cautioned. He wanted the church only to challenge him on the statements that he and other experts made. "There is something else I want from the church," he remarked. "I want to be assured that in my activities in the world I will not be separated from God's grace, even if the policies I advocate lead to disasters, which I know is not unlikely."[133] The ecclesiology was conservative Lutheranism. The authority ascribed to experts was a staple of neoconservatism, notwithstanding neoconservatism's denigrations of the New Class. The reference to likely disasters was an admission that few other neoconservatives would have made.

Having failed to get what he wanted from the church, however, Berger left the church behind. He reported that what he got was mostly feminist moralizing. The world of mainline Protestantism, he explained, "is a world completely foreign to me at this point, a world that, despite its continuing importance in my own society, barely attracts my attention and is nearly irrelevant to my ongoing concerns."[134] The central interest of his earlier life had fallen out of his life. Berger's shorthand explanation for the loss was that he "couldn't take the feminist crap." His more elaborate explanation was that the triumph of the New Class had established a monopoly of "left-liberal-liberationist politics" in mainline churches, and had driven him out.

The Noise of Solemn Assemblies contained the essential clue, for Berger, to what happened. His Barthian blast had complained that America's mainline churches sacralized American middle-class culture. Thirty years later, the mainliners were still baptizing their own arrangements. The only change was in the character of the culture that the churches endorsed. The culture of the old middle class still existed in the minds and habits of the traditional bourgeoisie, which was centered in the business community and the old professions. But the New Class had taken over the churches— as well as the media, the government, and the universities. The same churches that once sacralized the cultural values of the business class now legitimated their interests by promoting the New Class's liberal egalitarianism. The noise had changed in assemblies grown more snarling than somber.

Berger especially resented the change in manners. The face of bourgeois Protestantism was genial and tolerant, he recalled, reflecting the "ingenuous niceness" of the old American middle class. "That face now has a set and sour mien, an expression of permanent outrage," he claimed. Though he rarely wrote about feminism, he blamed the turn primarily on the rise of feminism. "Feminism more than anything else has set this tone in recent years," he lamented. "This grimly humorless ideology has established itself as an unquestioned orthodoxy throughout the mainline churches."[135] By exercising its power as the prevailing orthodoxy, feminism had stigmatized and excluded those who rejected what Berger called the rules of "Femspeak" and related "varieties of bullshit."[136] He counted himself among the exiles. "I don't relish this condition; [but] I can live with it," he reported.[137] He could not bear the grammar, the anger, or the politics of feminists in the churches or in academe. Having endured his share of conferences at which feminism was spoken, he would avoid further encounters when he could. The world of neoconservative conferences and think tanks would have to do.

7

Fractured Conservatisms:
The Politics of Culture and Empire

T he neoconservatives were always more diverse than their image. The blazing certainties and anathemas they proclaimed throughout the 1970s and 1980s often obscured their diversity. Like their conservative allies, the neoconservatives were united mostly by their anticommunism. The communist threat provided a focal point for their politics and a means to measure the political seriousness of others. The end of the Cold War magnified their disagreements and shattered their alliances. With the loss of the Right's anticommunist touchstone, the deepening splits within American conservatism and neoconservatism fanned liberal hopes that the Right was disintegrating. These splits were real—but so was the conservatism of America's mass political culture.

Having lost the touchstone of their previous unity, neoconservatives could not agree whether an alternative was necessary. Those who believed that an alternative was necessary could not agree what it should be. In the broadest terms, most neoconservatives believed that their movement should attack American culture at home and promote a Pax Americana abroad. Norman Podhoretz and Michael Novak promoted this two-sided crusade. They denied that American capitalism bore any significant responsibility for the country's physical or cultural decay. Irving Kristol was more sensitive to the connection, lamenting that American culture bore witness to capitalism's all-commodifying logic. For Kristol, as for Podhoretz and Novak, American mass culture was nothing to celebrate or export, but a sewer that degraded America's social achievements.

Peter Berger disputed the metaphor, however. For him, the "sewer" theme was an intellectualist hangover. To face up to modernity was to accept what modernization brought. Berger enthused that modernization was presently bringing American culture to the rest of the world. The

323

neoconservatives begrudged this victory, in his view, because they still hadn't relinquished their intellectual conceits. Mass culture offended their educated sensibilities. Their counter-intellectualism was incomplete. Berger noted that the harshest critics of American culture also wanted to export American democracy around the world. He shared neither position, and observed that the two arguments didn't fit together. Like Kristol, he wanted no part of an American crusade for global democracy. Unlike Kristol, he believed that neoconservatives should stop carping about the loss of traditions and values buried by commercial society. [1]

FOREIGN POLICY AND AMERICA'S GLOBAL MISSION

The collapse of the Soviet bloc broke neoconservatives into three main foreign policy factions, until the death of communism itself finally liquidated the movement's last faction of Cold War holdouts. Neoconservatives lost their last heavyweight Cold Warrior when Aleksandr Yakovlev told them that the Eastern Europeans were on their own. The implosion of the Soviet bloc later that year sealed Podhoretz's silence. In his stead, Frank Gaffney and Richard Perle poked at the ashes of totalitarianism. Gaffney and Perle wrote little, but appeared often on television. Their television careers reflected the influence that right-wing think tanks—which in their cases included the Heritage Foundation and the Center for Security Policy (Gaffney) and the American Enterprise Institute (Perle)—had secured over America's major media. In his appearances, Gaffney strenuously insisted that Reagan's endorsement of the START process was the worst strategic mistake by any American president since the Yalta accords. Five months after the Berlin Wall came down, Gaffney warned the Committee for the Free World that the Russians were still coming. The Soviets were closer to military preeminence in Europe than at any time since 1945, he announced. The warning evoked nostalgia and, perhaps, a few stifled giggles. Kristol mocked Gaffney from the podium. "Listening to Frank Gaffney, I thought I was listening to someone in a time warp," he remarked. It would require the botched Soviet coup of 1991 before Gaffney and Perle got their clocks fixed. [2]

Kristol and Jeane Kirkpatrick led the new neoconservatism's first main faction, which argued that the Cold War was over and that no substitute for it was needed. They urged a return to realpolitik. The crucial task for American foreign policy, in their view, was to unilaterally defend a relatively narrow conception of the national interest. Realists sought to secure international order by maintaining a balance of power among potential adversaries. They regarded foreign policy as a means of coping with a world in which conflict was inevitable. Kristol argued that it was not in America's interest to accept responsibility for the fate of Kashmir, or enforce the peace between India and Pakistan, or pour more money into the Philippines, or defend Lithuanian sovereignty. America's interest was to prevent the emergence of rival superpowers, form "attachments" (not sign treaties) with other democracies, and form relationships with other nations on a case-by-case basis. The United States should reward those countries that adopted the West's socioeconomic arrangements and be, at best, cool and correct toward those who did not.[3]

He eschewed any higher moral standard than this for American policy. American moralism was not to be encouraged or rechanneled, but assiduously restrained. American pieties notwithstanding, he observed, American policymakers already employed "as many standards as circumstances require—which is as it should be." American practice had always been more realistic than America's official pieties about foreign policy. In an age that no longer required ideological crusades, he argued, government officials needed to press this fundamental truism upon an overly pious electorate. America reacted more cautiously to Chinese repression that it would have reacted to Soviet repression, because America's Japanese ally strongly commended this approach. "There is nothing 'immoral' about such deference," Kristol asserted. He denied that America had "a special moral-political mission in the world, as we habitually think we do." He condemned the isolationist reluctance to use American power to promote America's interests, and he rejected liberal internationalism for its universalist conceits. "Nor am I thrilled to observe the sweeping popularity of American popular culture throughout the world," he declared. "I wish it were a lot less popular here at home, since it seems to me to be so recklessly subversive of the traditional ethos on which this democracy was founded and for so long sustained."[4]

Kirkpatrick advanced a similar foreign policy argument. In the early 1980s, her appropriation of Hannah Arendt's distinction between dictatorships and totalitarianism had provided the intellectual scaffolding for the Reagan administration's disavowal of Carter's human rights policy. In "Dictatorships and Double Standards," Kirkpatrick had argued that totalitarian regimes were qualitatively different from dictatorships, since totalitarian autocracies were protected from domestic pressures for social change. "The foreign policy of the Carter administration failed not for lack of good intentions but for lack of realism about the nature of traditional versus revolutionary autocracies and the relation of each to the American national interest," she wrote. Traditional dictatorships left in place the makings for dissent, reform, and democratic change. "They do not disturb the habitual rhythms of work and leisure, habitual places of residence, habitual patterns of family and personal relations," she explained. This was the key difference that human rights appeals typically overlooked. Communism obliterated traditional gods, taboos, and habits, and thus sealed its totalized tyranny over the lives of its victims. Traditional dictatorships retained the preconditions of social change, while communism destroyed them. Kirkpatrick argued that American alliances with noncommunist dictatorships were therefore strategically as well as morally justified. [5]

This argument fueled intense debates over American foreign policy in the early 1980s. Though the point was often obscured in the literature about her, Kirkpatrick generally couched her anticommunist polemics and even her appeals to human rights in the language of foreign policy realism. Her anticommunism was rooted in her conception of America's interests. She made few appeals to universalistic moral or ideological obligations. Though she often invoked the concept of human rights during her career as U. S. Permanent Representative to the United Nations, she did not claim that American foreign policy should be based on a human rights criterion. [6] Though she advocated using greater military force to fight communism, she eschewed the language of empire. Though she made blistering attacks on liberals who "blame America first," she did not believe that America had a special mission to protect or export democracy. When the Soviet Union turned out to be rather less sturdy than she had imagined, her largely unsuspected yearnings for a more chastened American role in the world were revealed. She was a realpolitiker.

It was not in America's interest, she argued, for America to mediate between Japan and India or between North and South Asia. It was not in America's interest to contain Japan's role in Asia or redesign the Soviet empire. "Americans do not know at this stage what is best for the Soviet people," she observed in 1990. "Any notion that the United States can manage the changes in that huge, multinational, developing society is grandiose. It is precisely the kind of thinking about foreign policy which Americans need to unlearn." She argued that the collapse of the Soviet empire permitted America to return to normalcy. "Today, when the Soviet Union has lost its political dynamism, when democracy is growing in strength, when Europe, Japan, Taiwan, Korea are strong and friendly, the United States is free to focus again on its own national interests without endangering the civilization of which it is a part," she contended. "That is a normal condition for nations." The twentieth century's great crusades against Nazism and communism were over, and the need for heroism had expired with them. America could become a normal country in a normal time. "With a return to 'normal' times, we can again become a normal nation—and take care of pressing problems of education, family, industry, and technology," Kirkpatrick urged. "It is time to give up the dubious benefits of superpower status and become again an unusually successful, open American republic."[7]

For most of the neoconservatives, however, this was not neoconservatism at all. It was a reworked paleoconservatism dressed up in the language of realpolitik and unilateralism. Most neoconservatives belonged to the second camp, as Midge Decter explained. "The great struggle in the neoconservative movement is going to be between the people who used to be called unilateralists like Irving who are now isolationists and us old interventionists who still think the U.S. has to be a strong and great military power, to keep things steady in the world," she declared.[8] Authentic neoconservatism kept the crusading spirit. It promoted not only democratic capitalism, but the democratic empire—in the name of a new ideological mission.

Joshua Muravchik issued the call before the Cold War was over. "The West knows little about ideological war," he observed in 1987. "But the place to start is with the assertion that democracy is our creed; that we believe all human beings are entitled to its blessings; and that we are prepared to do what we can to help others achieve it."[9] Muravchik later conceded that America's type of democracy was not necessarily the most suitable form of democracy for all nations. He joined most democratic globalists in emphasizing, however, that America should generally promote its own liberal capitalist variant of democracy. "We are the first universal nation," Ben Wattenberg claimed. " 'First' as in the first one, 'first' as in 'number one.' And 'universal' within our borders and globally."[10] America's uniquely universal character legitimized its interventionist foreign policy, he argued. Since the United States already represented what the rest of the world wanted or should want for itself, the proper business of American foreign policy was to "let freedom ring on a big brass bell labelled 'America.' "[11]

New ideological wars begin with new creeds, Muravchik observed. The democratic globalists thus created a new ideological grammar. The rhetoric of totalitarianism, Finlandization, present danger, fifth columnist, infiltration, and choke point went down the Orwellian memory hole; only "appeasement" survived the death of communism. The globalists would speak instead of neo-universalism, neo-Manifest Destinarianism, waging democracy, pro-democracy, democratic idealism, declinism, and unipolarism. Wattenberg explained that new ideological wars required new bumper stickers. "An American foreign policy, to be successful, must quicken the public pulse," he wrote. "Americans have a missionary streak, and democracy is our mission. The new sticker should read 'pro-democracy.' That's what it was before Lenin."[12]

He thus acknowledged the precedents, recalling that Woodrow Wilson pledged to make the world safe for democracy and that Theodore Roosevelt tried to export democracy. Wattenberg conceded that America's precommunist democratism "wasn't perfect policy, but American values were spread."[13] America was the only mythic nation, and its primary myth was Manifest Destiny. "Only Americans have the sense of mission—and gall—to engage in benign, but energetic, global cultural advocacy," he observed. "We are the most potent cultural imperialists in history, although generally constructive and noncoercive." He allowed that America's earlier Manifest Destinarianism "at times did go overboard, into distant geographic expansion and wild-eyed cultural imperialism." Neo-Manifest Destinarianism was more chastened. With the Communists out of the way, Wattenberg urged, America could return to its earlier mission of making the world look more like America, while accepting that America couldn't exactly clone the world in its image.[14] To begin, America could resume its long-interrupted battle against European decadence.

Wattenberg noted that the rise of communism interrupted the war between the Old and New Worlds, which he characterized as a fight between European feudalism and America's enterprising republicanism. "There was a rich and fine fight between values of the New World and the Old," he recounted. "The 'News' were winning, and we still are. Now, with the totalitarians out of the way, we ought to kick it into overdrive."[15] America's struggle for the world was a crusade to fulfill the destiny of America itself. Like most neoconservatives, he insisted that the war against communism was never merely a struggle to defeat communism; for America, it was primarily a crusade to shape the world's destiny. Morton Kondracke claimed that the Cold War was meant "to secure liberty for everyone, not just ourselves." The same struggle continued to serve American interests, Kondracke argued, because democracies didn't go to war with each other. American power deserved to be used for the purpose of exporting American democracy. As Wattenberg explained, "American taxpayers didn't put up trillions of dollars in the Cold War to create a few more Swedens."[16] Having won the Cold War, America was now required to do something with its victory. This was the historical moment to "go for the gold," he exhorted, remaking the world—so far as possible—in America's image.

In the globalists' view, this mission perfectly suited America's unparalleled cultural, military, political, and economic power. Like Muravchik,

Wattenberg was a Fellow at the American Enterprise Institute; he was also vice-chairman of the board of Radio Liberty and Radio Free Europe. His enthusiasm for waging democracy partly derived from this experience. "We have the biggest cultural arrows in the biggest quiver," he enthused. "These include our global entertainment monopoly, immigration, the spreading English language, the prime tourist destination, the best universities, the most powerful and far-flung military, an opportunity society, and a worldwide information operation."[17] To redeem America's global destiny, he prescribed increasing the National Endowment for Democracy budget by fifteen times and raising the budgets for the State Department, the U.S. Information Agency, foreign aid, and Radio Liberty and Radio Free Europe.[18]

The globalists generally denied that it was necessary to give primacy to America's democratic crusade or to the Pax Americana. Most of them claimed that any increase in American power and influence was simultaneously a boon for world democracy. American aggressiveness in foreign affairs was justified—even compelled—in their view by America's democratic character. Gregory Fossedal argued that the warrant for democratic globalism was drawn from the fundamental rights of humankind, on which American democracy was based. "The rights of mankind are not good or just because they promote democracy, or any other form of government; rather, democracy exists to promote and protect those rights, and as soon as it ceases to do so, it ceases to act in accordance with the principles of just government, of natural law," he asserted. Since rights were universal, he reasoned, Americans were obliged—if they believed in the existence of their own rights—to promote world democracy. "Whatever is peculiar to some is no right at all," he explained. "Whatever is a 'right' is universal. And what is universal certainly applies to American foreign policy."[19]

The "democratic imperative" was thus unavoidable for those who laid claim to their own rights. "There is no middle position to take in this matter," Fossedal instructed. "The rights of man are not a matter of multiple choice, but a true-or-false proposition. Without a universal right to self-government, republican democracy is merely a condition that happens to exist in some places and seems to have served some peoples well." Republican democracy may have produced superior economic growth and trial procedures, but "unless we start from some common notion of what is just and right, we cannot even say that economic growth is good or arbitrary trials bad," he contended. "We are left with a sturdy vessel, but no direction to sail it." Fossedal argued that a League of Democracies should be created to promote world democracy and replace many of the functions currently performed by the United Nations. A league of legitimate world governments would expand the force of international law among member states. "The League of Democracies would marry the most noble principles of Republican anticommunism and liberty with the highest Democratic ideals of peace and equality," he wrote. [20] Though some globalists dissented from the latter proposal, most of them shared Fossedal's assumption that promoting America and promoting democracy were the same thing. "A unipolar world is a good thing, if America is the uni," Wattenberg explained. [21]

This notion was taken from Charles Krauthammer. Throughout the 1980s, Krauthammer was neoconservatism's chief exponent of the democratic globalist faith. His influence derived, in part, from his sensitivity to the doctrine's apparent paradoxes. "There seems to be something self-contradictory about intervening on behalf of self-government," he aptly conceded, going to the heart of the matter. "It is a lot more straightforward to intervene the old-fashioned way: on behalf of the alleged superiority of the metropolitan civilization. At best, to intervene on behalf of democracy means leaving quickly. Occupation mocks the idea of self-government." He argued that these were not insuperable problems, however, for a pro-democratic interventionism. [22] He recalled that in 1954 the Eisenhower administration overthrew Guatemala's democratically elected government on shabby grounds. Jacobo Arbenz's land-reform policies were moderate by contemporary standards. More than three succeeding decades of vicious dictatorial governments was a high price for Guatemalans to pay for this particular American mistake. On the other hand, Krauthammer noted in the mid-1980s, the United States currently supported the Duarte government in El Salvador, "whose land-reform policies are not very different from Arbenz's." His first lesson followed: "Should the sins of thirty years ago in Guatemala discredit our policy today in El Salvador?"

His second lesson was drawn from America's most successful experiment in exporting democracy. It was apparent from America's relationship with Japan that democracy could be exported by force of arms, he observed. Japan proved that a self-respecting America could export its own political system. Krauthammer did not deny that imposed democracies flourished best if the conqueror's bayonets were quickly removed. But the point was that sometimes they could not be removed. America's nuclear-tipped bayonets were still in Germany and Japan forty years after World War II. "And though many Americans object to the cost, and some to the danger, there is no real opposition on principle," he noted. "There is no real case to be made that it contravenes our values to be stationing troops on German soil. Yet Germany is not ours. We have no colonial claim. Still, we do have a persuasive reason: we are needed to defend a democracy."[23]

America's obligation to defend the world's democracies thus provided a moral justification for American intervention. The moral claim was not sufficient, however, to require intervention. America was only compelled to intervene in the affairs of other nations when its own strategic interests were threatened. Foreign policy was not philanthropy. Philanthropists gave away their own money, Krauthammer noted, but statesmen were trustees; they spent the blood and treasure of others. Intervention therefore required both a moral justification and a strategic rationale. "If these criteria appear too general and all-encompassing, let me point out that they exclude, and are meant to exclude, considerations that tend to dominate American debates over intervention: international law, world public opinion, and the public sentiments of our own allies," he observed. America needed to break free from its tangle of self-imposed alliances, pieties, and guilt. Liberal internationalism was bankrupt. Krauthammer's crusade for world democracy would not be hampered by a League of Democracies that extended the force of international law. Multilateralism was a formula for tying America's hands.

He argued instead for "a kind of global unilateralism in the moral area" that blended Kristol's unilateralism with the globalist campaign to export democracy.

> We should be confident enough of our own values, and of our own ability to discern what actions abroad will promote them, to act accordingly without being bound by the verdict of others—like the World Court, whose composition and ideology is far less democratic than that of the United States Congress; like the U.N., according to which the fight against racism should have taken us by now to the beaches of Tel Aviv; or like the Organization of American States, once aptly described by Irving Kristol as "a kind of mini-United Nations where we can be voted down in only three languages, thereby saving translators' fees."[24]

He conceded that nationalist unilateralism blended uneasily with democracy. How could the leader of an alliance of democracies act alone? Global unilateralism seemed to defeat its own democratic purpose. Krauthammer argued in reply that America's allies were not free agents in the first place. "They are bound by weakness and fear," he observed. "They are subject to the kinds of threats and blackmail from which the United States, owing to its power, is immune." Consulting with America's allies was therefore useless, or worse, since the allies were prevented by their vulnerability from telling the truth. The positions they took—usually opposing American intervention—rarely represented their true interests. It was America's responsibility to gauge these interests by its own lights. This was the burden of the democratic empire.

His clinching point followed from the unavoidability of this burden. "Global unilateralism is not really a choice; it is an existing reality," he argued. "The European democracies, exhausted by two world wars, depleted and turned inward, did decide to place the ultimate responsibility for their safety in the hands of the United States. It is a fact, unpleasant perhaps, but a fact nonetheless." There was no realistic alternative; the United States was compelled to promote its own ideological and strategic interests unilaterally and to assume that other democracies would benefit from this policy. "An American foreign policy should be confident enough to define international morality in its own, American terms," Krauthammer declared. "Is that parochial? I think it is parochial to do otherwise. If we take our own ideas about democracy, rights, and self-government seriously, then it is the height of parochialism, and worse, to believe that these values are applicable only to a few largely white Western countries." The democratic faith was based on a universal creed, which engendered universal obligations.

Krauthammer cautioned that this did not mean that America was obliged to overthrow all of the world's dictatorships. The moral justification for intervention was necessary, but not sufficient. The United States was currently supporting guerrillas in Nicaragua but not in Haiti or South Africa because Haiti and South Africa failed the strategic test. "One doesn't intervene purely for justice," he explained. "One intervenes for reasons of strategy, and if justice permits. Neither Haiti nor South Africa is about to allow itself to be used for the projection of Soviet power; the same cannot said of Nicaragua."[25] The Cold War drew the boundaries for America's imperial idealism.

Krauthammer was a speechwriter for Walter Mondale during Mondale's term as vice president, but he became a neoconservative in the early 1980s. In the mid-1980s, he discovered the Reagan Doctrine. The Truman Doctrine had proclaimed America's commitment to anticommunist containment. The Nixon Doctrine leaned on allied regimes—like Iran under the Shah—to police their regions. The Carter Doctrine announced that America would use a rapid deployment force to defend Western interests unilaterally. The rapid deployment force never got off the drawing boards, however. In Reagan's 1985 State of the Union Address, Krauthammer heard a new doctrine buried beneath Reagan's boilerplate for a balanced budget amendment, school prayer, and the line-item veto: America would support anticommunist rebellions throughout the Third

World. Krauthammer conceded that there were precedents for such a policy, including Carter's arms shipments to Afghan rebels. What made the Reagan Doctrine a new departure in American foreign policy, however, was Reagan's vow to challenge the Soviet empire throughout its periphery. The United States would reverse Soviet expansionism by rolling back its Third World client states. Like the Nixon Doctrine, the Reagan Doctrine relied mostly on proxies. Unlike the Nixon Doctrine, however, "it supports not the status quo but revolution."[26] Though Reagan himself never invoked the phrase, Krauthammer enthused the following year that the Reagan Doctrine was becoming "the centerpiece of a revived and revised policy of containment."[27] The Reagan Doctrine resolved the Kennan–Burnham argument by saying yes to both containment and liberation. The Soviets would be contained in Europe and rolled back in the periphery, "where there is no threat of general war."[28]

Krauthammer defended his formulations of the Reagan Doctrine and the democratic globalist mission throughout the 1980s, insisting that America could remain a republic at home and operate as an empire abroad. He did not deny that American life "would be happier and more prosperous (less defense spending) and less riven by division" if the United States scaled back its foreign commitments.[29] Neither did he deny the isolationists' central claim, that maintaining America's empire "does encourage centralized authority, a military-industrial complex, the transfer of authority to the executive branch, and the imposition of secrecy on a wide range of government activities." He noted that left-wing isolationists emphasized the economic costs of empire, right-wing isolationists the costs to liberty. Both were right. The burdens of empire unavoidably effected "a diminution of democracy," he conceded.[30] These costs were worth bearing, however, for two reasons: to defeat communism and to promote the democratic idea. The democratic crusade was "an American vocation, for which we have long sacrificed blood and treasure," he observed. "The constraints on our democracy required for the running of an alliance are another form of sacrifice, a kind of foreign aid program in which the transfer is made in the coin of democratic practice rather than cash."[31] Democracy was a universal mission, and missionaries required, above all, a strong and self-confident faith. "If we believe democracy is good for us, then we must believe it will be good for others," he exhorted.[32]

He assumed that the struggles for world democracy and the Pax Americana were functionally the same thing. America's promotion of democracy served American interests and the interests of world democracy. He denied that there was any reason to give primacy to the democratic imperative or the American interest. The collapse of the Soviet bloc made Krauthammer reconsider this claim, however. During the very period in which many neoconservatives took up his crusade for world democracy, he began to argue that America's Cold War victory was changing the structure of the debate about waging democracy. "During the Cold War the United States has been involved in a struggle to preserve a *structure* of freedom in the world," he observed. "The necessary condition for what JFK called the 'success of liberty' was the defeat of those great forces—fascism and communism—which threatened the very idea of freedom and had the power and will to execute the threat."[33]

America had literally made the world safe for democracy by winning these victories, he argued. The mission to make democracy possible had been a historical absolute. American interests and American values compelled nothing less than a crusade to make democracy possible throughout the world. The mission to make democracy actual throughout the world, however, was another matter. "A great power undertakes great battles, because no one else can," he explained. "But with the great battle won, the question of whether to engage in the mop-up work is a very different one. A communist Nicaragua in isolation is far different from a communist Nicaragua as an outpost of the Soviet empire or as an outpost of communism as an armed creed." The strategic meaning of the outer Soviet empire was profoundly altered by the withering of the empire's metropolis. The collapse of the Soviet base made the Soviet-dominated periphery states suddenly unthreatening. Krauthammer observed that these regimes would probably disintegrate from their own contradictions. He argued that America should do whatever it could to accelerate the process. "But, unlike containment, that process of encouragement does not rise to the rank of defining purpose of American foreign policy," he asserted.[34]

His point was not to reject democratic globalism or embrace Kirkpatrick's realism. Americans had "no stomach and very little tolerance" for realpolitik, he explained. Henry Kissinger had proved the point more than once. In the post–Cold War context, however, waging democracy was mostly mop-up work. It was necessary, but uninteresting. America needed a higher mission than converting Third World nations to democracy, he argued. His prescription was to strive for universal dominion—a world order described, however problematically, by Francis Fukuyama. Fukuyama's celebrated article "The End of History" had proclaimed that the Hegelian end of history was presently occurring. The worldwide triumph of liberal democracy was not only bringing the West's ideological debates to a close, he argued; more importantly, it was creating a "common marketization of the world."[35] Krauthammer conceded that Fukuyama's announcement was premature. The worldwide triumph of liberal democracy was neither solidified nor inevitable. He argued that Fukuyama did sketch the most worthy vision for American policy, however. "America's purpose should be to steer the world away from its coming multipolar future toward a qualitatively new outcome—a unipolar world whose center is a confederated West," Krauthammer urged. America's mission was to work for "a super-sovereign West economically, culturally, and politically hegemonic in the world."[36]

Unipolarism assumed that community begets structure. Though the idea of a super-sovereign West replicated most of Krauthammer's earlier democratic globalist vision, unipolarism took a different approach to achieving it. Like the Reagan Doctrine, democratic globalism focused on the periphery, working to convert Third World nations to democracy. Unipolarism focused on the center. The death of communism changed the structure of America's obligations, Krauthammer argued. The primary aim of America's democratic crusade should not be to convert Third World nations to democracy, but to unify the industrial West. A strengthened Western center would serve American interests and "lead inexorably to the spread of democracy to the Second and Third worlds."

It was a top-down strategy. The crucial factor in politics, as Burnham taught, was always the character and strength of the elites. Unipolarism gave new meaning to Burnham's geopolitical ring image, however. Krauthammer initially emphasized the internationalist implications of unipolarism. He speculated that an increasingly unipolar world would diminish the role of national sovereignty. The super-sovereign West would now be in the center. "Around it would radiate in concentric circles, first, the Second World, the decommunizing states, dependent on the West for technology and finance," he explained. "As they liberalize economically and politically, they would become individually eligible for status as associate members of the unipolar center. The outer ring, even more dependent on the center, would consist of the developing states. Its graduates too (say, Korea, Brazil, Israel) might also eventually attach themselves to the center." Burnham's image of the world was thus exactly reversed, except that the New World Order would have a confederated West—rather than a single nation—at the center of the empire. The United States would have to subordinate its nationalistic interests to the interests of the Western alliance.[37]

In 1990, the Persian Gulf crisis blew the cover off this version of the New World Order, however. Krauthammer recognized during the early months of the crisis that the "confederated West" had become, at most, a useful fiction. The center of world power was not a super-sovereign West, he observed, but rather, the world's "unchallenged superpower, the

United States, attended by its Western allies." The conventional notion that Japan and Germany were rising to the status of great powers, he argued, was disproved in the closing months of 1990. Japan and Germany hid under the table after Iraq invaded Kuwait. England and France responded more forcefully to the crisis, but neither country possessed the economic base to become more than a second-rate power. The Gulf crisis brought into unmistakable focus the true geopolitical structure of the new order, Krauthammer claimed, which was "a single pole of world power that consists of the United States at the apex of the industrial West." The unipolar moment had arrived. Only the United States possessed the military, diplomatic, political, and economic power to shape events "in whatever part of the world it chooses to involve itself."[38]

He conceded that there was still "much pious talk" in America about multilateralism, collective security, and a larger role for the United Nations as a guarantor of world order. "But this is to mistake cause and effect, the United States and the United Nations," he contended. "The United Nations is guarantor of nothing. Except in a formal sense, it can hardly be said to exist." America's reigning pieties about national self-determination and international law forced American policymakers to cover up this fact with "pseudo-multilateral" gestures, he observed. "A dominant great power acts essentially alone, but, embarrassed at the idea and still worshiping at the shrine of collective security, [the United States] recruits a ship here, a brigade there, and blessings all around to give its unilateral actions a multilateral sheen."

Krauthammer argued that America needed to outgrow this pretense. The United States maintained its official pretense because many Americans only approved of military actions approved by the United Nations Security Council. Krauthammer professed not to comprehend the sentiment. "But to many Americans it matters," he observed. "It is largely for domestic reasons, therefore, that American political leaders make sure to dress unilateral action in multilateral clothing." With enough practice, he warned, they could begin to believe their own pretense—and thus endanger American interests.

Unipolarism fought on several fronts. It was inevitably assaulted by what Krauthammer called "the usual pockets of post-Vietnam liberal isolationism (e.g., the churches)." It was also forced to fight off the resurgence of Old Right isolationism, represented by Patrick Buchanan and Thomas Fleming, and to correct the illusions of the neoconservative realpolitikers, who wanted America to become a normal country in a normal time. Krauthammer replied that there was no such thing as a normal time. "The world does not sort itself out on its own," he admonished. In the nineteenth century, America was able to keep to itself because it was protected by two great oceans patrolled by the British Navy. But the British Navy was gone. He argued that the best prescription for the United States in a world that would never be normal was "American strength and will—the strength and will to lead a unipolar world, una-shamedly laying down the rules of world order and being prepared to enforce them."[39] The spirit of Burnham endured in the globalists' man-ifestos. "The new world order should be an assertion of American interests and values in the world, if necessary asserted unilaterally," Krauthammer announced. "Where possible, we should act in concert with others. Where not, we should proceed regardless."[40] With the traditional Right reverting to various forms of isolationism and realpolitik, only the neoconservatives were left to campaign for a new Pax Americana.

Neoconservatives criticized the Bush administration's conduct of the Persian Gulf War on several counts. Many reproached Bush for overindulg-ing America's multilateralist pretensions. Novak charged that Bush "tied Gulliver down with taut silken threads." Most of them later argued that Bush ended the war too soon and unforgivably turned his back on Iraq's Kurdish and Shiite rebels. A. M. Rosenthal compared America's initial abandonment of the Kurds to the Soviet troops who watched the Nazis massacre Polish resisters, in 1944, from the banks of the Vistula. "It is interesting how American politicians look into their own mirrors and decide that American voters are dolts devoid of memory or principle," Rosenthal bitterly remarked. "Still, it's terribly sad of course about those deported Iraqi mothers clutching dead babies in frontier mountains, and all that. Send them blankets."[41] The spectacle confirmed the globalists' belief that realpolitik was morally bankrupt. Their disgust with the war's conclusion did not prevent them from playing up the war's achievements, however. They rejoiced that their foreign policy vision was vindicated by America's war against Iraq. Though they criticized Bush for failing to acknowledge what he was doing, for ending the war too soon, and for abandoning the Kurds and Shiites, the globalists commended him for otherwise conducting the war in a manner that befitted the world's remaining superpower. The war advanced the Pax Americana, if not the cause of world democracy. They claimed that it also shredded the myth of America's imperial decline.

Paul Kennedy's theory of imperial decline especially offended most neoconservatives, as their repeated attacks on it revealed. In his best-selling work, *The Rise and Fall of the Great Powers*, Kennedy argued that America's vitality was threatened by the same pattern of imperial overcom-mitments that dragged down Imperial Spain in the early seventeenth century and the British Empire in the early twentieth century. America's military empire was created to protect the nation's increasingly far-flung economic interests and to take economic and strategic advantage of America's power. Like Spain and England, he argued, America had subsequently inherited a vast array of foreign commitments from a time when it held greater comparative political, economic, and military power. America's present network of foreign commitments was essentially fixed in 1945, Kennedy noted—at a time when the United States possessed more than 40 percent of the world's wealth and power. More than forty years later, America still had over 500,000 troops abroad—65,000 of them afloat—while holding a substantially reduced share of the world's wealth and power. The result was a condition he called "imperial overstretch." America's accumulated foreign interests and obligations had outstripped its relatively declining power. The dynamics were familiar to all historians of the rise and fall of empires. "Even as their relative economic strength is ebbing, the growing foreign challenges to their position have compelled them to allocate more and more of their resources into the military sector, which in turn squeezes out productive investment and, over time, leads to the downward spiral of slower growth, heavier taxes, deepening domestic splits over spending priorities, and a weakening capacity to bear the burdens of defense," he observed. [42]

America's relative decline was masked by its enormous military capabilities and by its success at internationalizing American capitalism and culture, Kennedy argued. In his view, the essential task for American policymakers was to manage smoothly America's relative decline to the status of "a very significant Power in a multipolar world." As Walter Lippmann famously remarked, the nation's commitments and the nation's power needed to be brought into balance. Kennedy concluded: "The tests before the United States as it heads toward the twenty-first century are certainly daunting, perhaps especially in the economic sphere; but the nation's resources remain considerable, if they can be properly organized, and if there is a judicious recognition of both the limitations and the opportunities of American power." [43]

This prescription was anathema to the heirs of Burnham and Hook. Neoconservatism's democratic globalists and unipolarists vehemently disputed Kennedy's description of the costs of empire. Krauthammer insisted that American power was not militarily overstretched at all. He noted that American defense spending averaged between 5 and 6 percent of GNP— nearly half of what it was in the early 1960s. Though Kennedy was right about America's declining economic strength, he allowed, this erosion was caused not by imperial overstretch, but by America's low savings rate, its inferior educational system, its deteriorating work habits, its stagnant economic productivity, and its "rising demand for welfare-state entitlements and new taste for ecological luxuries."[44] It was not America's military commitments that were making America poorer, but rather, something deeper within Americans themselves.

This was the crucial point for most neoconservatives. Novak asserted that Kennedy's theory of imperial overstretch "could not have been more wrong in predicting American decline." Kennedy aimed at the United States and hit the Soviet Union. Like Kennedy, Novak claimed, all the declinists were wrong. Their assumptions were false and their anti-imperialist biases controlled their interpretations of the data. The declinists were guilty of something worse than misreading the data, however. They were guilty of the unforgivable sin, the sin against the spirit. "They have unforgivably damaged our national morale, especially among the impressionable young in our colleges and universities," Novak charged. "It's wrong to steal hope for the future from the young, and to deprive them of the sense of belonging to a noble national experiment—the most universally attractive of our era."[45] It was also ridiculous to talk about imperial decline at the moment when most of the world was tuning in to American culture and trying to emulate America's political and economic systems. Novak observed that the Eastern Europeans, in particular, were looking in the right direction. "Regarding pluralism, the smaller, more homogeneous nation-states of Europe have less to teach than America does," he contended. "And about enterprise, initiative and risk, do Western European socialists or Americans have more to teach?"[46]

Wattenberg offered a biographical explanation for Kennedy's confusions in this area. "Kennedy doesn't really understand America," he observed. "He's an Englishman. He emigrated here as a young adult. My sense is that he hasn't got the whole message yet." Kennedy therefore persisted in offering his intellectual services to those who "want us to decline ourselves," Wattenberg explained. "They don't like being Number One."[47]

The "declinists" typically viewed the rise of Japan and Germany as an encroachment on America's superpower status. In their view, America's relative political and economic standing was declining as the losers of World War II steadily gained greater economic might. Most neoconservatives claimed that this schematism was too traditional to account for the legacy of the American empire, however. "The American empire is not like earlier European imperialisms," Wattenberg argued. "We have sought neither wealth nor territory. Ours is an imperium of values. We have sought to boost a community of ideas—political democracy, free market economics, and science and technology. These days those values are advancing, not eroding."[48]

Novak amplified the point. "The enduring American ideal has been to construct a *Novus Ordo Seclorum*—a new order of the ages—constituted along the lines of the three great liberties dear to the American experiment: political liberty, economic liberty and moral-cultural liberty," he observed. "Call this mysticism, if you like, or 'soft' power. But as you have watched Chinese students in Shanghai carry a replica of the U.S. Statue of Liberty, listened to a brewery worker in Prague quoting from Jefferson and watched dissidents in the fifteen republics of the U.S.S.R. voice dreams of new democracies, free economies and liberties of conscience, surely you have been tempted to think that this is the one kind of power most consistent with the purposes for which the U.S. was founded."[49] America's empire was designed to help other democracies become prosperous and to encourage other countries to become democracies. Seen in this light, neoconservatives argued, the rise of Japan and Germany was good news—especially since neither country rivalled America's military or diplomatic might.

The Persian Gulf War sealed the argument for most neoconservatives. On the day the bombing began, Podhoretz exulted that a quick American victory "would remoralize our whole country. Everyone would experience a new surge of confidence in America." The same week, Muravchik proclaimed that the war would redefine American politics, confirm America's "ideological supremacy," and demonstrate the worldwide supremacy of American military power. "The gulf war marks the dawning of the Pax Americana," he enthused. The bipolar world of the Cold War was a memory; America's victory in the Cold War had created the possibility of a unipolarist peace; and now the Gulf War was establishing the new order. The worldwide consolidation of the Pax Americana would bring the world "not only to the joys of jeans and rock and Big Macs," he predicted, "but also to our concept of how nations ought to be governed and to behave." Novak similarly welcomed the new Pax Americana immediately after the war ended. "This is the end of the decline," he proclaimed. "This is the decline of the declinists. The mother of all battles turned into the daughter of disasters for the declinists. For years, people are going to cite the lessons of the Persian Gulf." He later asserted that "there is now only one superpower. . . . While the rest of the world debated, the U.S. acted."[50] He found much company in celebrating the occasion.

The "declinists," however, were less impressed by America's ability to pulverize a tyrannical Third World desert nation. Kennedy observed that declining empires throughout history had often used military victories over lesser foes to prove their continued power. "The U.S. has been pouring $300 billion a year into defense throughout the '80s, so it was never a question of there being inadequate military power," he observed. "The argument was they were concentrating too much of their energy and resources on defense and neglecting the state of American technical education, infrastructure, indebtedness, high-tech competitiveness, erosion of the social fabric and other problems. To say a swift battlefield victory proves the declinists wrong is a total misinterpretation." In the early 1990s, a handful of neoconservatives reluctantly joined his side of the argument. Disdaining the political myth-making of his ideological allies, Edward Luttwak claimed that the "relentless erosion" of America's economic base was rapidly turning the United States into a Third World society. The cultural accompaniments of economic deterioration were already plainly evident in American society, he insisted. Americans increasingly accepted shoddy products, bureaucratic incompetence, and ugly cities with fatalistic detachment. Most neoconservatives disputed Luttwak's reading of America's world economic status while affirming his denunciations of American culture. The tactic of blaming America's problems on the decadence of the New Class had lost much of its polemical force after more than a decade of Reagan and Bush, however. In the century's closing years, neoconservatives would be pressed by the deterioration of America's socioeconomic position to defend their economy/culture dichotomy.[51]

THE CONSERVATIVE CRACK-UP

Neoconservatives disagreed among themselves whether America should fight for world democracy or for a narrower conception of its interests. The dissolution of the Soviet Union subsequently heightened these disagreements. A deeper rift over the same issue, however, occurred between most neoconservatives and their former allies on the traditional Right. Russell Kirk put the matter plainly in the closing months of the Cold War. The neoconservatives were often rash in their foreign pursuits, he contended, "pursuing a fanciful democratic globalism rather than the national interest of the United States." He was more inclined to resist foreign entanglements. He reported that it also seemed to him "as if some eminent Neoconservatives mistook Tel Aviv for the capital of the United States—a position they will have difficulty in maintaining, as matters drift in the Levant." The presumptuous universalisms of the neoconservatives were prescriptions for foreign policy disasters, he claimed. "They lead to the heaps of corpses of men who died in vain. We need to ask ourselves whether the Neoconservative architects of international policy are very different from the foreign policy advisors who surrounded Lyndon Johnson."[52]

The following year, Buchanan gave a further-right twist to the same sentiment. The neoconservatives were hyping "messianic globaloney," he complained. "We are not the world's policeman, nor its political tutor," he declared. "Whence comes this arrogant claim to determine how other nations should govern themselves, or face subversion by NED [the National Endowment for Democracy], the Comintern of the neo-cons?" Neoconservative chauvinism was not conservative. "Conservative principles do not sanction democracy worship," Buchanan explained. "It is liberal idolatry masquerading as conservative orthodoxy."[53]

Buchanan kept right-wing and left-wing isolationisms carefully separated. Right-wing isolationism was unabashedly nationalist. "What have the 'democracies' done for America lately?" Buchanan queried. He replied that the world's democracies had done far less for America than South Africa's and Chile's dictatorships—which liberals habitually condemned. He warned that if democratic globalism became official American policy, America's most reliable allies would be undermined. "Mr. Wattenberg's Mission Democracy is a prescription for endless and seditious meddling in the affairs of nations whose institutions are shaped by their own history, culture, traditions and values, not ours," Buchanan argued. He invoked America's pre-Wilsonian heritage. The American Idea was not "to go abroad in search of monsters to destroy," as John Quincy Adams famously declared. America was to be the well-wisher of freedom for all, but "the champion and vindicator only of her own."[54]

For more than a century, Buchanan noted, America resisted the siren's call of empire, until William McKinley received a divine command to take the Philippines. The American empire was launched. Two decades later, the United States joined an alliance of colonial empires to make the world safe for democracy. In the process, 100,000 Americans were killed "in places like the Argonne and Bellean Wood, in no small measure to vindicate the Germanophobia and Anglophilia of a regnant Yankee elite." The Great War for Democracy, in turn, produced Mussolini, Hitler, and Stalin—and confirmed the wisdom of America's founding fathers. America had no mission to remake the world in its image. In the succeeding fifty years, Buchanan observed, America had been "drained of wealth and power by wars, cold and hot." He conceded that much of America's loss of blood and treasure was necessary. "But America can only lead the world into the twenty-first century if she is not saddled down by all the baggage piled up in the twentieth," he argued.[55]

The standard for American foreign policy, for Buchanan, was defined by Walter Lippmann in 1943. "We must consider first and last the American national interest," Lippmann wrote. "If we do not, if we construct our foreign policy on some kind of abstract theory of rights and duties, we shall build castles in the air. We shall formulate policies which in fact the nation will not support with its blood, its sweat, and its tears." This was the ultimate problem with neoconservatism, Buchanan claimed. Krauthammer's new universalism "may set off onanistic rejoicing inside the Trilateral Commission," but it would set off alarm bells for ordinary Americans. The crusade for world democracy failed the ultimate test: Americans would never fight for it. A nationalistic American politics was needed that defined what *was* worth fighting for. "What we need is a new nationalism, a new patriotism, a new foreign policy that puts America first, and, not only first, but second and third as well," Buchanan urged.[56] While the United States prepared to intervene against Iraq, he complained that America was being stampeded into war by Israel and its neoconservative "amen corner." These sentiments fueled Buchanan's campaign for the Republican party presidential nomination in 1992.

This resurgence of Old Right isolationism in the late 1980s convinced the neoconservatives that their coalition with the traditional Right was finished. For several years, the neoconservatives had endured paleoconservative accusations that they were cunning, opportunistic, too ideological, not religious enough, and not really conservative. These complaints got their first public airing in 1981, when William F. Buckley, Jr., and other paleoconservatives promoted M. E. Bradford to be chairman of the National Endowment for the Humanities. A professor at the University of Dallas, Bradford was an anti-Lincoln, pro-Confederate enthusiast and former George Wallace supporter. He was also a considerably more accomplished scholar than William Bennett, a protégé of Kristol and Gertrude Himmelfarb, whom neoconservatives pushed for the post. At the height of the appointment struggle, the White House asked Russell Kirk if he would consider accepting the chairmanship, either temporarily or permanently, as a compromise between Bradford and Bennett. Kirk promptly declined the invitation and urged Reagan to appoint Bradford to the post. Kristol and others pressed hard for Bennett, however. They were joined at a critical point in the campaign by Buckley, who was convinced by neoconservative friends in New York to switch his support to Bennett. The neoconservatives won the campaign, and earned the Old Right's quietly nursed but deeply embittered resentment in the process. Bradford later charged that the neoconservatives defeated him by whispering that he was an anti-Semite. During Reagan's first term, the two camps gener-

ally kept their feud out of the newspapers—partly out of deference to
Reagan. Their coalition was severed during Reagan's second term, however, when the decline of their common enemy heightened the differences
between them.

In the last days of the Cold War, Krauthammer announced that the
crack-up of the conservative coalition was imminent. He explained that it
had never been easy to keep "all the strains of conservatism under one roof:
the libertarians and the cultural conservatives; the prewar isolationists and
the postwar interventionists; the paleoconservatives (conservative since
birth) and the neoconservatives (conservative since Vietnam, roughly)."
The communist enemy had kept these unlikely comrades under the same
tent, but as communism unraveled, so did its organized opposition. He
observed that in some respects, America appeared to be heading back to
the 1930s, when right-wing and left-wing isolationists marched together.
The collapse of communism was splintering the Reagan coalition and
creating even stranger coalitions in its place.[57]

An older echo also reverberated throughout the conservative crack-up.
The paleoconservatives repeatedly suggested that neoconservatives were
more loyal to Israel than to the United States. The "dual loyalty" charge
was a throwback to the 1940s, when Zionism was a liberal cause. Kirk's
suspicions were widely held among the Old Right. "What really animates
the neoconservatives, especially Irving Kristol, is the preservation of
Israel," he claimed. "That lies in back of everything." Paul Gottfried, a
Jewish conservative, continued, "I don't think one can differentiate the
neoconservatives from the very large Jewish composition of the movement, and the fact that many of the Jewish leaders of the movement broke
from the left precisely over the question of Israel and other Jewish issues
and therefore are going to take a very strong pro-Israeli position."
Gottfried noted that he happened to agree with this position; the difference was that "the neoconservatives would make it appear such no matter
what."[58]

Joseph Sobran clearly did dispute the pro-Israeli position. A syndicated columnist and senior editor of *National Review*, Sobran provoked
neoconservatives on numerous occasions with seemingly anti-Semitic
remarks against "the Jewish lobby," Zionism, the state of Israel, and *The
New York Times*. He argued that Israel was not a trustworthy American ally
and that America's Jewish-dominated elite media successfully manipulated
American feelings on the subject. He charged that *The New York Times*
supported America's military strike against Libya only because the attack
served Zionist interests. In April 1985, he wrote a series of columns that
defended Reagan's visit to Bitburg, complaining on one occasion that the

Times "really ought to change its name to *Holocaust Update.*" The following year, he equated the historic Christian persecution of Jews in Europe with alleged Jewish persecution of Christians. He described the viciously anti-Semitic and racist periodical *Instauration* as "often brilliant" and as the only "magazine in America that faces the harder facts about race." Sobran attacked feminists, gays, and black leaders with equal zeal, but these targets were fair game on the Right. He was slow to absorb the message that anti-Semitism was in a different category. Faced with increasingly enraged charges that his writings were anti-Semitic, he replied to his neoconservative critics, "If a Jew complains about Christians, Christians must be persecuting him. If a Christian complains about Jews, he is doing the persecuting—in the very act of complaining. It simply isn't fair."[59]

That did it. Several neoconservatives demanded that *National Review* do something about Sobran. In a widely circulated letter, Decter accused Sobran of being a "crude and naked anti-Semite." Buckley insisted in response that Sobran was not an anti-Semite, but conceded that his writings could give that impression to readers who didn't know him. Buckley and his editors therefore dissociated themselves from Sobran's "obstinate tendentiousness" on the subject, acknowledging that he had transgressed against "the structure of prevailing taboos respecting Israel." They sought to dampen the flames by forbidding Sobran from writing further about Israel. The bitterness remained deep on both sides, however. While conceding that Sobran had violated what Buckley called "the reigning protocols," the paleoconservatives believed that neoconservatives were committing commensurate offenses against them. Bradford charged that Decter's letter poisoned the waters between them. Kirk added that he was "very surprised at Midge Decter's intemperance. It seems that she would forbid any prudential discussion of these matters."[60]

These resentments simmered for the next two years, until Kirk's remark about neoconservatives mistaking Tel Aviv for the American capital rekindled the controversy. Decter called the statement "a bloody piece of anti-Semitism." Neoconservatives interpreted Kirk's comment as a revival of the dual loyalty smears of the 1940s, when conservatives accused the Roosevelt and Truman administrations of aiding the "international Jewish conspiracy." Kirk was stunned by their reaction. "They know very well I wasn't talking about *that*," he later insisted—but his surprise testified to the cultural gulf between the paleoconservatives and neoconservatives.[61]

The gulf widened the following spring. The alliance between the two conservatisms was symbolized, until then, by the existence of Richard John Neuhaus's New York–based Center on Religion and Society.

Neuhaus's outstanding quarterly journal, *This World*, and his Center's newsletter were funded by the paleoconservative Rockford Institute in Rockford, Illinois. The Rockford Institute's own journal, *Chronicles*, was edited by Thomas Fleming. In his March 1989 issue, Fleming argued that America's immigration policy was putting the nation "in danger of losing the entire concept of American citizenship." Cultural pluralism was not the most attractive legacy that Americans could leave to their children, he insisted. Stricter immigration quotas were urgently required, since a United States dominated by Third World immigrants would be a very different cultural and economic entity.[62]

The same issue of *Chronicles* offered unlikely praise for Gore Vidal, lauding him as "the champion of a distinctly American civilization, or what he thinks is left of it." Though Vidal was not exactly a conservative, the editors allowed, his writings on the American republic made him America's most worthy successor to Ralph Waldo Emerson, Robert Lowell, and William Dean Howells.[63] An article by novelist Bill Kauffman went further, calling Vidal a foe of empire who "offended all three pointy-heads of the regnant American political triangle: the Manhattan-Washington-based neoconservatives, the Manhattan-Washington-based New Class conservatives, and the Manhattan-Washington-based corporate-state socialists. In short, the power elite." Vidal was therefore repeatedly attacked by polemicists like Podhoretz, Kauffman observed, with "all the subtlety of the commode flush."[64]

Podhoretz was quick to respond. "Have you seen the latest issue of *Chronicles*?" he wrote to Neuhaus in mid-February. "Among other abominations (including a piece of nativist bigotry by the editor himself), it contains two—not one but two—hymns of praise to Gore Vidal." He was drawing the line. "I know an enemy when I see one, and *Chronicles* has become just that so far as I personally am concerned," Podhoretz declared.[65] The editor of *National Review*, John O'Sullivan, tried to explain Fleming's provocation. "Tom knew he would be annoying Norman and Midge," he said. "He was tweaking their noses. He didn't realize it would be taken as something more serious."[66] It was taken very seriously, however. Podhoretz later recalled that he couldn't abide the magazine's bigotry and couldn't believe that Neuhaus wanted to be associated with it, either.[67]

Neuhaus readily took sides, complaining that *Chronicles* was reviving long-forbidden bigotries and gratuitously attacking neoconservatives. The current issue was not only "xenophobic, racist and nativist," he charged, but filled with sneering gibes at neoconservatives and "pseudo-conservatives." The paleoconservatives were attacking his closest friends, including not only Podhoretz and Berger, but even Buckley. Their crowning offense was to elevate Vidal to the status of an authentic conservative. Vidal's writings unrelentingly skewered traditional values, the family, religion, and American foreign policy, Neuhaus observed, "while enthusiastically supporting abortion, the feminist agenda and homosexuality." To call him a conservative was, "in a word, grotesque."[68]

These complaints inspired numerous counteraccusations and a serious attempt to arrange an agreeable divorce between Neuhaus and Rockford. Neither party was willing to give up a $200,000 grant pledged to Neuhaus by the Bradley Foundation, however, and in May, Neuhaus found his belongings stuffed into garbage bags outside his New York office. His small-town midwestern sponsors had journeyed to New York, confiscated his files, and locked him out, leaving his staff in the rain. Neuhaus's eviction proved costly to the paleoconservatives. With his departure, Rockford promptly lost $750,000 from the Olin, Smith Richardson, and Bradley Foundations. *This World* was terminated while Neuhaus rounded up sponsors for a new institute, The Institute on Religion and Public Life, and a new journal, *First Things*.

His first issue settled an old score. His former allies and sponsors were only comfortable with governments led by men of tested genetic stock, Neuhaus noted. Like Henry Adams, they worried that America's republican legacy was being trashed by America's vulgar economic system and the unrefined immigrants it attracted. This was an old story, however. What was new was the concerted paleoconservative attempt to reinstate these bigotries into the nation's political discourse. "Beyond the paleo war against 'democratism,' one notes renewed attempts to invite back into the conservative movement a list of uglies that had long been consigned to the fever swamps," Neuhaus observed. "The list includes nativism, racism, anti-Semitism, xenophobia, a penchant for authoritarian politics, and related diseases of the *ressentiment* that flourishes on the marginalia of American life." It went without saying that such terms as racism and anti-Semitism could be abused to stifle discussion of legitimate issues, he said, but some conservatives apparently needed to be reminded that the evils signified by these terms were not "merely figments of the fevered liberal imagination."[69] The neoconservatives had reached the boundary of their rightward journey.

The paleoconservatives had more ironical explanations for their conflict with neoconservatives. Fleming argued that the neoconservatives were members of a New Class that wanted to expand government programs and share power with the Left. Their constant harping on the New Class was an example of projection. Their complaints about the moral intolerance and ultrasensitivity of the Left belonged to the same category. "Apparently, the first rule of the conservative coalition is that no magazine editor may ever publish anything without first checking with Norman Podhoretz, the Mrs. Grundy of the American right," Fleming announced. "Henceforth novelists are not to be judged on any but political standards, and those standards are set by *Commentary*." He claimed that none of the neoconservatives had identified anything in *Chronicles* that showed evidence of bigotry. They had fallen back, instead, "on the last resort of the calumniator: 'code words' and 'insensitivity.' " Fleming left the implication hanging: These were leftist sins. Right-wingers didn't accept the sensitivity code of the moral thought police. Neoconservatives only invoked the code when anti-Semitism was at issue. He noted that Decter had recently denounced the Bush administration's Middle East policy as a disaster and that she had characterized Bush's presidency as a "Philistine administration." She presumably was not criticizing Bush's arts policies, he observed. Neoconservatives increasingly reminded Fleming of conspiracy-theorists. "If they know where a man stands on nuclear energy, the Trilateral Commission, the Palestinians, or the gold standard, they can locate him precisely on the grid of their paranoia," he concluded.[70]

Kirk amplified this assessment. "The whole controversy was too ridiculous to be taken seriously, but that was our problem," he recalled. "We didn't take it seriously. The same thing kept happening. The neoconservatives would seize on some isolated remark of ours, get all worked up about it, and then blow it out of proportion." He declined to speculate on their motives. The more serious issue for him was the character of their politics. The neoconservatives were utilitarians in their view of society, he argued. "They are focused on the struggle for power, and are using power for their mundane purposes." In his view, they had little sense of the mundane order as a realm subordinate to the transcendent order. The paleoconservatives' hearts were in history, theology, and humane letters, he explained; neoconservatives were social scientists and activists, like the New Class liberals they derided. Like the liberals, their politics was therefore utilitarian, instrumental, self-promoting, and power-oriented. The modern battle between the conservatisms thus replayed the conflict between Burke and Bentham.[71]

Various attempts to mediate their dispute were offered.[72] These efforts were complicated by doctrinal splinterings on both sides, as paleoconservatives split into "Old Right," "paleolibertarian," Straussian, and other factions, and neoconservatives intensified their own already-considerable divisions. The rift was sealed by the Old Right's pecuniary grievances. Buchanan smoldered that the Right's major foundations had been captured "by neo-con staffers who are steering $30 million a year to front groups,

magazines, scholars and policy institutions who toe their party line."
Fleming similarly complained that neoconservatives had attained "a lock
on all money and the institutions created by the Right." He bitterly
claimed that neoconservatives controlled the Scaife, Olin, Smith Richardson, and Bradley Foundations. Gottfried summarized the Old Right's
resentments. "The neoconservatives created an enemy on the right by
vilification and exclusion," he explained. "The enemy lives increasingly for
revenge and is trying to subvert the neoconservative empire. Few old
rightists believe the foundations now run by neoconservatives will become
theirs as soon as their enemies fall. Far more likely such resources will go
to opera houses and other civic charities than to supporting old right
scholars. It is burning hate, not uncomplicated greed, that fuels the old
right war against the neoconservatives."[73]

THE CULTURE WAR AND
THE FUTURE OF THE MOVEMENT

Neoconservatives thus entered the 1990s as a splintering faction of a
disintegrating intellectual Right. On the level of mass politics, "conservatism" was declining, but still powerful. Among its intellectual elites, where
the movement's ideological contradictions were less tolerated, conservatism was a shambles. The unifying power of the totalitarian threat was
gone. Conservatives crusaded for America First and for American dominion over the world; they wanted to relinquish the empire and expand it;
they wanted to make America the universal nation and restrict immigration to America; they identified America's interests with Israel's and
resurrected the dual loyalty smears of the 1940s; they celebrated the
universality of American democracy and repudiated the imperialism of the
"democratists." At the height of the Right's faction fight, Stephen J.
Tonsor declared, "It has always struck me as odd, even perverse, that
former Marxists have been permitted, yes invited, to play such a leading
role in the Conservative movement of the twentieth century." He mused
that if Stalin had spared Trotsky's life, Trotsky would undoubtedly be
holed up at the Hoover Institution, writing neoconservative tracts for
Commentary. Neoconservatism was culturally unthinkable apart from the
history of modern Jewish intellectuals, he noted. The New York Intellectuals had come to conservatism with secular-ideological presuppositions.
This was the root of the problem. Trotsky's heirs had never made good
allies and never would, as long as they dithered in modernity's halfway
house.[74]

The crucial questions were broached at the Committee for the Free World's last hurrah, in April 1990. Could neoconservatives and paleoconservatives find enough common ground to fight the cultural wars of the 1990s? Could neoconservatives even continue to work with each other? Decter wistfully pressed both questions: "Are we a group of friends, a family?" she asked. "Or are we a long, sour marriage held together for the kids and now facing an empty nest?"[75] The same month, in her last appeal for financial support, she claimed that the death of communism had not ended the Committee's work. American freedom would not be secure, she admonished, as long as the media demoralized Americans "with their smug, lazy, ignorant misreporting," and America's schools inculcated racism through affirmative action and multiculturalism, and universities packaged anti-intellectual sophistries as learning, and America's arts and publishing industries demanded conformity to their culture-destroying conceits. As long as such conditions persisted, she promised, the Committee would continue to fight freedom's enemies. The culture war would keep the Committee going. The Family would hold together . . . until December, when the Committee for the Free World declared victory over "the spoiled brats of liberty" and went out of business.[76]

The epitaphs for neoconservatism came from all sides, and kept coming. Few observers believed that neoconservatism's culture war could sustain the movement. Kirk predicted that "within a very few years we will hear no more of the Neoconservatives." Some would revert to liberalism, some would become traditional conservatives, "and yet others' pert loquacity will have been silenced by the tomb," he claimed.[77] Christopher Hitchens argued that neoconservatism had lost the enemy on which it was dependent and therefore had outlived its usefulness to the conservative establishment. Sidney Blumenthal asserted that neoconservatism had no generations and was thus fated to fade away. "The neoconservatives may breed conservatives, who have never known the joy of disillusionment, but not neoconservatives," he explained. "Generational experience cannot be replicated."[78]

These arguments were echoed by certain neoconservatives who disliked their designation in the first place and never warmed to it afterward. Seymour Martin Lipset maintained that neoconservatism was losing what little coherence it had ever achieved. Like Daniel Bell and Nathan Glazer, Lipset emphasized that neoconservatives had never developed common beliefs on numerous domestic policy issues. The point was well taken. For all of their denunciations of America's educational decline and its promotion of welfare dependency, neoconservatives had never defined a distinctive, coherent, or common position on education or welfare policy. Lipset

contended that with the loss of the movement's anticommunist touchstone, neoconservatism was too diverse and ill-defined to survive as an
influential intellectual movement.[79]

The same argument, however, obtained against the traditional Right.
Though several of neoconservatism's most prominent advocates—such as
Lipset and Glazer—had never shown any interest in becoming part of a
movement, most neoconservatives did not share their distaste for movement politics. With few exceptions, contrary to Kirk's and Lipset's predictions, the neoconservatives neither returned to liberalism nor merged with
the paleoconservatives. They did not share the traditional Right's antipathy for the welfare state, or trade unionism, or the social sciences, or
modernity. With notable exceptions, they did not share the traditional
Right's ambivalence toward democracy or its nativist leanings. These
differences were loudly reaffirmed in the wake of the Cold War. Neoconservatives had reached the limits of their rightward pilgrimage, but most
of them were unlikely to turn back. Their task was to refashion neoconservatism. If the high tide of their movement had passed, their prospects as
a viable intellectual movement were brighter than the epitaphs suggested.

In 1952, the journal that epitomized alienated American intellectualism conducted the widely noted symposium "Our Country and Our
Culture." *Partisan Review* gave notice of a shifting sensibility in the country's
elite literary culture. Its editors announced, "The purpose of this symposium is to examine the apparent fact that American intellectuals now
regard America and its institutions in a new way." The New York Intellectuals were not impervious to the Zeitgeist. They confessed that they were
becoming less alienated from America. America's recent groundswell of
patriotic and assimilationist feeling was moving the forerunners of neoconservatism to reconsider their own Americanism. If they still opposed the
"philistine materialism" of their bourgeois country, they were, at least,
finally prepared to affirm that it was their country.[80] Their successors
would amplify the sentiment.

The major theorists of neoconservatism were raised to think of "the
Americans" as aliens. America belonged to and was defined by the WASPs.
Many of the neoconservatives applied to college just as their country's
doors were opening to them. Podhoretz entered Columbia in 1946 under
a 17 percent quota for Jews. To their own surprise, however, the neoconservatives prospered in the land of the Americans, and became its apologists. Their movement began as a counterprotest against a later generation
of ungrateful American children. The neoconservatives' revulsion for the
New Left's anti-American self-righteousness awakened their own unsuspected patriotism. Their own lives revealed the worthiness—even the

superiority—of the American idea. "I urge my readers to think back to their own families, circa 1935 or earlier," Michael Novak exhorted. "Were they from a privileged class? Or were they poor? Generation after generation, the poor have streamed to America and been lifted out of poverty."[81] The implicit call for gratitude was perhaps the movement's most compelling theme. It tapped the wellspring of American conservatism. It assured neoconservatism of a viable future, despite the movement's intellectual fragmentation. And it informed the neoconservatives' remaining domestic crusade, against the culture of the New Class.

Neoconservativism was held together by more than its anticommunism. All of the movement's major figures supported a minimal welfare state; all of them touted the superiority of capitalism and capitalist modernization; all of them vehemently condemned feminism, affirmative action, multiculturalism, and other adversary culture assaults on traditional Western values. Kristol recalled that Podhoretz and Decter chided him throughout the 1970s for his capitalist boosterism. For them, as for Novak, a residual identification with trade unionism and social democratic anticommunism had precluded any explicit apologetics for capitalism.[82] The American idea was bigger than democratic capitalism. The neoconservatives overcame their vestigial anticapitalism in the late 1970s, however. Many of them reassessed their friendships and made unexpected alliances. Their movement kept moving further Right. By the early 1980s, the movement's social democratic wing was a memory. Most of the earlier holdouts went on to surpass Kristol in their enthusiasm for free enterprise. If Kristol had given two cheers for capitalism, they would give four. The neoconservatives all became Americans. This conversion allowed them to give voice to certain quietly kept sentiments forbidden in progressive intellectual circles. For many neoconservatives, the experience of breaking ranks was a liberation from what they called "the tyranny of acceptable moral lines" and an opportunity to give free reign "to previously inhibited sentiments and ideas."[83]

Feminism was a chief target from the outset. Attacks on feminism became staples of neoconservative rhetoric. Though none of the movement's chief theorists wrote extensively on the subject, all of them gave free reign to their hostility for it. "Women's lib has swept over the past two decades like a tornado, leaving behind it a vast wreckage of broken and twisted lives," Podhoretz declared. In his telling, the legacy of feminism was "of children sacrificed to the 'needs' of their parents; of women driven literally crazy by bitterness and self-pity while being encouraged to see virtue and health in the indulgence of such feelings; of men emasculated by guilt and female bullying."[84]

The movement's chief publicists generally left supporting evidence to others. In their attempts to provide it, Decter, Michael Levin, Ruth Wisse, and Carol Iannone repeatedly portrayed feminists as self-absorbed New Class nihilists bent on destroying the family. The freedom demanded by feminists, Decter claimed, was the freedom demanded by spoiled children "and enjoyed by no one: the freedom from all difficulty."[85] She charged that by indulging this illusion in their children, Americans were "engaging in child sacrifice."[86] Feminist demands were not only infantile and destructive, but fraudulent. Decter revealed that when women spoke to each other "off-camera" about the men in their lives, they did not complain that men were manipulative or oppressive. They complained that men were wimps. "They tell stories that, without their being able themselves to pinpoint the difficulty, are stories of sickly vanity, of self-preoccupation, of fears and narcissistic anxieties—in other words, of unmanliness," she disclosed. It followed for her that feminism's on-camera complaints about male chauvinism and unequal treatment amounted to so much manipulative hypocrisy. The women's movement brought nothing but greater hypocrisy, bad faith, stupidity, and malevolence to American life—while making its purported beneficiaries miserable with self-pity. "All the demands for unneeded preference in admissions and hiring, all the absurd litigation, all the efforts at speech control and thought control, and most important, all the programs to manage and 'improve' the behavior of the men in her life, whether husband, boss, roommate or date, have left her more disaffected and more mentally self-indulgent than before," she contended.[87] This was less ironic than neoconservatism's critics often claimed. Decter began her career as a secretary for Elliott Cohen and worked to become an influential writer and social critic. Gertrude Himmelfarb and Brigitte Berger were eminent scholars, respectively, in English history and sociology. Decter and Himmelfarb kept their own names long before modern feminism institutionalized the practice. That these women and their husbands despised feminism was often thought to be odd, but was not. They made it without feminism. For them, the mere existence of a women's movement was demeaning.

Wisse explained the feeling. She reported that university deans frequently offered professorships to her and asked her to speak at their conferences. The offers kept coming because she was a woman, and universities were anxious to hire qualified women. The deans who courted her were apparently unaware of their "unspeakable rudeness" in looking for qualified women, she recounted. "Qualified women might be what a whoremaster assembles for his stable, a potentate for his harem, but an educator for his university?" The deans were looking for female professors only because the women's movement had shamed them into thinking that there was something wrong with hiring predominantly male professors. Through their efforts to attain greater freedom and equality for all women, feminists degraded the accomplishments of women who didn't need the women's movement. "By contriving to define me as a member of a handicapped species the women's movement has deprived me of my dignity and misrepresented my aims," Wisse charged. [88] That the women's movement had enhanced the dignity of millions of women by reducing the social barriers to their achievement was not, for her, a serious objection. It did not address her resentment at being lumped with her inferiors. Neither did it alleviate her anxiety that—like many black opponents of affirmative action—she was a beneficiary of affirmative action.

Neoconservatives traded on these potent feelings, arguing that affirmative action helped only those who didn't deserve their attainments and stigmatized those who did deserve them. Much of neoconservatism's considerable rhetorical power was attributable to its appeal to the fears of being stigmatized or reversely discriminated against. [89] Though affirmative action policies theoretically forbade reverse discrimination, neoconservatives insisted that affirmative action actually compelled it. Affirmative action policies compelled preference for women and minorities only when other relevant factors were relatively commensurate. Neoconservatives contended that the practice of affirmative action led inexorably, however, to racial, gender, and ethnic quotas. "There is only one item left on the so-called civil rights agenda and that is 'affirmative action,' defined in such a way as to mean racial and ethnic quotas," Kristol argued. He noted that affirmative action proponents always denied that their goal was to establish quotas. "They are lying," he wrote. "Blacks are overwhelmingly in favor of quotas, Hispanics mildly so, Asian-Americans not at all." But most working class whites were intensely opposed to quotas, he observed—and they outnumbered their opponents. [90] Neoconservatism endorsed the sentiments of this ostensible majority, and confirmed its worst suspicions about the machinations of civil rights proponents.

The extension of this debate to the curriculum struck a cultural nerve in the early 1990s. Neoconservative denunciations of multicultural education sparked a national mass media controversy over the scope and purpose of American education. Neoconservatives claimed that the movement for multicultural education concealed its true purpose under the cloak of its appeals to pluralism and diversity. Podhoretz charged that the effort to integrate works by women and minorities into courses on Western Civilization was a "brazen assault on the entire concept of the classics."

Multiculturalism was a "vulgar" plot to undermine Western civilization itself, he contended.[91]

Novak expanded on the same theme. "I do not like the herd instinct with which campuses have caved in on matters of race, feminism, and homosexuality," he declared.[92] The movement to make Western education less Eurocentric and male-dominated, to Novak, reflected a failure of nerve. Novak highlighted the curriculum overload problem that some multiculturalist prescriptions presented. Multiculturalists argued that American education needed to integrate a wider range of historical and cultural experiences into its definitions of "history," "literature," "philosophy," "religion," "sociology," and "political science." The problem with this prescription, Novak maintained, was that it made excessive demands on educators and students. In the name of making education more inclusive, multiculturalism threatened to make it poorer. "Will students ignorant of their own culture suddenly become learned in cultures far away?" Novak asked. "Which professors want to teach a core even they don't know?"[93] The questions were penetrating, raising issues at the center of contemporary debates about multiculturalism. The counsel to give up making the curriculum more inclusive and international fit oddly, however, with the neoconservative exhortation to face up to the modern world.

Podhoretz explained the sentiment behind neoconservatism's opposition to multicultural education. He recalled that when he was an undergraduate at Columbia, the classic texts of Western literature and philosophy were taught in two required courses. These courses shaped the rest of his student career and his life. They converted him to culture. "Before Columbia, I had never truly understood that I was the product of a tradition, that past ages had been inhabited by people like myself, and that the things they had done bore a direct relation to me and to the world in which I lived," he explained. Columbia instilled in him "a reverence toward Western civilization that was nothing short of religious in its intensity and that has lasted all my life." He argued that multiculturalism, however, destroyed the possibility of converting students to culture. To become converted to "culture"—that is, to the heritage of Western civilization—was to give oneself over to the languages and visions of the Western, white, male, Christian tradition. Nothing like his own experience was likely to be repeated, Podhoretz insisted, in a curriculum that integrated female and black writers into the mix.

Podhoretz acknowledged the irony of a Jew pointedly defending the traditional Western canon. He appealed to his own experience to refute those who claimed to feel excluded by the canon. When he was introduced to the classic texts of the West, he explained, "I felt that an inheritance of indescribable richness which in the past had often been inaccessible to my own people was now mine for the taking." Far from feeling excluded, he experienced his undergraduate education as an invitation to become part of an ongoing intellectual tradition. The invitation testified to the tradition's openness. Podhoretz therefore concluded that multiculturalist arguments were fraudulent. Multiculturalism met a nonexistent need. The real purpose of multicultural educators was not to enrich the curriculum, he argued, but "to carry forward the work of destruction begun by their radical forebears of the '60s."[94]

Neoconservatives rightly defended the richness and, in some respects, the inclusionary character of America's dominant cultural traditions. Multiculturalist appeals to diversity and freedom were already valorized, to a considerable extent, in the dominant Anglo/Germanic tradition that American education drew upon. Moreover, neoconservatives rightly criticized the more extreme forms of relativism that some multiculturalists promoted. Podhoretz had little difficulty finding inane quotations to support his contention that multiculturalism was nihilistic. As he suggested, those who could not explain why Shakespeare was superior to Jacqueline Susann had no business teaching literature. What he failed to explain—continuing with his own example—was why Maimonides and the Talmud didn't deserve a place in the curriculum. Podhoretz could not argue that Maimonides and the Talmud were intellectually inferior to Chaucer, Hobbes, or any of the canon's other foundational texts. These writings were not in the canon not because they were inferior, but because they were Jewish.[95] If Podhoretz was willing to swallow this arrangement, multiculturalists were not. They insisted that a true "common culture" could only be attained if American education opened itself to the voices of Jews, women, blacks, Native Americans, Asian Americans, and others.

The founding generation of neoconservatives never overcame their shock that many of America's privileged children turned against their country in the 1960s. Many neoconservatives found the antiwar movement more repulsive than America's incineration of Vietnam. The same overreactive revulsion was displayed in their subsequent attacks on the "feminization" and "multiculturalization" of American higher education. In their telling, modern American universities were overrun by hateful feminists, nihilistic deconstructionists, and ethnic tribalists conspiring to destroy the heritage of Western civilization through disingenuous appeals to "diversity" and "sensitivity."

Their argument was amplified by younger neoconservatives who barely remembered the 1960s. "Diversity, tolerance, multiculturalism,

pluralism—these phrases are perennially on the lips of university administrators," Dinesh D'Souza observed. "They are the principles and slogans of
the victim's revolution."[96] Roger Kimball declared that the multiculturalist
emphasis on pluralism and sensitivity "provides a graphic example of the
way in which the teaching of the humanities in our colleges and universities has been appropriated by special interests and corrupted by politics."[97]
The idea of a multicultural curriculum "nourished by disparate sources and
traditions" had been embraced not only by feminists and other New Class
radicals, he noted, but even by most deans of America's elite institutions,
including Henry Rosovsky, the former dean of Harvard University and
architect of Harvard's core curriculum. To neoconservatives, the turn
toward multiculturalism in the elite universities enshrined the cultural
ravages of the 1960s. It also provided an arresting enemy for a fractured
neoconservative movement.

Feminism and multiculturalism engendered new pedagogies, codes of
manners, and demands for student and faculty diversity at American
colleges and universities that neoconservatives repudiated. They especially opposed the antiharassment policies instituted by many universities
to censure offensive speech toward women and minorities. Neoconservatives argued that the demand for sensitivity toward the feelings of minorities had turned university administrators into thought police and repressed
actual diversity of thought and expression on America's campuses.[98] The
focal point of neoconservative criticism, however, was the multiculturalist
challenge to the curriculum. "Part of the rhetoric of 'pluralism' and
'diversity,' the elevation of multicultural experience cloaks the abandonment
of traditional humanistic culture," Kimball asserted. He contended that
multiculturalism was actually anticultural. "Notwithstanding the emanci-
pationist rhetoric that accompanies the term, 'multiculturalism' as used in
the academy today is not about recognizing genuine cultural diversity or
encouraging pluralism," he claimed. "It is about undermining the priority
of Western liberal values in our educational system and in society at
large."[99]

Since multiculturalism was not what it claimed to be, Kimball argued,
there was no reason to take multiculturalist arguments seriously. Kimball
built his argument against multiculturalism primarily by attacking the
motives of its proponents. He implied that if multiculturalists were serious
about enriching Western education, it would be necessary to take their
arguments seriously. Traditionalists were spared from this disagreeable
task, however, by the bad faith of their adversaries. Multiculturalists
focused on gender, race, and class not to enrich their disciplines with
neglected questions, but to "transform literature into a species of political

propaganda and virtue mongering." Since multiculturalism was actually "a convenient umbrella for the smorgasbord of radical ideologies regnant in the academy," Kimball argued, the multiculturalist challenge could be avoided. He gave short shrift to the movement's fundamental argument—that traditional American education ignored the histories and literature of women, minorities, and non-European cultures. "A swamp yawns open before us, ready to devour everything," he warned. "The best response to all this—and finally the only serious and effective response—is not to enter these murky waters in the first place. As Nietzsche observed, we do not refute a disease. We resist it."[100]

The metaphors were revealing. Modern dissatisfaction with an educational curriculum dominated by the discourses of privileged white European males was a sickness. Distinctions weren't necessary. The call for greater diversity was not to be debated, but fought off as one fought a disease. To recognize any form of multiculturalist criticism as a serious position was to get sucked into the swamp. Neoconservatives insisted that America's dominant Anglo/Germanic tradition already sanctioned as much cultural pluralism as American society could withstand. The imperative to become Americanized had not changed. America's various racial and ethnic groups would have to assimilate themselves to the dominant order, in which European history was far more important than the history of Africa or Asia. Multiculturalists replied, however, that the increasing numbers of culturally "unassimilated" Americans exposed the limitations and inadequacy of traditional American education.

Perhaps the most serious neoconservative attempt to address multiculturalist criticism was made by Diane Ravitch, who distinguished between what she called pluralistic and particularistic forms of multiculturalism. Ravitch recalled that for many years, American educators "attempted to neutralize controversies over race, religion, and ethnicity by ignoring them." Public secondary schools and universities tried to avoid divisive political and cultural issues, partly by teaching a sanitized historical narrative. "Race, religion, and ethnicity were presented as minor elements in the American saga; slavery was treated as an episode, immigration as a sidebar, and women were largely absent," she conceded. Textbooks concentrated on wars, national politics, and the policies of America's white, Anglo-Saxon, male leaders.

This formula was sustainable so long as minorities and women kept quiet or believed in the melting pot. Ravitch recounted that the traditional curriculum's focus on elites was complemented "by an assimilationist view of American society, which presumed that everyone in the American melting pot would eventually lose or abandon those ethnic characteristics that distinguished them from mainstream Americans." The cultural stirrings of the 1960s made this approach untenable, however. Multiculturalism was a product of the modern revival of racial, ethnic, and feminist consciousness.

Ravitch recalled that the first wave of multicultural textbooks in the 1960s added awkward sidebars about women, blacks, and ethnic minorities alongside the main narratives. (Religion was still carefully ignored, and still is.) Over the past generation, textbooks had increasingly incorporated multicultural content into increasingly sophisticated and inclusive narratives. "In contrast to the idea of the melting pot, which promised to erase ethnic and group differences, children now learn that variety is the spice of life," she noted. American education increasingly reflected the multicultural realities of American society and promoted cultural democracy, "a recognition that we must listen to a 'diversity of voices' in order to understand our culture, past and present." Like Nathan Glazer, she affirmed that this form of multiculturalism was based on sound scholarship and had enriched and enlivened American education on all levels. Ravitch explained that pluralistic multiculturalism "promotes a broader interpretation of the common American culture and seeks due recognition for the ways that the nation's many racial, ethnic, and cultural groups have transformed the national culture." She recognized, like Glazer, that traditional assimilationist pedagogies were particularly deficient in meeting the educational needs of American blacks, whose ancestors came to America in chains and whose parents were never fully incorporated into American life. Pluralistic multiculturalism sought a richer common culture, partly by devoting greater emphasis to the history of American racism. [101]

Pluralistic multiculturalism had recently spawned particularistic variants, however, that rejected the possibility or desirability of a common culture. "Advocates of particularism propose an ethnocentric curriculum to raise the self-esteem and academic achievement of children from racial and ethnic minority backgrounds," Ravitch observed. She cited numerous practical problems that this "unabashedly filiopietistic and deterministic" doctrine presented. How should history be taught to ethnically mixed groups? How should history be taught to groups lacking any claim to great inventions or discoveries? What were the limits to reducing history to ethnic propaganda? A larger problem transcended these objections, however. "Perhaps the most invidious implication of particularism is that racial and ethnic minorities are not and should not try to be part of American culture," she argued. "It implies that American culture belongs only to whose who are white and European; it implies that those who are neither white nor European are alienated from American culture by virtue of their race or ethnicity; it implies that the only culture they do belong to or can ever belong to is the culture of their ancestors, even if their families have lived in this country for generations."[102] The new particularism was not an advance on cultural pluralism, she claimed, but a tribalistic and often anti-intellectual distortion of it. To renounce the notion of a common culture was to undermine any society's struggle for attainable gains toward the common good.

Ravitch pressed the latter argument with considerable effectiveness and merit. Multiculturalist prescriptions raised many unanswered practical and theoretical questions about how to bring multiple cultural centers into interaction with each other. Ravitch's analysis and prescriptions had their own problems, however. Her distinction between pluralistic and particularistic multiculturalism and her emphasis on self-esteem were both misleading. To be worthy of its name, multiculturalism *had* to be pluralistic; by definition, it ruled out giving privilege to any particular group. Moreover, Ravitch's emphasis on self-esteem misrepresented the aims of most multicultural theorists, who viewed the question of self-esteem as secondary to the question of how to understand history from the perspective of more than one tradition or culture. That is, the question of truth, in its historical complexity and diversity, was the primary concern of multicultural theorists. To them, the common ground of Americanism was not any particular hegemonic culture, but the bond of democratic citizenship. [103]

Ravitch's generalizations against "particularism" implicitly dismissed any attempt to rethink the curriculum itself from the standpoint of feminist or multiculturalist criticism. Multicultural education needed to do more than "add women and stir." It was required to address the substantive critiques of the dominant tradition presented by feminist and multiculturalist perspectives. To take feminist and multiculturalist criticism seriously was not only to integrate more women and minorities into the curriculum, but to allow their perspectives on the dominant tradition to change the ways that history, society, and knowledge itself were understood. Ravitch's form of educational pluralism attempted to preempt such criticism. Her dehistoricized and (putatively) depoliticized concept of culture protected the dominant order from deeper criticism. Like virtually all neoconservatives, Ravitch dismissed feminist arguments that moved beyond the rhetoric of inclusion to critique remaining patriarchal assumptions, language, arguments, and pedagogies in American education. Her work nonetheless marked a considerable advance over most neoconservative discussions of feminism and multiculturalism. Her analysis of multiculturalism held up the possibility—like much of Glazer's work—of a type of neoconservatism that was empirical, judicious, generous in spirit, and disinclined to issue blanket condemnations.

Feminism and multiculturalism evoked more visceral reactions among most of neoconservatism's founders. Their counterintellectualism was rooted in their struggle to become Americans. In his elaborate account of his struggle to be accepted by America's WASP establishment, Podhoretz recalled that, in an earlier generation, the assimilation of vast numbers of ethnic immigrants made old WASP families feel that their country was being stolen from them. America's commitment to mass education and assimilation was creating a society with new centers of power, different manners, and different cultural values. These developments threatened the power and prestige of America's WASP elites. Podhoretz noted that Edmund Wilson had come from an old WASP family that felt deeply threatened by these changes in American society. It was difficult for Wilson's family, and for Wilson himself, to accept that mass education was reducing the prestige of their education and pedigree.

Podhoretz was a beneficiary of America's commitment to mass education. It was people like him who made the WASPs feel that they were being crowded out. Not long after he gained admission, however, he began to share their disdain for the riff-raff who came in with him. The Establishment was too accommodating; it accepted peaceniks, feminists, homosexuals, pot smokers, and multiculturalists. It gave titles and tenure to America's most insufferable critics. It accommodated black demands for an Afrocentric curriculum—though the Establishment had never catered to his own filiopiety. He had gone to schools where George Washington and Abraham Lincoln adorned the walls. He and his friends had made it in America without any special assistance from multiculturalist pedagogues. Why couldn't blacks do the same? How could any serious educator take feminist criticism seriously? Why was the Establishment debasing itself before the demands of America's underachievers and deviants? Podhoretz had once criticized Elliott Cohen for joining the American celebrants. He tartly observed that Cohen's *Commentary* attributed America's (presumably few) social defects to the human condition. The anti-Americanism of the New Left drove Podhoretz back to Cohen's boosterism, however, and beyond it. "What finally alienated me from the radical movement of the '60s was its hatred of America," he explained. "The New Left was not neutralist; the New Left was anti-American."[104] The failure of American liberals in the 1960s to repudiate the New Left's anti-Americanism drove him to the Right. American liberals were traumatized by Vietnam, maumaued by the Black Panthers, and unmanned by the women's movement.

Liberalism was perverted by guilt. Having struggled so hard for a place in the country's elite liberal culture, he resented that the guardians of liberalism gave the estate away.

Novak made a similar discovery. He made his early mark as a critic of the Catholic Church, switched to the New Left at the height of its influence, and discovered his ethnicity when his radicalism wore out. His pivotal bid for admission to the Establishment came in the form of a biting attack upon it. *The Rise of the Unmeltable Ethnics* defiantly told the WASPs to move over. Novak later downplayed the severity of his assault on the WASPs. His book was not meant to be taken literally, he claimed. It was merely a pitch for status recognition. He wanted the Establishment to make room, not to self-destruct. He was greatly saddened, after turning to Whiggery, to discover that the Establishment he had pilloried had not survived the 1960s. America's guardians "surrendered without a fight," he lamented. [105] They failed to defend America's heritage from its cultural enemies. Neoconservatism took up the fight against the feminization and multiculturalization of American culture.

James Nuechterlein described the etiology of America's feminized cultural sickness. The fatal weakness of the feminized imagination, he argued, was its defining reluctance to exercise power. The feminized mind always looked for ways to transcend or avoid power politics, and when it failed, it exercised power only with a bad conscience. Feminized politics therefore promoted "an ethic of noncoercion, a preference for emotion over rational analysis and for noncompetitive modes of social interaction, a focus on being rather than doing and on interpersonal relations as the primary preoccupation of the good life." [106]

He contended that the feminization factor had long distinguished American liberalism's two main historical streams from each other. Following the historical schematizations of Ann Douglas and Robert McElvaine, Nuechterlein traced the lineage of feminized liberalism from liberal Protestantism's Social Gospel to the "archetypal progressivism" of Jane Addams to the feminized reformism of Eleanor Roosevelt. [107] This highly moralistic tradition was spurned by the New Dealers and Old Leftists, who prided themselves on their lack of sentimentality. Roosevelt's gruff reformers shared more in common with Marxists like Hook and Burnham than with their feminized progressive forerunners. Nuechterlein recollected that realists such as Reinhold Niebuhr also belonged to the masculinized liberal tradition. Though Niebuhr remained a man of the Left throughout his life, "it would be impossible to find a less feminized imagination." Niebuhr's type of liberalism briefly dominated intellectual fashion during the early 1960s, when the Kennedy administration "virtually bristled with masculine assertiveness" and made no secret of its contempt for progressive moralism.

This was the liberalism that neoconservatives mourned. "For years I got angry with people who called me a neoconservative," Podhoretz recalled. "I was not a neoconservative, I said; I was a liberal. A certain kind of liberal: a real liberal, a genuine liberal, a 1950s liberal, or whatever. But to no avail."[108] Real liberalism was decimated in the 1960s by the Movement's feminist offspring. Nuechterlein explained that the triumph of feminization in the 1960s was engineered by modern feminism and sealed by the collapse of socialist and Keynesian ideologies. Feminism's language of morality and cooperation filled the void created by the Left's loss of hard beliefs. "Feminization has become a refuge for a Left in ideological crisis," he contended. Feminism provided a sustaining vocabulary for progressives while they struggled to replace their discredited ideologies and programs. He argued that the phenomenon was nowhere more apparent than in the mainline churches. The churches still occasionally invoked Niebuhr's name, but their statements on social issues recycled the very illusions about promoting cooperation, the common good, and alternatives to war that Niebuhr repudiated.[109]

Neoconservatives reinvoked Niebuhr's dichotomy between society's public and private realms, arguing that moral principles appropriate to the private realm had no direct bearing in the public realm. Politics was primarily about the struggle for power by groups generally unrestrained by morality. Nuechterlein claimed that feminized liberalism undermined society's struggle for justice by sentimentalizing the public realm. Feminism was a powerful force in American society not because it offered a usable social philosophy, but because its mixture of incoherent moral yearnings filled a vacuum in American life.

Carol Iannone extended the argument, charging that feminism was "a series of self-indulgent contradictions." Feminists claimed that women were the same as men and different from men, according to the ideological need of the moment, she argued. Women were strong and capable—and were also the slaves and victims of men. Feminists called themselves the humane and nurturing sex, "but can put their children in child care centers for ten hours a day." Feminists promoted choices for women, unless women chose the domestic role. Feminism was devoted to the common good, but "openly advocates dismantling the entire social order." Iannone recommended a frontal assault on feminism's purported absurdities. "Feminism rode into our cultural life on the coattails of the New Left but by now it certainly deserves its own place in the halls of intellectual barbarisms," she asserted.[110]

Neoconservatives would not take moral or political instruction from women who thought that a women's movement was needed. Though neoconservatives often described their opponents' views on other issues with polemically effective insight, their writings on feminism virtually never entered the experience or perspectives of feminist writers they denounced. Neoconservative writing on feminism was long on caricature, ridicule, and condemnation; it was uncomprehending as to why so many obviously intelligent and compassionate people would become feminists. The experiences of discrimination, exploitation, and abuse described by feminists were abruptly dismissed by neoconservatives as either unbelievable or childish. The differences between difference-oriented and equality-oriented feminisms were treated by neoconservatives as contradictions in feminism, as though feminism was a singular ideology. Feminist theorists repeatedly explained, however, that there was no such thing as "feminism," but rather, multiple feminist perspectives.[111]

Neoconservatives disagreed whether America's high culture should be included in their cultural war against feminism, multiculturalism, and New Class liberalism. Hilton Kramer's *New Criterion* defended the aesthetic achievements of modernism from "philistines" such as Kristol and Novak. Kramer denied that modernist high culture subverted the foundations of bourgeois democracy. Neoconservatives generally agreed, however, that their battle against the "adversary culture" was the defining political battle of the 1990s. The counterculture was not a product of modernization, but a disastrous assault upon it. "The counterculture discredited the intellectual vocation," Kramer argued. "It was their assault on the whole enterprise of high culture that created the polarity between serious criticism on the one hand and advocacy journalism on the other." Kramer resigned his position as chief art critic for *The New York Times* in 1982 to found *The New Criterion*. In one of his early editorials for the journal, he denounced the antiwar movement as an attack on authority and civilized values. "We are still living in the aftermath of the insidious assault on mind that was one of the most repulsive features of the radical movement of the '60s," he declared. He later found particular fault with television ads "in which the women are all so much smarter than the men" and with the media's relentless insistence on portraying women in men's jobs.[112]

Kramer's attacks on America's cultural decline were unsparing. In 1987, he spoke at a neoconservative conference devoted to the "Second Thoughts" of former radicals. Sponsored by the National Forum Foundation and financed by the Bradley and Olin Foundations, the conference was organized by the former editors of *Ramparts*, David Horowitz and Peter Collier, whose pilgrimages from communism to New Leftism to neoconservatism replicated an often-followed trajectory. Kramer was relegated to the evening panel of elders, presumably to congratulate the younger neoconservatives for mending their ways. Unlike Kristol and Podhoretz, however, he refused to play along. The day's proceedings had repulsed him. He thundered that younger neoconservatives still didn't understand the damage they had done. Kramer remarked that he was apparently the only person at the conference who had nothing to confess, having never associated with the Left. The younger neoconservatives had much to confess, however—and they weren't facing up to it. They were congratulating themselves for leaving the Left, but failing to repent for the destruction they had caused.

"Much as I admired certain things that were said in the discussion this morning, there was also that incredible smugness and vanity which was so suffocating to many of us in the '60s, all on parade again," he complained. The younger neoconservatives were failing to confront "the drug culture, the rock culture, the sexual revolution, the assault on the family and the middle class, the assault on high culture and the aggrandizement of popular culture, the devastation of the universities as the centers of cultural and intellectual life." These were the crucial issues. "Didn't anybody have any understanding of the wreckage that was left in the wake?" he asked. "The wreckage in family life and sexual life and academic life and intellectual life, in the whole structure of Western Culture? Well, you were all immoralists and we are now paying the price for the social agenda that your immoralism let loose." Thanks partly to them, American culture was in worse shape then than in the 1960s, "when you were all having such a wonderful time, being young and stupid," he scolded. "The difference between the '60s and the '80s is that the radicals in the '60s were on the outside beating on the doors, demonstrating, trying to get in. In the '80s they're on the inside running the institutions and that is a catastrophic difference."[113]

Neoconservatism after the Cold War—whether repentant or not—took its cue from this claim. The culture war was more like the Vietnam War than the Gulf War. The enemy was everywhere, entrenched, not always identifiable, and tenacious. The enemy was not only in the streets, but running the universities, the media, the churches, and the government. The task was daunting, especially because the moral and ideological basis on which a culture war might be waged was less apparent than was the case with anticommunism. "I don't know what to do about 'the culture,'" Podhoretz admitted. "I don't think any of us quite knows what to do. We have our own notions of how to go about it from day to day, conducting the argument, trying to persuade." He argued that the key was to be ready to make unexpected alliances and embrace "shocking" solutions "if we are ever to do anything about the corrupted and poisoned culture which in this country is our major problem."[114]

Neoconservatism was slow to elevate the culture war to preeminent significance. In 1982, George Gilder could still complain that "neoconservatives, in general, are afraid to fight on ERA, abortion, sex education, pornography, school prayer, and gay liberation." Neoconservatives were still too preoccupied with foreign policy, too devoted to their computer regressions, and too skittish about making alliances with the New Right to really fight America's cultural battles. They hadn't relinquished enough of their intellectual pretensions to make worthy allies of the Moral Majority, he explained. Gilder had no doubt that "at some future date, when these trends have reached some climax sufficiently catastrophic," neoconservatives would finally enter the trenches of the cultural struggle. "They will finally grant, in essence, that Ernest van den Haag and Billy Graham were right about pornography; that Anita Bryant knows more about homosexuality than does the American Association of Psychiatrists; that Phyllis Schlafly is better at defining national priorities than is Daniel Patrick Moynihan; that the Moral Majority is a more valuable and responsible movement in our politics than is the Coalition for a Democratic Majority." Until then, he warned, America's cultural Right would continue to lose America's most important battles.[115]

For neoconservatives, the sufficiently catastrophic climax turned out to be the death of communism. Many of them would begin to appreciate Gilder's lesson only after the New Right's social agenda became, by default, their own highest priority. The key to cultural warfare, as Decter explained, was to be willing insistently to proclaim and repeat a few simplistic truisms. This was Reagan's exemplary strength. Decter recalled that in 1976, when Reagan challenged Gerald Ford for the Republican nomination, most neoconservatives still didn't take Reagan seriously. Though they would later become "his passionate supporters," she recounted, it was difficult for them to take him seriously because of his lack of intellectual depth. They still hadn't overcome their intellectual conceits. "Though already deeply disaffected toward the liberals—of whatever party—they were still in the early stages of the process of stripping spiritual issues down to their simplicities and possibly a bit snobbish about their reluctance to push this process through to its end," she explained.[116] With the demise of the Soviet threat, neoconservatives increasingly joined Gilder in making the purgative reduction that cultural warfare required.

They applauded the Bush administration's censorial restrictions on the press during the Persian Gulf War. Their only complaint about the media's coverage of the war—or lack of it—was that the major media tried not to take sides. "Wherever I went during the third and fourth weeks of the Gulf war, people were angry at the media, particularly at CNN and Peter Arnett," Novak reported. "What antagonizes people so is that many correspondents talk as if they were 'above' being Americans," he explained. "They make themselves superior to the subjects of their stories, whether soldiers, generals or the President of the U.S. And they pretend even in wartime that they are neutral, above the fray, on Mount Olympus." Journalists typically replied that they weren't paid to be cheerleaders for their government, but to report the truth as objectively and independently as possible. "But this is phony," Novak retorted. "In their proud boast, 'We tell the truth to power,' they have forgotten something. The freedom to tell the truth depends on who is in power. Their freedom, as it did in World War II, rests on a victory for our side. What do they think? That UNESCO would fight for their right to be impartial?" Novak argued that when America's foreign correspondents woke up each morning, they should remind themselves, " 'My liberty to report the truth comes from the American republic—and from American military power. I am not neutral.' "[117]

The tone and the reasoning were characteristically neoconservative. Novak claimed to find the media's sanitized war coverage to be overly critical of America's war effort. With considerably greater justification, neoconservatives generally claimed to reflect popular American values. Their opposition to feminism, affirmative action, multiculturalism, and liberalism tapped powerful American sentiments. Their increasing willingness to take anti-intellectual postures in advancing these positions was a polemical asset. Their unabashed nationalism gave them towering rhetorical advantages over their liberal opponents. Their eagerness to defend corporate capitalism provided them with an unparalleled base of corporate-funded institutes and journals. Though most Americans were skittish about neoconservative designs for a new Pax Americana, neoconservatives successfully appealed, during the Gulf crisis, to America's Wilsonian self-image.

Neoconservatives' defense of "middle-class values" and their condemnations of America's universities and liberal churches made strong appeals to middle-class unease. The feeling that something had gone terribly wrong in American life was widely shared. Neoconservatism made an arguably justified claim to defend the values of an inarticulate majority. As Kristol explained, the essential task of neoconservatism was to tell the intellectuals why they were wrong, and the American people why they were right. The movement's future rests on its distinctive capacity to fulfill this mission.

8

Reconstructing Neoconservatism

The high-water mark for neoconservatism has undoubtedly passed. Neoconservatives are unlikely to regain the political influence and power they attained during Ronald Reagan's presidency. The dissolution of the Soviet Union has stripped neoconservatism of its unifying enemy and ended the world-historical phase of politicization by which neoconservatism was principally defined. At the outset of the 1990s, Michael Novak wistfully recalled that neoconservatives got used to winning during the previous decade. The 1990s would be defined by issues less favorable to neoconservative interests. Neoconservatives rode to power in the 1980s with a conservative administration that claimed it was "morning in America." Despite the stunning collapse of Soviet communism, no one claimed in the 1992 presidential campaign that it was morning in America. American resentment over the costs of unemployment, the costs and availability of health care, the corruption of America's political system, the ravages of racial injustice, and the disintegration of America's cities and infrastructure created a strikingly different mood in American politics. Americans no longer feared the Soviet threat, but worried that Japan and Germany had won the Cold War. Neoconservatives called for America to project its power aggressively throughout the world, but with episodic exceptions, most Americans were less eager to shoulder the burdens of empire. Neoconservative ideology lost much of its coherence and energy in the process. The movement's inability to forge a lasting alliance with the paleoconservative Right further hampered its capacity to reach a larger audience.

Neoconservatism nonetheless fills a long-remarked vacuum in American politics. A country as conservative and as open to social and economic modernization as the United States should have an intellectual Right that

368

defends existing arrangements. Such a conservatism would defend what Irving Kristol calls "the conservative Welfare State" and forcefully promote America's national interests. It would identify with the tradition of liberal democratic modernity—the tradition of Montesquieu, Hume, Madison, and Tocqueville. It would appeal not to the traditional Right's religious-based principles of tradition, hierarchy, and prescription, but to the Whig principles of individual liberty, enterprise, and opportunity. It would defend capitalism and the welfare state; democracy and the role of elites; modernity and traditional morality. It would oppose modern liberalism's endorsement of group rights and affirmative action in the name of liberal democratic individualism.

America's liberal intelligentsia long claimed to want a worthy right-wing opposition. In 1950, Lionel Trilling complained in *The Liberal Imagination* that American conservatism consisted of "irritable mental gestures which seek to resemble ideas." Notwithstanding the emergence of a new generation of conservative intellectuals in the succeeding decade, Trilling's New York Intellectual acquaintances would repeatedly dismiss American conservatives with the same characterization. America's conservative intellectuals weren't intellectuals at all, but reactionary neurotics. The few serious thinkers among them were isolated individuals, representing nothing. Neither did the presence of former leftists such as James Burnham, Max Eastman, and Will Herberg make the Right intellectually respectable to America's reigning intelligentsia. The long-awaited intellectual opposition that liberal intellectuals claimed to be looking for emerged only when many of the key complainants—including Trilling, Hook, Kristol, and Norman Podhoretz—themselves moved to the Right. They did not convert to existing conservatism, but rather created an alternative to it.

Their movement's greatest strength was the militant anticommunism it inherited from the Old Left. The neoconservatives' insistence on the leftist patrimony of their anticommunism was amply justified, and it explained much of their animus for the cultural revolutions of the 1960s. Nothing that neoconservatives claimed about the tyranny, mendacity, brutality, or squalor of communism was unknown to Norman Thomas or disbelieved by most of his socialist comrades. In the 1930s, Thomas repeatedly condemned the ruling Soviet dictatorship and personally struggled with the question whether, under any circumstance, an alliance with Communists in the struggle against fascism could be justified.[1] During World War II, Thomas spoke against his country's sudden infatuation with Stalin and ridiculed the absurdly idealized portraits of Soviet life that were appearing in America's mass media. He spoke out against the Soviet massacre of Polish prisoners of war in the Katyn Forest in 1940, when the story was generally treated by the media and the U.S. State Department as Nazi propaganda. He denounced Franklin Roosevelt's concessions to Stalin at Cairo and Teheran and condemned Roosevelt's abandonment of Eastern Europe at Yalta. The war had begun "ostensibly to guarantee the integrity of Poland," he observed. It ended by selling out Eastern Europe. America's social democrats later condemned the Potsdam agreements for the same reason. As Thomas explained, Potsdam "represented a triumph of vengeance and stupidity and in its inevitable application by the triumphant Kremlin turned eastern and central Europe over to the communists."[2] Thomas traced the primary causes of the Cold War to the Soviet conquest of Eastern Europe, the Berlin blockade, and Stalin's rejection of American proposals for disarmament and control of atomic energy. The fellow-travelers disgusted him. He spent most of his 1948 presidential campaign attacking Henry Wallace's communist-dominated Progressive party campaign, and he proclaimed for the rest of his life that "the evidence of the essential evil of communism is strong."[3]

The neoconservatives justifiably regarded themselves as heirs to this tradition. Their writings on the Cold War repeatedly returned to the same historical benchmarks and resurrected Thomas's criticisms of them. Their portrait of the Soviet empire recycled the commonplaces of the anti-Stalinist Old Left. The Soviet enemy described by Thomas, Burnham, Shachtman, Hook, and Harry Overstreet had not changed, they insisted. It had only grown larger, more fearsome, and more directly threatening. The reality of the Soviet threat was widely discounted in America only because most Americans secretly feared Soviet might. The intellectuals, especially, cowered before the Soviet empire. Neoconservatism revived much of the rhetoric of the Old Left in reaction, summoning America to take the fight to the Soviets. Like many of the Old Leftists themselves, however, neoconservatives retained only Thomas's anticommunism. Thomas's antimilitarism, his commitment to economic and social democracy, his unwavering opposition to dictatorships of all kinds, his egalitarianism, his passion for racial justice, and his profound concern for the poor and oppressed would have little place in the Old Left's last mutation.

In the mid-1960s, Shachtman and his followers supported America's war in Vietnam with a patchwork of Marxist arguments and a distinction taken from Hannah Arendt's theory of totalitarianism. They turned Arendt's distinction between dictatorial and totalitarian regimes into a foreign policy double standard. Faced with a choice between watching Third World nations fall to communism or supporting existing dictatorships, Shachtman argued, the United States needed to support ruling governments until democratic forces emerged within these countries. A novel rationale was thus offered for traditional American policy. Totalitarian communist regimes obliterated the political, cultural, and economic preconditions of democracy. The Shachtmanites claimed that communist regimes thus exterminated opposition forces far more successfully than rightist dictatorships. Communism destroyed civil society and extinguished all preexisting democratic and traditional habits. Though both kinds of tyranny used terror to enforce conformity, communist regimes were distinctive for their capacity to enslave their populations and suffocate dissent.[4]

Shachtman never claimed that communist regimes were invulnerable to domestic opposition or that no communist government would ever accept democratic reforms. It would be left to the neoconservatives to take the argument this far. "The transition to totalitarian rule is by definition irrevocable except in the case of some cataclysm like a world war," Jean-François Revel announced. By definition, totalitarian states made their victims unable to remember a society different from their own, or unable even to think or dream of one. "Nostalgia for the past and the utopian dream of the future are both beyond their reach," Revel wrote. "Such people can no longer imagine either past or future."[5] For Podhoretz, this explained why there was not "the slightest possibility that even the most minimal degree of civil or political liberty will ever be allowed under Communism."[6] The prisoners of totalitarianism lacked not only any means to resist their rulers, but even any capacity to dream of resisting them. Jeane Kirkpatrick turned these assurances into a foreign policy doctrine. America needed to make its peace with the world's authoritarian tyrannies, she argued, because these regimes at least preserved the social preconditions for reform. In the Soviet bloc, the preconditions for reform had been erased. Arendt had described the Nazi and Stalinist concentration camps as the defining models of totalitarianism. Neoconservatives insisted that ruling regimes in Hungary, Czechoslovakia, Poland, and even Yugoslavia were descendants of the Stalinist model.

They portrayed the center of the totalitarian empire as a towering, expanding, internally unchangeable monolith. Burnham's depiction of the Soviet threat was reproduced with fearsome self-certainty. Neoconservatives demanded a massive military build-up and a new interventionist foreign policy on the basis of this portrait. Revel argued that the strengths of the totalitarian system gave Soviet leaders immense advantages over their democratic opponents. He repeatedly insisted that Soviet communism was stronger than liberal democracy because liberalism permitted too much internal criticism.[7] Podhoretz claimed that Soviet military strength and strategic geopolitical power surpassed America's. Richard Pipes warned that Soviet leaders were preparing to fight and win a nuclear war. American military spending doubled between 1980 and 1985 on the basis of these claims. Neoconservatives would later argue that the collapse of the Soviet bloc owed much to Reagan's military build-up, which purportedly convinced Soviet leaders that they couldn't afford to perpetuate the arms race. Neoconservatives claimed that Reagan's Star Wars initiative, in particular, pushed the arms race into areas in which the Soviets were inferior and economically unable to compete.

These claims were not without merit. The pace of Soviet communism's disintegration was, quite possibly, accelerated by the pressure of heightened American military spending in the 1980s. In their eagerness to attribute the dissolution of the Cold War to Reagan's militarism, however, neoconservatives exaggerated the impact of Reagan's spending increases and, more importantly, underestimated the importance of Reagan's disarmament initiatives and his personal commitment to abolishing nuclear weapons.

As early as 1983, the chief of the Soviet General Staff, Marshal Nikolai Ogarkov, was telling former American officials that the Cold War was over because of Soviet economic and technological backwardness. Ogarkov explained that with its rigid authoritarian structures, the Soviet Union was incapable of competing with societies that made computers widely available. The failure of the Soviet system was already understood by some high-ranking Soviet officials before Mikhail Gorbachev took power. [8]

During the early 1980s, while a burgeoning peace movement insistently rejected the deterrence system and brought pressure on the Reagan administration and Congress to freeze the nuclear arms race, neoconservative hardliners disdained the peace movement and regarded nuclear weapons as necessary instruments of statecraft. Some neoconservatives even talked about winning nuclear wars.

In his own way, Reagan adopted both positions. He increased military spending and called the Soviet Union an evil empire, but he also embraced much of the rhetoric and spirit of the peace movement. During his first term, he frequently expressed his abhorrence of nuclear weapons and envisioned, in 1983, a world in which these weapons would be "banished from the face of the earth." With the ascension of Gorbachev to the Soviet presidency in 1985, Reagan was given the opportunity to show that his anti-nuclearism was not mere pious rhetoric. In November 1985, Reagan's reassertion of his antinuclear vision at the Geneva summit convinced Gorbachev that nuclear disarmament was a genuine possibility. The following year, Reagan and Gorbachev stunned the world at the Reyjavík summit by announcing that they had nearly agreed to a comprehensive ban on nuclear weapons. Neoconservatives regarded the summit as a narrow escape from what James Schlesinger scathingly called Reagan's "casual utopianism"; Podhoretz referred to the summit afterward as "the Reyjavík comedy." In the face of vehement opposition by many of his neoconservative supporters, however, Reagan pressed on with his disarmament initiatives and committed the United States, in 1987, to its first genuine nuclear disarmament treaty. Podhoretz and many other neoconservatives (though not all of them) inveighed against the Treaty on Intermediate-range Nuclear Forces (INF), claiming that Reagan's disarmament initiatives amounted to surrender. Reagan was selling out America and calling it peace, Podhoretz complained. In fact, however, Reagan's negotiations with Gorbachev marked the beginning of the end of the Cold War. The Cold War was defused much more by the antinuclearism that neoconservatives opposed than by the military buildup they supported.[9]

Neoconservatives not only grossly overestimated the political strength and efficiency of Soviet bloc totalitarianism, they equally overestimated Soviet geopolitical force and economic strength. They thus demanded enormous military increases to outstrip a largely fantasized opponent. The United States was the world's leading creditor nation when Reagan's military build-up began, providing the largest source of capital for national economies throughout the world. By the end of Reagan's presidency, the United States was the world's largest debtor nation. America's dominant economic position in the world was squandered virtually overnight, partly as a consequence of David Stockman's unintended "giant fiscal syllogisms." Neoconservatives typically responded that even with a doubled military budget, American defense spending represented only 6 percent of GNP. America still sold enough videocassettes and Big Macs to afford its military outlays. The appeal to this relativizing macroeconomic statistic, however, masked the consequences of militarization. America's GNP was large enough to dwarf any conceivable military expenditure. Neoconservatives relativized the significance of Reagan's budget deficits with the same argument, even after Reagan tripled the national debt.

The relevant question was not whether American military spending was 5 or 7 percent of the GNP of a largely service-based economy, but the extent to which dramatically heightened military spending in the 1980s crowded out vital national investments in infrastructure, education, housing, soft-energy hardware, full employment, and other economic and social needs. Federal aid to education was slashed by a third while workforce training and retraining were gutted. While Japanese and German resources were devoted primarily to commercial research and development, 75 percent of American research was military-related, contributing decisively to America's trade deficits. America spent more than $2 trillion on the military in the 1980s without raising the money to pay for it, leaving debts that devoured nearly half of every subsequent tax dollar. Neoconservatives failed to address the economic and social costs of America's remilitarization during a period when the United States lost vital economic markets to East Asian and European countries. They ignored evidence that Reagan's military build-up occurred too quickly for the American economy to absorb. They harshly rejected the argument that it was militarily unneccesary. The Reagan military budgets sent a fantastic-ally expensive message to a Soviet leadership that, in any case, could not have indefinitely ignored its disintegrating economic base. In an increas-ingly internationalized world economy, the gross inferiority of the Soviet economic system was too obvious even for Soviet leaders to ignore. A more realistic assessment of the Soviet threat could have allowed America to husband its resources. Neoconservative polemics against "appeasement" made such an assessment politically impossible during the Reagan presi-dency. [10]

The loss of the movement's catalyzing enemy split most neoconserva-tives into realist and globalist/unipolarist camps, with a few individuals—such as Peter Berger and William Bennett—seeking a middle position. The Persian Gulf War brought out the differences between these perspectives, while also revealing the deeper agreements between them. Virtually all of the neoconservatives supported President Bush's decision to go to war; nearly all of them tweaked him for overindulging America's multilateralist pretensions during the preparations for it; and all of them exulted that America's victory would quash isolationist sentiment in the United States. The war's aftermath quickly brought out the differences between them. The realpolitikers supported Bush's initial attempt to stay out of Iraq's domestic turmoil; the globalists were appalled by Bush's refusal to assist the rebel Kurds and Shiites in Iraq immediately after the war.

"We intervened in the Gulf to prevent a belligerent, powerful, anti-Western tyrant from dominating that oil-rich area," Kristol wrote. "It was (and is) in our national interest that this not happen." Driving Saddam Hussein from Kuwait was also in the national interests of America's principal allies in the region, he noted. America didn't go to war for the moralistic reasons its leaders felt compelled to proffer. The United States needed to prevent a thug from controlling 40 percent of the world's oil. America's allies had the same interest, which they generally advanced without resorting to the rhetoric of "abstract moralism and high sentimen-talism" that prevailed in the United States. Kristol observed that this difference granted powerful advantages to America's allies at the war's end.

America's Middle East allies wanted the United States to stay out of Iraq because their interests would be threatened by a dismembered Iraq. They were not moved by the plight of the Kurds, since Kurdish nationalism threatened their own sovereignty. For that straightforward reason, they urged the United States not to become sentimental about the Kurds. "As for the unfortunate Kurds, it is their bad luck that their 20 million are divided among Turkey, Syria, Iraq, Iran and the Soviet Union, none of which wishes to encourage the idea that a united 'Kurdistan' could ever come into existence," Kristol remarked. These countries had enough ethnic problems already.[11]

"So there it is," Kristol shrugged. Bush's initial abandonment of the Iraqi Kurds and Shiites had looked bad at first, but this was only because America's ingrained moralism made its leaders "hopelessly inept" at explaining perfectly sensible policies. America's chief interest after the war was to preserve the integrity of Iraq. The best strategy for preserving Iraq, Kristol argued, was the cautiously noninterventionist course that Bush had chosen. It was hoped that Iraq's military would eventually depose Hussein, but preserving Iraqi sovereignty was more important to the United States and its allies. The alternative was to send American troops to Baghdad, either to keep existing rebellions in check or to tripartition Iraq against the wishes of America's allies. "Neither alternative is attractive, since each could end up committing us to govern Iraq," Kristol concluded. "And no civilized person in his right mind wants to govern Iraq."[12]

By this characteristic reckoning, the globalists had lost their minds. The snobbish tone of the realpolitikers offended them. A. M. Rosenthal recalled that Bush had exhorted the Iraqi people to overthrow Hussein. "It is shameful to pretend that the rebels could then expect we would fail to issue the command that would protect them from annihilation," he contended. Bush's claim to this effect was disgraceful. Rosenthal further insisted that resuming the war would serve American interests. "A monumental camouflage of reality is taking place," he charged. The Kurds and Shiites were slaughtered immediately after the war by Hussein, who remained in power because America's foreign policy establishment worshiped its own balance-of-power idol. So long as Hussein remained in power, he argued, it would be suicidal for any freedom movement in the world to trust the Bush administration's word. That reality needed to be factored into the realists' calculations.[13]

In Rosenthal's view, America's abandonment of the Iraqi rebels during the war's immediate aftermath confirmed the utter bankruptcy of realism. He acidly observed that the Bush administration only believed in democracy "for designated parts of the world, mostly where it is already in place."

American policy was elsewhere shaped by a paralyzing fear of morality. Realism was self-defeating. The record gave ample testimony to the realists' lack of real solutions or vision. "For many years now, the 'realists' have dominated American foreign policy, particularly on the Middle East," Rosenthal observed. He claimed that democratic gains in the Middle East would be impossible so long as State Department realpolitikers appeased the region's tyrants and coddled its oil sheiks. "Just see where realpolitik has gotten us in the Mideast: Iran in the hands of religious fanatics, Syria and Libya ruled under terrorist fascism, Saddam Hussein still in power, marauding—and a million Iraqi refugees clawing for food, crying out their hunger and betrayal," he argued. [14]

Realism was cynical, provincial, and accommodating. The democratic globalist faith was moral, universal, and militant. By choosing opportunism over democratic principle, the realists repeatedly showed themselves to be too smart by half. Podhoretz bitterly observed that Bush's call for a New World Order "was revealed in the aftermath of the war as nothing but a meatless bone thrown to the neo-Wilsonians." A genuine New World Order would require an American administration that believed in its right to replace Middle Eastern thugs, he argued, rather than merely defang them. Rosenthal appealed to Aleksandr Solzhenitsyn. "I tell you: Interfere more and more," Solzhenitsyn had written. "We beg you to come and interfere." Democratic globalism was a willing response to this plea. The globalists disagreed whether America's alliances with dictatorships could be justified. Rosenthal took a minority view, arguing that the United States should break its relationships with Third World dictatorships, or at least refuse to support them financially. The globalists agreed, however, that America was morally obliged to heed the call "that rises from the graves of those who were shot, butchered, strangled or incinerated, quietly, without interference." [15]

The dissolution of the Soviet Union elicited similar arguments. The realpolitikers argued that America should play down the issues of democracy and minority rights in its dealings with the former Soviet republics. The democratic globalists countered that America should push hard for the creation of democratic institutions and polities throughout the former Soviet Union. Charles Krauthammer's unipolarism drew distinctions on the latter commitment. America should encourage democracy throughout the new Commonwealth of Independent States, he argued, but should push for it only in Russia. Since Russia was the only Commonwealth republic with the potential to become a world power, it was "therefore the only state that requires a full U.S. commitment to total democratization and pacification." The other republics were mere ex-colonies. Apart from their nuclear weapons, they posed no threat to American interests. The time for hardball had therefore arrived for dealing with this remaining threat, Krauthammer wrote. American unipower needed to be used to compel the Kazakhs, Ukrainians, and Belarussians to dismantle their nuclear weapons. Economic aid and diplomatic support for these states would be linked to this demand.[16]

America's approach to Russia, however, needed to respect Russia's greater potential strength. Krauthammer proposed a cooptation strategy in which America would pursue a military alliance with the Russian republic. This strategy would advance both of America's crucial goals in the region: It would preempt the formation of a possible geopolitical rival, and it would accelerate America's drive "to inherit the Soviet empire." The foreign policy mission of the United States was to use American power aggressively to reshape the world according to America's military, political, and economic interests. An aggressive foreign policy was not merely a means to an end, Krauthammer claimed, but a good in itself. It was the only honorable posture for any great power that believed in itself. For the world's remaining superpower, anything less than a vigorously interventionist foreign policy would be shameful. Krauthammer bitterly complained at the end of 1991 that American policy was being shaped by a president who had no beliefs at all. Bush's capacity for foreign policy aggressiveness had apparently been used up during the Gulf War. He was now backing away from more important challenges. The opportunity to inherit the Soviet empire was being thrown away by a president who only wanted to relive the Gulf War and preserve the status quo. If there was no such thing as a normal time, and there was no such thing as a good time for America to reduce its imperial commitments, the present time was particularly unsuited for such sentiments. Krauthammer exhorted Bush to stir up his courage and take the risk of believing in something.[17]

Most neoconservatives were crusaders. They were not temperamentally suited for the kind of conservatism that merely tended to society's arrangements. Most of them were disinclined for the same reason to believe that a culture war was enough. It was axiomatic for them that America needed a foreign policy mission that served its most expansive international visions. The United States was obliged to wage an economic, political, and military crusade for world democracy. Woodrow Wilson once proclaimed that America "has the infinite privilege of fulfilling her destiny and saving the world." The globalists and unipolarists exulted in the early 1990s that the Wilsonian moment had arrived. "For our nation, this is the opportunity of a lifetime," Joshua Muravchik exhorted. "Our failure to exert every possible effort to secure this outcome would be unforgivable. If we succeed, we will have forged a Pax Americana unlike any previous peace, one of harmony, not of conquest. Then the twenty-first century will be the American century by virtue of the triumph of the humane idea born in the American experiment."[18]

Muravchik called this new Wilsonianism "democratic idealism." The realists shuddered. The differences between the realists and democratic globalists should not be exaggerated, however. Both camps were unilateralist; both asserted that America needed to "accept its responsibilities" as the world's remaining imperial power. Kristol worried that most Americans were not prepared "to accept those imperial responsibilities that history has thrust upon us."[19] He did not doubt that America's interests would compel frequent interventions in the future, however. History's assignments were not to be shunned. The globalists issued the same prescription in the name of world democracy, the New World Order, and/or the Pax Americana. Novak urged that the number of "three-sided social systems" in the world could be increased dramatically if the United States employed its power for this purpose. America could enlarge the number of countries that featured capitalist economies, democratic political systems, and conservative cultural systems. "The new world order means a world of individual nations shaped more and more on the threefold model pioneered for all other nations by the American experiment," he claimed. "And it also means a world more reliant than ever on the twofold American capacity for quick decision and power projection on an international scale."[20] If the realists backed off from crusading for three-sided social systems, they agreed that the world's remaining empire would need to project its power more forcefully throughout the world in the future. Whether in the name of the national interest or the New World Order or both, whether seeking them or not, America was certain to find more of John Quincy Adams's "monsters abroad" that needed to be destroyed.

The globalists welcomed this prospect by appealing to their country's missionary impulse. They were not chastened by the legacy of the last great American crusade for world democracy, which stirred and partly created the nationalist resentments that produced World War II. Muravchik's manifesto for democratic globalism, Exporting Democracy, recounted the entire story of American interventionism as a struggle for world democracy. It gave short shrift to America's imperial maneuvers and its support for dictatorships in Guatemala, Haiti, Iran, Vietnam, Chile, Panama, El Salvador, and elsewhere. While claiming that American culture was a moral sewer and a national disgrace, while conceding that America's economic position in the world had seriously declined, while confirming that America's educational system was badly failing, while noting that America's prisons were stuffed beyond capacity, while acknowledging that America's cities were violent, ugly, and degraded, the globalists nonetheless insisted that American democracy and capitalism set the standards by which other nations should be judged. The globalists compellingly observed that democracies didn't go to war with each other, that democracies had the world's best human rights records, and that the ideals of political freedom, self-determination, and equality of opportunity were best attained or only attainable through democracy. The rhetorical power of democratic globalism derived from these truisms and from the globalists' effective critique of the moral bankruptcy of realism. The death of communism provided extraordinary opportunities for American policymakers to redeem Wilson's world-embracing vision for his country. As Berger maintained, however, the globalists failed to explain by what right the United States was justified in arrogating to itself "the national mission to promote this particular form of government at all times and in all places."[21] The ideals of freedom and self-determination were incompatible with political, economic, or cultural imperialism. The first Wilsonianism revealed the limits of foreign policy. The truisms invoked by neoconservatives provided the basis for a worthy effort to nurture democratic values and institutions in the world. To build these truisms into a policy crusade for "world democracy," however, was to bring on the law of unintended consequences with an explosive vengeance. Democratic values did not take root in societies through manipulation, coercion, or blackmail; they could only be imposed on other societies in distorted forms.

The globalists pointed to the Japanese precedent to argue that democracy *could* be imposed from the outside—if only by a conquering army. Some of them wanted similarly to impose democracy on Iraq—an ethnically divided nation with little national consciousness and no tradition of democratic politics or culture whatsoever. The globalists typically regarded the complexities of history, ethnicity, pluralism, and nationalism as subordinate to their own moral and ideological convictions about the superiority of American democracy. Their crusade for world democracy would be the next epochal test of American will. Having convinced themselves that they won the Cold War through will power and moral conviction, they wanted to carry the same mission to less advanced parts of the world.

Novak and Gregory Fossedal added economic arguments to the globalist appeal, contending that capitalism and democracy supported and promoted each other through each stage of their development.[22] The claim that democracy fostered economic development in its take-off phase was empirically unwarranted, however. As Berger observed, much of the evidence favored the opposite thesis.[23] The only existing examples of successful Third World modernization disconfirmed the democratic capitalist thesis. There was solid evidence for the claim that successful economic development often created democratizing pressures. Novak's insistence on the point was amply justified. His attribution of an inherent democratizing logic to capitalism, however, was far more problematic. Capitalism did not necessarily promote democracy, and democracy did not necessarily promote economic development. Democratic gains typically produced demands for entitlement systems that threatened further economic growth. Novak's opposition to Left-liberal movements was rational in this context. The Western democracies became democracies not through the "natural logic of capitalism," as Novak claimed, but through the efforts of democratizing social forces that he routinely denigrated. American democracy expanded not as a product of the "dynamic balance of emergent democratic capitalism," but primarily through the struggles of working-class, unionist, minority, and reformist movements. Successful modernization in East Asia confirmed the point throughout the 1980s. Four decades of successful economic modernization in the East Asian Pacific Rim failed to produce a democratic trend. Democratic gains will be made in East Asia not when the logic of capitalism finally asserts itself, but when organized democratizing forces finally wrench concessions from East Asia's economic and governmental elites. It is possible, as these elites fear, that the creation of what Mancur Olson calls "distributional coalitions" in the Pacific Rim could then reduce rates of economic growth in the region.[24]

Neoconservatives made exaggerated claims for capitalism partly for rhetorical reasons. As Kristol explained, the language of politics "is itself of the utmost political significance." Though conservatives had long bewailed the debasement and vulgarization of political discourse, he observed, it was the neoconservatives who did something about it. "Liberals and socialists have, over recent decades, made a highly successful takeover bid, so that the words we unthinkingly use end up being *their* words, with *their* connotations, insinuating the exclusive legitimacy of *their* way of looking at the world," he wrote. Such terms as "disadvantaged" and "underprivileged," for example, had "been inserted into our everyday parlance." Kristol contended that these were loaded terms that insinuated egalitarian values into American discourse. Their insertion into everyday language made it possible for radicals to manipulate America's public debate. "You don't have to be a socialist or a social-democrat in the U.S. today, arguing explicitly for extensive equality," he argued. "You can be a 'liberal' focusing public attention on the 'disadvantaged' and 'underprivileged.' This latter position is so much more convenient."[25]

Neoconservatives fought this conspiracy with one of their own. Kristol observed that "capitalism" had acquired a positive connotation among intellectuals only in the past generation. "Such usage is no accident, but resulted from a conspiracy among a handful of neoconservative intellectuals—Michael Novak, Peter Berger, George Gilder, Norman Podhoretz and (I am pleased to say) myself," he recalled. "We did not like 'free enterprise,' with its Darwinian connotations, and 'market economy' we felt was too narrow. So we decided, after considerable debate and some misgivings, to be belligerent and to take the term 'capitalism,' a term invented and used by socialists, as our own. We were tired of being accused of supporting capitalism. Henceforth, we would advocate it. It has worked, though it has taken a while."[26]

It worked partly because neoconservatives were schooled in ideological warfare. Their rhetorical methods derived from the Marxist Left, where bad manners were the norm. Robert Lekachman once observed that while Podhoretz's first volume of memoirs was "indiscreet and mean-spirited," the tone of the second was "almost unbelievably vindictive." Like their Stalinist and Trotskyist forebears, many neoconservatives traded on a stigmatizing rhetoric that impugned the loyalties and character of their opponents. Diana Trilling commented ruefully on the carryover.

> Neoconservatives such as Joseph Epstein, Norman Podhoretz, and Hilton Kramer, all of them editors of important periodicals, are not so young but that they have to be fully aware of the irreparable damage that was done to the cultural and even the political life of this country by their Stalinist forebears who, instead of honorably debating issues, poisoned the intellectual atmosphere with lies and invective. By what process of self-hallucination do they now persuade themselves that just because they operate from an opposite premise, the anti-Communist premise, they do us any better service with such methods?[27]

The movement's chief publicists responded that only the language and tactics of class warfare would suffice in a class war. The echoes of their Trotskyist heritage reverberated throughout their attacks on the New Class. In the 1930s and 1940s, many of America's leading Stalinists were well-bred WASPs with Ivy League degrees. Alfred Kazin once recalled of them that after graduating from Harvard or Yale, they became Marxists and "worried in the *New Masses* whether Proust should be read after the Revolution and why there should be no simple proletarians in the novels of André Malraux."[28] He also recalled that he held them in deepest contempt. The sentiment was widely shared among the New York Intellectuals, whose disgust with high-society leftism informed their own anti-Stalinism. The same disgust would later resurface in the neoconservatives' bitter polemics against the New Class.

Though all of them appealed to the concept, neoconservatives never settled on a definition of the New Class. Some definitions restricted the notion to liberal intellectuals; others added liberal activists and the major media; others added government bureaucrats, social workers, consultants, and educational administrators; others added lawyers, foundation directors, engineers, psychologists, and nearly all academics; others distinguished between experts (good) and intellectuals (bad); others added liberal judges, doctors, entrepreneurs, medical administrators, and executives to the list.

If the New Class was a "muddled concept," as Daniel Bell contended, the muddle did not diminish the concept's polemical force. [29] The electoral strength of the American Right partly depended on its capacity to make working-class voters resent the media, academics, and the government rather than America's business and financial elites. American election campaigns assiduously reinforced this message. In the 1988 presidential campaign, the archetypal scion of the WASP upper class attacked his Democratic opponent for being associated with the so-called "liberal elite." Two decades of neoconservative and New Right polemics against the New Class reached their apogee. The malleable nature of the New Class idea provided neoconservatives with an adaptable weapon. Neoconservatism traded not only on its leftist past, but on the rhetoric of American populism. It spoke not only the language of democracy and progress, but of populist resentment. Though the concept of the New Class was a product of anarchist and Trotskyist history, its use by neoconservatives appropriated longstanding American populist resentments against nonproducing elites. Neoconservatism turned populism's traditional attacks on business and financial elites against an alternative list of alleged parasites.

Neoconservatism cut the heart out of populism, however. Neoconservatives gave a free ride to the business and financial elites who controlled America's investment process. They justified the corporate class's leveraged buy-outs and greenmail, and defended the managerial prerogatives of technocratic elites no longer bound to community, cultural, or even national loyalties. They rationalized America's regressive tax code and its worsening maldistribution of wealth. They deflected responsibility for America's social and economic decay onto America's cultural elites. Novak lamented the corrupting influence of television on American life—and claimed that television was corrupting because it was controlled by the Left. "The bad guy on television is always the business executive," he explained. "The New Class insinuates its leftist contempt for traditional values into the culture through its control of the media."[30]

The notion that the so-called New Class was using its purported control over the media to wage a class struggle against the corporate sector, however, ignored the fact that the media was part of the corporate establishment. The television networks were themselves commercial enterprises utterly dependent on advertising revenue. They existed primarily to gather audiences for their advertisers. Media images of reality were shaped primarily by the media's own institutional need to stimulate consumption. The moral corruption and narcissism that neoconservatives condemned in American society thus owed more to commercial imperatives than to the failures of some fictionally autonomous "culture." Commercial society relentlessly provoked and manipulated consumer desires for success, excitement, novelty, and immediate gratification. It bombarded individuals with sexually charged messages and images not because the "New Class" conspired to destroy morality, but because unrelenting titillation promoted consumption. The neoconservatives' strictures against the cultural failings of America's churches and schools were not so much mistaken as futile, given their refusal to address the structural causes of commercial society's moral and social ravages.

Commercially dominated societies separated the moral meaning of freedom from the ends for which individuals exercised their rights. In classical liberal theory, these ends remained private, ensuring the predominance of the economic system over other spheres. This inheritance was anticipated more than two hundred years ago by a chief celebrant of the emerging capitalist order. While the material benefits of a commercially oriented society were not to be doubted, David Hume observed, the acquisitive spirit that commercial society engendered was "insatiable, perpetual, universal, and directly destructive of society."[31] The original Whigs had few illusions about the cultural contradictions of capitalism. Their modern followers rejected all challenges to capitalist economics while themselves rejecting capitalist culture. Having thrown off the Marxist economism of their forebears, they insisted that America's moral and cultural deformities were separable from its economic system. Most neoconservatives condemned what they described as an erosion of moral values under modernity. Their denunciations were rarely lacking in eloquence or substance. It was primarily under the pressure of the business civilization they celebrated, however, that the communities of memory that once sustained these values were being eviscerated.

Neoconservatives viewed families, churches, and voluntary associations as structures that mediated between individuals and the state. They powerfully condemned the encroachments of the state on civil society, arguing that New Class idealism bred increased dependency on the state and eroded traditional moral habits. They claimed that the continuing expansion of state power encouraged individuals to forsake their individual moral responsibilities and undermined the roles of families, churches, and voluntary associations. No comparable intellectual movement condemned the moral ravages of modernity with such force. Their critiques of the state and their calls for strengthening civil society were frequently compelling. Neoconservatism made numerous converts on the basis of this unarguably powerful theme. The problem was that civil society was undermined in America not only by the state, but more importantly by the market. Mediating structures confronted not only the often-overreaching arm of the modern bureaucratic state, but the relentlessly desacralizing and commodifying force of the market. Notwithstanding Novak's redefinition of capitalism, the chief difference between modern industrial capitalism and previous market economies was capitalism's transformation of labor and land into commodities. The great historian of the rise of capitalism, Karl Polanyi, recounted the legacy of commercial society's commodification of labor. "To separate labor from other activities of life and to subject it to the laws of the market was to annihilate all organic forms of existence and to replace them by a different type of organization, an atomistic and individualistic one," he observed. The "great transformation" wrought by modern capitalism produced a society that "could not exist for any length of time without annihilating the human and natural substance of society."[32]

Neoconservatives bewailed the cultural consequences of this inheritance. They used religious arguments persuasively in their criticisms of sexual promiscuity, the breakdown of family ties, and the erosion of traditional cultural values. They found more difficulty, however, making constructive religious claims beyond these carefully chosen themes. The neoconservatives were too theologically diverse to make common theologically based arguments and too utilitarian to make the effort. Kristol longed for a religious establishment that sacralized the existing social order and reconciled individuals to "the world as it is." More pointedly than Kristol, Podhoretz identified with a form of Jewish faith—but the form was an unabashedly heretical survivalism that enshrined a neoconservative version of Jewish political interests with ultimate significance. Novak returned to a theologically conservative form of Catholicism, while urging the church to promote democratic capitalism. Berger maintained that theological conservatism was untenable, while claiming that the church should stay out of politics. Neoconservatives agreed that modern Christianity and Judaism were politically moralistic, overly prophetic, and invidiously feminized; they did not agree, however, on the role that religious institutions should play in society or on what theological basis they should act. Neoconservative attempts to enlist religion in the culture war foundered on these disagreements. While condemning the atomizing nihilism of modern society, neoconservatives failed to recognize its chief socioeconomic causes. While bemoaning the decline of religion under modernity, neoconservatives themselves rarely appealed to a transcendent source of meaning or virtue.

The movement's most representative spokesman in the 1970s was Kristol. Virtually every commentary on neoconservatism during this period focused on Kristol's arsenal of Whiggish arguments, his polemical style, his attacks on the New Class, and his fundraising exploits. His remark that a neoconservative was a liberal who had been mugged by reality set the tone. His appeals for corporate support gave notice that neoconservatism would not be a passing intellectual fad. The corporate sector needed its own intellectuals to help it expose, refute, and defund the New Class, he insisted. While railing against the self-aggrandizing opportunism of the New Class, neoconservatives built their own elaborate infrastructure of corporate-funded think tanks, foundations, journals, and lobbying agencies. Kristol informed corporate executives that they didn't know how to think politically or defend themselves ideologically. He assured them that traditional conservatives couldn't help with either task. Only the neoconservatives had the requisite background, training, politics, and temperament for the job. Neoconservatives alone knew how to unmask the class interests of middle-class liberalism. David Bazelon, who revived the notion of the New Class in the 1960s, later remarked that Kristol gave new meaning to New Class careerism. "We're very easy to buy," Bazelon observed. "He opened up a new career line."[33]

The battle lines of neoconservatism's war against the New Class were drawn by Podhoretz. "In trying to dislodge the old order, the New Class was using its own young people as commandos, sending them out into the streets to clash with the enemy's troops (the police and the National Guard) while the 'elders' directed the grand strategy from behind the lines and engaged in less dangerous forms of political warfare against the established power," he explained. "And not the least effective form of this warfare was to identify their side with the youth, thus implying that they were the fabled wave of the future."[34] Podhoretz managed to take this account utterly seriously while conceding its fancifulness. The predominant form of neoconservatism in the 1980s was represented by his writings and his magazine. His exertions against the New Class heightened Kristol's battlefield rhetoric and expanded the movement's list of cultural enemies. His militant anticommunism flattened the ambiguities in Kristol's blend of anticommunism and realpolitik. *Commentary's* domestic crusades were extensions of its war against world communism. More emphatically than Kristol, Podhoretz conceived neoconservatism as an intellectual and political movement. More ardently than Kristol, he devoted his energies to building the movement. The demise of neoconservatism's principal enemy, the Soviet Union, left Podhoretz anxious to redirect the movement's energies. He called for an intensified culture war and a refashioned American crusade for world democracy. His own contributions to the movement's new face, however, would diminish precipitously. He would be reduced mostly to attacks on feminists and anti-Zionists. Like many of his contributors, he was ill-prepared for a world that lacked a devouring totalitarian threat.

Neoconservatism in its third decade moved between Novak's democratic capitalist enthusiasms and Berger's more chastened case for capitalist modernization. Unlike most neoconservatives, Berger lacked the missionary spirit. He shared Kristol's distaste for foreign crusades as well as Kristol's reluctance to equate neoconservatism with an ideology of democratic capitalism. Though he concurred with the movement's disregard for feminism and multiculturalism, he did not share its commitment to cultural warfare. His variant of neoconservatism was the movement's ultimate fall-back position. It resolved not to remake the world or transform American culture, but merely to defend the superiority of bourgeois capitalism in a world of limited possibilities. For Berger, the empirical evidence for capitalism's superiority was sufficient. To argue for the moral or political promise of democratic capitalism was to hold up another falsifiable vision. It was to fight Marxism with a reverse-Marxism. Having witnessed the death of Marxism, he believed that neoconservatism should break the Marxist mold and reconcile itself to modernity's trade-offs.

Some variant of this argument—whether called "neoconservatism" or not—is bound to endure in American political culture. In its least-common-denominator form, neoconservatism has become inevitable. As a movement that endorses a socioeconomic system envied by much of the world, neoconservatism has a viable future. America has long needed an intellectual conservatism that defends the establishment that is really there. During the 1980s, more than a few disillusioned Swedophiles and former liberals became neoconservatives. They were chastened by what Nathan Glazer called the limits of social policy. For them, neoconservatism was a corrective retrenchment from the welfare state's overreaching commitments. Neoconservatism would promote entrepreneurial freedom from the state and instruct Americans on the limits of what government could do for them. They would not dispute America's need for social insurance, but would vigorously resist government attempts to break down America's maldistribution of wealth. E. M. Forster once remarked that the critical need in modern societies is to "combine the new economy and the old morality."[35] More than any of its rival traditions, neoconservatism meets this need.

Neoconservatism will not remain a vital intellectual movement on the strength of this agenda alone, however. Those who care most about saving neoconservatism as a movement—Novak, Podhoretz, Midge Decter, Richard John Neuhaus, Joshua Muravchik, and Hilton Kramer—appreciate the importance of refashioning its ideology. Their battlefield rhetoric serves this purpose. Neoconservatism did not begin merely to defend existing arrangements or to curtail the expansion of the welfare state. It will not engender generations on that basis alone. "Fighting American culture" and "exporting American democracy" are projects for a movement in search of a higher cause. Neoconservative attacks on feminism, multiculturalism, gay rights, affirmative action, school busing, the liberal churches, the pathologies of welfare dependency, and the New Class have formidable intellectual and emotional power in a society where cultural politics constantly trumps the politics of distribution. Americans incessantly debate the politics of abortion, sexuality, school prayer, and the pledge of allegiance while barely noticing multibillion-dollar bank scandals, the diversion of public resources to private development, and tax policies that worsen America's maldistribution of wealth. Neoconservatism's new emphasis on "culture wars" trades upon this disposition.

Neoconservatism emerged at the historical moment when working- and middle-class Americans could no longer expect to live better than their parents. America's decline as a world economic power cost Jimmy Carter his second presidential term and propelled most neoconservatives to support not only Ronald Reagan's anticommunism, but Reaganomics. To explain to Americans why their country was in economic decline, neoconservatives joined Reagan in blaming "labor elites" that strangled American productivity, a New Class that benefited from expanded government, and a welfare class that was addicted to government largesse. The image of a burgeoning welfare class that physically and economically threatened other Americans lurked behind most neoconservative rhetoric about the "culture of poverty." *Commentary* made the latter point no less stridently than the Reagan and Bush presidential campaigns. American liberals coddled America's criminal class (which was disproportionately black) and welfare class (which was also disproportionately black) and discriminated against white Americans (through affirmative action). In an age of diminishing economic expectations, the charge of reverse discrimination carried powerful overtones. Bush's 1988 presidential campaign manipulated these themes with notable success. Neoconservatives revived the rhetoric of democratic individualism in a society that increasingly distrusted liberal solutions to America's racial, educational, and urban problems. Their call for a new Pax Americana tapped powerful, though more ambiguous, sentiments in American life. Neoconservatism's survival as an intellectual movement rested on its capacity to refashion itself around these substantial concerns.

Though many neoconservatives promoted "democratic capitalism," none of them supported efforts to make capitalism more democratic by breaking down the overconcentration of corporate stock ownership, or expanding the cooperative sector, or promoting community land trusts. While they repeatedly condemned the social ravages of welfare dependency, they did not call for accelerated federal investments in worker education, retraining, or full-employment planning. While they assailed the erosion of America's economic position throughout the 1980s, neoconservatives refrained from tracking where the money went. They were silent about the failure of America's corporate elite to make productive investments in America's future. They were notably silent about the half-trillion-dollar cost of the savings and loan debacle, and about the orgy of mergers and leveraged buy-outs that left America's corporate economy buried in debt. An earlier neoconservative movement—the one that included Daniel Moynihan, Daniel Bell, and Seymour Martin Lipset—would not have faced America's collapsing infrastructure and industrial base with so little to say. The neoconservatism that embraced Reagan's economic policy was subsequently reduced—like Reagan and Bush—to ritualistic calls for further cuts in the capital gains tax. Having aligned themselves with a corporate elite that squandered much of its investment capital on shell-games, greenmail, and speculation in the 1980s, neoconservatives strained to blame the consequences of Reaganomics on its opponents. In a society now forced to live with these consequences, the triumphant rhetoric of the 1980s has diminishing force.

It also distinguishes most neoconservatives from Democratic party reformers who took up the cause, in the mid-1980s, that neoconservatives relinquished in their lurch to the Right. Throughout the 1970s, neoconservatives identified themselves as realistic liberals who sought to moderate their party's ultra-liberalism. Some of them became Republicans after they concluded that McGovernism was surviving George McGovern's colossal 1972 electoral defeat; others became Republicans out of disgust with the Carter administration; others were attracted to Reagan's nationalism and his anticommunism. In 1985, after the Democracts lost forty-nine states in another electoral landslide and long after most neoconservatives had become Reagan supporters, a new Democratic organization led by Sam Nunn, Richard Gephardt, Bill Clinton, Charles Robb, and Al Gore was launched to fulfill the task that neoconservatives had abandoned. This organization, the Democratic Leadership Council (DLC), criticized the national Democratic party's identification with welfare state liberalism and called for a Democratic politics that emphasized personal responsibility, economic growth and competition, and a strong defense. In 1990, Clinton became the organization's chairman. His subsequent ascension to the top of the Democratic party's 1992 presidential ticket, and his selection of Gore as his running mate, symbolized the DLC's success in bringing the national party to a more chastened liberalism. At the same time, Clinton beckoned neoconservatives to return to the Democratic fold. The party had learned its lessons, he assured them. He would not sell out America or make the Democratic party hostage to special interests the way his predecessors had.

To those neoconservatives who had never felt comfortable supporting Republicans, Clinton made a compelling pitch to come home. He told them that there was room in the Democratic party for neoconservative nationalism, interventionism, capitalism, and cultural conservatism. He respected neoconservatives and took them seriously. His appeal was convincing to Richard Schifter, a neoconservative and former human rights official in the Reagan and Bush administrations, who joined the Clinton team as a foreign policy adviser and enlisted neoconservative support for Clinton. Several veterans of the Coalition for a Democratic Majority, including Peter Rosenblatt and David Ifshin, also joined the Clinton team. Clinton made particular gains with neoconservatism's democratic globalist wing. Citing America's urgent need to "overcome the isolationist temptation," neoconservatives such as Samuel Huntington, Edward Luttwak, Penn Kemble, Martin Peretz, Stephen Morris, Joshua Muravchik, and Aaron Wildavsky supported Clinton and claimed that he would promote an aggressive foreign policy "infused with democratic spirit." "What's kept me in the Republican voting column is foreign policy," Muravchik explained. "But on foreign policy, Clinton's stands are preferable to Bush's. On what I care about—human rights and promoting democracy, keeping some sense of ideals in our foreign policy—Clinton is more amenable than Bush." Clinton's call for a more aggressive foreign policy appealed to democratic globalists in a period when American policymakers faced difficult decisions about intervening or shaping events in such places as Croatia, Bosnia, Burma, and Haiti. The inertia of the Bush administration and Bush's notorious lack of a political vision or defining set of beliefs drove many neoconservatives to reconsider their party affiliation in the early 1990s. They perceived that neoconservatism itself stood to gain greater influence and viability if it could re-establish its role in the Democratic party. Ben Wattenberg spoke for many of them when he welcomed Clinton's ascendency and his overtures to the neoconservatives, while reserving judgment on Clinton's seriousness. "To get the Reagan Democrats back, Clinton's got to show he's not just going to talk the talk, he'll walk the walk," Wattenberg noted. [36]

Many neoconservatives, however, had moved too far to the Right to support Clinton under any circumstance. For most of the movement's best known proponents, especially Kristol, Podhoretz, Jeane Kirkpatrick, William Bennett, Linda Chavez, and Elliott Abrams, the possibility of returning to the Democratic column was ruled out. For numerous others, including Novak and George Weigel, the prospect was tantalizing, but unlikely. They were suspicious of Clinton, fearing that he would be another Carter. They were repelled by the tasks and the company that returning "home" would bring. The Democratic party was no longer home to them, even though some still called themselves Democrats. Novak was particularly repulsed by Clinton's "grotesque" rhetoric on abortion. Vice President Quayle's chief of staff, William Kristol, spoke for many neoconservatives when he announced, "Any neocon who drifts back to the Democratic Party is a pseudo-neocon." For Kristol, as for his father, neoconservatism had become too conservative to reclaim a place in the Democratic party. Most neoconservatives stuck with Bush in 1992, though they did so, as Podhoretz explained of himself, "not only with no pleasure, but with great distaste."[37]

With Clinton's election to the presidency, the factional intraparty disputes of the Carter period were promptly reproduced. Wattenburg declared that the Democratic party was split between two chief opposing forces, which he called the Scoop Jackson party and the Jesse Jackson party. Though Clinton tried to hold these (and other) factions together, neoconservatives insisted that he needed to choose between them. He specifically needed to restrain federal spending, stimulate economic growth, stifle the liberal interest groups, and fulfill his campaign promise to forge what Clinton called a pro-democratic "global alliance as united and steadfast as the global alliance that defeated Communism." Neoconservatives worried at the outset of his presidency that Clinton was a domestic policy wonk, that he had no passion for foreign policy, and that he was too eager to please everyone. Their attitude toward his administration would depend chiefly upon his willingness to oppose liberal interests and pursue an aggressive foreign policy.

If America's war in Vietnam had unleashed only an antiwar movement, neoconservatism would not have emerged as a phenomenon worth naming. Neoconservatism drew its converts from the Movement's various offspring. The Movement eventually challenged not only the moral legitimacy of America's intervention in Vietnam, but the legitimacy of America's established elites, the overreaching power of the military-industrial complex, the evils of American racism and sexism, and the environmental ravages of modern industrialism. The Movement produced currents that challenged hierarchy at every turn. The exhortation to question authority was taken seriously by movements unimagined by the liberalism of the 1950s.

Neoconservatism began as an attempt to discredit these challenges to bourgeois society. Neoconservatives complained at first that liberalism had lost its mind. Their efforts to refute the social movements of the 1960s and early 1970s preoccupied their early attention. Neoconservatives attacked some of these movements—especially feminism—with vengeful persistence. They rejected others out of hand. Throughout the 1970s and 1980s, *Commentary* failed to publish a single serious article on the environmental crisis. Neoconservatives routinely treated the depletion of the ozone shield and the deforestation of the Third World not as serious issues, but as last resorts trumped up by a desperate Left. With the collapse of socialism, they explained, the Left had retreated to feminism, multiculturalism, and environmentalism. Having lost its substantive beliefs, the Left traded on mush.

Among the first observers to weigh the meaning of neoconservatism was James Burnham. In 1972, Burnham appreciatively noted that neoconservatives were united in their rejection of liberalism, "which they find both intellectually bankrupt and, by and large, pragmatically sterile." He cautioned that they were also united, however, by their retention of what he called the "emotional gestalt" or sensibility of liberalism. Burnham admired the spirit with which neoconservatives were taking up the struggle for the world. He observed that they were not, however, becoming conservatives. They were not prepared to take up the Old Right's battles against modernity and the welfare state.

Burnham didn't blame them for this. Many of the Right's long-cherished beliefs were "if not quite bankrupt, more and more obviously obsolescent," he conceded. Though he continued to identify with the traditional Right, he could understand why neoconservatives wanted to create a new conservatism. His hope was that neoconservatives and the Old Right would converge to form an "integral" conservatism shorn of liberal affectations and conservative anachronisms. The defining political struggle of the next generation, he argued, would pit the aggressive, forward-marching, growth-oriented forces against the "let Nature be" types who wanted disarmament, reduced consumption, and reduced energy output. [38]

For Burnham, this was the crucial divide in modern politics. He conceded that the old conservatism was intellectually unprepared to lead America's struggle against the politics of feminization, environmentalism, and decline. He welcomed the new conservatives to the battle. He admired their aggressive spirit and appreciated their intellectual trajectories, which so closely resembled his own. In subsequent years, he indulged their unacknowledged appropriation of his ideas. He lived to see the neoconservatives, the traditional Right, and the New Right work together. He lived to find himself lionized by a triumphant Right coalition. He did not live to see the coalition fall apart or to witness the revival of Old Right isolationism. The latter development would have turned his stomach—and possibly driven him to join forces with those who still believed in struggling for the world. In that event, he would have found himself finally conserving the establishment that was actually there. In the early 1940s, he had predicted that Germany, Japan, and the United States would soon attain hegemonic power over the world. In the early 1990s, neoconservatives would call the fulfillment of this prediction the end of history. Whether their movement could survive the loss of a world-embracing ideological war was a question that he would have regarded— like most of them—as a test of their will and self-confidence.

Neoconservatism was distinctive partly because liberal intellectuals took it seriously. The distinction was noted ruefully by paleoconservatives. "Liberal intellectuals have designated the neoconservatives as the official conservative opposition," Paul Gottfried observed. His explanation for the choice was that liberals wanted to spare themselves the necessity of arguing with authentic conservatives. [39] If Gottfried's explanation smacked of *ressentiment*, his complaint nonetheless went to the heart of the conflict between the conservatisms and confirmed the distinctive role of neoconservatism in American politics. Neoconservatives opposed feminism, affirmative action, multiculturalism, and modern liberalism without the baggage of a racist and nativist past. They understood that American conservatism needed to speak the language of democracy. They were committed, far more than paleoconservatives, to conserve and defend the

American system that actually existed. They defended what they called "the American reality" and pointedly dissociated themselves from "those of a reactionary bent who imagine themselves superior to that reality."[40]

Neoconservatism derived its considerable rhetorical power from its opposition to a liberal intelligentsia associated with minority rights, feminism, expanded government, and foreign policy weakness. Most neoconservatives turned to the Right at the same time and for the same reasons that millions of white ethnics and middle-class taxpayers began, in the late 1960s, to vote Republican. The guilt-ridden anti-Americanism and cultural politics of the New Politics generation drove them into alliances with their former opponents. The social engineering of America's policymaking class—which kept most of its own children out of the school busing programs—created a backlash among many of those directly affected by affirmative action and busing schemes. The impression that America's liberal intelligentsia exalted minority rights over the needs and interests of America's majority gave liberalism an ugly odor to many Americans. Neoconservatives expressed their feelings with considerable eloquence and effectiveness.

In 1968, James Q. Wilson stoutly defended inner-city whites from the charge of racism, arguing that white anger at the black underclass was not racially motivated, but was based on the perception that poor blacks refused to abide by reasonable standards of social behavior.[41] Wilson would later make a revealing characterization of his own social views. He reported that for a long time, he had doubted that he should be counted among the neoconservatives because he lacked the presumably requisite background. "I didn't know what a Trotskyite was until Dan Bell explained it to me," he recalled. He finally reconciled himself to the designation when he grasped that neoconservatism was essentially an intellectualized expression of popular American beliefs. "I am struck by the relationship between my opinions, which I am told are neoconservative, and popular opinions," he remarked. "That relationship is formed by my own experiences, not in the eating halls of CCNY, but on the playing fields of David Starr Jordan High School in Long Beach, California."[42] The plausibility of this conclusion suggested that neoconservatism was likely to have generations.

To those who claimed that neoconservatism had no generations, neoconservatives pointed to numerous proponents younger than the Kristol and Podhoretz generations working in academe and their own institutes. Some of them, such as Muravchik, Neuhaus, Novak, Carl Gershman, Penn Kemble, Scott McConnell, and Ronald Radosh, came to neoconservatism from the Left. A larger number, including Kimball,

Nuechterlein, Carol Iannone, Krauthammer, Wilson, Elliott Abrams, Bernard Aronson, Bruce Bawer, Robert Benne, William Bennett, Chester Finn, Dan Himmelfarb, Edward Luttwak, and George Weigel, came to neoconservatism from inheritance or from moderately liberal backgrounds. A sizable group of younger neoconservatives, including Mary Eberstadt, Steven Bryan, Douglas Feith, Allan Gerson, and Robert Kagen, acquired their political contacts and education while working for the Reagan administration. Several neoconservatives, including William Kristol, Bernard Aronson, Constance Horner, Diane Ravitch, and Paul Wolfowitz, became key officials in the Bush administration, while others, including Richard Perle, Kenneth Adelman, and Jeane Kirkpatrick, served as unofficial advisers to Vice President Quayle.

To those who claimed that neoconservatism was fated to lose its corporate sponsors, neoconservatives effectively replied that no evidence for this often-predicted drop-off existed. Though neoconservatives had less control over certain foundations than their embittered Old Right antagonists often alleged, their highly beneficial ties to such institutions as the Olin, Scaife, Bradley, and Smith Richardson foundations were plainly evident. Neoconservative conquests in the financial arena pointed to a decisive financial-ideological realignment in the American Right. Notwithstanding Burnham's efforts to internationalize America's traditional Right, the Old Right was predominantly protectionist and isolationist. Patrick Buchanan sought to revive this tradition in his 1992 presidential campaign.

Neoconservative internationalism was better suited to promote the interests and world view of modern corporations. In this area, neoconservatives needed to make adjustments of their own to make further gains. Much of America's global corporate class remained wary of the neoconservatives, who were too nationalistic and ideological to serve the interests of an increasingly internationalized corporate sector. America's corporate establishment was generally more comfortable with the toned-down pragmatism of the Trilateral Commission (which contained only a handful of neoconservatives) and the prescriptions of bestselling futurists than with neoconservative procapitalism. This reality would require neoconservatives to modulate their ideological preoccupations in a deideologized global market. If they found difficulties in making the adjustment, they were at least better suited for modernity's next stage than their former allies in the paleoconservative Right. The world-embracing neoconservatism of the American Enterprise Institute offered more to America's business class than the Heritage Foundation—which coped with the problem by enlisting neoconservatives into its ranks.

The promise of neoconservatism remains unredeemed in the early 1990s, but attainable. Neoconservatism attempts to fill a long-observed void in American politics. A generation before neoconservatism emerged, Peter Viereck argued that a genuine American conservatism would conserve the American roots and social institutions that were really there. What generally passed for conservatism in America, Viereck contended throughout the 1950s and early 1960s, was a pseudoconservatism that variously recycled imported European ideologies, a fantasized Southern-agrarian past, and the populist bigotries of McCarthyism. A genuine American conservatism would offer a third way between the boosters of big business who mistakenly called themselves conservatives and the "neo-Populist barn-burners" who followed Joseph McCarthy and Huey Long. [43] It would also offer an alternative, he argued later, to the rootless and abstract conservatism exemplified by Russell Kirk's "unhistorical appeal to history." Kirk's "traditionless worship of tradition" was not an American conservatism, he insisted, but a contrivance of Anglophiliac nostalgia. [44]

Viereck contended that a genuine American conservatism would appeal to the semi-aristocratic Whig tradition of Madison and The Federalist. It would revere the American constitution, take a gradualist approach to politics, uphold traditional mores, and protect the executive branch from outside mob pressures. Following the example of the Constitutional Convention of 1787, an American conservatism would conserve America's roots and defend its existing institutions, blending Lockean liberalism and Burkean conservatism. The American experience was based on the complementarity of moderate liberalism and moderate conservatism, Viereck explained, while European politics was based on the difference between extreme liberalism and extreme conservatism. The conservatism that America needed would understand the difference. It would prefer Washington and Calhoun over Jefferson and Jackson, but would not dissociate itself from the Jeffersonian tradition. It would be anticommunist, but opposed to McCarthyism. It would uphold the Lockean rights pertaining to private property, but accept many of the economic reforms of the New Deal as a Burkean bulwark against socialism. It would restrain state power while recognizing with Burke that a state "without the means of some change is without the means of its conservation." It would splinter Coleridge's organic unity of society while taking measures to counteract modernity's atomization of society. It would promote capitalism while also supporting trade unionism. [45] A genuine American conservatism would be a new thing that preserved what was actually old and most valuable in the American experience.

These arguments got Viereck expelled from the conservative movement of his time. A generation later, he undoubtedly would have shunned
the ideological zeal and polemical harshness of those who carried out
much of his project. Neoconservatism is not altogether what he had in
mind. It does not speak in the tones he considered endemic to authentic
conservatism. It is too militaristic and too obsequious toward big business
to meet his tests for true conservatism. If neoconservatism is not yet the
reflective, deeply rooted, American conservatism that Viereck sought,
however, it remains, in the century's last decade, the most serious and
still-promising effort of its kind that Americans are likely to see. For the
same reason, neoconservatives offer the most instructive opposition that
any reconstructed progressive politics is likely to encounter.

Notes

Notes to Chapter 1

1. Michael Harrington, interview with author, May 27, 1988.
2. Michael Harrington, *Fragments of the Century* (New York: Saturday Review Press, 1973), p. 145.
3. Bogdan Denitch, interview with author, April 30, 1991.
4. Cf. Social Democrats, U.S.A, "For the Record: The Report of Social Democrats, U.S.A. on the Resignation of Michael Harrington and His Attempt to Split the American Socialist Movement," undated and unpublished position paper, pp. 1–36; Maurice Isserman, *If I Had a Hammer . . . : The Death of the Old Left and the Birth of the New Left* (New York: Basic Books, 1987), pp. 57–75.
5. Harrington, *Fragments of the Century*, pp. 195–196.
6. Denitch, interview with author, April 30, 1991.
7. Harrington, *Fragments of the Century*, p. 224.
8. Harrington, interview with author, May 27, 1988.
9. For a collection of early critiques of neoconservatism, most of which first appeared in *Dissent*, see Lewis A. Coser and Irving Howe, eds., *The New Conservatives: A Critique from the Left* (New York: New American Library, 1977). For a discussion of neoconservatism's origins that emphasizes (and exaggerates) the "labeling" phenomenon, see Seymour Martin Lipset, "Neoconservatism: Myth and Reality," *Society* 25, no. 5 (July/August 1988): 33–36.
10. Michael Harrington, "The New Class and the Left," in *The New Class?* ed. B. Bruce-Biggs (New Brunswick, N.J.: Transaction Books, 1979), p. 137.
11. Irving Kristol, *Reflections of a Neoconservative: Looking Back, Looking Ahead* (New York: Basic Books, 1983), pp. 75–76.
12. Michael Novak, *Will It Liberate? Questions about Liberation Theology* (New York: Paulist Press, 1986), pp. 47–48.
13. Norman Podhoretz, "New Vistas for Neoconservatives," *Washington Post*, August 4, 1988.
14. Quoted in Jürgen Habermas, *The New Conservatism: Cultural Criticism and the*

Historians' Debate, ed. and trans. S. W. Nicholsen (Cambridge: MIT Press, 1989), p. 24.

15. Peter Steinfels, "Michael Novak and his ultrasuper democraticapitalism," *Commonweal* 110, no. 1 (January 14, 1983): 11.

16. Habermas, *New Conservatism*, p. 24.

17. On the New York Intellectuals, see Terry A. Cooney, *The Rise of the New York Intellectuals: Partisan Review and Its Circle, 1934–1945* (Madison: University of Wisconsin Press, 1986); Alan M. Wald, *The New York Intellectuals: The Rise and Decline of the Anti-Stalinist Left from the 1930s to the 1980s* (Chapel Hill: University of North Carolina Press, 1987); Richard H. Pells, *The Liberal Mind in a Conservative Age: American Intellectuals in the 1940s and 1950s* (New York: Harper & Row, 1985); William Barrett, *The Truants: Adventures among the Intellectuals* (New York: Anchor Press, 1982); William Phillips, *A Partisan View: Five Decades of the Literary Life* (New York: Stein & Day, 1983); Alexander Bloom, *Prodigal Sons: The New York Intellectuals and Their World* (New York: Oxford University Press, 1986); Neil Jumonville, *Critical Crossings: The New York Intellectuals in Postwar America* (Berkeley: University of California Press, 1991).

18. Norman Podhoretz, interview with author, June 12, 1990.

19. Cf. Jeane Kirkpatrick, "Dictatorships and Double Standards," *Commentary* 68, no. 5 (November 1979).

20. Michael Massing, "Trotsky's Orphans: From Bolshevism to Reaganism," *New Republic* 196, no. 25 (June 22, 1987): 18–22.

21. On this theme, see Charles R. Kesler, "Jeane Kirkpatrick: Not Quite Right," *National Review* 34, no. 21 (October 29, 1982): 1341–1343; Adam Meyerson, "Welfare State Conservatism" (interview with Jeane Kirkpatrick), *Policy Review* 44 (Spring 1988): 2–6.

22. Quoted in Sidney Blumenthal, *The Rise of the Counter-Establishment: From Conservative Ideology to Political Power* (New York: Harper & Row), 1988, p. 154.

23. Russell Kirk, *The Neoconservatives: An Endangered Species*, The Heritage Lectures, no. 178 (Washington, D.C.: Heritage Foundation, 1988), pp. 1–10.

24. Stephen J. Tonsor, "Why I Too Am Not a Neoconservative," *National Review* 38, no. 11 (June 20, 1986): 55.

25. Paul Gottfried and Thomas Fleming, *The Conservative Movement* (Boston: Twayne Publishers, 1988), p. 73.

26. Clyde Wilson, "The Conservative Identity," *Intercollegiate Review* 21, no. 3, (Spring 1986): 66. This declaration was quoted repeatedly in the conservatives' offensive against neoconservatism. See Jeffrey Hart, "Gang Warfare in Chicago," *National Review* 38, no. 10 (June 6, 1986): 32; Gottfried and Fleming, *Conservative Movement*, p. 71.

27. Cf. James Burnham, *The Managerial Revolution: What Is Happening in the World* (New York: John Day, 1941); Milovan Djilas, *The New Class: An Analysis of the Communist System* (New York: Praeger, 1957).

28. Cf. Joseph Schumpeter, *Capitalism, Socialism and Democracy* (1942; reprint, New York: Harper & Brothers, 1950), pp. 131–155; F. A. Hayek, "The Intellectuals and Socialism," *University of Chicago Law Review,* Spring 1949.

29. David T. Bazelon, "The New Class," *Commentary* 42, no. 2 (August 1966); reprinted in Bazelon, *Power in America: The Politics of the New Class* (New York: New American Library, 1967), p. 308.

30. Cf. Bazelon, "The New Class" and "The Liberal American," in *Power in America,* pp. 309–332, 333–359.

31. Michael Harrington, *Toward a Democratic Left: A Radical Program for a New Majority* (New York: Macmillan, 1968), pp. 282–291.

32. Michael Novak, "Needing Niebuhr Again," *Commentary* 54, no. 3 (September 1972): 60–62.

33. Cf. Peter Steinfels, *The Neoconservatives: The Men Who Are Changing America's Politics* (New York: Simon & Schuster), 1979.

34. Cf. Daniel Bell, *The Cultural Contradictions of Capitalism* (New York: Basic Books, 1978), pp. xi–xv; Dinesh D'Souza, "Paddy, We Hardly Knew Ye: Daniel Patrick Moynihan Was Once the Great Neoconservative Hope," *Policy Review* 28 (Spring 1984): 42–49.

35. Cf. Daniel Patrick Moynihan, "The Professionalization of Reform," *Public Interest* 1 (Fall 1965): 6–16; Moynihan, *Maximum Feasible Misunderstanding* (New York: Free Press, 1970); Nathan Glazer, "The Limits of Social Policy," *Commentary* 52, no. 3 (September 1971); Glazer, "Reform Work, Not Welfare," *Public Interest* 40 (Summer 1975); Michael Crozier, Samuel P. Huntington, and Joji Watanuki, *The Crisis of Democracy: A Report on the Governability of Democracies to the Trilateral Commission* (New York: New York University Press, 1975).

36. Cf. George Gilder, "In Defense of Capitalists," *Commentary* 70, no. 6 (December 1980): 42–45; Gilder, "Welfare's 'New Consensus': The Collapse of the American Family," *Public Interest* 87 (Fall 1987): 20–25; Charles Murray, "The Two Wars Against Poverty: Economic Growth and the Great Society," *Public Interest* 69 (Fall 1982): 3–16; Murray, "Helping the Poor: A Few Modest Proposals," *Commentary* 79, no. 5 (May 1985): 27–34; Murray, "In Search of the Working Poor," *Public Interest* 89 (Fall 1987): 3–19; Murray, "The Coming of Custodial Democracy," *Commentary* 86, no. 3 (September 1988): 19–24.

37. Cf. Daniel Patrick Moynihan, "How America Blew It," *Newsweek,* December 10, 1990, p. 14; Moynihan, *Family and Nation* (New York: Harcourt Brace Jovanovich, 1986), pp. 86–101, 124–194.

38. Cf. Arch Puddington, "Jesse Jackson, the Blacks and American Foreign Policy," *Commentary* 77, no. 4 (April 1984); Carl Gershman, "The Rise and Fall of the New Foreign Policy Establishment," *Commentary* 70, no. 1 (July 1980); Penn Kemble, "The Democrats and the Kissinger Report," *Commentary* 77, no. 3 (March 1984); Joshua Muravchik, "Maximum Feasible Containment," *New Republic* 196, no. 22 (June 1, 1987).

39. Quoted in James Atlas, "The Changing World of New York Intellectuals," *New York Times Magazine,* August 25, 1985, p. 76.

Notes to Chapter 2

1. *Toward an American Revolutionary Labor Movement: A Statement of Programmatic Orientation by the American Workers Party* (New York: Provisional Organizing Committee of the American Workers Party, 1934), pp. 23–24.

2. Sidney Hook, *Towards the Understanding of Karl Marx: A Revolutionary Interpretation* (New York: John Day, 1933), p. 69.

3. Ibid., p. 114. Cf. Sidney Hook, *From Hegel to Marx: Studies in the Intellectual Development of Karl Marx* (New York: John Day, 1936), pp. 272–286.

4. Hook, *Towards the Understanding of Karl Marx*, p. 256.

5. Ibid., pp. 278–305.

6. Sidney Hook, "Why I Am a Communist: Communism without Dogmas," *Modern Monthly* 8, no. 3 (April 1934): 165.

7. Cf. Sidney Hook, "Workers' Democracy," *Modern Monthly* 8, no. 8 (October 1934).

8. Sidney Hook, *Out of Step: An Unquiet Life in the Twentieth Century* (New York: Carroll & Graf, 1987), p. 204; William Barrett, *The Truants: Adventures among the Intellectuals* (New York: Anchor Press, 1982), p. 89. On the origins of American Trotskyism, see Theodore Draper, *American Communism and Soviet Russia* (New York: Viking Press, 1960), pp. 357–376. On American Trotskyist leaders of the 1930s and 1940s, see Alan M. Wald, *The New York Intellectuals: The Rise and Decline of the Anti-Stalinist Left from the 1930s to the 1980s* (Chapel Hill: University of North Carolina Press, 1987), pp. 91–97, 164–192.

9. James Burnham and Philip Wheelwright, *Introduction to Philosophical Analysis* (New York: Henry Holt, 1932).

10. Cf. James Burnham, "On Defining Poetry," *Symposium* 1, no. 2 (April 1930): 221–230; Burnham, "Progress and Tradition," *Symposium* 1, no. 3 (July 1930): 349–360; Burnham, "Trying to Say," *Symposium* 2, no. 1 (January 1931): 51–59; Burnham, review of *The History of the Russian Revolution* by Leon Trotsky, *Symposium* 3, no. 2 (July 1932).

11. James Burnham, "Marxism and Esthetics," *Symposium* 4, no. 1 (January 1933): 3–29.

12. James Burnham, "Comment," *Symposium* 4, no. 4 (October 1933): 403–413. For an excellent discussion of Burnham's career from which I have drawn background information, see John P. Diggins, *Up from Communism: Conservative Odysseys in American Intellectual History* (New York: Harper & Row, 1975), pp. 163–169.

13. Quoted in Diggins, *Up from Communism*, p. 169.

14 Ibid., pp. 172–173. On the Trotskyists' manipulation of the Socialist party, see Daniel Bell, *Marxian Socialism in the United States* (1952; reprint, Princeton: Princeton University Press, 1967), pp. 174–176.

15. Cf. Leon Trotsky, *Their Morals and Ours: Marxist Versus Liberal Views on Morality* (New York: Pathfinder Press, 1973) (includes Trotsky's "Their Morals and Ours," *New International* 4, no. 6 [June 1938]; and John Dewey's "Means and Ends," *New International* 4, no. 8 [August 1938]); Dwight Macdonald, "Once More: Kronstadt," *New International* 4, no. 7 (July 1938): 211–214; Diggins, *Up*

from Communism, pp. 183–184; Mikhail Heller and Aleksandr M. Nekrich, *Utopia in Power: The History of the Soviet Union from 1917 to the Present*, trans. Phyllis B. Carlos (New York: Summit Books, 1986), pp. 107–110.

16. "Violence, For and Against" (symposium), *Common Sense* 7, no. 1 (January 1938): 19–21; quoted in Diggins, *Up from Communism*, p. 183.

17. James Burnham and Max Shachtman, "Intellectuals in Retreat," *New International* 5, no. 1 (January 1939): 5.

18. Cf. Sidney Hook, "Reflections on the Russian Revolution," *Southern Review*, Winter 1938–39, pp. 452–470. Hook believed, however, that the connections between Leninism and Stalinism were being overdrawn in the current moral denunciations of the Kronstadt massacre. The suppression of the Kronstadt sailors was unnecessarily savage, he allowed, but no more savage than Cromwell's or Sherman's actions under similar circumstances. Cf. Hook, "As a (Marxist) Professor Sees It," *Common Sense* 7, no. 1 (January 1938): 23.

19. Cf. Eugene Lyons, *Assignment in Utopia* (New York: Harcourt, Brace, and Co., 1937), p. 640.

20. Burnham and Shachtman, "Intellectuals in Retreat," p. 13.

21. Ibid., p. 14.

22. "Manifesto of the Committee for Cultural Freedom," reprinted in Hook, *Out of Step*, pp. 271–272.

23. For accounts of these debates, see Eugene Lyons, *The Red Decade* (1940; reprint, New York: Arlington House, 1970), pp. 345–349; Hook, *Out of Step*, pp. 259–271; Paul Berman, "The Last True Marxist Is a Neoconservative," *Voice Literary Supplement* 24 (March 1984): 10–12; David Caute, *The Fellow-Travellers: A Postscript to the Enlightenment* (New York: Macmillan, 1973), pp. 75–76.

24. Cf. Leon Trotsky, "The USSR in War," *New International* 5, no. 11 (November 1939): 325–332 (reprinted in Trotsky, *In Defense of Marxism: Against the Petty-Bourgeois Opposition* [New York: Merit Publishers, 1965], pp. 3–21; and in *The Basic Writings of Trotsky*, ed. Irving Howe [New York: Random House, 1963], pp. 305–314); Trotsky, "The Twin-Stars: Hitler–Stalin," "The World Situation and Perspectives," and "Stalin after the Finnish Experience," in *Writings of Leon Trotsky (1939–40)*, ed. Naomi Allen and George Breitman (New York: Pathfinder Press, 1973), pp. 113–124, 139–157, 160–164; Isaac Deutscher, *The Prophet Outcast: Trotsky, 1929–1940* (New York: Vintage Books, 1965), pp. 457–462.

25. James Burnham, "Science and Style: A Reply to Comrade Trotsky," reprinted in Trotsky, *In Defense of Marxism*, pp. 187–206.

26. Quoted in Adam Westoby, Introduction to *The Bureaucratization of the World* by Bruno Rizzi, trans. Adam Westoby (1939; reprint, New York: Free Press, 1985), p. 30.

27. Cf. Karl Marx, "On Bakunin's *Statism and Anarchy*," in *Karl Marx: Selected Writings*, ed. David McLellan (Oxford: Oxford University Press, 1977), pp. 561–563; Leszek Kolakowski, *Main Currents of Marxism: Its Rise, Growth, and Dissolution*, vol. 1, *The Founders*, trans. P. S. Falla (Oxford: Clarendon Press, 1978), pp. 246–256; George Woodcock, *Anarchism: A History of Libertarian Ideas and Movements* (Cleveland: World Publishing, 1962).

28. Cf. Max Nomad, *Rebels and Renegades* (1932; reprint, Freeport, N.Y.: Books for Libraries Press, 1968); Nomad, *Apostles of Revolution* (1939; reprint, New York: Collier Books, 1961).

29. Quoted in Leon Trotsky, "Not a Workers' and Not a Bourgeois State?" in *Writings of Leon Trotsky (1937–38)* (New York: Pathfinder Press, 1970), pp. 60–71. Burnham and Carter's amendment was published in *Socialist Workers Party Bulletin* 2 (1937).

30. Trotsky, "Not a Workers' and Not a Bourgeois State?" pp. 64–67.

31. Ibid., pp. 61–67; cf. Leon Trotsky, "Once Again on the 'Crisis of Marxism,'" in *Writings of Leon Trotsky (1938–39)* (New York: Pathfinder Press, 1974), pp. 204–206; Trotsky, "Bureaucratism and the Revolution" and "Is the Bureaucracy a Ruling Class?" in *Basic Writings of Trotsky*, pp. 170–177, 216–222; Trotsky, "A Petty-Bourgeois Opposition in the Socialist Workers Party," reprinted in Trotsky, *In Defense of Marxism*, pp. 43–62.

32. Bruno Rizzi, *The Bureaucratization of the World*, trans. Adam Westoby (1939; reprint, New York: Free Press, 1985), p. 50.

33. Ibid., p. 56.

34. Leon Trotsky, "The USSR in War," reprinted in Trotsky, *In Defense of Marxism*, p. 10.

35. Max Shachtman, untitled essay written in 1940, reprinted in Shachtman, *Bureaucratic Revolution: The Rise of the Stalinist State* (New York: Ronald Press, 1962); also reprinted under the title "Stalinism: A New Social Order" in *Essential Works of Socialism*, ed. Irving Howe (New Haven: Yale University Press, 1976), pp. 526–546. Cf. Leon Trotsky, "Socialism in a Separate Country?" printed as Appendix 2 in Trotsky, *The History of the Russian Revolution*, trans. Max Eastman (1932; reprint, New York: Monad Press, 1980), pp. 378–418; Trotsky, "A Letter to Max Shachtman," reprinted in Trotsky, *In Defense of Marxism*, pp. 37–41. Trotsky's critique of Shachtman and Burnham's appropriation of the theory of bureaucratic collectivism is contained in "The USSR in War," reprinted in Trotsky, *In Defense of Marxism*, pp. 3–21.

36. On Shachtman's later career and his theory of bureaucratic collectivism, see Julius Jacobson, "The Two Deaths of Max Shachtman," *New Politics* 10, no. 2 (Winter 1973): 96–99; Tom Kahn, "Max Shachtman: His Ideals and His Movement," *New America* 10, no. 22 (November 16, 1972): 5; Irving Howe, *A Margin of Hope: An Intellectual Autobiography* (New York: Harcourt Brace Jovanovich, 1982), pp. 40–55; Michael Harrington, *Fragments of the Century* (New York: Saturday Review Press, 1972), pp. 67–75; Maurice Isserman, *If I Had a Hammer . . . : The Death of the Old Left and the Birth of the New Left* (New York: Basic Books, 1987), pp. 37–75; Wald, *New York Intellectuals*, pp. 182–192, 280–284.

37. James Burnham, "Letter of Resignation of James Burnham from the Workers Party," reprinted in Trotsky, *In Defense of Marxism*, pp. 207–211.

38. James Burnham, *The Managerial Revolution: What Is Happening in the World* (New York: John Day, 1941), p. 7.

39. The first to accuse Burnham of plagiarizing Rizzi's book was Joseph Hansen, a leading Trotskyist official and secretary/bodyguard for Trotsky.

Hansen's review of *The Managerial Revolution* (in June 1941) was written in the bitter aftermath of Burnham's resignation from the Trotskyist movement, however. His assumption that Burnham obtained a copy of *La Bureaucratisation du Monde* before writing his own book was never proven. Though Rizzi conducted a brief correspondence with Burnham in the early 1950s, he angrily maintained for the rest of his life that Burnham plagiarized his book. Max Nomad similarly charged that Burnham, though "a professor of ethics," gave no credit to his predecessors— including Machajski and himself. See Nomad, *Aspects of Revolt* (New York: Bookman Associates, 1959), p. 15; Daniel Bell, "The Strange Tale of Bruno R.," *New Leader* 42, no. 35 (September 28, 1959): 19; Westoby, Introduction to *Bureaucratization of the World*, pp. 24–26.

40. Burnham, *Managerial Revolution*, p. 73.

41. Ibid., p. 201.

42. Ibid., pp. 172–176.

43. Ibid., p. 246.

44. James Burnham, "The Sixth Turn of the Communist Screw," *Partisan Review* 11, no. 3 (Summer 1944): 366.

45. Burnham, *Managerial Revolution*, p. 36.

46. Quoted in Diggins, *Up from Communism*, p. 305; citation from James Burnham, "Is Democracy Possible?" in *Whose Revolution? A Study of the Future Course of Liberalism in the United States*, ed. Irving DeWitt Talmadge (Westport, Conn.: Hyperion Press, 1941), pp. 187–217.

47. James Burnham, *The Machiavellians: Defenders of Freedom* (New York: John Day, 1943), p. 208.

48. Ibid., p. 225.

49. Ibid., pp. 228–229.

50. Ibid., p. 242.

51. Ibid., p. 269.

52. Cf. Diggins, *Up from Communism*, pp. 312–315; Sheldon Wolin, *Politics and Vision: Continuity and Innovation in Western Political Thought* (Boston: Little Brown, 1960), p. 217; J.G.A. Pocock, "Machiavelli in the Liberal Cosmos," *Political Theory* 13, no. 4 (November 1985): 559–574.

53. Diggins, *Up from Communism*, p. 191.

54. James Burnham, "Lenin's Heir," *Partisan Review* 12, no. 1 (Winter 1945): 64, 72.

55. Ibid., pp. 66–67.

56. Ibid., pp. 61–62.

57. Cf. Lionel Abel, "Stalin's Advocate," *Politics* 2, no. 5 (May 1945): 146–148; Dwight Macdonald, "Beat Me Daddy," *Partisan Review* 12, no. 2 (Spring 1945): pp. 181–187.

58. Burnham, "Lenin's Heir," p. 70.

59. Macdonald, "Beat Me Daddy," pp. 181–187.

60. For an account of his conversion, see Dwight Macdonald, *Memoirs of a Revolutionist: Essays in Political Criticism* (New York: Farrar, Straus & Cudahy, 1957), pp. 17–31.

61. George Orwell, "Second Thoughts on James Burnham" (1946), reprinted in Orwell, *Collected Essays* (London: Secker & Warburg, 1961), pp. 382–383.

62. Ibid., pp. 370, 381.

63. Ibid., pp. 389–392.

64. James Burnham, *The Struggle for the World* (New York: John Day, 1947), p. 7.

65. Ibid., pp. 5–7.

66. Ibid., pp. 9–13.

67. Ibid., p. 59.

68. Ibid., p. 53.

69. Ibid., pp. 96–108.

70. Ibid., pp. 183–184.

71. Ibid., pp. 136–143.

72. Ibid., p. 182.

73. Ibid., p. 248.

74. James Burnham, *The Coming Defeat of Communism* (New York: John Day, 1949), p. 27.

75. On the counter-conference by Hook's group ("Americans for Intellectual Freedom") and the founding of the American Committee for Cultural Freedom, see Peter Coleman, *The Liberal Conspiracy: The Congress for Cultural Freedom and the Struggle for the Mind of Postwar Europe* (New York: Free Press, 1989), pp. 5–8; Alexander Bloom, *Prodigal Sons: The New York Intellectuals and Their World* (New York: Oxford University Press, 1986), pp. 259–264; Hook, *Out of Step*, pp. 382–396.

76. Coleman, *Liberal Conspiracy*, pp. 30–32; Hook, *Out of Step*, pp. 432–444.

77. Quoted in William L. O'Neill, *A Better World: The Great Schism: Stalinism and the American Intellectuals* (New York: Simon & Schuster, 1982), p. 298.

78. Arthur M. Schlesinger, Jr., *The Vital Center: The Politics of Freedom* (Boston: Houghton Mifflin, 1949); Michael Harrington, "Liberalism—A Moral Crisis: The Committee for Cultural Freedom," *Dissent* 2, no. 2 (Spring 1955): 114–115, 121–122; Irving Howe, "This Age of Conformity," *Partisan Review* 21, no. 1 (January/February 1954) (reprinted in Howe, *Steady Work: Essays in the Politics of Democratic Radicalism, 1953–1966* [New York: Harcourt, Brace & World, 1966], pp. 324–329); Richard H. Pells, *The Liberal Mind in a Conservative Age: American Intellectuals in the 1940s and 1950s* (New York: Harper & Row, 1985), pp. 339–345.

79. Cf. Medford Evans, *The Secret Fight for the A-Bomb* (Chicago: Henry Regnery, 1953). For Burnham's own account of the evidence for scientific espionage, see James Burnham, *The Web of Subversion: Underground Networks in the U.S. Government* (New York: John Day, 1954).

80. Quoted in Diggins, *Up from Communism*, p. 329.

81. James Burnham, "Notes on the CIA Shambles," *National Review* 19, no. 11 (March 21, 1967).

82. Rahv quoted in Barrett, *The Truants: Adventures among the Intellectuals*, p. 195.

83. Cf. Norman Podhoretz, *The Present Danger: Do We Have the Will to Reverse the*

Decline of American Power? (New York: Simon & Schuster, 1980), pp. 17–24, 96–101; Michael Novak, "Mr. X Abandons Containment: George Kennan Loses His Nerve," *Catholicism in Crisis* 4, no. 4 (April 1986): 28–31.

84. X [George Kennan], "The Sources of Soviet Conduct," *Foreign Affairs* 25, no. 4 (July 1947): 576.

85. Ibid., pp. 579–580.

86. James Burnham, *Containment or Liberation? An Inquiry into the Aims of United States Foreign Policy* (New York: John Day, 1953), pp. 32–43 (quote on p. 38).

87. Text quoted in David Mayers, *George Kennan and the Dilemmas of U.S. Foreign Policy* (New York: Oxford University Press, 1988), p. 99.

88. All of Burnham's books contain Machiavellian asides about the tactics of political rule, and his approach to domestic politics remained essentially Machiavellian. See James Burnham, *Congress and the American Tradition* (Chicago: Henry Regnery, 1959).

89. Burnham, *Containment or Liberation?* p. 48. For Burnham's assessment of what he called the "Kennan–de Gaulle–Morgenthau–Lippmann approach," see James Burnham, *The War We Are In: The Last Decade and the Next* (New Rochelle, N.Y.: Arlington House, 1967), pp. 61–63.

90. Burnham, *Containment or Liberation?* pp. 42–43.

91. Ibid., pp. 41–42.

92. Ibid., pp. 217–218.

93. Arthur M. Schlesinger, Jr., "Middle-Aged Man with a Horn," *New Republic* 128, no. 11 (March 16, 1953): 16–17; cited in Diggins, *Up from Communism*, p. 331.

94. James Burnham, "The President and the Professor," *National Review* 1, no. 2 (November 26, 1955): 27–28.

95. Cf. Burnham, *The War We Are In*, pp. 53–60; Burnham, "Sino-Soviet Sense and Nonsense," *National Review* 14, no. 2 (January 15, 1963): 16; Burnham, "Nikita Krushchev: Maoist," *National Review* 16, no. 30 (July 28, 1964): 644.

96. James Burnham, "Who Shall Be Master?" *National Review* 16, no. 32 (August 11, 1964): 688.

97. James Burnham, "Sighting the Target," *National Review* 2, no. 31 (December 22, 1956); cf. Burnham, *The War We Are In*, pp. 114–116.

98. Cf. Frank Meyer, *The Conservative Mainstream* (New Rochelle, N.Y.: Arlington House, 1969), pp. 319–327; Burnham, *The War We Are In*, p. 108.

99. Burnham, *The War We Are In*, pp. 128–130; Burnham, "The Choking Point," *National Review* 12, no. 12 (March 27, 1962): 203.

100. James Burnham, "Toujours, La Sale Guerre," *National Review* 14, no. 4 (January 29, 1963): 60.

101. James Burnham, "Who Gives a Whoop?" *National Review* 14, no. 14 (April 9, 1963): 279.

102. James Burnham, "Crumbling Line," *National Review* 16, no. 24 (June 16, 1964): 493.

103. James Burnham, "The Perils of Under-Simplification," *National Review* 16, no. 36 (September 8, 1964).

104. James Burnham, "Why Rhodesia?" *National Review* 29, no. 32 (August 19, 1977): 935.

105. James Burnham, "The Kissinger–Sonnenfeldt Doctrine: III," *National Review* 28, no. 21 (June 11, 1976): 611.

106. Quoted in Richard Brookhiser, "James Burnham: A Hard Man to Snooker," *National Review* 37, no. 25 (December 31, 1985): 63.

107. Cf. James Burnham, "The Whipping Boys Club," *National Review* 23, no. 23 (January 25, 1976); Burnham, "Do-Good as Foreign Policy," *National Review* 29, no. 1 (January 7, 1977): 23.

108. Burnham, *The War We Are In*, p. 61.

109. On Burnham's recognition in later life, see John B. Judis, "Apocalypse Now and Then," *New Republic* 197, no. 9 (August 31, 1987): 29; Sidney Blumenthal, "Dateline Washington: The Conservative Crackup," *Foreign Policy* 69 (Winter 1987–88): 169–170.

110. Hook, *Out of Step*, p. 605.

111. Burnham's *The Web of Subversion* was reissued by the John Birch Society in 1961 in its American Opinion series.

112. Hook, *Out of Step*, pp. 600–601.

113. James Burnham, *Suicide of the West: An Essay on the Meaning and Destiny of Liberalism* (1964; reprint, Washington, D.C.: Regnery Gateway, 1985), p. 150.

114. Cf. Sidney Hook, "Stanford Documents: An Open Letter to the Stanford University Faculty Senate," *Partisan Review* 55, no. 4 (Fall 1988): 653–659; Hook, *Out of Step*, p. 598.

115. Arthur Schlesinger, Jr., "A Life at the Barricades," *New Republic* 196, no. 18 (May 4, 1987): 30–31.

Notes to Chapter 3

1. Quoted in Sidney Blumenthal, *The Rise of the Counter-Establishment: From Conservative Ideology to Political Power* (New York: Harper & Row, 1988), p. 154.

2. Quoted in Alexander Bloom, *Prodigal Sons: The New York Intellectuals and Their World* (New York: Oxford University Press, 1986), p. 372.

3. David Stockman, *The Triumph of Politics: How the Reagan Revolution Failed* (New York: Harper & Row, 1986). Stockman subsequently reduced Kristol to a purveyor of "intellectual sophistry" (p. 405). For Kristol's rebuttal, see Irving Kristol, "The David I Knew," *Wall Street Journal*, May 9, 1986.

4. For accounts of the careers of Kristol's classmates, see Alan M. Wald, *The New York Intellectuals: The Rise and Decline of the Anti-Stalinist Left from the 1930s to the 1980s* (Chapel Hill: University of North Carolina Press, 1987); Richard H. Pells, *The Liberal Mind in a Conservative Age: American Intellecuals in the 1940s and 1950s* (New York: Harper & Row, 1985); Neil Jumonville, *Critical Crossings: The New York Intellectuals in Postwar America* (Berkeley: University of California Press, 1991); and Irving Howe, "The New York Intellectuals: A Chronicle and Critique," *Commentary* 46, no. 4 (October 1968): 29–51.

5. Bloom, *Prodigal Sons*, p. 36; Irving Howe, *A Margin of Hope: An Intellectual Autobiography* (San Diego: Harcourt Brace Jovanovich, 1982), p. 12.

6. Howe, *A Margin of Hope*, p. 56.

7. Quoted in Walter Goodman, "Irving Kristol: Patron Saint of the New Right," *New York Times Magazine*, December 6, 1981, p. 200.

8. Irving Kristol, "Memoirs of a Trotskyist," *New York Times Magazine*, January 23, 1977; reprinted in Kristol, *Reflections of a Neoconservative: Looking Back, Looking Ahead* (New York: Basic Books, 1983), p. 12.

9. Howe, *A Margin of Hope*, p. 34; Peter Coleman, *The Liberal Conspiracy: The Congress for Cultural Freedom and the Struggle for the Mind of Postwar Europe* (New York: Free Press, 1989), p. 62.

10. Kristol, *Reflections of a Neoconservative*, p. 5.

11. Cf. William Ferry, "Other People's Nerve," *Enquiry* 1, no. 4 (May 1943): 3–6.

12. Kristol, *Reflections of a Neoconservative*, p. 4.

13. Irving Kristol, interview with author, March 21, 1990.

14. Irving Kristol, "Second Thoughts: A Generational Perspective," in *Second Thoughts: Former Radicals Look Back at the Sixties*, ed. Peter Collier and David Horowitz (Lanham, Md.: Madison Books, 1989), p. 184.

15. Kristol, interview with author, March 21, 1990.

16. Cf. Irving Kristol, "Adam and I: A Story," *Commentary* 2, no. 5 (November 1946): 448–451; Kristol, "In Hillel's Steps," *Commentary* 3, no. 2 (February 1947): 191–192 (review of Victor Gollancz, *In Darkest Germany*); Kristol, "The Myth of the Supra-Human Jew: The Theological Stigma," *Commentary* 4, no. 2 (August 1947): 226–233.

17. Michael Harrington, "The Committee for Cultural Freedom," *Dissent* 2, no. 2 (Spring 1955): 116.

18. Irving Kristol, "The New York Intellectuals," *Commentary* 47, no. 1 (January 1969): 14.

19. Irving Kristol, " 'Civil Liberties': 1952—A Study in Confusion," *Commentary* 13, no. 3 (March 1952): 233–234.

20. Ibid., p. 236.

21. It is often forgotten that even the *Nation* was not monolithic on the subject. While the front of the magazine regularly featured the fellow-traveling procommunist politics of Freda Kirchway, Carey McWilliams, and J. Alvarez del Vayo, the cultural section featured anti-Stalinists such as Clement Greenberg and Randall Jarrell.

22. Kristol, " 'Civil Liberties': 1952," p. 231.

23. Cf. Norman Thomas, *A Socialist's Faith* (New York: W. W. Norton, 1951), pp. 36–47.

24. Norman Thomas, "Letters from Readers: 'Civil Liberties': 1952," *Commentary* 13, no. 5 (May 1952): 492–493.

25. Kristol, " 'Civil Liberties': 1952," p. 236.

26. Ibid., p. 233.

27. Cf. Alan Barth, *The Loyalty of Free Men* (New York: Viking Press, 1951),

pp. 23–30 (quotation on p. 24); Joseph Rauh, "Letters from Readers: 'Civil Liberties': 1952," *Commentary* 13, no. 5 (May 1952): 493–494.

28. Kristol, " 'Civil Liberties': 1952," p. 234.

29. Rauh, "Letters from Readers: 'Civil Liberties': 1952," p. 494.

30. Irving Kristol, "Mr. Kristol Comments," *Commentary* 13, no. 5 (May 1952): 500.

31. Arthur Schlesinger, Jr., "Letters from Readers: Liberty and the Liberal," *Commentary* 13, no. 7 (July 1952): 83.

32. Ibid., p. 84.

33. Kristol, " 'Civil Liberties': 1952," p. 231; cf. Kristol, "Liberty and the Communists," *Partisan Review* 19, no. 4 (July/August 1952): 493–496.

34. Cf. William L. O'Neill, *A Better World: The Great Schism: Stalinism and the American Intellectuals* (New York: Simon & Schuster, 1982), pp. 138–211; Pells, *Liberal Mind in a Conservative Age*, pp. 96–147.

35. Cf. Coleman, *Liberal Conspiracy*, p. 17.

36. Ibid., p. 27.

37. The main *New York Times* article reporting CIA funding of the Congress appeared on April 27, 1966, and contained only a brief reference to *Encounter*. CIA subsidies to *Encounter* ran from 1953 to 1964, and subsidies to the Congress continued until 1966. For accounts of the reporting of this story, see Harrison E. Salisbury, *Without Fear or Favor: The New York Times and its Times* (New York: Times Books, 1980), pp. 514–528; Jason Epstein, "The CIA and the Intellectuals," *New York Review of Books* 8, no. 7 (April 20, 1967).

38. Daniel Bell, "Liberal Anti-Communism Revisited" (symposium), *Commentary* 44, no. 3 (September 1967): 36–39.

39. Papers delivered at the Milan Conference in 1955, for example, included Raymond Aron's "Nations and Ideologies," Michael Polanyi's "On Liberalism and Liberty," and "Stuart Hampshire's "In Defense of Radicalism," published respectively in the January, March, and August 1955 issues of *Encounter*. For an insider's account of the Congress's conferences in the 1950s, see Bell, "Liberal Anti-Communism Revisited."

40. For an excellent overview of the Congress's publications, see Coleman, *Liberal Conspiracy*, pp. 81–102, 183–197.

41. Irving Kristol, "After the Apocalypse," *Encounter* 1, no. 1 (October 1953): 1 (unsigned editorial).

42. Quoted in Coleman, *Liberal Conspiracy*, p. 74.

43. Ibid., pp. 74–75.

44. Quoted in Bloom, *Prodigal Sons*, p. 266.

45. Quoted in O'Neill, *A Better World*, p. 304.

46. The Congress's European leaders often complained about what they regarded as the simplistic belligerence of "the obnoxious Americans" in the ACCF. For discussions of the complaint, see Coleman, *Liberal Conspiracy*, pp. 159–170; Hook, *Out of Step*, pp. 423–431.

47. Cf. Bloom, *Prodigal Sons*, p. 266; Coleman, *Liberal Conspiracy*, p. 76.

48. Diana Trilling, *We Must March My Darlings: A Critical Decade* (New York: Harcourt Brace Jovanovich, 1978), pp. 60–61.

49. Cf. Letters Section, *The New York Times*, May 9, 1966; the editorial appeared the following day.

50. The *Encounter* attack on O'Brien appeared in the "R" Column (written by Goronwy Rees) in *Encounter* 27, no. 2 (August 1966): 41–44. The key sections of O'Brien's lecture (published in *Book Week*) were fully reprinted in Rees's article.

51. Cf. Sol Stern, "NSA and the CIA: A Short Account of International Student Politics and the Cold War with Particular Reference to the NSA, CIA, Etc.," *Ramparts* 5, no. 9 (March 1967): 29–38. In its June 1967 issue, *Encounter* published an apology to O'Brien that read, in part, "We acknowledge that this article contained implications against the character and integrity of Dr. O'Brien which were unwarranted and we wish unreservedly to withdraw them and to apologise to Dr. O'Brien for having made them" (p. 49). For accounts of this episode, see Christopher Lasch, "The Cultural Cold War: A Short History of the Congress for Cultural Freedom," in *Towards a New Past: Dissenting Essays in American History*, ed. Barton Bernstein (New York: Pantheon, 1968), 322–359; and Coleman, *Liberal Conspiracy*, pp. 219–234 (Josselson quotation on p. 226).

52. Thomas Braden, "I'm Glad the CIA Is 'Immoral,' " *Saturday Evening Post*, May 20, 1967, p. 10.

53. Peter Steinfels, *The Neoconservatives: The Men Who Are Changing America's Politics* (New York: Simon & Schuster, 1979), p. 85; Kristol quoted in Bloom, *Prodigal Sons*, p. 267.

54. Quoted in Bloom, *Prodigal Sons*, p. 267.

55. Stephen Spender, "Liberal Anti-Communism Revisited" (symposium), *Commentary* 44, no. 3 (September 1967): 73.

56. Kristol later dismissed Braden's article as the work of a "publicity-hungry columnist." Cf. Irving Kristol, "The Way We Were," *National Interest* 17 (Fall 1989): 72.

57. Irving Kristol, "Memoirs of a 'Cold Warrior,' " *New York Times Magazine*, February 11, 1968; reprinted in Kristol, *Reflections of a Neoconservative*, p. 16.

58. Ibid., p. 17.

59. Ibid., pp. 17–18.

60. Steinfels, *The Neoconservatives*, p. 87.

61. Quoted in Goodman, "Irving Kristol: Patron Saint of the New Right," p. 202; and Bloom, *Prodigal Sons*, p. 328.

62. Kristol, interview with author, March 21, 1990.

63. Michael Harrington, *The Other America: Poverty in the United States* (New York: Macmillan, 1962), p. 202.

64. Daniel Bell and Irving Kristol, "What Is the Public Interest?" *Public Interest* 1 (Fall 1965): 4.

65. Cf. Nathan Glazer, "Housing Problems and Housing Policies," *Public Interest* 7 (Spring 1967): 21–51; Aaron Wildavsky, "The Political Economy of Efficiency," *Public Interest* 8 (Summer 1967): 30–48; James Q. Wilson, "The

Bureaucracy Problem," *Public Interest* 6 (Winter 1967): 3–9; Wilson, "The Urban Unease: Community vs. City," *Public Interest* 12 (Summer 1968): 25–39.

66. Daniel P. Moynihan, "A Crisis of Confidence," *Public Interest* 7 (Spring 1967): 3–10; John H. Bunzel, "Black Studies at San Francisco State," *Public Interest* 13 (Fall 1968): 22–38.

67. Kristol, interview with author, March 21, 1990.

68. Steinfels, *The Neoconservatives*, pp. 95–96.

69. Cf. Irving Kristol, "The Politics of 'Stylish Frustration,' " *New Leader* 46, no. 7 (April 1, 1963): 9–11; Kristol, "One Man, One Vote," *New Leader* 46, no. 13 (June 24, 1963): 12–14; Kristol, "Age of the Remittance-Man," *New Leader* 46, no. 16 (August 5, 1963): 10–11; Kristol, "Facing the Facts in Vietnam," *New Leader* 46, no. 20 (September 30, 1963): 7–8; Kristol, "On Literary Politics," *New Leader* 47, no. 20 (August 3, 1964): 10–11; Kristol, "The Poverty of Equality," *New Leader* 48, no. 5 (March 1, 1965): 15–16.

70. Joseph Epstein, "The New Conservatives: Intellectuals in Retreat," in *The New Conservatives: A Critique from the Left*, ed. Lewis A. Coser and Irving Howe (New York: New American Library, 1977), pp. 22–23.

71. Kristol, "Facing the Facts in Vietnam," pp. 7–8.

72. Irving Kristol, "A New Isolationism? Letter from New York," *Encounter* 26, no. 6 (June 1966): 52.

73. Ibid.

74. Ibid.

75. Irving Kristol, "Teaching In, Speaking Out: The Controversy over Viet Nam," *Encounter* 25, no. 2 (August 1965): 66, 68.

76. Ibid., p. 67.

77. Ibid., p. 68.

78. Ibid.

79. Kristol, "Facing the Facts in Vietnam," p. 8. Cf. Kristol, "New Right, New Left," *Public Interest* 4 (Summer 1966).

80. Irving Kristol, "American Intellectuals and Foreign Policy," *Foreign Affairs* 45, no. 4 (July 1967); reprinted in Kristol, *On the Democratic Idea in America* (New York: Harper & Row, 1972), p. 88.

81. Kristol, "Teaching In, Speaking Out," p. 69.

82. Kristol, "American Intellectuals and Foreign Policy," *Foreign Affairs* 45 (July 1967); reprinted in Kristol, *On the Democratic Idea in America*, p. 69.

83. Ibid., pp. 69–74.

84. Cf. Irving Kristol, "The Adversary Culture of Intellectuals," *Encounter* 53, no. 4 (October 1979); reprinted in Kristol, *Reflections of a Neoconservative*, pp. 27–42; and Kristol, "The Troublesome Intellectuals," *Public Interest* 2 (Winter 1966).

85. Lionel Trilling, *Beyond Culture* (New York: Scribner's, 1955), pp. 14–15.

86. Cf. David Bazelon, *Power in America: The Politics of the New Class* (New York: New American Library, 1967); B. Bruce-Biggs, ed., *The New Class?* (New Brunswick, N.J.: Transaction Books, 1979).

87. Irving Kristol, "Business and the 'New Class,' " *Wall Street Journal*, 1970;

reprinted in Kristol, *Two Cheers for Capitalism* (New York: Basic Books, 1978), p. 28.

88. Ibid., pp. 29–30.

89. Irving Kristol, "About Equality," *Commentary* 54, no. 5 (November 1972); reprinted in Kristol, *Two Cheers for Capitalism*, p. 177.

90. Irving Kristol, "On Corporate Capitalism in America," *Public Interest* 41 (Fall 1972): 124–141; reprinted in *The American Commonwealth—1976*, ed. Nathan Glazer and Irving Kristol (New York: Basic Books, 1976); Kristol, *Two Cheers for Capitalism* (quotation on p. 16); Kristol, *Reflections of a Neoconservative* (quotation on p. 212).

91. Kristol, *Two Cheers for Capitalism*, p. 16; Kristol, *Reflections of a Neoconservative*, p. 212.

92. Vosol Rogat, "I'm All Right, Dick," *New York Review of Books* 19, no. 4 (September 21, 1972): 6–8; cited in Steinfels, *The Neoconservatives*, p. 106.

93. Kristol, "About Equality," in *Two Cheers for Capitalism*, p. 177.

94. Ibid., p. 184.

95. For an exaggerated neo-Hegelian form of a similar argument, see Francis Fukuyama, "The End of History?" *National Interest* 16 (Summer 1989): 3–18.

96. Cf. Michael Walzer, *Spheres of Justice: A Defense of Pluralism and Equality* (New York: Basic Books, 1983), pp. 3–30; Walzer, "Nervous Liberals," *New York Review of Books* 26, no. 15 (1979); reprinted in Walzer, *Radical Principles: Reflections of an Unreconstructed Democrat* (New York: Basic Books, 1980), pp. 92–106.

97. Kristol, "About Equality," in *Two Cheers for Capitalism*, p. 183.

98. Walzer, *Spheres of Justice*, p. xiii; cf. Walzer, "In Defense of Equality," in *The New Conservatives: A Critique from the Left*, ed. Coser and Howe, pp. 108–114.

99. Steinfels, *The Neoconservatives*, p. 88.

100. Irving Kristol, "On Corporate Philanthropy," *Wall Street Journal*, March 21, 1977; reprinted as American Enterprise Institute pamphlet no. 65 (Washington, D.C.: American Enterprise Institute, April 1977); also reprinted in Kristol, *Two Cheers for Capitalism*, pp. 143–144.

101. Irving Kristol, "On 'Economic Education,'" in *Two Cheers for Capitalism*, pp. 100–101.

102. Irving Kristol, "Conservatives' Greatest Enemy May Be the GOP," *Wall Street Journal*, February 20, 1990; cf. Kristol, "American Universities in Exile," *Wall Street Journal*, June 17, 1986.

103. Kristol, "On Corporate Philanthropy," in *Two Cheers for Capitalism*, p. 145.

104. Blumenthal, *Rise of the Counter-Establishment*, p. 148.

105. Goodman, "Irving Kristol: Patron Saint of the New Right," p. 207.

106. Wanniski quoted in Blumenthal, *Rise of the Counter-Establishment*, p. 148; Weigel quoted in Jacob Weisberg, "Hunter Gatherers," *New Republic* 205, no. 10 (September 2, 1991): 15. On Kristol's corporate connections, see John S. Saloma III, *Ominous Politics: The New Conservative Labyrinth* (New York: Hill & Wang, 1984), pp. 9–11, 34–35, 42, 65; Goodman, "Irving Kristol: Patron Saint of the New Right," p. 207; Jon Wiener, "Dollars for Neocon Scholars: The Olin Money

Tree," *Nation* 250, no. 1 (January 1, 1990): 12–14; Geoffrey Norman, "The Godfather of Neoconservatism (and His Family)," *Esquire* 91, no. 3 (February 13, 1979): 37–38.

107. Blumenthal, *Rise of the Counter-Establishment*, pp. 148, 159; Wiener, "Dollars for Neocon Scholars," p. 12.

108. Kristol, interview with author, March 21, 1990.

109. Cf. Irving Kristol, "Confessions of a True, Self-Confessed—Perhaps the Only—'Neoconservative,'" *Public Opinion* 2, no. 5 (October/November 1979); reprinted in Kristol, *Reflections of a Neoconservative*, pp. 73–77.

110. Blumenthal, *Rise of the Counter-Establishment*, pp. 147–148; cf. Irving Kristol, "The Trouble with Republicans," *Wall Street Journal*, August 22, 1988.

111. Kristol, *Reflections of a Neoconservative*, pp. xiv–xv.

112. Cf. Steinfels, *The Neoconservatives*, pp. 188–194.

113. Kristol, *Reflections of a Neoconservative*, p. xiv.

114. Cf. Michael Oakeshott, *Rationalism in Politics* (New York: Basic Books, 1962); Oakeshott, *On Human Conduct* (Oxford: Clarendon Press, 1975); Paul Franco, "Michael Oakeshott as Liberal Theorist," *Political Theory* 18, no. 3 (August 1990): 411–436.

115. Kristol, *Reflections of a Neoconservative*, pp. ix, x.

116. Ibid., p. x.

117. Ibid., p. vi.

118. Ibid., p. xi.

119. Irving Kristol, "What Is a Liberal — Who Is a Conservative?" *Commentary* 62, no. 3 (September 1976).

120. Irving Kristol, "Adam Smith and the Spirit of Capitalism," in *The Great Ideas Today: 1976*, ed. Robert M. Hutchins and Mortimer J. Adler (Chicago: Encyclopedia Britannica, 1976); reprinted in Kristol, *Reflections of a Neoconservative*, pp. 168–169.

121. Kristol, *Reflections of a Neoconservative*, p. xi.

122. Kristol, "Adam Smith and the Spirit of Capitalism," in *Reflections of a Neoconservative*, p. 169.

123. Irving Kristol, "'When Virtue Loses All Her Loveliness'—Some Reflections on Capitalism and the 'Free Society,'" *Public Interest* 21 (Fall 1970); reprinted in Kristol, *On the Democratic Idea in America*, pp. 96–97, and Kristol, *Two Cheers for Capitalism*, pp. 261–262.

124. Robert Glasgow, "Interview with Irving Kristol," *Psychology Today* 7, no. 9 (February 4, 1974): 80; Kristol, "Adam Smith and the Spirit of Capitalism," pp. 175–176.

125. Kristol, "Adam Smith and the Spirit of Capitalism," p. 173.

126. Ibid., p. 176.

127. Adam Smith, *An Inquiry into the Nature and Causes of the Wealth of Nations*, ed. Edwin Cannan (Chicago: University of Chicago Press, 1976), pp. 309–338.

128. Kristol, "Adam Smith and the Spirit of Capitalism," p. 154.

129. Cf. Robert Bellah, "The Economics Pastoral, a Year Later," *Commonweal* 114, no. 22 (December 18, 1987): 739–740.

130. Adam Smith, *The Theory of Moral Sentiments*, ed. D. D. Raphael and A. L. Macfie (Indianapolis, Ind.: Liberty Classics, 1982), pp. 312–313.

131. Ibid., p. 223.

132. Ibid., p. 220. For a more extended discussion of Kristol's interpretation of the "Anglo-Scottish Enlightenment," see Nicholas Xenos, "Neoconservatism Kristolized," *Salmagundi* 74–75 (Spring/Summer 1987): 138–149.

133. Harold Laski, *The Rise of Liberalism: The Philosophy of a Business Civilization* (New York: Harper & Brothers, 1936), pp. 204–205.

134. Kristol, "Adam Smith and the Spirit of Capitalism," pp. 160–161.

135. Cf. Xenos, "Neoconservatism Kristolized," p. 146.

136. Irving Kristol, "Some Personal Reflections on Economic Well-Being and Income Distribution," in *The American Economy in Transition*, ed. Martin Feldstein (Chicago: University of Chicago Press, 1980); reprinted in Kristol, *Reflections of a Neoconservative*, p. 200.

137. Irving Kristol, "Pornography, Obscenity, and the Case for Censorship," *New York Times Magazine*, March 28, 1971; reprinted in Kristol, *On the Democratic Idea in America*, p. 41, and Kristol, *Reflections of a Neoconservative*, p. 50.

138. Ibid.

139. Ibid., p. 42 and p. 51.

140. Irving Kristol, "Post-Watergate Morality: Too Good for Our Good?" *New York Times Magazine*, November 14, 1976, p. 35.

141. Irving Kristol, "End Game of the Welfare State," *Wall Street Journal*, September 11, 1989.

142. Kristol, "The Trouble with Republicans."

143. Irving Kristol, "The Spiritual Roots of Capitalism and Socialism," in *Capitalism and Socialism: A Theological Inquiry*, ed. Michael Novak (Washington, D.C.: American Enterprise Institute, 1979); reprinted as "Christianity, Judaism, and Socialism" in Kristol, *Reflections of a Neoconservative*, p. 315.

144. For Voegelin's discussion of Christianity, gnosticism, and the "gnostic nature of modernity," see Eric Voegelin, *The New Science of Politics* (Chicago: University of Chicago Press, 1952), pp. 107–132.

145. Kristol, "Christianity, Judaism, and Socialism," p. 318.

146. Ibid., p. 317.

147. Ibid., p. 320.

148. Ibid., p. 326.

149. Kristol, interview with author, March 21, 1990.

150. Kristol, "Christianity, Judaism, and Socialism," p. 318.

151. Kristol, interview with author, March 21, 1990.

152. Kristol, "Christianity, Judaism, and Socialism," p. 323.

153. Ibid., p. 326.

154. Irving Kristol, "Foreign Policy in an Age of Ideology," *National Interest* 1 (Fall 1985): 6–15.

155. Irving Kristol, "Diplomacy vs. Foreign Policy in the United States," *Wall Street Journal*, April 15, 1982; reprinted in Kristol, *Reflections of a Neoconservative*, p. 229.

156. Ibid.

157. Irving Kristol, "Our Incoherent Foreign Policy," *Wall Street Journal*, October 15, 1980; reprinted in Kristol, *Reflections of a Neoconservative*, p. 234.

158. Kristol, "Diplomacy vs. Foreign Policy in the United States," pp. 229–230.

159. Kristol, "Our Incoherent Foreign Policy," p. 234.

160. Kristol, "Diplomacy vs. Foreign Policy in the United States," p. 229.

161. Irving Kristol, "Now What for U.S. Client States?" *Wall Street Journal*, March 3, 1986; cf. Kristol, " 'Global Unilateralism' and 'Entangling Alliances,' " *Wall Street Journal*, February 3, 1986.

162. Kristol, "Foreign Policy in an Age of Ideology," pp. 7–8.

163. Ibid., p. 7.

164. Ibid., p. 11.

165. Kristol, " 'Global Unilateralism' and 'Entangling Alliances' "; Irving Kristol, "U.S. Foreign Policy Has Outlived Its Time," *Wall Street Journal*, January 21, 1988.

166. Kristol, "Foreign Policy in an Age of Ideology," p. 13.

167. Irving Kristol, " 'Human Rights': The Hidden Agenda," *National Interest* 6 (Winter 1986–87): 8.

168. Ibid., p. 6.

169. Ibid.

170. Kristol, "Foreign Policy in an Age of Ideology," p. 12.

171. Ibid. Cf. Irving Kristol, "The New Liberal Isolationism," *Wall Street Journal*, August 11, 1987; Kristol, "Why a Debate over Contra Aid?" *Wall Street Journal*, April 11, 1986.

172. Kristol, "Foreign Policy in an Age of Ideology," p. 13.

173. Cf. Irving Kristol, "Does NATO Exist?" *Washington Quarterly*, Autumn 1979, reprinted in Kristol, *Reflections of a Neoconservative*, pp. 236–247; Kristol, "Exorcising the Nuclear Nightmare," *Wall Street Journal*, March 12, 1980, reprinted in Kristol, *Reflections of a Neoconservative*, pp. 248–252; Kristol et al., "Should the U.S. Stay in NATO?" *Harper's* 268, no. 1604 (January 1984); Kristol, "NATO Edges Toward the Moment of Truth," *Wall Street Journal*, April 14, 1987.

174. Kristol, "Foreign Policy in an Age of Ideology," p. 13.

175. Ibid.

176. Irving Kristol, "Nuclear NATO: A Moment of Truth," *Wall Street Journal*, July 9, 1987.

177. Ibid. Cf. Kristol, "U.S. Foreign Policy Has Outlived Its Time."

178. Irving Kristol, "Taking Glasnost Seriously," *Wall Street Journal*, December 8, 1987. Cf. Alain Bescancon, "Gorbachev Without Illusions," *Commentary* 85, no. 4 (April 1988); Angelo Codevilla, "Is There Still a Soviet Threat?" *Commentary* 86, no. 5 (November 1988).

179. Irving Kristol, "The Soviets' Albatross States," *Wall Street Journal*, July 22, 1988.

180. Ibid.

181. Irving Kristol, "Bush Must Fight the GOP Energy Shortage," *Wall Street*

Journal, December 21, 1988. Cf. Kristol, "A Smug NATO Is Letting Germany Secede," *Wall Street Journal,* May 2, 1989.

182. Irving Kristol, "Sometimes It's Over Before It's Over," *Wall Street Journal,* December 1, 1989; Kristol, "The Map of the World Has Changed," *Wall Street Journal,* January 3, 1990.

183. Kristol, "The Map of the World Has Changed."

184. Irving Kristol, "In Search of Our National Interest," *Wall Street Journal,* June 7, 1990. Cf. Kristol, "Defining Our National Interest," *National Interest* 21 (Fall 1990): 18–19.

185. Irving Kristol, "Bush Is Right about Lithuania," *Wall Street Journal,* April 11, 1990. Cf. Kristol, "Defining Our National Interest," pp. 16–25.

186. Kristol, "In Search of Our National Interest."

187. Irving Kristol, "There's No 'Peace Process' in Mideast," *Wall Street Journal,* February 19, 1988.

188. Irving Kristol, "Who Needs Peace in the Middle East?" *Wall Street Journal,* July 21, 1989.

189. Kristol, "There's No 'Peace Process' in Mideast"; Kristol, "Who Needs Peace in the Middle East?"

190. Kristol, interview with author, March 21, 1990.

191. Ibid.

192. Irving Kristol, "Hoover, Nixon, Carter . . . Bush?" *Wall Street Journal,* October 8, 1990.

193. Irving Kristol, "After the War, What?" *Wall Street Journal,* February 22, 1991.

194. Cf. Irving Kristol, "The Missing Social Agenda," *Wall Street Journal,* January 26, 1987.

195. Theodore Draper, *A Present of Things Past: Selected Essays* (New York: Hill & Wang, 1990), p. 262.

196. Kristol, "Foreign Policy in an Age of Ideology," p. 8.

Notes to Chapter 4

1. Francis X. Clines, "U.S. Neo-Conservatives Taunt 'Evil' in Its Habitat," *New York Times,* June 21, 1989.

2. Quoted in Merle Miller, "Why Norman and Jason Aren't Talking," *New York Times Magazine,* March 26, 1972, p. 104.

3. Lionel Trilling, "Our Country and Our Culture," *Partisan Review* 19, no. 3 (May/June 1952): 324.

4. Norman Podhoretz, *Making It* (New York: Random House, 1967), pp. 73–79.

5. Norman Podhoretz, *The Bloody Crossroads: Where Literature and Politics Meet* (New York: Simon & Schuster, 1986), pp. 73–74.

6. Podhoretz, *Making It,* p. 83.

7. Ibid., p. 146.

8. Ibid., p. 147.

9. Ibid., p. 149.

10. Norman Podhoretz, "Literature and the 'Spiritual Crisis,' " *Commentary* 16, no. 2 (August 1953): 150.

11. Ibid., pp. 150–151.

12. Ibid., p. 151.

13. Norman Podhoretz, "Sholom Aleichem: Jewishness Is Jews," *Commentary* 16, no. 3 (September 1953): 261–263.

14. Norman Podhoretz, "The Language of Life," *Commentary* 16, no. 4 (October 1953), 380.

15. Ibid., p. 382.

16. Podhoretz, *Making It*, p. 167. Cf. Norman Podhoretz, "Southern Claims," *Partisan Review* 21, no. 1 (January/February 1954); Podhoretz, "Symbolism and/or Literature," *Partisan Review* 21, no. 3 (May/June 1954).

17. Norman Podhoretz, "William Faulkner and the Problem of War," *Commentary* 18, no. 3 (September 1954): 227; reprinted in Podhoretz, *Doings and Undoings: The Fifties and After in American Writing* (New York: Noonday Press, 1964), pp. 13–24.

18. Ibid, p. 232.

19. Podhoretz, *Making It*, p. 96.

20. Ibid., p. 191.

21. Ibid., p. 222.

22. Ibid., pp. 230–231.

23. Ibid., p. 242.

24. Ibid., p. 253.

25. Podhoretz, *Doings and Undoings*, p. 111.

26. Norman Podhoretz, "The Know-Nothing Bohemians," *Partisan Review* 25, no. 2 (Spring 1958); reprinted in Podhoretz, *Doings and Undoings*, pp. 143–158.

27. Podhoretz, *Making It*, p. 254.

28. Cf. Norman Podhoretz, "Edmund Wilson: The Last Patrician, I," *Reporter* 19, no. 11 (December 25, 1958); Podhoretz, "Edmund Wilson: The Last Patrician, II, *Reporter* 20, no. 1 (January 8, 1959); both reprinted in Podhoretz, *Doings and Undoings*, pp. 30–50.

29. Cf. Norman Podhoretz, "Norman Mailer: The Embattled Vision," *Partisan Review* 26, no. 3 (Summer 1959); reprinted in Podhoretz, *Doings and Undoings*, pp. 179–204. Podhoretz's reconsideration of Bellow is reprinted in *Doings and Undoings*, pp. 205–227.

30. Norman Podhoretz, The Issue, *Commentary* 29, no. 2 (February 1960): a.

31. Elliott Cohen, "An Act of Affirmation: Editorial Statement," *Commentary* 1, no. 1 (November 1945): 1; Podhoretz, *Making It*, p. 295.

32. Podhoretz, The Issue (February 1960): 184.

33. Norman Podhoretz, The Issue, *Commentary* 29, no. 4 (April 1960): a.

34. Ibid., p. 368.

35. Podhoretz, *Doings and Undoings*, p. 111.

36. Norman Podhoretz, *Breaking Ranks: A Political Memoir* (New York: Harper & Row, 1979), p. 53.

37. See, e.g., Christopher Hitchens, "A Modern Medieval Family," *Mother Jones* 11, no. 5 (July/August 1986): 54.

38. Norman Podhoretz, "The Cold War and the West: A Symposium," *Partisan Review* 29, no. 1 (Winter 1962): 62.

39. Podhoretz, *Making It*, pp. 334–337.

40. Norman Podhoretz, "My Negro Problem—And Ours," *Commentary* 35, no. 2 (February 1963): 93; reprinted in Podhoretz, *Doings and Undoings*, pp. 354–371.

41. Ibid., pp. 97–98.

42. Ibid., p. 97.

43. Podhoretz, *Making It*, p. 343.

44. Podhoretz, "My Negro Problem," p. 100.

45. Ibid., p. 101.

46. Morton Weitzner, "Letters from Readers," *Commentary* 35, no. 4 (April 1963): pp. 342–343.

47. Cf. E. F. Schumacher, "A Humanistic Guide to Foreign Aid," *Commentary* 32, no. 5 (November 1961); Schumacher, "Economism," *Commentary* 36, no. 1 (July 1963): 81–84.

48. The text of Moynihan's paper, "The Negro Family: The Case for National Action," is reprinted in *The Moynihan Report and the Politics of Controversy*, ed. Lee Rainwater and William L. Yancey (Cambridge: MIT Press, 1967), pp. 39–124.

49. Podhoretz, *Breaking Ranks*, p. 141.

50. Alexander Bloom, *Prodigal Sons: The New York Intellectuals and Their World* (New York: Oxford University Press, 1986), p. 323; Sidney Blumenthal, *The Rise of the Counter-Establishment: From Conservative Ideology to Political Power* (New York: Harper & Row, 1988), p. 137.

51. Cf. Moshe Decter, William Appleman Williams, George Lichtheim, and Staughton Lynd, "The Origins of the Cold War: An Exchange," *Commentary* 31, no. 2 (February 1961); Sidney Hook, H. Stuart Hughes, Hans J. Morgenthau, and C. P. Snow, "Western Values and Total War: An Exchange," *Commentary* 32, no. 4 (October 1961).

52. H. Stuart Hughes, "The Strategy of Deterrence: A Dissenting Statement," *Commentary* 31, no. 3 (March 1961): 185–192; Hook et al., "Western Values and Total War," pp. 279, 281–282.

53. Podhoretz, *Breaking Ranks*, pp. 197–200.

54. Cf. Miller, "Why Norman and Jason Aren't Talking," p. 108.

55. Jason Epstein, "The CIA and the Intellectuals," *New York Review of Books* 8, no. 7 (April 20, 1967): 20.

56. Podhoretz, *Making It*, pp. 262–263.

57. Ibid., pp. 352–354.

58. Wilfrid Sheed, "*Making It* in the Big City," *Atlantic Monthly* 221, no. 4 (April 1968): 97–102; William Phillips, "The World According to Norman," *Partisan Review* 47, no. 3 (1980): 336; Edgar Z. Friedenberg, "Du cote de chez Podhoretz," *New York Review of Books* 10, no. 2 (February 1, 1968): 12–13;

Norman Mailer, "Up the Family Tree," *Partisan Review* 35, no. 2 (Spring 1968): 237, 245.

59. Podhoretz, *Breaking Ranks*, p. 267.

60. Quoted in Miller, "Why Norman and Jason Aren't Talking," p. 106.

61. Cf. Hans J. Morgenthau, "Asia: The American Algeria," *Commentary* 32, no. 1 (July 1961); Morgenthau, "Vietnam: Another Korea?" *Commentary* 33, no. 5 (May 1962); Morgenthau, "The Impotence of American Power," *Commentary* 36, no. 5 (November 1963).

62. Cf. Staughton Lynd, "How the Cold War Began," *Commentary* 30, no. 5 (November 1960): 379–389; Decter et al., "Origins of the Cold War," pp. 142–159.

63. Quoted in Jack Newfield, *A Prophetic Minority* (New York: Signet Books, 1967), p. 148; Paul Hollander, *Political Pilgrims: Travels of Western Intellectuals to the Soviet Union, China, and Cuba* (New York: Harper Colophon Books, 1983), p. 273.

64. Podhoretz, *Breaking Ranks*, pp. 188–190.

65. Cf. "Liberal Anti-Communism Revisited" (symposium), *Commentary* 44, no. 3 (September 1967); Epstein, "CIA and the Intellectuals," pp. 16, 20, 29.

66. Tom Kahn, "The Problem of the New Left," *Commentary* 42, no. 1 (July 1966); Bayard Rustin, " 'Black Power' and Coalition Politics," *Commentary* 42, no. 3 (September 1966); Nathan Glazer, "The New Left and Its Limits," *Commentary* 46, no. 1 (July 1968); Diana Trilling, "On the Steps of Low Library: Liberalism and the Revolution of the Young," *Commentary* 46, no. 5 (November 1968); Kahn, "Why the Poor Peoples' Campaign Failed," *Commentary* 46, no. 3 (September 1968).

67. Cf. Robert Heilbroner, "Counterrevolutionary America," *Commentary* 43, no. 4 (April 1967); Michael Harrington, "Voting the Lesser Evil," *Commentary* 45, no. 4 (April 1968); Irving Howe, "The Culture of Modernism," *Commentary* 44, no. 5 (November 1967); Howe, "The New York Intellectuals: A Chronicle and a Critique," *Commentary* 46, no. 4 (October 1968); Norman Mailer, "The Battle of the Pentagon," *Commentary* 45, no. 4 (April 1968); Noam Chomsky, "Vietnam, the Cold War and Other Matters," *Commentary* 48, no. 4 (October 1969).

68. Norman Podhoretz, "A Note on Vietnamization," *Commentary* 51, no. 5 (May 1971): 6–9; Nathan Glazer, "Vietnam: The Case for Immediate Withdrawal," *Commentary* 51, no. 5 (May 1971): 33–37.

69. Norman Podhoretz, "Reflections on Earth Day," *Commentary* 49, no. 6 (June 1970): 26.

70. Podhoretz, *Breaking Ranks*, p. 306.

71. Samuel McCracken, "Quackery in the Classroom," *Commentary* 52, no. 4 (October 1971); Dorothy Rabinowitz, "The Radicalized Professor," *Commentary* 50, no. 1 (July 1970); Rabinowitz, "The Activist Cleric," *Commentary* 50, no. 3 (September 1970); Midge Decter, "The Liberated Woman," *Commentary* 50, no. 4 (October 1970); Arlene Croce, "Sexism in the Head," *Commentary* 51, no. 3 (March 1971); Dennis H. Wrong, "The Case of the 'New York Review,' " *Commentary* 50, no. 5 (November 1970): 49–63.

72. Irving Kristol, "Urban Civilization and Its Discontents," *Commentary* 50,

no. 1 (July 1970); Nathan Glazer, "On Being Deradicalized," *Commentary* 50, no. 4 (October 1970).

73. Michael Novak, "Needing Niebuhr Again," *Commentary* 54, no. 3 (September 1972); Jeane Kirkpatrick, "The Revolt of the Masses," *Commentary* 55, no. 2 (February 1973).

74. Podhoretz, *Breaking Ranks*, p. 307.

75. Ibid., p. 320.

76. Cf. Norman Podhoretz, "Adversaries or Critics?" *Commentary* 51, no. 3 (March 1971); Podhoretz, "Liberty and the Intellectuals," *Commentary* 52, no. 5 (November 1971); Podhoretz, "Liberty and the Liberals," *Commentary* 52, no. 6 (December 1971); Podhoretz, "Is It Good for the Jews?" *Commentary* 53, no. 2 (February 1972); Podhoretz, "The Intellectuals and the Pursuit of Happiness," *Commentary* 55, no. 2 (February 1973); Podhoretz, "Vietnam and Collective Guilt," *Commentary* 55, no. 3 (March 1973).

77. Norman Podhoretz, "What the Voters Sensed," *Commentary* 55, no. 1 (January 1973): 6.

78. Ibid., p. 6.

79. Norman Podhoretz, "The Present Danger," *Commentary* 69, no. 3 (March 1980): 33; reprinted in modified form in Podhoretz, *The Present Danger: Do We Have the Will to Reverse the Decline of American Power?* (New York: Simon & Schuster, 1980).

80. Norman Podhoretz, "Making the World Safe for Communism," *Commentary* 61, no. 4 (April 1976): 40; reprinted in modified form in Podhoretz, *Present Danger.*

81. Ibid., p. 37.

82. Ibid., pp. 40–41.

83. Norman Podhoretz, "The Culture of Appeasement," *Harper's* 255, no. 1529 (October 1977): 32; reprinted in modified form in Podhoretz, *Present Danger.*

84. Quoted in Blumenthal, *Rise of the Counter-Establishment*, p. 128.

85. Podhoretz, "Making the World Safe for Communism," p. 37.

86. Podhoretz, "Culture of Appeasement," p. 29.

87. Ibid., p. 30.

88. Ibid., p. 31.

89. Ibid., pp. 29–31.

90. Podhoretz, "Present Danger," pp. 36–38.

91. Ibid., p. 37.

92. Ibid., p. 38.

93. Norman Podhoretz, "The Neo-Conservative Anguish over Reagan's Foreign Policy," *New York Times Magazine*, May 2, 1982, p. 97.

94. David Stockman, *The Triumph of Politics: How the Reagan Revolution Failed* (New York: Harper & Row, 1986), pp. 108–109.

95. Robert Tucker, "The Middle East: Carterism Without Carter?" *Commentary* 72, no. 3 (September 1981): 27–36.

96. Podhoretz, "Neo-Conservative Anguish over Reagan's Foreign Policy," p. 33.

97. Ibid., pp. 96–98.

98. X [George F. Kennan], "The Sources of Soviet Conduct," *Foreign Affairs* 25, no. 4 (July 1947): 578.

99. George F. Kennan, *The Nuclear Delusion: Soviet–American Relations in the Atomic Age* (New York: Pantheon Books, 1983).

100. Norman Podhoretz, *Why We Were in Vietnam* (New York: Simon & Schuster, 1983), p. 210.

101. Podhoretz, "Present Danger," pp. 28, 40.

102. Podhoretz, "Making the World Safe for Communism," p. 38.

103. Norman Podhoretz, "The Future Danger," *Commentary* 71, no. 4 (April 1981): 35.

104. Cf. Stephen Cohen, *Sovieticus: American Perceptions and Soviet Realities* (New York: W. W. Norton, 1985); Cohen, *Rethinking the Soviet Experience: Politics and History since 1917* (New York: Oxford University Press, 1985); Jerry Hough, *Soviet Leadership in Transition* (Washington, D.C.: Brookings Institution, 1980); Hough, *The Struggle for the Third World: Soviet Debates and American Options* (Washington, D.C.: Brookings Institution, 1986); Hough, *Russia and the West: Gorbachev and the Politics of Reform* (New York: Simon & Schuster, 1988).

105. Podhoretz, "Future Danger," p. 39. Though Podhoretz developed a more sympathetic opinion of Henry Kissinger after Kissinger left office, he continued to argue that during his term in office, Kissinger's view of the Soviet Union mistakenly minimized the ideological factor and overemphasized the importance of Russian geography, history, and culture. Cf. Norman Podhoretz, "Kissinger Reconsidered," *Commentary* 73, no. 6 (June 1982): 19–28; reprinted in Podhoretz, *Bloody Crossroads*, pp. 139–166.

106. Cf. Podhoretz, *Present Danger*, pp. 96–101.

107. Cf. Podhoretz, "Making the World Safe for Communism," pp. 38–39; Jean-François Revel, "Can the Democracies Survive?" *Commentary* 77, no. 6 (June 1984); Jeane Kirkpatrick, *Dictatorships and Double Standards: Rationalism and Reason in Politics* (New York: American Enterprise Institute/Simon & Schuster, 1982), pp. 96–138.

108. Kennan, *Nuclear Delusion*, pp. xix, 74.

109. Norman Podhoretz, "Appeasement by Any Other Name," *Commentary* 76, no. 1 (July 1983): 33.

110. Ibid., p. 37.

111. Ibid., p. 34.

112. Ibid., pp. 36–38.

113. Cf. David Johnston, "Elliott Abrams Admits His Guilt to Two Counts in Contra Cover-Up," *New York Times*, October 8, 1991; Max Singer, "Losing Central America," *Commentary* 82, no. 1 (July 1986): 11–14; Penn Kemble and Arturo J. Cruz, Jr., "How the Nicaraguan Resistance Can Win," *Commentary* 82, no. 6 (December 1986): 19–29; L. Gordon Crovitz, "Crime, the Constitution, and the Iran/Contra Affair," *Commentary* 84, no. 4 (October 1987): 23–30; Mark Falcoff, "Making Central America Safe for Communism," *Commentary* 85, no. 6 (June 1988): 17–24; Elliott Abrams, "The Deal in Central America," *Commentary* 87, no. 5 (May 1989); Editorial, "Lying in State," *Nation* 244, no. 24 (June 20, 1987): 835.

114. Cf. Richard Pipes, "Why the Soviet Union Thinks It Could Fight and Win a Nuclear War," *Commentary* 64, no. 1 (July 1977); Edward Luttwak, "Why We Need More 'Waste, Fraud, and Mismanagement' in the Pentagon," *Commentary* 73, no. 2 (February 1982); Luttwak, "A New Arms Race?" *Commentary* 70, no. 3 (September 1980); Walter Laqueur, "Reagan and the Russians," *Commentary* 73, no. 1 (January 1982); Laqueur, "What We Know about the Soviet Union," *Commentary* 75, no. 2 (February 1983); Laqueur, "Glasnost and Its Limits," *Commentary* 86, no. 1 (July 1988).

115. Robert Jastrow, "Why Strategic Superiority Matters," *Commentary* 75, no. 3 (March 1983); Patrick Glynn, "Why an American Arms Build-Up Is Morally Necessary," *Commentary* 77, no. 2 (February 1984); Angelo Codevilla, "Is There Still a Soviet Threat?" *Commentary* 86, no. 5 (November 1988).

116. Pipes, "Why the Soviet Union Thinks It Could Fight and Win a Nuclear War," pp. 24–26.

117. Ibid., pp. 26–31.

118. Ibid., pp. 30–34.

119. Cf. Richard Pipes, "How to Cope with the Soviet Threat," *Commentary* 78, no. 2 (August 1984); Pipes, "Team B: The Reality Behind the Myth," *Commentary* 82, no. 4 (October 1986); Edward Luttwak, "How to Think about Nuclear War," *Commentary* 74, no. 2 (August 1982); Robert Jastrow, "The War Against 'Star Wars,' " *Commentary* 78, no. 6 (December 1984); Angelo Codevilla, "How SDI Is Being Undone from Within," *Commentary* 81, no. 5 (May 1986); Eugene V. Rostow, "Why the Soviets Want an Arms Control Agreement, and Why They Want It Now," *Commentary* 83, no. 2 (February 1987); Patrick Glynn, "Reagan's Rush to Disarm," *Commentary* 85, no. 3 (March 1988).

120. Bernard Avishai, "Breaking Faith: *Commentary* and the American Jews," *Dissent* 28, no. 2 (Spring 1981): 237.

121. Theodore Draper, "Israel and World Politics," *Commentary* 44, no. 2 (August 1967): 40.

122. Amos Elon, "Letter from the Sinai Front," *Commentary* 44, no. 2 (August 1967): 68.

123. Avishai, "Breaking Faith," p. 247.

124. Arthur Hertzberg, "Israel and American Jewry," *Commentary* 44, no. 2 (August 1967): 69.

125. Ibid., pp. 72–73.

126. Arthur Hertzberg, *The Zionist Idea: A Historical Analysis and Reader* (New York: Atheneum, 1982), p. 95.

127. Podhoretz, "My Negro Problem—And Ours," p. 101.

128. Emil L. Fackenheim, "Jewish Faith and the Holocaust: A Fragment," *Commentary* 46, no. 2 (August 1968): 31–32.

129. Ibid., p. 35.

130. Hertzberg, "Israel and American Jewry," p. 72.

131. Ibid., p. 71.

132. Fackenheim, "Jewish Faith and the Holocaust," p. 35.

133. Norman Podhoretz, interview with the author, June 12, 1990.

134. Norman Podhoretz, "A Certain Anxiety," *Commentary* 52, no. 2 (August 1971): 6.

135. Ibid., pp. 6–10. Cf. Norman Podhoretz, "The Tribe of the Wicked Son," *Commentary* 51, no. 2 (February 1971): 6–10; Podhoretz, "What Is Anti-Semitism? An Open Letter to William F. Buckley, Jr.," *Commentary* 93, no. 2 (February 1992): 15–20.

136. Norman Podhoretz, "Is It Good for the Jews?" p. 12.

137. Ibid.

138. Cf. Podhoretz, "A Certain Anxiety," pp. 8–10; Podhoretz, "Is It Good for the Jews?" pp. 12–14; Irving Kristol, "The Political Dilemma of American Jews," *Commentary* 78, no. 1 (July 1984): 23–29; Kristol, "Liberalism and American Jews," *Commentary* 86, no. 4 (October 1988): 19–23.

139. Norman Podhoretz, "J'Accuse," *Commentary* 74, no. 3 (September 1982): 28–29. Cf. Podhoretz, "The State of World Jewry," *Commentary* 76, no. 6 (December 1983): 37–45; Podhoretz, "Israel: A Lamentation from the Future," *Commentary* 87, no. 3 (March 1989): 15–21; Podhoretz, "New Guises for Old Anti-Semitism," *New York Post*, June 10, 1986.

140. Podhoretz, "J'Accuse," p. 28.

141. Gore Vidal, "The Empire Lovers Strike Back," *Nation* 242, no. 11 (March 22, 1986): 350, 353.

142. Midge Decter, "The Boys on the Beach," *Commentary* 70, no. 3 (September 1980): 48.

143. Norman Podhoretz, "AIDS in Plain English," *New York Post*, September 24, 1985. Cf. Podhoretz, "The Plain Truth about AIDS," *New York Post*, October 27, 1987.

144. Norman Podhoretz, "A Day in the Decline of America," *New York Post*, March 25, 1986.

145. Editorial, "Patriotic Gore," *New Republic*, April 28, 1986, pp. 8–9; Irving Howe, "Ugly Stuff at the *Nation*," *Dissent* 33, no. 3 (Summer 1986): 271–275; Arthur Hertzberg, "Screaming Rhetoric" (letter), *Nation* 242, no. 17 (May 3, 1986): 628; cf. Editorial, "The Vidal Exemption," *National Review* 38, no. 10 (June 6, 1986): 20.

146. Norman Podhoretz, "The Hate that Dare Not Speak Its Name," *Commentary* 82, no. 5 (November 1986): 25, 27; Podhoretz, "Anti-Semitism in the 'Nation,' " *New York Post*, May 6, 1986.

147. Podhoretz, *Breaking Ranks*, p. 300.

148. Podhoretz, interview with author, June 12, 1990.

149. Daniel Patrick Moynihan, "Joining the Jackals: The U.S. at the U.N., 1977–1988," *Commentary* 71, no. 2 (February 1981): 23–31.

150. Norman Podhoretz, "Ganging Up on Israel," *New York Post*, March 22, 1988. Cf. Podhoretz, "Israel's 'Friends'—There They Go Again," *New York Post*, March 26, 1985; Podhoretz, "With 'Friends' Like This . . . ," *New York Post*, December 22, 1987.

151. Podhoretz, "Ganging Up on Israel."

152. Norman Podhoretz, "A Sure Road to Mideast War," *New York Post*,

December 20, 1988. Cf. Podhoretz, "Israel's Dangerous Alternatives," *New York Post*, November 3, 1987; Podhoretz, "New Front in Forty-Year War Against Israel," *New York Post*, January 12, 1988; Podhoretz, "Israel's Impossible Trap," *New York Post*, February 2, 1988; Podhoretz, "Slouching Toward a PLO State," *New York Post*, February 14, 1989.

153. Norman Podhoretz, "The Reagan Road to Detente," *Foreign Affairs* 63, no. 3 (1985): 463–464.

154. Norman Podhoretz, "Reagan's Forbidden Truths," *New York Post*, October 29, 1985; Podhoretz, "How Reagan Succeeds as a Carter Clone," *New York Post*, October 7, 1986. Cf. Podhoretz, "Nixon, The Ghost of Detente Past," *New York Post*, November 5, 1985; Podhoretz, "Reagan—The Crippled Hawk," *New York Post*, June 25, 1985; Podhoretz, "The Madness of Arms Control," *New York Post*, October 1, 1985.

155. Podhoretz, "How Reagan Succeeds as a Carter Clone"; Podhoretz, "Reagan: A Case of Mistaken Identity," *New York Post*, August 6, 1985.

156. Podhoretz, "What if Reagan Were President?" *New York Post*, April 29, 1986.

157. Norman Podhoretz, "The Courage of Reagan's Convictions," *New York Post*, June 3, 1986; Podhoretz, "Gorbachev's Salami Tactics," *New York Post*, October 20, 1987. Cf. Podhoretz, "Moscow's Double Missile Trap," *New York Post*, September 22, 1987; Podhoretz, "What the Soviets Really Want," *New York Post*, November 19, 1985.

158. Norman Podhoretz, "The Danger Is Greater than Ever," *New York Post*, December 1, 1987; Podhoretz, "Gorbachev's Salami Tactics."

159. Norman Podhoretz, "Reagan's Reverse Rollback," *New York Post*, November 10, 1987. Cf. Podhoretz, "The Myth of Our Military Buildup," *New York Post*, September 30, 1986.

160. Podhoretz, "Gorbachev's Salami Tactics." Cf. Podhoretz, "Propping Up the Soviet Empire," *New York Post*, July 15, 1986.

161. Podhoretz, "The Danger Is Greater than Ever." Cf. Podhoretz, "From Containment to Appeasement," *New York Post*, June 18, 1985.

162. Norman Podhoretz, "Peace, Peace, When there Is No Peace," *New York Post*, February 16, 1988; Podhoretz, "The Danger Is Greater than Ever"; Podhoretz, "Reagan Was Right the First Time," *New York Post*, June 7, 1988.

163. Podhoretz, interview with author, June 12, 1990; Podhoretz, "Gorbachev Wins One for Lenin," *New York Post*, December 13, 1988.

164. Podhoretz, "Gorbachev Wins One for Lenin"; Podhoretz, "Munich and Gorbachev: The Lesson Is Still Valid," *New York Post*, October 4, 1988.

165. Norman Podhoretz, "Now for the Left-Wing Dictators," *New York Post*, March 4, 1986; Podhoretz, "Peace, Peace, When there Is No Peace."

166. Podhoretz, "Present Danger," p. 37; quoted in Podhoretz, "Gorbachev Wins One for Lenin."

167. Podhoretz, "Gorbachev Wins One for Lenin." Cf. Podhoretz, "Gorbachev's Reforms Stop at the Border," *New York Post*, May 5, 1987; Podhoretz, "Munich and Gorbachev: The Lesson Is Still Valid."

168. Cf. Jeane Kirkpatrick, "Moscow's Anti-American Reformer" (syndicated column) October 17, 1988, reprinted in Kirkpatrick, *The Withering Away of the Totalitarian State . . . and Other Surprises,* (Washington, D.C.: American Enterprise Institute, 1990), pp. 38–41; Aleksandr Yakovlev, *On the Edge of the Abyss: From Truman to Reagan, the Doctrine and Realities of the Nuclear Age* (Moscow: Progress Publishers, 1985).

169. Podhoretz, interview with author, June 12, 1990.

170. Cf. Norman Podhoretz, "Do Not Go Gentle into the Night," *New York Post,* March 18, 1986.

171. Podhoretz, interview with author, June 12, 1990.

172. Ibid.

173. Cf. James Cone, *A Black Theology of Liberation,* (Philadelphia: J. B. Lippincott, 1970), pp. 32–33; Juan Luis Segundo, *The Liberation of Theology,* trans. John Drury (Maryknoll, N.Y.: Orbis Books, 1976), pp. 25–34.

174. Cf. Ben Wattenberg, "Neo-Manifest Destinarianism," *National Interest* 21 (Fall 1990); Charles Krauthammer, "Universal Dominion: Toward a Unipolar World," *National Interest* 18 (Winter 1989–90); Joshua Muravchik, "Maximum Feasible Containment," *New Republic* 196, no. 22 (June 1, 1987): 23–25; Gregory A. Fossedal, *The Democratic Imperative: Exporting the American Revolution* (New York: Basic Books, 1989).

175. Cf. Norman Podhoretz, "Right about Everything, Wrong about Nothing?" *Encounter* 75, no. 1 (July/August 1990): 9–11; Norman Podhoretz, "A Statement on the Persian Gulf Crisis," *Commentary* 90, no. 5 (November 1990): 17–20.

176. Norman Podhoretz, "Enter the Peace Party," *Commentary* 91, no. 1 (January 1991): 19.

177. Ibid., p. 21.

178. Norman Podhoretz, "In Israel, With Scuds and Patriots," *Commentary* 91, no. 4 (April 1991): 20–21.

179. Cf. Norman Podhoretz, "America and Israel: An Ominous Change," *Commentary* 93, no. 1 (January 1992): 21–25. In June 1992, *Commentary* launched a new feature, "Israel Watch," which was devoted to "countering the stepped-up ideological and political war against Israel" that followed the Gulf War.

180. Phillips, "World According to Norman," p. 336.

181. Cf. Norman Podhoretz, "Rape in Feminist Eyes," *Commentary* 92, no. 4 (October 1991): 29–35.

182. Norman Podhoretz, "The Terrible Question of Aleksandr Solzhenitsyn," *Commentary* 79, no. 2 (February 1985): 17–24.

183. Norman Podhoretz, "If Orwell Were Alive Today," *Harper's* 266, no. 1592 (January 1983): 37; reprinted in Podhoretz, *Bloody Crossroads,* pp. 50–68.

184. Podhoretz, "Camus and His Critics," in *Bloody Crossroads,* pp. 47–49.

185. Norman Podhoretz, "An Open Letter to Milan Kundera," *Commentary* 78, no. 4 (October 1984): 38–39; reprinted in Podhoretz, *Bloody Crossroads,* pp. 167–183.

186. Sidney Blumenthal, *Our Long National Daydream: A Political Pageant of the Reagan Era* (New York: Harper & Row, 1988), p. 202.

187. Cf. Podhoretz, "Rape in Feminist Eyes"; Podhoretz, "America and Israel: An Ominous Change"; Podhoretz, "Buchanan and the Conservative Crackup," *Commentary* 93, no. 5 (May 1992): 30–34; Podhoretz, "What Is Anti-Semitism? An Open Letter to William F. Buckley, Jr.," *Commentary* 93, no. 2 (February 1992): 15–20.

Notes to Chapter 5

1. Michael Novak, "Errand into the Wilderness," in *Political Passages: Journeys of Change Through Two Decades, 1968–1988*, ed. John H. Bunzel (New York: Free Press, 1988), p. 248.

2. Michael Novak, "Engagement but No Security," *Commonweal* 108, no. 2 (January 30, 1981), p. 45; Novak, interview with author, March 20, 1990.

3. Michael Novak, "The Game's Not Over," *Forbes* 146, no. 4 (August 20, 1990): 56; Novak, "Engagement but No Security," p. 45; Novak, *Confession of a Catholic*, (San Francisco: Harper & Row, 1983), p. 12.

4. Novak, interview with author, March 20, 1990; Novak, "Orthodoxy vs. Progressive Bourgeois Christianity," in *Once a Catholic: Prominent Catholics and Ex-Catholics Discuss the Influence of the Church in Their Lives and Work*, ed. Peter Occhiogrosso (Boston: Houghton Mifflin, 1987), pp. 121–124.

5. James Finn, "The Evolving Thought of Michael Novak," *National Review* 38, no. 25 (December 31, 1985): 109.

6. See Michael Novak, *The Tiber Was Silver: A Novel of Spiritual Adventure in Modern Rome* (New York: Doubleday, 1961).

7. Cf. Michael Novak, *The Open Church: Vatican II, Act II* (New York: Macmillan, 1964); Novak, "Catholic Education and the Idea of Dissent," *Commonweal* 76, no. 5 (April 27, 1962).

8. Novak, "Engagement but No Security," p. 44.

9. Michael Novak, *Belief and Unbelief: A Philosophy of Self-Knowledge* (New York: Macmillan, 1965), pp. 189, 192.

10. Reprinted in expanded form in Michael Novak, *A Time to Build* (New York: Macmillan, 1967), pp. 405–412.

11. Ibid., p. 421; Michael Novak, "Stumbling into War and Stumbling Out," in Robert McAfee Brown, Abraham J. Heschel, and Michael Novak, *Vietnam: Crisis of Conscience* (New York: Association Press, 1967), pp. 38, 47.

12. Michael Novak, *A Theology for Radical Politics* (New York: Herder & Herder, 1969), pp. 25, 79.

13. Ibid., pp. 28, 60.

14. Ibid., pp. 74, 81.

15. Ibid., p. 67.

16. Ibid., pp. 66–68.

17. Michael Novak, *"Story" in Politics*, (New York: Council on Religion and International Affairs, 1970), p. 40.

18. Novak, "Errand into the Wilderness," p. 251.

19. Novak, "Engagement but No Security," p. 44.

20. Michael Novak, *Naked I Leave* (New York: Macmillan, 1970).

21. Michael Novak, *The Experience of Nothingness* (New York: Harper & Row, 1970), pp. 51–64.

22. Michael Novak, *Ascent of the Mountain, Flight of the Dove: An Invitation to Religious Studies* (New York: Harper & Row, 1971), pp. 134, 73.

23. Michael Novak, *The Rise of the Unmeltable Ethnics: Politics and Culture in the Seventies* (New York: Macmillan, 1971), pp. 126, 249–253.

24. Ibid., pp. 115, 285.

25. Novak, "Errand into the Wilderness," p. 257.

26. Novak, *Rise of the Unmeltable Ethnics*, p. 248.

27. Ibid., p. 254.

28. Garry Wills, review of *The Rise of the Unmeltable Ethnics: Politics and Culture in the Seventies*, by Michael Novak, in *New York Times Book Review*, April 23, 1972, pp. 27–28.

29. Novak, "Errand into the Wilderness," p. 258.

30. Novak, *Ascent of the Mountain, Flight of the Dove*, p. 153.

31. Michael Novak, *Choosing Our King: Powerful Symbols in Presidential Politics* (New York: Macmillan, 1974), p. 291.

32. Michael Novak, "Against 'Affirmative Action,' " *Commonweal* 100, no. 5 (April 5, 1974): 102, 118; Novak, "Errand into the Wilderness," p. 260.

33. Michael Novak, "Needing Niebuhr Again," *Commentary* 54, no. 3 (September 1972), p. 52.

34. Reinhold Niebuhr, *Moral Man and Immoral Society* (1932; reprint, New York: Scribner's, 1960), p. xx; quoted in Novak, "Needing Niebuhr Again."

35. David T. Bazelon, *Power in America: The Politics of the New Class* (New York: New American Library, 1967); Michael Harrington, *Toward a Democratic Left: A Radical Program for a New Majority* (New York: Macmillan, 1968).

36. Harrington, *Toward a Democratic Left*, p. 290.

37. Quoted in Harrington, *Toward a Democratic Left*, p. 289; and Novak, "Needing Niebuhr Again," p. 60.

38. Harrington, *Toward a Democratic Left*, pp. 282–291.

39. Novak, "Needing Niebuhr Again," p. 60.

40. Ibid., p. 61.

41. Novak, interview with author, March 20, 1990.

42. Michael Novak, *The Spirit of Democratic Capitalism* (New York: American Enterprise Institute/Simon & Schuster, 1982), p. 24.

43. Michael Novak, *The Joy of Sports* (New York: Basic Books, 1976), p. 61. Cf. Novak, *The Guns of Lattimer* (New York: Basic Books, 1978); Novak, *In Praise of Cynicism (or) When the Saints Go Marching Out* (Bloomington, Ind.: Poynter Center, 1975). For a more extensive discussion of Novak's ruminations on sports,

see J. David Hoeveler, Jr., *Watch on the Right: Conservative Intellectuals in the Reagan Era* (Madison: University of Wisconsin Press, 1991), pp. 247–251.

44. Novak, "Orthodoxy vs. Progressive Bourgeois Christianity," p. 130; Novak, "A Closet Capitalist Confesses," *Wall Street Journal*, April 20, 1976. Cf. Novak, "Capitalism, Socialism, and Democracy: A Symposium," *Commentary* 65, no. 4 (April 1978): 63–64.

45. Novak, "Errand into the Wilderness," p. 260.

46. Ibid., p. 254.

47. Michael Novak, "A Switch to Reagan: For a Strong America," *Commonweal* 107, no. 19 (October 24, 1980): 588–591.

48. Michael Novak, *The American Vision: An Essay on the Future of Democratic Capitalism* (Washington, D.C.: American Enterprise Institute, 1978), pp. 1, 24.

49. Novak, "A Switch to Reagan," pp. 589–591.

50. Novak, "Errand into the Wilderness," p. 260.

51. Daniel Bell, *The Cultural Contradictions of Capitalism* (New York: Basic Books, 1978), p. 10.

52. Cf. Novak, *Spirit of Democratic Capitalism*, pp. 14–16, 49–67; Novak, "Seven Theological Facets," in *Capitalism and Socialism: A Theological Inquiry*, ed. Novak (Washington: D.C.: American Enterprise Institute, 1979), pp. 112–113.

53. Novak, *Spirit of Democratic Capitalism*, p. 14.

54. Ibid., pp. 14–15.

55. Ibid., p. 15.

56. Bell, *The Cultural Contradictions of Capitalism*, p. xii.

57. Michael Novak, "Class, Culture and Society," review of *The Winding Passage: Essays and Sociological Journeys, 1960–1980*, by Daniel Bell, *Commentary* 72, no. 1 (July 1981): 72.

58. Friedrich A. Hayek, "Why I Am Not a Conservative," postscript to *The Constitution of Liberty* (Chicago: University of Chicago Press, 1960), pp. 400–411.

59. Novak, "Errand into the Wilderness," p. 254.

60. Novak, *Confession of a Catholic*, pp. 115–118; Novak, "Errand into the Wilderness," pp. 254–255, 269–272; Novak, *Freedom with Justice: Catholic Social Thought and Liberal Institutions* (San Francisco: Harper & Row, 1984), pp. 16–17; Novak, "Free Persons and the Common Good," in *The Common Good and U.S. Capitalism*, ed. Oliver F. Williams and John W. Houck (Lanham, Md.: University Press of America, 1987), pp. 238–240; Novak, *Will It Liberate? Questions about Liberation Theology* (New York: Paulist Press, 1986), p. 35; Novak, "The Return of the Catholic Whig," *First Things* 1 (March 1990): 38; Novak, *This Hemisphere of Liberty: A Philosophy of the Americas* (Washington, D.C.: American Enterprise Institute, 1990), p. 9.

61. Peter Steinfels, "Michael Novak and his ultrasuper democraticapitalism," *Commonweal* 110, no. 1 (January 14, 1983): 13.

62. Novak, *This Hemisphere of Liberty*, p. 11.

63. Louis Hartz, *The Liberal Tradition in America: An Interpretation of American*

Political Thought since the Revolution (New York: Harcourt Brace Jovanovich, 1955), p. 93.

64. Novak, *This Hemisphere of Liberty*, p. 8.

65. Novak, "Free Persons and the Common Good," p. 240.

66. Novak, *Spirit of Democratic Capitalism*, p. 89.

67. Novak, *Confession of a Catholic*, p. 117.

68. Hartz, *Liberal Tradition in America*, p. 110; quoted in Arthur M. Schlesinger, Jr., *The Age of Jackson* (Boston: Little, Brown, 1945), p. 271. Cf. Michael Novak, "Not Only the Rich Are Capitalists Now," *Forbes* 144, no. 5 (September 4, 1989); Novak, "Capitalist Liberation," *Forbes* 144, no. 6 (September 18, 1989).

69. Hartz, *Liberal Tradition in America*, pp. 111–112.

70. Cf. James MacGregor Burns, *The Vineyard of Liberty* (New York: Alfred A. Knopf, 1982), p. 433.

71. Hartz, *Liberal Tradition in America*, pp. 205–206.

72. Ibid., p. 208.

73. Michael Novak, "The Old Virtues," review of *The Way of the WASP: How It Made America, and How It Can Save It, So to Speak*, by Richard Brookhiser, *Commentary* 91, no. 3 (March 1991): 54.

74. Novak, *Spirit of Democratic Capitalism*, p. 359.

75. Michael Novak, *Toward a Theology of the Corporation*, (Washington, D.C.: American Enterprise Institute, 1981), pp. 41–43.

76. Ibid., p. 39. Cf. Michael Novak, "Business Should Speak Up," *Forbes* 143, no. 9 (May 1, 1989).

77. Novak, *This Hemisphere of Liberty*, p. 10.

78. Novak, interview with author, March 20, 1990.

79. Michael Novak, "Boredom, Virtue, and Democratic Capitalism," *Commentary* 88, no. 3 (September 1989): 35.

80. Cf. Michael Novak, "Mediating Institutions: The Communitarian Individual in America," *Public Interest* 68 (Summer 1982); Novak, "Habits of the Left-Wing Heart," *National Review* 37, no. 12 (June 28, 1985): 36.

81. Novak, "Boredom, Virtue, and Democratic Capitalism," p. 35.

82. Michael Novak, "Defining the U.S. System," *Washington Times*, April 28, 1989.

83. Novak, *This Hemisphere of Liberty*, p. 28.

84. Novak, "Boredom, Virtue, and Democratic Capitalism," p. 36. Cf. Novak, " 'Built Wiser than They Knew': The Constitution and the Wealth of Nations," *Crisis* 5, no. 5 (May 1987); Novak, "The Mind-Centered System," *Forbes* 143, no. 3 (February 6, 1989).

85. Novak, *This Hemisphere of Liberty*, p. 44.

86. Novak, "Boredom, Virtue, and Democratic Capitalism," p. 36. Cf. Novak, "The Virtue of Enterprise: The Discovery of a 'Right to Economic Initiative' Could Revolutionize Catholic Social Thought," *Crisis* 7, no. 5 (May 1989).

87. Novak, *Spirit of Democratic Capitalism*, p. 15.

88. C.B. Macpherson, *The Real World of Democracy* (Toronto: Canadian Broadcasting Corporation, 1965), p. 9.

89. Steinfels, "Michael Novak and his ultrasuper democraticapitalism," pp. 14–15; John C. Cort, "The Social Thought of Michael Novak: At Odds with the Principles of Catholic Social Thought," *New Oxford Review* 55, no. 9 (November 1988): 8–9; Russell Kirk, *The Neoconservatives: An Endangered Species*, Heritage Lectures, no. 178 (Washington, D.C.: Heritage Foundation, 1988), pp. 6–7.

90. Novak, "Defining the U.S. System"; Novak, letter to *New Oxford Review* 55, no. 6 (July/August 1988).

91. Steinfels, "Michael Novak and his ultrasuper democraticapitalism," p. 14; Cort, "Social Thought of Michael Novak," pp. 8–9; Novak, letter to *New Oxford Review*.

92. Novak, letter to *New Oxford Review*. Cf. Novak, "A Phrase with a Winning Ring," *Forbes* 144, no. 3 (August 7, 1989); Novak, *This Hemisphere of Liberty*, p. 106.

93. Novak, *Will It Liberate?* pp. 13–153.

94. Quoted in Robert McAfee Brown, "Liberation as Bogeyman," review of *Will It Liberate? Questions about Liberation Theology*, by Michael Novak, *Christianity and Crisis* 47, no. 5 (April 6, 1987): p. 124.

95. Michael Novak, "The Case Against Liberation Theology," *New York Times Sunday Magazine*, October 21, 1984, p. 51; expanded and reprinted in *Will It Liberate?* pp. 13–32. Cf. Novak, "Liberation Theology on the Move," *National Review* 37, no. 18 (September 20, 1985).

96. Novak, *Spirit of Democratic Capitalism*, pp. 299–307.

97. Cf. Raul Prebisch, *The Economic Development of Latin America and Its Principal Problems* (New York: United Nations, 1950); Andre Gunder Frank, *Capitalism and Underdevelopment: Historical Studies of Chile and Brazil* (New York: Monthly Review Press, 1967); Frank, *Dependent Accumulation and Underdevelopment* (New York: Monthly Review Press, 1979); Fernando Henrique Cardoso and Enzo Falleto, *Dependency and Development in Latin America* (Berkeley: University of California Press, 1979); and Gabriel Palma, "Dependency: A Formal Theory of Underdevelopment or a Methodology for the Analysis of Concrete Situations of Underdevelopment?" *World Development*, July/August 1978, pp. 881–924.

98. Cited in Novak, *Spirit of Democratic Capitalism*, p. 279.

99. Ibid.

100. Novak, *Will It Liberate?* p. 129. Cf. Novak, "Why Latin America Is Poor," *Forbes* 143, no. 8 (1989); Novak, "Liberation Theology in Practice," *Thought* 59, no. 233 (June 1984).

101. Novak, *Spirit of Democratic Capitalism*, pp. 281, 275, 285.

102. Cf. Gustavo Gutierrez, *A Theology of Liberation: History, Politics, and Salvation*, trans. Sr. Caridad Inda and John Eagleson (Maryknoll, N.Y.: Orbis Books, 1973), pp. 87, 95; Leonardo Boff, *Liberating Grace*, trans. John Drury (Maryknoll: N.Y.: Orbis Books, 1979), pp. 65–78.

103. Cf. Michael Klare, *American Arms Supermarket* (Austin: University of Texas Press, 1984), pp. 1–25.

104. Novak, *Will It Liberate?* pp. 25–26, 49–50; Novak, "A Malthusian

Vision," *Forbes* 145, no. 10 (May 14, 1990); Novak, "Markets Make People Smile," *Forbes* 145, no. 8 (April 16, 1990).

105. Cf. Nicholas Eberstadt, "No Democratic Trend in East Asia," *Wall Street Journal*, July 18, 1989; Walden Bello and Stephanie Rosenfeld, "Dragons in Distress: The Crisis of the NICs," *World Policy Journal* 7, no. 3 (Summer 1990): 431–468.

106. Novak, *This Hemisphere of Liberty*, pp. 49–61.

107. Cf. Andre Gunder Frank, "Can the Debt Bomb Be Defused?" *World Policy Journal* 1, no. 4 (Summer 1984): 723–743; Hugo Assmann, "Democracy and the Debt Crisis," *This World* 14 (Spring/Summer 1986): 83–98; Robert E. Wood, "Making Sense of the Debt Crisis," *Socialist Review* 81, no. 15 (1985): 7–33; James S. Henry, "Where the Money Went: Third World Debt Hoax," *New Republic* 194, no. 15 (April 14, 1986): 20–23.

108. Fernando Fajnzylber, *Estrategia Industrial y Empresas Internacionales: Posicion relativa de America y Brasil* (Rio de Janeiro: United Nations, CEPAL, November 1970), p. 65; Richard J. Barnet and Ronald E. Muller, *Global Reach: The Power of the Multinational Corporations* (New York: Simon & Schuster, 1974), pp. 152–153.

109. Cf. Peter Evans, *Dependent Development: The Alliance of Multinational, State and Local Capital in Brazil* (Princeton: Princeton University Press, 1979); Aldo Ferrer, "The Structure of the World Economy: Southern Perspectives," in *The Structure of the World Economy and the Prospects for a New International Economic Order*, ed. E. Lazlo and J. Kurtzman (New York: Pergamon Press, 1982); E.V.K. FitzGerald, "Aspects of Finance Capital in Latin America," in *Economic Imperialism in Latin America*, ed. C. Abel and C. Lewis (London: London University Press, 1983); Richard Newfarmer and W. Mueller, *Multinational Corporations in Brazil and Mexico: Structural Sources of Economic and Noneconomic Power*, prepared for the Senate Sub-Committee on Multinationals (Washington, D.C.: U.S. Government Printing Office, 1975).

110. Novak, *Spirit of Democratic Capitalism*, p. 14.

111. Michael Novak, "Public Theology and the Left: What Happens after Reagan?" *Christian Century* 105, no. 15 (May 4, 1988): 454. Cf. Novak, "Why Latin America Is Poor."

112. Novak, *Will It Liberate?* p. 5.

113. Ibid.

114. Novak, *This Hemisphere of Liberty*, pp. 55–56.

115. Octavio Paz, "After the Cultural Delirium" (interview), *Encounter* 67, no. 2 (July/August, 1986): 66.

116. For discussions of this development, see Paul Sigmund, *Liberation Theology at the Crossroads: Democracy or Revolution?* (New York: Oxford University Press, 1990); Arthur F. McGovern, *Liberation Theology and Its Critics: Toward an Assessment* (Maryknoll, N.Y.: Orbis Books, 1989).

117. Novak, *Will It Liberate?* p. 5.

118. Cf. José Miranda, *Marx and the Bible: A Critique of the Philosophy of Oppression*, trans. John Eagleson (Maryknoll, N.Y.: Orbis Books, 1974); Miranda, *Communism in the Bible*, trans. Robert R. Barr (Maryknoll, N.Y.: Orbis Books, 1982).

119. Cf. McGovern, *Liberation Theology and Its Critics*, pp. 156–176; John R. Pottenger, *The Political Theory of Liberation Theology: Toward a Reconvergence of Social Values and Social Science* (Albany: State University of New York Press, 1989), pp. 99–129; Michael Novak, "Are You Sleeping Well, Fidel?" *Forbes* 145, no. 3 (February 5, 1990); Novak, "Liberation from Liberation Theology," *Forbes* 143, no. 10 (May 15, 1989); Novak, *Will It Liberate?* pp. 13–32; Novak, "Liberation Theology—What's Left," *First Things* 14 (June/July 1991): 10–12.

120. Cf. George V. Pixley, *God's Kingdom: A Guide for Biblical Study* (Maryknoll, N.Y.: Orbis Books, 1981); Jon Sobrino, *Christology at the Crossroads: A Latin American Approach*, trans. John Drury (Maryknoll, N.Y.: Orbis Books, 1978); Sobrino and Juan Hernandez Pico, *Theology of Christian Solidarity*, trans. Phillip Berryman (Maryknoll, N.Y.: Orbis Books, 1985).

121. Cf. Gustavo Gutierrez, *We Drink from Our Own Wells: The Spiritual Journey of a People*, trans. Matthew J. O'Connell (Maryknoll, N.Y.: Orbis Books, 1984); Leonardo Boff, *Ecclesiogenesis: The Base Communities Reinvent the Church*, trans. Robert R. Barr (Maryknoll, N.Y.: Orbis Books, 1986); Alvaro Barreiro, *Basic Ecclesial Communities: The Evangelization of the Poor*, trans. Barbara Campbell (Maryknoll, N.Y.: Orbis Books, 1982); Guillermo Cook, *The Expectation of the Poor: Latin American Basic Ecclesial Communities in Protestant Perspective* (Maryknoll, N.Y.: Orbis Books, 1985).

122. Novak, *Will It Liberate?* p. 3.

123. Ibid., p. 243.

124. Ibid., p. 9.

125. Novak, *Experience of Nothingness*, p. 100.

126. Cf. Peter L. Berger and Michael Novak, *Speaking to the Third World: Essays on Democracy and Development* (Washington, D.C.: American Enterprise Institute, 1985), pp. 31–59; Novak, "What Became of the Ugly American?" *Forbes* 145, no. 9 (April 30, 1990); Novak, "Markets Make People Smile."

127. On the "universality" of Western culture, see Michael Novak, "After Socialism, What?" *Forbes* 144, no. 1 (July 10, 1989).

128. Novak, *Spirit of Democratic Capitalism* pp. 253–254.

129. Ibid., p. 334.

130. Novak, *Will It Liberate?* p. 175.

131. Ibid., p. 192.

132. Ibid., p. 176.

133. Cf. Rudolf Meidner, *Employee Investment Funds: An Approach to Collective Capital Formation* (London: George Allen & Unwin, 1978); John D. Stephens, *The Transition from Capitalism to Socialism* (Atlantic Highlands, N.J.: Humanities Press, 1980); Robert A. Dahl, *A Preface to Economic Democracy* (Berkeley: University of California Press, 1985); Jon Elster and Karl Ove Moene, eds., *Alternatives to Capitalism* (Cambridge: Cambridge University Press, 1989).

134. Novak, "Public Thelogy and the Left," p. 455.

135. Novak, *Spirit of Democratic Capitalism*, p. 112.

136. Novak, *Spirit of Democratic Capitalism*, pp. 189–210; Novak, "The Twilight of Socialism," *Catholicism in Crisis* 1, no. 9 (August 1983): 1–2.

137. On America's "broker state" model, see Gar Alperovitz and Jeff Faux, *Rebuilding America: A Blueprint for the New Economy* (New York: Pantheon Books, 1984); Samuel Bowles, David M. Gordon, and Thomas E. Weisskopf, *Beyond the Wasteland: A Democratic Alternative to Economic Decline* (Garden City, N.Y.: Anchor Press, 1983); Michael Harrington, *Decade of Decision: The Crisis of the American System* (New York: Simon & Schuster, 1980).

138. Charles E. Lindblom, *Politics and Markets: The World's Political-Economic Systems* (New York: Basic Books, 1977), p. 356.

139. Novak, *Spirit of Democratic Capitalism*, pp. 176–181.

140. Ibid., p. 178.

141. Cf. Michael Quarry, *Employee Ownership and Corporate Performance* (Oakland: National Center for Employee Ownership, 1986); Frank Lindenfeld and Joyce Rothschild-Whitt, eds., *Workplace Democracy and Social Change* (Boston: Porter Sargent, 1982); John F. Witte, *Democracy, Authority, and Alienation in Work* (Chicago: University of Chicago Press, 1980), pp. 130–150; J. Maxwell Elden, "Political Efficacy at Work" *American Political Science Review* 75 (March 1981): 43–58; Joseph R. Blasi, *Employee Ownership: Revolution or Ripoff?* (Cambridge, Mass.: Ballinger, 1988); Branko Horvat, Mihailo Markovic, and Rudi Supek, eds., *Self-Governing Socialism*, 2 vols. (White Plains, N.Y.: M. E. Sharpe, 1975); Thomas H. Naylor, "Redefining Corporate Motivation, Swedish Style," *Christian Century* 107, no. 18 (May 30–June 6, 1990): 566–570.

142. Cf. Martin Carnoy and Derek Shearer, *Economic Democracy: The Challenge of the 1980s* (White Plains, N.Y.: M. E. Sharpe, 1980); Alec Nove, *The Economics of Feasible Socialism* (London: George Allen & Unwin, 1983); Allen Buchanan, *Ethics, Efficiency, and the Market* (Totowa, N.J.: Rowman & Allanheld, 1985); Graham Wooton, *Workers, Unions and the State* (London: Routledge & Kegan Paul), 1986.

143. Novak, "Errand into the Wilderness," pp. 263–264. On the relationships between religion, utopianism, and political vision, see Michael Novak, "Religion and Liberty: From Vision to Politics," *Christian Century* 105, no. 21 (July 6–13, 1988): 635–638.

144. Michael Novak, "Making Deterrence Work," *Catholicism in Crisis* 1, no. 1 (November 1982).

145. Michael Novak, "Moral Clarity in the Nuclear Age," *Catholicism in Crisis* 1, no. 4 (March 1983); reprinted in *National Review* 35, no. 6 (April 1, 1983). For a thoughtful critique of Novak's argument, see J. M. Cameron, *Nuclear Catholics and Other Essays* (Grand Rapids, Mich.: William B. Eerdmans, 1989), pp. 60–74.

146. Michael Novak, *Moral Clarity in the Nuclear Age* (Nashville: Thomas Nelson, 1983), p. 42.

147. National Conference of Catholic Bishops, *The Challenge of Peace: God's Promise and Our Response* (Washington, D.C.: United States Catholic Conference, 1983).

148. Novak, *Clarity in the Nuclear Age*, p. 121.

149. Michael Novak, "Born-Again Bishops," *National Review* 34, no. 15 (August 6, 1982): 960. Cf. Novak, "Why the Church Is Not Pacifist," *Catholicism in Crisis* 2, no. 7 (June 1984).

150. Michael Novak, "On Democratic Capitalism," *National Review* 36, no. 2 (October 29, 1982): 1351. Cf. Novak, "Prince-Bishop Economics," *National Review* 35, no. 4 (March 4, 1983): 260; Novak, "Theology and Economics," *National Review* 36, no. 2 (February 10, 1984): 40.

151 Novak, "Twilight of Socialism," p. 2.

152. Lay Commission on Catholic Social Teaching and the U.S. Economy, *Toward the Future* (New York: Lay Commission, 1984), p. 58.

153. National Conference of Catholic Bishops, *Economic Justice for All: Catholic Social Teaching and the U.S. Economy* (Washington, D.C.: United States Catholic Conference, 1986); reprinted in *Origins* (Washington, D.C.: National Catholic News Service, November 27, 1986), nos. 85–94.

154. Michael Novak, "Toward Consensus: Suggestions for Revising the First Draft," *Catholicism in Crisis* 3, no. 4 (March 1985): 9–10.

155. Ibid., p. 5; quotation from Novak, interview with author, March 20, 1990.

156. Michael Novak, "Economic Rights: The Servile State," *Catholicism in Crisis* 3, no. 10 (October 1985): 8.

157. David Hollenbach, *Claims in Conflict: Retrieving and Renewing the Catholic Human Rights Tradition* (New York: Paulist Press, 1979).

158. Novak, "Economic Rights," p. 10. Cf. Novak, "Socialists Circle Bishops," *National Review* 37, no. 6 (April 5, 1985): 46; Novak, "Polarizing Catholics?" *National Review* 37, no. 22 (November 15, 1985): 46; Novak, "Blaming America: A Comment on Paragraphs 202–204 of the First Draft," *Catholicism in Crisis* 3, no. 8 (July 1985): 12–16.

159. Novak, "Economic Rights," p. 10.

160. Ibid., p. 8.

161. Michael Novak, "The Christian Vision of Economic Life," *Catholicism in Crisis* 3, no. 12 (December 1985): 27.

162. Ibid., p. 29.

163. Ibid.

164. Michael Novak, interview with author, June 19, 1992.

165. Novak, "Economic Rights," p. 13.

166. David Hollenbach, "The Growing End of an Argument," *America* 153, no. 16 (November 30, 1985): 365.

167. Michael Novak, *Free Persons and the Common Good* (Lanham, Md.: Madison Books, 1989), p. 155.

168. Cf. John Rawls, *A Theory of Justice* (Cambridge, Mass.: Harvard University Press, 1971); Ronald Dworkin, *Taking Rights Seriously* (Cambridge, Mass.: Harvard University Press, 1977); Amy Gutmann, *Liberal Equality* (Cambridge: Cambridge University Press, 1980); William A. Galston, *Justice and the Human Good* (Chicago: University of Chicago Press, 1980); Bruce A. Ackerman, *Social Justice in the Liberal State* (New Haven: Yale University Press, 1980).

169. Cf. Michael J. Sandel, *Liberalism and the Limits of Justice* (Cambridge: Cambridge University Press, 1982); Alasdair MacIntyre, *After Virtue: A Study in Moral Theory* (Notre Dame, Ind.: University of Notre Dame Press, 1981); Michael

Walzer, *Spheres of Justice: A Defense of Pluralism and Equality* (New York: Basic Books, 1983).

170. David Hollenbach, "Liberalism, Communitarianism and the Bishops' Pastoral Letter on the Economy," *Annual of the Society of Christian Ethics 1987* (Washington, D.C.: Georgetown University Press), pp. 19–23. Cf. Hollenbach, "Justice as Participation: Public Moral Discourse and the U.S. Economy," in *Community in America: The Challenge of "Habits of the Heart,"* ed. Charles H. Reynolds and Ralph V. Norman (Berkeley: University of California Press, 1988), pp. 217–229; Hollenbach, *Justice, Peace and Human Rights: American Catholic Social Ethics in a Pluralistic Context* (New York: Crossroad, 1989), pp. 104–106.

171. Novak, *Free Persons and the Common Good,* p. 158; Novak, "Twilight of Socialism," p. 2.

172. Novak, "Virtue of Enterprise," p. 21.

173. Novak, *This Hemisphere of Liberty,* p. 38; Novak, "A Papal 'Yes' to Capitalism," *Forbes* 147, no. 11 (May 27, 1991): 182–183.

174. Novak, *Free Persons and the Common Good,* p. 86.

175. Cf. Milton Friedman, *Capitalism and Freedom* (Chicago: University of Chicago Press, 1962); John Hospers, *Libertarianism* (Los Angeles: Nash, 1971). Perhaps the most sophisticated defense of libertarianism is Robert Nozick's *Anarchy, State, and Utopia* (New York: Basic Books, 1974). Nozick has since rejected the hyperindividualistic notion of the self on which this book's argument was based, however. Cf. Robert Nozick, *The Examined Life: Philosophical Meditations* (New York: Simon & Schuster, 1989).

176. Friedrich A. Hayek, *Law, Legislation and Liberty,* vol. 2, *The Mirage of Social Justice* (Chicago: University of Chicago Press, 1976).

177. Cf. Novak, "Return of the Catholic Whig," p. 42.

178. Novak, *Free Persons and the Common Good,* p. 80.

179. Michael Novak, "The Rights and Wrongs of 'Economic Rights': A Debate Continued," *This World* 17 (Spring 1987): 47.

180. Cf. Michael Novak, "St. Thomas for the Twenty-First Century," *Catholicism in Crisis* 2, no. 3 (March 1984); Novak, "Dissent in the Church," *Catholicism in Crisis* 4, no. 1 (January 1986); Novak, "Not Yet: Biblical Realism and Power Politics," *Catholicism in Crisis* 2, no. 8 (July 1984); Novak, *Confession of a Catholic.*

181. Novak, *Rise of the Unmeltable Ethnics,* p. xv.

182. Cf. Novak, *A Time to Build,* pp. 79–96, 215–372.

183. Michael Novak, "Democracy and Human Rights," in Berger and Novak, *Speaking to the Third World,* p. 33.

184. Brown, "Liberation as Bogeyman," p. 124.

185. Novak, *Confession of a Catholic,* p. 13.

186. Ibid., pp. 193–198.

187. Michael Novak, "Woman Church Is Not Mother Church," *Catholicism in Crisis* 2, no. 3 (February 1984): 20–21.

188. Ibid., p. 21. Cf. Elaine Pagels, *The Gnostic Gospels* (New York: Vintage Books, 1979).

189. Novak, "Orthodoxy vs. Progressive Bourgeois Christianity," p. 127.

190. Cf. Michael Novak, "New Questions for Humanists," in *The Denigration of Capitalism: Six Points of View*, ed. Novak (Washington, D.C.: American Enterprise Institute, 1979), p. 57; Novak, "Changing the Paradigms: The Cultural Deficiencies of Capitalism," in *Democracy and Mediating Structures: A Theological Inquiry*, ed. Novak (Washington, D.C.: American Enterprise Institute, 1980), p. 193.

191. Novak, *Confession of a Catholic*, pp. 178–181.

192. Cf. Ibid., p. 180; Novak, *Free Persons and the Common Good*, pp. 158, 161.

193. Cf. Novak, *Freedom with Justice*, p. xiv; Novak, *Confession of a Catholic*, p. 117; Novak, "Reinhold Niebuhr: Model for Neoconservatives," *Christian Century* 103, no. 3 (January 22, 1986): 70.

194. Novak, "Seven Theological Facets," pp. 117–118. Cf. Novak, "Not Yet: Biblical Realism and Power Politics."

195. Novak, *Will It Liberate?* p. 56.

196. Novak, *This Hemisphere of Liberty*, p. 70.

197. Michael Novak, presentation of "Wealth and Virtue: The Development of Christian Economic Teaching," delivered at the American Enterprise Institute Religion and Economics Seminar, March 20, 1990; Novak, interview with author, March 20, 1990; Novak, *Will It Liberate?* pp. 56–57.

198. Novak, interview with author, March 20, 1990.

199. Novak, *Spirit of Democratic Capitalism*, p. 185.

200. Novak, interview with author, March 20, 1990.

201. Peter Steinfels, "Does Capitalism Equal Pluralism Equal Democracy?" *Commonweal* 110, no. 3 (February 11, 1983): 81.

202. Novak, "Changing the Paradigms," p. 199.

203. Michael Novak, "The Revolt Against Our Public Culture," *National Review* 36, no. 8 (May 4, 1984): 48.

204. Novak, interview with author, March 20, 1990.

205. Michael Novak, "The Left Still Owns American Culture," *Forbes* 145, no. 5 (March 5, 1990): 118.

206. Novak, interview with author, March 20, 1990.

207. Novak, "Reinhold Niebuhr: Model for Neoconservatives," p. 71.

208. Cf. Frederick R. Strobel, *Upward Dreams, Downward Mobility: The Economic Decline of the Middle Class* (Lanham, Md.: Rowman & Littlefield, 1992).

209. Novak, "Not Only the Rich Are Capitalists Now," p. 98.

210. Cf. Jon Wiener, "Dollars for Neocon Scholars," *Nation* 250, no. 1 (January 1, 1990): 13.

Notes to Chapter 6

1. Peter L. Berger, "Two Paradoxes," *National Review* 24, no. 18 (May 12, 1972): 510; reprinted in Berger, *Facing Up to Modernity: Excursions in Society, Politics, and Religion* (New York: Basic Books, 1977), pp. 107–117 (quotation on p. 115).

2. Peter L. Berger, "From Secularity to World Religions," *Christian Century* 97, no. 2 (January 16, 1980): 44.

3. Peter L. Berger, *The Noise of Solemn Assemblies: Christian Commitment and the Religious Establishment in America* (Garden City, N.Y.: Doubleday, 1961), pp. 92–93.

4. Ibid., pp. 98–99, 102–103.

5. Ibid., p. 115.

6. Ibid., pp. 116–117.

7. Ibid., p. 118.

8. Cf. Dietrich Bonhoeffer, *Letters and Papers from Prison*, ed. Eberhard Bethge (New York: Macmillan, 1972), pp. 278–282, 324–329, 360–362.

9. Peter L. Berger, *The Precarious Vision: A Sociologist Looks at Social Fictions and the Christian Faith* (Garden City, N.Y.: Doubleday, 1961), p. 177.

10. Ibid., p. 180.

11. Cf. Harvey Cox, *The Secular City: Urbanization and Secularization in Theological Perspective* (New York: Macmillan, 1965).

12. Peter L. Berger, *Invitation to Sociology: A Humanistic Perspective* (Garden City, N.Y.: Anchor Books, 1963), pp. 91–92.

13. Ibid., p. 55.

14. Ibid., pp. 142–144.

15. Cf. Jean-Paul Sartre, *Anti-Semite and Jew*, ed. Paul Morihien (New York: Schocken, 1948).

16. Berger, *Precarious Vision*, p. 159.

17. Berger, *Invitation to Sociology*, p. 145.

18. Ibid., pp. 175–176.

19. Peter L. Berger and Thomas Luckmann, *The Social Construction of Reality: A Treatise in the Sociology of Knowledge* (New York: Doubleday, 1966), pp. 186–188.

20. Berger, *Invitation to Sociology*, pp. 5–6.

21. Berger and Luckmann, *Social Construction of Reality*, p. 187.

22. Peter L. Berger, *The Sacred Canopy: Elements of a Sociological Theory of Religion* (Garden City, N.Y.: Doubleday, 1967), p. 3.

23. Ibid., p. 4.

24. Ibid., pp. 19, 25.

25. Ibid., p. 27.

26. Ibid., p. 27.

27. Ibid., pp. 149–150.

28. Ibid., p. 156.

29. Ibid., p. 165.

30. Peter L. Berger, *A Rumor of Angels: Modern Society and the Rediscovery of the Supernatural* (Garden City, N.Y.: Doubleday, 1969), p. ix.

31. Herman Kahn and Anthony J. Wiener, *The Year 2000: A Framework for Speculation on the Next Thirty-three Years* (New York: Macmillan, 1967), p. 7. For a strikingly similar perspective, this time offered as an account of the "American" world view, see Henry Steele Commager, *The American Mind: An Interpretation of American Thought and Character since the 1880s* (New Haven: Yale University Press, 1950).

32. Berger, *Rumor of Angels*, pp. 8–17.

33. Ibid., p. 44.

34. Ibid., p. 3.

35. Cf. Rudolf Bultmann, "New Testament and Mythology," in *Kerygma and Myth: A Theological Debate*, ed. Hans Werner Bartsch, trans. Reginald H. Fuller (London: S.P.C.K., 1954), pp. 1–44.

36. Berger, *Rumor of Angels*, p. 57.

37. Ibid., pp. 53–72.

38. Ibid., p. 84.

39. Ibid., p. 88.

40. Peter L. Berger, interview with author, September 26, 1990.

41. Ibid.

42. Richard J. Neuhaus, "The Thorough Revolutionary," in Peter L. Berger and Richard John Neuhaus, *Movement and Revolution* (Garden City, N.Y.: Doubleday, 1970), p. 127.

43. Ibid., pp. 215–236.

44. Peter L. Berger, "Between System and Horde: Personal Suggestions to Reluctant Activists," in Berger and Neuhaus, *Movement and Revolution*, pp. 13–19, 50, 63.

45. Ibid., p. 71.

46. Ibid., p. 21.

47. Ibid., p. 16.

48. Ibid., p. 43.

49. Ibid., pp. 44–46.

50. Ibid., p. 62.

51. Berger, "Two Paradoxes," pp. 507–508; reprinted in Berger, *Facing Up to Modernity*, pp. 108–111.

52. Ibid., p. 510 and p. 114.

53. Ibid., p. 510 and p. 113.

54. Peter L. Berger, *Pyramids of Sacrifice: Political Ethics and Social Change* (New York: Basic Books, 1974), p. 13.

55. Ibid., p. 46.

56. Ibid., p. 48.

57. Ibid., p. 54.

58. Peter L. Berger, "Underdevelopment Revisited," *Commentary* 78, no. 1 (July 1984): 42.

59. Berger, *Pyramids of Sacrifice*, pp. 217–218.

60. Ibid., p. 208.

61. Peter L. Berger, "The Greening of American Foreign Policy," *Commentary* 61, no. 3 (March 1976): 23; reprinted in slightly edited form in Berger, *Facing Up to Modernity*, pp. 95–106 (quotation on p. 96).

62. Ibid., p. 24 and p. 98. Cf. Peter L. Berger, "The Socialist Myth," *Public Interest* 44 (Summer 1976); reprinted in Berger, *Facing Up to Modernity*, pp. 56–69.

63. Berger, "Greening of American Foreign Policy," pp. 25–26 and pp. 101–102.

64. Ibid., p. 26 and p. 103.

65. Ibid., p. 27 and p. 105.

66. Berger, interview with author, September 26, 1990.

67. Berger, *Pyramids of Sacrifice*, p. 54.

68. Cf. Peter L. Berger and Philip Marcus, eds., *The Arithmetic of Justice: Capitalism and Equality in America* (Washington, D.C.: University Press of America, 1986); Berger and Marcus, eds., *Capitalism and Equality in the Third World* (Washington, D.C.: University Press of America, 1986). These volumes are collections of papers presented at Berger's Seminar on Modern Capitalism.

69. Peter L. Berger, "Progress Report—June 1990" (report to donors of the Institute for the Study of Economic Culture, Boston University), p. 4.

70. Berger, "Underdevelopment Revisited," p. 42.

71. Ibid., pp. 42–43; Peter L. Berger, "Speaking to the Third World," *Commentary* 72, no. 4 (October 1981): 32; reprinted in Peter L. Berger and Michael Novak, *Speaking to the Third World: Essays on Democracy and Development* (Washington, D.C.: American Enterprise Institute, 1985), p. 11.

72. Peter L. Berger, "Democracy for Everyone?" *Commentary* 76, no. 3, (September 1983): 33.

73. Peter L. Berger, *The Capitalist Revolution: Fifty Propositions about Prosperity, Equality, and Liberty* (New York: Basic Books, 1986), pp. 141–150. Cf. William W. Lockwood, *The Economic Development of Japan: Growth and Structural Change, 1868–1938* (Princeton: Princeton University Press, 1954), pp. 78–150.

74. Berger, *Capitalist Revolution*, p. 149.

75. Ibid., p. 157.

76. Cf. K. M. Panikkar, *Asia and Western Dominance* (New York: Collier Books, 1969), pp. 153–162; Michael Schaller, *The American Occupation of Japan: The Origins of the Cold War in Asia* (New York: Oxford University Press, 1985).

77. Berger, *Capitalist Revolution*, p. 129.

78. Ibid., p. 130.

79. Berger, "Speaking to the Third World," p. 34. Discussion of "Underdevelopment Revisited" quoted in Michael Novak, ed., *Liberation Theology and the Liberal Society* (Washington, D.C.: American Enterprise Institute, 1987), p. 93.

80. Cf. Bernard S. Silberman, *Ministers of Modernization: Elite Mobility in the Meiji Restoration* (Tuscon: University of Arizona Press, 1964); Sakakibara Eisuke and Noguchi Yukio, "Organization for Economic Reconstruction," in *Inside the Japanese System: Readings in Contemporary Society and Political Economy*, ed. Daniel I. Okimoto and Thomas P. Rohlen (Stanford: Stanford University Press, 1988), pp. 43–54; Jon Livingston, Joe Moore, and Felicia Oldfather, eds., *Imperial Japan, 1800–1945* (New York: Pantheon Books, 1973), pp. 105–335; W. G. Beasley, *The Rise of Modern Japan* (New York: St. Martin's Press, 1990), pp. 54–83, 243–277.

81. Cf. Richard J. Samuels, *The Business of the Japanese State: Energy Markets in Comparative and Historical Perspective* (Ithaca, N.Y.: Cornell University Press, 1987), pp. 257–290; Karel von Wolferen, *The Enigma of Japanese Power: People and Politics in a Stateless Nation* (New York: Vintage Books, 1990), pp. 25–49; John Foster and Charles Woolfson, "Corporate Reconstruction and Business Unionism: The Lessons of Caterpillar and Ford," *New Left Review* 174 (March/April 1989);

Ezra F. Vogel, *Japan as Number One* (New York: Harper & Row, 1979), pp. 97–157.

82. Alice H. Amsden, "Third World Industrialization: 'Global Fordism' or a New Model?" *New Left Review* 182 (July/August 1990): 16.

83. Berger, *Capitalist Revolution*, p. 158. Cf. Seung-Hee Kim, "Economic Development of South Korea," in *Government and Politics of Korea*, ed. Sejia Kim and Chang Hyun Cho (Silver Spring, Md.: Research Institute on Korean Affairs, 1972), pp. 148–175; Jung-en Woo, *Race to the Swift: State and Finance in Korean Industrialization* (New York: Columbia University Press, 1991); Peter A. Petri, "Korea's Export Niche: Origins and Prospects," *World Development*, January 1988, pp. 47–68; Kyong-Dong Kim, *Man and Society in Korea's Economic Growth* (Seoul: Seoul National University Press, 1984).

84. Berger, *Capitalist Revolution*, p. 159.

85. For discussions of the cultural foundations of power and authority in contemporary East Asia, see Lucian W. Pye, *Asian Power and Politics: The Cultural Dimensions of Authority* (Cambridge, Mass.: Harvard University Press, 1985); Robert Christopher, *The Japanese Mind* (New York: Fawcett Columbine, 1983); Frank Gibney, *Japan: The Fragile Superpower* (New York: New American Library, 1985); Brian Kelly and Mark London, *The Four Little Dragons* (New York: Simon & Schuster, 1989).

86. Cf. Nicholas Eberstadt, "No Democratic Trend in East Asia," *Wall Street Journal*, July 18, 1989; Claudia Rosett, "Secrets of Singapore's Leninist Order," *Wall Street Journal*, November 7, 1990; Michio Morishima, "Confucianism as a Basis for Capitalism," in *Inside the Japanese System*, ed. Okimoto and Rohlen, pp. 36–38; Pye, *Asian Power and Politics*, pp. 31–89.

87. Berger, interview with author, September 26, 1990.

88. Michael Novak, *Will It Liberate? Questions about Liberation Theology* (New York: Paulist Press, 1986), pp. 4–6.

89. Berger, interview with author, September 26, 1990.

90. Ibid. See also Michael Novak, ed., *Liberation Theology and the Liberal Society* (Washington, D.C.: American Enterprise Institute, 1987), pp. 97–100.

91. Berger, *Capitalist Revolution*, p. 156.

92. Walden Bello and Stephanie Rosenfeld, "Dragons in Distress: The Crisis of the NICs," *World Policy Journal* 7, no. 3 (Summer 1990): 434–435.

93. Berger, *Capitalist Revolution*, p. 146. Cf. Michio Morishima, *Why Japan Has Succeeded: Western Technology and the Japanese Ethos* (New York: Cambridge University Press, 1982).

94. Bello and Rosenfeld, "Dragons in Distress," pp. 435–436.

95. Ibid., pp. 443–447; Hla Myint, *Southeast Asia's Economy: Development Policies in the 1970s* (New York: Praeger Publishers, 1972), pp. 58–72.

96. Cf. Bill Moyers, *A World of Ideas: Conversations with Thoughtful Men and Women about American Life Today and the Ideas Shaping Our Future* (New York: Doubleday, 1989), p. 492.

97. Cf. Christopher Lasch, "The American 80's: Disaster or Triumph?" *Commentary* 90, no. 3 (September 1990): 23–24; Lasch, "The Communitarian

Critique of Liberalism," in *Community in America: The Challenge of 'Habits of the Heart,'* ed. Charles H. Reynolds and Ralph V. Norman (Berkeley: University of California Press, 1988), pp. 173–184; Jeffrey Stout, "Liberal Society and the Languages of Morals," in *Community in America*, ed. Reynolds and Norman, pp. 127–146.

98. Peter L. Berger and Richard John Neuhaus, *To Empower People: The Role of Mediating Structures in Public Policy* (Washington, D.C.: American Enterprise Institute, 1977), p. 6.

99. Ibid., p. 15.

100. Ibid., p. 21.

101. Ibid., pp. 22–23.

102. Ibid., p. 44.

103. On communitarian theory, see Amitai Etzioni, "Liberals and Communitarians," *Partisan Review* 57, no. 2 (Spring 1990): 215–227; Ken Anderson, Paul Piccone, Fred Siegel, and Michael Taves, "Roundtable on Communitarianism," *Telos* 76 (Summer 1988): 2–32; Michael Walzer, "The Communitarian Critique of Liberalism," *Political Theory* 18, no. 1 (February 1990): 6–23.

104. Richard B. Madden, "The Large Business Corporation as a Mediating Structure," in *Democracy and Mediating Structures: A Theological Inquiry*, ed. Michael Novak (Washington, D.C.: American Enterprise Institute, 1980), pp. 106–117.

105. Tom Kahn, "Organized Labor as a Mediating Structure," in *Democracy and Mediating Structures*, ed. Novak, pp. 125–134.

106. Cf. Lasch, "Communitarian Critique of Liberalism"; Michael J. Sandel, *Liberalism and the Limits of Justice* (Cambridge: Cambridge University Press, 1982); Michael Walzer, *Spheres of Justice: A Defense of Pluralism and Equality* (New York: Basic Books, 1983); Robert Bellah et al., *The Good Society* (New York: Alfred A. Knopf, 1991); Benjamin Barber, *Strong Democracy: Participatory Politics for a New Age* (Berkeley: University of California Press, 1984): Harry C. Boyte, *CommonWealth: A Return to Citizen Politics* (New York: Free Press, 1989).

107. Berger, *Capitalist Revolution*, p. 85.

108. Quoted in Novak, ed., *Liberation Theology and the Liberal Society*, p. 105.

109. Berger, interview with author, September 26, 1990. Cf. Berger, "Capitalism: The Continuing Revolution," *First Things* 15 (August/September 1991): 24–25.

110. Cf. Oskar Lange and F. M. Taylor, *On the Economic Theory of Socialism,* (1931; reprint, New York: McGraw-Hill, 1964).

111. Cf. Ludwig von Mises, *Socialism: An Economic and Sociological Analysis,* trans. J. Kahane (1936; reprint, Indianapolis: Liberty Classics, 1981), pp. 229–245.

112. Berger, *Capitalist Revolution*, p. 190.

113. On worker ownership in the United States, see Len Krimerman and Frank Lindenfeld, "Contemporary Workplace Democracy in the United States: Taking Stock of an Emerging Movement," *Socialism and Democracy* 11 (September 1990): 109–139; Severyn T. Bruyn and James Meehan, eds., *Beyond State and*

Market: New Directions in Community Development (Philadelphia: Temple University Press, 1987); Thomas H. Naylor, "Redefining Corporate Motivation, Swedish Style," *Christian Century* 107, no. 18 (May 30/June 6, 1990): 566–570; Joseph Blasi, *Employee Ownership: Revolution or Ripoff?* (Cambridge, Mass.: Ballinger, 1988); Steven Bloom, *Employee Ownership and Firm Performance* (Cambridge, Mass.: Harvard University Press, 1986); Karl Frieden, *Workplace Democracy and Productivity* (Washington, D.C.: National Center for Economic Alternatives, 1980).

114. On the Mondragon cooperatives, see Henk Thomas and Chris Logan, *Mondragon: An Economic Analysis* (London: George Allen & Unwin, 1982); W. Whyte and Kathleen K. Whyte, *Making Mondragon* (Ithaca, N.Y.: ILR Press, 1988); Keith Bradley and Alan Gelb, *Cooperation at Work: The Mondragon Experience* (London: Heinemann Educational Books, 1984).

115. Cf. Rudolf Meidner, *Employee Investment Funds: An Approach to Collective Capital Formation* (London: George Allen & Unwin, 1978); Meidner, "A Swedish Union Proposal for Collective Capital Sharing," in *Eurosocialism and America: Political Economy for the 1980s,* ed. Nancy Lieber (Philadelphia: Temple University Press, 1982); Meidner and Anna Hedborg, *Model Schweden* (Frankfurt: Campus Verlag, 1984).

116. Berger, interview with author, September 26, 1990.

117. Berger, *Capitalist Revolution,* p. 203.

118. Peter L. Berger and Brigitte Berger, "Our Conservatism and Theirs," *Commentary* 82, no. 4 (October 1986): 63.

119. Ibid., p. 65. For an extended discussion, see Peter L. Berger, Brigitte Berger, and Hansfried Kellner, *The Homeless Mind: Modernization and Consciousness* (New York: Vintage Books, 1974).

120. Cf. Max Weber, "Politics as a Vocation," in *Weber: Selections in Translation,* ed. W. G. Runciman, trans. Eric Matthews (Cambridge: Cambridge University Press, 1978), pp. 212–225; Martin Luther, "Temporal Authority: To What Extent It Should Be Obeyed," in *Martin Luther's Basic Theological Writings,* ed. Timothy F. Lull (Minneapolis: Fortress Press, 1989), pp. 655–703; Peter L. Berger, "Moral Judgment and Political Action," *This World* 21 (Spring 1988): 4–7, 15–18.

121. Peter L. Berger and Richard John Neuhaus, eds., *Against the World for the World: The Hartford Appeal and the Future of American Religion* (New York: Seabury, 1976).

122. Peter L. Berger, *The Heretical Imperative: Contemporary Possibilities of Religious Affirmation* (Garden City, N.Y.: Anchor Press, 1979), p. xiv.

123. Berger, "From Secularity to World Religions," p. 44.

124. Berger, *Heretical Imperative,* pp. 133–134.

125. Cf. Ibid., pp. 127–135; Peter L. Berger, "The Other Side of God—Problem and Agenda," in *The Other Side of God: A Polarity in World Religions,* ed. Berger (Garden City, N.Y.: Anchor Books, 1981), pp. 3–27. For a discussion of Berger's "inductive option," see George Pepper, "Peter Berger: Modernization and Religion," *Cross Currents* 38, no. 4 (Winter 1988–89): 448–456.

126. Peter L. Berger, "Different Gospels: The Social Sources of Apostasy," *This World* 17 (Spring 1987): 12–13.

127. Ibid., p. 11. Cf. Peter L. Berger, "The First Freedom," *Commentary* 86, no. 6 (December 1988): 64–67.

128. Quoted in Richard John Neuhaus, ed., *Confession, Conflict, and Community* (Grand Rapids, Mich.: William B. Eerdmans, 1986), pp. 73–74. Cf. Peter L. Berger, "Can the Bishops Help the Poor?" *Commentary* 79, no. 2 (February 1985): 31–35.

129. Peter L. Berger, "The Concept of Mediating Action," in *Confession, Conflict, and Community*, ed. Neuhaus, p. 11.

130. Peter L. Berger, "Democracy for Everyone?" pp. 31–36 (quotation on p. 36); Berger, interview with author, September 26, 1990.

131. Berger, interview with author, September 26, 1990.

132. Michael Harrington confessed that reading the repeated "value free" claims in *The Capitalist Revolution* put him "in a constant state of irritation punctuated by occasional gusts of anger." Cf. Harrington's review in *Commonweal* 113, no. 18 (October 24, 1986): 558, 568–569.

133. Quoted in Neuhaus, ed., *Confession, Conflict, and Community*, p. 70.

134. Peter L. Berger, "Reflections of an Ecclesiastical Expatriate," *Christian Century* 107, no. 30 (October 24, 1990): 964.

135. Ibid., p. 135. Cf. Peter L. Berger, "Worldly Wisdom, Christian Foolishness," *First Things* 5 (August/September 1990): 19; Berger, "Religion in Post-Protestant America," *Commentary* 81, no. 5 (May 1986): 41–46.

136. Peter L. Berger and Brigitte Berger, *The War over the Family: Capturing the Middle Ground* (Garden City, N.Y.: Anchor Press, 1983), p. 52.

137. Berger, "Reflections of an Ecclesiastical Expatriate," p. 969. For an elaboration of Berger's disaffection from modern liberal Protestantism, see Berger, *A Far Glory: The Quest for Faith in an Age of Credulity* (New York: Free Press, 1992).

Notes to Chapter 7

1. Peter Berger, interview with author, September 26, 1990.

2. Quoted in John B. Judis, "The Conservative Crackup," *American Prospect* 3 (Fall 1990): 35. Cf. Frank Gaffney, "A Layman's Guide to Fixing the INF Treaty," *National Review* 40, no. 5 (March 18, 1988): 44–45.

3. Irving Kristol, "Defining Our National Interest," *National Interest* 21 (Fall 1990): 23.

4. Ibid., p. 24.

5. Jeane J. Kirkpatrick, "Dictatorships and Double Standards," *Commentary* 68, no. 5 (November 1979); reprinted in Kirkpatrick, *Dictatorships and Double Standards: Rationalism and Reason in Politics* (New York: American Enterprise Institute, 1982), p. 49.

6. Cf. Jeane J. Kirkpatrick, *Legitimacy and Force*, vol. 1, *Political and Moral Dimensions* (New Brunswick, N.J.: Transaction Books, 1988), pp. 85–190.

7. Jeane J. Kirkpatrick, "A Normal Country in a Normal Time," *National Interest* 21 (Fall 1990): 44. Cf. Kirkpatrick, "Beyond the Cold War," *Foreign Affairs*

69, no. 1 (1990): 1–16; Kirkpatrick, *The Withering Away of the Totalitarian State . . . and Other Surprises* (Washington, D.C.: American Enterprise Institute, 1990), pp. 172–174, 268–270.

8. Quoted in Judis, "Conservative Crackup," p. 36.

9. Joshua Muravchik, "Maximum Feasible Containment," *New Republic* 196, no. 22 (June 1, 1987): 25.

10. Joshua Muravchik, *Exporting Democracy: Fulfilling America's Destiny* (Washington, D.C.: American Enterprise Institute, 1991), pp. 67–68; Ben J. Wattenberg, *The First Universal Nation: Leading Indicators and Ideas about the Surge of America in the 1990s* (New York: Free Press, 1991), p. 24.

11. Wattenberg, *First Universal Nation*, p. 20.

12. Ibid., p. 196.

13. Ibid.

14. Ben J. Wattenberg, "Neo-Manifest Destinarianism," *National Interest* 21 (Fall 1990): 52.

15. Ibid., pp. 51–52.

16. Morton Kondracke, "The Democracy Gang," *New Republic* 201, no. 1 (November 6, 1989): 18, 20; Wattenberg, "Neo-Manifest Destinarianism," p. 51.

17. Wattenberg, "Neo-Manifest Destinarianism," p. 52.

18. Wattenberg, *First Universal Nation*, p. 196.

19. Gregory A. Fossedal, *The Democratic Imperative: Exporting the American Revolution* (New York: Basic Books, 1989), p. 219.

20. Ibid., pp. 220, 237.

21. Wattenberg, "Neo-Manifest Destinarianism," p. 54.

22. Charles Krauthammer, "When to Intervene," *New Republic* 192, no. 18 (May 6, 1985): 10.

23. Ibid., p. 10.

24. Ibid., pp. 10–11.

25. Ibid.

26. Charles Krauthammer, "The Reagan Doctrine," *Time* 125, no. 13 (April 1, 1985): 54–55. Cf. Jeane J. Kirkpatrick, "The Reagan Doctrine," in Kirkpatrick, *Legitimacy and Force: Political and Moral Dimensions*, pp. 422–446.

27. Charles Krauthammer, "The Poverty of Realism," *New Republic* 194, no. 7 (February 17, 1986): 15.

28. Ibid., p. 16.

29. Charles Krauthammer, "Divided Superpower," *New Republic* 195, no. 25 (December 22, 1986): 16.

30. Krauthammer, "The Price of Power," *New Republic* 196, no. 6 (February 9, 1987): 23. Cf. Krauthammer, *Cutting Edges: Making Sense of the Eighties* (New York: Random House, 1985), pp. 148–160.

31. Krauthammer, "Price of Power," p. 24.

32. Krauthammer, "When to Intervene," p. 11.

33. Charles Krauthammer, "Universal Dominion: Toward a Unipolar World," *National Interest* 18 (Winter 1989): 47.

34. Ibid., p. 48.

35. Francis Fukuyama, "The End of History?" *National Interest* 16 (Summer 1989): 3–18.

36. Krauthammer, "Universal Dominion," pp. 48–49.

37. Ibid., p. 49.

38. Charles Krauthammer, "The Unipolar Moment," *Foreign Affairs* 70, no. 1 (1991): 23.

39. Ibid., pp. 25–33.

40. Charles Krauthammer, "The Lonely Superpower," *New Republic* 205, no. 5 (July 29, 1991): 27.

41. Michael Novak, "Moiling, Muddling, and Malaise," *Forbes*, November 26, 1991; A. M. Rosenthal, "America at the Vistula," *New York Times*, April 9, 1991. Cf. Rosenthal, "How to Lose the Peace," *New York Times*, March 12, 1991; Rosenthal, "Why the Betrayal?" *New York Times*, April 2, 1991.

42. Paul Kennedy, *The Rise and Fall of the Great Powers: Economic Change and Military Conflict from 1500 to 2000* (New York: Vintage Books, 1987), p. 533.

43. Ibid., pp. 534–535.

44. Krauthammer, "Unipolar Moment," p. 26.

45. Michael Novak, "What Became of the Ugly American?" *Forbes* 145, no. 9 (April 30, 1990): 120.

46. Michael Novak, "The Game's Not Over," *Forbes* 146, no. 4 (August 20, 1990): 56.

47. Wattenberg, *First Universal Nation*, pp. 188, 202.

48. Ibid., pp. 188–189.

49. Novak, "The Game's Not Over," p. 56.

50. Norman Podhoretz, "In Israel, With Scuds and Patriots," *Commentary* 91, no. 4 (April 1991): 20; Joshua Muravchik, "At Last, Pax Americana," *New York Times*, January 24, 1991. Novak quoted in Peter Applebome, "At Home, War Healed Several Wounds," *New York Times*, March 4, 1991. See also Michael Novak, "Pax Americana," *Forbes* 147, no. 9 (April 29, 1991): 121.

51. Kennedy quoted in Applebome, "At Home, War Healed Several Wounds." See also Edward N. Luttwak, "Is America on the Way Down? Yes," *Commentary* 93, no. 3 (March 1992): 15–21.

52. Russell Kirk, *The Neoconservatives: An Endangered Species*, Heritage Lectures, no. 178 (Washington, D.C.: Heritage Foundation, 1988), pp. 5–7.

53. Patrick J. Buchanan, "Has Cold War's End Doomed Conservative Unity?" *Detroit News*, September 26, 1989. For similar views, see Clyde Wilson, "Global Democracy and American Tradition," *Intercollegiate Review* 24, no. 1 (Fall 1988): 3–14; Claes G. Ryn, "The Democracy Boosters," *National Review* 41, no. 5 (March 24, 1989): 30–32, 52. The lasting impression left by the democratic globalists, Ryn argued, was self-satisfaction: "With champions like these, democracy does not need enemies."

54. Buchanan, "Has Cold War's End Doomed Conservative Unity?"

55. Patrick J. Buchanan, "America First—And Second, and Third," *National Interest* 19 (Spring 1990): 81.

56. Ibid., pp. 77, 82.

57. Charles Krauthammer, "Has Cold War's End Doomed Conservative Unity?" *Detroit News*, September 26, 1989.

58. John B. Judis, "The Conservative Wars: Paleocons versus Neocons," *New Republic* 195, no. 8 (August 11 & 18, 1986): 16.

59. Cf. Joseph Sobran, Universal Press Syndicate Columns, April 22, 1986, and May 8, 1986; quoted in Judis, "Conservative Wars," p. 18; and William F. Buckley, Jr., "In Search of Anti-Semitism," *National Review* 43, no. 24 (December 30, 1991): 20–31.

60. William F. Buckley, Jr., "Notes and Asides: Joe Sobran and Anti-Semitism," *National Review* 38, no. 12 (July 4, 1986): 19–20; Bradford and Kirk quoted in Judis, "Conservative Wars," p. 18. Kirk quote corrected in interview with author, July 16, 1992. Sobran was angered by Buckley's declaration, but agreed to abide by it. He sought Buckley's approval for two subsequent columns on the Middle East and then avoided the subject altogether until September 1990, when he claimed that Bush's response to the Gulf crisis was primarily motivated by his desire to help Israel. Sobran's elaborations on this theme eventually moved Buckley to ask for his resignation as senior editor of *National Review*, where he was reassigned as a "critic at large." Cf. Buckley, "In Search of Anti-Semitism," pp. 28–31.

61. Russell Kirk, interview with author, October 19, 1989.

62. Thomas Fleming, "The Real American Dilemma," *Chronicles* 13, no. 3 (March 1989): 8–11.

63. Katherine Dalton, "The Native American," *Chronicles* 13, no. 3 (March 1989): 37.

64. Bill Kauffman, "Gnawing Away at Vidal," *Chronicles* 13, no. 3 (March 1989): 46.

65. Quoted in Robert Moynihan, "Thunder on the Right," *Thirty Days*, September 1989, pp. 69–70.

66. Ibid., p. 69.

67. Norman Podhoretz, interview with author, June 12, 1990.

68. Quoted in Moynihan, "Thunder on the Right," p. 69.

69. Richard John Neuhaus, "Democratic Conservatism," *First Things* 1 (March 1990): 65.

70. Thomas Fleming, "The Closing of the Conservative Mind," *Chronicles* 13, no. 9 (September 1989): 12.

71. Kirk, interview with author, October 19, 1989.

72. Cf. Ernest Van Den Haag, "The War Between Paleos and Neos," *National Review* 41, no. 3 (February 24, 1989): 21–23; Dan Himmelfarb, "Conservative Splits," *Commentary* 85, no. 5 (May 1988): 54–58; Jeffrey Hart, "Gang Warfare in Chicago," *National Review* 38, no. 10 (June 6, 1986); Eugene B. Meyer, "The Case for Tolerance," *National Review* 38, no. 13 (July 18, 1986): 45.

73. Buchanan and Fleming quoted in David Frum, "The Conservative Bully Boy," *American Spectator* 24, no. 7 (July 1991): 12; Gottfried quoted in Moynihan, "Thunder on the Right," p. 68.

74. Stephen J. Tonsor, "Why I Too Am Not a Neoconservative," *National Review* 38, no. 11 (June 20, 1986): 55.

75. Quoted in Christopher Hitchens, "How Neoconservatives Perish: Good-bye to 'Totalitarianism' and All That," *Harper's* 281, no. 1682 (July 1990): 66.

76. Fundraising letter from Midge Decter, Committee for the Free World, April 1990. Cf. Decter, "An Announcement, a Thank-you, and a Prayer," *Contentions*, December 1990.

77. Kirk, *Neoconservatives: An Endangered Species*, p. 5.

78. Hitchens, "How Neoconservatives Perish," pp. 65–70; Sidney Blumenthal, *The Rise of the Counter-Establishment: From Conservative Ideology to Political Power* (New York: Harper & Row, 1988), p. 165.

79. Seymour Martin Lipset, "Neoconservatism: Myth and Reality," *Society* 25, no. 5 (July/August 1988): 29–37.

80. "Our Country and Our Culture" (symposium), *Partisan Review* 19, no. 3 (May/June 1952): 282.

81. Michael Novak, *Will It Liberate? Questions about Liberation Theology* (New York: Paulist Press, 1986), p. 35.

82. Podhoretz, interview with author, June 12, 1990; Michael Novak, interview with author, March 20, 1990. Cf. Novak, "Capitalism, Socialism, and Democracy: A Symposium," *Commentary* 65, no. 4 (April 1978): 64.

83. Michael Novak, "Engagement but No Security," *Commonweal* 108, no. 2 (January 30, 1981): 45; Norman Podhoretz, *Breaking Ranks: A Political Memoir* (New York: Harper & Row, 1979), p. 320.

84. Norman Podhoretz, "The Disaster of Women's Lib," *New York Post*, August 18, 1987.

85. Midge Decter, "The Liberated Woman," *Commentary* 50, no. 4 (October 1970): 44.

86. Midge Decter, "For the Family: Millions of Americans Have Been Engaging in Child Sacrifice," *Policy Review* 27 (Winter 1984): 44–45.

87. Midge Decter, "Liberating Women: Who Benefits?" *Commentary* 77, no. 3 (March 1984): 36; Decter, "Farewell to the Woman Question," *First Things* 14 (June/July 1991): 9.

88. Ruth R. Wisse, "Living with Women's Lib," *Commentary* 86, no. 2 (August 1988): 45.

89. Cf. Nathan Glazer, *Affirmative Discrimination: Ethnic Inequality and Public Policy* (New York: Basic Books, 1975); Edward C. Banfield, *The Unheavenly City Revisited* (Boston: Little, Brown, 1974).

90. Irving Kristol, "What Won, and What Lost, in 1990," *Wall Street Journal*, November 16, 1990.

91. Norman Podhoretz, " 'Hey, Hey, Ho Ho, Western Culture's Got to Go,' " *New York Post*, January 26, 1988. Cf. Jerry Adler, et al., "Taking Offense," *Newsweek* 116, no. 26 (December 24, 1990); Paul Gray, "Whose America?" *Time* 138, no. 1 (July 8, 1991): 12–17; Fred Siegel, "The Cult of Multiculturalism," *New Republic* 204, no. 7 (February 18, 1991): 34–40; Josh Ozersky, "The Enlightenment Theology of Political Correctness," *Tikkun* 6, no. 4 (July/August 1991): 35–39; Arthur Schlesinger, Jr., *The Disuniting of America: Reflections on a Multicultural Society* (New York: Whittle Books, 1991).

92. Michael Novak, "Thought Police," *Forbes* 146, no. 7 (October 1, 1990): 212.

93. Michael Novak, "Our Uneducated Graduates," *Forbes* 144, no. 11 (November 13, 1989): 96.

94. Podhoretz, " 'Hey, Hey, Ho Ho, Western Culture's Got to Go.' "

95. Cf. Sidney Hook, "Stanford Documents: An Open Letter to the Stanford University Faculty Senate," *Partisan Review* 55, no. 4 (1988): 653–659; Hook, "Civilization and Its Malcontents," *National Review* 41, no. 19 (October 13, 1989): 30–33; Thomas Short, " 'Diversity' and 'Breaking the Disciplines': Two New Assaults on the Curriculum," *Academic Questions* 1 (Summer 1988): 6–29.

96. Dinesh D'Souza, *Illiberal Education: The Politics of Race and Sex on Campus* (New York: Free Press, 1991), p. 17.

97. Roger Kimball, *Tenured Radicals: How Politics Has Corrupted Our Higher Education* (New York: Harper & Row, 1990), p. 3.

98. Cf. D'Souza, *Illiberal Education,* pp. 124–156; Eugene D. Genovese, "Heresy, Yes—Sensitivity, No," *New Republic* 204, no. 15 (April 15, 1991): 30–35.

99. Kimball, *Tenured Radicals,* p. 192.

100. Ibid., p. 204.

101. Diane Ravitch, "Multiculturalism: E Pluribus Plures," *American Scholar* 59, no. 3 (Summer 1990): 338–340. Cf. Nathan Glazer, "In Defense of Multiculturalism," *New Republic* 205, no. 10 (September 2, 1991): 18–22.

102. Ravitch, "Multiculturalism: E Pluribus Plures," pp. 340–341.

103. Cf. Molefi Kete Asante, *The Afrocentric Idea* (Philadelphia: Temple University Press, 1987); Elizabeth Minnich, *Transforming Knowledge* (Philadelphia: Temple University Press, 1991); Chicago Cultural Studies Group, "Critical Multiculturalism," *Critical Inquiry* 18, no. 3 (Spring 1992): 530–555.

104. Norman Podhoretz, "Second Thoughts: A Generational Perspective," in *Second Thoughts: Former Radicals Look Back at the Sixties,* ed. Peter Collier and David Horowitz (Lanham, Md.: Madison Books, 1989), p. 193.

105. Michael Novak, "The Old Virtues," review of *The Way of the WASP: How It Made America, and How It Can Save It, So To Speak,* by Richard Brookhiser, *Commentary* 91, no. 3 (March 1991): 54.

106. James Nuechterlein, "The Feminization of the American Left," *Commentary* 84, no. 5 (November 1987): 43.

107. Cf. Ann Douglas, *The Feminization of American Culture* (New York: Anchor Press, 1988); Robert S. McElvaine, *The Great Depression: America 1929–1941* (New York: New York Times Books, 1985).

108. Podhoretz, "Second Thoughts," p. 194.

109. Nuechterlein, "Feminization of the American Left," pp. 45–46.

110. Carol Ianonne, "The Feminist Confusion," in *Second Thoughts,* ed. Collier and Horowitz, pp. 150–153; cf. Ianonne, "The Barbarism of Feminist Scholarship," *Intercollegiate Review* 23, no. 1 (Fall 1987): 35–41.

111. Cf. Alison M. Jagger and Paula S. Rothenberg, eds., *Feminist Frameworks* (New York: McGraw-Hill, 1984); bell hooks, *Feminist Theory: From Margin to Center*

(Boston: South End Press, 1984); Linda J. Nicholson, ed., *Feminism/Postmodernism* (New York: Routledge, 1990).

112. Quoted in James Atlas, "The Changing World of New York Intellectuals," *New York Times Magazine*, August 25, 1985, p. 52; second quotation in symposium discussion, "The Changing Culture of the University: The Impact of the Media," *Partisan Review* 58, no. 2 (Spring 1991): 239.

113. Hilton Kramer, "Second Thoughts: A Generational Perspective," in *Second Thoughts*, ed. Collier and Horowitz, p. 176.

114. Podhoretz, "Second Thoughts," p. 195.

115. George Gilder, "Why I Am Not a Neo-Conservative," *National Review* 34, no. 4 (March 5, 1982): 218–220.

116. Midge Decter, "Ronald Reagan and the Culture War," *Commentary* 91, no. 3 (March 1991): 46.

117. Michael Novak, "A Phony Objectivity," *Forbes* 147, no. 6 (March 18, 1991): 70–71.

Notes to Chapter 8

1. Cf. Norman Thomas, *The Choice Before Us: Mankind at the Crossroads* (New York: Macmillan, 1934), pp. 63–82, 162–199.

2. Norman Thomas, *A Socialist's Faith* (New York: W. W. Norton, 1951), p. 67.

3. Ibid.; Norman Thomas, *The Prerequisites for Peace* (New York: W. W. Norton, 1959), p. 3.

4. Michael Harrington, interview with author, May 27, 1988. Cf. Harrington, *Fragments of the Century* (New York: Saturday Review Press, 1973), pp. 207–211; Julius Jacobson, "The Two Deaths of Max Shachtman," *New Politics* 10, no. 2 (Winter 1973); Hannah Arendt, *The Origins of Totalitarianism* (New York: Harcourt, Brace, 1951).

5. Jean-François Revel, *The Totalitarian Temptation* (New York: Doubleday, 1977), p. 26.

6. Norman Podhoretz, "Making the World Safe for Communism," *Commentary* 61, no. 4 (April 1976): 38.

7. Cf. Jean-François Revel, *How Democracies Perish* (New York: Harper & Row, 1985); Revel, *The Flight from Truth: The Reign of Deceit in the Age of Information* (New York: Random House, 1992).

8. Leslie H. Gelb, "Who Won the Cold War?" *New York Times*, August 20, 1992.

9. Cf. Daniel Deudney and G. John Ikenberry, "Who Won the Cold War?" *Foreign Policy* 87 (Summer 1992): 123–138.

10. Cf. Benjamin M. Friedman, *Day of Reckoning: The Consequences of American Economic Policy* (New York: Vintage Books, 1989); Franklyn Holzman, "Administration Misrepresentations of Soviet Military Spending," and Gene R. LaRocque, "Preparing to Fight a Nuclear War . . . The Reagan Arms Budget," in *Defense Sense: The Search for a Rational Military Policy*, ed. Ronald V. Dellums et al. (Cambridge,

Mass.: Ballinger, 1983), pp. 96–105, 109–124; Mary Kaldor, *The Baroque Arsenal* (New York: Hill and Wang, 1981).

11. Irving Kristol, "Tongue-Tied in Washington," *Wall Street Journal*, April 15, 1991.

12. Ibid.

13. A. M. Rosenthal, "America at the Vistula," *New York Times*, April 9, 1991.

14. A. M. Rosenthal, "The Fear of Morality," *New York Times*, April 16, 1991.

15. Norman Podhoretz, "After the Cold War," review of *America's Purpose: New Visions of U.S. Foreign Policy*, ed. Owen Harries, *Commentary* 92, no 1 (July 1991): 56; Aleksandr Solzhenitsyn, *Warning to the West* (New York: Farrar, Straus & Giroux, 1976), p. 48, quoted in Rosenthal, "The Fear of Morality." Closing quotation from Rosenthal.

16. Charles Krauthammer, "Aid, Trade: Nuclear Republics Need Not Apply," *Detroit News*, December 24, 1991.

17. Charles Krauthammer, "Bush Turns His Back on the Few Beliefs He Had," *Detroit News*, December 31, 1991.

18. Joshua Muravchik, *Exporting Democracy: Fulfilling America's Destiny* (Washington, D.C.: American Enterprise Institute, 1991), p. 227.

19. Kristol, "Tongue-Tied in Washington."

20. Michael Novak, "Pax Americana," *Forbes* 147, no. 9 (April 29, 1991): 52.

21. Peter L. Berger, "The Democratic Imperative," review of *The Democratic Imperative: Exporting the American Revolution*, by Gregory A. Fossedal, *American Spectator* 22, no. 7 (July 1989): 45.

22. Cf. Gregory A. Fossedal, *The Democratic Imperative: Exporting the American Revolution* (New York: Basic Books, 1989), pp. 178–213.

23. Berger, "Democratic Imperative," p. 45. Cf. Berger, "Underdevelopment Revisited: Discussion," in *Liberation Theology and the Liberal Society*, ed. Michael Novak (Washington, D.C.: American Enterprise Institute, 1987), pp. 87–105; Berger, *The Capitalist Revolution: Fifty Propositions about Prosperity, Equality, and Liberty* (New York: Basic Books, 1986), pp. 115–139.

24. Cf. Nick Eberstadt, "No Democratic Trend in East Asia," *Wall Street Journal*, July 18, 1989; Mancur Olson, *The Rise and Decline of Nations: Economic Growth, Stagflation, and Social Rigidities* (New Haven: Yale University Press, 1982), pp. 41–73.

25. Irving Kristol, "The War of the Words," *Wall Street Journal*, June 6, 1987.

26. Ibid.

27. Robert Lekachman, "Mean to Me," review of *Breaking Ranks: A Political Memoir*, by Norman Podhoretz, *Nation* 229, no. 15 (November 10, 1979), pp. 469–470; Diana Trilling, Letter to the Editor, *New Republic* 189, No. 27, (December 31, 1983): 40.

28. Alfred Kazin, *Starting Out in the Thirties* (1962; reprint, New York: Cornell University Press, 1989), pp. 4–5.

29. Daniel Bell, "The New Class: A Muddled Concept," in *The New Class?* ed. B. Bruce-Biggs (New Brunswick, N.J.: Transaction Books, 1979).

30. Michael Novak, interview with author, March 20, 1990.

31. Quoted in Christopher Lasch, "Conservatism Against Itself," *First Things* 2 (April 1990): 20.

32. Karl Polanyi, *The Great Transformation: The Political and Economic Origins of Our Time* (1944; reprint, Boston: Beacon Press, 1957), pp. 163, 3.

33. Quoted in Barbara Ehrenreich, *Fear of Falling: The Inner Life of the Middle Class* (New York: HarperCollins, 1989), p. 158.

34. Norman Podhoretz, *Breaking Ranks: A Political Memoir* (New York: Harper & Row, 1979), pp. 288–289.

35. E. M. Forster, *Two Cheers for Democracy* (New York: Harcourt, Brace, 1951), p. 57.

36. Fred Barnes, "They're Back! Neocons for Clinton," *New Republic* 207, no. 6 (August 3, 1992): 12–14.

37. Michael Novak, interview with author, August 6, 1992; Barnes, "They're Back!"

38. James Burnham, "Selective, Yes. Humanism, Maybe," *National Review* 24, no. 18 (May 12, 1972): 516.

39. Paul Gottfried, "A View of Contemporary Conservatism," *Intercollegiate Review* 21, no. 3 (Spring 1986): 20.

40. James Nuechterlein, "The Paleo's Paleo," review of *The Conservative Constitution*, by Russell Kirk, *First Things* 15 (August/September 1991): 46.

41. James Q. Wilson, "The Urban Unease: Community vs. City," *Public Interest* 12 (Summer 1968): 25–39.

42. James Q. Wilson, "Neoconservatism: Pro and Con" (symposium), *Partisan Review* 47, no. 4 (1980): 508.

43. Peter Viereck, "The Revolt Against the Elite," in *The Radical Right*, ed. Daniel Bell (New York: Doubleday, 1963), pp. 135–154.

44. Peter Viereck, "The Philosophical 'New Conservatism'—1962," in *The Radical Right*, ed. Bell, p. 158.

45. Ibid., pp. 155–173.

Bibliography

Abel, Lionel. *The Intellectual Follies: A Memoir of the Literary Venture in New York and Paris.* New York: W. W. Norton, 1984.

Abrams, Elliott. "The Deal in Central America." *Commentary* 87, no. 5 (May 1989).

Alperovitz, Gar, and Jeff Faux. *Rebuilding America: A Blueprint for the New Economy.* New York: Pantheon Books, 1984.

Amsden, Alice H. *Asia's Next Giant: South Korea and Late Industrialization.* Oxford: Oxford University Press, 1989.

———. "Third World Industrialization: 'Global Fordism' or a New Model?" *New Left Review* 182 (July/August 1990).

Arendt, Hannah. *The Origins of Totalitarianism.* New York: Harcourt, Brace, 1951.

Ashford, Nigel. "The Neo-Conservatives." *Government and Opposition* 16, no. 3 (1981).

Assmann, Hugo. "Democracy and the Debt Crisis." *This World* 14, (Spring/Summer 1986).

Atlas, James. "The Changing World of New York Intellectuals." *New York Times Magazine,* August 25, 1985.

Avishai, Bernard. "Breaking Faith: *Commentary* and the American Jews." *Dissent* 28, no. 2 (Spring 1981).

———. *The Tragedy of Zionism: Revolution and Democracy in the Land of Israel.* New York: Farrar Straus Giroux, 1985.

Bane, Mary Jo. "Is the Welfare State Replacing the Family?" *Public Interest* 70 (Winter 1983).

Banfield, Edward. *The Unheavenly City Revisited.* Boston: Little, Brown, 1974.

Barrett, William. *The Truants: Adventures among the Intellectuals.* New York: Anchor Press, 1982.

Barth, Alan. *The Loyalty of Free Men.* New York: Viking Press, 1951.

Barzun, Jacques. *The Culture We Deserve.* Middletown, Conn.: Wesleyan University Press, 1989.

Bauer, P. T. *Equality, the Third World, and Economic Delusion.* Cambridge, Mass.: Harvard University Press, 1981.

451

Bazelon, David. *Power in America: The Politics of the New Class.* New York: New American Library, 1967.

Beasley, W. G. *The Rise of Modern Japan.* New York: St. Martin's Press, 1990.

Bell, Daniel. *The Coming of Post-Industrial Society: A Venture in Social Forecasting.* New York: Basic Books, 1973.

————. *The Cultural Contradictions of Capitalism.* New York: Basic Books, 1976.

————. *The End of Ideology: On the Exhaustion of Political Ideas in the Fifties.* New York: Free Press, 1960.

————. *The Winding Passage: Essays and Sociological Journeys, 1960–1980.* Cambridge, Mass.: Abt Books, 1980.

————, ed. *The Radical Right.* New York: Doubleday, 1963.

Bellah, Robert. *The Broken Covenant: American Civil Religion in Time of Trial.* New York: Seabury Press, 1975.

Bello, Walden, and Stephanie Rosenfeld. "Dragons in Distress: The Crisis of the NICs," *World Policy Journal* 7, no. 3 (Summer 1990).

Benne, Robert. "The Church and Politics: Four Possible Connections." *This World* 25 (Spring 1989).

————. *The Ethic of Democratic Capitalism: A Moral Reassessment.* Philadelphia: Fortress Press, 1981.

Berger, Peter L. "Are Human Rights Universal?" *Commentary* 64, no. 3 (September 1977).

————. "Can the Bishops Help the Poor?" *Commentary* 79, no. 2 (February 1985).

————. "Capitalism and the Disorders of Modernity." *First Things* 9 (January 1991).

————. "Capitalism: The Continuing Revolution." *First Things* 15 (August/September 1991).

————. *The Capitalist Revolution: Fifty Propositions about Prosperity, Equality, and Liberty.* New York: Basic Books, 1986.

————. "The Concept of Mediating Action." In *Confession, Conflict, and Community,* ed. Richard J. Neuhaus. Grand Rapids, Mich.: William B. Eerdmans, 1986.

————. "Democracy for Everyone?" *Commentary* 76, no. 3 (September 1983).

————. "Different Gospels: The Social Sources of Apostasy." *This World* 17 (Spring 1987).

————. "Empirical Testings." *This World* 22 (Summer 1988).

————. *Facing Up to Modernity: Excursions in Society, Politics, and Religion.* New York: Basic Books, 1977.

————. *A Far Glory: The Quest for Faith in an Age of Credulity.* New York: Free Press, 1992.

————. "The First Freedom." *Commentary* 86, no. 6 (December 1988).

————. "From Secularity to World Religions." *Christian Century* 97, no. 2 (January 16, 1980).

————. "The Greening of American Foreign Policy." *Commentary* 61, no. 3 (March 1976). Reprinted in Berger, *Facing Up to Modernity.*

————. *The Heretical Imperative: Contemporary Possibilities of Religious Affirmation.* Garden City, N.Y.: Anchor Press, 1979.

——. "Human Development and Economic Alternatives." *Crisis* 5, no. 10 (November 1987).

——. "Human Rights and American Foreign Policy: A Symposium." *Commentary* 72, no. 5 (November 1981).

——. *Invitation to Sociology: A Humanistic Perspective.* Garden City, N.Y.: Anchor Books, 1963.

——. "The Moral Crisis of Capitalism." In *Corporations and the Common Good*, ed. Robert B. Dickie and Leroy S. Rouner. Notre Dame, Ind.: University of Notre Dame Press, 1986.

——. *The Noise of Solemn Assemblies: Christian Commitment and the Religious Establishment in America.* Garden City, N.Y.: Doubleday, 1961.

——. *The Precarious Vision: A Sociologist Looks at Social Fictions and the Christian Faith.* Garden City, N.Y.: Doubleday, 1961.

——. *Pyramids of Sacrifice: Political Ethics and Social Change.* New York: Basic Books, 1974.

——. "Reflections of an Ecclesiastical Expatriate." *Christian Century* 107, no. 30 (October 24, 1990).

——. "Religion in Post-Protestant America." *Commentary* 81, no. 5 (May 1986).

——. *A Rumor of Angels: Modern Society and the Rediscovery of the Supernatural.* Garden City, N.Y.: Doubleday, 1969.

——. *The Sacred Canopy: Elements of a Sociological Theory of Religion.* Garden City, N.Y.: Doubleday, 1967.

——. "The Socialist Myth." *Public Interest* 44 (Summer 1976). Reprinted in Berger, *Facing Up to Modernity.*

——. "Speaking to the Third World." *Commentary* 72, no. 4 (October 1981).

——. "Two Paradoxes." *National Review* 24, no. 18 (May 12, 1972).

——. "Underdevelopment Revisited." *Commentary* 78, no. 1 (July 1984).

——. "Worldly Wisdom, Christian Foolishness." *First Things* 5 (August/September 1990).

——, ed. *The Capitalist Spirit: Toward a Religious Ethic of Wealth Creation.* San Francisco: ICS Press, 1990.

——, ed. *The Human Shape of Work.* New York: Macmillan, 1964.

——, ed. *Marxism and Sociology: Views from Eastern Europe.* New York: Appleton, 1969.

——, ed. *The Other Side of God: A Polarity in World Religions.* Garden City, N.Y.: Anchor Books, 1981.

Berger, Peter L., and Brigitte Berger, "Our Conservatism and Theirs." *Commentary* 82, no. 4 (October 1986).

——. *Sociology: A Biographical Approach.* New York: Basic Books, 1972.

——. *The War over the Family: Capturing the Middle Ground.* Garden City, N.Y.: Anchor Press, 1983.

Berger, Peter L., Brigitte Berger, and Hansfried Kellner. *The Homeless Mind: Modernization and Consciousness.* New York: Vintage Books, 1974.

Berger, Peter L., and Bobby Godsell. "Fantasies about South Africa." *Commentary* 84, no. 1 (July 1987).

Berger, Peter L., and Thomas Luckmann. *The Social Construction of Reality: A Treatise in the Sociology of Knowledge.* New York: Doubleday, 1966.

Berger, Peter L., and Richard J. Neuhaus. *Movement and Revolution.* Garden City, N.Y.: Doubleday, 1970.

————. *To Empower People: The Role of Mediating Structures in Public Policy.* Washington, D.C.: American Enterprise Institute, 1977.

————, eds. *Against the World for the World: The Hartford Appeal and the Future of American Religion.* New York: Seabury Press, 1976.

Berger, Peter L., and Michael Novak. *Speaking to the Third World: Essays on Democracy and Development.* Washington, D.C.: American Enterprise Institute, 1985.

Berman, Paul. "The Last New Leftists." *New Republic* 200, no. 17 (April 24, 1989).

————. "The Last True Marxist Is a Neoconservative." *Voice Literary Supplement* 24 (March 1984).

Bescancon, Alain. "Gorbachev Without Illusions." *Commentary* 85, no. 4 (April 1988).

Bishop, Joseph. "Carter's Last Capitulation." *Commentary* 71, no. 3 (March 1981).

Blasi, Joseph R. *Employee Ownership: Revolution or Ripoff?* Camridge, Mass.: Ballinger, 1988.

Bloom, Alexander. *Prodigal Sons: The New York Intellectuals and Their World.* New York: Oxford University Press, 1986.

Blumenthal, Sidney. "Dateline Washington: The Conservative Crackup." *Foreign Policy* 69 (Winter 1987–88).

————. *Our Long National Daydream: A Political Pageant of the Reagan Era.* New York: Harper & Row, 1988.

————. *Pledging Allegiance: The Last Campaign of the Cold War.* New York: Harper-Collins, 1990.

————. *The Rise of the Counter-Establishment: From Conservative Ideology to Political Power.* New York: Harper & Row, 1988.

Boff, Leonardo. *Ecclesiogenesis: The Base Communities Reinvent the Church.* Translated by Robert R. Barr. Maryknoll, N.Y.: Orbis Books, 1986.

Boyte, Harry C. *CommonWealth: A Return to Citizen Politics.* New York: Free Press, 1989.

Braden, Thomas. "I'm Glad the CIA Is 'Immoral.'" *Saturday Evening Post,* May 20, 1967.

Bradford, M. E. *The Reactionary Imperative: Essays Literary and Political.* Peru, Ill.: Sherwood Sugden, 1990.

Bradley, Keith, and Alan Gelb. *Cooperation at Work: The Mondragon Experience.* London: Heinemann Educational Books, 1984.

Brookhiser, Richard. "James Burnham: A Hard Man to Snooker." *National Review* 37, no. 25 (December 31, 1985).

Brown, Robert McAfee. "Reinhold Niebuhr: His Theology in the 1980s." *Christian Century* 103, no. 3 (January 22, 1986).

Brown, Robert McAfee, Abraham J. Heschel, and Michael Novak. *Vietnam: Crisis of Conscience.* New York: Association Press, 1967.

Bruce-Biggs, B., ed. *The New Class?* New Brunswick, N.J.: Transaction Books, 1979.

Brzezinski, Zbigniew. "Beyond Chaos: What the West Must Do." *National Interest* 19 (Spring 1990).

Buchanan, Allen. *Ethics, Efficiency, and the Market.* Totowa, N.J.: Rowman & Allanheld, 1985.

Buchanan, Patrick. "America First—And Second, and Third." *National Interest* 19 (Spring 1990).

Buckley, William F., Jr., ed. *American Conservative Thought in the Twentieth Century.* Indianapolis: Bobbs-Merrill, 1970.

Buckley, William F., Jr., and Charles R. Kesler, eds. *Keeping the Tablets: Modern American Conservative Thought.* New York: Harper & Row, 1988.

Bukovsky, Vladimir. "Will Gorbachev Reform the Soviet Union?" *Commentary* 82, no. 3 (September 1986).

Bunzel, John H. "Black Studies at San Francisco State." *Public Interest* 13 (Fall 1968).

———, ed. *Political Passages: Journeys of Change Through Two Decades, 1968–1988.* New York: Free Press, 1988.

Burnham, James. *The Coming Defeat of Communism.* New York: John Day, 1949.

———. *Containment or Liberation? An Inquiry into the Aims of United States Foreign Policy.* New York: John Day, 1952.

———. "Lenin's Heir." *Partisan Review* 12, no. 1 (Winter 1945).

———. *The Machiavellians: Defenders of Freedom.* New York: John Day, 1943.

———. *The Managerial Revolution: What Is Happening in the World.* New York: John Day, 1941.

———. *The Struggle for the World.* New York: John Day, 1947

———. *Suicide of the West: An Essay on the Meaning and Destiny of Liberalism.* 1964. Reprint. Washington, D.C.: Regnery Gateway, 1985.

———. *The War We Are In: The Last Decade and the Next.* New Rochelle, N.Y.: Arlington House, 1967.

———. *The Web of Subversion: Underground Networks in the U.S. Government.* New York: John Day, 1954.

Burnham, James, and Max Shachtman. "Intellectuals in Retreat." *New International* 5, no. 1 (January 1939).

Burnham, James, and Philip Wheelwright. *Introduction to Philosophical Analysis.* New York: Henry Holt, 1932.

Cameron, J. M. *Nuclear Catholics and Other Essays.* Grand Rapids, Mich.: William B. Eerdmans, 1989.

Cardoso, Fernando Henrique, and Enzo Falleto. *Dependency and Development in Latin America.* Berkeley: University of California Press, 1979.

Carnoy, Martin, and Derek Shearer. *Economic Democracy: The Challenge of the 1980s.* White Plains, N.Y.: M. E. Sharpe, 1980.

Caute, David. *The Fellow-Travellers: A Postscript to the Enlightenment.* New York: Macmillan, 1973.

Chase, James, et al. "What Are the Consequences of Vietnam?" *Harper's* 270, no. 1619 (April 1985).

Chomsky, Noam. "Vietnam, the Cold War and Other Matters." *Commentary* 48, no. 4 (October 1969).

Christopher, Robert. *The Japanese Mind.* New York: Fawcett Columbine, 1983.

Codevilla, Angelo. "Eastern Europe: Is Olof Palme the Wave of the Future?" *Commentary* 89, no. 3 (March 1990).

———. "Is There Still a Soviet Threat?" *Commentary* 86, no. 5 (November 1988).

Cohen, Arthur. "The Myth of the Judeo-Christian Tradition." *Commentary* 48, no. 5 (November 1969).

Cohen, Stephen F. *Rethinking the Soviet Experience: Politics and History since 1917.* New York: Oxford University Press, 1985.

———. *Sovieticus: American Perceptions and Soviet Realities.* New York: W. W. Norton, 1985.

Coleman, John. "Development of Catholic Social Teaching." *Origins*, January 4, 1981.

Coleman, Peter. *The Liberal Conspiracy: The Congress for Cultural Freedom and the Struggle for the Mind of Postwar Europe.* New York: Free Press, 1989.

Collier, Peter, and David Horowitz. "Another 'Low Dishonest Decade' on the Left." *Commentary* 83, no. 1 (January 1987).

———. *Destructive Generation: Second Thoughts about the Sixties.* New York: Summit Books, 1989.

———. "McCarthyism: The Last Refuge of the Left." *Commentary* 85, no. 1 (January 1988).

———, eds. *Second Thoughts: Former Radicals Look Back at the Sixties.* Lanham, Md.: Madison Books, 1989.

Colville, John. "How the West Lost the Peace in 1945." *Commentary* 80, no. 3 (September 1985).

Committee for the Free World. *Our Country and Our Culture.* New York: Orwell Press, 1983.

Conant, Oliver. "Culture and the Neoconservatives." *Dissent* 34, no. 2 (Spring 1987).

Cooney, Terry A. *The Rise of the New York Intellectuals: Partisan Review and Its Circle, 1934–1945.* Madison: University of Wisconsin Press, 1986.

Cort, John C. "The Social Thought of Michael Novak: At Odds with the Principles of Catholic Social Thought." *New Oxford Review* 55, no. 9 (November 1988).

Coser, Lewis, Oscar Gass, Hans J. Morgenthau, and Arthur Schlesinger, Jr. "America and the World Revolution: A Round Table Discussion." *Commentary* 36, no. 4 (October 1963).

Coser, Lewis, and Irving Howe, eds. *The New Conservatives: A Critique from the Left.* New York: New American Library, 1977.

Croce, Arlene. "Sexism in the Head." *Commentary* 51, no. 3 (March 1971).

Cuddihy, John Murray. *The Ordeal of Civility: Freud, Marx, Lévi-Strauss, and the Jewish Struggle with Modernity.* 1974. Reprint. Boston: Beacon Press, 1987.

Dahl, Robert A. *A Preface to Economic Democracy.* Berkeley: University of California Press, 1985.

Decter, Midge. "The Boys on the Beach." *Commentary* 70, no. 3 (September 1980).

———. "Kennedyism." *Commentary* 49, no. 1 (January 1970).

———. "The Liberated Woman." *Commentary* 50, no. 4 (October 1970).

———. "Liberating Women: Who Benefits?" *Commentary* 77, no. 3 (March 1984).

———. "Looting and Liberal Racism." *Commentary* 64, no. 3 (September 1977).

———. *The New Chastity and Other Arguments Against Women's Liberation.* New York: Coward, McCann & Geoghegan, 1972.

———. "The Professor and the L-Word." *Commentary* 87, no. 2 (February 1989).

———. "Ronald Reagan and the Culture War." *Commentary* 91, no. 3 (March 1991).

Decter, Moshe, William Appleman Williams, George Lichtheim, and Staughton Lynd, "The Origins of the Cold War: An Exchange." *Commentary* 31, no. 2 (February 1961).

Diggins, John P. *Up from Communism: Conservative Odysseys in American Intellectual History.* New York: Harper & Row, 1975.

Dionne, E. J. *Why Americans Hate Politics.* New York: Simon & Schuster, 1991.

Dorrien, Gary J. *The Democratic Socialist Vision.* Totowa, N.J.: Rowman & Littlefield, 1986.

———. *Reconstructing the Common Good: Theology and the Social Order.* Maryknoll, N.Y.: Orbis Books, 1990.

Douglas, Ann. *The Feminization of American Culture.* New York: Anchor Press, 1988.

Draper, Theodore. *American Communism and Soviet Russia.* New York: Viking Press, 1960.

———. "The American Crisis: Vietnam, Cuba, and the Dominican Republic." *Commentary* 43, no. 1 (January 1967).

———. "The Fantasy of Black Nationalism." *Commentary* 48, no. 3 (September 1969).

———. "Israel and World Politics." *Commentary* 44, no. 2 (August 1967).

———. "Neoconservative History." *New York Review of Books,* April 24, 1986.

———. *Present History.* New York: Random House, 1983.

———. *A Present of Things Past: Selected Essays.* New York: Hill & Wang, 1990.

———. "Vietnam and American Politics." *Commentary* 45, no. 3 (March 1968).

Drucker, Peter. *The Age of Discontinuity: Guidelines to Our Changing Society.* New York: Alfred A. Knopf, 1969.

D'Souza, Dinesh. *Illiberal Education: The Politics of Race and Sex on Campus.* New York: Free Press, 1991.

———. "Paddy, We Hardly Knew Ye: Daniel Patrick Moynihan Was Once the Great Neoconservative Hope." *Policy Review* 28 (Spring 1984).

Eberstadt, Nick. "The Latest Myths about the Soviet Union." *Commentary* 83, no. 5 (May 1987).

Ehrenreich, Barbara. *Fear of Falling: The Inner Life of the Middle Class.* New York: HarperCollins, 1989.

Elon, Amos. "Letter from the Sinai Front." *Commentary* 44, no. 2 (August 1967).

Epstein, Barbara. "The Reagan Doctrine and Right-Wing Democracy." *Socialist Review* 19, no. 1 (January/March 1989).

Epstein, Joseph. *The Middle of My Tether: Familiar Essays.* New York: W. W. Norton, 1983.

———. *Once More Around the Block: Familiar Essays.* New York: W. W. Norton, 1987.

———. *Plausible Prejudices: Essays on American Writing.* New York: W. W. Norton, 1985.

———. "The Rise of the Verbal Class." *Harper's* 268, no. 1606 (March 1984).

Evans, Peter. *Dependent Development: The Alliance of Multinational, State and Local Capital in Brazil.* Princeton: Princeton University Press, 1979.

Fackenheim, Emil. "Jewish Faith and the Holocaust: A Fragment." *Commentary* 46, no. 2 (August 1968).

———. *Quest for Past and Future: Essays in Jewish Theology.* Bloomington: Indiana University Press, 1968.

Fajnzylber, Fernando. *Estrategia Industrial y Empresas Internacionales: Posicion relativa de America y Brasil.* Rio de Janeiro: United Nations, CEPAL, November 1970.

Falcoff, Mark. "Making Central America Safe for Communism." *Commentary* 85, no. 6 (June 1988).

———. "Nicaraguan Harvest." *Commentary* 80, no. 1 (July 1985).

Ferrer, Aldo. "The Structure of the World Economy: Southern Perspectives." In *The Structure of the World Economy and the Prospects for a New International Economic Order,* ed. E. Lazlo and J. Kurtzman. New York: Pergamon Press, 1982.

Finn, Chester E. " 'Affirmative Action' under Reagan." *Commentary* 73, no. 4 (April 1982).

———. "Quotas and the Bush Administration." *Commentary* 92, no. 5 (November 1991).

Finn, James. "The Evolving Thought of Michael Novak." *National Review* 38, no. 25 (December 31, 1985).

FitzGerald, E. V. K. "Aspects of Finance Capital in Latin America." In *Economic Imperialism in Latin America,* ed. C. Abel and C. Lewis. London: London University Press, 1983.

Fleming, Thomas. "The Closing of the Conservative Mind." *Chronicles* 13, no. 9 (September 1989).

———. "The Real American Dilemma." *Chronicles* 13, no. 3 (March 1989).

Flick, Rachel. "The New Feminism and the World of Work." *Public Interest* 71 (Spring 1983).

Fossedal, Gregory A. *The Democratic Imperative: Exporting the American Revolution.* New York: Basic Books, 1989.

Francis, Samuel. "Letter from Washington: Left, Right, Up, Down." *Chronicles* 13, no. 9 (September 1989).

Frank, Andre Gunder. "Can the Debt Bomb Be Defused?" *World Policy Journal* 1, no. 4 (Summer 1984).

———. *Capitalism and Underdevelopment: Historical Studies of Chile and Brazil.* New York: Monthly Review Press, 1967.

—————. *Dependent Accumulation and Underdevelopment.* New York: Monthly Review Press, 1979.

Frankel, Charles. "The New Egalitarianism and the Old." *Commentary* 56, no. 3 (September 1973).

Frieden, Karl. *Workplace Democracy and Productivity.* Washington, D.C.: National Center for Economic Alternatives, 1980.

Friedman, Benjamin M. *Day of Reckoning: The Consequences of American Economic Policy.* New York: Vintage Books, 1989.

Friedman, Milton. *Capitalism and Freedom.* Chicago: University of Chicago Press, 1962.

Fukuyama, Francis. "The End of History?" *National Interest* 16 (Summer 1989).

Galbraith, John Kenneth. "A Hard Case." *New York Review of Books,* April 20, 1978.

—————. *The New Industrial State.* Boston: Houghton Mifflin, 1967.

Gall, Norman. "Latin America: The Church Militant." *Commentary* 49, no. 4 (April 1970).

Gass, Oscar. "China and the United States." *Commentary* 34, no. 5 (November 1962).

—————. "Vietnam—Resistance or Withdrawal?" *Commentary* 37, no. 5 (May 1964).

Gershman, Carl. "The Rise and Fall of the New Foreign Policy Establishment." *Commentary* 70, no. 1 (July 1980).

—————. "The World According to Andrew Young." *Commentary* 66, no. 2 (August 1978).

Gerson, Allan. *The Kirkpatrick Mission: Diplomacy Without Apology: America at the United Nations, 1981–1985.* New York: Free Press, 1991.

Gibney, Frank. *Japan: The Fragile Superpower.* New York: New American Library, 1985.

Gilder, George. "In Defense of Capitalists." *Commentary* 70, no. 6 (December 1980).

—————. *Wealth and Poverty.* New York: Basic Books, 1981.

—————. "Why I Am Not a Neo-Conservative." *National Review* 34, no. 4 (March 5, 1982).

Glazer, Nathan. *Affirmative Discrimination: Ethnic Inequality and Public Policy.* New York: Basic Books, 1975.

—————. "Blacks, Jews, and the Intellectuals." *Commentary* 47, no. 4 (April 1969).

—————. "In Defense of Multiculturalism." *New Republic* 205, no. 10 (September 2, 1991).

—————. "The Limits of Social Policy." *Commentary* 52, no. 3 (September 1971).

—————. "The New Left and Its Limits." *Commentary* 46, no. 1 (July 1968).

—————. "On Being Deradicalized." *Commentary* 50, no. 4 (October 1970).

—————. "The Peace Movement in America . . . 1961." *Commentary* 31, no. 4 (April 1961).

—————. "Reform Work, Not Welfare." *The Public Interest* 40 (Summer 1975).

—————. *Remembering the Answers: Essays on the American Student Revolt.* New York: Basic Books, 1970.

———. "The Social Policy of the Reagan Administration: A Review." *Public Interest* 75 (Spring 1984).

———. "Vietnam: The Case for Immediate Withdrawal." *Commentary* 51, no. 5 (May 1971).

———. "Why Isn't There More Equality?" *This World* 6 (Fall 1983).

Glynn, Patrick. "The Dangers Beyond Containment." *Commentary* 88, no. 2 (August 1989).

———. "Reagan's Rush to Disarm." *Commentary* 85, no. 3 (March 1988).

———. "Why an American Arms Build-Up Is Morally Necessary." *Commentary* 77, no. 2 (February 1984).

Goodman, Walter. "Irving Kristol: Patron Saint of the New Right." *New York Times Magazine*, December 6, 1981.

Gottfried, Paul. "A View of Contemporary Conservatism." *Intercollegiate Review* 21, no. 3 (Spring 1986).

Gottfried, Paul, and Thomas Fleming. *The Conservative Movement*. Boston: Twayne Publishers, 1988.

Gouldner, Alvin W. *The Future of Intellectuals and the Rise of the New Class*. New York: Seabury, 1979.

Grant, George. *Technology and Empire: Perspectives on North America*. Toronto: House of Anansi, 1969.

Gray, Colin S. "Keeping the Soviets Landlocked: Geostrategy for a Maritime America." *National Interest* 4 (Summer 1986).

Gremillion, Joseph, ed. *The Gospel of Peace and Justice: Catholic Social Teaching since Pope John XXIII*. Maryknoll, N.Y.: Orbis Books, 1976.

Grenier, Richard. *Capturing the Culture: Film, Art and Politics*. Washington, D.C.: Ethics and Public Policy Center, 1990.

Greve, Michael. "Why 'Defunding the Left' Failed." *Public Interest* 89 (Fall 1987).

Gutierrez, Gustavo. *A Theology of Liberation: History, Politics, and Salvation*. Translated by Sr. Caridad Inda and John Eagleson. Maryknoll, N.Y.: Orbis Books, 1973.

———. *We Drink from Our Own Wells: The Spiritual Journey of a People*. Translated by Matthew J. O'Connell. Maryknoll, N.Y.: Orbis Books, 1984.

Gutmann, David. "The Palestinian Myth." *Commentary* 60, no. 4 (October 1975).

Habermas, Jürgen. *The New Conservatism: Cultural Criticism and the Historians' Debate*. Edited and translated by S. W. Nicholsen. Cambridge, Mass.: MIT Press, 1989.

Halberstam, David. "Getting the Story in Vietnam." *Commentary* 39, no. 1 (January 1965).

Hamburger, Joseph. *Macaulay and the Whig Tradition*. Chicago: University of Chicago Press, 1976.

Harap, Louis. "*Commentary* Moves to the Right." *Jewish Currents* 25, no. 11 (December 1971).

Harap, Nigel. "Right-Wing Intellectuals and Jews." *Jewish Currents* 34, no. 6 (June 1980).

Harries, Owen. "A Primer for Polemicists." *Commentary* 78, no. 3 (September 1984).
——. "The Rise of American Decline." *Commentary* 85, no. 5 (May 1988).
Harrington, Michael. "The Committee for Cultural Freedom." *Dissent* 2, no. 2 (Spring 1955).
——. *Decade of Decision: The Crisis of the American System*. New York: Simon & Schuster, 1980.
——. *Fragments of the Century*. New York: Saturday Review Press, 1973.
——. *The Other America: Poverty in the United States*. New York: Macmillan, 1962.
——. *Toward a Democratic Left: A Radical Program for a New Majority*. New York: Macmillan, 1968.
——. *The Twilight of Capitalism*. New York: Simon & Schuster, 1976.
Harrison, Lawrence E. *Underdevelopment Is a State of Mind: The Latin American Case*. Lanham, Md.: Madison Books, 1985.
Hart, Jeffrey. "Gang Warfare in Chicago." *National Review* 38, no. 10 (June 6, 1986).
Hartz, Louis. *The Liberal Tradition in America: An Interpretation of American Political Thought since the Revolution*. New York: Harcourt Brace Jovanovich, 1955.
Hayek, Friedrich A. *The Constitution of Liberty*. Chicago: University of Chicago Press, 1960.
——. *Law, Legislation and Liberty*. Vol. 1, *Rules and Order*. Chicago: University of Chicago Press, 1973.
——. *Law, Legislation and Liberty*. Vol. 2, *The Mirage of Social Justice*. Chicago: University of Chicago Press, 1976.
——. *The Road to Serfdom*. 1944. Reprint. Chicago: University of Chicago Press, 1972.
——. *Studies in Philosophy, Politics and Economics*. Chicago: University of Chicago Press, 1967.
Heilbroner, Robert. "Counterrevolutionary America." *Commentary* 43, no. 4 (April 1967).
Hertzberg, Arthur. "Israel and American Jewry." *Commentary* 44, no. 2 (August 1967).
——. "Reagan and the Jews." *New York Review of Books*, January 31, 1985.
——, ed. *The Zionist Idea: A Historical Analysis and Reader*. 1959. Reprint. New York: Atheneum, 1982.
Himmelfarb, Dan. "Conservative Splits." *Commentary* 85, no. 5 (May 1988).
——. "Freedom, Virtue, and the Founding Fathers." *Public Interest* 90 (Winter 1988).
Himmelfarb, Gertrude. *The New History and the Old: Critical Essays and Reappraisals*. Cambridge, Mass.: Harvard University Press, 1987.
Himmelfarb, Milton. "Are Jews Becoming Republican?" *Commentary* 72, no. 2 (August 1981).
Hinkelammert, Franz J. *The Ideological Weapons of Death: A Theological Critique of Capitalism*. Translated by Phillip Berryman. Maryknoll, N.Y.: Orbis Books, 1986.

Hitchcock, James. "The Catholic Bishops, Public Policy, and the New Class." *This World* 9 (Fall 1984).

Hitchens, Christopher. "How Neoconservatives Perish: Good-bye to 'Totalitarianism' and All That." *Harper's* 281, no. 1682 (July 1990).

———. "A Modern Medieval Family." *Mother Jones* 11, no. 5 (July/August 1986).

Hoeveler, J. David, Jr. *Watch on the Right: Conservative Intellectuals in the Reagan Era.* Madison: University of Wisconsin Press, 1991.

Hollander, Paul. *Political Pilgrims: Travels of Western Intellectuals to the Soviet Union, China, and Cuba.* New York: Harper Colophon Books, 1983.

Hollenbach, David. *Claims in Conflict: Retrieving and Renewing the Catholic Human Rights Tradition.* New York: Paulist Press, 1979.

———. "The Growing End of an Argument." *America* 153, no. 16 (November 30, 1985).

———. "Justice as Participation: Public Moral Discourse and the U.S. Economy." In *Community in America: The Challenge of "Habits of the Heart,"* ed. Charles H. Reynolds and Ralph V. Norman. Berkeley: University of California Press, 1988.

———. *Justice, Peace, and Human Rights: American Catholic Social Ethics in a Pluralistic Context.* New York: Crossroad, 1988.

———. "Liberalism, Communitarianism and the Bishops' Pastoral Letter on the Economy." *Annual of the Society of Christian Ethics, 1987.* Washington, D.C.: Georgetown University Press, 1987.

———. *Nuclear Ethics: A Christian Moral Argument.* New York: Paulist Press, 1983.

Hook, Sidney. *From Hegel to Marx: Studies in the Intellectual Development of Karl Marx.* New York: John Day, 1936.

———. *Marxism and Beyond.* Totowa, N.J.: Rowman & Littlefield, 1983.

———. "On Being a Jew." *Commentary* 88, no. 4 (October 1989).

———. *Out of Step: An Unquiet Life in the Twentieth Century.* New York: Carroll & Graf, 1987.

———. *Paradoxes of Freedom.* Buffalo, N.Y.: Prometheus Books, 1987.

———. *The Quest for Being and Other Studies in Naturalism and Humanism.* New York: St. Martin's Press, 1961.

———. *Revolution, Reform, and Social Justice.* New York: New York University Press, 1975.

———. *Towards the Understanding of Karl Marx: A Revolutionary Interpretation.* New York: John Day, 1933.

Hook, Sidney, H. Stuart Hughes, Hans J. Morgenthau, and C. P. Snow. "Western Values and Total War: An Exchange." *Commentary* 32, no. 4 (October 1961).

Horowitz, David. "Nicaragua: A Speech to My Former Comrades on the Left." *Commentary* 81, no. 6 (June 1986).

———. "Still Taking the Fifth." *Commentary* 88, no. 1 (July 1989).

Hospers, John. *Libertarianism.* Los Angeles: Nash, 1971.

Hough, Jerry. *Russia and the West: Gorbachev and the Politics of Reform.* New York: Simon & Schuster, 1988.

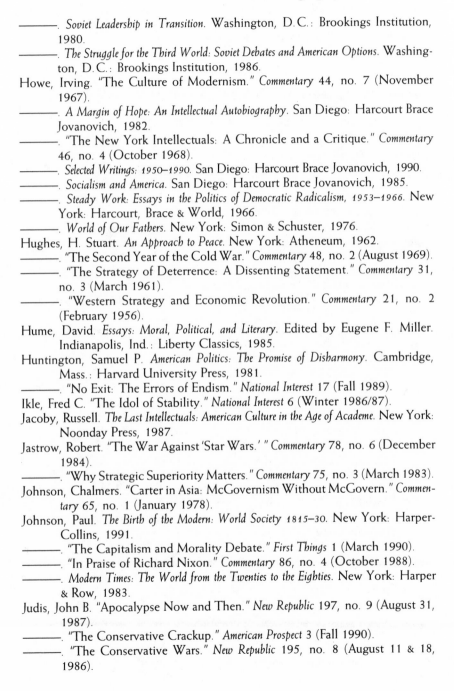

——. *Soviet Leadership in Transition*. Washington, D.C.: Brookings Institution, 1980.

——. *The Struggle for the Third World: Soviet Debates and American Options*. Washington, D.C.: Brookings Institution, 1986.

Howe, Irving. "The Culture of Modernism." *Commentary* 44, no. 7 (November 1967).

——. *A Margin of Hope: An Intellectual Autobiography*. San Diego: Harcourt Brace Jovanovich, 1982.

——. "The New York Intellectuals: A Chronicle and a Critique." *Commentary* 46, no. 4 (October 1968).

——. *Selected Writings: 1950–1990*. San Diego: Harcourt Brace Jovanovich, 1990.

——. *Socialism and America*. San Diego: Harcourt Brace Jovanovich, 1985.

——. *Steady Work: Essays in the Politics of Democratic Radicalism, 1953–1966*. New York: Harcourt, Brace & World, 1966.

——. *World of Our Fathers*. New York: Simon & Schuster, 1976.

Hughes, H. Stuart. *An Approach to Peace*. New York: Atheneum, 1962.

——. "The Second Year of the Cold War." *Commentary* 48, no. 2 (August 1969).

——. "The Strategy of Deterrence: A Dissenting Statement." *Commentary* 31, no. 3 (March 1961).

——. "Western Strategy and Economic Revolution." *Commentary* 21, no. 2 (February 1956).

Hume, David. *Essays: Moral, Political, and Literary*. Edited by Eugene F. Miller. Indianapolis, Ind.: Liberty Classics, 1985.

Huntington, Samuel P. *American Politics: The Promise of Disharmony*. Cambridge, Mass.: Harvard University Press, 1981.

——. "No Exit: The Errors of Endism." *National Interest* 17 (Fall 1989).

Ikle, Fred C. "The Idol of Stability." *National Interest* 6 (Winter 1986/87).

Jacoby, Russell. *The Last Intellectuals: American Culture in the Age of Academe*. New York: Noonday Press, 1987.

Jastrow, Robert. "The War Against 'Star Wars.'" *Commentary* 78, no. 6 (December 1984).

——. "Why Strategic Superiority Matters." *Commentary* 75, no. 3 (March 1983).

Johnson, Chalmers. "Carter in Asia: McGovernism Without McGovern." *Commentary* 65, no. 1 (January 1978).

Johnson, Paul. *The Birth of the Modern: World Society 1815–30*. New York: Harper-Collins, 1991.

——. "The Capitalism and Morality Debate." *First Things* 1 (March 1990).

——. "In Praise of Richard Nixon." *Commentary* 86, no. 4 (October 1988).

——. *Modern Times: The World from the Twenties to the Eighties*. New York: Harper & Row, 1983.

Judis, John B. "Apocalypse Now and Then." *New Republic* 197, no. 9 (August 31, 1987).

——. "The Conservative Crackup." *American Prospect* 3 (Fall 1990).

——. "The Conservative Wars." *New Republic* 195, no. 8 (August 11 & 18, 1986).

Jumonville, Neil. *Critical Crossings: The New York Intellectuals in Postwar America.* Berkeley: University of California Press, 1991.

Kahn, Tom. "The Problem of the New Left." *Commentary* 42, no. 1 (July 1966).

――――. "Why the Poor Peoples' Campaign Failed." *Commentary* 46, no. 3 (September 1968).

Kauffman, Bill. "Gnawing Away at Vidal." *Chronicles* 13, no. 3 (March 1989).

Kazin, Alfred. *Starting Out in the Thirties.* 1962. Reprint. Ithaca, N.Y.: Cornell University Press, 1989.

Kemble, Penn. "The Democrats and the Kissinger Report." *Commentary* 77, no. 3 (March 1984).

――――, ed. *After the Cold War and the Gulf War: A New Moment in America?* New York: Freedom House, 1991.

Kemble, Penn, and Arturo J. Cruz, Jr. "How the Nicaraguan Resistance Can Win." *Commentary* 82, no. 6 (December 1986).

Kemp, Jack. *An American Renaissance.* New York: Harper & Row, 1979.

Kennan, George. *Memoirs: 1925–1950.* Boston: Atlantic–Little, Brown, 1967.

――――. *Memoirs: 1950–1963.* Boston: Atlantic–Little, Brown, 1972.

――――. *The Nuclear Delusion: Soviet–American Relations in the Atomic Age.* New York: Pantheon Books, 1983.

―――― [X, pseud.]. "The Sources of Soviet Conduct." *Foreign Affairs* 25, no. 4 (July 1947).

Kennedy, Paul. *The Rise and Fall of the Great Powers: Economic Change and Military Conflict from 1500 to 2000.* New York: Vintage Books, 1987.

Kesler, Charles R. "Jeane Kirkpatrick: Not Quite Right." *National Review* 34, no. 21 (October 29, 1982).

Kimball, Roger. *Tenured Radicals: How Politics Has Corrupted Our Higher Education.* New York: Harper & Row, 1990.

Kirk, Russell. *The Conservative Mind: From Burke to Eliot.* 1953. Reprint. Chicago: Henry Regnery, 1987.

――――. *The Cultural Conservatives.* The Heritage Lectures. Washington, D.C.: Heritage Foundation, 1988.

――――. "Eliot and a Christian Culture." *This World* 24 (Winter 1989).

――――. *The Neoconservatives: An Endangered Species.* Heritage Lectures, no. 178. Washington, D.C.: Heritage Foundation, 1988.

――――. *The Popular Conservatives.* Heritage Lectures, Washington, D.C.: Heritage Foundation, 1988.

――――. *The Roots of American Order.* LaSalle, Ill.: Open Court, 1974.

Kirkpatrick, Jeane J. "Beyond the Cold War." *Foreign Affairs* 69, no. 1 (1990).

――――. "Dictatorships and Double Standards." *Commentary* 68, no. 5 (November 1979).

――――. *Dictatorships and Double Standards: Rationalism and Realism in Politics.* New York: American Enterprise Institute/Simon & Schuster, 1982.

――――. "How the PLO Was Legitimized." *Commentary* 88, no. 1 (July 1989).

――――. *Legitimacy and Force.* Vol. 1, *Political and Moral Dimensions.* New Brunswick, N.J.: Transaction Books, 1988.

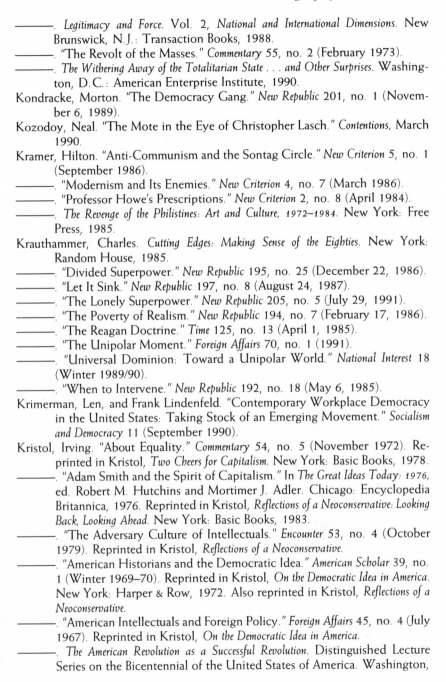

———. *Legitimacy and Force.* Vol. 2, *National and International Dimensions.* New Brunswick, N.J.: Transaction Books, 1988.

———. "The Revolt of the Masses." *Commentary* 55, no. 2 (February 1973).

———. *The Withering Away of the Totalitarian State . . . and Other Surprises.* Washington, D.C.: American Enterprise Institute, 1990.

Kondracke, Morton. "The Democracy Gang." *New Republic* 201, no. 1 (November 6, 1989).

Kozodoy, Neal. "The Mote in the Eye of Christopher Lasch." *Contentions,* March 1990.

Kramer, Hilton. "Anti-Communism and the Sontag Circle." *New Criterion* 5, no. 1 (September 1986).

———. "Modernism and Its Enemies." *New Criterion* 4, no. 7 (March 1986).

———. "Professor Howe's Prescriptions." *New Criterion* 2, no. 8 (April 1984).

———. *The Revenge of the Philistines: Art and Culture, 1972–1984.* New York: Free Press, 1985.

Krauthammer, Charles. *Cutting Edges: Making Sense of the Eighties.* New York: Random House, 1985.

———. "Divided Superpower." *New Republic* 195, no. 25 (December 22, 1986).

———. "Let It Sink." *New Republic* 197, no. 8 (August 24, 1987).

———. "The Lonely Superpower." *New Republic* 205, no. 5 (July 29, 1991).

———. "The Poverty of Realism." *New Republic* 194, no. 7 (February 17, 1986).

———. "The Reagan Doctrine." *Time* 125, no. 13 (April 1, 1985).

———. "The Unipolar Moment." *Foreign Affairs* 70, no. 1 (1991).

———. "Universal Dominion: Toward a Unipolar World." *National Interest* 18 (Winter 1989/90).

———. "When to Intervene." *New Republic* 192, no. 18 (May 6, 1985).

Krimerman, Len, and Frank Lindenfeld. "Contemporary Workplace Democracy in the United States: Taking Stock of an Emerging Movement." *Socialism and Democracy* 11 (September 1990).

Kristol, Irving. "About Equality." *Commentary* 54, no. 5 (November 1972). Reprinted in Kristol, *Two Cheers for Capitalism.* New York: Basic Books, 1978.

———. "Adam Smith and the Spirit of Capitalism." In *The Great Ideas Today: 1976,* ed. Robert M. Hutchins and Mortimer J. Adler. Chicago: Encyclopedia Britannica, 1976. Reprinted in Kristol, *Reflections of a Neoconservative: Looking Back, Looking Ahead.* New York: Basic Books, 1983.

———. "The Adversary Culture of Intellectuals." *Encounter* 53, no. 4 (October 1979). Reprinted in Kristol, *Reflections of a Neoconservative.*

———. "American Historians and the Democratic Idea." *American Scholar* 39, no. 1 (Winter 1969–70). Reprinted in Kristol, *On the Democratic Idea in America.* New York: Harper & Row, 1972. Also reprinted in Kristol, *Reflections of a Neoconservative.*

———. "American Intellectuals and Foreign Policy." *Foreign Affairs* 45, no. 4 (July 1967). Reprinted in Kristol, *On the Democratic Idea in America.*

———. *The American Revolution as a Successful Revolution.* Distinguished Lecture Series on the Bicentennial of the United States of America. Washington,

D.C.: American Enterprise Institute, 1973. Reprinted in Kristol, *Reflections of a Neoconservative.*

————. " 'Capitalism' and 'The Free Society': A Reply." *Public Interest* 22 (Winter 1971).

————. "Capitalism, Socialism, and Nihilism." *Public Interest* 31 (Spring 1973). Reprinted in Kristol, *Two Cheers for Capitalism.*

————. "Civil Disobedience Is Not Justified by Vietnam." *New York Times Magazine,* November 26, 1967.

————. " 'Civil Liberties': 1952—A Study in Confusion." *Commentary* 13, no. 3 (March 1952).

————. "Class and Sociology: The Shadow of Marxism." *Commentary* 24, no. 4 (October 1957).

————. "Confessions of a True, Self-Confessed—Perhaps the Only—'Neoconservative.' " *Public Opinion* 2, no. 5 (October/November 1979). Reprinted in Kristol, *Reflections of a Neoconservative.*

————. "Decentralization for What?" *Public Interest* 11 (Spring 1968).

————. "Defining Our National Interest." *National Interest* 21 (Fall 1990).

————. "Deterrence." *Commentary* 32, no. 1 (July 1961).

————. "Does NATO Exist?" *Washington Quarterly,* Autumn 1979. Reprinted in Kristol, *Reflections of a Neoconservative.*

————. "Don't Count Out Conservatism." *New York Times Magazine,* June 14, 1987.

————. "The Essence of Capitalism." Review of *Polity and Economy: An Introduction to the Principles of Adam Smith,* by Joseph Cropsey. *Encounter* 9, no. 5 (November 1957).

————. "Facing the Facts in Vietnam." *New Leader* 46, no. 20 (September 30, 1963).

————. "A Foolish American Ism—Utopianism." *New York Times Magazine,* November 14, 1971. Reprinted as "Utopianism and American Politics" in Kristol, *On the Democratic Idea in America.*

————. "Foreign Policy in an Age of Ideology." *National Interest* 1 (Fall 1985).

————. "The Future of American Jewry." *Commentary* 92, no. 2 (August 1991).

————. "High, Low, and Modern: Some Thoughts on Popular Culture and Popular Government." *Encounter* 15, no. 2 (August 1960).

————. " 'Human Rights': The Hidden Agenda." *National Interest* 6 (Winter 1986/87).

————. "Ideology and Supply-Side Economics." *Commentary* 71, no. 4 (April 1981).

————. "Is the Urban Crisis Real?" *Commentary* 50, no. 5 (November 1970).

————. "Last of the Whigs." Review of *The Constitution of Liberty,* by Friedrich Hayek. *Commentary* 29, no. 4 (April 1960).

————. "Learning to Live with the *N.S. & N.*" *Encounter* 21, no. 2 (August 1963).

————. "Liberalism and American Jews." *Commentary* 86, no. 4 (October 1988).

————. "Liberty and the Communists." *Partisan Review* 19, no. 4 (July/August 1952).

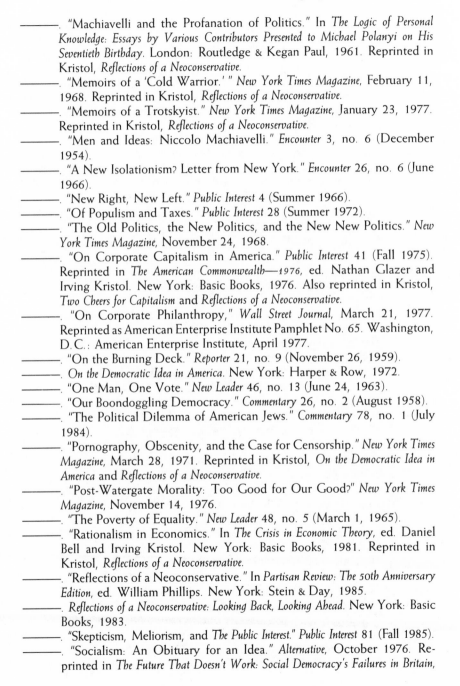

————. "Machiavelli and the Profanation of Politics." In *The Logic of Personal Knowledge: Essays by Various Contributors Presented to Michael Polanyi on His Seventieth Birthday*. London: Routledge & Kegan Paul, 1961. Reprinted in Kristol, *Reflections of a Neoconservative*.

————. "Memoirs of a 'Cold Warrior.'" *New York Times Magazine*, February 11, 1968. Reprinted in Kristol, *Reflections of a Neoconservative*.

————. "Memoirs of a Trotskyist." *New York Times Magazine*, January 23, 1977. Reprinted in Kristol, *Reflections of a Neoconservative*.

————. "Men and Ideas: Niccolo Machiavelli." *Encounter* 3, no. 6 (December 1954).

————. "A New Isolationism? Letter from New York." *Encounter* 26, no. 6 (June 1966).

————. "New Right, New Left." *Public Interest* 4 (Summer 1966).

————. "Of Populism and Taxes." *Public Interest* 28 (Summer 1972).

————. "The Old Politics, the New Politics, and the New New Politics." *New York Times Magazine*, November 24, 1968.

————. "On Corporate Capitalism in America." *Public Interest* 41 (Fall 1975). Reprinted in *The American Commonwealth—1976*, ed. Nathan Glazer and Irving Kristol. New York: Basic Books, 1976. Also reprinted in Kristol, *Two Cheers for Capitalism* and *Reflections of a Neoconservative*.

————. "On Corporate Philanthropy," *Wall Street Journal*, March 21, 1977. Reprinted as American Enterprise Institute Pamphlet No. 65. Washington, D.C.: American Enterprise Institute, April 1977.

————. "On the Burning Deck." *Reporter* 21, no. 9 (November 26, 1959).

————. *On the Democratic Idea in America*. New York: Harper & Row, 1972.

————. "One Man, One Vote." *New Leader* 46, no. 13 (June 24, 1963).

————. "Our Boondoggling Democracy." *Commentary* 26, no. 2 (August 1958).

————. "The Political Dilemma of American Jews." *Commentary* 78, no. 1 (July 1984).

————. "Pornography, Obscenity, and the Case for Censorship." *New York Times Magazine*, March 28, 1971. Reprinted in Kristol, *On the Democratic Idea in America* and *Reflections of a Neoconservative*.

————. "Post-Watergate Morality: Too Good for Our Good?" *New York Times Magazine*, November 14, 1976.

————. "The Poverty of Equality." *New Leader* 48, no. 5 (March 1, 1965).

————. "Rationalism in Economics." In *The Crisis in Economic Theory*, ed. Daniel Bell and Irving Kristol. New York: Basic Books, 1981. Reprinted in Kristol, *Reflections of a Neoconservative*.

————. "Reflections of a Neoconservative." In *Partisan Review: The 50th Anniversary Edition*, ed. William Phillips. New York: Stein & Day, 1985.

————. *Reflections of a Neoconservative: Looking Back, Looking Ahead*. New York: Basic Books, 1983.

————. "Skepticism, Meliorism, and *The Public Interest*." *Public Interest* 81 (Fall 1985).

————. "Socialism: An Obituary for an Idea." *Alternative*, October 1976. Reprinted in *The Future That Doesn't Work: Social Democracy's Failures in Britain*, ed. R. Emmett Tyrell, Jr. Garden City, N.Y.: Doubleday, 1977. Also reprinted in Kristol, *Reflections of a Neoconservative*.

————. "Social Sciences and Law." In *The Great Ideas Today, 1962*, ed. Robert M. Hutchins and Mortimer J. Adler. Chicago: Encyclopedia Britannica, 1962.

————. "Some Personal Reflections on Economic Well-Being and Income Distribution." In *The American Economy in Transition*, ed. Martin Feldstein. Chicago: University of Chicago Press, 1980. Reprinted in Kristol, *Reflections of a Neoconservative*.

————. "The Spirit of '87." *Public Interest* 86 (Winter 1987).

————. "The Spiritual Roots of Capitalism and Socialism." In *Capitalism and Socialism: A Theological Inquiry*, ed. Michael Novak. Washington, D.C.: American Enterprise Institute, 1979. Reprinted as "Christianity, Judaism, and Socialism" in Kristol, *Reflections of a Neoconservative*.

————. "Taxes, Poverty, and Equality." *Public Interest* 37 (Fall 1974). Reprinted in Kristol, *Two Cheers for Capitalism*.

————. "Teaching In, Speaking Out: The Controversy over Viet Nam." *Encounter* 25, no. 2 (August 1965).

————. "Toward a Restructuring of the University." *New York Times Magazine*, December 8, 1968. Reprinted in Kristol, *On the Democratic Idea in America*.

————. "Toward Pre-emptive War?" *Reporter* 20, no. 10 (May 14, 1959).

————. "The Troublesome Intellectuals." *Public Interest* 2 (Winter 1966).

————. *Two Cheers for Capitalism*. New York: Basic Books, 1978.

————. "The Underdeveloped Profession." *Public Interest* 6 (Winter 1967).

————. "Urban Civilization and Its Discontents." *Commentary* 50, no. 1 (July 1970). Reprinted in Kristol, *On the Democratic Idea in America*.

————. "Utopianism, Ancient and Modern." *Imprimus* 2 (April 1973). Reprinted in Kristol, *Two Cheers for Capitalism*.

————. "The Way We Were." *National Interest* 17 (Fall 1989).

————. "What's Bugging the Students." *Atlantic Monthly* 216, no. 5 (November 1965).

————. " 'When Virtue Loses All Her Loveliness'—Some Reflections on Capitalism and 'The Free Society.' " *Public Interest* 21 (Fall 1970). Reprinted in Kristol, *On the Democratic Idea in America* and *Two Cheers for Capitalism*.

Kristol, Irving, et al. "Should the U.S. Stay in NATO?" *Harper's* 26 , no. 1604 (January 1984).

Lange, Oskar, and F. M. Taylor. *On the Economic Theory of Socialism*. 1931. Reprint. New York: McGraw-Hill, 1964.

Laqueur, Walter. " 'Eurocommunism' and Its Friends." *Commentary* 62, no. 2 (August 1976).

————. "Glasnost and Its Limits." *Commentary* 86, no. 1 (July 1988).

————. "How Real Is Arab Nationalism?" *Commentary* 23, no. 4 (April 1957).

————. "The Psychology of Appeasement." *Commentary* 66, no. 4 (October 1978).

————. "Reagan and the Russians." *Commentary* 73, no. 1 (January 1982).

————. "The Specter of Finlandization." *Commentary* 64, no. 6 (December 1977).

———. "What We Know about the Soviet Union." *Commentary* 75, no. 2 (February 1983).

———. "The World and President Carter." *Commentary* 65, no. 2 (February 1978).

Lasch, Christopher. *The Agony of the American Left.* New York: Alfred A. Knopf, 1969.

———. "Conservatism Against Itself." *First Things* 2 (April 1990).

———. "The Cultural Cold War: A Short History of the Congress for Cultural Freedom." In *Towards a New Past: Dissenting Essays in American History,* ed. Barton Bernstein. New York: Pantheon Books, 1968.

———. *The Culture of Narcissism: American Life in an Age of Diminishing Expectations.* New York: W. W. Norton, 1978.

———. "Engineering the Good Life: The Search for Perfection." *This World* 26 (Summer 1989).

———. "The New Class Controversy." *Chronicles* 14, no. 6 (June 1990).

———. *The New Radicalism in America (1889–1963): The Intellectual as a Social Type.* New York: Alfred A. Knopf, 1965.

———. *The True and Only Heaven: Progress and Its Critics.* New York: W. W. Norton, 1991.

Laski, Harold. *The Rise of Liberalism: The Philosophy of a Business Civilization.* New York: Harper & Brothers, 1936.

Lay Commission on Catholic Social Teaching and the U.S. Economy. *Toward the Future.* New York: Lay Commission, 1984.

Lenkowsky, Leslie. "Welfare Reform and the Liberals." *Commentary* 67, no. 3 (March 1979).

Levin, Michael. "Comparable Worth: The Feminist Road to Socialism." *Commentary* 78, no. 3 (September 1984).

———. *Feminism and Freedom.* New Brunswick, N.J.: Transaction Books, 1987.

———. "The Feminist Mystique." *Commentary* 70, no. 6 (December 1980).

Lewis, Arthur. *The Theory of Economic Growth.* London: George Allen & Unwin, 1955.

Lichtheim, George. "The Cold War in Perspective." *Commentary* 37, no. 6 (June 1964).

———. *Collected Essays.* New York: Viking Press, 1974.

———. *The Concept of Ideology and Other Essays.* New York: Random House, 1967.

Lindblom, Charles E. *Politics and Markets: The World's Political-Economic Systems.* New York: Basic Books, 1977.

Lindenfeld, Frank, and Joyce Rothschild-Whitt, eds. *Workplace Democracy and Social Change.* Boston: Porter Sargent, 1982.

Lipset, Seymour Martin. "The Death of the Third Way." *National Interest* 20 (Summer 1990).

———. "Neoconservatism: Myth and Reality." *Society* 25, no. 5 (July/August 1988).

Lipset, Seymour Martin, and William Schneider. "Carter vs. Israel: What the Polls Reveal." *Commentary* 64, no. 5 (November 1977).

Livingston, Jon, Joe Moore, and Felicia Oldfather, eds. *Imperial Japan, 1800–1945.* New York: Pantheon Books, 1973.

Lockwood, William W. *The Economic Development of Japan: Growth and Structural Change, 1868–1938.* Princeton: Princeton University Press, 1954.

Loury, Glenn C. "Black Dignity and the Common Good." *First Things* 4 (June–July 1990).

———. "The Moral Quandary of the Black Community." *Public Interest* 79 (Spring 1985).

Luttwak, Edward. "Defense Reconsidered." *Commentary* 63, no. 3 (March 1977).

———. "From Geopolitics to Geo-Economics." *National Interest* 20 (Summer 1990).

———. "Gorbachev's Strategy, and Ours." *Commentary* 88, no. 1 (July 1989).

———. "How to Think about Nuclear War." *Commentary* 74, no. 2 (August 1982).

———. "A New Arms Race?" *Commentary* 70, no. 3 (September 1980).

———. "The Shape of Things to Come." *Commentary* 89, no. 6 (June 1990).

———. "Ten Questions about Salt II." *Commentary* 68, no. 2 (August 1979).

———. "Why Arms Control Has Failed." *Commentary* 65, no. 1 (January 1978).

———. "Why We Need More 'Waste, Fraud and Mismanagement' in the Pentagon." *Commentary* 73, no. 2 (February 1982).

Lynd, Staughton. "How the Cold War Began." *Commentary* 30, no. 5 (November 1960).

Lynn, Kenneth S. *The Air-Line to Seattle: Studies in Literary and Historical Writing about America.* Chicago: University of Chicago Press, 1983.

Lyons, Eugene. *Assignment in Utopia.* New York: Harcourt, Brace, and Co., 1937.

McConnell, Scott. "Resurrecting the New Left." *Commentary* 84, no. 4 (October 1987).

———. "Vietnam and the 60's Generation: A Memoir." *Commentary* 79, no. 6 (June 1985).

McCracken, Samuel. "Apocalyptic Thinking." *Commentary* 52, no. 4 (October 1971).

———. "Quackery in the Classroom." *Commentary* 49, no. 6 (June 1970).

Macdonald, Dwight. *Discriminations: Essays and Afterthoughts.* New York: Grossman Publishers, 1974.

———. *Memoirs of a Revolutionist: Essays in Political Criticism.* New York: Farrar, Straus & Cudahy, 1957.

McGovern, Arthur F. *Liberation Theology and Its Critics: Toward an Assessment.* Maryknoll, N.Y.: Orbis Books, 1989.

MacIntyre, Alasdair. *After Virtue: A Study in Moral Theory.* Notre Dame, Ind.: University of Notre Dame Press, 1981.

Mailer, Norman. "The Battle of the Pentagon." *Commentary* 45, no. 4 (April 1968).

Mander, John. "In Defense of the 50's." *Commentary* 48, no. 3 (September 1969).

Mannheim, Karl. *Man and Society in an Age of Reconstruction.* New York: Harcourt, Brace & World, 1940.

Mayers, David. *George Kennan and the Dilemmas of U.S. Foreign Policy.* New York: Oxford University Press, 1988.

Meidner, Rudolf. *Employee Investment Funds: An Approach to Collective Capital Formation.* London: George Allen & Unwin, 1978.

Meyer, Frank. *The Conservative Mainstream*. New Rochelle, N.Y.: Arlington House, 1968.

Miller, Merle. "Why Norman and Jason Aren't Talking." *New York Times Magazine*, March 26, 1972.

Milstein, Tom. "A Perspective on the Panthers." *Commentary* 50, no. 3 (September 1970).

Mises, Ludwig von. *Socialism: An Economic and Sociological Analysis*. 1932. Reprint. Translated by J. Kahane. Indianapolis, Ind.: Liberty Classics, 1981.

Molnar, Thomas. "Modernity." *This World* 23 (Fall 1988).

Morgenthau, Hans J. "Asia: The American Algeria." *Commentary* 32, no. 1 (July 1961).

———. "The Impotence of American Power." *Commentary* 36, no. 5 (November 1963).

———. "The Perils of Political Empiricism." *Commentary* 34, no. 1 (July 1962).

———. "Vietnam: Another Korea?" *Commentary* 33, no. 5 (May 1962).

Morley, Jefferson. "The Washington Intellectual." *New Republic* 195, no. 8 (August 11 & 18, 1986).

Moynihan, Daniel P. *Coping: On the Practice of Government*. New York: Vintage Books, 1975.

———. *Family and Nation*. New York: Harcourt Brace Jovanovich, 1986.

———. "Joining the Jackals: The U.S. at the U.N., 1977–1988." *Commentary* 71, no. 2 (February 1981).

———. *Maximum Feasible Misunderstanding*. New York: Free Press, 1970.

———. "The Negro Family: The Case for National Action." In *The Moynihan Report and the Politics of Controversy*, ed. Lee Rainwater and William L. Yancy. Cambridge, Mass.: MIT Press, 1967.

———. *The Politics of a Guaranteed Income*. New York: Random House, 1973.

———. "The Politics of Human Rights." *Commentary* 64, no. 2 (August 1977).

———. "The United States in Opposition." *Commentary* 59, no. 3 (March 1975).

———. "Zionism, the United Nations and American Foreign Policy." *Catholicism in Crisis* 2, no. 5 (April 1984).

Moynihan, Robert. "Thunder on the Right." *Thirty Days*, September 1989.

Muller, Jerry Z. "Capitalism: The Wave of the Future." *Commentary* 86, no. 6 (December 1988).

Muravchik, Joshua. "Dictatorships and Single Standards." *Crisis* 8, no. 2 (February 1990).

———. *Exporting Democracy: Fulfilling America's Destiny*. Washington, D.C.: American Enterprise Institute, 1991.

———. "Glasnostrums." *New Republic* 200, no. 5 (January 30, 1989).

———. "Gorbachev's Intellectual Odyssey." *New Republic* 202, no. 10 (March 5, 1990).

———. "How I Got Smart: A Young Marxist Throws in the Towel." *Crisis* 6, no. 6 (June 1988).

———. "Maximum Feasible Containment." *New Republic* 196, no. 22 (June 1, 1987).

———. "Nicaragua's Slow March to Communism." *This World* 13 (Winter 1986).

Murray, Charles. "The Coming of Custodial Democracy." *Commentary* 86, no. 3 (September 1988).

——. *Losing Ground: American Social Policy, 1950–1980.* New York: Basic Books, 1984.

Nash, George H. *The Conservative Intellectual Movement in America since 1945.* New York: Basic Books, 1976.

National Conference of Catholic Bishops. *Economic Justice for All: Catholic Social Teaching and the U.S. Economy.* Reprinted in *Origins*. Washington: D.C.: National Catholic News Service, November 27, 1986.

Naylor, Thomas H. "Redefining Corporate Motivation, Swedish Style." *Christian Century* 107, no. 18 (May 30–June 6, 1990).

Neuhaus, Richard John. *The Catholic Moment: The Paradox of the Church in the Postmodern World.* New York: Harper & Row, 1987.

——. "Democratic Conservatism." *First Things* 1 (March 1990).

——. *The Naked Public Square: Religion and Democracy in America.* Grand Rapids, Mich.: William B. Eerdmans, 1984.

——. "Prophets with Tenure." *Commentary* 84, no. 1 (July 1987).

——. "The Theonomist Temptation." *First Things* 3 (May 1990).

——. *Time Toward Home: The American Experiment as Revelation.* New York: Seabury Press, 1975.

——, ed. *Confession, Conflict, and Community.* Grand Rapids, Mich.: William B. Eerdmans, 1986.

Neuhaus, Richard John, George Weigel, and Michael Novak. "America Is Not a Secular Society." *Thirty Days*, June 1989.

Newfield, Jack. *A Prophetic Minority.* New York: Signet Books, 1967.

Niebuhr, Reinhold. *An Interpretation of Christian Ethics.* 1935. Reprint. New York: Harper & Row, 1963.

——. *Moral Man and Immoral Society.* New York: Scribner's, 1932.

Nisbet, Robert. *Conservatism: Dream and Reality.* Minneapolis: University of Minnesota Press, 1986.

——. *The Present Age: Progress and Anarchy in Modern America.* New York: Harper & Row, 1988.

——. "The Pursuit of Equality." *Public Interest* 35 (Spring 1974).

——. *The Quest for Community.* New York: Oxford University Press, 1953.

——. *Twilight of Authority.* New York: Oxford University Press, 1975.

Norman, Edward. *Christianity and the World Order.* Oxford: Oxford University Press, 1979.

Norman, Geoffrey. "The Godfather of Neoconservatism (and His Family)." *Esquire* 91, no. 3 (February 13, 1979).

Novak, Michael. "Against 'Affirmative Action.'" *Commonweal* 100, no. 5 (April 5, 1974).

——. *All the Catholic People: Where Did All the Spirit Go?* New York: Herder & Herder, 1971.

——. "American Catholicism after the Council." *Commentary* 40, no. 2 (August 1965).

———. *The American Vision: An Essay on the Future of Democratic Capitalism.* Washington, D.C.: American Enterprise Institute, 1978.

———. "Arms and the Church." *Commentary* 73, no. 3 (March 1982).

———. *Ascent of the Mountain, Flight of the Dove: An Invitation to Religious Studies.* New York: Harper & Row, 1971.

———. *Belief and Unbelief: A Philosophy of Self-Knowledge.* New York: Macmillan, 1965.

———. "Beyond 'Populorum Progressio': John Paul II's 'Economic Initiative.' " *Crisis* 6, no. 3 (March 1988).

———. "Blaming America: A Comment on Paragraphs 202–204 of the First Draft." *Catholicism in Crisis* 3, no. 8 (July 1985).

———. *A Book of Elements: Reflections on Middle-Class Days.* New York: Herder & Herder, 1972.

———. "Boredom, Virtue, and Democratic Capitalism." *Commentary* 88, no. 3 (September 1989).

———. "'Built Wiser than They Knew': The Constitution and the Wealth of Nations." *Crisis* 5, no. 5 (May 1987).

———. "Can a Christian Work for a Corporation? The Theology of the Corporation." In *The Judeo-Christian Vision and the Modern Corporation,* ed. Oliver Williams and John Houck. Notre Dame, Ind.: University of Notre Dame Press, 1982.

———. "The Case Against Liberation Theology." *New York Times Sunday Magazine,* October 21, 1984.

———. "The Catholic Anticapitalist Bias." Introduction to *Catholicism, Protestantism and Capitalism,* by Amintore Fanfani. Notre Dame, Ind.: University of Notre Dame Press, 1984.

———. "Catholic Education and the Idea of Dissent." *Commonweal* 76, no. 5 (April 27, 1962).

———. *Choosing Our King: Powerful Symbols in Presidential Politics.* New York: Macmillan, 1974.

———. "The Christian Vision of Economic Life." *Catholicism in Crisis* 3, no. 12 (December 1985).

———. "Class, Culture and Society." Review of *The Winding Passage: Essays and Sociological Journeys, 1960–1980,* by Daniel Bell. *Commentary* 72, no. 1 (July 1981).

———. "The Communitarian Individual in America." *Public Interest* 68 (Summer 1982).

———. *Confession of a Catholic.* San Francisco: Harper & Row, 1983.

———. "Crime and Character." *This World* 14 (Spring/Summer 1986).

———. "The Danger of Egalityranny." *American Spectator* 15, no. 8 (August 1982).

———. "The Development of Nations." *This World* 22 (Summer 1988).

———. "The Disaster of Vatican II." *Notre Dame Magazine,* October 1982.

———. "Dissent in the Church." *Catholicism in Crisis* 4, no. 1 (January 1986).

———. "Economic Rights: The Servile State." *Catholicism in Crisis* 3, no. 10 (October 1985).

————. "Engagement but No Security." *Commonweal* 108, no. 2 (January 30, 1981).

————. "Errand into the Wilderness." In *Political Passages: Journeys of Change Through Two Decades, 1968–1988*, ed. John H. Bunzel, New York: Free Press, 1988.

————. *The Experience of Nothingness*. New York: Harper & Row, 1970.

————. *Freedom with Justice: Catholic Social Thought and Liberal Institutions*. San Francisco: Harper & Row, 1984.

————. "Free Persons and the Common Good." In *The Common Good and U.S. Capitalism*, ed. Oliver F. Williams and John W. Houck. Lanham, Md.: University Press of America, 1987.

————. *Free Persons and the Common Good*. Lanham, Md.: Madison Books, 1989.

————. "The Greening of a Con-III-Man." *Commonweal* 93, no. 10 (December 4, 1970.

————. *The Guns of Lattimer*. New York: Basic Books, 1978.

————. *Human Rights and the New Realism: Strategic Thinking in a New Age*. New York: Freedom House, 1986.

————. "In Eastern Europe, Little Things Count." *Christian Century* 106, no. 38 (December 13, 1989).

————. *The Joy of Sports*. New York: Basic Books, 1976.

————. "Liberation Theology and the Pope." *Commentary* 67, no. 6 (June 1979).

————. "Liberation Theology in Practice." *Thought* 59, no. 233 (June 1984).

————. "Liberation Theology in the Americas: The Romance and the Reality." *New Catholic World* 229, no. 1373 (September/October 1986).

————. "Making Deterrence Work." *Catholicism in Crisis* 1, no. 1 (November 1982).

————. "Mediating Institutions: The Communitarian Individual in America." *Public Interest* 68 (Summer 1982).

————. "Mr. X Abandons Containment: George Kennan Loses His Nerve." *Catholicism in Crisis* 4, no. 4 (April 1986).

————. *Moral Clarity in the Nuclear Age*. Nashville: Thomas Nelson, 1983.

————. *Naked I Leave*. New York: Macmillan, 1970.

————. "Narrative and Ideology." *This World* 23 (Fall 1988).

————. "Needing Niebuhr Again," *Commentary* 54, no. 3 (September 1972).

————. "The New Science." *National Review* 39, no. 13 (July 17, 1987).

————. "Not Yet: Biblical Realism and Power Politics." *Catholicism in Crisis* 2, no. 8 (July 1984).

————. "On Achieving Genuine Disagreement." *Thirty Days*, October 1989.

————. "On Democratic Capitalism." *National Review* 36, no. 2 (October 29, 1982).

————. *The Open Church: Vatican II, Act II*. New York: Macmillan, 1964.

————. "Ordinary People." *National Interest* 5 (Fall 1986).

————. "Orthodoxy vs. Progressive Bourgeois Christianity." In *Once a Catholic: Prominent Catholics and Ex-Catholics Discuss the Influence of the Church on Their Lives and Work*, ed. Peter Occhiogrosso. Boston: Houghton Mifflin, 1987.

————. "Political Economy and Christian Conscience." *Journal of Ecumenical Studies* 24, no. 3 (Summer 1987).

————. "The Politics of John Paul II." *Commentary* 68, no. 6 (December 1979).

————. *Politics: Realism and Imagination.* New York: Herder & Herder, 1971.

————. "The Presidency and Professor Schlesinger." *Commentary* 57, no. 2 (February 1974).

————. "Public Theology and the Left: What Happens after Reagan? *Christian Century* 105, no. 15 (May 4, 1988).

————. "Race and Truth." *Commentary* 62, no. 6 (December 1976).

————. "Reinhold Niebuhr: Model for Neoconservatives." *Christian Century* 103, no. 3 (January 22, 1986).

————. "Religion and Liberty: From Vision to Politics." *Christian Century* 105, no. 21 (July 6–13, 1988).

————. "The Religion of Paul Tillich." *Commentary* 43, no. 4 (April 1967).

————. "The Return of the Catholic Whig." *First Things* 1 (March 1990).

————. "The Revolt Against Our Public Culture." *National Review* 36, no. 8 (May 4, 1984).

————. "The Rich, the Poor and Reaganomics." *First Things* 12 (April 1991).

————. "The Rich, the Poor and the Reagan Administration." *Commentary* 76, no. 2 (August 1983).

————. "The Rights and Wrongs of 'Economic Rights': A Debate Continued." *This World* 17 (Spring 1987).

————. *The Rise of the Unmeltable Ethnics: Politics and Culture in the Seventies.* New York: Macmillan, 1971.

————. "Schindler's Conversion: The Catholic Right Accepts Pluralism," *Communio* 19, no. 1 (Spring 1992): 145–163.

————. *The Spirit of Democratic Capitalism.* New York: American Enterprise Institute/Simon & Schuster, 1982.

————. *"Story" in Politics.* New York: Council on Religion and International Affairs, 1970.

————. *Taking Glasnost Seriously: Toward an Open Soviet Union.* Washington, D.C.: American Enterprise Institute, 1988.

————. "Theologians and Economists: The Next Twenty Years." *This World* 3 (Winter 1984).

————. *A Theology for Radical Politics.* New York: Herder & Herder, 1969.

————. *This Hemisphere of Liberty: A Philosophy of the Americas.* Washington, D.C.: American Enterprise Institute, 1990.

————. "Three Porcupines of Pluralism." *This World* 19 (Fall 1987).

————. *The Tiber Was Silver: A Novel of Spiritual Adventure in Modern Rome.* New York: Doubleday, 1961.

————. *A Time to Build.* New York: Macmillan, 1967.

————. *Toward a Theology of the Corporation.* Washington, D.C.: American Enterprise Institute, 1981.

————. "Toward Consensus: Suggestions for Revising the First Draft." *Catholicism in Crisis* 3, no. 4 (March 1985).

————. "The Twilight of Socialism." *Catholicism in Crisis* 1, no. 9 (August 1983).

————. "An Underpraised and Undervalued System: The Creed of Democratic Capitalism." *Worldview,* July/August 1977.

————. "Up from Underdevelopment." *Commentary* 78, no. 3 (September 1984).

————. "The Virtue of Enterprise: The Discovery of a 'Right to Economic Initiative' Could Revolutionize Catholic Social Thought." *Crisis* 7, no. 5 (May 1989).

————. "Welfare's 'New Consensus': Sending the Right Signals." *Public Interest* 89 (Fall 1987).

————. "Where the Second Draft Errs." *America* 154, no. 2 (January 18, 1986).

————. "Why the Church Is Not Pacifist." *Catholicism in Crisis* 2, no. 7 (June 1984).

————. *Will It Liberate? Questions about Liberation Theology.* New York: Paulist Press, 1986.

————. "Woman Church Is Not Mother Church." *Catholicism in Crisis* 2, no. 3 (February 1984).

————, ed. *Capitalism and Socialism: A Theological Inquiry.* Washington, D.C.: American Enterprise Institute, 1979.

————, ed. *Democracy and Mediating Structures: A Theological Inquiry.* Washington, D.C.: American Enterprise Institute, 1980.

————, ed. *The Denigration of Capitalism: Six Points of View.* Washington, D.C.: American Enterprise Institute, 1979.

————, ed. *The Experience of Marriage.* New York: Macmillan, 1964.

————, ed. *Growing Up Slavic in America.* Bayville, N.Y.: EMPAC, 1976.

————, ed. *Liberation South, Liberation North.* Washington, D.C.: American Enterprise Institute, 1981.

————, ed. *Liberation Theology and the Liberal Society.* Washington, D.C.: American Enterprise Institute, 1987.

Novak, Michael, and John W. Cooper, eds. *The Corporation: A Theological Inquiry.* Washington, D.C.: American Enterprise Institute, 1981.

Novak, Michael, and Gordon Green. "Poverty Down, Inequality Up?" *Public Interest* 83 (Spring 1986).

Novak, Michael, and Michael P. Jackson, eds. *Latin America: Dependency or Interdependence?* Washington, D.C.: American Enterprise Institute, 1985.

Novak, Michael, Richard Neuhaus, and George Weigel. "America Is Not a Secular Society." *Thirty Days,* June 1989.

Nove, Alec. *The Economics of Feasible Socialism.* London: George Allen & Unwin, 1983.

Nozick, Robert. *The Examined Life: Philosophical Meditations.* New York: Simon & Schuster, 1989.

Nuechterlein, James. "A Farewell to Civil Rights." *Commentary* 84, no. 2 (August 1987).

————. "The Feminization of the American Left." *Commentary* 84, no. 5 (November 1987).

————. "Neoconservatism and Irving Kristol." *Commentary* 78, no. 2 (August 1984).

Oakeshott, Michael. *Rationalism in Politics.* New York: Basic Books, 1962.

Okimoto, Daniel I., and Thomas P. Rohlen, eds. *Inside the Japanese System: Readings in Contemporary Society and Political Economy.* Stanford: Stanford University Press, 1988.

O'Neill, William L. *A Better World: The Great Schism: Stalinism and the American Intellectuals.* New York: Simon & Schuster, 1982.

Orwell, George. *Collected Essays.* London: Secker & Warburg, 1961.

Ozersky, Josh. "The Enlightenment Theology of Political Correctness." *Tikkun* 6, no. 4 (July/August 1991).

Palma, Gabriel. "Dependency: A Formal Theory of Underdevelopment or a Methodology for the Analysis of Concrete Situations of Underdevelopment?" *World Development,* July/August 1978.

Panikkar, K. M. *Asia and Western Dominance.* New York: Collier Books, 1969.

Patterson, Orlando. *Ethnic Chauvinism: The Reactionary Impulse.* New York: Stein & Day, 1978.

Pavlischek, Keith, "The Ethics and Economics of 'Workplace Democracy': A Response to the Catholic Bishops." *This World* 21 (Spring 1988).

Paz, Octavio. *One Earth, Four or Five Worlds: Reflections on Contemporary History.* Translated by Helen R. Lane. New York: Harcourt Brace Jovanovich, 1985.

Pells, Richard H. *The Liberal Mind in a Conservative Age: American Intellectuals in the 1940s and 1950s.* New York: Harper & Row, 1985.

Phillips, Kevin. *The Politics of Rich and Poor: Wealth and the American Electorate in the Reagan Aftermath.* New York: Random House, 1990.

Phillips, William. *A Partisan View: Five Decades of the Literary Life.* New York: Stein & Day, 1983.

———. "The World According to Norman." *Partisan Review* 47, no. 3 (1980).

Phillips, William, and Philip Rahv, eds. *The New Partisan Reader 1945–1953.* New York: Harcourt Brace, 1953.

———. *The Partisan Reader 1934–1944: An Anthology.* New York: Dial Press, 1946.

Pipes, Daniel. "Can the Palestinians Make Peace?" *Commentary* 89, no. 4 (April 1990).

———. "How Important Is the PLO?" *Commentary* 75, no. 4 (April 1983).

Pipes, Richard. "Gorbachev's Russia: Breakdown or Crackdown?" *Commentary* 89, no. 3 (March 1990).

———. "How to Cope with the Soviet Threat." *Commentary* 78, no. 2 (August 1984).

———. "Soviet Global Strategy." *Commentary* 69, no. 4 (April 1980).

———. "Team B: The Reality Behind the Myth." *Commentary* 82, no. 4 (October 1986).

———. "Why the Soviet Union Thinks It Could Fight and Win a Nuclear War." *Commentary* 64, no. 1 (July 1977).

Podhoretz, Norman. "The Abandonment of Israel." *Commentary* 62, no. 1 (July 1976).

———. "Achilles in Left Field." *Commentary* 15, no. 3 (March 1953).

———. "America and Israel: An Ominous Change." *Commentary* 93, no. 1 (January 1992).

————. "Appeasement by Any Other Name." *Commentary* 76, no. 1 (July 1983).

————. *The Bloody Crossroads: Where Literature and Politics Meet.* New York: Simon & Schuster, 1986.

————. *Breaking Ranks: A Political Memoir.* New York: Harper & Row, 1979.

————. "A Certain Anxiety." *Commentary* 52, no. 2 (August 1971).

————. "The Culture of Appeasement." *Harper's* 255, no. 1529 (October 1977).

————. *Doings and Undoings: The Fifties and After in American Writing.* New York: Noonday Press, 1964.

————. "Edmund Wilson: The Last Patrician, I." *Reporter* 19, no. 11 (December 25, 1958).

————. "Edmund Wilson: The Last Patrician, II." *Reporter* 20, no. 1 (January 8, 1959).

————. "Enter the Peace Party." *Commentary* 91, no. 1 (January 1991).

————. "The Future Danger." *Commentary* 71, no. 4 (April 1981).

————. "Handing Nicaragua over to Reds." *New York Post*, April 30, 1985.

————. "Hannah Arendt on Eichmann: A Study in the Perversity of Brilliance." *Commentary* 36, no. 3 (September 1963).

————. "The Hate that Dare Not Speak Its Name." *Commentary* 82, no. 5 (November 1986).

————. "In Israel, With Scuds and Patriots." *Commentary* 91, no. 4 (April 1991).

————. "Israel: A Lamentation from the Future." *Commentary* 87, no. 3 (March 1989).

————. "J'Accuse." *Commentary* 74, no. 3 (September 1982).

————. "The Jew as Bourgeois." *Commentary* 21, no. 2 (February 1956).

————. "Jewish Culture and the Intellectuals." *Commentary* 19, no. 5 (May 1955).

————. "Kissinger Reconsidered." *Commentary* 73, no. 6 (June 1982).

————. "The Know-Nothing Bohemians." *Partisan Review* 25, no. 2 (Spring 1958).

————. "Literature and the 'Spiritual Crisis.' " *Commentary* 16, no. 2 (August 1953).

————. *Making It.* New York: Random House, 1967.

————. "Making the World Safe for Communism." *Commentary* 61, no. 4 (April 1976).

————. "My Negro Problem—And Ours." *Commentary* 35, no. 2 (February 1963).

————. "The Neo-conservative Anguish over Reagan's Foreign Policy." *New York Times Magazine*, May 2, 1982.

————. "The New American Majority." *Commentary* 71, no. 1 (January 1981).

————. "The New Nationalism and the Election." *Public Opinion* 3, no. 1A (February/March 1980).

————. "The New Nihilism and the Novel." *Partisan Review* 25, no. 4 (Fall 1958).

————. "Norman Mailer: The Embattled Vision." *Partisan Review* 26, no. 3 (Summer 1959).

————. "An Open Letter to Milan Kundera." *Commentary* 78, no. 4 (October 1984).

————. "The Present Danger." *Commentary* 69, no. 3 (March 1980).

————. *The Present Danger: Do We Have the Will to Reverse the Decline of American Power?* New York: Simon & Schuster, 1980.

————. "Rape in Feminist Eyes." *Commentary* 92, no. 4 (October 1991).

————. "The Reagan Road to Detente." *Foreign Affairs* 63, no. 3 (1985).

————. "Right about Everything, Wrong about Nothing?" *Encounter* 75, no. 1 (July/August 1990).

————. "Sholom Aleichem: Jewishness Is Jews." *Commentary* 16, no. 3 (September 1953).

————. "The State of World Jewry." *Commentary* 76, no. 6 (December 1983).

————. "A Statement on the Persian Gulf Crisis." *Commentary* 90, no. 5 (November 1990).

————. "Symbolism and/or Literature." *Partisan Review* 21, no. 3 (May/June 1954).

————. "The Terrible Question of Aleksandr Solzhenitsyn." *Commentary* 79, no. 2 (February 1985).

————. "What Is Anti-Semitism? An Open Letter to William F. Buckley, Jr." *Commentary* 93, no. 2 (February 1992).

————. *Why We Were in Vietnam.* New York: Simon & Schuster, 1983.

————. "William Faulkner and the Problem of War." *Commentary* 18, no. 3 (September 1954).

Polanyi, Karl. *The Great Transformation: The Political and Economic Origins of Our Time.* 1944. Reprint. Boston: Beacon Press, 1957.

Prebisch, Raul. *The Economic Development of Latin America and Its Principal Problems.* New York: United Nations, 1950.

Puddington, Arch. "Are Things Getting Better in Eastern Europe?" *Commentary* 76, no. 2 (August 1983).

————. "Jesse Jackson, the Blacks and American Foreign Policy." *Commentary* 77, no. 4 (April 1984).

————. "Life under Communism Today." *Commentary* 87, no. 2 (February 1989).

Pye, Lucian W. *Asian Power and Politics: The Cultural Dimensions of Authority.* Cambridge, Mass.: Harvard University Press, 1985.

Raab, Earl. "The Black Revolution and the Jewish Question." *Commentary* 47, no. 1 (January 1969).

Rabinowitz, Dorothy. "The Activist Cleric." *Commentary* 50, no. 3 (September 1970).

————. "The Radicalized Professor." *Commentary* 50, no. 1 (July 1970).

Revel, Jean-François, *The Flight from Truth: The Reign of Deceit in the Age of Information.* New York: Random House, 1992.

————. "Hastening the Death of Communism." *Commentary* 88, no. 4 (October 1989).

————. *How Democracies Perish.* New York: Harper & Row, 1985.

————. "Is Communism Reversible?" *Commentary* 87, no. 1 (January 1989).

————. *The Totalitarian Temptation.* New York: Doubleday, 1977.

Riesman, David. *Individualism Reconsidered.* New York: Free Press, 1964.

Rizzi, Bruno. *The Bureaucratization of the World*. Translated by Adam Westoby. 1939. Reprint. New York: Free Press, 1985.

Roberts, Paul Craig. "The Breakdown of the Keynesian Model." *Public Interest* 52 (Summer 1978).

Rostow, Eugene. "The Case Against Salt II." *Commentary* 67, no. 2 (February 1979).

————. "Why the Soviets Want an Arms Control Agreement, and Why They Want It Now." *Commentary* 83, no. 2 (February 1987).

Rostow, W. W. *The Stages of Economic Growth: A Non-Communist Manifesto*. Cambridge: Cambridge University Press, 1960.

Rustin, Bayard. " 'Black Power' and Coalition Politics." *Commentary* 42, no. 3 (September 1966).

Rustin, Bayard, and Carl Gershman. "Africa, Soviet Imperialism and the Retreat of American Power." *Commentary* 64, no. 4 (October 1977).

Ryn, Claes G. "The Democracy Boosters." *National Review* 41, no. 5 (March 24, 1989).

Saloma, John S., III. *Ominous Politics: The New Conservative Labyrinth*. New York: Hill & Wang, 1984.

Samuels, Richard J. *The Business of the Japanese State: Energy Markets in Comparative and Historical Perspective*. Ithaca, N.Y.: Cornell University Press, 1987.

Sandel, Michael J. *Liberalism and the Limits of Justice*. Cambridge: Cambridge University Press, 1982.

Schaller, Michael. *The American Occupation of Japan: The Origins of the Cold War in Asia*. New York: Oxford University Press, 1985.

Schambra, William. "Progressive Liberalism and American 'Community.' " *Public Interest* 80 (Summer 1985).

Schindler, David. "The One, True American Religion." *Thirty Days*, June 1989.

————. "U.S. Catholicism: A 'Moment of Opportunity'?" *Thirty Days*, May 1989.

Schlesinger, Arthur M., Jr. *The Age of Jackson*. Boston: Little, Brown, 1945.

————. *The Cycles of American History*. Boston: Houghton Mifflin, 1986.

————. *The Disuniting of America: Reflections on a Multicultural Society*. New York: Whittle Books, 1991.

————. *The Vital Center: The Politics of Freedom*. Boston: Houghton Mifflin, 1949.

Schorr, Alvin. "The Ideology of Entitlements." *Public Interest* 87 (Spring 1987).

Schumpeter, Joseph. *Capitalism, Socialism and Democracy*. 1942. Reprint. New York: Harper & Brothers, 1950.

Seabury, Paul. "Yalta and the Neoconservatives." *Commentary* 82, no. 2 (August 1986).

Seltzer, Robert, "Judaism According to Emil Fackenheim." *Commentary* 86, no. 3 (September 1988).

Shapiro, Edward. "Conservatism and Its Discontents." *The World and I*, September 1986.

Shaw, Peter. *The War Against the Intellect: Episodes in the Decline of Discourse*. Iowa City: University of Iowa Press, 1989.

Sheed, Wilfrid. "*Making It* in the Big City." *Atlantic Monthly* 221, no. 4 (April 1968).

Siegel, Fred. "The Cult of Multiculturalism." *New Republic* 204, no. 7 (February 18, 1991).

Sigmund, Paul. *Liberation Theology at the Crossroads: Democracy or Revolution?* New York: Oxford University Press, 1990.

Silberman, Bernard S. *Ministers of Modernization: Elite Mobility in the Meiji Restoration.* Tucson: University of Arizona Press, 1964.

Silver, Isidore. "What Flows from Neo-Conservatism." *Nation* 225, no. 2 (July 9, 1977).

Singer, Max. "Losing Central America." *Commentary* 82, no. 1 (July 1986).

Smith, Adam. *An Inquiry into the Nature and Causes of the Wealth of Nations.* Edited by Edwin Cannan. Chicago: University of Chicago Press, 1976.

———. *The Theory of Moral Sentiments.* Edited by D. D. Raphael and A. L. Macfie. Indianapolis, Ind.: Liberty Classics, 1976.

Sobrino, Jon. *Christology at the Crossroads.* Translated by John Drury. Maryknoll, N.Y.: Orbis Books, 1978.

Solotaroff, Theodore. "Irving Howe—The Socialist Imagination." *Commentary* 37, no. 6 (June 1964).

Sowell, Thomas. "Affirmative Action: A Worldwide Disaster." *Commentary* 88, no. 6 (December 1989).

———. *Knowledge and Decisions.* New York: Basic Books, 1980.

Spender, Stephen. "Liberal Anti-Communism Revisited." *Commentary* 44, no. 3 (September 1967).

Steel, Ronald. "The 'Yellow Peril' Revisited." *Commentary* 43, no. 6 (November 1967).

Steinfels, Peter. "Does Capitalism Equal Pluralism Equal Democracy?" *Commonweal* 110, no. 3 (February 11, 1983).

———. "Michael Novak and his ultrasuper democraticapitalism." *Commonweal* 110, no. 1 (January 14, 1983).

———. *The Neoconservatives: The Men Who Are Changing America's Politics.* New York: Simon & Schuster, 1979.

———. "Neoconservative Theology." *Democracy* 2, no. 2 (April 1982).

Stern, Sol. "NSA and the CIA: A Short Account of International Student Politics and the Cold War with Particular Reference to the NSA, CIA, Etc." *Ramparts* 5, no. 9 (March 1967).

Stockman, David. "The Social Pork-Barrel." *Public Interest* 39 (Spring 1975).

———. *The Triumph of Politics: How the Reagan Revolution Failed.* New York: Harper & Row, 1986.

Strauss, Leo. *Natural Right and History.* Chicago: University of Chicago Press, 1953.

———. *The Rebirth of Classical Political Rationalism.* Chicago: University of Chicago Press, 1989.

Szamuely, George. "The Intellectuals and the Cold War." *Commentary* 88, no. 6 (December 1989).

Talmage, Frank. "Christian Theology and the Holocaust." *Commentary* 60, no. 4 (October 1975).

Talmon, J. L. *The Origins of Totalitarian Democracy*. New York: Frederick Praeger, 1960.

———. "Uniqueness and Universality of Jewish History." *Commentary* 24, no. 1 (July 1957).

Teachout, Terry. *Beyond the Boom: New Voices on American Life, Culture and Politics*. New York: Poseidon Press, 1990.

Thomas, Henk, and Chris Logan. *Mondragon: An Economic Analysis*. London: George Allen & Unwin, 1982.

Thomas, Norman. *A Socialist's Faith*. New York: W. W. Norton, 1951.

———. *The Test of Freedom*. New York: W. W. Norton, 1954.

Thurow, Lester. *Generating Inequality*. New York: Basic Books, 1975.

Tonsor, Stephen J. "Why I Too Am Not a Neoconservative." *National Review* 38, no. 11 (June 20, 1986).

Trilling, Diana. "On the Steps of Low Library: Liberalism and the Revolution of the Young." *Commentary* 46, no. 5 (November 1968).

———. *We Must March My Darlings: A Critical Decade*. New York: Harcourt Brace Jovanovich, 1978.

Trilling, Lionel. *The Liberal Imagination*. New York: Scribner's, 1950.

Trotsky, Leon. *The Basic Writings of Trotsky*. Edited by Irving Howe. New York: Random House, 1963.

———. *In Defense of Marxism: Against the Petty-Bourgeois Opposition*. New York: Merit Publishers, 1965.

———. *Their Morals and Ours: Marxist Versus Liberal Views on Morality*. New York: Pathfinder Press, 1973.

———. *Writings of Leon Trotsky*. 4 vols. Edited by Naomi Allen and George Breitman, New York: Pathfinder Press, 1970–74.

Tucker, Robert W. "Exemplar or Crusader? Reflections on America's Role." *National Interest* 5 (Fall 1986).

———. "Isolation and Intervention." *National Interest* 1 (Fall 1985).

———. "Lebanon: The Case for the War." *Commentary* 74, no. 4 (October 1982).

———. "The Middle East: Carterism Without Carter?" *Commentary* 72, no. 3 (September 1981).

———. "Vietnam: The Final Reckoning." *Commentary* 59, no. 5 (May 1975).

Ulam, Adam. "The Cold War According to Kennan." *Commentary* 55, no. 1 (January 1973).

Van Den Haag, Ernest. "The War Between Paleos and Neos." *National Review* 41, no. 3 (February 24, 1989).

———, ed. *Capitalism: Sources of Hostility*. Washington, D.C.: Heritage Foundation, 1979.

Van Toai, Doan. "Vietnam: How We Deceived Ourselves." *Commentary* 81, no. 3 (March 1986).

Viereck, Peter. "The Philosophical 'New Conservatism'—1962." In *The Radical Right*, ed. Daniel Bell (New York: Doubleday, 1963).

———. "The Revolt Against the Elite." In *The Radical Right*, ed. Daniel Bell (New York: Doubleday, 1963).

————. *Shame and Glory of the Intellectuals*. Boston: Houghton Mifflin, 1953.

Voegelin, Eric. *The New Science of Politics*. Chicago: University of Chicago Press, 1952.

Vogel, Ezra F. *Japan as Number One*. New York: Harper & Row, 1979.

Wald, Alan M. *The New York Intellectuals: The Rise and Decline of the Anti-Stalinist Left from the 1930s to the 1980s*. Chapel Hill: University of North Carolina Press, 1987.

Walzer, Michael. "The Communitarian Critique of Liberalism." *Political Theory* 18, no. 1 (February 1990).

————. "The Obligations of Oppressed Minorities." *Commentary* 49, no. 5 (May 1970).

————. *Radical Principles: Reflections of an Unreconstructed Democrat*. New York: Basic Books, 1980.

————. *Spheres of Justice: A Defense of Pluralism and Equality*. New York: Basic Books, 1983.

Wattenberg, Ben J. *The First Universal Nation: Leading Indicators and Ideas about the Surge of America in the 1990s*. New York: Free Press, 1991.

————. "Neo-Manifest Destinarianism." *National Interest* 21 (Fall 1990).

Wattenberg, Ben, and Richard Scammon. "Black Progress and Liberal Rhetoric." *Commentary* 55, no. 4 (April 1973).

Weigel, George S. "John Courtney Murray and the Catholic Human Rights Revolution." *This World* 15 (Fall 1986).

————. *Tranquillitas Ordinis: The Present Failure and Future Promise of American Catholic Thought on War and Peace*. New York: Oxford University Press, 1987.

Weisberg, Jacob. "Hunter Gatherers." *New Republic* 205, no. 10 (September 2, 1991).

Weiss, Philip. "Going to Extremes." *Harper's* 267, no. 1602 (November 1983).

Whyte, W., and Kathleen K. Whyte. *Making Mondragon*. Ithaca, N.Y.: ILR Press, 1988.

Wiener, Jon. "Dollars for Neocon Scholars: The Olin Money Tree." *Nation* 250, no. 1 (January 1, 1990).

Wildavsky, Aaron. "The Political Economy of Efficiency." *Public Interest* 8 (Summer 1967).

————. *The Rise of Radical Egalitarianism*. Washington, D.C.: American University Press, 1991.

Williams, Oliver F., and John W. Houck, eds. *The Common Good and U.S. Capitalism*. Lanham, Md.: University Press of America, 1987.

Wilson, Clyde. "The Conservative Identity." *Intercollegiate Review* 21, no. 3 (Spring 1986).

————. "Global Democracy and American Tradition." *Intercollegiate Review* 24, no. 1 (Fall 1988).

Wilson, James Q. "The Bureaucracy Problem." *Public Interest* 6 (Winter 1967).

————. "Liberalism Versus Liberal Education." *Commentary* 53, no. 6 (June 1972).

————. " 'Policy Intellectuals' and Public Policy." *Public Interest* 64 (Summer 1981).

————. "The Urban Unease: Community vs. City." *Public Interest* 12 (Summer 1968).

Winchell, Mark Royden. *Neoconservative Criticism: Norman Podhoretz, Kenneth S. Lynn and Joseph Epstein.* Boston: Twayne Publishers, 1991.

Winik, Jay. "The Neoconservative Reconstruction." *Foreign Affairs* 73 (Winter 1988–89).

Wisse, Ruth. "The Delegitimation of Israel." *Commentary* 74, no. 1 (July 1982).

————. "Israel and the Intellectuals: A Failure of Nerve?" *Commentary* 85, no. 5 (May 1988).

————. "Jewish Guilt and Israeli Writers." *Commentary* 87, no. 1 (January 1989).

————. "Living with Women's Lib." *Commentary* 86, no. 2 (August 1988).

Witte, John F. *Democracy, Authority, and Alienation in Work.* Chicago: University of Chicago Press, 1980.

Wolferen, Karel von. *The Enigma of Japanese Power: People and Politics in a Stateless Nation.* New York: Vintage Books, 1990.

Woo, Jung-en. *Race to the Swift: State and Finance in Korean Industrialization.* New York: Columbia University Press, 1991.

Wooton, Graham. *Workers, Unions and the State.* London: Routledge & Kegan Paul, 1986.

Wrong, Dennis H. "The Case of the 'New York Review.' " *Commentary* 50, no. 5 (November 1970).

Xenos, Nicholas. "Neoconservatism Kristolized." *Salmagundi* 74–75 (Spring/Summer 1987).

Zasloff, Joseph. "The Problem of South Viet Nam." *Commentary* 33, no. 2 (February 1962).

Index

Novak, Michael: antiwar sympathies of, 210–13; Clinton campaign and, 390; Cold War collapse and, 198, 323; *Commentary* contributions of, 165; democratic globalism and, 379–80; dissolution of neoconservatism and, 11, 352, 368; early life, 207–8; Hook's influence on, 64; intellectual background of, 8; Kennedy's unipolarism refuted by, 339–40; liberation theology questioned by, 237–45; multiculturalism attacked by, 355, 362; neoconservative origins and, 7, 16–18; New Class emergence and, 14–15; news media criticized by, 366–67, 382–83; on economic vs. political rights, 245–57, 302; Persian Gulf War and, 340–41; transition to conservatism, 219–24; "unmeltable ethnics" theory of, 215–19; Whig tradition and, 207–8, 224–37; writings of, 165, 208–10, 213–15, 257–64

Novak, Richard, 209

Novus Ordo Seclorum, 229–30, 340

Nozick, Robert, 434n.175

nuclear weapons, 372–74; Burnham's ideology and, 46–47; Podhoretz's defense of, 172–76, 182–84

Nuechterlein, James, 362–63

Nunn, Sam, 389

Oakeshott, Michael, 103–4

objectivization, Berger's theory of, 273–74

O'Brien, Conor Cruise, 84–85, 409n.51

Odets, Clifford, 28, 50

Office of Strategic Services, 44, 61

Ogarkov, Nikolai, 372

Olin Foundation, 12, 102, 321, 347, 349, 364, 394

Olson, Mancur, 380

Oppenheimer, Robert, 53

Orbis, 9

Organization of American States, 116–17, 122, 130–31

Orthodox Judaism, 203; Kristol's ideology and, 112–15; Podhoretz and, 134–35

Orwell, George, 42–43, 173, 205

O'Sullivan, John, 346

Overstreet, Harry, 2, 370

Owen, Wilfred, 172

paleoconservatives, 11–13; dissolution of neoconservatism and, 343–49; foreign policy and, 327

Palestinians: Kristol's foreign policy analysis and, 127–29; Podhoretz on, 196

Panichas, George, 12

Pareto, Vilfredo, 37–39

Park Chung Hee, 300–301

Partisan Review, The, 8–9, 159; Burnham's writings in, 40–41, 63; *Commentary* and, 72–73; dissolution of neoconservatism and, 351; funding shortages of, 84; Kristol influenced by, 70–71; Lasky's contributions to, 79–81; Podhoretz's contributions to, 140, 149

Pax Americana, 91–92, 203–6; neoconservatives' support of, 323–24, 329–41

Paz, Octavio, 243

Peace Corps, 212

Peretz, Martin, 9, 389

Perle, Richard, 10, 170, 176, 324

Persian Gulf crisis: culture of appeasement and, 172–76; dissolution of neoconservatism and, 374–75; media suppression during, 366–67; New World Order ideology and, 335–38, 340

Phillips, William, 8, 28, 51, 159; Podhoretz and, 137, 205–6

Pipes, Richard, 10, 182–84, 371–72

Pluralism, Berger's discussion of, 316–22

Podhoretz, Julius, 134

Podhoretz, Norman: affirmative action policies and, 191–96; Carter administration and, 167–74; *Commentary* editorship, 137–45; culture of appeasement disparaged by, 164–84, 371–72; disaffection with left, 155–64; dissolution of neoconservatives and, 346–49, 390; early education, 134–35; feminism attacked by, 352–55; on Gorbachev and Cold War collapse, 197–206, 323; homosexuality criticized by, 194–96; Hook's influence on, 64; literary criticism of, 137–38, 143–46; military career, 140–41; multiculturalism attacked by, 355–56, 361–63; neoconservative origins and, 7, 15–18; New Class and, 15, 385–86; New York Intellectuals and, 9; on Persian Gulf crisis, 340, 376; opposition to arms limitation talks, 373–